Third Edition

Management Fundamentals

Concepts • Applications • Skill Development

Robert N. Lussier, Ph.D.

Springfield College
Springfield, Massachusetts

THOMSON

SOUTH-WESTERN

Australia · Canada · Mexico · Singapore · Spain · United Kingdom · United States

THOMSON

SOUTH-WESTERN

Management Fundamentals, Third Edition
Robert N. Lussier

VP/Editorial Director:
Jack W. Calhoun

VP/Editor-in-Chief:
Dave Shaut

Executive Editor:
John Szilagyi

Developmental Editor:
Leslie Kauffman, LEAP Publishing Services

Sr. Marketing Manager:
Rob Bloom

Production Project Manager:
Starratt E. Alexander

Manager of Technology, Editorial:
Vicki True

Technology Project Editor:
Kristen Meere

Web Coordinator:
Karen L. Schaffer

Manufacturing Coordinator:
Doug Wilke

Production House:
Stratford Publishing Services, Inc.

Printer:
Quebecor World Versailles
Versailles, Kentucky

Art Director:
Anne Marie Rekow

Cover and Internal Design:
Craig Ramsdell, Ramsdell Design

Cover Images:
Getty Images; David Madison, Photographer

Photography Manager:
Deanna Ettinger

Photo Researcher:
Susan Van Etten

Library of Congress Control Number:
2005927136

For more information about our products, contact us at:

Thomson Learning Academic Resource Center

1-800-423-0563

Thomson Higher Education
5191 Natorp Boulevard
Mason, OH 45040
USA

To my wife, Marie, and our six children:

Jesse, Justin, Danielle, Nicole, Brian, and Renee

Brief Contents

Contents

Preface xv
About the Author 1

PART 1: MANAGING IN A GLOBAL INTERNET ENVIRONMENT

PART 2: PLANNING

PART 3: ORGANIZING

PART 4: LEADING

PART 5: CONTROLLING

Preface

In his book *Power Tools*, John Nirenberg asks: "Why are so many well-intended students learning so much and yet able to apply so little in their personal and professional lives?" The world of management has changed and so should how it is taught. Increasing numbers of students want more than just an understanding of the concepts of management. They also want skills they can use in their everyday life at work. It's not enough to learn about management; they want to learn how to *be* managers. This is why I wrote this book.

COMPETITIVE ADVANTAGES

I personally developed the total package to have the following competitive advantages:

- A unique "**how-to-manage**" approach.
- Nine types of high-quality **application materials** using the concepts to develop critical-thinking skills.
- Five types of high-quality **skill-builder exercises** to develop management skills that can be utilized in students' professional and personal lives.
- A comprehensive **video** package, including 11 Behavior Model Videos and 6 Video Cases.
- A **flexible** package. With all these features, instructors can design the course by selecting the features that meet their needs.
- A **lower price** to students than major competitors.

Integration

Based on my experience teaching management courses for more than 25 years, I created course materials that develop students into managers. As the title of this book implies, it involves a balanced, three-pronged approach to the curriculum:

- a clear understanding of management **concepts;**
- the **application** of management concepts for critical thinking in the real world; and
- the development of management **skills.**

I wrote this text and its supporting ancillary package to support these three distinct but integrated parts. This text follows a management functions approach covering all the traditional concepts and current topics. The applications develop students' critical-thinking skills as they require them to apply specific concepts to their own work experience (part-time, summer, or full-time), to short situations, and to cases. In addition, this text meets the challenge of the AACSB and SCANS call for skills development. Since I wrote almost every exercise and application in the package, the material is completely integrated to create a seamless experience in the classroom.

Flexibility

Because these three key elements of concepts, applications, and skills are integrated throughout the chapters, you won't find them in broad general sections. However, they are identified clearly and are delineated in some detail for your reference in this preface. Recognizing the diverse needs of students and faculty, they can be used flexibly to fit any classroom. Instructors can create their course by using only features that fit with their objectives.

CONCEPTS

This text covers all key management topics and concepts. It is comprehensive in scope as shown by the detailed learning outcomes at the front of each chapter. Each outcome is reinforced and identified throughout the chapter. Key terms are highlighted in red to emphasize the vocabulary of management for students.

Systems Integration

Businesses today no longer operate in traditional departments isolated by function. To understand management, students must understand the interrelationships of the various business functions. The text is written from this perspective. The business is shown as a system; managers work within a system of relationships. The text focuses on viewing the organization as a whole and the interrelationship of its parts.

Current Management Issues

Because this text takes an integrated approach to the subject of management, it is not cluttered with extraneous boxes. Instead, current topics as described by the AACSB, such as globalization, diversity, ethics and social responsibility, quality, productivity, and participative management and teams, are covered throughout the chapters.

End-of-Chapter Material Reinforcement of Concepts

Each chapter ends with a Chapter Summary, which includes a glossary. The summary reinforces every Learning Outcome. The unique glossary enables the readers to quiz themselves on the definitions, making it an active glossary. In addition, at least ten Review and Discussion Questions that support and reinforce the key conceptual learnings appear in the chapter.

Product Support Web Site

The product support Web site, http://lussier.swlearning.com, has information for both professors and students. Students can take interactive quizzes, quiz themselves on glossary terms, and download the PowerPoint slides to use as study tools.

Test Bank (Assessment of Concepts)

Over half of the questions in the test bank (print and electronic) assess student knowledge of the managerial concepts taught in the text. In addition, every question identifies the chapter outcome that it tests.

APPLICATIONS

Powerful learning takes place when theory is put within the context of the real world. Using this text, students are challenged to apply the concepts they learn to actual business situations, especially as they have experienced them personally. Students must think critically as they apply specific concepts to their own work experience, short situations, and cases.

Ideas on Management Opening Case and InfoTrac

At the beginning of each chapter, information about an actual manager and organization is presented. The case is followed by four to eight questions, new to this edition, to get students involved. Throughout the chapter, the answers to the questions are given to illustrate how the organization actually uses the text concepts to create opportunities and solve problems through decision making. An icon like that in the margin here appears in the margin where the opening case is applied in the text. The students get a real-world example illustrated extensively throughout the chapter beginning with the opening pages. As appropriate, an Internet address referring students to that company's Web site is provided, allowing students to do further research on the organization. Use of the Internet is optional.

Also new to this edition is the integration of InfoTrac into the opening cases. Students can use Infotrac's fast and easy search tools to find relevant news and analytical information among the tens of thousands of articles in the database—updated daily and going back as far as four years—all at a single Web site. Sample article numbers are given to get students started with their search.

Company Examples

New to this edition are extended, yet concise, company examples to illustrate how companies use the text concepts. There are over 120 altogether, with an average of eight per chapter. Text concepts come alive as students see how actual organizations use them to succeed. Companies featured include Microsoft, the New York Yankees, Nike, eBay, Yahoo!, Google, MTV, Blockbuster, Intel, Wal-Mart, Dell Computer, and Apple, among many others. The organization names are highlighted throughout the text.

DIFFERENTIATION STRATEGY

With a differentiation strategy, a company stresses its advantage over its competitors.[69] **Nike, Ralph Lauren, Calvin Klein**, and others place their names on the outside of their products to differentiate them from those of the competition. Differentiation strategy somewhat resembles the prospecting strategy. According to **Coca-Cola**, the three keys to selling consumer products are differentiation, differentiation, differentiation, which it achieves with its scripted name logo and contour bottle.

Work Applications

Open-ended questions called Work Applications require students to explain how the text concepts apply to their own work experience; there are over 160 of these scattered throughout the text. Student experience can be present, past, summer, full-time, or part-time employment. The questions help students bridge the gap between theory and their real world.

Applying the Concept

Every chapter contains a series of three to six Applying the Concept boxes that require the student to determine the management concept being illustrated in a specific short example. There are 15 to 25 objective questions per chapter for development of student critical-thinking skills.

WorkApplication2

Describe the kinds of interactions you have had with the human resources department of an organization you work for or have worked for.

Applying The Concept 2

Corporate Growth Strategies

Identify the type of growth strategy described by each statement.

a. concentration
b. forward integration
c. backward integration
d. related diversification
e. unrelated diversification

_____ 6. Sears buys a tool manufacturer to make its Craftsman tools.
_____ 7. General Motors buys the Sea World theme park.
_____ 8. The Gap opens a new retail store in a mall.
_____ 9. Lee opens stores to sell its clothes.
_____10. Gateway, a computer manufacturer, produces printers.

Join the Discussion: Ethics and Social Responsibility Dilemmas

New to this edition are 39 ethical dilemma boxed items, with two to three included per chapter. Many of the dilemmas include information from companies such as Gap, National Highway Traffic Safety Administration

(NHTSA), Kazaa, Monsanto, Arthur Andersen, Global Crossing, SAP, and jetBlue Airways. Each dilemma has two to four questions for class discussion.

Join the Discussion | Ethics & Social Responsibility

Factory Conditions

1. Should Gap let local authorities monitor its factory conditions?
2. Is it ethical and socially responsible for Gap to revoke contracts, causing poor workers to lose their jobs?
3. Is it ethical and socially responsible to Gap's stockholders to pay higher labor costs than necessary, thus possibly reducing profits and their dividends?

Gap, the subject of the opening case in Chapter 1, has 3,000 factories in about 50 countries, making clothes for its Gap, Old Navy, and Banana Republic clothing-store chains. Gap is the largest specialty-apparel retailer, with over $15 billion in sales. Many companies, including Gap, have been criticized for not monitoring factory conditions. To address the criticism, the firm set standards for its manufacturers. In 2003, Gap revoked its contracts with 136 factories for persistent or severe violations of standards.[30]

End-of-Chapter (Objective) Cases

Following the review questions, students are presented with another actual manager and organization. The student learns how the manager/organization applies the management concepts from that chapter. Each case is followed by 9-10 multiple-choice questions and some open-ended questions. The questions require the student to apply management practices and concepts to the actual organization. The InfoTrac Web site address is provided, allowing students to do further research on the organization. Use of the Internet is optional.

Chapters 2 through 15 also include cumulative case questions. Cumulative questions relate case material to concepts from prior chapters. Thus, students continually review and integrate concepts from previous chapters.

Video Cases

Student learning is enhanced by seeing actual managers tackling real management problems within their workplaces. The Lussier package contains six video cases provided free to adopters. Each video case centers around the decisions made by managers from the topic of a given chapter. Video Cases are integrated at the end of six chapters. All Video Cases have supporting print material for both instructors and students, including a brief description and critical-thinking questions.

Video Case

TIMBERLAND

About Timberland

This video on Timberland deals with a broad array of issues associated with the company's business environment. In particular, the video shows vividly how Timberland shares its culture and ethics with its customers, its employees, its shareholders, and the community. The ways in which managers at Timberland build culture and make clear what Timberland stands for are very well documented in this short clip.

View the Video (10–15 minutes)

View the accompanying video on Timberland in class or at *http://lussier.swlearning.com*.

Read the Case

New Hampshire–based Timberland builds its products to last—"to withstand the elements of nature." But Timberland is striving to build something more permanent than just high-quality footwear and clothing. It's trying to make the world a better place in which to live and work.

Timberland recognizes its responsibility to be profitable for investors and employees. The company has recently

reported 20 consecutive quarters of record-level revenue and improved earnings. Timberland also considers its employees as critical to its success and has appeared numerous times on *Fortune* magazine's list of the best companies to work for. With repeated news reports about exploitation of foreign workers at other companies, Timberland monitors its offshore factories every 8 to 12 weeks to ensure that workers are paid decent wages, provided periodic work breaks, and not required to work excessive overtime.

Through its daily efforts to manage its operations better than the day before, Timberland maintains its edge as a productive and profitable business.

Answer the Questions

1. Describe how Timberland managers handle some of the external environmental factors discussed in the chapter.
2. How well does Timberland manager Ken Freitas (former vice president for social enterprise) communicate what Timberland stands for?
3. Would you like to work at Timberland? Why or why not?

Test Bank (Assessment of Application Ability) and Instructor's Manual (Reinforcement of Applications)

The Test Bank contains application questions that include true/false and multiple-choice questions, learning outcomes questions, work application questions, questions similar to "applying the concept" questions, and review and discussion questions. The Instructor's Manual contains detailed answers for all of the text application features.

SKILLS

The difference between learning about management and learning to be a manager is the acquisition of skills. This text focuses on skill development to students can use what they learn on the job. The skill material is integrated throughout the text, but instructors can choose how to incorporate the material into their classroom experience—individually or as groups, inside the class or as outside group projects. Instructors can also determine the extent to which they want to use behavior modeling as the basis for skill development in their classroom, if at all.

Students can actually develop a skill that can be used on the job. The features listed in the following paragraphs include true skill building, such as step-by-step models, skill-builder exercises, and behavior model videos. Other features support skill building, such as self-assessments and group exercises.

Step-by-Step Models

The book contains 25 detailed sets of how-to steps for handling day-to-day management functions. They are integrated into the context of the chapter or skill-building exercise being taught. For example, models teach students how to set objectives and priorities, how to handle a complaint, and how to discipline an employee. This feature directly teaches students how to be managers.

Skill Builders

Each chapter contains two or three Skill Builders, all of which have been class-tested to be the best found in any text in the market. Full support of 36 activities can be found in the Instructor's Manual including detailed information, timing, answers, and so on. All exercises and their uses are optional in the classroom. There are three primary types of exercise:

A. Individual Focus: Seventeen exercises (47%) are those in which participants are required to make individual decisions prior to or during class. These answers can be shared in class for discussion, or the instructor may elect to go over recommended answers.
B. Group Focus: Eight exercises (22%) are those in which participants discuss the material presented and may select group answers.
C. Role-Play Focus: Eleven exercises (31%) are those in which participants are presented with a model and given the opportunity to use the model, usually in groups of three.

Behavior Model Videos

To reinforce the development of skills for students, the Lussier package includes 11 Behavior Model Videos, unique to the management curriculum. The videos demonstrate managers successfully performing common management

Behavior **Modeling**
DECISION-MAKING STYLES

The scenario for this chapter features Richard, a human resources director, meeting with a supervisor, Denise, to discuss training changes. The video illustrates four management styles.

Objective
To better understand four management decision-making styles.

View the Video (13 minutes)
View the accompanying video in class or at *http://lussier.swlearning.com*. As you view each of the four scenes, identify the management decision-making style being used by the manager in each scene (autocratic, consultative, participative, or empowerment).

Scene 1. _____

Scene 2. _____

Scene 3. _____

Scene 4. _____

Apply It
What did I learn from this exercise? How will I use this knowledge in the future?

_____

_____

functions such as handling complaints, delegating tasks, and conducting job interviews. Students learn from watching the videos and/or using them in conjunction with the Skill Builders. Material in the text integrates the videos into the chapters. Ideas for using all videos are detailed in the Instructor's Manual.

Self-Assessments

Scattered throughout the text are 21 Self-Assessments, with at least one per chapter. Students complete these assessments to gain personal knowledge. All information for completing and scoring the assessments is contained within the text. Self-knowledge leads students to an understanding of how

Self-Assessment

What Motivates You?

Following are 12 job factors that contribute to job satisfaction. Rate each according to how important it is to you by placing a number from 1 to 5 on the line before each factor.

Very Important	Somewhat important	Not important
5 ———————— 4 ———————— 3 ———————— 2 ———————— 1		

_____ 1. An interesting job I enjoy doing

_____ 2. A good boss who treats people fairly

_____ 3. Getting praise and other recognition and appreciation for the work that I do

_____ 4. Satisfying interpersonal interactions on the job

_____ 5. The opportunity for advancement

_____ 6. A prestigious or high-status job

_____ 7. Job responsibility that gives me freedom to do things my way

_____ 8. Good working conditions (safe environment, nice office, cafeteria, etc.)

_____ 9. The opportunity to learn new things

_____10. Sensible company rules, regulations, procedures, and policies

_____11. A job I can do well and succeed at

_____12. Job security

Indicate below how you rated each factor.

Motivating Factors	_Maintenance Factors_
1. ____	2. ____
3. ____	4. ____
5. ____	6. ____
7. ____	8. ____
9. ____	10. ____
11. ____	12. ____
____	Total points ____

Add each column vertically. Are motivators or maintenance factors more important to you?

they can and will operate as managers in the real world. Many of the assessments are tied to exercises within the book, thus enhancing the impact of the activities.

Product Support Web Site

The product support Web site, http://lussier.swlearning.com, contains the Behavior Model Video clips for student viewing.

Test Bank (Assessment of Skill Development) and Instructor's Manual (Reinforcement of Skills)

Skill Builders in the text have reinforcement and assessment questions in the corresponding Test Bank chapter, a unique feature of the Lussier text package. The Instructor's Manual contains detailed answers for all of the skills features in the text, including timing, information, answers, logistics for instructor use, and follow-up questions for student debriefing. The manual also explains how to test on skill building.

ANCILLARY SUPPORT

Just as businesses must be integrated across functions and departments for success, text and ancillary material must also be integrated to create the optimum student learning experience. Many of our key supplements have been described to you as part of the support for our three-pronged approach to the management curriculum. The following paragraphs describe all elements of the text package, which are designed to create a successful classroom environment.

Instructor's Manual (0-324-22607-1)

The Instructor's Manual was written to ensure that every faculty member would receive complete integrated support for teaching. The manual contains the following for each chapter of the book: a detailed outline for lecture enhancement, Work Application Student Sample Answers, Review and Discussion Question Answers, Applying the Concept Answers, Objective Case and Video Case Question Answers, Instructions on Use of Videos, and Skill Builder Ideas (including set-up and timing). The Instructor's Manual also includes ideas on how to use the special features of the text in the classroom with emphasis on creating an interactive learning environment. Written by the author, Robert N. Lussier, Springfield College.

Test Bank (0-324-22608-X)

A unique feature of the text package is a comprehensive Test Bank that is structured around the three-pronged approach of the book: concepts, applications, and skills. Questions assessing each aspect of student learning in these three areas are delineated and included for each chapter. No other book on the market attempts to assess student skill development. Written by the author, Robert N. Lussier, Springfield College, and Molly Pepper, Gonzaga University.

ExamView® Testing Software (0-324-22610-1)

All questions from the printed Test Bank are available in ExamView®, an easy-to-use test-creation program compatible with both Word and Macintosh operating systems.

PowerPoint™

Teaching transparencies are available in electronic format for a more flexible and professional presentation in the classroom.

Behavior Model Videos (VHS 0-324-32190-2, DVD 0-324-32189-9)

To reinforce the development of skills for students, the Lussier package includes 11 Behavior Model Videos, unique to the management curriculum. The videos demonstrate managers successfully performing common management functions, such as handling complaints, delegating tasks, and conducting job interviews. Students learn from watching the videos and/or using them in conjunction with the Skill Builders. Material in the text integrates the videos into the chapters. Ideas for using all videos are detailed in the Instructor's Manual.

Video Cases (VHS 0-324-32190-2, DVD 0-324-32189-9)

Accompanying and integrated within the text are six Video Cases. Each case centers around topics key to management understanding within a profile of a real business organization solving real-world problems. These video cases add variety in the classroom presentation and stimulate students to learn about organizations, teams, and management.

Instructor's Resource CD-ROM (0-324-22609-8)

Get quick access to the Instructor's Manual, Test Bank, ExamView, and PowerPoint slides from your desktop via one CD-ROM.

Product Support Web Site

The dedicated *Management Fundamentals* Web site, http://lussier.swlearning. com, offers broad online support. Log on for additional quizzes, downloadable ancillaries, and more.

InfoTrac College Edition

With InfoTrac College Edition, students can receive anytime, anywhere online access to a database of full-text articles from hundreds of popular and scholarly periodicals, such as *Newsweek, Fortune, Entrepreneur, Journal of Management,* and *Nation's Business,* among others. InfoTrac is a great way to expose students to online research techniques, with the security that the content is academically based and reliable. An InfoTrac College Edition subscription card is packaged free with new copies of the *Management Fundamentals,* third edition, text. For more information, visit http://info-trac.thomsonlearning.com.

Our Feature Presentation: Management
(0-324-28281-8)

Our Feature Presentation: Management adds excitement and relevance to management through selected film scenes from popular film releases. This unique product combines a workbook with actual film clips on CD and Video, eliminating the need to purchase or rent costly videos. The *Management Fundamentals*, 3e Instructor's Manual includes a correlation guide that matches the *Our Feature Presentation: Management* film clips with the text chapters. Film provides your students a visual portrayal of abstract management concepts and provides inexperienced students a greater feeling of reality and connection to the topic. Further, there are many unique aspects of film such as editing, sound, framing, and focusing techniques that make it a powerful communication device that often goes beyond what we can experience in reality. Equally powerful are the reactions of the varied responses of the viewer that can spark lively debate. Register for access to the videos online at http://featurepresentation.swlearning.com.

The Business & Company Resource Center

Put a complete business library at your fingertips with **The Business & Company Resource Center**. The BCRC is a premier online business research tool that allows you to seamlessly search thousands of periodicals, journals, references, financial information, industry reports, company histories, and much more.

- The **BCRC** is conveniently accessible from anywhere with an Internet connection, allowing students to access information at school, at home, or on the go.
- The **BCRC** is a powerful and time-saving research tool for students—whether they are completing a case analysis, preparing for a presentation or discussion, creating a business plan, or writing a reaction paper.
- Instructors can use the **BCRC** like an online coursepack, assigning readings and research-based homework without the inconvenience of library reserves, permissions, and printed materials.

The Business & Company Resource Center is available as an optional package item with Management Fundamentals, 3e. To learn more about BCRC, contact your local Thomson representative and visit *http://bcrc.swlearning.com*.

SUMMARY OF KEY INNOVATIONS

My goal is to make both students and instructors successful in the classroom by providing learning features that not only teach about management but also help students become managers. Here are the special ways in which this is done:

- The three-pronged approach to the curriculum: concepts, applications, and skills.
- Assessment of this approach through a three-section Test Bank: concepts, applications, and skills.
- Flexibility—use any or all of the features that work for you!
- Unique skill-builder exercises that develop skills for use on the job.

- An unsurpassed video package: 11 Behavior Model Videos and 6 Video Cases.
- Cumulative case questions.

Changes to the Third Edition

I am really excited about this new edition, as I have totally updated it.

- The number of references has increased from slightly more than 1,000 to over 1,400. Other than the classic references, such as motivation and leadership theories, over 85 percent of the references are new to this edition and from 2000–2004.
- Every opening case is new and now includes questions, which are answered throughout the chapter.
- A new InfoTrac feature has been added to the opening case in each chapter.
- Ten of the 15 end-of-chapter cases are new.
- Thirty-nine new Ethics and Social Responsibility dilemmas, with two to four questions each for class discussion, have been added.
- Over 120 new, extended, yet concise, company examples have been added.
- Six new Video Cases have been added.
- Four new Self-Assessments (previously known as Self-Assessment Exercises in last edition) have been added.
- Three new Skill Builders (previously known as Skill-Building Exercises in last edition) have been added.
- Two new appendices (Career Management and Networking, and Written Communication) have been added.

CHAPTER 1. There is new opening section—Why Study Management?—to help the students understand the importance of the course and how they can benefit from the book. The prior Managing in the Global Internet Environment section has been renamed New Workplaces Issues and Challenges, and expanded greatly. Knowledge management has been added as a new key term.

CHAPTER 2. The Self-Assessment on ethical behavior has been changed to include a wider variety of examples of unethical behavior, and has been moved from the end of the chapter to within the chapter. The Business Ethics section has been expanded to include subsections for How Personality Traits and Attitudes, Moral Development, and the Situation Affect Ethical Behavior, and How People Justify Unethical Behavior.

CHAPTER 3. The chapter has been reorganized so that the Business Practices of Global Companies section from last edition has been moved to become a subsection of the Taking a Business Global section. The countries of the European Union have been updated to include the current 25 countries.

CHAPTER 4. There are two new subsections that have been added to the chapter: Decision Making in the Global Village, and Ethics and Social Responsibility in Decision Making. A new section on Vroom's Participative Decision-Making Model has been added, including a new key term—participative decision-making model. A new Work Application, Applying the

Concept, and Skill Builder have been added on Vroom's participative decision-making model.

CHAPTER 5.   The chapter has been reorganized so that the Standing Plans versus Single-Use Plans and Contingency Plans subsections have been moved to near the end of the chapter, under the new Operational Planning section. There is a new Self-Assessment on effective planning.

CHAPTER 6.   There is a new overview of the chapter and a new Exhibit 6-1.

CHAPTER 7.   Last edition's Managing Change section has been split into two sections: Change, which now includes a subsection on Forms of Change (incremental and radical), and Managing Change. MIS has been changed to just IS. Creating urgency has been added to the list of ways to overcome resistance to change. From the Innovation section, a discussion of quality, which overlaps Chapters 2 and 15, has been cut. From the Organizational Development section, the subsection on Organizational Development Interventions has been reorganized by level of focus—from individual, to group, to organizational. The topic of grid OD has been dropped, and large-group intervention, also a new key term, has been added in its place.

CHAPTER 8.   There is a new Exhibit 8-2 that describes federal laws related to human resource management. A new discussion of outsourcing the HR function has been added, with an example. There is a new Self-Assessment on career development. The appendix on Career Management and Networking is new. Students can develop a career plan and learn how to network to find a job and advance in their career.

CHAPTER 9.   There is a new brief discussion of obesity.

CHAPTER 10.   There is a new Self-Assessment that measures how much of a team player you are. There is new coverage of global virtual teams, which has also been added as a new key term.

CHAPTER 11.   The name of the chapter has been changed to reflect new coverage of information technology and information systems, moved here from last edition's Chapter 15. An appendix on Written Communications is new. Students can review grammar and complete exercises to improve their writing skills.

CHAPTER 12.   The discussion of reinforcement for attendance and punctuality has been cut.

CHAPTER 13.   Servant leadership has been added as a behavioral contemporary perspective. The Vroom's Normative Leadership Model subsection has been updated and moved to Chapter 4.

CHAPTER 14.   There is a new Self-Assessment on coaching. The Productivity section has been moved to Chapter 15.

CHAPTER 15. The material on information technology has been moved to Chapter 11. The Productivity section from Chapter 14 has been moved to this chapter, and the title of the chapter has been revised to reflect the organizational changes. There is increased coverage of supply chain management, which has also been added as a new key term. A section on the balanced scorecard has been added, which is also a new key term. There is a new Self-Assessment that reviews all of these concepts in previous Self-Assessments and puts them together, with a new Skill Builder based on the new Self-Assessment.

ACKNOWLEDGMENTS

The authorship of a publishing project of this magnitude is only one aspect of a complex process. Many hardworking individuals gave great effort to create this text and package. I wish to express my gratitude to many of these key contributors, especially the fine people at Thomson/South-Western. Having worked with a number of major publishers over the years, South-Western is the best. Specifically, I would like to thank my executive editor, John Szilagyi; my marketing manager, Rob Bloom; my developmental editor, Leslie Kauffman of LEAP Publishing Services, Inc.; my production editor, Starratt Alexander; my art director, Anne Marie Rekow; my technology project manager, Kristen Meere; and my Web coordinator, Karen Schaffer.

Thanks to my mentor and coauthor of many publications, Joel Corman, for his advice and encouragement during and after my graduate education at Suffolk University. I am grateful to Dr. Abbas Nadim, Dr. David Morris, and Dr. Judith Neal, doctoral faculty at the University of New Haven. Thanks, Dr. Nadim (Ph.D., Wharton School; protégé of Russell Ackoff), for educating me in the ways of systems theory, which is used throughout this book; Dr. Morris, for influencing the development of more exhibits that integrate the material through the use of visuals; and Dr. Neal, for influencing the three-pronged approach.

In addition, the reviewers of the project provided me with great ideas and inspiration for writing. The reviewers overwhelmingly confirmed the basic philosophical premise behind the book—teaching students how to be managers—and I am very grateful for their valuable input:

Jeff Belsky,
Pittsburgh Technical Institute

Jerry L. Bennett,
University of North Texas

Trini Callava,
Miami Dade College

Frederick T. Dehner,
Langara College

Louann Hofheins Cummings,
Bossier Parish Community College

Jeffrey Galbraith,
West Shore Community College

Trish Haigood,
South Arkansas Community College

Peter D. Hechler,
Massachusetts Bay Community College

Don Hill,
Aurora University

Sarah Holding,
Texas State Technical College

Mohammad Idrees,
South Piedmont Community College

Thomas O. Jones, Jr.,
Greensboro College

Thomas Kappock,
Malaspina University

George Kelley,
Citrus College

Janet Kuser Komarnicki,
Fisher College

L.F. Maxwell,
Cambridge College

Robert O'Keefe (student),
St. Cloud State University

Susan Peterson,
Scottsdale Community College

Alex Pomnichowski,
Ferris State University

Cynthia Ruszkowski,
Illinois State University

Norman L. Shlager,
Erie Community College

Judy D. Smith,
University of Central Arkansas

Robert Smolin,
Greenfield Community College

Tim Sylvester,
Glendale Community College

Kenneth R. Tillery,
Middle Tennessee State University

Neil Trotta,
Fisher College

Laura Valerius,
Seattle University

Dale Weaver,
West Virginia University

Thomas Voigt, Jr.,
Western Kentucky University

Nat B. White, Jr.,
California State University, Los Angeles

Patricia Wyatt,
Rivier College

I hope everyone who uses this text enjoys teaching from these materials as I do.

Robert N. Lussier
Springfield College

CONTACT ME WITH FEEDBACK

I wrote this book for you. Let me know what you think of it. More specifically, how can it be improved? I will respond to your feedback. If I use your suggestion for improvement, your name and college will be listed in the acknowledgments section of the next edition.

Dr. Robert Lussier
Management Department
Springfield College
Springfield, MA 01109
413-748-3202
rlussier@spfldcol.edu

About the Author

Robert N. Lussier is a professor of management at Springfield College and has taught management for more than 25 years. He has developed some innovative and widely copied methods for applying concepts and developing skills that can be used in one's personal and professional life. He was the director of Israel Programs and taught there. Other international experiences include Namibia and South Africa.

Dr. Lussier is a prolific writer, with over 250 publications to his credit. His articles have been published in the *Academy of Entrepreneurship Journal, Business Horizons, Business Journal, Entrepreneurial Executive, Entrepreneurship Theory and Practice, Journal of Business & Entrepreneurship, Journal of Business Strategies, Journal of Management Education, Journal of Small Business Management, Journal of Small Business Strategy, SAM Advanced Management Journal,* and others.

When not writing, he consults to a wide array of commercial and nonprofit organizations. In fact, some of the material in the book was developed for such clients as Baystate Medical Center, Coca-Cola, Friendly Ice Cream, Institute of Financial Education, Mead, Monsanto, Smith & Wesson, the Social Security Administration, the Visiting Nurses Association, and YMCAs.

Dr. Lussier holds a bachelor of science in business administration from Salem State College, two master's degrees in business and education from Suffolk University, and a doctorate in management from the University of New Haven.

Learning Outcomes

After studying this chapter, you should be able to:

1. Describe a manager's responsibility. **PAGE 6**

2. List and explain the three management skills. **PAGE 9**

3. List and explain the four management functions. **PAGE 11**

4. Identify the three management role categories. **PAGE 13**

1: Managing

5. List the hierarchy of management levels. **PAGE 15**

6. Describe the three different types of managers. **PAGE 16**

7. Describe the differences among management levels in terms of skills needed and functions performed. **PAGE 18**

8. Define the following **key terms:**

manager
manager's resources
performance
management skills
technical skills
human and communication skills
conceptual and decision-making
   skills
management functions

planning
organizing
leading
controlling
management role categories
levels of management
types of managers
knowledge management

Ideas on Management

at Gap

Husband-and-wife team Donald and Doris Fisher started the Gap in 1969, when they opened a store on Ocean Avenue in San Francisco, California, to sell jeans, records, and tapes. Less than a decade later, in 1976, the Gap went public. Don Fisher remained chairman of the board until May 2004, but Millard Drexler, hired in the early 1980s and later named president, then CEO, ushered in a new wave of growth by buying Banana Republic, going international, and launching Gap's retail empire with GapKids. Drexler retired after 19 years and was succeeded as CEO by Paul Pressler in 2002.

Today Gap Inc. is a leading international specialty retailer offering casual clothing, accessories, and personal care products for men, women, children, and babies under three brand names: Gap (which includes Gap, GapKids, babyGap, GapBody, and Gap Outlet), Banana Republic, and Old Navy. Gap Inc. has more than 4,200 stores located in the United States, the United Kingdom, Canada, France, Japan, and Germany, and it employs 165,000 people.

© Daniel Acker/Bloomberg News/Landov

Gap Inc. has a customer-driven culture and reputation. In other words, all Gap employees view focusing on the customer as the most important part of their jobs. Evidence of this dedication is Gap's policy of greeting each customer at the door to make him or her feel welcome and to determine how the staff can help. All store managers work the floor and are evaluated and promoted according to how well they deal with customers. Gap has a promotion policy that enables talented, hard-working managers to move ahead, but the competition for advancement is no cakewalk. Those who are willing to relocate can climb the corporate ladder more rapidly.

I O M

1. **What resources does Gap use to sell its merchandise?**
2. **What management functions are performed at Gap stores?**
3. **What levels and types of managers have careers at Gap?**
4. **How does Gap meet new workplace issues and challenges?**

You'll find answers to these questions about management at Gap throughout the chapter, and you will also learn about Gap manager Bonnie Castonguary and her experiences in managing several stores for this casual-look retailer.

To learn more about Gap businesses, visit the company's corporate Web site at *http://www.gapinc.com,* or log on to InfoTrac® College Edition at *http://infotrac.thomsonlearning.com,* where you can locate articles on all aspects of Gap businesses. It's worth taking a glance at InfoTrac now, if you haven't done so already, just to get a sense of what you'll find on the site and how its search functions work. To get started, take a look at the recent profile of Millard Drexler from *WWD,* which brilliantly captures his genius in taking the Gap forward from a single store. Use the advanced search option to key in record number A111196907, and you're off.

Source: Information for the case was taken from Gap's Web site at *http://www.gapinc.com,* accessed February 19, 2004.

3

WHY STUDY MANAGEMENT?

It's natural at this point to be thinking "What can I get from this book?" or "What's in it for me?" These common questions are seldom asked or answered directly. The short answer is that the better you can work with people—and this is what most of this book is about—the more successful you will be in both your personal and your professional lives.[1] Obviously, the study of management applies directly to your professional life. If you are a manager, or want to be a manager someday, the need for good management skills is self-evident. Even if you are not interested in being a manager, you still need management skills to succeed in today's workplace. The old workplace, in which managers simply told employees what to do, is gone. Very likely, you will be expected to become a partner in managing your organization through participative management.[2] You may work in a team and share in decision making and other management tasks.[3] Employers want to hire employees who can participate in managing the firm,[4] and they are training nonmanagers to perform management functions.[5]

The study of management also applies directly to your personal life. You communicate with and interact with people every day; you make personal plans and decisions, set goals, prioritize what you will do, and get others to do things for you. Are you ever in conflict with family and friends, and do you ever feel stressed? This book can help you develop management skills that you can apply in all of those areas. In this chapter, you will learn what management is all about, and we will begin the discussion of how you can develop your management skills.

WHAT IS A MANAGER'S RESPONSIBILITY?

This interview with Bonnie Castonguary, a store manager for Gap, provides an overview of the manager's job and responsibility.

Q: When did you start with the Gap, and what was your progression to your present job as store manager?

A: I started in November of 1990 as a store manager in training. In September of 1991 I replaced a woman on maternity leave as acting store manager. In January of 1992 I had my first store. In August of 1993 and October of 1994, I was promoted to larger stores with more sales volume. In 1997, I was promoted to manager of [a] Gap outlet store. . . . My next career advancement is to general manager . . . I would still be in one store, but I would assist the district manager by overseeing other stores in my district.

Q: Briefly describe your job.

A: The Gap's two-page "Position Overview Store Management" form, which also contains a detailed summary for each level of management, presents this general summary: "The Store Management team manages the sales, operations, and personnel functions of the store to ensure maximum profitability and compliance with company procedures. The Team includes Assistant Managers, Associate Managers, the Store Manager, and/or the General Manager." [See Exhibit 1-1 for Castonguary's description of a typical Monday.]

Exhibit 1-1 *A Day in the Life of a Manager*

8:00 A.M.
- Enter the store and walk the sales floor to ensure a proper closing took place the night before.
- Project the payroll cost for the week as a percentage of my forecasted sales, and call it in.
- Perform opening procedures on the controller (computer that records sales transactions and inventory count for all cash registers in the store).

8:30 A.M.
- Walk the sales floor with staff and assign projects for them to create new displays for merchandise during the day (create a "to do" list for employees and myself).

9:00 A.M.
- Before the store opens, call voice mail for messages left by other store managers or my boss, the district manager.
- Make business telephone calls for the day.

9:30 A.M.
- Assign sales associates to store zones.
- Put money in computer cash register drawers.

10:00 A.M.
- Open the store.
- Make sure sales associates are in their zones on the floor for proper floor coverage.
- Make sure everyone who enters the store is greeted and has his or her needs determined.
- Provide floor coverage. (Help out as needed—greet customers, assist customers with sales, stock shelves, assist at the changing room, etc.)

12:00 P.M.
- Do business analysis for previous month from operating statement and gross margin reports.

12:30 P.M.
- Provide floor coverage as needed for staggered employee breaks.

1:30–2:30 P.M. My break, then:
- Prepare customer request transfers (merchandise our store has but other stores do not have) to be delivered. Enter transfers into computer and get merchandise.

3:00 P.M.
- Leave for district meeting.

3:15 P.M.
- Drop off transfers and pick up another store manager; continue on to district meeting.

4:00 P.M.
- Meeting is conducted by district manager with the seven general and store managers. Meeting begins with discussion of the following topics:
  Previous week's sales, previous week's payroll, payroll projections for next month (cost as a percentage of sales), cleanliness, and standards of the stores.
  New information items, mail, general discussion, questions, etc.
- Meeting ends with a walk-through of the store at which the meeting is held. During a walk-through, the host store manager discusses new display ideas that the other store managers may want to use. In addition, the other store managers give the host manager ideas for improving the store visually. In other words, this is a time to share ideas that will help all team members in the Gap district.

6:00 P.M.
- Call my store to see how sales are going for the day, then leave for home.

Q: What do you like best about being a manager?

A: You don't have time to get bored on the job because you are always doing something different.

Q: What do you like least about being a manager?

A: Dealing with difficult performance problems of employees and customers, and always being on call. When I'm not at work, I'm still on call when there are problems at the store. This could mean going to the store at 2:00 A.M. to shut off the alarm.

Q: What advice would you give to college graduates without any full-time work experience who are interested in a management career after graduation?

A: You need to be dedicated and hardworking. You must take great pride in your work. You have to be willing to take on a lot of responsibility. Remember, your employees are always looking to you to set the example; when you make a mistake (which you will do), it affects your staff. You have to be a self-starter. As a store manager you have to motivate employees, but your boss is not around much to motivate you.

Learning Outcome 1
Describe a manager's responsibility.

A **manager** *is responsible for achieving organizational objectives through efficient and effective utilization of resources. Efficient* means doing things right so as to maximize the utilization of resources. *Effective* means doing the right thing in order to attain an objective; a manager's effectiveness reflects the degree to which he or she achieves objectives. *The* **manager's resources** *are human, financial, physical, and informational.*

HUMAN RESOURCES

Human resources are people. Managers are responsible for getting the job done through employees. People are the manager's most valuable resource.[6] Throughout this book, we will focus on how managers work with employees to accomplish organizational objectives.

FINANCIAL RESOURCES

Most managers have a budget stating how much it should cost to operate their department/store for a set period of time. In other words, a budget defines the financial resources available.

PHYSICAL RESOURCES

Getting the job done requires effective and efficient use of physical resources. Managers are responsible for keeping equipment in working condition and for making sure that necessary materials and supplies are available. Deadlines might be missed and present sales and future business lost if physical resources are not available and used and maintained properly.

INFORMATIONAL RESOURCES

Managers need information technology.[7] Information continues to increase in importance as a means of increasing the speed of doing business in a competitive global environment.[8]

WorkApplication1

Describe the specific resources used by a present or past boss. Give the manager's job title and department.

_____

_____

_____

_____

_____

The level of organizational **performance** *is based on how effectively and efficiently managers utilize resources to achieve objectives.* Managers are responsible for and evaluated on how well they meet organizational objectives through effective and efficient utilization of resources.

Successful managers are committed to improving performance.[9] Selecting the right resources—being effective—and using them efficiently results in high levels of performance.[10] Without capable management, resources will remain underutilized and never become productive.[11] The trend today is to set ambitious objectives and to achieve them with fewer resources.[12]

The Gap has 165,000 human resources to help in the sale of its merchandise. In order to acquire financial resources to expand, the Gap sold stock and took out loans. Castonguary has a budget for her store, as do managers at all Gap stores, and she is responsible for sales revenues gained when customers use cash and credit cards. Physical resources of the Gap include more than 4,200 stores, and each store has fixtures to display its merchandise. The Gap's major information system is its controller (a computer system), which stores information from all Gap stores that can be retrieved by Gap managers. When Castonguary was checking her voice mail and e-mail, making calls, giving employees directions on setting up displays, attending the district meeting, and participating in the store walk-through, she was using informational resources. The Gap's growth from one store to more than 4,200 represents a high level of performance.

I
O
M

WHAT DOES IT TAKE TO BE A SUCCESSFUL MANAGER?

Now that you have an idea of what management is, let's focus on some of the qualities and skills necessary to be a successful manager.

Management Qualities

Over the years, numerous researchers have attempted to answer the question "What does it take to be a successful manager?" In a *Wall Street Journal* Gallup survey, 782 top executives in 282 large corporations were asked,

WorkApplication2
Identify a specific manager, preferably one who is or was your boss, and explain what makes him or her successful or unsuccessful. Give examples.

Self-Assessment

Management Traits

The following 15 questions relate to some of the qualities needed to be a successful manager. Rate yourself on each item by indicating with a number (1–4) how well each statement describes you.

4___ The statement does not describe me at all.

3___ The statement somewhat describes me.

2___ The statement describes me most of the time.

1___ The statement describes me very accurately.

(Continued)

Self-Assessment

Management Traits   (Continued)

_____ 1. I enjoy working with people. I prefer to work with others rather than working alone.

_____ 2. I can motivate others. I can get people to do things they may not want to do.

_____ 3. I am well liked. People enjoy working with me.

_____ 4. I am cooperative. I strive to help the team do well, rather than to be the star.

_____ 5. I am a leader. I enjoy teaching, coaching, and instructing people.

_____ 6. I want to be successful. I do things to the best of my ability to be successful.

_____ 7. I am a self-starter. I get things done without having to be told to do them.

_____ 8. I am a problem-solver. If things aren't going the way I want them to, I take corrective action to meet my objectives.

_____ 9. I am self-reliant. I don't need the help of others.

_____10. I am hardworking. I enjoy working and getting the job done.

_____11. I am trustworthy. If I say I will do something by a set time, I do it.

_____12. I am loyal. I do not do or say things to intentionally hurt my friends, relatives, or coworkers.

_____13. I can take criticism. If people tell me negative things about myself, I give them serious thought and change when appropriate.

_____14. I am honest. I do not lie, steal, or cheat.

_____15. I am fair. I treat people equally. I don't take advantage of others.

_____ Total score (add numbers on lines 1–15; the range of possible scores is 15–60)

In general, the lower your score, the better your chances of being a successful manager. You can work on improving your integrity (items 11–15), industriousness (items 6–10), and ability to get along with people (items 1–5) both in this course and in your personal life. As a start, review the traits listed here. Which ones are your strongest and weakest ones? Think about how you can improve in the weaker areas, or even better, write out a plan.

"What are the most important traits for success as a supervisor?"[13] Before you read what these executives replied, complete the Self-Assessment on management traits above to find out if you have what it takes to become a successful manager.

The executives in the Gallup survey identified integrity, industriousness, and the ability to get along with people as the three most important traits for successful managers. Other necessary traits included business knowledge, intelligence, leadership ability, education, sound judgment, ability to communicate, flexibility, and ability to plan and set objectives.

—————— Learning Outcome 2 ——————
List and explain the three management skills.

Management Skills

All employees today need good management skills.[14] Because management skills are so important, the focus of this book is on skill building. If you work at it, you can develop your management skills through this course.[15]

For our purposes, **management skills** *include (1) technical, (2) human and communication, and (3) conceptual and decision-making skills.* You should work to develop these three kinds of skills to be an effective administrator.[16]

TECHNICAL SKILLS

Technical skills *involve the ability to use methods and techniques to perform a task.* When managers are working on budgets, for example, they may need computer skills in order to use spreadsheet software such as Lotus 1-2-3 or Excel. Most employees are promoted to their first management position primarily because of their technical skills.[17] Technical skills vary widely from job to job;[18] therefore, this course does not focus on developing these skills.

HUMAN AND COMMUNICATION SKILLS

Human and communication skills *reflect the ability to work with people in teams.* You need a balance of technical and human skills.[19] Without communication skills, you cannot be an effective team member or manager.[20] Bill Gates, cofounder of Microsoft, advises students to learn to work with people.[21] How well you get along with employees will affect your management success.[22] Throughout this book, you will learn how to work with a diversity of people, improve communication skills, motivate and lead others, manage teams, develop power and political skills, manage conflict, and improve employee performance.

CONCEPTUAL AND DECISION-MAKING SKILLS

Conceptual and decision-making skills *center around the ability to understand abstract ideas and select alternatives to solve problems.* Another term for conceptual skills is *systems thinking,* or the ability to understand an organization/department as a whole while also being aware of the interrelationships among its parts.[23] As businesses compete in a continually diversifying global Internet environment, creative analysis, or *critical thinking,* is vital to resolving conflict and solving problems.[24] Throughout this book, you will learn how to develop your conceptual and decision-making skills. Review the management skills in Exhibit 1-2; then complete Applying the Concept 1.

Joe Torre is the manager of the **New York Yankees** baseball team. Although the success of the Yankees is based on multiple factors, Torre's management skills clearly play an important part in the team's success. Torre has the technical skills necessary to win ball games, and he helps his players develop their technical skills to their full potential. He also has the

Exhibit 1-2
Management Skills

Management Skills

Identify each ability as being one of the following types of management skills:

a. technical

b. human and communication

c. conceptual and decision-making

_____ 1. The ability to see things as a whole and as the interrelationship of their parts.

_____ 2. The ability to motivate employees to do a good job.

_____ 3. The ability to perform departmental jobs such as data entry in a computer.

_____ 4. The ability to determine what's going wrong and correct it.

_____ 5. The ability to write memos and letters.

WorkApplication3

Select a manager, preferably one who is or was your boss, and state the specific management skills he or she uses on the job.

_____

_____

_____

_____

conceptual skills to understand how each player's performance affects the team's performance, and he has made good decisions about which players to sign. However, his human and communication skills are what set him apart from other coaches. Torre puts his players first. He knows his players as individuals and treats each of them with fairness, respect, and trust—which he calls the three elements of productive work relationships. Torre does not give a lot of motivational team speeches, and he does not use fear, manipulation, or public humiliation to motivate and control his players. He relies more on one-to-one communication. He watches, listens, and tries to understand the players and work with them individually to solve any problems.[25]

Supervisory Ability

Professor Edwin Ghiselli conducted a study to determine the traits that contribute to success as a manager.[26] Ghiselli identified six traits as important, although not all are necessary for success. These six traits, in reverse order of importance, include (6) initiative, (5) self-assurance, (4) decisiveness, (3) intelligence, (2) need for occupational achievement, and (1) supervisory ability. The number-one trait, supervisory ability, includes skills in planning, organizing, leading, and controlling. These four areas of supervisory ability are more commonly referred to as the *management functions*, which you will learn about in the next section.

WHAT DO MANAGERS DO?

Having discussed what a manager is responsible for and what it takes to be a successful manager, our next question is "What do managers do?" In this section, you will learn about the four functions performed by managers and the three roles that all managers play.

Management Functions

A manager plans, organizes, leads, and controls resources to achieve organizational objectives through others.[27] If managers run a machine, wait on customers, or put up a store display, they are performing nonmanagement or employee functions. *The four* **management functions** *include the following:*

- *Planning*
- *Organizing*
- *Leading*
- *Controlling*

PLANNING

Planning is typically the starting point in the management process.[28] To be successful, organizations need a great deal of planning.[29] People in organizations need goals and the plans to achieve them.[30] **Planning** *is the process of setting objectives and determining in advance exactly how the objectives will be met.* The ability to perform the planning function requires conceptual and decision-making management skills.

ORGANIZING

To be successful requires organization.[31] A manager must design and develop an organizational system to implement the plans.[32] **Organizing** *is the process of delegating and coordinating tasks and allocating resources to achieve objectives.* An important part of coordinating human resources is to assign people to various jobs and tasks.[33] An important part of organizing, sometimes listed as a separate function, is staffing. *Staffing* is the process of selecting, training, and evaluating employees. The ability to organize involves a blend of conceptual and decision-making skills and human and communication skills.

LEADING

A manager must lead employees as they perform their daily tasks.[34] **Leading** *is the process of influencing employees to work toward achieving objectives.* Managers must communicate the objectives to employees and motivate them to achieve those objectives.[35]

CONTROLLING

Not all employees do the things they say they will do. Therefore, objectives will not be met without follow-through.[36] **Controlling** *is the process of establishing and implementing mechanisms to ensure that objectives are achieved.* An important part of controlling is measuring progress toward the achievement of an objective and taking corrective action when necessary.[37] The ability to control is based on conceptual and decision-making and human and communication skills.

Growing the Gap from one store to over 4,200 took lots of planning. Bonnie Castonguary has to plan displays and schedule employees. The entire Gap chain has an organizational structure based on territory, and each Gap store has its own organization. Castonguary has full responsibility for selecting, training, and evaluating

WorkApplication4
Identify a specific manager, preferably one who is or was your boss, and give examples of how that person performs each of the four management functions.

her store's employees. **The Gap would not have had such great success without effectively leading employees by motivating them. Controlling is also important at the Gap. Not all stores have been successful, and some have been closed after not making the target profit level. Castonguary is consistently taking corrective action with inventory to make sure her store has the right products available in the right quantities.**

Nonmanagement Functions

All managers perform the four functions of management as they get work done through employees. However, many managers perform nonmanagement, or employee, functions as well. For example, Bonnie Castonguary spent from 10:00 to 12:00 and 12:30 to 1:30 primarily waiting on customers, which is a nonmanagement function. Many managers are called *working managers* because they perform both management and employee functions.

The Systems Relationship among the Management Functions

The management functions are not steps in a linear process. Managers do not usually plan, then organize, then lead, and then control.[38] The functions are distinct yet interrelated.[39] Managers often perform them simultaneously. In addition, each function depends on the others.[40] For example, if you start with a poor plan, the objective will not be met even if things are well organized, led, and controlled. Or, if you start with a great plan but are poorly organized or lead poorly, the objective may not be met. Plans without controls are rarely implemented effectively. Exhibit 1-3 illustrates the interrelationship of management skills and functions. Remember that the management functions are based on setting objectives (planning) and achieving them (through organizing, leading, and controlling).

ApplyingTheConcept 2

Management Functions

Indicate which type of function the manager is performing in each situation.

a. planning   d. controlling

b. organizing   e. nonmanagement

c. leading

_____ 6. The manager is showing an employee how to set up a machine for production.

_____ 7. The manager is determining how many units were produced during the first half of the shift.

_____ 8. An employee has been absent several times. The manager is discussing the situation and trying to get the employee to improve attendance.

_____ 9. The manager is conducting a job interview to fill the position of a retiring employee.

_____10. The manager is fixing a broken machine.

Exhibit 1-3 *Management Skills and Functions*

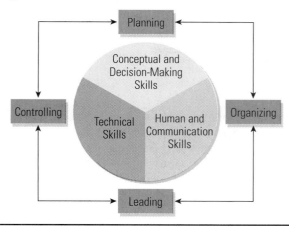

Learning Outcome 4
Identify the three management role categories.

Management Roles

Managers have a set of distinct roles.[41] A *role* is a set of expectations of how one will behave in a given situation. Henry Mintzberg identified ten roles that managers embody as they accomplish management functions. Studies have supported Mintzberg's management role theory.[42] Mintzberg grouped these roles into three **management role categories**:[43]

- *Interpersonal roles*
- *Informational roles*
- *Decisional roles*

INTERPERSONAL ROLES

Interpersonal roles include figurehead, leader, and liaison. When managers play interpersonal roles, they use their human and communication skills as they perform management functions. Managers play the figurehead role when they represent the organization or department in ceremonial and symbolic activities. The manager of the Gap store where Bonnie Castonguary attended the district meeting played the figurehead role when she greeted visitors and gave them a tour of the store. Managers play the leader role when they motivate, train, communicate with, and influence others. Throughout the day, Castonguary performed the leader role as she directed employees to maintain floor coverage. Managers play the liaison role when they interact with people outside of their unit to gain information and favors. Castonguary was a liaison at the district meeting, which included the store walk-through.

INFORMATIONAL ROLES

Informational roles include monitor, disseminator, and spokesperson. When managers play informational roles, they use their human and communication skills. Managers play the monitor role when they read and talk to others to receive information. Bonnie Castonguary was continually monitoring the store

WorkApplication5
Identify a specific manager, preferably one who is or was your boss, and give examples of how that person performs roles in each of the three management role categories. Be sure to identify at least one of the three or four roles in each category.

to ensure full floor coverage. Managers play the disseminator role when they send information to others. Castonguary played the disseminator role when she was at the district meeting. Managers play the spokesperson role when they provide information to people outside the organization. Castonguary played the spokesperson role when she made business calls in the morning and gave the interview to the author of this book.

DECISIONAL ROLES

Decisional roles include entrepreneur, disturbance handler, resource allocator, and negotiator. When managers play decisional roles, they use their conceptual and decision-making management skills. Managers play the entrepreneur role when they innovate and initiate improvements. Bonnie Castonguary played this role when she had the staff set up new displays to help improve store sales. Managers play the disturbance-handler role when they take corrective action during disputes or crisis situations. Castonguary had to deal with a customer who was not satisfied that an employee would not give a cash refund for

---

Applying The Concept 3

Management Roles

Identify each of the managerial activities as part of one of the three role categories:

a. interpersonal role

b. informational role

c. decisional role

_____ 11. The manager discusses the new union contract with union representatives.

_____ 12. The manager shows an employee how to fill out a form.

_____ 13. The manager reads the *Wall Street Journal* while having coffee first thing in the morning.

_____ 14. The manager develops new total quality management (TQM) techniques.

_____ 15. The sales manager discusses a complaint with a customer.

Exhibit 1-4 *Ten Roles Managers Play*
Managers play various roles as necessary while performing their management functions so as to achieve organizational objectives.

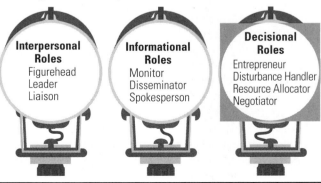

Interpersonal Roles	Informational Roles	Decisional Roles
Figurehead	Monitor	Entrepreneur
Leader	Disseminator	Disturbance Handler
Liaison	Spokesperson	Resource Allocator
		Negotiator

merchandise returned. Managers play the resource-allocator role when they schedule, request authorization, and perform budgeting and programming activities, as when Castonguary allocated sales associates to zones on the floor. Managers perform the negotiator role when they represent their department or organization during nonroutine transactions to gain agreement and commitment. Castonguary played the negotiator role when she made business calls to outside contractors.

Exhibit 1-4 illustrates the three categories of management roles.

Learning Outcome 5
List the hierarchy of management levels.

DIFFERENCES AMONG MANAGERS

There are many differences in levels of management, types of managers, management skills needed, management functions performed, roles played, and the functions of managers in large businesses versus small businesses and for-profit versus not-for-profit businesses.

The Three Levels of Management

The three **levels of management** *are top managers, middle managers, and first-line managers*; these are also called strategic, tactical, and operational. The three levels relate to each other as described here. See Exhibit 1-5 for an illustration of the three levels of management and operative employees.

TOP MANAGERS

Top managers—people in executive positions—have titles such as chief executive officer (CEO), president, or vice president. Most organizations have relatively

Exhibit 1-5 *Management Levels and Functional Areas*

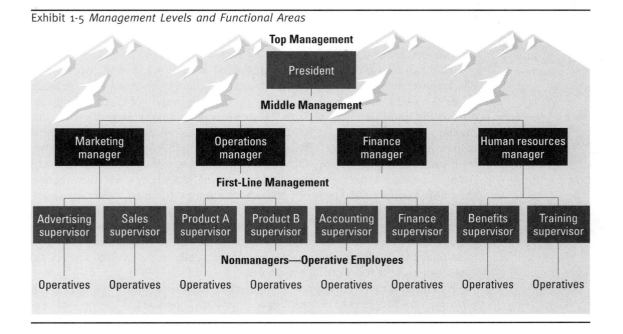

WorkApplication6

Identify the three levels of management in a specific organization by level and title. Be sure to give the organization's name.

_____

_____

_____

_____

few top management positions. Top managers are responsible for managing an entire organization or major parts of it. They develop and define the organization's purpose, objectives, strategies, and long-term plans.[44] They report to other executives or boards of directors and supervise the activities of middle managers.

MIDDLE MANAGERS

People in middle management positions have titles such as sales manager, branch manager, or department head. Middle managers are responsible for implementing top management's strategy by developing short-term operating plans. They generally report to executives and supervise the work of first-line managers.

FIRST-LINE MANAGERS

Examples of titles of first-line managers are crew leader, supervisor, head nurse, and office manager. These managers are responsible for implementing middle managers' operational plans. They generally report to middle managers. Unlike those at the other two levels of management, first-line managers do not supervise other managers; they supervise operative employees.

NONMANAGEMENT OPERATIVE EMPLOYEES

Operative employees are the workers in an organization who do not hold management positions. They report to first-line managers. They make the products, wait on customers, perform repairs, and so on.

— Learning Outcome 6 —
Describe the three different types of managers.

Types of Managers

WorkApplication7

Identify which type of boss you have now or have had previously. If that person is or was a functional manager, be sure to specify the functional tasks of the department.

_____

_____

_____

_____

The three types of managers are general managers, functional managers, and project managers. Top-level and some middle managers are _general managers_ because they supervise the activities of several departments that perform different activities. Middle and first-line managers are often _functional managers_ who supervise the completion of related tasks.

The four most common functional areas include marketing, operations/production, finance/accounting, and human resources/personnel management, as shown in Exhibit 1-5. A marketing manager is responsible for selling and advertising products and services. A production manager is responsible for making a product such as a Ford Mustang, whereas an operations manager is responsible for providing a service such as a loan by Bank America. (However, both product and service organizations now use the broader term _operations_.) An accounting manager is responsible for keeping records of sales and expenses (accounts receivable and payable) and determining profitability, whereas a financial manager is responsible for obtaining the necessary funds and investments. The term _finance_ is commonly used to mean both accounting and financial activities. A human resources manager (known in the past as a _personnel manager_) is responsible for forecasting future employee needs and recruiting, selecting, evaluating, and compensating employees.

A _project manager_ coordinates employees and other resources across several functional departments to accomplish a specific task, such as to develop and produce a new breakfast cereal for Kellogg's or a new aircraft at Boeing.

Join the Discussion   Ethics & Social Responsibility

Executive Compensation

1. Do top executives deserve to make 200 times as much as the average worker?
2. Is it ethical for managers to take large pay increases while laying off employees?
3. Are companies being socially responsible when paying executives premium compensation?

Executive management skill has a direct impact on the success of a firm. Top executives should be paid well; after all, if it weren't for effective CEOs, many companies would not be making the millions of dollars in profits they make each year. Top executives deserve a piece of the pie they help create. *Business Week*'s 2000 compensation survey reported that the average yearly total compensation for CEOs of the 362 largest U.S. public companies was $12.4 million.

Executive compensation is based on multiple factors. Valuable managerial skills seem to be the most important factor in how much executives make. Firm size and performance also affect compensation, as does the power of the executive to influence pay. Managers' compensation can also be negatively affected by company performance: Consider the CEO of **Tyco**, who faced a 12 percent decrease in total compensation, based on stock value, when the value of the company stock fell 71 percent in 2002—yet he still made $82 million that year, and was the second highest-paid executive in the United States.

Top executives have been criticized for getting richer as employees get poorer. For example, when **American Airlines** was about to go bankrupt, top executives negotiated special pension protection worth $41 million for themselves while pilots, mechanics, and flight attendants were asked to agree to take pay and benefits cuts averaging around 23 percent. In 1989, CEOs of U.S. companies were paid 56 times as much as the average worker; in 2002, they were paid 200 times as much. How much did your pay, and that of your family members, increase during those 10 years?

Sources: S. A. Zahra, "*The Practice of Management*: Reflections on Peter F. Drucker's Landmark Book," *Academy of Management Executive* (2003), Vol. 17, No. 3, pp. 16–23; J. G. Combs and M. S. Skill, "Managerialist and Human Capital Explanations for Key Executive Pay Premiums: A Contingency Perspective," *Academy of Management Journal* (2003), Vol. 46, No. 1, pp. 63–73; A. Gupta, "The Death of Shame," *Mid-American Journal of Business* (2003), Vol. 18, No. 3.

The Gap has all three levels of managers. The CEO and VPs are top-level managers, the regional and store managers are middle managers, and the assistant store managers are first-line managers. Gap's CEO is a general manager, and the company has managers for each of the functional areas, as well as purchasing and promotions/advertising, which are important functions for the Gap. Gap also uses project managers when opening new stores and developing new product lines, such as GapBody and Old Navy Maternity. As a store manager, Bonnie Castonguary is a middle manager supervising assistant store managers, but she is also a first-line manager, as she supervises operative employees. Castonguary is a general manager, as she is responsible for all activities in her store. However, she is personally involved in all the functional areas, with strong support from headquarters.

Describe the differences among management levels in terms of skills needed and functions performed.

Differences in Management Skills

All managers need technical, human and communication, and conceptual and decision-making skills. However, the relative importance of these types of skills varies with the level of management.[45] At all three levels of management, the need for human and communication skills remains fairly constant. However, top-level managers have a greater need for conceptual and decision-making skills, whereas first-line managers have a greater need for technical skills. Middle managers tend to need all three skills, but the mix required differs somewhat from organization to organization.

Differences in Management Functions

All managers perform the four management functions: planning, organizing, leading, and controlling. However, the time spent on each function varies with the level of management. First-line managers spend more time leading and controlling, middle-level managers spend equal time on all four functions, and top managers spend more time planning and organizing.

Exhibit 1-6 summarizes the primary skills needed and functions performed at each of the three management levels.

Large-Business versus Small-Business Managers

Bonnie Castonguary works for a large organization—Gap Inc. Her independent store resembles a small business, but it has the support of a large organization. Exhibit 1-7 lists some of the differences between large and small businesses. However, these are general statements; many large and small businesses share certain characteristics. Most large businesses, including Gap Inc., started as small businesses.

Managers of For-Profit versus Not-for-Profit Organizations

Is the manager's job the same in for-profit and not-for-profit organizations? Although some noteworthy differences exist, the answer is basically yes. All managers need management skills, perform management functions, and play

Exhibit 1-6 *Skills Needed and Functions Performed at Different Management Levels*

Management Level	Primary Management Skills Needed	Primary Management Functions Performed
Top	Conceptual and Human Skills	Planning and Organizing
Middle	Balance of all three	Balance of all four
First-Line	Technical and Human Skills	Leading and Controlling

Exhibit 1-7 *Differences between Large and Small Businesses*

Functions and Roles	Large Business	Small Business
Planning	Commonly have formal written objectives and plans with a global business focus.	Commonly have informal objectives and plans that are not written with a global focus.
Organizing	Tend to have formal organization structures with clear policies and procedures, with three levels of management. Jobs tend to be specialized.	Tend to have informal structures without clear policies and procedures, with fewer than three levels of management. Jobs tend to be more general.
Leading	Managers tend to be more participative, giving employees more say in how they do their work and allowing them to make more decisions.	Entrepreneurs tend to be more autocratic and want things done their ways, often wanting to make the decisions.
Controlling	Tend to have more sophisticated computerized control systems.	Tend to use less sophisticated control systems and to rely more on direct observation.
Important management roles	Resource allocator.	Entrepeneur and spokesperson.

management roles regardless of the organization type. Bonnie Castonguary works for a for-profit business. Government employees work for the public (not-for-profit) sector.

Two primary areas of difference between for-profit and not-for-profit organizations relate to measuring performance and staffing. The primary measure of performance in for-profit organizations is bottom-line profit. Not-for-profit organizations have no universal measure of performance. The United Way, Boy Scouts and Girl Scouts, a library, and a state's department of motor vehicles have different performance measurements. In addition, for-profit organizations pay all workers. In many not-for-profit organizations, some of the workers are unpaid volunteers.

Applying The Concept 4

Differences among Management Levels

Identify the level of management in the following five instances:

a. top

b. middle

c. first-line

_____ 16. Supervises the operative employees.

_____ 17. Has greater need for conceptual skills than for technical skills.

_____ 18. Spends more time leading and controlling.

_____ 19. Reports to an executive.

_____ 20. Needs a balance of management skills and performs all of the management functions.

Throughout this text, you will read about and practice management skills that are universally valuable to all organizations.

NEW WORKPLACE ISSUES AND CHALLENGES

In the appendix to this chapter, you can learn about the history of management. However, the modern workplace is quite different from those studied by early management scientists. We now discuss the issues and challenges facing today's managers in "the new workplace." Contemporary concepts and terms are briefly introduced here and are discussed in detail throughout the book.

Technology and Speed

Technology, especially computers and the Internet, has changed the way we conduct business and the speed at which we transact it. Computer pioneers don't agree on who started the Internet, but an early prototype was created in the late 1960s by the Defense Advanced Research Projects Agency (DARPA), an agency of the U.S. Department of Defense. Scientists at DARPA are working to improve the Internet so that 100 million U.S. homes will be able to access it at 100 megabytes a second, which is more than 100 times faster than current high-speed connections.[46] More than half of professionals responding to a 2003 survey said their productivity decreases when they are away from their computer and cannot access e-mail.[47] Laptop computers, cell phone features, and other Internet connection devices help today's managers maintain their productivity.

E-business is work done by using electronic linkages (including the Internet) between employees, partners, suppliers, and customers. Much e-business is done within an organization between employees using an *intranet*. *E-commerce* is more narrowly defined as business exchanges or transactions that occur electronically. Exhibit 1-8 illustrates business-to-business (B2B),

Exhibit 1-8 *E-Commerce*

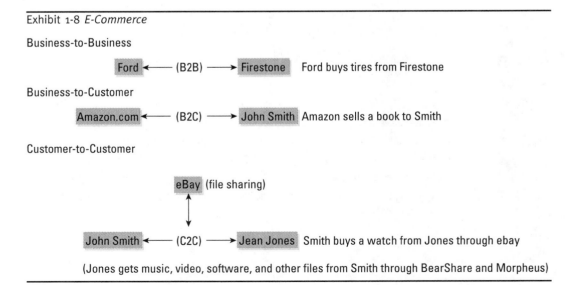

Business-to-Business

Ford ←— (B2B) —→ Firestone   Ford buys tires from Firestone

Business-to-Customer

Amazon.com ←— (B2C) —→ John Smith   Amazon sells a book to Smith

Customer-to-Customer

eBay (file sharing)

John Smith ←— (C2C) —→ Jean Jones   Smith buys a watch from Jones through ebay

(Jones gets music, video, software, and other files from Smith through BearShare and Morpheus)

business-to-customer (B2C), and customer-to-customer (C2C) transactions. Most B2B transactions are done through electronic data interchange (EDI) networks.

Globalization and Diversity

Technological advances in transportation and communication have made it easier to conduct business all over the world. E-business and e-commerce are global; in fact, in the next few years, around 80 percent of all Internet users will be outside of the United States.[48]

As businesses compete globally, they have merged to become larger. For example, many large grocery chain stores today, including Stop and Shop, are foreign-owned. If an organization is not conducting business in other countries, it is most likely competing with global companies.

Companies competing globally have to act locally.[49] People around the world are different, and while the world population continues to grow to over 6 billion people, there isn't a major country in the world where the white population is growing; it's declining globally. As global companies increase and minority populations continue to grow, diversity becomes more of a factor in business decisions.

Based on market value, **General Electric** was the largest public company in the world, for the fourth year in a row, in 2003.[50] Former CEO Jack Welch led GE through globalization for two decades, and although he did not use e-mail himself until 1999, he realized that e-business should be used to reinvent and transform GE in the 21st century, and it has.[51] GE is not only purchasing goods electronically, it is digitizing every function it can, including buying airline tickets. GE used to process more than 3 million paper invoices a year, but now most invoices and payments are done electronically. GE estimates that conducting e-business saves the company over a billion dollars a year.[52]

Wal-Mart is the third largest company in the world.[53] Wal-Mart uses its tremendous power to get the best deals globally. It invests heavily in technology to keep costs and prices low. Wal-Mart uses an EDI network to transmit sales data from stores' cash registers to its many merchandise suppliers and to automatically order shipments of products to restock stores' shelves. Wal-Mart also sells products through its online store at *http://www.walmart.com.*

Knowledge, Learning, Quality, and Continuous Improvement

In the competitive global market, customers are demanding higher-quality products and lower prices. To survive and succeed in this environment, firms must work on continuous improvement of the products they sell and of the processes they use to run their business.[54] Knowledge is the key: Today, knowledge is considered a foundation of a business's competitive advantage.[55] Knowledge allows managers to take advantage of opportunities and to solve problems.[56]

Recall that information is one of the four management resources. Information is a foundation for knowledge.[57] Knowledge workers are critical thinkers who spend a good part of their day creating, processing, interpreting, and using information to create value.[58] To be successful, managers must be able to use knowledge to make things happen; this ability is known as *competency*.[59]

The *learning organization* gives information to all employees to develop knowledge. Such organizations use teams to share and develop knowledge, and they empower all employees to continuously improve themselves and the organization.

Knowledge Management

How do you view education and learning? If you think that once you graduate, that's the end of it, you'd better change your view. If you want to succeed in the new workplace, you need to focus on learning throughout your career.[60] But just learning isn't enough; it's important to move to the next level of knowledge through applying what you learn.[61] **Knowledge management** *involves everyone in an organization in sharing knowledge and applying it to continuously improve products and processes.*

Most students are weak at applying the concepts they learn.[62] Employers and educators say that students ought to be able to apply the principles learned in class on the job and that the gap between learning and practical application needs to be closed.[63] Management guru Russell Ackoff says that being taught is a lousy way to learn; students need to learn how to learn.[64] You need to be able to learn on your own, because in today's workplace, managers are too busy to teach you everything, and they expect you to be able to work on your own with minimal supervision.

Author John Nirenberg asks, "Why are so many well-intended students learning so much and yet able to apply so little of what they learn on the job and in their personal life?"[65] There are two major reasons. First, very few textbooks really focus on applying concepts and developing skills. Simply reading texts and listening to lectures and discussions tends to result in little ability to apply what is learned. Researchers have found that the most effective way to develop knowledge is to teach students concepts and then have them apply the concepts to develop management skills.[66] That is the approach this book uses.

Another reason many students cannot apply what they learn on the job is that they fail to take responsibility for their learning and apply it in their professional and personal lives.[67] How much time and effort do you put into applying what you learn? Research has shown that you can develop your management skills if you work at it.[68]

Change, Creativity, Innovation, and Entrepreneurship

Knowledge management requires that people *change* in order to continually improve. The speed of change in modern business has increased because of globalization and changes in technology. It has been said that change is the only constant.[69] Change is necessary for survival and success.[70] Whatever a company did to become an industry leader is never enough to keep it there.[71] Firms that don't manage knowledge well will lose customers to companies that do. For example, **IBM** lost PC software business to **Microsoft**, as the case at the end of the chapter explains in more detail.

Creativity is coming up with new ideas for improvements, and *innovation* is implementing those ideas.[72] Creative ideas that are not used are of no value to an organization. Thus, knowledge management is about generating creative ideas and using them through innovation. *Entrepreneurs* are known for being creative and innovative. It's common for an entrepreneur to start a small company (**Cape Cod Potato Chips** or **Smart Food Popcorn**), and later to be bought out by a large company (**Frito-Lay**). Large companies recognize the need to be entrepreneurial, and they even use the term *corporate entrepreneurship*.[73] An executive at the global company **GlaxoSmithKline** put it this way, "We need to be big and small at the same time."[74]

Participative Management, Empowerment, and Teams

As noted in the beginning of this chapter, successful companies are using participative management, as they empower employees to share in performing management functions by working in teams.[75] Learning organizations manage knowledge well by empowering these teams to be creative and innovative.

Ethics and Social Responsibility

Ethics and social responsibility are topics that are not new to management textbooks. However, with the recent criminal and unethical behavior at **WorldCom, Enron, Global Crossing, Tyco, Waste Management, Arthur Andersen, Credit Suisse First Boston**, and other large firms, business ethics has been a hot topic in the media.[76] As a result, more than half (54 percent) of Americans have low or very low confidence in the honesty and integrity of CEOs and CFOs (chief financial officers); astonishingly, only 8 percent hold top business leaders in high regard. As a result, business school deans are considering a greater emphasis on ethics in the curriculum.[77] Each chapter in this book includes a number of Join the Discussion features on ethics and social responsibility, such as the one below.

Join the Discussion Ethics & Social Responsibility

Virtual Internships

1. What are the benefits of virtual internships to employers and to interns?
2. Should a student be given college credit for a virtual internship, or should he or she receive only pay without credit—a part-time job?
3. Is it ethical and socially responsible to use interns instead of regular employees?
4. Will the use of virtual interns become the norm, or will the practice fade?

You are familiar with the traditional internship model, in which a student works at an organization to gain experience and perhaps a full-time job after graduation. With today's Internet technology, more and more companies are hiring virtual interns, who work from their college computers. Virtual interns do a variety of tasks, including secretarial work, software and Web site development, and information technology (IT) projects. Most virtual interns never even set foot inside the organization's facilities.

Nataly Kogan, 27, and Avi Spivack, 25, co-founded **Natavi Guides**, a New York small business, in 2002, to publish guidebooks for students. Natavi hires virtual interns to write stories, and locates people by posting openings with career

(Continued)

(Continued)

offices at more than 30 universities nationwide. When Natavi posted an opening at Columbia University, it received 100 résumés in an hour. Kogan estimates that Natavi saved $100,000 in overhead during the first year in business by not having to furnish office space, computers, and other equipment to interns who rarely if ever came to the office. If virtual interning grows large enough, it could change the workplace by creating a generation of employees who expect to be judged by the work they complete instead of the number of hours they work. In other words, they'll expect to be treated like free agents.

Networking and Boundaryless Relationships

The term *networking* refers to two types of networks. Computer networks and other *electronic networks* connect machines for e-business or e-commerce, as illustrated in Exhibit 1-8. The second type of network is *relationship networks* between people, which are just as important.[78] These kinds of networks are related, because people use machine networks to develop human relationships. Successful businesses realize the need to foster close working relationships among their employees and with their customers, suppliers, and anyone else with whom employees interact regularly.[79] New workplace networks are boundaryless. Employees in today's workplace may not all be located at a single physical site (a plant or office building, for example), and there is no longer a clear distinction between who is in and outside the firm. For example, a team developing a new product can be made up of a company's employees, its customers, its suppliers, and even competitors from several countries. Former CEO Jack Welch, an evangelist of boundarylessness, stated that a boundaryless attitude led ordinary employees at GE to achieve extraordinary things.[80] Sharing knowledge and innovating globally through the use of boundaryless network technologies involving diverse people are challenging aspects of today's managerial environment.

Michael Dell started his entrepreneurial career from his college dorm room. He founded **Dell Computer** in 1984 with $1,000 and a vision—to sell computer systems directly to customers, cutting out wholesalers and retailers. Today he is still chairman and CEO, and Dell sells computers to businesses of all sizes as well as to indvidual customers. Dell sells more personal computers every year than any other company in the world, and it is the 30th largest company in the world.[81]

Michael Dell revolutionized B2C with what he calls *virtual integration*. Dell innovated the use of end-to-end digital supply-chain networks to take orders from customers, buy components from suppliers, coordinate with manufacturing partners, and ship customized products directly to customers. Dell specializes in assembling and shipping customized orders, and the company is boundaryless in multiple ways. For example, Dell tells the manufacturers of its computer parts the number of components to be delivered every morning. Dell does not even stock its own monitors. Dell tells the shipper (UPS and others) to come to Austin, Texas, to pick up the computers, to go to the Sony factory in Mexico to pick up the corresponding monitors, and to match them up and deliver them. Through virtual integration, Dell employs 44,300 team members and indirectly employs more than 80,000 people.[82]

The Gap was started by an entrepreneurial couple, the Fishers. The Gap grew from one store to more than 4,200 through participative management, by empowering its employees to be creative and innovative. The Gap also focuses on continuing improvement, as it offers quality products, which it constantly changes, and distinctive brands. Gap is a global and boundaryless company with corporate operations all around the world and stores in all 50 states and five countries. Gap uses the technology of e-business, including B2C selling through the Internet. Online sales were less than 5 percent of total U.S. retail spending in 2003, but represented more than $12 billion between Thanksgiving and Christmas alone.[83] The Gap is after a share of this market, and it opened its online Gap store, *http://www.gap.com*, in 1997, *http://www.gapkids.com* and *http://www.babygap.com* in 1998, *http://www.BananaRepublic.com* in 1999, and *http://www.oldnavy.com* in 2000. Knowledge management at Gap takes place through sharing of ideas for products and how to display and sell them. Gap has solid electronic and relationship networks with its suppliers. Teams work together to create new designs. The Gap is considered an ethical company. Here is its social responsibility statement, taken from its Web site at *http://www.gapinc.com*:

> *Gap Inc. is committed to having a positive impact in the communities where we do business. This commitment means supporting and volunteering with organizations that address the needs of youth and neighborhoods. It means working to ensure that the garment workers who produce our clothes are treated with dignity and respect. And it means minimizing our effect on the environment.*

OBJECTIVES OF THE BOOK

This book takes a "how-to" approach to management, as research has shown that knowledge is more likely to be implemented when it is acquired from learning by doing rather than from learning by reading, listening, or thinking.[84] As indicated by its subtitle, "Concepts, Applications, and Skill Development," this book uses a three-pronged approach, with these objectives:

- To teach you the important concepts of management
- To develop your ability to apply the management concepts through critical thinking
- To develop your management skills in your personal and professional lives

The book offers some unique features to further each of these three objectives, as summarized in Exhibit 1-9.

Management Concepts

Throughout this book, you will learn management concepts and see how they relate to organizational success, as well as to the difficulties and challenges managers face. Your knowledge of management concepts is vital to your success as a manager. This book offers the six features listed in Exhibit 1–9 to help you learn management concepts.

Exhibit 1-9 *Features of This Book's Three-Pronged Approach*

Features That Present Important Concepts	• Text discussions of management research • Step-by-step behavior models • Learning Outcome statements • Key terms • Chapter summaries and glossaries • Review and discussion questions
Features That Help You Apply What You Learn	• Opening cases • Organizational examples • Work Applications • Applying the Concept • Objective cases • Video cases • Ethics and Social Responsibility features • Internet exercises
Features That Foster Skill Development	• Self-assessments • Behavior Modeling videos • Behavior Modeling training • Skill Builder exercises

Application of Management Concepts

Understanding theory and concepts is essential before moving to the next level: applying the concepts. If you don't understand the concepts, how can you develop the critical thinking skills you need to apply them? As shown in Exhibit 1-9, this book offers eight features to help you develop the critical thinking skills you will need to apply the concepts.

Development of Management Skills

The third and highest-level objective is to develop the management skills that you can use in your personal and professional lives, as both a leader and a follower. You can develop your management skills. This book offers four features to help you do so.

PRACTICE

Most of the successful leaders in large companies have had extensive leadership training. A major concern of those who plan training is making sure that trainees can apply the training on the job.[85] As with just about everything in life, you cannot become skilled by simply reading about or trying something once. The great football coach Vince Lombardi said that leaders are made by effort and hard work. If you want to develop your management skills, you must not only learn the concepts in this book, but also practice with the applications and skill-building exercises. But most important, to be successful, you need to practice using your skills in your personal and professional lives.

Flexibility

This book has so many features that it is unlikely that all of them can be covered in class during a one-semester course. Your instructor will select the features that best meet the course objectives and the amount of class time available, but you may want to cover some or all of the other features on your own or with the assistance of others outside class.

Organization of the Book

This book is organized into five parts, with Part One covering the introductory information, and Parts Two through Five covering the four functions of management discussed in this chapter. The next two chapters in Part One discuss the global environment. Part Two, which covers planning, includes two chapters and an appendix. Part Three on organizing has three chapters and an appendix. Part Four covers leading and includes five chapters and an appendix. Finally, Part Five, which covers controlling, contains two chapters.

Take advantage of the companion Web site for *Management Fundamentals*, where you will find a broad array of resources to help you maximize what you learn in class:

- Try a quiz
- View chapter videos
- Download slides
- Boost your vocabulary
- Work through an Internet exercise
- Find related links

Take a look for yourself at *http://lussier.swlearning.com.*

Chapter Summary

1. Describe a manager's responsibility.

A manager is responsible for achieving organizational objectives through efficient and effective use of resources. *Efficient* means doing things right, and *effective* means doing the right thing. The manager's resources include human, financial, physical, and informational resources.

2. List and explain the three management skills.

The three management skills are technical, human and communication, and conceptual and decision-making skills. Technical skills involve the ability to use methods and techniques to perform a task. Human and communication skills reflect the ability to work with people in teams. Conceptual and decision-making skills center around the ability to understand abstract ideas and select alternatives to solve problems.

3. List and explain the four management functions.

The four management functions are planning, organizing, leading, and controlling. Planning is the process of setting objectives and determining in advance exactly how the objectives will be met. Organizing is the process of delegating and coordinating tasks and allocating resources to achieve objectives. Leading is the process of influencing employees to work toward achieving objectives. Controlling is the process of establishing and implementing mechanisms to ensure that the organization achieves its objectives.

4. Identify the three management role categories.

Managers play the interpersonal role when they act as figurehead, leader, or liaison. Managers play the informational role when they act as monitor, disseminator, or spokesperson. Managers play the decisional role when they act as entrepreneur, disturbance handler, resource allocator, or negotiator.

5. List the hierarchy of management levels.

The three hierarchy levels are top managers (e.g., operations executive), middle managers (e.g., marketing manager), and first-line managers (e.g., accounting supervisor).

6. Describe the three different types of managers.

A general manager supervises the activities of several departments or units that perform different activities. Functional managers supervise related activities such as marketing, operations, finance, and human resources management. A project manager coordinates employees and other resources across several functional departments to accomplish a specific task.

7. Describe the differences among management levels in terms of skills needed and functions performed.

Top managers have a greater need for conceptual and decision-making skills than first-line managers. Middle managers have a need for all three skills. First-line managers have a greater need for technical skills than top managers.

8. Complete each of the following statements using one of this chapter's key terms.

A _____ is responsible for achieving organizational objectives through efficient and effective utilization of resources.

The _____ include human, financial, physical, and informational.

The level of organizational _____ is based on how effectively and efficiently managers use resources to achieve objectives.

_____ include technical, human and communication, and conceptual and decision-making skills.

_____ involve the ability to use methods and techniques to perform a task.

_____ reflect the ability to work with people in teams.

_____ reflect the ability to understand abstract ideas and select alternatives to solve problems.

The four _____ include planning, organizing, leading, and controlling.

_____ is the process of setting objectives and determining in advance exactly how the objectives will be met.

_____ is the process of delegating and coordinating tasks and resources to achieve objectives.

_____ is the process of influencing employees to work toward achieving objectives.

_____ is the process of establishing and implementing mechanisms to ensure that objectives are achieved.

The _____ include interpersonal, informational, and decisional.

There are three _____: top managers, middle managers, and first-line managers.

There are three _____: general, functional, and project.

_____ involves everyone in an organization in sharing knowledge and applying it to continuously improve products and processes.

Key **Terms**

conceptual and decision-making
   skills, 9
controlling, 11
human and communication skills, 9
knowledge management, 22
leading, 11

levels of management, 15
management functions, 11
management role categories, 13
management skills, 9
manager, 6
manager's resources, 6

organizing, 11
performance, 7
planning, 11
technical skills, 9
types of managers, 16

Review and **Discussion** Questions

1. What is management, and why is it important to learn about management?
2. What are the three management skills? Do all managers need these skills?
3. What are the four functions of management? Do all managers perform all four functions?
4. What are the three management roles? Do all managers perform all three roles?
5. What are the three types of managers? Is there really a difference among them?
6. Is it more important for managers to be efficient or effective? Can you be both?
7. When a good employee is promoted to management, (a) to which management level is the person typically promoted, and (b) how do the person's skills and functions change with the job promotion?

8. When an employee is promoted to a management position, should the organization provide the employee with some type of training? Why or why not?
9. Should a course on principles of management focus on teaching students about management or on teaching students to be managers? Explain your answer.
10. Can students really develop their management skills through a college course? Why or why not?
11. Which of the current trends in managing in the global Internet environment through information technology would you say is the most important for managers today? Why?
12. Do you believe that management theory is as precise as theory in physics and chemistry? Should it be? Explain.

Objective **Case**

In 1975, Bill Gates and Paul Allen founded Microsoft, based on their vision of using a new technology to change the way business was done and to benefit and transform society. In their view, the future was in computer software, not hardware. At the time, IBM saw its business as primarily selling mainframe computers; the company's mission later expanded to include the sale of PC hardware. Bill Gates convinced IBM to use Microsoft software to operate its PCs. Unlike Microsoft, IBM did not manage knowledge well. Although IBM eventually realized the value of developing its own PC operating systems and software, the company did not have much success. Even when IBM acquired Lotus Development Corporation in 1995 in an effort to add software (Lotus Notes, Lotus 1-2-3, Ami Pro) to its product line, the company was too late to catch up with Microsoft. And over the years, with competition from IBM clones, IBM continued to lose PC market share to competitors; eventually the company's share of the PC market dropped below 5 percent. Today, IBM sells more computer parts to competitors than PCs. As you probably know, Microsoft Windows and other Microsoft operating systems and office software dominate the market. By managing knowledge well, Microsoft passed IBM to become the world's second-largest company in 2003, based on market value; IBM was 12th.

Over the past 30 years, Microsoft has been a technology leader in transforming the way people work, play, and communicate. In June 2003, Microsoft changed its mission statement to reflect its diversity. Microsoft's Web site at *http://www.microsoft.com* presents the company's mission statement and describes its seven core business units:

Microsoft's mission: To enable people and businesses throughout the world to realize their full potential.

Microsoft's core business units:

- Windows Client, including the Microsoft® Windows® XP desktop operating system, Windows 2000, and Windows Embedded operating system
- Information Worker, including Microsoft Office, Microsoft Publisher, Microsoft Visio®, Microsoft Project, and other stand-alone desktop applications
- Business Solutions, encompassing Great Plains and Navision business process applications and bCentral™ business services
- Servers and Tools, including the Microsoft Windows Server System™ integrated server software, software developer tools, and MSDN®
- Mobile and Embedded Devices, featuring mobile devices, including the Windows Powered Pocket PC, the Mobile Explorer micro browser, and the Windows Powered Smartphone software platform

- MSN, including the MSN® network, MSN Internet Access, MSNTV, MSN Hotmail®, and other Web-based services
- Home and Entertainment, including Microsoft Xbox®, consumer hardware and software, online games, and the Microsoft TV platform

Bill Gates stepped down as CEO of Microsoft to focus on product development. His current title is Chairman, Chief Software Architect. Gates is consistently ranked as the richest man in the world, and depending on the stock price of Microsoft, his personal wealth has been estimated to be as high as $70 billion. In his book *Business @ the Speed of Thought*, Gates argues that instant access to information is the key to knowledge management. He says that most organizations don't maximize new technology, they don't manage knowledge well, because they have the wrong mindset about how information should be handled and distributed within an organization. Gates suggests that one way to improve knowledge management is by giving all employees access to a majority of organizational information, except personnel records and private compensation and benefits information of employees. He sees the information flow as being as important as the flow of blood through the body.

Chairman Bill Gates, known as a demanding boss, has consistently encouraged creativity and recognized employee achievements. He demands that his colleagues be well-informed, logical, vocal, and thick-skinned. Employees often spend long hours interacting in teams. Teams that develop and market programming languages must present their ideas at the so-called "Bill" meeting. During Bill meetings, Gates often interrupts presentations to question facts and assertions. He is known to shout criticism and challenges at team members, who are expected to stand up to him with good answers.

Bill Gates actively participates in and coordinates small units devoted to functional areas such as programming and marketing, but he delegates authority to managers to run their departments. Each part of the company is independent, yet Gates is the glue that holds it all together.

Source: Information for this case was taken from Bill Gates, *Business @ the Speed of Thought* (New York: Warner Books, 2000) and from the Microsoft Web site at *http://www.microsoft.com*, accessed January 12, 2004.

Go to the Internet for the latest news and information about Microsoft. You can learn what is currently being written about Microsoft in today's business press by logging on to InfoTrac® College Edition at *http://infotrac.thomsonlearning.com* and using its advance search functions.

_____ 1. Which type of resource played the most important role in the success of Microsoft?

    a. human   c. financial

    b. physical   d. informational

_____ 2. Which of the management skills is stressed most in the case study?

    a. technical

    b. human and communication

    c. conceptual and decision-making

_____ 3. Which of the management functions is stressed most in the case study?

    a. planning   c. leading

    b. organizing   d. controlling

_____ 4. Bill Gates's participation in and coordination of small units and his delegation of authority to managers to run their departments are examples of the _____ management function.

    a. planning   c. leading

    b. organizing   d. controlling

_____ 5. Which primary management role did Bill Gates use to achieve success?

    a. interpersonal–leader

    b. informational–monitor

    c. decisional–negotiator

_____ 6. Bill Gates is at which level of management?

    a. top

    b. middle

    c. first-line

_____ 7. Which type of manager is Bill Gates?

    a. general

    b. functional

    c. project

_____ 8. Bill Gates has greater need for which skills?

    a. technical rather than conceptual

    b. conceptual rather than technical

    c. a balance of both

_____ 9. How does Bill Gates spend most of his time?

    a. planning and organizing

    b. leading and controlling

    c. a balance of both a and b

_____10. Would Ghiselli agree that Bill Gates has supervisory ability?

    a. yes

    b. no

11. Give examples of some of the tasks Bill Gates performs in each of the four management functions.

12. Give examples of some of the tasks Bill Gates performs in each of the three management roles.

13. Do you think you would like to work for Bill Gates? Explain your answer.

14. Are Bill Gates and Microsoft ethical and socially responsible?

Video Case

LE MERIDIEN

About Le Meridien

Le Meridien is a chain of 125 luxury hotels operating in 55 countries. Premium service is the key to the success of this chain, and the role that managers play in ensuring that employees deliver the highest levels of service are well documented in this video. The dynamic nature of management is particularly evident, as cameras follow assistant manager Bob van den Oord through a typical day. The video includes many vivid examples of managers setting a direction, then standing back to allow employees to exercise their discretion and training.

View the Video (10–15 minutes)

View the video on Le Meridien in class or at *http://lussier.swlearning.com*.

Read the Case

At Le Meridien Hotel in Boston, a manager's work is never done. Bob van den Oord, assistant general manager of the hotel, arrives before 8:00 A.M. and does a walk-through of the entire hotel. By 9:30, all managers—including Bob—are assembled for the daily operational meeting, in which everyone reports briefly on the hotel's activities for the past 24 hours. By 9:45, the meeting is over, and all managers return to their posts.

Bob van den Oord fulfills all the four management functions every day he's on the job. He manages by walking around. "It's a good tool to see what's going on," he says. "I like [walking around], the staff likes it, and guests like to see management around as well."

Le Meridien in Boston—a single hotel in a huge organization—is itself a complex organization, hosting more than 100,000 visitors each year. "It's hard work, but it's fun," Bob notes. Of his staff, he says, "We're all in it together."

Answer the Questions

1. How does Bob van den Oord embody the four management functions?

2. Which management skill—technical, human and communication, or conceptual and decision making—does Bob van den Oord seem to use most?

3. How many different management levels and types of managers are evident in the video?

Skill **Builder** 1
COMPARING MANAGEMENT SKILLS

Recall the best supervisor or boss you ever worked for and the worst one you ever worked for. Compare these two people by writing brief notes in the chart below about each person's management skills and ability to perform the four management functions.

Management Skills and Functions	Best Supervisor or Boss	Worst Supervisor or Boss
Technical		
Human and Communication		
Conceptual and Decision Making		
Planning		
Organizing		
Leading		
Controlling		

Based on your own experiences with a good boss and a poor one, what do you believe are the key differences between good and poor managers?

Apply It (2–4 minutes)

What did I learn from this exercise? How will I use this knowledge in the future?

_____

_____

_____

Skill Builder 2

MANAGEMENT STYLES

Objectives

To learn your preferred management style and how to match a situation to an appropriate management style.

Assess Your Preferred Management Style

Following are 12 situations. Select the one alternative that most closely describes what you would do in each situation. Don't be concerned with trying to pick the right answer;

select the alternative you would really use. Circle a, b, c, or d. (Ignore the C _____ preceding each situation and the S _____ following each answer choice; these will be explained later.)

C _____ 1. Your rookie crew seems to be developing well. Their need for direction and close supervision is diminishing. What do you do?

    a. Stop directing and overseeing performance unless there is a problem. S _____

    b. Spend time getting to know them personally, but make sure they maintain performance levels. S _____

    c. Make sure things keep going well; continue to direct and oversee closely. S _____

    d. Begin to discuss new tasks of interest to them. S _____

C _____ 2. You assigned Jill a task, specifying exactly how you wanted it done. Jill deliberately ignored your directions and did it her way. The job will not meet the customer's standards. This is not the first problem you've had with Jill. What do you decide to do?

    a. Listen to Jill's side, but be sure the job gets done right. S _____

    b. Tell Jill to do it again the right way and closely supervise the job. S _____

    c. Tell her the customer will not accept the job and let Jill handle it her way. S _____

    d. Discuss the problem and solutions to it. S _____

C _____ 3. Your employees work well together and are a real team; the department is the top performer in the organization. Because of traffic problems, the president has approved staggered hours for departments. As a result, you can change your department's hours. Several of your workers are in favor of changing. What action do you take?

    a. Allow the group to decide the hours. S _____

    b. Decide on new hours, explain why you chose them, and invite questions. S _____

    c. Conduct a meeting to get the group members' ideas. Select new hours together, with your approval. S _____

    d. Send out a memo stating the hours you want. S _____

C _____ 4. You hired Bill, a new employee. He is not performing at the level expected after a month's training. Bill is trying, but he seems to be a slow learner. What do you decide to do?

    a. Clearly explain what needs to be done and oversee his work. Discuss why the procedures are important; support and encourage him. S _____

    b. Tell Bill that his training is over and it's time to pull his own weight. S _____

    c. Review task procedures and supervise his work closely. S _____

    d. Inform Bill that his training is over and that he should feel free to come to you if he has any problems. S _____

C _____ 5. Helen has had an excellent performance record for the last five years. Recently you have noticed a drop in the quality and quantity of her work. She has a family problem. What do you do?

    a. Tell her to get back on track and closely supervise her. S _____

    b. Discuss the problem with Helen. Help her realize that her personal problem is affecting her work. Discuss ways to improve the situation. Be supportive and encourage her. S _____

    c. Tell Helen you're aware of her productivity slip and that you're sure she'll work it out soon. S _____

    d. Discuss the problem and solution with Helen and supervise her closely. S _____

C _____ 6. Your organization does not allow smoking in certain areas. You just walked by a restricted area and saw Joan smoking. She has been with the organization for ten years and is a very productive worker. Joan has never been caught smoking before. What action do you take?

    a. Ask her to put the cigarette out; then leave. S _____

    b. Discuss why she is smoking and what she intends to do about it. S _____

    c. Give her a lecture about not smoking and check up on her in the future. S _____

    d. Tell her to put the cigarette out, watch her do it, and tell her you will check on her in the future. S _____

C _____ 7. Your employees usually work well together with little direction. Recently a conflict between Sue and Tom has caused problems. What action do you take?

    a. Call Sue and Tom together and make them realize how this conflict is affecting the department. Discuss how to resolve it and how you will check to make sure the problem is solved. S _____

    b. Let the group resolve the conflict. S _____

    c. Have Sue and Tom sit down and discuss their conflict and how to resolve it. Support their efforts to implement a solution. S _____

    d. Tell Sue and Tom how to resolve their conflict and closely supervise them. S _____

C ___ 8. Jim usually does his share of the work with some encouragement and direction. However, he has migraine headaches occasionally and doesn't pull his weight when this happens. The others resent doing Jim's work. What do you decide to do?

    a. Discuss his problem and help him come up with ideas for maintaining his work; be supportive. S ___

    b. Tell Jim to do his share of the work and closely watch his output. S ___

    c. Inform Jim that he is creating a hardship for the others and should resolve the problem by himself. S ___

    d. Be supportive but set minimum performance levels and ensure compliance. S ___

C ___ 9. Barbara, your most experienced and productive worker, came to you with a detailed idea that could increase your department's productivity at a very low cost. She can do her present job and this new assignment. You think it's an excellent idea. What do you do?

    a. Set some goals together. Encourage and support her efforts. S ___

    b. Set up goals for Barbara. Be sure she agrees with them and sees you as being supportive of her efforts. S ___

    c. Tell Barbara to keep you informed and to come to you if she needs any help. S ___

    d. Have Barbara check in with you frequently so that you can direct and supervise her activities. S ___

C ___ 10. Your boss asked you for a special report. Frank, a very capable worker who usually needs no direction or support, has all the necessary skills to do the job. However, Frank is reluctant because he has never done a report. What do you do?

    a. Tell Frank he has to do it. Give him direction and supervise him closely. S ___

    b. Describe the project to Frank and let him do it his own way. S ___

    c. Describe the benefits to Frank. Get his ideas on how to do it and check his progress. S ___

    d. Discuss possible ways of doing the job. Be supportive; encourage Frank. S ___

C ___ 11. Jean is the top producer in your department. However, her monthly reports are constantly late and contain errors. You are puzzled because she does everything else with no direction or support. What do you decide to do?

    a. Go over past reports, explaining exactly what is expected of her. Schedule a meeting so that you can review the next report with her. S ___

    b. Discuss the problem with Jean and ask her what can be done about it; be supportive. S ___

    c. Explain the importance of the report. Ask her what the problem is. Tell her that you expect the next report to be on time and error-free. S ___

    d. Remind Jean to get the next report in on time without errors. S ___

C ___ 12. Your workers are very effective and like to participate in decision making. A consultant was hired to develop a new method for your department using the latest technology in the field. What do you do?

    a. Explain the consultant's method and let the group decide how to implement it. S ___

    b. Teach the workers the new method and supervise them closely as they use it. S ___

    c. Explain to the workers the new method and the reasons it is important. Teach them the method and make sure the procedure is followed. Answer questions. S ___

    d. Explain the new method and get the group's input on ways to improve and implement it. S ___

To determine your preferred management style, circle the letter you selected for each situation.

	Autocratic	Consultative	Participative	Empowerment
1.	c	b	d	a
2.	b	a	d	c
3.	d	b	c	a
4.	c	a	d	b
5.	a	d	b	c
6.	d	c	b	a
7.	d	a	c	b
8.	b	d	a	c
9.	d	b	a	c
10.	a	c	d	b
11.	a	c	b	d
12.	b	c	d	a
Totals	___	___	___	___

Now add up the number of circled items per column. The column with the most items circled suggests your preferred management style. Is this the style you tend to use most often?

Your management style flexibility is reflected in the distribution of your answers. The more evenly distributed the numbers, the more flexible your style. A total of 1 or 0 for any column may indicate a reluctance to use that style.

Learn More about Management Styles

According to contingency theorists, there is no best management style for all situations. Instead, effective managers adapt their styles to individual capabilities or group situations.

Manager–Employee Interactions. Managers' interactions with employees can be classified into two distinct categories: directive and supportive.

- *Directive behavior.* The manager focuses on directing and controlling behavior to ensure that tasks get done and closely oversees performance.
- *Supportive behavior.* The manager focuses on encouraging and motivating behavior without telling the employee what to do. The manager explains things and listens to employee views, helping employees make their own decisions by building up confidence and self-esteem.

As a manager you can focus on directing (getting the task done), supporting (developing relationships), or both.

Employee Capability. There are two distinct aspects of employee capability.

- *Ability.* Do employees have the knowledge, experience, education, skills, and training to do a particular task without direction?
- *Motivation.* Do the employees have the confidence to do the task? Do they want to do the task? Are they committed to performing the task? Will they perform the task without encouragement and support?

Employee capability may be measured on a continuum from low to outstanding. As a manager, you assess each employee's capability level and motivation.

- *Low.* The employees can't do the task without detailed directions and close supervision. Employees in this category are either unable or unwilling to do the task.
- *Moderate.* The employees have moderate ability and need specific direction and support to get the task done properly. The employees may be highly motivated but still need direction.
- *High.* The employees have high ability but may lack the confidence to do the job. What they need most is support and encouragement to motivate them to get the task done.
- *Outstanding.* The employees are capable of doing the task without direction or support.

Most people perform a variety of tasks on the job. It is important to realize that employee capability may vary depending on the specific task. For example, a bank teller may handle routine transactions with great ease but falter when opening new or special accounts. Employees tend to start working with low capability, needing close direction. As their ability to do the job increases, managers can begin to be supportive and probably cease close supervision. As a manager, you must gradually develop your employees from low to outstanding levels over time.

Four Management Styles. The four situational management styles are autocratic, consultative, participative, and empowerment.

- An *autocratic style* is highly directive and less concerned with building relationships. The autocratic style is appropriate when interacting with low-capability employees. When interacting with such employees, give very detailed instructions describing exactly what the task is and when, where, and how to perform it. Closely oversee performance and give some support. The majority of time with the employees is spent giving directions. Make decisions without input from the employees.
- A *consultative style* involves highly directive and highly supportive behavior and is appropriate when interacting with moderately capable employees. Give specific instructions and oversee performance at all major stages of a task. At the same time, support the employees by explaining why the task should be performed as requested and answering their questions. Work on relationships as you explain the benefits of completing the task your way. Give fairly equal amounts of time to directing and supporting employees. When making decisions, you may consult employees, but retain the final say. Once you make the decision, which can incorporate employees' ideas, direct and oversee employees' performance.
- A *participative style* is characterized by less directive but still highly supportive behavior and is appropriate when interacting with employees with high capability. When interacting with such employees, spend a small amount of time giving general directions and a great deal of time giving encouragement. Spend limited time overseeing performance, letting employees do the task their way while focusing on the end result. Support the employees by encouraging them and building up their self-confidence. If a task needs to be done, don't tell them how to do it; ask them how they will accomplish it. Make decisions together or allow employees to make decisions subject to your limitations and approval.
- An *empowerment style* requires providing very little direction or support for employees and is appropriate when interacting with outstanding employees. You should let them know what needs to be done and answer their questions, but it is not necessary to oversee their performance. Such employees are highly motivated and need little, if any, support. Allow them to make their own decisions, subject to your approval. Other terms for empowerment are *laissez-faire* and *hands off*. A manager who uses this style lets employees alone to do their own thing.

Apply Management Styles

Return to the portion of the exercise where you assessed your preferred management style. Identify the employee capability level for each item; indicate the capability level by placing a number from 1 to 4 on the line marked "C" before each item. (1 indicates low capability; 2, moderate capability; 3, high capability; and 4, outstanding capability.) Next, indicate the management style represented in each answer choice by placing the letter A (Autocratic), C (Consultative), P (Participative), or E (Empowerment) on the line marked "S" following each answer choice. Will your preferred management style result in the optimum performance of the task?

Let's see how you did by looking back at the first situation.

C _____ 1. Your rookie crew seems to be developing well. Their need for direction and close supervision is diminishing. What do you do?

   a. Stop directing and overseeing performance, unless there is a problem. S _____
   b. Spend time getting to know them personally, but make sure they maintain performance levels. S _____
   c. Make sure things keep going well; continue to direct and oversee closely. S _____
   d. Begin to discuss new tasks of interest to them. S _____

- As a rookie crew, the employees' capability started at a low level, but they have now developed to the moderate level. If you put the number 2 on the C line, you were correct.
- Alternative a is E, the empowerment style, involving low direction and support. Alternative b is C, the consultative style, involving both high direction and high support.

Alternative c is A, the autocratic style, involving high direction but low support. Alternative d is P, the participative style, involving low direction and high support (in discussing employee interests).

- If you selected b as the management style that best matches the situation, you were correct. However, in the business world there is seldom only one way to handle a situation successfully. Therefore, in this exercise, you are given points based on how successful your behavior would be in each situation. In situation 1, b is the most successful alternative because it involves developing the employees gradually; answer b is worth 3 points. Alternative c is the next best alternative, followed by d. It is better to keep things the way they are now than to try to rush employee development, which would probably cause problems. So c is a 2-point answer, and d gets 1 point. Alternative a is the least effective because you are going from one extreme of supervision to the other. This is a 0-point answer because the odds are great that this approach will cause problems that will diminish your management success.

The better you match your management style to employees' capabilities, the greater are your chances of being a successful manager.

Apply It

What did I learn from this skill-building experience? How will I use this knowledge in the future?

_____

_____

Your instructor may ask you to do Skill Builder 2 in class in a group. If so, the instructor will provide you with any necessary information or additional instructions.

Skill Builder 3
GETTING TO KNOW YOU

Objectives
1. To get acquainted with some of your classmates
2. To gain a better understanding of what the course covers
3. To get to know more about your instructor

Procedure 1 (5–8 minutes)
Break into groups of five or six, preferably with people you do not know. Have each member tell his or her name and two or three significant things about himself or herself.

Then ask each other questions to get to know each other better.

Procedure 2 (4–8 minutes)
Can everyone in the group address every other person by name? If not, have each member repeat his or her name. Then each person in the group should repeat the names of all the group members, until each person knows everyone's first name.

Discussion

What can you do to improve your ability to remember people's names?

_____

_____

_____

Procedure 3 (5–10 minutes)

Elect a spokesperson for your group. Look over the following categories and decide on some specific questions you would like your spokesperson to ask the instructor from one or more of the categories. The spokesperson will not identify who asked the questions. You do not have to have questions for each area.

- *Course expectations*. What do you expect to cover or hope to learn from this course?

- *Doubts or concerns*. Is there anything about the course that you don't understand?
- *Questions about the instructor*. List questions to ask the instructor in order to get to know him or her better.

Procedure 4 (10–20 minutes)

Each spokesperson asks the instructor one question at a time until all questions have been answered. Spokespeople should skip questions already asked by other groups.

Apply It

What did I learn from this experience? How will I use this knowledge in the future?

_____

_____

APPENDIX A

A Brief History of Management

Learning Outcomes

After studying this appendix, you should be able to:

1. State the major similarities and differences between the classical and behavioral theorists. PAGE 37

2. Describe how systems theorists and contingency theorists differ from classical and behavioral theorists. PAGE 40

3. Define the following **key terms**:

classical theorists
behavioral theorists
management science theorists

systems theorists
sociotechnical theorists
contingency theorists

—————— Learning Outcome 1 ——————
State the major similarities and differences between the classical and behavioral theorists.

There are two primary reasons why you should be concerned about the history of management: to better understand current developments and to avoid repeating mistakes. Early literature on management was written by management practitioners who described their experiences and attempted to extrapolate basic principles. More recent literature comes from researchers. There are different classifications of management approaches, or schools of management thought. In this appendix you will learn about five management theories: the classical, behavioral, management science, systems, and contingency theories.

CLASSICAL THEORY

The **classical theorists** *focus on the job and management functions to determine the best way to manage in all organizations.* In the early 1900s, managers began an organized approach to increasing performance by focusing on the efficiency of managing jobs. This focus later changed to a concern for managing departments and organizations. Scientific management stressed job efficiency through the development of technical skills, while administrative theory stressed rules and the structure of the organization.

Scientific Management

Frederick Winslow Taylor (1856–1915), an engineer known as the Father of Scientific Management, focused on analyzing jobs and redesigning them so that they could be accomplished more efficiently. As he searched for the best way to maximize performance, he developed "scientific management" principles, including the following:

1. Develop a procedure for each element of a worker's job.
2. Promote job specialization.
3. Select, train, and develop workers scientifically.
4. Plan and schedule work.
5. Establish standard methods and times for each task.
6. Use wage incentives such as piece rates and bonuses.[1]

Frank Gilbreth (1868–1924) and his wife Lillian Gilbreth (1878–1972) used time and motion studies to develop more efficient work procedures. Their work was popularized in a book entitled *Cheaper by the Dozen* (and later two movies and a television comedy of the same name)—which described their application of scientific management practices to their family of 12 children. When Frank died, the children ranged in age from 2 to 19 years old. Lillian continued her work as a consultant but changed the focus of her work to become a pioneer in industrial psychology. Lillian became a professor of management at Purdue University and is commonly referred to as the First Lady of Management.

Another person who made important contributions to scientific management was Henry Gantt (1861–1919). He developed a method for scheduling work over a period of time that is still widely used today. You will learn how to develop a Gantt chart in Chapter 5.

Administrative Theory

Henri Fayol (1841–1925) was a French engineer who is sometimes referred to as the Father of Modern Management. Fayol was a pioneer in the study of the principles and functions of management. He made a clear distinction between operating and managerial activities. Fayol identified five major functions of management: planning, coordinating, organizing, controlling, and commanding. In addition to his five management functions, Fayol also developed 14 principles that are still used today.[2] Most principles of management textbooks are organized on the basis of the functions of management.

Two other contributors to administrative management are Max Weber (1864–1920) and Chester Barnard (1886–1961). Max Weber was a German sociologist who developed the *bureaucracy concept*. The aim of his concept of bureaucracy was to develop a set of rules and procedures to ensure that all employees were treated fairly. Chester Barnard studied authority and power distributions in organizations. He raised awareness of the informal organization—cliques and naturally occurring social groupings within formal organizations.

Mary Parker Follett (1868–1933) stressed the importance of people rather than engineering techniques. Follett contributed to administrative theory by emphasizing the need for worker participation, conflict resolution, and shared goals. The trend today is toward increasingly higher levels of employee participation. Barnard and Follett's contributions led to the development of behavioral theory.

Many companies still use classical management techniques successfully today. McDonald's system of fast-food service is one good example of a company that uses these techniques. Managers at Monsanto also use classical techniques, such as time and motion studies and organization principles that you will learn about in Chapter 6. Large organizations that are downsizing to cut costs by laying off employees and becoming more efficient are using a classical management approach.

BEHAVIORAL THEORY

The **behavioral theorists** *focus on people to determine the best way to manage in all organizations.* In the 1920s, management writers began to question the classical approach to management and changed their focus from the job itself to the people who perform the job. Like the classicists, behaviorists were looking for the best way to manage in all organizations. However, the behavioral approach to management stressed the need for human skills rather than technical skills.

Elton Mayo (1880–1949) pioneered the *human relations* movement. Mayo headed a group of Harvard researchers in conducting the Hawthorne studies, a landmark series of studies of human behavior in Western Electric's Hawthorne plant (Cicero, Illinois) from 1927 to 1932. Like Taylor, Mayo wanted to increase performance; however, he viewed determining the best work environment as the means to this end. Mayo's research suggested that a manager's treatment of people had an important impact on their performance. In other words, treating people well and meeting their needs frequently results in increased performance. The *Hawthorne effect* refers to the phenomenon that just studying people affects their performance.[3]

Abraham Maslow (1908–1970) developed the *hierarchy of needs* theory.[4] Maslow is one of the earliest researchers to study motivation, and motivation is still a major area of research. You will learn more about Maslow's hierarchy of needs and other motivation theories in Chapter 12.

Douglas McGregor (1906–1964) developed *Theory X* and *Theory Y*. McGregor contrasted the two theories, based on the assumptions that managers make about workers. Theory X managers assume that people dislike work and that only if managers plan, organize, and closely direct and control their work will workers perform at high levels. Theory Y managers assume that people like to work and do not need close supervision. McGregor did not give specific details on how to manage; he suggested a reorientation in managerial thinking.[5]

Behaviorists believed that happy employees would be productive. However, later research suggested that a happy worker is not necessarily a productive worker. As you can see, the classical and behavioral theories are very different, yet both kinds of theorists claim that their approach is the best way to manage in all organizations.

The behavioral approach to management is still evolving and being used in organizations. The current term for studying people at work is the *behavioral science approach*, which draws from economics, psychology, sociology, and other disciplines. Most of the material in the chapters in Parts 3 and 4 is based on behavioral science research. Managers all over the globe use behavioral sciences in dealing with people.

MANAGEMENT SCIENCE

*The **management science theorists** focus on the use of mathematics to aid in problem solving and decision making.* During World War II, a research program began to investigate the applicability of quantitative methods to military and logistics problems. After the war, business managers began to use management science (math). Some of the mathematical models are used in the areas of finance, management information systems (MIS), and operations management. The use of computers has led to an increase in the use of quantitative methods by managers all over the globe. Because management science stresses decision-making skills and technical skills, it is more closely aligned with classical management theory than with behavioral theory. You will learn more about management science in the chapters in Parts 2 and 5. Management science is not commonly used in organizing and leading.

Learning Outcome 2

Describe how systems theorists and contingency theorists differ from classical and behavioral theorists.

INTEGRATIVE PERSPECTIVE

The integrative perspective has three components: systems theory, sociotechnical theory, and contingency theory.

Systems Theory

*The **systems theorists** focus on viewing the organization as a whole and as the interrelationship of its parts.* In the 1950s, management theorists attempted to integrate the classical, behavioral, and management science theories into a holistic view of the management process. Systems theorists began by assuming that an organization is a system that transforms inputs (resources) into outputs (products and/or services).

According to Russell Ackoff, the commonly used classical approach to problem solving is a reductionist process. Managers tend to break an organization into its basic parts (departments), understand the behavior and properties of the parts, and add the understanding of the parts together to understand the whole. They focus on making independent departments operate as efficiently as possible. According to systems theorists, the reductionist approach cannot yield an understanding of the organization, only knowledge of how it works. Because the parts of a system are interdependent, even if each part is independently made to perform as efficiently as possible, the organization as a whole may not perform as effectively as possible. For example, all-star athletic teams are made up of exceptional players. But because such players have not played together as a team before, the all-star team may not be able to beat an average team in the league.[6]

Systems theory stresses the need for conceptual skills in order to understand how an organization's subsystems (departments) interrelate and contribute to the organization as a whole. For example, the actions of the marketing, operations, and financial departments (subsystems) affects each other; if the quality of the product goes down, sales may decrease, causing a decrease in finances. Before managers in one department make a decision, they should consider the interrelated effects it will have on the other departments. The organization is a system (departments), just as the management process is a system (planning, organizing, leading, and controlling), with subsystems (parts of departments) that affect each other. So, in other words, when you have a problem to solve, do not break it into pieces; focus on the whole.

According to Harold Koontz, Daniel Katz, Robert Kahn, and others, the systems approach recognizes that an organization is an open system because it interacts with, and is affected by, the external environment.[7] For example, government laws affect what an organization can and cannot do, the economy affects the organization's sales, and so on. You will learn more about open systems and the organizational environment in Chapter 2.

Over the years, systems theory lost some of its popularity. However, today one of the major trends is toward total quality management (TQM), which takes a systems approach to management. You will learn more about TQM in Chapters 2, 7, and 15.

Sociotechnical Theory

The **sociotechnical theorists** *focus on integrating people and technology.* Sociotechnical theory was formulated during the 1950s and 1960s, by Eric Trist, Ken Bamforth, Fred Emery, and others.[8] They realized, as today's managers do, that a manager must integrate both people and technology. To focus on one to the exclusion of the other leads to lower levels of performance. Much of current behavioral science work is in agreement with sociotechnical theory.

Contingency Theory

The **contingency theorists** *focus on determining the best management approach for a given situation.* In the 1960s and 1970s, management researchers wanted to determine how the environment and technology affected the organization.

Tom Burns and George Stalker conducted a study to determine how the environment affects a firm's organization and management systems. They identified two different types of environments: stable (where there is little change) and innovative (great changes). The researchers also identified two types of management systems: mechanistic (similar to bureaucratic classical theory) and organic (nonbureaucratic, similar to behavioral theory). They concluded that in a stable environment, the mechanistic approach works well, whereas in an innovative environment, the organic approach works well.[9]

Joan Woodward conducted a study to determine how technology (the means of producing products) affects organizational structure. She found that organizational structure did change with the type of technology. Woodward concluded that the mechanistic or classical approach worked well with mass-production technology (such as that of an automobile assembly line), whereas the organic or behavioral approach worked well with small-batch (custom-made) products and long-run process technology (such as for refining crude oil).

COMPARING THEORIES

Exhibit A reviews the theories covered in this appendix. Throughout this book, you will learn to take an integrative perspective using systems and contingency theories, combined with some management science, to ensure that you maximize development of your management skills. For example, Skill Builder 1 at the end of Chapter 1, uses a contingency approach.

Exhibit A *Comparing Theories*

Classical	Behavioral	Management Science	Systems Theory	Sociotechnical Theory	Contingency Theory
Attempts to develop the best way to manage in all organizations best by focusing on the jobs and structure of the firm.	Attempts to develop a single best way to manage in all organizations by focusing on people and making them productive.	Recommends using math (computers) to aid in problem solving and decision making.	Manages by focusing on the organization as a whole and the interrelationship of its departments, rather than on individual parts.	Recommends focusing on the integration of people and technology.	Recommends using the theory or the combination of theories that meets the given situation.

Appendix Summary

1. State the major similarities and differences between the classical and behavioral theorists.

Both classical and behavioral theorists wanted to find the best way to manage in all organizations. However, the classicists focused on the job and management functions, whereas the behaviorists focused on people.

2. Describe how systems theorists and the contingency theorists differ from classical and behavioral theorists.

The classical and behavioral and the systems theorists differ in the way they conceptualize the organization and its problems. The classical and behavioral theorists use a reductionist approach by breaking the organization into its component parts to understand the whole (sum of parts = whole). Systems theorists look at the organization as a whole and the interrelationship of its parts to understand the whole (whole = interrelationship of parts).

The classical and behavioral theorists seek the best management approach in all organizations. The contingency theorists propose that there is no best approach for all organizations; they seek to determine which management approach will work best in a given situation.

3. Complete each of the following statements using one of this appendix's key terms:

The _____ focus on the job and management functions to determine the best way to manage in all organizations.

The _____ focus on people to determine the best way to manage in all organizations.

The _____ focus on the use of mathematics to aid in problem solving and decision making.

The _____ focus on viewing the organization as a whole and as the interrelationship of its parts.

The _____ focus on integrating people and technology.

The _____ focus on determining the best management approach for a given situation.

Key **Terms**

behavioral theorists, 39

classical theorists, 37

contingency theorists, 41

management science theorists, 40

sociotechnical theorists, 41

systems theorists, 40

Learning Outcomes

After studying this chapter, you should be able to:

1. Explain the five internal environmental factors: management and culture, mission, resources, systems process, and structure. PAGE 46

2. List and explain the need for the two primary principles of total quality management (TQM). PAGE 49

3. Describe the three levels of organizational culture and their relationship to each other. PAGE 51

4. Describe how the nine external environmental factors—customers, competitors, suppliers, labor force, shareholders, society, technology, economies, and governments—can affect the internal business environment. PAGE 54

2: Environment: Culture, Ethics, and Social Responsibility

5. Compare the three levels of moral development. PAGE 63

6. Explain the stakeholders' approach to ethics. PAGE 66

7. Define the following **key terms**:

internal environment
organizational culture
mission
stakeholders
systems process
quality
customer value
total quality management (TQM)

levels of culture
symbolic leaders
learning organization
external environment
ethics
stakeholders' approach to ethics
social responsibility

Ideas on Management
at Ford and General Motors

Henry Ford founded the Ford Motor Company in 1903, at the dawn of the American automotive industry. Ten years later, in 1913, he revolutionized automotive technologies by introducing the moving assembly line. A century later, the company markets its portfolio of automotive brands—Ford, Lincoln, Mercury, Mazda, Volvo, Jaguar, Land Rover, and Aston Martin—in more than 150 countries, employing over 350,000 people worldwide.

Founded five years after Henry Ford launched his venture, General Motors (GM), like Ford, grew throughout the twentieth century by acquiring independent carmakers. Today, GM remains the world's largest automotive corporation despite impressive share gains among its rivals. GM's present lineup of vehicle brands consists of Buick, Cadillac, Chevrolet, GMC, Holden, Hummer, Opel, Pontiac, Saab, Saturn, and Vauxhall. GM employs nearly 340,000 people around the world and operates manufacturing facilities in 32 countries. It sells vehicles in more than 190 markets.

© Bloomberg News/Landov

For 2005, GM's Chevy division is rolling out a 6-liter, 400-horsepower Corvette that goes from 0 to 60 mph in 4.3 seconds, with a top speed of 180 mph. Meanwhile, Ford is upgrading its Mustang to a 300-horsepower engine that goes from 0 to 60 mph in 5.3 seconds, with a top speed of 150 mph.

I O M

1. Who is the top manager at Ford and GM, and what is Ford's mission?
2. What makes up the Ford culture, and what drives it?
3. What is GM's worldwide ranking in terms of sales of light vehicles, and which of the company's competitors are also its partners?
4. What is included in the Ford Motor Company Standards of Corporate Conduct?
5. How is GM socially responsible?

To learn more about Ford and GM, visit their Web sites at *http://www.ford.com* and *http://www.gm.com* or log on to InfoTrac® College Edition at *http://infotrac.thomsonlearning.com* to read about the latest competitive strategies undertaken by Ford and GM at home and abroad. Use the advanced search option to key in one of four record numbers (A111975901, A104021395, A112553034, or A110036069) and sample the news regarding these companies' latest struggles and triumphs.

Source: Information for the opening case was taken from the Ford and GM Web sites at *http://www.ford.com* and *http://www.gm.com*, accessed May 13, 2004.

Learning Outcome 1

Explain the five internal environmental factors: management and culture, mission, resources, systems process, and structure.

THE INTERNAL ENVIRONMENT

For-profit and nonprofit organizations are created to produce products and/or services for customers.[1] *The organization's* **internal environment** *includes the factors that affect its performance from within its boundaries.* They are called internal factors because they are within the organization's control, as opposed to external factors, which are outside the organization's control.[2] The five internal environmental factors that we'll talk about in this section are management and culture, mission, resources, the systems process, and structure.

Management and Culture

Managers are responsible for the organization's performance.[3] They perform the functions of planning, organizing, leading, and controlling.[4] Top managers often receive credit for the success or failure of the organization because they have control over their behavior, even though the success or failure of a business is also affected by the external environment.[5] Clearly, however, FedEx would not be the success it is today without its founder and CEO, Frederick W. Smith.

Managers are also responsible for linking employees to the organizational culture.[6] *An* **organizational culture** *consists of the values, beliefs, and assumptions about appropriate behavior that members of an organization share.* The concept of an organizational culture is an approach to understanding how organizations function; its culture gives meaning to an organization's way of doing things.[7] Think of the culture as the organization's personality. Members of an organization need to understand its culture.[8]

This entire book focuses on how to manage. Because culture is such an important part of management,[9] we will discuss it in more detail after we have discussed the other four internal environmental factors.

Mission

The organization's **mission** *is its purpose or reason for being.* Developing the mission is top management's responsibility.[10] Managers with vision adapt the organization's mission by offering products in demand by customers.[11] Managers must develop and convey missions with clear objectives.[12]

When you see or hear the name **FedEx**, what do you think of? If you said overnight delivery, you are only partly correct. FedEx does deliver around 5 million packages daily, but today's FedEx is a family of companies that offers a global network of specialized services—transportation, information, international trade support, and supply-chain services—covering more than 210 countries and employing 210,000 people. On December 30, 2003, FedEx acquired **Kinko's**, to expand its global presence in that chain's 1,200 stores.

According to FedEx's new mission statement, "FedEx Corporation will produce superior financial returns for its shareowners by providing high value-added logistics, transportation, and related information services through focused operating companies. Customer service requirements will be met in the highest quality manner appropriate to each market segment served. FedEx Corporation will strive to develop mutually rewarding relationships with its

WorkApplication1

For each work application in this chapter, use a different organization, or several different ones, for your examples.
State the mission of an organization, preferably an organization you work for or have worked for.

employees, partners, and suppliers. Safety will be the first consideration in all operations. Corporate activities will be conducted to the highest ethical and professional standards."[13]

William Clay Ford, Jr. is the chairman and CEO of Ford Motor Company. Ford's vision is "to become the world's leading consumer company for automotive parts and services." Ford's mission: "We are a global family with a proud heritage, passionately committed to providing personal mobility for people around the world. We anticipate consumer need and deliver outstanding products and services that improve people's lives."

A company's mission statement should include objectives that allow for measurement and evaluation of performance.[14] It should state how the organization differs from its competitors. What unique advantage does the organization have to offer customers?[15] The mission should be relevant to all stakeholders.[16] **Stakeholders** *are people whose interests are affected by organizational behavior.* Among a company's stakeholders are employees, shareholders, customers, suppliers, and the government.[17] More about these stakeholders appears throughout this chapter.

The mission is an expression of the ends the organization strives to attain. The other internal environmental factors are considered the means to achieve the ends. Exhibit 2-1 illustrates how all factors of the internal environment are means to achieving the organization's mission. Note that managers develop the mission and set objectives, but the managers are a means to the end. As a manager, you may not write the mission statement, but you will be responsible for helping to achieve it.

Resources

As stated in Chapter 1, organizational resources include human, financial, physical, and informational. Human resources are responsible for achieving the organization's mission and objectives.[18] FedEx has thousands of employees delivering millions of packages daily worldwide. Physical resources at FedEx include aircraft and ground vehicles. Financial resources are necessary to purchase and maintain the physical resources and to pay employees. Informational resources include the FedEx computer system. As a manager, you will be responsible for using these four types of resources to achieve your organization's mission.

Systems Process

The **systems process** *is the method used to transform inputs into outputs.* The systems process has four components:

1. *Inputs.* Inputs are an organization's resources (human, financial, physical, and informational) that are transformed into products or services. At FedEx, the primary input is the millions of packages to be delivered worldwide daily.
2. *Transformation.* Transformation is the conversion of inputs into outputs. At FedEx, the packages (input) go to the hub (transformation), where they are sorted for delivery.
3. *Outputs.* Outputs are the products or services offered to customers. At FedEx, the packages are delivered to customers; the service of package delivery is FedEx's output.
4. *Feedback.* Feedback provides a means of control to ensure that the inputs and transformation process are producing the desired results. FedEx uses computers to gain feedback by tracking packages to help ensure that they are delivered on time.

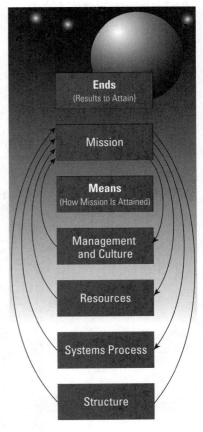

Exhibit 2-1
Internal Environmental Means and Ends

WorkApplication2

Illustrate the systems process for an organization you work for or have worked for.

_____

_____

_____

_____

Exhibit 2-2 _The Systems Process_

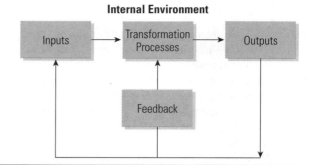

Managers with a systems perspective view the organization as a process rather than as separate departments for finance, marketing, operations, and human resources.[19] The focus is on the interrelationship of all of these functions as the inputs are converted into outputs.[20] See Exhibit 2-2 for an illustration of the systems process.

WorkApplication3

Identify the quality and value of a product you purchased recently.

_____

_____

_____

_____

_____

QUALITY

Quality is an internal factor because it is within the control of the organization. _Customers determine_ **quality** _by comparing a product's actual functioning to their requirements to determine value._ **Customer value** _is the perceived benefit of a product, used by customers to determine whether or not to buy the product._ Customers don't simply buy a product itself. They buy the benefit they expect to derive from that product. Value is what motivates us to buy products. When the author of this book bought a computer and software, it was not for the equipment itself; it was for the benefit of being able to compose the manuscript for the book using word-processing software.

—————————————— **Learning** Outcome **2** ——————————————
List and explain the need for the two primary principles of total quality management (TQM).

TOTAL QUALITY MANAGEMENT (TQM)

TQM is the commonly used term for stressing quality within an organization.[21] TQM uses a systems perspective because it is not a program for one department, but a responsibility of everyone in an organization.[22] **Total quality management (TQM)** *is the process that involves everyone in an organization focusing on the customer to continually improve product value.* The two primary principles of TQM are (1) to focus on delivering customer value and (2) to continually improve the system and its processes.[23] The Japanese term for continuous improvement is *kaizen.* You will learn more about quality and TQM in Chapter 15.

Structure

Structure refers to the way in which an organization groups its resources to accomplish its mission.[24] As discussed in Chapter 1, an organization is a system structured into departments such as finance, marketing, production, human resources, and so on. Each of these departments affects the organization as a whole, and each department is affected by the other departments. Organizations structure resources to transform inputs into outputs. All of an organization's resources must be structured effectively to achieve its mission. As a manager, you will be responsible for part of the organization's structure. You will learn more about organizational structure in Chapters 6 through 8. See Exhibit 2-3 for a review of the components of the internal environment.

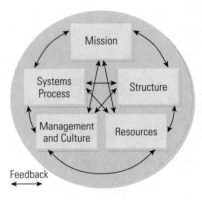

Exhibit 2-3
Components of the Internal Environment

Join the Discussion Ethics & Social Responsibility

Downsizing and Part-Time Workers

1. Is downsizing ethical and socially responsible?
2. Is using part-time employees rather than full-time ones ethical and socially responsible?

As firms struggle to compete in the global economy, many have downsized. *Downsizing* is the process of cutting resources to get more done with less and thereby increase productivity. Primarily, cuts are made in human resources, and many laid-off factory workers find their jobs have disappeared for good. With downsizing, many firms are using new structures that have fewer levels of management. In some firms, the positions formerly held by full-time employees are filled by part-time workers. Using part-time employees saves companies money because such employees do not receive any benefits (e.g., health insurance), in contrast to full-time employees, who are entitled to benefits. **Wal-Mart** is known for maintaining a very high ratio of part-time to full-time employees, as a way of keeping costs down. Wal-Mart's policy of using mostly part-time workers at minimum or near-minimum wage is one of the reasons the chain can offer lower prices.

(Continued)

Join the Discussion Ethics & Social Responsibility

(Continued)

    Wal-Mart has recently been expanding its sales of grocery items, competing directly with supermarket chains. Most supermarket chain employees are unionized and receive good wages and benefits. In 2003 and 2004, supermarket workers in California went on strike to keep their health care benefits. Negotiators on the side of management claimed that the chains could not afford to continue to offer the level of benefits that strikers were asking for, because the chains had to compete with Wal-Mart's low grocery prices.

Sources: W. F. Cascio, "Strategies for Responsible Restructuring," *Academy of Management Executive* (2002), Vol. 16, No. 3, pp. 80–81; C. Ansberry, "Laid-Off Factory Workers Find Jobs Are Drying Up for Good," *Wall Street Journal* (July 21, 2003), p. A1; J. Child and R. G. McGrath, "Organizations Unfettered: Organizational Form in an Information-Intensive Economy," *Academy of Management Journal* (2001), Vol. 44, No. 6, pp. 1135–1146.

ORGANIZATIONAL CULTURE

Fostering the right organizational culture is one of the most important responsibilities of a chief executive.[25] Management needs to be involved in establishing the shared values, beliefs, and assumptions so that employees know how to behave.[26] CEO Ronald DeFeo of **Terex Corporation** says that top management has to establish practical values in the organization, things that people can relate to that are common across nationalities.[27] However, at the same time, culture plays a major role in shaping managers' behavior. Examples of aspects of organizational culture include the casual dress and long workdays of **Microsoft**; the rigid work rules and conservative dress code at the **Bank of America**; the emphasis at **Southwest Airlines** on fun and excitement, which founder Herb Kelleher explains in an orientation video set to rap music; and FedEx's People-Service-Profit philosophy and its goal to ensure time-certain delivery.

In this section, we will discuss how employees learn organizational culture, the three levels of culture, strong and weak cultures, managing and changing cultures, and organizational learning.

Learning the Organization's Culture

Organizational culture is primarily learned through observing people and events in the organization.[28] There are five artifacts of organizational culture, which are important ways that employees learn about it:[29]

1. *Heroes*, such as founders Tom Watson of IBM, Sam Walton of Wal-Mart, Herb Kelleher of Southwest Airlines, Frederick Smith of FedEx, and others who have made outstanding contributions to their organizations.
2. *Stories*, often about founders and others who have made extraordinary efforts, such as Sam Walton visiting every Wal-Mart store yearly, or someone driving through a blizzard to deliver a product or service. Public statements and speeches can also be considered stories.

3. *Slogans*, such as McDonald's Q, S, C, V (or Quality, Service, Cleanliness, and Value).
4. *Symbols*, such as plaques, pins, jackets, or a Mary Kay Cosmetics pink Cadillac. Symbols convey meaning.
5. *Ceremonies*, such as awards dinners for top achievers at Mary Kay Cosmetics.[30]

Learning Outcome 3

Describe the three levels of organizational culture and their relationship to each other.

Three Levels of Culture

*The three **levels of culture** are behavior, values and beliefs, and assumptions.* Exhibit 2-4 illustrates the three levels of culture.

LEVEL 1. BEHAVIOR

Behavior includes the observable things that people do and say, or the actions employees take. *Artifacts* result from behavior and include written and spoken language, dress, material objects, and the organization's physical layout. Heroes, stories, slogans, symbols, and ceremonies are all part of behavior-level culture. The behavior level is also called the *visible level*. Values, beliefs, and assumptions are considered the *invisible level*, as you cannot actually observe them.

LEVEL 2. VALUES AND BELIEFS

Values represent the way people believe they ought to behave,[31] and beliefs represent "if-then" statements: "If I do X, then Y will happen." Values and beliefs provide the operating principles that guide decision making and shape the behavior that result in level 1 culture. Values and beliefs cannot be observed directly; we can only infer from people's behavior what they value and believe.

Although organizations use heroes, stories, symbols, and ceremonies to convey the important values and beliefs, the slogan is critical to level 2 culture. A *slogan* expresses key values. Slogans are part of organizational mission statements, while a philosophy (People-Service-Profit) is a formal statement of values and beliefs.

LEVEL 3. ASSUMPTIONS

Assumptions are values and beliefs that are so deeply ingrained that they are considered unquestionably true. Because assumptions are shared, they are rarely discussed. They serve as an "automatic pilot" to guide behavior. In fact, people often feel threatened when assumptions are challenged. If you question employees on why they do something, or suggest a change, they often respond with statements like "That's the way it's always been done." Assumptions are often the most stable and enduring part of culture and are difficult to change.

Notice that behavior is at the top of the diagram in Exhibit 2-4. Assumptions and values and beliefs affect behavior, not the other way around; in other words, cause and effect work from the bottom up.

WorkApplication4

Identify the cultural heroes, stories, symbols, slogans, and ceremonies for an organization you are/were a member of.

_____

_____

_____

_____

Exhibit 2-4
Three Levels of Organizational Culture

Strong and Weak Cultures

WorkApplication5

Describe the organizational culture at all three levels for a firm you work for or have worked for. Does the organization have a strong or a weak culture?

_____

_____

_____

_____

_____

Organizational cultural strength is characterized by a continuum from strong to weak. Organizations with strong cultures have employees who subconsciously know the shared assumptions; consciously know the values and beliefs; agree with the shared assumptions, values, and beliefs; and behave as expected.[32] Organizations with many employees who do not behave as expected have weak cultures. When employees do not agree with the generally accepted shared values, they may become rebels and fight the culture.

Fortune magazine has an annual edition covering "Most Admired Companies" that have the characteristics of strong organizational culture. Companies with strong cultures include **Amdahl, Boeing, Dana Corporation, Emerson Electric, Fluor, IBM, Johnson & Johnson, Marriott, Procter & Gamble,** and **3M.**

The primary benefits of a strong culture include easier communication and cooperation. Employees exhibit unity of direction, and consensus is easier to reach. The primary disadvantage is the threat of becoming stagnant.

Managing, Changing, and Merging Cultures

Symbolic leaders *articulate a vision for an organization and reinforce the culture through slogans, symbols, and ceremonies.* They may also tell stories and draw people's attention to heroes. Herb Kelleher at Southwest Airlines is often cited as an example of a great symbolic leader. FedEx's Fred Smith is also a symbolic leader. Symbolic leaders manage, change, and merge cultures.

Organizational culture can be managed by drawing attention to heroes and using stories, symbols, slogans, and ceremonies.[33] If any of these five elements of a strong culture are missing or weak, top management can work

---

Applying The Concept 2

Strong and Weak Cultures

Identify whether each statement reflects an organization with a strong or weak culture.

a. strong culture

b. weak culture

_____ 6. "Walking around this department during my job interview, I realized I'd have to wear a jacket and tie every day."

_____ 7. "I'm a little tired of hearing about how our company founders conducted business. We all know the stories, so why do people keep telling them?"

_____ 8. "I've never attended a meeting with people who all seem to act the same. I guess I can just be me rather than trying to act in an acceptable manner to others."

_____ 9. "It's hard to say what is really important because management says quality is important, but they force us to work at too fast a pace and they know we send out defective products just to meet orders."

_____ 10. "I started to tell this ethnic joke and the other employees all gave me a dirty look."

to strengthen the culture.[34] However, strengthening an organizational culture is not a program with a starting and ending date; it is an ongoing process.

Organizational cultures often need to be changed to ensure organizational success.[35] However, changing cultures is not easy. Organizations that have successfully changed cultures include the **City of San Diego, Fiat, Ford, GM, Pacific Mutual, Polaroid, Procter & Gamble, Tektronix,** and **TRW, Inc.**

A key strategy that big businesses use to compete in the global environment is to take part in mergers and acquisitions. However, almost one-half of acquired companies are sold within five years, and 90 percent of mergers never live up to expectations—**DaimlerChrysler** and **Pharmacia & Upjohn** are prime examples. One of the major reasons for failure is the inability to integrate the organizational cultures.

To successfully change or merge cultures, a strong symbolic leader is needed. The new or merged cultural vision must generate excitement that employees can share.[36] The leader must also continue to give public statements and speeches about the new slogan and use symbols and ceremonies to reinforce implementation of the new or merged culture.

Bill Gates appointed his longtime friend and VP Steve Ballmer to replace him as CEO of Microsoft, so that Gates could focus on product development. Motivated by Jack Welch's autobiography, *Jack: Straight from the Gut*, Ballmer reorganized Microsoft into seven core units over a 20-month period. (See the case at the end of Chapter 1 for a list of the seven units.) At the same time, Ballmer realized he had to fix a major flaw in Microsoft's corporate culture. Microsoft was strong in product development and sales, but weak in financial management. Microsoft had invested billions to expand into diverse businesses, but it lacked a clear sense of how well each venture was performing financially. Now each of the seven units has strong financial measures in place. Executives set financial targets, handle budgeting, and measure performance of their units.

Microsoft also changed another element affecting its culture. It stopped offering entrepreneurial stock options, which made many early employees millionaires, and replaced these incentives with stock awards, which provide earnings even when the stock is falling. Steve says these changes are not going to remake Microsoft's culture quickly.[37]

Learning Organizations

Learning has been defined as the detection and correction of errors; individual learning enables organizational learning.[38] In order to learn in the workplace, you must understand the organizational culture in which you work and the other cultures you interact with.[39] Is your organization a learning organization?[40] You should understand the relationship between knowledge management and the learning organization. *A* **learning organization** *has a culture that values sharing knowledge so as to adapt to the changing environment and continuously improve.* Solving problems is critical to continuous improvement in learning organizations.

Learning organizations use information technology (IT) to manage knowledge, but IT is only part of what contributes to making them learning organizations. Through IT, knowledge, rather than being hoarded, is shared across the organization to increase the performance of business units and the entire organization.[41] TQM also uses IT, and thus TQM can be incorporated within the learning organization.[42]

CREATING A LEARNING ORGANIZATION

The learning organization is not a program with steps to follow. The learning organization is a philosophy or attitude about what an organization is and about the role of employees; it is part of the organizational culture.

Creating a learning organization requires changes in many areas and demands strong leadership, a team-based structure, employee empowerment, open information, a participative strategy, and a strong adaptive culture.[43] A strong adaptive culture is created through effective leadership, often by a symbolic leader; however, everyone helps to create learning by participating in open sharing of information. Teams are empowered to create and share knowledge. These six characteristics of learning organizations are interrelated through the systems effect, as each one affects all the others.

Ford has a strong culture, which is driven by its slogan, "Quality Is Job One." Ford's mission, values, and guiding principles are expressed in one sentence: "Quality comes first—to achieve customer satisfaction, the quality of our products and services must be our number-one priority." Ford has adopted the concept of Total Quality Excellence (TQE), emphasizing the importance of quality in everything the company does. Several values influence Ford's organizational culture:

- **Our business is driven by our customer focus, creativity, resourcefulness, and entrepreneurial spirit.**
- **We are an inspired, diverse team. We respect and value everyone's contribution. The health and safety of our people are paramount.**
- **We are a leader in environmental responsibility. Our integrity is never compromised and we make a positive contribution to society.**
- **We constantly strive to improve in everything we do. Guided by these values, we provide superior returns to our shareholders.**

Learning Outcome 4

Describe how the nine external environmental factors—customers, competitors, suppliers, labor force, shareholders, society, technology, economies, and governments—can affect the internal business environment.

THE EXTERNAL ENVIRONMENT

The organization's **external environment** *includes the factors outside its boundaries that affect its performance.* Although managers can control the internal environment, they have very limited influence over what happens outside the organization. The nine major external factors are customers, competition, suppliers, labor force/unions, shareholders, society, technology, the economy, and governments. The first five are known as *task factors*, and the other four are known as *general factors*.

Customers

Customers have more power today than ever before, as they have a major effect on the organization's performance through their purchase of products.[44] Without customers, there is no need for an organization. Effective managers realize the need to offer customers products of value to them.[45] Continually improving customer value is often the difference between success and failure in business.[46] Customer value changes over time, and if products don't change with it, companies lose customers to competitors.[47] Changing tastes dented Campbell's canned-soup sales, so Campbell developed new soups to compete with popular ready-to-serve soups.

IS CUSTOMER SERVICE IMPORTANT?

A study revealed that organizations with high service strategies have higher market share and return on sales than organizations with low service strategies.[48] So there is no question that service has an economic impact.[49] Service is an important part of value. This, among other reasons, is why TQM focuses on creating customer value.[50] The better you are at creating customer value, the more successful your management career will be.

Competition

Organizations must compete for customers. Competitors' strategic moves affect the performance of the organization. FedEx was the first to offer overnight delivery by 10:30 A.M., but its primary competitor, **United Parcel Service (UPS)**, was first to introduce overnight delivery by 8:30 A.M., followed by same-day delivery. FedEx now matches UPS's services in order to keep its customers.

Another important area of customer value is pricing. When a competitor changes prices, firms tend to match prices to keep customers; for example, the prices of Compaq, Dell, Gateway, Hewlett Packard (HP), and IBM computers have all declined over the past decade. Competition is increasing as the global economy expands.

Effective managers develop missions with strategies that offer a unique advantage over the competition. **Domino's Pizza** offered free delivery guaranteed within 30 minutes (this time limit was later changed), and took business away from **Pizza Hut** and others. Now, because of the competition, Pizza Hut and others also offer free delivery.

Time-based competition, which focuses on increasing the speed of going from product idea to delivery to customers, is a current trend in the global business environment.

Exhibit 2-5 presents the worldwide ranking, by sales volume, of companies that manufacture light vehicles (as of October 2003). Note that the exhibit lists global competitors. U.S. automakers lost market share to foreign rivals in 2003.[51]

WorkApplication6

Give an example of how one firm's competitors have affected that business.

_____

_____

_____

_____

_____

IOM

Exhibit 2-5 *Light Vehicle Sales*

Company	Sales (Jan.–Oct. 2003)
General Motors	8,790,000
Ford	7,600,000
Toyota	6,901,000
DaimlerChrysler	6,050,000
Renault/Nissan	5,420,000
Volkswagen	5,060,000
PSA	3,230,000
Honda	3,000,000
Suzuki	2,350,000
Hyundai	2,250,000

Source: "Race Leaders," *Wall Street Journal* (December 8, 2003), p. A1.

Although these automakers compete, they also collaborate to help each other. "The GM Group of global partners includes Fiat Auto SpA of Italy, Fuji Heavy Industries Ltd., Isuzu Motors Ltd., and Suzuki Motor Corp. of Japan, which are involved in various product, power train, and purchasing collaborations. In addition, GM is the largest shareholder in GM Daewoo Auto and Technology Co. of South Korea. GM also collaborates on technology with BMW AG of Germany and Toyota Motor Corp. of Japan, and shares vehicle manufacturing ventures with several automakers around the world, including Toyota, Suzuki, Shanghai Automotive Industry Corp. of China, AVTOVAZ of Russia, and Renault SA of France." (*http://www.gm.com*, accessed May 13, 2004)

The future growth of the auto industry is in China. **Toyota** is pushing hard in China, as it hopes to take the number-one spot away from competitor and partner GM. Executive Akio Toyoda, grandson of the founder of Toyota, is in charge of expansion into China, and he said, "There's no future for us globally if we mess up in China." However, GM is not about to give up its number-one spot without a fight. In fact, GM currently controls about 35 percent of sales in China, compared to Toyota's 2 percent.[52] Can Toyota overtake GM?

Suppliers

An organization's resources often come from outside the firm. Organizations buy land, buildings, machines, equipment, natural resources, and component parts from suppliers. Therefore, an organization's performance is affected by suppliers. General Motors built the Saturn plant and developed a separate Saturn dealership network to sell its cars. However, in its first year, because of production problems, Saturn dealers received only half of their allocation of cars. The dealers' performance was adversely affected. To be an effective manager, you need to realize the importance of suppliers and develop close working relationships with them.[53]

Labor Force

The employees of an organization have a direct effect on its performance. Management recruits human resources from the available labor force outside its boundaries. The firm's mission, its structure, and its systems process are major determining factors of the capability levels employees need to meet objectives. The skills needed by FedEx employees differ from those needed by the employees of Gap and high-tech firms, and there is a labor shortage in some industries.

Unions also provide employees for the organization. Unions are considered an external factor because they become a third party when dealing with the organization. Most UPS employees are members of the Teamsters Union, whereas FedEx employees do not have a major union. A union has the power to strike. When a union strikes, revenues and wages are lost.

Shareholders

The owners of a corporation, known as *shareholders*, have a significant influence on management.[54] Most shareholders of large corporations are generally not involved in the day-to-day operation of the firm, but they do vote for the directors of the corporation. The board of directors is also generally not involved in the day-to-day operation of the firm. However, it hires and fires top management. The top manager reports to the board of directors. If the organization does not perform well, managers can be fired.[55]

Society

Members of society may also exert pressure on the management of an organization.[56] Individuals and groups have formed to pressure business for changes. People who live in the same area with a business do not want it to pollute the air or water or otherwise abuse the natural resources. Societal pressures have brought about tougher pollution requirements. Tuna companies used to kill dolphins when catching tuna. However, because of societal pressure, many companies now put claims on tuna fish cans stating that they are "dolphin safe." Society is pressuring business to be socially responsible and ethical. **Monsanto** was pressured because of its bioengineered agricultural products, and **Nike** because of its sweatshop tactics that exploited employees.[57]

Technology

As discussed in Chapter 1, technological change is a fact of life in today's world, and the rate of technological change will continue to increase. Few organizations operate today as they did even a decade ago. Products not envisioned a few years ago are now being mass-produced. Computers and the Internet have changed the speed and the manner in which organizations conduct and transact business.[58] Computers are often a major part of a firm's systems process.

The Internet and the virtual office are blurring roles in the supply chain and giving small companies the chance to work with and compete against large businesses on an even footing.[59] The Internet is creating global opportunities for many organizations. For example, Ford backed the use of the Internet by giving 400,000 employees computers so that they can go online from home.[60] Companies that do not use the Internet or are slow to change face the threat of losing business to competitors. New technology creates opportunities for some companies and is a threat to others.

FedEx prides itself in using technology. FedEx was the first to develop a hub system that enabled overnight delivery and a real-time tracking system for all packages. On the other hand, the fax machine and e-mail created a threat for FedEx, offering instant delivery of text material.

WorkApplication7

Give an example of how technology has affected one or more organizations, preferably one you work for or have worked for.

_____

_____

_____

_____

_____

The Economy

No organization has control over economic growth, inflation, interest rates, foreign exchange rates, and so on, yet these things have a direct impact on organizational performance. In general, as measured by gross domestic product (GDP), businesses do better when the economy is growing than during times of decreased economic activity, or recession.[61]

During periods of inflation, businesses experience increased costs, which cannot always be passed along to consumers. This results in decreased profits. When interest rates are high, it costs more to borrow money, which may affect profits. Foreign exchange rates affect businesses both at home and abroad. (We'll see how in Chapter 3.) An understanding of economics, and more important, global economics, can help you to advance to top-level management.

Governments

National, state, and local governments all set laws and regulations that businesses must obey. These laws remain basically intact through generations of political turnover, even though their interpretations, guidelines, and enforcement do depend heavily on the government officials of the time.[62] The government environment is sometimes referred to as the political and legal environment.[63]

The auto industry has been required to decrease the amount of pollution cars emit. Airlines have been told to decrease the noise level of their planes. Businesses can no longer dump their waste in waterways. The Occupational Safety and Health Administration (OSHA) sets safety standards that must be met. Pharmaceutical companies cannot market drugs without Food and Drug Administration (FDA) approval. The Americans with Disabilities Act (ADA) compelled businesses to change many employment practices. In other words, to a large extent, business may not do whatever it wants to do; the government tells business what it can and cannot do.[64]

Governments create both opportunities and threats for businesses. A number of years ago, the state of Maine changed the legal drinking age from 21 to 18. Dick Peltier opened a bar targeted at the 18- to 20-year-old group that became very successful. However, a few years later, the state increased the legal drinking age. Dick lost his business virtually overnight. **Allstate Insurance** left the state of Massachusetts because of the unfavorable government environment there.

To learn more about the U.S. federal government, visit one or more of its many Web sites:

Federal Trade Commission, *http://www.ftc.gov*
Government Printing Office, *http://www.gpo.gov*

Applying The Concept 3

The External Environment

Identify which external environmental factor is referred to in each statement.

a. customers   d. labor force   g. technology
b. competition   e. shareholders   h. governments
c. suppliers   f. society   i. economy

_____11. "Procter & Gamble has developed a new biodegradable material to replace the plastic liner on its diapers so that they don't take up landfill space for so long."

_____12. "At one time, AT&T was the only long-distance company, but then MCI, Sprint, and others came along and have taken away some of its customers."

_____13. "I applied for a loan to start my own business, but I might not get it because money is tight these days, even though interest rates are high."

_____14. "The owners of the company have threatened to fire the CEO if the business does not improve this year."

_____15. "Management was going to sell our company to PepsiCo, but the government said that would be in violation of antitrust laws. What will happen to our company now?"

Internal Revenue Service, *http://www.irs.ustreas.gov*
Library of Congress, *http://www.loc.gov*
Securities and Exchange Commission, *http://www.sec.gov*
Department of Commerce, *http://www.doc.gov*
Treasury Department, *http://www.ustreas.gov*
Environmental Protection Agency, *http://www.epa.gov*
A great place to find demographic information on potential customers is the Census Bureau Web site: *http://www.census.gov*.

Chaos and Interactive Management

In many industries, the environment is changing at an incredibly fast pace.[65] Operating in such an environment is commonly referred to as being "in chaos." Today's managers must be able to thrive on chaos. But at the same time, change should be interactive.

According to Russell Ackoff, unlike reactive managers (who make changes only when forced to by external factors) and responsive managers

---

Join the Discussion Ethics & Social Responsibility

Auto Fuel Efficiency

1. Are the automakers being ethical and socially responsible by taking advantage of loopholes in the law to classify one-half of their vehicles as light trucks?
2. Should society be concerned about fuel efficiency? Should people use fuel efficiency as a major criterion when buying a car?
3. Should the government be involved in setting fuel efficiency standards? If yes, should it change the current standards? How?

The **National Highway Traffic Safety Administration (NHTSA)** is responsible for setting fuel efficiency standards for cars and light trucks. However, NHTSA has been criticized because the fuel economy of new vehicles in the United States has been falling since 1988, even as the country continues to depend on foreign oil. NHTSA has actually increased its standards over the years: 2005 model cars must average 27.5 miles per gallon (mpg); light trucks must average 21 mpg.

NHTSA advocates claim that the automakers are taking advantage of loopholes in the current laws. For example, one-half of all vehicles sold in the United States, including the PT cruiser, are classified as light trucks, to avoid the need to achieve higher fuel efficiency. Also, heavy SUVs (over 8,500 pounds) including the Hummer H2, are not subject to fuel efficiency standards.

If the NHTSA changed the definition of light trucks, automakers would have to spend a lot of money to reengineer their SUVs to make them more efficient; these expenditures would cut into profits. Also, some people fear that the automakers would dramatically decrease the weight of their vehicles, making them less safe. So SUV rollover accidents could increase, which could also cause more accidents to small vehicles.

Source: S. Power, "Rules Regulating Gasoline Mileage Face an Overhaul," *Wall Street Journal* (December 22, 2003), p. A1.

(who try to adapt to the environment by predicting and preparing for change before they are required to do so), interactive managers design a desirable future and invent ways of bringing it about.[66] They believe they are capable of creating a significant part of the future and controlling its effects on them. They try to prevent threats, not merely prepare for them, and to create opportunities, not merely exploit them. Rather than reacting or responding, interactive managers make things happen for their benefit and for that of their stakeholders.[67] In the early 1970s, people believed that overnight delivery was not possible, but this did not stop Frederick Smith from making overnight delivery a reality with Federal Express. Do you have any great ideas for a new business or a way to help an existing business create customer value?

As a business grows, the complexity of its internal and external environments increases. The major factor increasing the complexity of the environment is the globalization of markets.[68] For a review of the organizational environment, see Exhibit 2-6.[69] Think about the complexity of FedEx's environment. FedEx does business worldwide. Therefore, it has to follow the rules and regulations of different governments in countries with different economies, labor forces, societies, and so on. In the next chapter, you will learn about conducting business in a global environment.

Exhibit 2-6 *The Organizational Environment*

Feedback

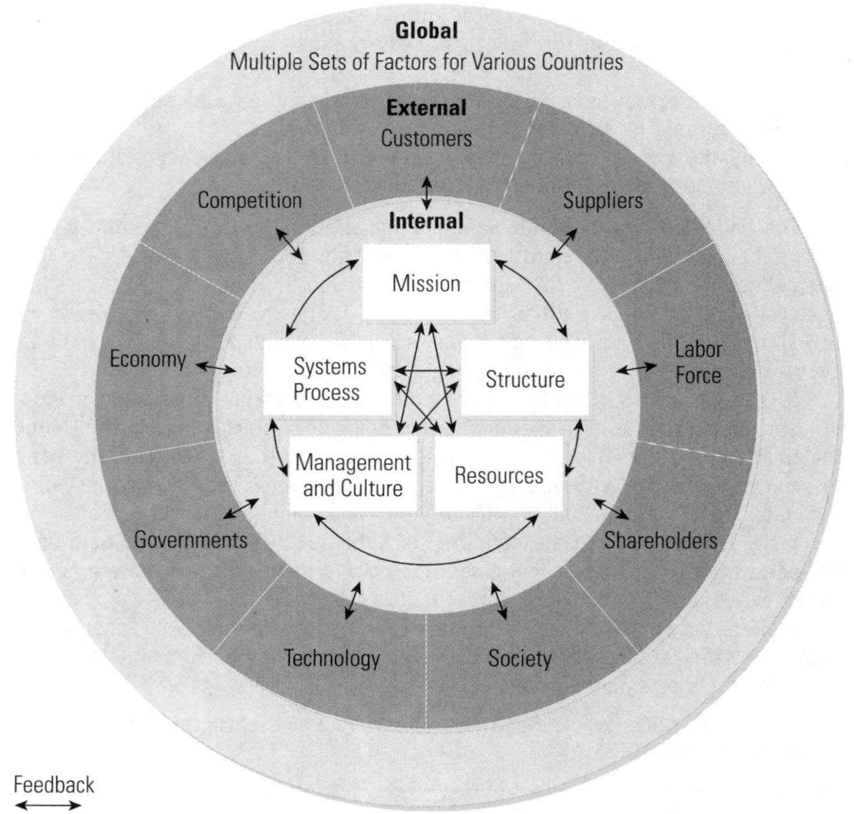

BUSINESS ETHICS

As we discussed in Chapter 1, Americans' trust in corporations has been strained because of criminal and unethical behavior by executives at numerous firms. The loss of public trust threatens the very integrity of capitalism.[70] To help restore confidence, the Sarbanes-Oxley Act was passed to tighten the laws affecting business ethics, and most companies have reexamined their ethics policies.[71]

Ethics *are the standards of right and wrong that influence behavior.* Right behavior is considered ethical, and wrong behavior is considered unethical. Government laws and regulations are designed to govern business behavior. However, ethics go beyond legal requirements. What is considered ethical in one country may be unethical in another. It is not always easy to distinguish between ethical and unethical behavior, such as accepting a gift (ethical) versus taking a bribe (unethical). In this section, we'll discuss ethics and ethical management. First, complete the Self-Assessment that follows to determine how ethical your behavior is.

Self-Assessment

How Ethical Is Your Behavior?

For this exercise, you will respond to the same set of statements twice. The first time you read them, focus on your own behavior and the frequency with which you behave in certain ways. On the line before each statement number, place a number from 1 to 4 that represents how often you do that behavior (or how likely you would be to do it):

Frequently			Never
1	2	3	4

The numbers allow you to determine your level of ethics. You can be honest, as you will not tell others in class your score. *Sharing ethics scores is not part of the exercise.*

Next, go through the list of statements a second time, focusing on other people in an organization that you work for now or one you have worked for. Place an O on the line after the number of each statement if you have observed someone doing this behavior; place an R on the line if you reported this behavior within the organization or externally: O = observed, R = reported.

In College

_____ 1._____ Cheating on homework assignments

_____ 2._____ Cheating on exams

_____ 3._____ Submitting as your own work papers that were completed by someone else

On the Job

_____ 4._____ Lying to others to get what you want or to stay out of trouble

_____ 5._____ Coming to work late, leaving work early, taking long breaks/lunches and getting paid for them

_____ 6._____ Socializing, goofing off, or doing personal work rather than doing the work that you are getting paid to do

_____ 7._____ Calling in sick to get a day off when you are not sick

_____ 8._____ Using an organization's phone, computer, Internet access, copier, mail, or car for personal use

_____ 9._____ Taking home company tools or equipment without permission for personal use

_____ 10._____ Taking home organizational supplies or merchandise

_____ 11._____ Giving company supplies or merchandise to friends or allowing them to take them without saying anything

_____ 12._____ Applying for reimbursement for expenses for meals, travel, or other expenses that weren't actually incurred

(Continued)

How Ethical Is Your Behaviour   (Continued)

_____13._____ Taking spouse or friends out to eat or on business trips and charging their expenses to the organizational account

_____14._____ Accepting gifts from customers/suppliers in exchange for giving them business

_____15._____ Cheating on your taxes

_____16._____ Misleading a customer to make a sale, such as promising rapid delivery dates

_____17._____ Misleading competitors to get information to use to compete against them, such as pretending to be a customer/supplier

_____18._____ Planting something that makes you look good, like weapons of mass destruction so you get reelected

_____19._____ Selling more of a product than the customer needs in order to get the commission

_____20._____ Spreading rumors about coworkers or competitors to make yourself look better, so as to advance professionally or to make more sales

_____21._____ Lying for your boss when asked or told to do so

_____22._____ Deleting information that makes you look bad or changing information to make yourself look better

_____23._____ Allowing yourself to be pressured, or pressuring others, to sign off on documents that contain false information

_____24._____ Allowing yourself to be pressured, or pressuring others, to sign off on documents you haven't read, knowing they may contain information or describe decisions that might be considered inappropriate

_____25._____ If you were to give this assessment to a coworker with whom you do not get along, would she or he agree with your answers? If your answer is yes, write a 4 on the line before the statement number; if your answer is no, write a 1 on the line.

After completing the second phase of the exercise (indicating whether you have observed or reported any of the behaviors), list any other unethical behaviors you have observed. Indicate if you reported the behavior using R.

26. _____

27. _____

28. _____

Note: This self-assessment is not meant to be a precise measure of your ethical behavior. It is designed to get you thinking about ethics and about your behavior and that of others from an ethical perspective. All of these actions are considered unethical behavior in most organizations.

Another ethical aspect of this exercise is your honesty when rating your behavior. How honest were you?

Scoring: To determine your ethics score, add up the numbers for all 25 statements. Your total will be between 25 and 100. Place the number that represents your score on the continuum below. The higher your score, the more ethical your behavior.

25 30 40 50 60 70 80 90 100
Unethical   Ethical

Does Ethical Behavior Pay?

Ethical behavior _is_ worthwhile. Research studies have reported a positive relationship between ethical behavior and leadership effectiveness.[72] And unethical behavior is damaging on many levels. At the societal level, unethical behavior creates a negative image of big business. The unethical behavior of those at **Enron** and other companies cost many organizations and people a great deal of money directly, but it also hurt everyone who had invested in the stock market, and the general economy, as the unethical behavior contributed to the bear market. At the organizational level, Enron is no longer the company it was, and its auditor, Arthur Andersen, lost many of its clients and had to sell parts of its business as a result of the unethical behavior. At the individual level, you may say that former Enron CEO Kenneth Lay and others made millions from their unethical behavior. However, these top executives had already made millions through honest behavior; their unethical behavior sent some of them to prison, and they may never hold high-level positions again. With all the negative media coverage, unethical leaders' lives will never be the same. Undoubtedly, greed has destroyed leaders.[73] Mahatma Gandhi called business without morality a sin.

Values and ethics are vitally important to effective leadership.[74] Having strong ethics means having integrity, and people trust others they believe have integrity. Today, employees don't assume that they can trust managers, and a survey found that most respondents do not have a great deal of trust in management.[75] A broken promise or a lie results in a loss of trust that's extremely difficult to regain.[76] Do you have good relationships with people who lie to you? If you want to have good relationships, you have to be ethical.

How Personality Traits and Attitudes, Moral Development, and the Situation Affect Ethical Behavior

PERSONALITY TRAITS AND ATTITUDES

In Chapter 9, you will learn more about personality. For now, you probably already realize that because of their personalities, some people have a higher level of ethics than others, as integrity is considered a personality trait. Unfortunately, a culture of lying and dishonesty is infecting American business and society, as these behaviors have become more acceptable.[77] Some people lie deliberately, based on the attitude that lying is no big deal; some people don't even realize that they are liars.[78]

—————————————— Learning Outcome 5 ——————————————
Compare the three levels of moral development.

MORAL DEVELOPMENT

A second factor affecting ethical behavior is *moral development*, which refers to distinguishing right from wrong and choosing to do the right thing. People's ability to make ethical choices is related to their level of moral development.

There are three levels of personal moral development, as outlined in Exhibit 2-7. At the first level, the *preconventional* level, a person chooses right and wrong behavior based on self-interest and the likely consequences of the behavior (reward or punishment). Those whose ethical reasoning has advanced to the second, *conventional* level, seek to maintain expected standards and live up to the expectations of others. Those at the third level, the *postconventional* level, make an effort to define moral principles for themselves, regardless of leaders' or groups' ethics.

Although most of us have the potential to reach the third, or postconventional, level of moral development, only about 20 percent of people reach this level. Most people behave at the conventional level, while some do not advance beyond the first, or preconventional, level. What level of moral development do you consider yourself to have reached? What can you do to further develop your ethical behavior?

WorkApplication8

Give an example from an organization where you work or have worked, of behavior at each of the three levels of moral development.

————————————————
————————————————
————————————————
————————————————
————————————————

Exhibit 2-7 *Levels of Moral Development*

Level	Description of Behavior	Examples
1. Preconventional level	Self-interest motivates behavior; a person acts to meet his or her own needs or gain rewards and follows rules or obeys authority only to avoid punishment. Leaders at this level often are autocratic toward others and use their position to gain personal advantages.	"I lie to customers to sell more products and get bigger commission checks."
2. Conventional level	Behavior is motivated by the desire to live up to others' expectations. It is common to copy the behavior (ethical or otherwise) of leaders or of those in one's group. Peer pressure is used to enforce group norms. Lower-level managers at this level of moral development tend to use a leadership style similar to those of higher-level managers.	"I lie to customers because the other sales reps do it, too."
3. Postconventional level	Behavior is motivated by universal principles of right and wrong, regardless of the expectations of leaders or one's group. A person seeks to balance self-interest with the interests of others and the common good. People at this level will follow ethical principles even if doing so violates the law and risks social rejection, economic loss, or physical punishment. Leaders at this level of moral development tend to be visionary and committed to serving others while empowering followers to also attain this level of morality.	"I don't lie to customers because it's wrong to do so." Martin Luther King, Jr. broke what he considered to be unjust laws and spent time in jail in his quest for universal dignity and justice.

THE SITUATION

A third factor affecting ethical behavior is the situation. Unsupervised people in highly competitive situations are more likely to engage in unethical behavior. Unethical behavior occurs more often when there is no formal ethics policy or code of ethics and when unethical behavior is not punished; unethical behavior is especially prevalent when it is rewarded.[79] People are also less likely to report unethical behavior (blow the whistle) when they perceive the violation as not being serious or when they are friends of the offender.[80]

How People Justify Unethical Behavior

Most people understand right and wrong behavior and have a conscience. So why do good people do bad things? Most often, when people behave unethically, it is not because they have some type of character flaw or were born bad. Few people see themselves as unethical. We all want to view ourselves in a positive manner. Therefore, when we do behave unethically, we often justify the behavior to protect our *self-concept* so that we don't have a guilty conscience or feel remorse. Let's discuss several thinking processes used to justify unethical behavior.

Moral justification is the process of reinterpreting immoral behavior in terms of a higher purpose. The terrorists who struck the United States on September 11, 2001, killed innocent people, as do suicide bombers in Israel and elsewhere—yet they believe their killing is for the good and that they will go to heaven for their actions. People who behave unethically (lie about a competitor to hurt its reputation, fix prices, steal confidential information, etc.) say that they do so for the good of the organization or its employees. People at the preconventional and conventional levels of moral development more commonly use the following justifications.

- **Displacement of responsibility** is the process of blaming one's unethical behavior on others. "I was only following orders, my boss told me to inflate the figures." In a response to one survey, 53 percent of employees said they would be willing to misrepresent financial information if asked to by a supervisor.[81]
- **Diffusion of responsibility** occurs when those in a group behave unethically and no one person is held responsible. "We all take bribes/kickbacks; it's the way we do business." or "We all take merchandise home (steal)." As noted earlier in the discussion of conventional morality, peer pressure is used to enforce group norms.
- **Advantageous comparison** is the process of comparing oneself to others who are worse. "I only call in sick when I'm not a few times a year; Tom and Ellen do it all the time." "We pollute less than our competitors do."
- **Disregard or distortion of consequences** is the process of minimizing the harm caused by the unethical behavior. "No one will be hurt if I inflate the figures, and I will not get caught. And if I do, I'll just get a slap on the wrist anyway." Was this the case at Enron?
- **Attribution of blame** is the process of claiming the unethical behavior was caused by someone else's behavior. "It's my coworker's fault that I repeatedly hit him and put him in the hospital. He called me a [blank]—so I had to hit him."
- **Euphemistic labeling** is the process of using "cosmetic" words to make the behavior sound acceptable. "Terrorist group" sounds bad, but "freedom fighter" sounds justifiable. "Misleading" or "covering up" sounds better than lying to others.

WorkApplication9

Give at least two organizational examples of unethical behavior and the justification that was used in each instance.

_____

_____

_____

_____

Simple Guides to Ethical Behavior

Every day in your personal and professional lives, you face decisions in which you can make ethical or unethical choices. You make your choices based on your past learning experiences with parents, teachers, friends, managers, coworkers, and so forth. These experiences together contribute to what many refer to as the conscience, which helps you choose right from wrong in a given situation. Following are some guides that can help you make the right decisions.

GOLDEN RULE

Everybody is familiar with the Golden Rule: "Do unto others as you want them to do unto you," or "Don't do anything to anyone that you would not want someone to do to you." Following the Golden Rule will help you to be ethical.

FOUR-WAY TEST

Rotary International developed a four-way test to guide one's thoughts and behavior in business transactions. The four questions are (1) Is it the truth? (2) Is it fair to all concerned? (3) Will it build goodwill and better friendship?

(4) Will it be beneficial to all concerned? When making a decision, if you can answer yes to these four questions, your potential course of action is probably ethical.

———————————— Learning Outcome 6 ————————————
Explain the stakeholders' approach to ethics.

STAKEHOLDERS' APPROACH TO ETHICS

Under the **stakeholders' approach to ethics**, *when making decisions, you try to create a win-win situation for all relevant stakeholders so that everyone benefits from the decision.* You can ask yourself one simple question to help you determine if your decision is ethical from a stakeholders' approach: "Would I be proud to tell relevant stakeholders my decision?" If you would be proud to tell relevant stakeholders your decision, it is probably ethical. If you would not be proud to tell others your decision or you keep rationalizing it, the decision may not be ethical. If you are unsure whether a decision is ethical, talk to your boss, higher-level managers, ethics committee members, and other people with high ethical standards.[82] If you are reluctant to ask others for advice on an ethical decision because you may not like their answers, the decision may not be ethical.

Unfortunately, sometimes decisions must be made that do not benefit all stakeholders. For example, if business is slow, a layoff may be necessary. Usually, the employees who get laid off do not benefit from the decision. Many large companies that permanently lay off employees offer severance pay and outplacement services to help the employees get other jobs.

Managing Ethics

An organization's ethics are based on the collective behavior of its employees. If each individual is ethical, the organization will be ethical. The starting place for ethics is you. Are you an ethical person? The Self-Assessment earlier in this chapter will help you answer this question. From the management perspective, managers should establish guidelines for ethical behavior, set a good example, and enforce ethical behavior.

CODES OF ETHICS

Codes of ethics, also called *codes of conduct*, state the importance of conducting business in an ethical manner and provide guidelines for ethical behavior.[83] Most large businesses have written codes of ethics.

Ford has a 25-page booklet, which is also on its Web site (*http://www.ford.com*) and is entitled "Ford Motor Company Standards of Corporate Conduct," to help its employees be ethical. The standards are broken into sections covering a number of topics:

- **Compliance with laws and Ford policy**
- **Government and legal inquiries and investigations**
- **Antitrust policy and compliance guide**
- **Dealing with suppliers and customers and other potential conflicts of interest (gifts and favors)**
- **Dealing with governments and government employees (domestic and foreign)**
- **Political contributions and activities**
- **Securities trading**

- **Product safety and quality**
- **Environmental matters**
- **Health and safety policy**
- **Employment policies**
- **Confidential information**
- **Intellectual property**
- **Information management**
- **Customer complaints**
- **Use of company vehicles**

The conclusion includes a toll-free number to call with any questions or to report violations anonymously.

TOP MANAGEMENT SUPPORT AND EXAMPLE

It is the responsibility of management from the top down to develop codes of ethics, to ensure that employees are instructed on what is and what is not considered ethical behavior, and to enforce ethical behavior.[84] However, the primary responsibility is to lead by example. Employees tend to look to managers, especially top managers, for examples of behavior. If managers are not ethical, employees will not be ethical. The CEO has to be the model for ethical standards; managers will treat customers and workers fairly if the CEO does.

ENFORCING ETHICAL BEHAVIOR

If employees are rewarded rather than punished for their unethical behavior, they will conduct unethical business practices. Many organizations have developed ethics committees that act as judges and juries to determine if unethical behavior has been conducted and what the punishment should be for violating company policy. More companies are establishing ethics offices, with a director or vice president who reports directly to the CEO, to establish ethics policies, listen to employees' complaints, conduct training, and investigate abuses such as sexual harassment.[85]

As a means of enforcing ethical behavior, employees should be encouraged to become internal whistle-blowers.[86] *Whistle-blowing* occurs when employees expose what they believe to be unethical behavior by their fellow employees. Whistle-blowing should begin internally, and information should go up the chain of command. If nothing is done, then the whistle-blower can go outside the organization as a last resort.[87] According to the law and ethics, whistle-blowers should not suffer any negative consequences.

Would you report unethical behavior by fellow employees to your boss or upper-level managers? If upper-level managers engage in, or support, unethical behavior, would you go outside the organization to report it? It is not easy to say whether you would be a whistle-blower unless you are in a specific situation—but some day you may be faced with that decision.

The **Boeing Company** is best known as an aerospace giant making commercial aircraft for the global airline industry and for being the largest defense contractor dealing with the U.S. government. However, these are only two of Boeing's seven business units (Air Traffic Management, Boeing Capital, Commercial Airplanes, Commexion by Boeing, Integrated Defense Systems, Phantom Works, and Shared Services Group). In addition, the company has ten subsidiaries.

WorkApplication10

Select a business and identify how it manages ethics.

_____

_____

_____

_____

Boeing has had ethics problems in the past, and the board of directors and CEO Phil Condit are working to improve ethical behavior within the company. To send the message that unethical behavior will not be tolerated, the board unanimously voted to fire its Chief Financial Officer (CFO) Michael Sears, who had been with Boeing for 34 years and was considered a possible successor to become CEO. Boeing alleged that Sears had violated company policy by communicating with Darleen Druyun to discuss her potential employment while she was still negotiating contracts with Boeing on behalf of the Pentagon.[88]

CEO Phil Condit is clearly giving top-management support to ethics and is enforcing ethical standards by sending the message to all employees that they can get fired for unethical behavior.

SOCIAL RESPONSIBILITY

Ethics and social responsibility are closely related. **Social responsibility** *is the conscious effort to operate in a manner that creates a win-win situation for all stakeholders.* Ethical behavior is often socially responsible, and vice versa. In this section, we'll discuss social responsibility to stakeholders and why it pays to be socially responsible.

Social Responsibility to Stakeholders

Companies have a responsibility to try to create a win-win situation for external stakeholders, as well as internal stakeholders—employees.[89] For customers, the company must provide safe products and services with customer value. For society, the company should improve the quality of life, or at least not destroy the environment.[90] Senior executives of large global corporations acknowledge their responsibility to control pollution. The company must

WorkApplication11

Select a business and identify how it is socially responsible on a specific issue.

_____

_____

_____

_____

_____

Applying The Concept 4

Stakeholders

Identify which kind of stakeholder is referred to in each statement.

a. employees   d. competitors

b. customers   e. suppliers

c. society   f. government

_____ 16. "We are going to fight that utility company to stop it from putting a nuclear power plant in our town."

_____ 17. "I bought this cigarette. It exploded in my face when I lit it, causing me injury."

_____ 18. "The town board is very political, so you have to play games if you want to get a liquor license."

_____ 19. "I'm sorry to hear your retail sales are down; we will have to cut back our production."

_____ 20. "I bid on the job, but PIP's got the contract to print the material."

compete fairly with competitors. Through technology, the company should develop new ways of increasing customer value and the quality of life. The company must work with suppliers in a cooperative manner. It must abide by the laws and regulations of government. The company must strive to provide equal-employment opportunities for the labor force. It must be financially responsible in relation to the economy. The company must provide shareholders with a reasonable profit. It must provide employees with safe working conditions with adequate pay and benefits.[91]

Does It Pay to Be Socially Responsible?

Various researchers have tried to determine the relationship between social responsibility and financial performance. However, results have been inconsistent.[92] Although there is no clear link between social responsibility and profits, it is certainly true that social responsibility does not hurt performance, but scandals *do* hurt corporate reputations, which can hurt sales.[93] Social responsibility does benefit many stakeholders in many different ways.

Ben Cohen and Jerry Greenfield started **Ben & Jerry's Homemade, Inc.** with a $12,000 investment ($4,000 of which was borrowed) in 1978 in a renovated gas station in Burlington, Vermont. Ben & Jerry's has a reputation as a leader in corporate social responsibility. Ben and Jerry ran the company with a dual focus on profit and social responsibility, giving 7.5 percent of its profits for socially responsible activities. Ben and Jerry have been popular active speakers on the importance of corporate social responsibility, and have stated that social responsibility helped Ben & Jerry's become the company it is today.

Ben and Jerry no longer run the company, but its current mission has three parts: product mission, economic mission, and social mission. Social responsibility remains very important to the company. The company's Web site gives information about Ben & Jerry's longtime commitment to maintaining Vermont's employment and manufacturing base and to paying workers a livable wage with complete benefits; to buying milk from Vermont family farmers who agree not to use growth hormones on their cows; to contributing over $1.1 million annually to Ben & Jerry's Foundation and employee-led Community Action Teams; and to providing opportunities to disadvantaged persons. In addition, Ben & Jerry's supports environmental efforts to fight global warming, programs to register voters, and various programs to promote world peace.[94]

SOCIAL AUDIT

A *social audit* is a measure of a firm's social behavior. Many large businesses set social objectives and try to measure whether they have met the objectives. Many large corporations include a social audit in their annual report.

GM prides itself on its social responsibility. It conducts regular social audits. At its Web site, *http://www.gm.com*, GM has an entire section called "GMability: Citizenship and Responsibility," which is devoted to corporate responsibility and offers downloadable sustainability reports. GMability contains links to discussions of leadership and vision, and to information on economics, the environment, the workplace, the community, education, and product safety, among others.

I
O
M

Join the Discussion Ethics & Social Responsibility

TV and Movie Sex and Violence

1. How do TV and movies influence societal values? (Consider that many children watch as many as five hours of TV per day.)
2. Do TV shows and movies that include sex and violence reflect current religious and societal values?
3. Should the FCC regulate television, and if yes, how far should it go? Should it make CBS tone down the sex and violence, or take shows like *CSI* off the air?
4. Is it ethical and socially responsible to portray women as sex objects?

Over the years, various social activist groups, including the Parents Television Council, National Viewers and Listeners Association, and the National Coalition Against Censorship, have taken stances for and against censorship of sex and violence on TV and in the movies. People call for more censorship to protect children from seeing sex and violence, while others don't want censorship at all, on the grounds that it violates free speech guarantees.

The Federal Communications Commission (FCC) has the power to regulate television broadcasts. In response to societal pressure, in December 2003, the FCC was considering imposing a more severe form of regulation and the possible termination of specific television programs containing explicit sex and violence—among them *CSI* (CBS).

Advocates for less regulation state that TV shows like *CSI* are shown late at night while children should not be watching. However, advocates of regulation point out that many daytime soap operas include sexual content and that cable stations show reruns of major network shows in the day and early evening when children are watching. For example, many *Seinfeld* episodes had sexual themes, and the show was not aired until 9:00 P.M., but now it's shown on cable stations at all hours.

Source: Information taken from the Federal Communications Commission Web site at *http://www.fcc.gov*, accessed January 3, 2004.

The message of this chapter boils down to this: As a manager, you are going to have to manage the organization's internal environment (including its organizational culture) while interacting with its external environment to create a win-win situation for stakeholders through ethical and socially responsible leadership.

Take advantage of the companion Web site for Management Fundamentals, where you will find a broad array of resources to help you maximize what you learn in class:

- Try a quiz
- View chapter videos
- Download slides
- Boost your vocabulary
- Work through an Internet exercise
- Find related links

Take a look for yourself at *http://lussier.swlearning.com.*

Chapter Summary

1. Explain the five internal environmental factors: management and culture, mission, resources, systems process, and structure.

Management refers to the people responsible for an organization's performance. Mission is the organization's purpose or reason for being. The organization has human, physical, financial, and informational resources to accomplish its mission. The systems process is the method of transforming inputs into outputs as the organization accomplishes its mission. Structure refers to the way in which the organization groups its resources to accomplish its mission.

2. List and explain the need for the two primary principles of total quality management (TQM).

The two primary principles of TQM are (1) to focus on delivering customer value and (2) to continually improve the system and its processes. To be successful, businesses must continually offer value to attract and retain customers. Without customers, you don't have a business.

3. Describe the three levels of organizational culture and their relationship to each other.

Level 1 of culture is behavior—the actions employees take. Level 2 is values and beliefs. Values represent the way people believe they ought to behave and beliefs represent if-then statements. Level 3 is assumptions—values and beliefs that are deeply ingrained as unquestionably true. Values, beliefs, and assumptions provide the operating principles that guide decision making and behavior.

4. Describe how the nine external environmental factors— customers, competitors, suppliers, labor force, shareholders, society, technology, economies, and governments—can affect the internal business environment.

Customers decide what products the business offers, and without customer value there are no customers or business. Competitors' business practices often have to be duplicated in order to maintain customer value. Poor-quality inputs from suppliers result in poor-quality outputs without customer value. Without a qualified labor force, products and services will have little or no customer value. Shareholders, through an elected board of directors, hire top managers and provide directives for the organization. Society pressures business to perform or not perform certain activities, such as pollution control. The business must develop new technologies, or at least keep up with them, to provide customer value. Economic activity affects the organization's ability to provide customer value. For example, inflated prices lead to lower customer value. Governments set the rules and regulations that business must adhere to.

5. Compare the three levels of moral development.

At the lowest level of moral development, the preconventional, behavior is motivated by self-interest and people seek rewards and attempt to avoid punishment. At the second level, the conventional, behavior is motivated by a desire to meet group expectations and to fit in by copying others' behavior. At the highest level, the postconventional, behavior is motivated by a desire to do the right thing, at the risk of alienating the group. The higher the level of moral development, the more ethical is one's behavior.

6. Explain the stakeholders' approach to ethics.

Managers who use the stakeholders' approach to ethics create a win-win situation for the relevant parties affected by the decision. If you are proud to tell relevant stakeholders about your decision, it is probably ethical. If you are not proud to tell stakeholders, or if you keep rationalizing the decision, it may not be ethical.

7. Complete each of the following statements using one of this chapter's key terms.

The organization's _____ includes the factors that affect the organization's performance from within its boundaries.

_____ is the shared values, beliefs, and assumptions about how an organization's members should behave.

The organization's _____ is its purpose or reason for being.

_____ are people whose interests are affected by organizational behavior.

The _____ is the method for transforming inputs into outputs.

Customers determine _____ by comparing how a product functions when it is used to what they require a product to do, to determine value.

_____ is the perceived benefits of a product, used by customers to determine whether or not to buy the product.

_____ is a process that involves everyone in an organization focusing on the customer to continually improve product value.

_____ are behavior, values and beliefs, and assumptions.

_____ articulate a vision for an organization and reinforce the culture through slogans, symbols, and ceremonies.

A _____ has a culture that values sharing knowledge so as to adapt to the changing environment and continuously improve.

The organization's _____ includes the external factors that affect its performance.

_____ are the standards of right and wrong that influence behavior.

Using the _____, when making decisions you try to create a win-win situation for all relevant stakeholders so that everyone benefits from the decision.

_____ is the conscious effort to operate in a manner that creates a win-win situation for all stakeholders.

Key Terms

customer value, 48

ethics, 61

external environment, 54

internal environment, 46

learning organization, 53

levels of culture, 51

mission, 46

organizational culture, 46

quality, 48

social responsibility, 68

stakeholders, 47

stakeholders' approach to ethics, 66

symbolic leaders, 52

systems process, 47

total quality management (TQM), 49

Review and Discussion Questions

1. Do you believe that most organizations focus on creating customer value? Explain.
2. Do you think that all organizations should use TQM? Explain your answer.
3. What is the relationship between management and mission, resources, the systems process, and structure? Which of these internal factors are ends, and which are means?
4. What major technology change has had the greatest impact on the quality of your life?
5. Which of the five artifacts, or important ways that employees learn about organizational culture, is the most important?
6. What is the difference between a strong and a weak organizational culture, and which is preferable?
7. What is symbolic leadership? Is it important?
8. What is a learning organization? Should a manager create one?
9. Do you believe that ethical behavior will pay off in the long run?
10. Do you have your own guide to ethical behavior that you follow now? Will you use one of the guides from the text? If yes, which one and why?
11. Can ethics be taught and learned?
12. Do you believe that companies benefit from being socially responsible? Why or why not?
13. As a CEO, what level of social responsibility would you use?

Objective Case

THE STATE OF FLORIDA

Storms have long battered beaches in the state of Florida, and local projects to repair them have, from time to time, generated more than their share of controversy. Everyone in Florida is critically aware of the links between healthy beaches, healthy tourism, and a healthy economy, but are the efforts to keep Florida beaches in shape creating more problems than they solve?

In addition to suffering storm damage, beaches on the state's west coast are also victims of man-made disturbances. Pollution in the Gulf of Mexico is a chronic problem. Another threat is runoff from land developed to house the nearly 5 million people who have settled along the Gulf over the past 20 years. The state's agricultural industry contributes its share of problems in the form of pesticides that make their way into several major rivers that flow into the Gulf. Heavy industry in other states bordering the Gulf also takes its toll. Carcinogens such as dioxin are in the water, and mercury has

been found in fish, leading many health agencies to issue warnings that people should limit their intake.

Pasco County, located north of Pinellas County, has polluted water. In some areas, human waste can be seen floating in the water. Boats dump sewage, and some homes are not hooked up to the sewer system. Yet signs warning people to stay out of the water are not always posted, some observe, for fear of driving away tourists. Is this ethical? The tourism industry, obviously, is big business in Florida, and no one wants the state's tourism dollars to diminish.

On November 4, 2003, voters in Manalapan agreed that owners of oceanfront property should take over ownership and repair of 1.6 miles of seawall that the town had built in the 1960s and 1980s. Before the vote, the town charter had required the town to maintain the seawall at public expense.

Beach "renourishment" is the process of restoring sand to beaches where it has washed away. The U.S. Army Corps of Engineers leads efforts throughout Florida to dredge sand from other places and relocate it to depleted beaches; the Corps spent $75 million from 1992 through 2002. In addition to the money spent by Army engineers, state and local sources authorized another $52.5 million for beach maintenance during the same period. But not all approve of these sand relocation efforts. Some, including state park rangers, are on record as saying that they are against beach renourishment, preferring to let nature take its course.

Renourishment, although it counteracts nature's course of eroding the beaches, helps to keep shores sandy, and sandy beaches bring tourists to Florida's shores. Nearly all of Florida's mainland beaches are resupplied with sand to protect the state's all-important tourism industry. In Pinellas County alone, home to Clearwater and St. Petersburg, the state reaped $2.6 billion in expenditures from visitors in 2003. Statewide, tourism generates $50 billion annually.

Florida beaches, a huge tourism draw, are consistently ranked among the nation's top beaches. *National Geographic Travel* magazine conducted an online poll in 2003 that ranked several beaches in Florida among the top 10 in the United States, including Fort DeSoto Park in Pinellas County. Yet, "a battle persists within the coastal scientific community between retreat and structuring," said Nicole Elko, coastal coordinator for Pinellas County's Department of Environmental Management. The state considers beach renourishment as a form of infrastructure maintenance, along with the repairing and resurfacing of roads.

The costs and benefits of beach renourishment are difficult to pin down, thus making the politics of renourishment rather complex. U.S. Congressman Bill Young (R-Florida) is the chairman of the House Appropriations Committee, and he has consistently backed federal funds for renourishment of Florida beaches, which Presidents Clinton and Bush have opposed.

The state of Florida reaped $886.7 million in federal dollars for renourishment between 1923 and 2001. This amount was the second highest received by any state in the nation. Only New Jersey, the recipient of $1 billion in federal money, outpaced Florida.

Critics of the renourishment program focus on two areas: the impact of renourishment on wildlife and natural resources and the benefits reaped by individual homeowners of expensive waterfront property. Should homeowners in affluent enclaves benefit from federally funded programs to maintain beaches? In the past year, the Florida Department of Environmental Protection dismissed a challenge to Boca Raton's central beach renourishment project, allowing city officials to push ahead with plans to add sand to the beach north of the Boca Raton inlet.

To learn more about beach renourishment in Florida, log on to InfoTrac® College Edition at *http://infotrac.thomsonlearning.com* and use the advanced search function.

_____ 1. The focus of this case is on which internal environmental factor in Florida?

    a. management and culture   d. systems process
    b. mission   e. structure
    c. resources

_____ 2. What kind of organizational resource do beaches in the state of Florida represent?

    a. human   c. physical
    b. informational   d. financial

_____ 3. What part of the external environment do tourists represent in this case?

    a. suppliers   d. labor force
    b. competitors   e. government
    c. customers

_____ 4. What part of the external environment do beaches in other states represent in this case?

    a. shareholders   d. labor force
    b. competitors   e. suppliers
    c. customers

_____ 5. The state of Florida requested help from which external environmental factor?

    a. government   d. labor force
    b. competitors   e. suppliers
    c. customers

_____ 6. Renourishment led by the U.S. Army Corps of Engineers is an example of which external environmental factor?

    a. government   d. labor force
    b. competitors   e. suppliers
    c. customers

_____ 7. A decision not to post signs to warn swimmers about polluted water is likely to be made by someone at the _____ level of moral development.

    a. postconventional
    b. conventional
    c. preconventional

_____ 8. The term "renourishment" may be considered by some people a form of _____, a method of justifying unethical behavior.

    a. displacement of responsibility
    b. diffusion of responsibility
    c. advantageous comparison
    d. disregard or distortion of consequences
    e. attribution of blame
    f. euphemistic labeling

_____ 9. Which group would be considered a stakeholder in this case?

    a. government   d. residents
    b. businesses   e. all of these are stakeholders
    c. tourists

_____ 10. Is the federal government practicing socially responsible behavior by helping the state of Florida renourish its beaches?

    a. yes
    b. no

11. Is the state of Florida creating a threat for the beach environment?

12. Is it ethical for the state to pay for renourishment in areas where people own the beachfront property?

Cumulative Case Questions

13. What primary management skill does the U.S. Army Corps of Engineers provide? (Chapter 1)

14. Which management functions are needed for the renourishment of Florida beaches? (Chapter 1)

Video Case

TIMBERLAND

About Timberland

This video on Timberland deals with a broad array of issues associated with the company's business environment. In particular, the video shows vividly how Timberland shares its culture and ethics with its customers, its employees, its shareholders, and the community. The ways in which managers at Timberland build culture and make clear what Timberland stands for are very well documented in this short clip.

View the Video (10–15 minutes)

View the accompanying video on Timberland in class or at *http://lussier.swlearning.com*.

Read the Case

New Hampshire–based Timberland builds its products to last—"to withstand the elements of nature." But Timberland is striving to build something more permanent than just high-quality footwear and clothing. It's trying to make the world a better place in which to live and work.

Timberland recognizes its responsibility to be profitable for investors and employees. The company has recently reported 20 consecutive quarters of record-level revenue and improved earnings. Timberland also considers its employees as critical to its success and has appeared numerous times on *Fortune* magazine's list of the best companies to work for. With repeated news reports about exploitation of foreign workers at other companies, Timberland monitors its offshore factories every 8 to 12 weeks to ensure that workers are paid decent wages, provided periodic work breaks, and not required to work excessive overtime.

Through its daily efforts to manage its operations better than the day before, Timberland maintains its edge as a productive and profitable business.

Answer the Questions

1. Describe how Timberland managers handle some of the external environmental factors discussed in the chapter.
2. How well does Timberland manager Ken Freitas (former vice president for social enterprise) communicate what Timberland stands for?
3. Would you like to work at Timberland? Why or why not?

Skill **Builder** 1

THE ORGANIZATIONAL ENVIRONMENT AND MANAGEMENT PRACTICES ANALYSIS

Preparing for Skill Builder 1

For this exercise you will select a specific organization, preferably one you work for or have worked for, and answer the questions as they relate to the business you have selected. You may contact people in the organization to get your answers. Write your answers to all questions.

The Internal Environment

1. Identify the top managers and briefly discuss their leadership style.
2. State the organization's mission.
3. Identify some of the organization's major resources.

4. Explain the organization's systems process. Discuss how the organization ensures quality and customer value.
5. Identify the organization's structure by listing its major departments.

The External Environment

In answering this section's questions, be sure to state how each of these external factors affects the organization.

6. Identify the organization's target customers.
7. Identify the organization's major competitors.
8. Identify the organization's major suppliers.
9. What labor force does the organization primarily recruit from?
10. Does the organization have shareholders? Is its stock listed on one of the three major stock exchanges? If yes, which one?
11. How does the organization affect society, and vice versa?
12. Describe some of the past, present, and future technologies of the organization's industry. Is the organization a technology leader?
13. Identify the governments that affect the organization. List some of the major laws and regulations affecting the business.
14. Explain how the economy affects the organization.

Culture

15. Does the organization use all five artifacts to teach culture? Explain which are used and how.
16. Describe the culture at all three levels. Is it a strong or a weak culture?
17. Is the firm creating a learning organization? Explain why or why not.

Ethics

18. Does the organization have any guides to ethical behavior? If yes, explain.
19. How does the organization manage ethics? Does it have a code of ethics? If so, what does the code cover? Does top management lead by good ethical example? Are ethical behaviors enforced? If so, how?

Apply It

What did I learn from this experience? How will I use this knowledge in the future?

_____

_____

Your instructor may ask you to do this Skill Builder in class in a group. If so, the instructor will provide you with any necessary information or additional instructions.

Skill Builder 2

ETHICS AND WHISTLE-BLOWING

Preparing for Skill Builder 2

For this exercise, first complete the Self-Assessment in the chapter (page 61).

Discussion Questions

1. Who is harmed and who benefits from the unethical behaviors in items 1–3?
2. For items 4–24, select the three (circle their numbers) you consider the most unethical. Who is harmed by and who benefits from these unethical behaviors?
3. If you observed unethical behavior but didn't report it, why didn't you report the behavior? If you did blow the whistle, what motivated you to do so? What was the result?

4. As a manager, it is your responsibility to uphold ethical behavior. If you know employees are doing any of these unethical behaviors, will you take action to enforce compliance with ethical standards?
5. What can you do to prevent unethical behavior?
6. As part of the class discussion, share any of the other unethical behaviors you observed and listed.

Apply It

What did I learn from this experience? How will I use this knowledge in the future?

_____

_____

Learning Outcomes

After studying this chapter, you should be able to:

1. Discuss the role of technology in the global village. PAGE 79

2. State the difference between a domestic, an international, and a multinational business. PAGE 83

3. List the six activities that make a business a global one, in order from lowest to highest cost and risk. PAGE 84

4. Describe some differences in the business practices of large multinational corporations and small international companies. PAGE 88

3: The Global Environment and Entrepreneurship

5. Explain the difference between an entrepreneur and an intrapreneur. PAGE 91

6. Describe how global diversity affects the management functions. PAGE 101

7. Define the following **key terms:**

ethnocentrism	new venture
global village	entrepreneurs
international business	intrapreneurs
multinational corporation (MNC)	small business
global sourcing	competitive advantage
joint venture	first-mover advantage
direct investment	business plan

Ideas on Management
at Amazon.com

E-commerce pioneer Jeff Bezos launched Amazon.com as an online bookstore in July 1995. In its first 30 days, the business recorded sales in all 50 U.S. states and 45 other countries. Impressive! Today, Amazon.com is a Fortune 500 company with 95,000 employees. Its mission is to become the most customer-centric company in the world, to build a place where consumers around the globe can find and discover anything they might want to buy online. During the 2003 holiday season, Amazon logged a one-day record of 2.1 million orders (twenty-four for every second of the day worldwide) and shipped more than one million packages. By the end of December 2003, the company reached a milestone by achieving its first billion-dollar quarter and posting its first annual profit.

In its quest to provide the best buying experience on the Internet, Amazon has expanded its list of product offerings well beyond books to include apparel and accessories, electronics, sporting goods, gourmet food, computers, computer hardware and software, kitchenware and home furnishings, music, DVDs, videos, cameras and photo equipment, toys, video games and electronics, cell phones and service, tools and hardware, magazine subscriptions, and outdoor living items.

© AP/Wide World Photos

IOM

1. How is Amazon.com classified in the global village, and how does Amazon.com use technology?
2. With which companies does Amazon.com have alliances, and how did it go global?
3. How did Jeff Bezos become an entrepreneur and select the new venture? What is Amazon.com's competitive advantage? Was the company a first-mover?
4. How does Amazon.com meet the needs of a diverse global customer base?

Answers to these questions about management at Amazon.com are embedded throughout the chapter, where you will learn more about Amazon's journey toward profitability and its growing worldwide reach.

To learn more about Amazon.com, visit the company's Web site at *www.amazon.com* or log on to InfoTrac® College Edition at *http://infotrac.thomsonlearning.com*, where you will find articles on all aspects of Amazon.com's management practices, including the latest developments in e-business. For example, the Spring 2004 issue of *CFO: The Magazine for Senior Financial Executives* examines Amazon's business fundamentals and assesses its capacity to sustain profitability and expand globally. You can locate this article by keying in record number A114603229 in InfoTrac's advanced search option.

Source: Information for the opening case and answers to questions within the chapter were taken from the Amazon.com Web site at *http://www.amazon.com*, accessed January 20, 2004.

THE GLOBAL ENVIRONMENT

Today's managers—and students of management—cannot afford to underestimate the importance of the global environment to business. The CEOs of some major corporations have stated that globalization is the number-one challenge of business leaders in the 21st century.[1] Management guru Peter Drucker said there will be two kinds of managers—those who think globally and those who are unemployed.[2] We live and do business in a world without boundaries.[3] As discussed and illustrated in Chapter 2 (Exhibit 2-6), the global business environment is complex, with multiple stakeholders.[4] In this section, we will discuss ethnocentrism, the role of technology and the Internet, the external environmental factors of the economy and governments, and how businesses in the global village are classified.

Ethnocentrism Is Out and "Made in America" Is Blurred

Parochialism means having a narrow focus, or seeing things solely from one's own perspective. **Ethnocentrism** *is regarding one's own ethnic group or culture as superior to others.* Thus, a parochial view is part of ethnocentrism. Successful managers of large companies headquartered in the United States (including **Coca-Cola, FedEx, Ford, GE**, and **3M**, to name just a few) are not ethnocentric; they don't view themselves simply as American companies, but rather as companies conducting business in a global environment. If they can buy or make better or cheaper materials, parts, or products in another country, they do so.[5] Businesspeople now commonly conduct business with people of other cultures and countries, sometimes by working in transnational teams composed of members of the same company from multiple countries.[6] If you are ethnocentric, you will not work well with diverse groups, and your chances of career success will be limited.

Many consumers subscribe to the idea behind "Buy American," but few know the country of origin of the products they regularly buy. Look at the labels in your clothes and you will realize that most clothing is not made in America. Did you know that although **Nike** is an American company, most of its clothes and sneakers are not made in the United States, or that **Ford**, which is also an American company, makes some of its cars in Mexico? Many of the parts for a Ford Crown Victoria are made in other countries, including Mexico (seats, windshields, and fuel tanks), Japan (shock absorbers), Spain (electronic engine controls), Germany (antilock-brake systems), and England (key axle parts). So if you buy Nike clothes and sneakers or a Crown Victoria, are you buying American? On the other hand, the Nissan Altima or Maxima is a Japanese car manufactured by a French-owned company, possibly at a plant in Tennessee. Are you getting the picture of the global environment?

Complete the Self-Assessment on page 79 to see if you know the country of origin of the products listed. But also remember that many foreign companies and people own stock in American companies, and vice versa. Country of origin is increasingly blurred.

——————————— Learning Outcome 1 ———————————
Discuss the role of technology in the global village.

The Role of Technology and the Internet in the Global Village

Technology, particularly transportation and communications technology (the Internet), has made it possible to travel to multiple countries in the same day and to communicate instantly with most of the world. In other words, technology has changed the way business is conducted in the global village.[7] *The* **global village** *refers to companies conducting business worldwide without boundaries*. The word *village* implies something small and emphasizes that the world, although very large, is becoming smaller through technology. Not only are diverse cultures interacting more and more frequently, but customer values (Chapter 2) are becoming similar. Through travel and mass media communications, people all over the world see and come to want the same products. Coca-Cola and the McDonald's Big Mac are examples.

E-COMMERCE/E-BUSINESS

As discussed in Chapter 1, e-business and e-commerce are critically important in the global village. Some 605.6 million people worldwide use the Internet;

WorkApplication1

Give one or more examples of how an organization uses the Internet.

——————————————
——————————————
——————————————
——————————————
——————————————

Self-Assessment

Country of Origin of Products

For each item, determine the country of origin. If your answer is the United States, place a check in the left-hand column. If it's another country, write the name of the country in the right-hand column.

Product	United States	Other (list country)
1. Shell gasoline	_____	_____
2. Nestlé candy	_____	_____
3. Unilever Dove soap	_____	_____
4. Nokia camera	_____	_____
5. L'Oreal cosmetics	_____	_____
6. Samsung cell phones	_____	_____
7. Columbia Records	_____	_____
8. Aiwa stereos	_____	_____
9. Bayer aspirin	_____	_____
10. Chrysler Jeep	_____	_____

1. Shell is owned by Royal Dutch/Shell of the Netherlands. 2. Nestlé is headquartered in Switzerland. 3. Unilever is British. 4. Nokia is a Finnish company. 5. L'Oreal is French. 6. Samsung is South Korean. 7, 8. Columbia Records and Aiwa (Sony) are Japanese. 9. Bayer is German. 10. Daimler is German and it owns Chrysler, which is American.[8]

How many did you get correct? (Count item 10 as either.)

Join the Discussion Ethics & Social Responsibility

Buy American

1. Is it ethical and socially responsible to buy foreign products?

You most likely have heard the slogan "Buy American." Many labor unions urge Americans to buy products made in the United States, because that helps retain jobs for American workers. On the other hand, some Americans ask why they should buy American products if they cost more or their quality of style is not as good as that of foreign-made products. But as you've seen, it isn't always easy for consumers to know the country of origin of many products they buy.

Europe leads the way, with 190.91 million users, but as the list below shows, there are many millions of users worldwide.[9]

- Asia and Pacific Rim countries   187.24 million Internet users
- Canada and United States   182.67 million Internet users
- Latin America   33.35 million Internet users
- Africa   6.31 million Internet users
- Middle East   5.12 million Internet users

Hewlett-Packard (HP) realizes the importance of the Internet, and that is where it sees its future. The HP vision is to combine business units and help consumers and businesses use the Internet.[10] In 2002, HP merged with Compaq Computer Corporation to create a powerful team of 140,000 employees in 178 countries, doing business in more than 40 currencies and using more than 10 languages. Today, HP uses business and technology solutions to enable more people to participate in the world economy via information technology. HP ranks number one among global companies in the production of computer printers, scanners, disk storage systems, printer servers, storage-area network systems, notebook PCs, and desktop PC supplies.[11]

WIRELESS COMMUNICATION

With the increasing popularity of wireless communications devices such as cellular phones, the notion of the "Web in your pocket" is rapidly becoming a compelling solution to speeding communication and business. India-born Hatim Tyabji founded **Saraide** to help further the convergence between the Internet and wireless communications; Saraide delivers a wide range of wireless Internet services to customers throughout the global village.[12] E-business is making the virtual organization an increasingly dominant business mode.[13]

We have discussed two external environmental factors, society and technology, so let's now focus on the economy and the government. As we do, keep in mind the complexity of globalization. Every country in which a firm does business has its own economic and governmental environment. So, for example, FedEx deals with hundreds of different economies and governments.

The Economic Environment

The economic environment includes level of economic development, infrastructure, and exchange rates.

ECONOMIC DEVELOPMENT

The level of economic development varies widely across the globe.[14] Countries are commonly classified, based on wealth, as either "developed" (United States and Canada, Western Europe, Japan) or "developing." The less developed countries are generally located in Asia, Africa, and South America.

INFRASTRUCTURE

An important indicator of economic development is infrastructure. *Infrastructure* refers to a country's physical facilities, including transportation (airports, highways, railroads, public transportation), communications (telephone and mass media), and utilities (power plants). Developed countries have well-developed infrastructures, while developing countries are still working to build strong infrastructures. Companies that are in the business of developing infrastructure, such as **United Technologies** (producers of jet engines, heating and cooling systems, and elevators), have global business opportunities. The Internet helps to overcome poor infrastructure, but telephone lines and computers are often scarce in developing countries. However, with wireless communications using the Internet, the speed of development may increase. As a manager taking a business global (the topic of the next section), you must consider a country's infrastructure when deciding whether to do business there.

EXCHANGE RATES

The *exchange rate* is how much of one country's currency you get for another country's. Your own currency is considered strong when you get more of another country's currency than you give up in the exchange, and weak when you get less. As an American traveling to other countries, a strong dollar gives you greater buying power, as you get more for your money. However, when a U.S. business conducts foreign trade, the opposite is true. When the dollar is weak, foreign goods are more expensive in the United States, and when it is strong, foreign goods are less expensive. Thus, a weak dollar helps to create opportunities for American global businesses.[15]

Exchange rate fluctuations can have a major impact on profitability.[16] For example, suppose you are selling a product in Japan for 8,000 yen. With an exchange rate of 8 yen to 1 dollar, you get $1,000 (8,000 [yen selling price] divided by 8 [8 yen = $1]) for each product you sell. Suppose that this price and exchange rate give you a 25 percent profit margin. Now let's see what happens with the extreme fluctuations in exchange rates that sometimes occur:

- If the exchange rate becomes 6 yen to 1 dollar, the yen is strong (and the dollar is weak). When you exchange the yen for dollars, you get $1,333.33 (8,000 [yen selling price] divided by 6 [6 yen = $1]) for each product you sell.
- Now let's make the dollar strong (and the yen weak). If the exchange rate goes to 10 yen to the dollar, you get $800 (8,000 [yen selling price] divided by 10 [10 yen = $1]).

You can either change your yen selling price to maintain your 25 percent profit margin or make more or less based on the exchange rate. Now think about the complexity of FedEx doing business in over 100 currencies.

The Governmental Environment

Every country has its own laws and regulations that the global business must follow. Three important aspects of the governmental environment include political instability, political risk, and government trade agreements.

POLITICAL INSTABILITY

In dealing with some countries, businesses face the possibility of *political instability*, or potential riots, revolutions, civil disorder and wars, and frequent changes in governments.[17] Imagine starting a business in another country and then a civil war breaks out and interrupts your business, or the government then changes many of the laws and regulations on how you conduct business.

POLITICAL RISK

Global businesses also face the *political risk* of loss of assets, earning power, or management control due to political events in a country's government. In extreme cases, when government power has changed hands, as in Cuba, governments have taken over foreign companies, or made them leave, without any remuneration. Imagine starting a business in another country and having the government take everything away from you without giving you a cent.

Political instability and risk are important considerations in doing global business.[18] As with most investments, the greater the risk, the higher the return or loss. Operating in developed countries is relatively risk-free; however, there are fewer opportunities for many products than in developing countries. Most of the large global businesses are taking the risks; investment in China, for example, is viewed as having great potential.[19]

WORLD TRADE ORGANIZATION (WTO)

Organizations and governments are working together to develop free trade between countries. The **World Trade Organization (WTO)** establishes and enforces world trade laws. The WTO is an international organization to which over 100 countries belong. It works to develop general agreements between all members and acts as a mediator between member countries that cannot resolve differences, as when one country feels another is using unfair practices. A WTO panel can order unfair practices stopped or allow the country claiming unfair practices to retaliate.

Some countries, including China and Russia, have been very lax about stopping corruption. Some countries, such as the United States and countries in Europe, are trying to eliminate corruption and standardize ethics. For example, giving a gift worth $200 may be customary in Asia, but such a gift could be considered a bribe in the United States.[20]

The largest European trade alliance is the European Union (EU), formerly called the European Community, which consists of 25 member states: Austria, Belgium, Cyprus, Czech Republic, Denmark, Estonia, Finland, France, Germany, Greece, Hungary, Ireland, Italy, Latvia, Lithuania, Luxembourg, Malta, the Netherlands, Poland, Portugal, Slovakia, Slovenia, Spain, Sweden, and the United Kingdom. Since late 1992, the EU has been a single market without national barriers to travel, employment, investment, and trade. EU members have developed a single currency (the euro) to create an Economic and Monetary Union (EMU). Europeans in EU countries from Portugal to Finland use the new currency. The euro makes conducting business and traveling much easier in this trading bloc.

Exhibit 3-1 *Trading Blocs*

The North American Free Trade Agreement (NAFTA) was created in 1993 and implemented in 1994; the United States–Canada agreement was expanded to include Mexico. As many as 20,000 separate tariffs are expected to be eliminated to allow free trade among member countries. There are plans to expand NAFTA to include alliances with Central and South America. This will create the Free Trade Area of the Americas (FTAA) with 850 million people. In April 2001, leaders of the 33 democratic nations of the Western Hemisphere agreed to open markets by 2005,[21] and as many as 36 nations may participate. Visit *http://www.ftaa-alca.org* for updated information on FTAA.

Asia and the Pacific Rim (China, Hong Kong, Indonesia, Japan, Korea, Malaysia, the Philippines, Singapore, Taiwan, and Thailand) comprise an important trade area. The six-member Association of Southeast Asian Nations (ASEAN) is a trade agreement between Brunei, Indonesia, Malaysia, the Philippines, Singapore, and Thailand that includes 330 million people. ASEAN created a free trade area in 2003 that limits *tariffs* (a tax on imports) to no more than 5 percent of the cost of a product. For updated information, visit *http://www.aseansec.org*. The Asia-Pacific Economic Cooperation (APEC) is a broader agreement between Australia, Canada, China, Hong Kong, Japan, New Zealand, South Korea, Taiwan, the United States, and members of ASEAN. For updated information, visit *http://www.apecsec.org.sg*. Exhibit 3-1 illustrates these trading blocs.

Learning Outcome 2

State the difference between a domestic, an international, and a multinational business.

Classifying Businesses in the Global Village

Since the early 1990s, the question asked by managers has not been "Should the business go global?" but rather "How do we go global and how fast?"[22] The primary reason for conducting business globally is to increase sales and profits. If you start a *domestic business* (a business conducted in only one country) in the United States, you have around 281 million people as potential customers. If you expand to buy and sell inputs and outputs in Canada and Mexico (NAFTA countries), you increase your population market to over 400 million. At this point, you have an international business. *An* **international business** *is based primarily in one country but transacts business in other countries.* If you expand by setting up business operations in one of the EU countries and transact business throughout the EU, you have over 440 million more potential customers for a total of over 825 million. Go to China and India, with populations of over 1 billion each, and your market is up to around 3 billion people, about one-half of the world's population of 6 billion people. When you have significant operations (an established place of business at home and in at least one other country and sales outside your home country of 25 percent or more), you have a multinational or global business.[23]

A **multinational corporation (MNC)** *has significant operations in more than one country.* Larger MNCs that do business in many countries and have sales outside their home countries exceeding 50 percent include **Aflac, Avon, Citicorp, Coca-Cola, Colgate, Dow Chemical, Exxon, Gillette, Hewlett-Packard, IBM, Mobil, Motorola, NCR, Rhône-Poulenc Rorer, Texaco,** and **Xerox. Nestlé** is based in Vevy, Switzerland, but over 98 percent of the company's revenues and over 95 percent of its assets originate from or are located outside of Switzerland. You may never start your own global business, but you may become an international manager. An *international manager* manages across a number of countries and cultures simultaneously. It is common for MNCs to send managerial employees overseas, and such *expatriation* typically enhances career progression.[24]

As a startup business, Amazon.com used the Internet to conduct business. In its first 30 days, the company shipped orders from the United States to 45 countries, making it an international business and a global leader in e-business and e-commerce right from the start. Today, Amazon.com is a multinational corporation (MNC), operating additional Web sites in six other countries: Austria, Canada, France, Germany, Japan, and the United Kingdom. All these sites are linked through the main site in the United States. The link between the main computer in the United States and one in each other country allows a customer to use the same password and e-mail address on all seven sites. Thus, Amazon.com allows sharing of knowledge globally.

WorkApplication2

Classify a business you work for or have researched as domestic, international, or multinational. If the business is international or an MNC, list some of the countries where it does business.

_____

_____

_____

_____

_____

Learning Outcome 3

List the six activities that make a business a global one, in order from lowest to highest cost and risk.

TAKING A BUSINESS GLOBAL

A domestic business can become a global one through any of six activities: global sourcing, importing and exporting, licensing, contracting, joint ventures, and direct investment. Exhibit 3-2 presents these methods in order by cost and risk and indicates what types of companies tend to use them.

Exhibit 3-2 *Taking a Business Global*

Lowest Cost and Risk ⟶				Highest Cost and Risk
Importing/Exporting	Licensing	Contracting	Joint Ventures	Direct Investment
Characteristic of International Business ⟶				Characteristic of Multinational Corporations

Note that global sourcing can be used alone (at low cost/risk), but is commonly used in tandem with other global strategies.

Global Sourcing

Global sourcing *is the use of worldwide resources.* It is also called *outsourcing.*[25] Global managers look worldwide for the best deal on inputs and a location for transforming inputs into outputs. **General Motors (GM)** and **Ford** use material, supplies, and parts from other countries in their U.S.-made cars. One of the effects of the passage of NAFTA was that it allowed U.S. companies to take advantage of low-cost Mexican labor through *maquiladoras,* or light-assembly plants located in Mexico, near the U.S. border. Both international corporations and MNCs are increasing their use of global sourcing.[26] As an international manager, you will need to scan the globe, not just the United States, for the best deals.

For several years, companies such as Nike have used cheap, unskilled overseas labor to make their labor-intensive products; most clothes sold in the United States are made outside the country.[27] However, a more recent trend is for companies, including **Lehman** and **Bear Sterns Financial**, to send higher paying knowledge jobs overseas to India and China.[28] Indian tech companies are recruiting people from the United States and Europe to compete with such companies.[29]

IBM is the 12th-largest company in the world.[30] IBM strives to lead in the invention, development, and manufacture of the industry's most advanced information technologies, including computer systems, software, storage systems, and microelectronics. IBM translates these advanced technologies into value for its customers through professional solutions, services, and consulting businesses worldwide.[31]

In late 2003, IBM announced that to cut costs, it would move the work of as many as 4,730 programmers to India, China, and elsewhere. In the United States, these workers typically make $75,000 to $100,000 a year. IBM can hire software engineers with a bachelor's or even a master's degree from a top technical university in India for $10,000 to $20,000 a year. Replaced U.S. workers are expected to train their overseas replacements, after which they will be offered another job within the company within 60 days, while IBM holds down hiring.[32]

A programmer in China with three to five years' experience costs about $12.50 an hour, including salary and benefits; a similar worker in the United States costs IBM $56 an hour. With these outsourcing efforts, IBM expects to save $168 million annually starting in 2006. IBM also stated that it expects to add 15,000 jobs worldwide in 2004, with 5,000 of them in the United States, thereby raising its global employment to 330,000.[33]

Importing and Exporting

When *importing*, a domestic firm buys products from foreign firms and sells them at home. **Pier 1 Imports** and U.S. auto dealerships that sell Japanese and German cars are examples of importing companies. When *exporting*, a domestic firm sells its products to foreign buyers. Ford, for example, exports cars to Japanese dealerships.

Licensing

Under a *licensing* agreement, one company allows another to use its assets (intellectual property), such as a brand name, trademark, a particular technology, a patent, or a copyright. For a fee, **Walt Disney** allows companies around the world to make all kinds of products using Mickey Mouse and other characters. **Oracle's** earnings rose 15 percent on sales of new licenses of its software. However, part of the revenue increase was a consequence of the weak dollar.[34]

A common form of licensing is a *franchise*, in which the franchiser provides a combination of trademark, equipment, materials, training, managerial guidelines, consulting advice, and cooperative advertising to the franchisee for a fee and a percentage of the revenues. **McDonald's, Pizza Hut, Subway**, and **Holiday Inn**, for example, have franchise operations all over the world.

Contracting

With *contract manufacturing*, a company has a foreign firm manufacture the goods that it sells as its own. **Sears** uses this approach in Latin America and Spain. Contract manufacturers make products with the Sears name on them, and Sears sells them in its stores. With *management contracting*, a company provides management services for a foreign firm. **Hilton** operates hotels all over the world for local owners. All kinds of contract services can be provided.

Joint Venture

*A **joint venture** is created when firms share ownership of a new enterprise.* **Toyota** and **GM** have a joint venture in California. The two firms share the costs and risk, but both lose some control over how business is conducted and must share the rewards. A *strategic alliance* is an agreement that does not necessarily involve shared ownership.

Over half of America's fastest-growing companies have teamed with others to improve products or create new ones. To be more competitive with **FedEx, UPS** entered a joint venture with the New Zealand company **Fliway Transport Group**. The new venture is called UPS-Fliway (NZ) Ltd.

Direct Investment

Direct investment *is the construction or purchase of operating facilities (subsidiaries) in a foreign country.* Ford and GM have production facilities in Europe, but the auto industry uses a combination of joint ventures and direct investments. The auto industry trend is to make cars closer to where they are sold. In its pursuit of global expansion, FedEx made direct investments by purchasing 20 different companies. Clearly, FedEx is a MNC.

WorkApplication3
Select a business and identify its globalization strategy.

_____

_____

_____

_____

_____

The Role of the Internet in Taking a Business Global

The Internet and e-commerce make global sourcing and importing and exporting much easier. B2B transactions speed the ordering and processing of goods and services worldwide through networks of computers. The Internet and wireless communications are speeding up the communication process and allowing more informed and faster decision making about contracting and joint ventures. In addition, the Internet improves coordination and control between headquarters and subsidiaries.

Many large companies depend on alliances for a significant portion of their annual revenues and research needs; IBM receives more than one-third of its revenues from alliances of various types.[35] Allied firms need to balance cooperation and competition, as the toughest competitor can be a great ally.[36] Rather than compete head-on with rival bookstore Borders Group, Inc., Amazon.com established an e-commerce agreement. Amazon.com provides Borders Group with technology services, site content, product selection, and customer service for the co-branded "Borders Teamed with Amazon.com" (Borders.com) and "Waldenbooks Teamed with Amazon.com" (Waldenbooks.com) Web sites. Amazon.com receives a percentage of sales transacted through the sites. The home page of Amazon.com's Web site lists featured partners for whom Amazon sells products, through what are often called *store fronts*. In a sense, an individual consumer

IOM

Applying The Concept 1

Taking a Business Global

Identify which activity of global businesses is described in each statement:

a. outsourcing
b. importing/exporting
c. licensing
d. contracting
e. joint venture
f. direct investment

_____ 1. Burger King allows a Chinese businessperson to open a Burger King in Beijing.

_____ 2. Springfield College offers its degree programs in Israel at the Health and Behavioral Sciences College, which provides the facilities and administrative support.

_____ 3. GE makes its Whirlpool appliances in its factory in Europe.

_____ 4. Dell makes its computers in the United States and sells them online to people in France.

_____ 5. The Stop & Shop supermarket chain has a Canadian company make potato chips packaged under the Stop & Shop brand name for sale in its U.S. stores.

_____ 6. Wilson Sporting Goods buys the rubber for basketballs from Brazil.

_____ 7. Amazon.com buys a warehouse in Spain through which it distributes books ordered from the United States by customers in the EU.

_____ 8. The Children's Television Network gives a Mexican company the right to make its Sesame Street character puppets.

_____ 9. Philips in France makes TVs using speakers from Japan.

_____10. Town Fair Tires in the United States buys tires from Bridgestone in Japan for retail sale.

IOM

can become a partner with Amazon.com. You can set up a link on "Sell Your Stuff," and Amazon.com will list your item, sell it for you, and collect payment and send you the profits (minus a commission, of course).

Amazon.com started out as a global company, by using the Internet and exporting books to other countries. It outsources shipping and other functions and imports and exports products. Its Web sites in Austria, Canada, France, Germany, Japan, and the United Kingdom are operated in those countries as direct investments.

--- Learning Outcome 4 ---

Describe some differences in the business practices of large multinational corporations and small international companies.

Business Practices of Global Companies

Although both multinational corporations and small international companies compete in the global environment, they use different business practices, based on size and resources.[37] There are six major business practices that differ in global companies listed in Exhibit 3-3 and discussed below.[38]

GLOBAL MANAGEMENT TEAM

Leading MNCs have top-level managers who are foreign nationals and subsidiaries managed by foreign nationals. Cross-culturally trained managers travel frequently to the countries in which their firms do business. The fast management track now leads overseas; global companies want top managers who have been around the world.[39] Small businesses often can't afford to hire foreign managers, but some use consultants and agents.

GLOBAL STRATEGY

In an MNC, there is one strategy for the entire company, not one per subsidiary. Worldwide coordination attains economies of scale, but still allows a country manager to respond to local consumer needs and counter local competition. Global strategy utilizes direct investment, joint ventures, and

Exhibit 3-3 *Practices of Global Companies*

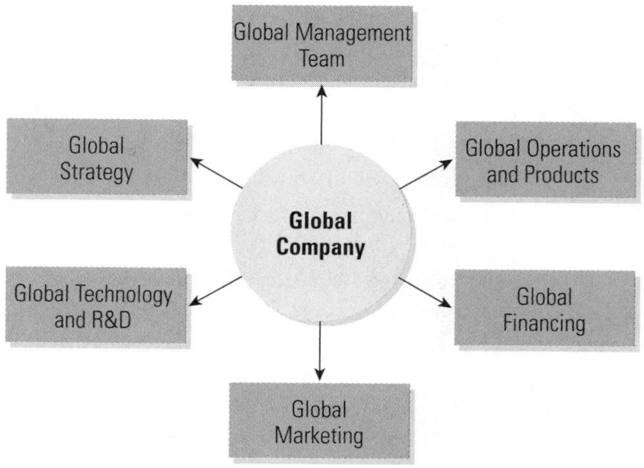

strategic alliances. The common small business global strategies are outsourcing and importing and exporting.

GLOBAL OPERATIONS AND PRODUCTS

MNCs have standardized operations worldwide to attain economies of scale, and they make products to be sold worldwide, not just in local markets. In the mid-1990s, Ford sold different cars in Europe and the United States with different operating equipment. However, Ford's stated goal was to have the same type of facilities producing cars that would be sold in NAFTA, EU, and other countries. Unit headquarters are placed in the country with the best resources to do the job, rather than in the home country. Small businesses can sell standard global products, but they commonly use contractors and exporting.

GLOBAL TECHNOLOGY AND R&D

Technology and research and development (R&D) are centralized in one country, rather than duplicated at each subsidiary, to develop world products. Global sourcing of technology and R&D is used.[40] Small businesses are creative, though they have limited funds for R&D. But they are often quick to adopt new technology.[41]

GLOBAL FINANCING

MNCs search world markets to get the best rates and terms when borrowing money for the long term; short-term financing is largely arranged in individual countries using local financial institutions. Product prices are quoted in foreign currencies, rather than the home currency. MNCs sell stock in their subsidiary to the people in the country where the subsidiary is located. They manage currency exchange—as well as global purchasing, currency hedging, currency risk exposure, and other important corporate functions—on an international basis.

Many small business owners turn to the Export-Import Bank (Ex-Im Bank) when they are ready to go global. The Ex-Im Bank is a government agency responsible for aiding the export of U.S. goods and services through a variety of loan guarantees and insurance programs. Besides using the Ex-Im Bank, a small business may be able to get a loan in the country in which it plans to do business. This should be a consideration when selecting a country in which to do business.

GLOBAL MARKETING

Global products and marketing are adapted for local markets.[42] When McDonald's went to India, it had a problem. Can you guess what it was? You're right: The cow is sacred in India, and most people there will not eat an all-beef patty. So McDonald's sells its Big Mac in India, but without any beef. Advertisements are often developed by local agencies.

Products used to be developed in the home market and then brought to other countries later, but the trend is toward global introduction of products (time-based competition). Many products are now introduced and distributed globally. For example, the latest Harry Potter book was translated into multiple languages, and all of the different editions were sold globally on the same day. Small international businesses can use export management companies, agents, and distributor services to conduct their marketing. In addition, small business managers can attend trade shows, network through trade centers, and advertise in industry publications.

WorkApplication4
Select a company and identify as many of its global business practices as you can.
_____
_____
_____
_____
_____

Applying The Concept 2

Global Practices

Identify each practice as more likely to be used by large or small global companies:

a. large MNCs

b. small international companies

_____11. Have their own operating facilities in many countries.

_____12. Develop a product in one country and then bring the product to other countries.

_____13. Use importing and exporting to operate globally.

_____14. Include foreign nationals among their top-level managers.

_____15. Develop the latest technology through R&D.

Join the Discussion Ethics & Social Responsibility

File Sharing

1. Is it ethical and socially responsible for people to download music, movies, or software for free, which prevents recording, film, or software companies and artists from getting any royalties?

2. Is it ethical and socially responsible for **Kazaa** and others to give people the means to download music, movies, or software for free?

The file-share industry provides software for customer-to-customer (C2C) downloading of files from a Web site. Kazaa is a leading C2C file-share company, with over 15 million downloads every month worldwide. At any given time, there are about 4 million users online with Kazaa, most between the ages of 17 and 35.

Music companies and an industry watch group, the Recording Industry Association of America (RIAA), which represents musicians, are trying to sue Kazaa for copyright infringement and shut the company down. The music companies complain that they are losing profits and that musicians are losing royalties as people download music for free, which violates copyright law. The RIAA is also suing individuals who have downloaded music from Kazaa and other file-sharing Web sites.

Kazaa's parent company is **Sharman Networks** in Sydney, Australia, but most of its users are outside of Australia. There is no Australian law against file sharing, and managers at Kazaa do not believe the company should be sued in the U.S. court system. It would be hard to close Kazaa, because it does not have a central database of music, as Napster did. Kazaa's managers do not believe the company is doing anything wrong, but Kazaa is moving toward having all customers pay for downloads.

Source: "Kazaa CEO Goes on the Defensive," *USA Today* (November 17, 2003), p. 6.

ENTREPRENEURSHIP

Business is often described as a jungle, but are you ready for the untamed wilderness of entrepreneurship in the global village?[43] Entrepreneurships, especially those in the high-tech industries, have assumed a prominent role.[44] We discussed some of the differences between large and small businesses in management functions and roles in Chapter 1; in this section, we will discuss new venture creation by entrepreneurs and intrapreneurs and see how such businesspeople select, plan for, control, and finance new ventures. Before we begin, have you ever wondered what qualities entrepreneurs have?[45] Complete the Self-Assessment to discover whether you have entrepreneurial qualities.

—————————— **Learning** Outcome 5 ——————————
Explain the difference between an entrepreneur and an intrapreneur.

New Venture Entrepreneurs and Intrapreneurs

A **new venture** *is a new business or a new line of business.* For example, when Jeff Bezos started Amazon.com to sell books, it was a new business venture; when Amazon.com offered customer auction services, it was a new line of business. **Entrepreneurs** *commonly start a new small business venture.* **Intrapreneurs** *commonly start a new line of business within a large organization.* Intrapreneurs are also called *corporate entrepreneurs.* In essence, intrapreneurs commonly start and run a small business within a large organization, often as a separate business unit.[46] Both entrepreneurs and intrapreneurs are highly motivated to create something new.[47]

DEFINING SMALL AND LARGE BUSINESSES

There are many different definitions of *small business.* A useful one is from the Small Business Administration (SBA): *A* **small business** *is independently owned and operated, is not dominant in its field, and has annual receipts not in excess of $500,000.* A business that does not meet these three criteria is not technically a small business. Large businesses commonly are publicly owned (sell stock to the general public), are dominant competitors in their field, have sales of more than half a million dollars, and have 500 or more employees.

There are about 23 million small businesses in the United States.[48] An estimated 80 percent of these are family businesses.[49] African American men are 50 percent and Hispanic American men are 20 percent more likely than white men to start a business.[50] More women are also starting businesses, and the number will grow by 4 percent annually from 2003 through 2006.[51]

RISK TAKING BY ENTREPRENEURS AND INTRAPRENEURS

A major difference between entrepreneurs and intrapreneurs is risk taking. Entrepreneurs commonly risk personal assets, as they finance part or all of their business and run the risk of losing their investment. Some entrepreneurs have lost their life savings, retirement investments, homes, cars, and other assets. Often, they quit their jobs to start their new businesses and cannot go back if the business fails; they risk a dependable salary for potential profits, which usually take a few years to earn and may never come.

Self-Assessment

Entrepreneurial Qualities

Have you ever thought about starting your own business? This exercise gives you the opportunity to determine whether you have entrepreneurial qualities. Each item below presents two statements describing opposite ends of a spectrum of attitudes or behavior. Below each pair of statements is a six-point scale, with each end corresponding to one of the given statements and several positions in between. After reading the two statements for each item, place a check mark on the point on the scale that best represents where you see yourself on the spectrum. Answer the questions honestly, you will not be required to share your answers during class.

1. I have a strong desire to be independent— to do things my way and to create something new.   I like following established ways of doing things.

  6   5   4   3   2   1

2. I enjoy taking reasonable risks.   I avoid taking risks.

  6   5   4   3   2   1

3. I avoid making the same mistakes twice.   I often repeat my mistakes.

  6   5   4   3   2   1

4. I can work without supervision.   I need supervision to motivate me to work.

  6   5   4   3   2   1

5. I seek out competition.   I avoid competition.

  6   5   4   3   2   1

6. I enjoy working long, hard hours.   I enjoy taking it easy and having plenty of personal time.

  6   5   4   3   2   1

7. I am confident of my abilities.   I lack self-confidence.

  6   5   4   3   2   1

8. I need to be the best and to be successful.   I'm satisfied with being average.

  6   5   4   3   2   1

9. I have a high energy level.   I have a low energy level.

  6   5   4   3   2   1

10. I stand up for my rights.   I let others take advantage of me.

  6   5   4   3   2   1

Scoring: Add up the numbers below your check marks. The total will be between 10 and 60. Note where your score fits on the continuum of entrepreneurial qualities below.

Strong 60——50——40——30——20——10 Weak

Entrepreneurship is clearly not for everyone. Generally, the higher/stronger your entrepreneurial score, the better your chance of being a successful entrepreneur. However, simple paper-and-pencil surveys are not always good predictors. If you had a low score but really want to start a business, you may be successful. But, realize that you don't have all the typical entrepreneurial qualities. (Interestingly, around 66 percent of entrepreneurs are firstborn children.[52])

However, most entrepreneurs attempt to minimize their personal risk.[53] Intrapreneurs commonly have no risk of personal investment, as the large business provides the financing, and if the venture fails, they can usually return to their prior job or a similar one. Intrapreneurs also maintain their salary and often get a raise and/or part of the profits. However, like entrepreneurs, intrapreneurs usually work long hours. Although entrepreneurs take greater risks than intrapreneurs, their reward (like their loss) is usually greater, as the profits are theirs.

THE ENTREPRENEURIAL SPIRIT
Large businesses are clearly trying to be more entrepreneurial by taking advantage of opportunities, often by outsourcing and encouraging intrapreneurs. 3M and GE are well known for intrapreneurship and encouraging risk taking. One of 3M's goals is to have 25 percent of sales coming from products that did not exist five years ago. Thus, 3M and GE are constantly seeking new intrapreneurial ventures.

Contributions of Entrepreneurs

Entrepreneurs provide three major contributions to society: innovation, job creation and economic growth, and support of large businesses.

INNOVATION
Much of the creativity and innovation in society comes from entrepreneurs; the Goliaths of business have always looked to the Davids for new innovations.[54] Large businesses commonly acquire small businesses to gain innovations. Entrepreneurs working alone invented the transistor radio, the photocopy machine, instant photography, the personal computer, and the jet engine. Entrepreneurs also used others' ideas to give society the pocket calculator, power steering, automatic transmissions, air conditioning, and the 19-cent ballpoint pen, just to name a few innovations.

JOB CREATION AND ECONOMIC GROWTH
More than 600,000 new businesses are started in the United States each year. Small businesses employ 57.1 million workers—more than half of all private sector jobs—and create more than half of the nonfarm private sector gross domestic product (GDP).[55] Around 40 percent of the tax dollars collected by the Internal Revenue Service (IRS) comes from small businesses and self-employed taxpayers.[56]

SUPPORT OF LARGE BUSINESS
Small businesses are the primary suppliers and distributors of products for large businesses.[57] For example, GM buys materials from more than 25,000 suppliers, most of which are small businesses. GM also distributes its cars through small independent dealerships. As noted earlier, global outsourcing is on the increase, and much of it is being done by small businesses. Almost all large businesses started small and grew successfully.

Selecting the New Venture

Entrepreneurs (and intrapreneurs) possess a high degree of creativity and are responsible individuals who desire to work independently and be their own boss.[58] The first step to entrepreneurship is to select the new venture or the industry in which the business will compete.[59] Successful entrepreneurs select ventures with good growth potential (many buyers, few competitors) and profit opportunities.[60]

A survey revealed that nearly half of new venture ideas stem from previous work experience.[61] Experience helps entrepreneurs to envision creative (new and better) ways of operating a venture and also provides a network of personal, professional, and market contacts to ease entry into the field.

(Intrapreneurs also often start new lines of business that relate to the business they are already in.) Another 15 percent of entrepreneurs stated that they evaluated other businesses that were making mistakes or doing something well to capitalize on. Jiffy Lube and McDonald's both started as small businesses that were bought by companies that expanded corporate operations and opened franchises. Eleven percent of entrepreneurs looked for a new market niche or a segment of the market that had been overlooked. For example, rather than compete with Wal-Mart on price, many successful entrepreneurs have started specialty retail stores that focus on offering more variety and better service at higher profit margins.[62] Specialty retail, services, and wholesale are industries with many successful entrepreneurs; entrepreneurs have also done well in specialty manufacturing that does not require mass production. Seven percent of entrepreneurs systematically searched for an opportunity, while 5 percent got their ideas from a hobby or just talking to friends and colleagues.

COMPETITIVE ADVANTAGE

A **competitive advantage** *specifies how an organization offers unique customer value.* It answers the questions: What makes us different from the competition? Why should a person buy our product rather than the products of our competitors?[63] A sustainable competitive advantage is not easily duplicated.[64] Low prices (Wal-Mart), location (local day-care centers), convenience (Amazon.com), or brand (Coca-Cola) can provide a competitive advantage.

A related concept is **first-mover advantage**, which refers to *offering a unique customer value before competitors do so.*[65] For example, Pizza Hut had a competitive advantage for pizza restaurant dining. When Domino's started, it did not compete directly with restaurants; it made free delivery its competitive advantage, gaining the first-mover advantage over competitors. But free delivery was easily duplicated, so Domino's lost its unique competitive advantage. Jiffy Lube also lost some of its competitive advantage through duplication.

A recent survey revealed that the five strategies most commonly used by small business entrepreneurs are (1) creating a competitive advantage, (2) maintaining innovation, (3) lowering the costs of developing and/or maintaining one's venture, (4) defending an existing product/service, and (5) creating a first-mover advantage.[66]

If you like to do things your way, you may be a successful entrepreneur/intrapreneur.[67] If you decide to try, select a new venture in a growth industry with a competitive advantage and clearly state it in your business plan. If you do consider starting a business, be sure to answer two questions: What will make my business different from the competition's? Why should a person buy my product or service rather than the competition's? If you don't have answers to these questions, you will not have a competitive advantage, and you may not be able to get enough customers to have a successful business.

The Business Plan

A **business plan** *is a written description of a new venture—its objectives and the steps for achieving them.* Writing a business plan forces you to crystallize your thinking about what you must do to start your new venture before investing

WorkApplication5

Does the company you work for (or one you have worked for) have a competitive advantage? If yes, what is it? If not, how is this company the same as its competitors?

time and money in it.[68] The well-prepared business plan answers the following questions:

1. What is the purpose and mission of this business?
2. What products (goods and/or services) will the business provide? Who is in the target market?
3. Who are my competitors?
4. What is my competitive advantage? How will my business be successful?
5. How much money do I need to get started?
6. Where do I secure the money to finance the new venture?
7. What are the potential revenues, expenses, and profits?
8. How do I control the business?
9. What are possible expansion plans?[69]

THE BUSINESS PLANNING PROCESS

The first step in planning a business is to select a new venture based on marketing research. In completing this first step, you will find answers to questions 1–4. Through marketing research, you investigate the competition and select products based on your competitive advantage. You also need to forecast sales to determine growth and profit potential. (In Skill Builder 1 at the end of the chapter, you will select a new venture and answer questions 1–4 without extensive marketing research and sales forecasting.) Based on your marketing research, you are ready to write the business plan. Exhibit 3-4 presents sections that are commonly included in a business plan.

Jeff Bezos was a successful computer programmer on Wall Street in 1994. However, his entrepreneurial spirit and his knowledge of the growth of Internet use—about 2300 percent per month at the time—led him to quit his job and start his own business using the Internet. He made a list of items that he thought could be sold over the Internet. He came up with 20 items, including music, magazines, software, and books. Jeff Bezos eventually selected books, because of the volume of the product available—there are 1.5 million English-language books in print, and 3 million in all languages worldwide.

Jeff Bezos had a vision of creating the world's largest bookstore, which would be difficult to copy in any other format. He moved to Seattle, Washington, to start Amazon.com. Bezos developed a competitive advantage with his use of the Internet to offer a wide variety of products at low cost. He had a first-mover advantage, but he went far beyond his original idea of selling books, as Amazon.com continues to offer more products and services.

IOM

SOURCES OF ASSISTANCE IN PLANNING, STARTING, AND OPERATING THE NEW VENTURE

Entrepreneurs have never had a better friend than the Internet. There are plenty of Web sites dedicated to providing you with the information you need to develop a business plan, to start up your new business, and to operate it as it grows and becomes established.[70] Many entrepreneurs today use business-planning software; essentially, you answer preset questions and provide financial data, and the software completes your business plan. The two Web sites in Exhibit 3-4 and those listed below provide specific business-planning information.

• *Palo Alto Software, http://www.bplans.com.* This site offers a model of the business-planning process with an excellent narrative and more than 50 examples of business plans from actual firms. You will also find many links to other sites.

Exhibit 3-4 *Information Commonly Included in a Business Plan*[71]

- **Executive Summary.** Although presented first, this section is written after the rest of the business plan has been completed.

- **Introduction.** This section describes the business, answering these questions: What is the business? What goods or services does the business provide? Who are the business's competitors? What is the business's competitive advantage? It also introduces key managers and describes the legal form of the business (sole proprietorship, partnership, or corporation) and the type of business (an existing business, new start-up, franchise, or a new line).

- **Location and Layout.** Where will business be conducted, and how will the facilities be organized?

- **Operations.** This section describes the systems process for transforming inputs into outputs.

- **Marketing.** This section describes the marketing mix of the four Ps for the business: (1) products to be sold, (2) place products will be sold, (3) price of products, and (4) promotion to let target customers know about your products. (You can take a marketing quiz at *http://www.marketingangel.com.*)

- **Human Resources.** How many employees will the business need, and how will it recruit and hire them?

- **Accounting.** How will the business keep records? The business plan should include a three-year projection (*pro forma*) for three important financial reports: balance sheet, income statement, and cash flow. The accounting plan indicates the company's potential revenues, expenses, and profits. Potential creditors (people who will lend you money, assets, and inventory) and investors (co-owners with you) generally require projected financial statements.

- **Controls.** This section describes the mechanisms to ensure that objectives are achieved.

- **Financing.** The financial plan specifies how much money and other assets will be required to start and operate the new venture and where the financing will come from. (Tips and strategies for finding funding sources can be found at *http://www.growco.com.* As a general rule, you should not start a new venture unless you can operate the business for one year without drawing money from the business for personal expenses. In other words, you need to live for a year without a salary. Paying rent, car payments, and so on with business profits during first years is rarely possible, and doing so can cause your business to run out of funds and close.)

- *Small Business Administration (SBA), http://www.sba.gov/starting-business/planning/basic.html.* The SBA provides a detailed business plan outline as well as other excellent materials that illustrate strategic planning for a small business. In addition to online help, the SBA offers three free management assistance programs: Service Corps of Retired Executives (SCORE), Small Business Institute (SBI), and Small Business Development Centers (SBDC). You can find out more about these three services at the SBA Web site, *http://www.sba.gov.*

- The Minority Business Development Agency (MBDA), *http://www.mbda.gov.*

GLOBAL DIVERSITY

Managers from different countries do not see the world in quite the same way because they come from different cultures. Cultural values and beliefs are often unspoken and taken for granted; we tend to expect people to behave as we do. However, to be successful in the global village, managers need to be sensitive to other cultures. In fact, companies seek employees who are aware of and sensitive to other cultures. Global companies are also training employees in language, local customs, and local business practices so they can be successful in the global market.[72] As a global manager, you need to be flexible and adapt to other ways of behaving; you cannot expect others to change for you.

The world is undergoing profound cultural changes that are reshaping the relationship between employer and employee.[73] In this section, we will discuss global diversity in culture, work-related values, and management functions.

Cultural Diversity

Exhibit 3-5 illustrates some of the many areas in which cultures differ: customs, attitudes toward time, the work ethic, pay, laws and politics, and ethics. As you read this section, keep in mind that it offers generalities, to which there are always exceptions. The examples in the text are not meant to illustrate "right" or "wrong" behavior, but rather cross-cultural differences that affect human relations and management.

DIVERSITY IN CUSTOMS

Customs determine the accepted way of conducting business. For example, the Japanese place a high priority on human relations, participative management, and teamwork. If you try to be an individual star, you will not be successful in Japan. If you are very outspoken, you will be considered impolite. If you refuse to be involved in receiving and giving gifts, you will offend Japanese people. Many Japanese companies start the day with exercises and company cheers. If you do not actively participate, you will be an outsider.

In Europe, management has many cultural aspects that involve interpersonal rituals and protocols. For example, power and politics are important in the United States, but they are even more important in France. It is important for a French manager to be seen as holding great power. Teamwork is less important in France than in some other countries.

Exhibit 3-5 *Global Diversities*

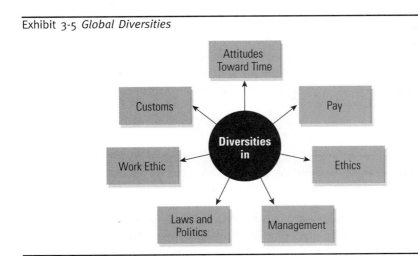

Americans prefer to speak face-to-face from a greater distance than people of most other countries. If you back away or turn to the side of a person you're speaking with, the person may feel the need to follow you and create a dance, and you may be considered cold and standoffish. During face-to-face communications, Latin American tend to touch each other more than North Americans do.

Gestures vary from country to country. For example, Americans prefer eye contact. However, young Puerto Ricans tend to look down as a mark of respect when speaking to adults. In Australia, making the V sign with the hand is considered an obscenity rather than a sign of victory. Former President George Bush found this out after flashing the V sign to Australian crowds in 1992.

DIVERSITY IN ATTITUDES TOWARD TIME

Americans typically view time as a valuable resource that is not to be wasted, and socializing at work is often considered a waste of time. However, it would be considered impolite to start a business meeting with Latin Americans without engaging in a certain amount of relaxed small talk. If you try to rush business deals without slowly developing personal relationships with Japanese managers, you will not be successful in obtaining Japanese business accounts.

American and Swiss businesspeople usually expect you to be precisely on time for an appointment. However, if you arrive on time for an appointment with a manager in other countries, you may be kept waiting for an hour. In some countries, most people who are due to attend a meeting will be late, and some may not show up at all. If you get angry at people for being late, you could harm human relations.

DIVERSITY IN WORK ETHIC

The work ethic—the view of work as a central interest and a desirable goal in life—varies all over the world. Generally, the Japanese have a stronger work ethic than Americans and Europeans. This strong work ethic and the acceptance of automation have made many Japanese plants the most productive in the world. Although there is not much difference in work ethic between Americans and Europeans, Americans are more productive, even though Europeans are usually better trained. In terms of number of hours worked, Americans work more hours than those in many other cultures.[74]

Americans are relatively good at extracting value from poorly prepared workers, which is important when working with illiterate people all over the world. However, in some cultures, managers and employees have little interest in being productive. These relaxed attitudes do not do much for the bottom line of global businesses.

DIVERSITY IN PAY

Americans, in general, are no longer the world's highest-paid employees. The Japanese and Europeans have caught up and earn as much as Americans. Employees in developing countries are paid much less than employees in developed countries.

Pay systems also must vary in some countries to meet employee values. One of the trends in American pay has been pay for performance. However, some countries value being paid for loyalty and following orders. Paying a salary works well in some countries, but not in others.

Join the Discussion Ethics & Social Responsibility

Bribes

1. Is it ethical and socially responsible to pay bribes?
2. Should the manager have paid the bribe to get the phone installed?

An American businessperson working in a foreign country complained to a local telephone manager that the technician showed up and asked for a bribe before installing the phone. The businessperson refused, so the telephone worker left without installing the phone. The telephone company manager told the businessperson that the matter would be investigated, for a fee.

DIVERSITY IN LAWS AND POLITICS

The legal and political environment becomes increasingly complex for the multinational company that does business all over the world. Health and safety laws are generally more protective of employees in developed countries than in developing countries. Labor laws also vary widely from country to country. Western European nations offer good benefits, including a required four- to six-week vacation, paid holidays, and sick and family leave. It is also easier to terminate employees in some countries than in others.

In some countries, government structure and politics are much more stable than in others. Recall our discussion of political instability and risk.

DIVERSITY IN ETHICS

When conducting global business, you must rethink business ethics. In the United States and other countries, it is illegal to take and give bribes for doing business. However, in many countries, paying bribes is a standard part of doing business.

Diversity in Work-Related Values

Geert Hofstede studied 116,000 IBM employees in 40 countries and identified four dimensions of national value systems that influence working relationships among organizational employees: individualism and collectivism, high and low power distance, high and low uncertainty avoidance, and achievement and relationship orientations. We will examine each of these, as well as their implications for management.[75]

INDIVIDUALISM AND COLLECTIVISM

Individualism reflects the value of a loosely knit social framework in which people take care of themselves and their immediate families. Individualistic countries include Australia, Canada, France, Great Britain, and the United States. *Collectivism* reflects the value of a tightly knit social framework in which people take care of each other and organizations take care of employees' interests. Collectivist countries include Costa Rica, Ecuador, Guatemala, Japan, Mexico, Panama, and Thailand.

HIGH AND LOW POWER DISTANCE

Societies that value *high power distance* accept inequity of authority among institutions, organizations, and people. Employees respect managers, as ranks and titles are important. Countries that value high power distance include France, India, Malaysia, Mexico, Panama, the Philippines, and Thailand. Countries that value *low power distance*, or equality, include Austria, Costa Rica, Denmark, Germany, Israel, Sweden, and the United States.

HIGH AND LOW UNCERTAINTY AVOIDANCE

People in cultures that exhibit *high uncertainty avoidance* like to avoid uncertainty and risk. They prefer lots of rules and regulations to ensure certainty and conformity of behavior. High uncertainty avoidance countries include Costa Rica, France, Greece, Japan, Mexico, Portugal, and Uruguay. *Low uncertainty avoidance* cultures accept uncertainty and ambiguity, and thus risk and nonconformity. Low uncertainty avoidance countries include Australia, India, Jamaica, Singapore, Sweden, and the United States.

ACHIEVEMENT AND RELATIONSHIP ORIENTATION

Achievement orientation refers to valuing achievement, heroism, assertiveness, competition, and material success. Countries where people have more of an achievement orientation include Austria, Germany, Mexico, and the United States. *Relationship orientation* refers to valuing relationships, cooperation, and group decision making. Countries with more of a relationship orientation include Costa Rica, Denmark, France, Norway, Sweden, and Thailand.[76]

MANAGERIAL IMPLICATIONS

Hofstede has provided a framework for managing in the global village. National culture has a major impact on employees' work-related values and attitudes and thus should affect the way organizations manage. In countries that are more like the United States (such as Australia, Canada, and England), American managers have fewer adjustments to make, whereas countries with

WorkApplication6

Give an example of cultural diversity you have encountered, preferably at work.

_____

_____

_____

_____

_____

Applying The Concept 3

Work-Related Values

Identify the work-related value exemplified by each statement.

a. individualism
b. collectivism
c. high power distance
d. low power distance
e. high uncertainty avoidance
f. low uncertainty avoidance
g. achievement orientation
h. relationship orientation

_____ 16. Employees are afraid of change and get nervous and stressed just talking about the possibility of it.

_____ 17. Monetary incentives are what motivate employees to achieve high levels of success.

_____ 18. The athletes seem to prefer sports like soccer and basketball to sports like golf and track and field.

_____ 19. Managers place great importance on status symbols such as the executive dining room, reserved parking spaces, and big offices.

_____ 20. Employees like having their boss do their performance appraisals; they don't want their peers involved.

cultures that are quite different from that of the United States (such as China, India, and Japan) require greater adjustment. The U.S. culture is individualistic, with low power distance. Similar values are found in Australia, Canada, England, the Netherlands, and New Zealand. Countries that are collectivist with high power distance include Colombia, Pakistan, the Philippines, Singapore, and Venezuela. Thus, American managers who work in these countries, or deal with people from them, need training on the foreign culture in order to successfully adjust. The United States is also low in uncertainty avoidance and high on achievement orientation, as are Australia, Canada, England, India, Ireland, New Zealand, and South Africa. Countries high on uncertainty avoidance and high on relationship orientation include Chile and Portugal.

In taking a business global, particularly when using strategic alliances and joint ventures, managing cultures is critical to success. One study of a seven-nation sample revealed that people in cultures that value relationship orientation, collectivism, and uncertainty avoidance have an appreciation for cooperative strategies.[77] Clearly, as a global manager you need to be able to work with a wide range of people.[78]

————————————————— Learning Outcome 6 —————————————————
Describe how global diversity affects the management functions.

Diversity in Management Functions

What works well in the United States does not necessarily work in other countries. To successfully manage globally, the international manager must plan, organize, lead, and control according to the characteristics of the culture of the country where he or she is working.[79] Global companies can compile a general set of principles that their managers can follow, but cannot detail everything. With restaurants in 119 countries, **McDonald's** has employment practices and philosophies that are, in essence, similar around the world. However, this does not mean that McDonald's implements these practices the same way from one country to the next. To do so would be unfair and culturally inappropriate.[80]

Let's discuss the need for diversity in each of the management functions.[81] Keep in mind that we are talking in general terms. As in the United States, specific organizations and employees in any country can and do vary.

PLANNING AND DECISION MAKING

People in collectivist, low power, low uncertainty avoidance, and relationship-oriented societies generally prefer to be involved in planning and decision making. Although the United States does not fit this profile perfectly, participation in planning and decision making is clearly on the increase in the United States, as well as in other countries throughout the world. High power distance and high uncertainty avoidance can lead employees to want managers to develop very clear plans and make the decisions. In fact, in Mexico, it is considered a sign of weakness to even explain why a decision was made. Conversely, people in Arab and African nations expect to be involved in planning and decision making. However, employees in developing nations often need basic skills training and are not capable of participating in planning and decision making without being trained.

ORGANIZING AND STAFFING

Employees in cultures with high power distance and high uncertainty avoidance want clear lines of authority and well-defined jobs with rules and regulations. Employees in collectivist and relationship-oriented societies expect great teamwork and group-based (rather than individual) rewards and pay; they also want greater job security and more benefits. Thus, a trip or other incentive for the salesperson with the highest sales works well in the individualistic United States but not in collectivist Japan. Management–labor relations also vary globally. In France and Israel, management–labor relations are more competitive than in the United States, whereas in Japan they are more cooperative.

LEADING

People in collectivist, low power distance, and relationship-oriented cultures want a participative leadership style based on relationship development. Employees in the Arab world, Asia, and Latin America expect managers to take a personal interest in them and to visit with them socially; managers must also be very careful in criticizing employees, as criticism contributes to a loss of self-respect and brings dishonor to the individual and his or her entire family. Individualistic, high power distance, and high uncertainty avoidance cultures are more open to autocratic leadership styles. Cultures with low power distance and low uncertainty avoidance prefer more informal communications that bypass the formal lines of communications, whereas cultures at the opposite end of the spectrum prefer formal communications that follow a chain of command.

CONTROLLING

Employees in high power distance and high uncertainty avoidance cultures prefer clear standards and controls. In an individualistic culture, the manager is usually the one responsible for enforcing the controls, such as rules and expected behavior. The manager may also do a fair share of the group's work. In collectivist societies, on the other hand, the group more commonly enforces the controls. It is difficult to fire employees for poor performance in some collectivist societies, including Mexico and Indonesia.

THE GLOBAL LEARNING ORGANIZATION

The complex global village clearly has a diversity of cultures, and successful MNCs are global learning organizations that value sharing of knowledge in order to adapt to the changing environment. One of the reasons Japanese MNCs have been so successful globally is that their culture encourages learning and adaptability. In Asia, teaching and learning are generally highly regarded, and the role of a manager is understood to be that of teacher or facilitator, who is responsible for helping employees to learn and improve.

I O M

Amazon.com started as an international business, but it did not meet the needs of a diverse global customer base, as it had only one Web site, in English and based in the United States. However, over the years, the company developed separate Web sites that are operated in six other countries in multiple languages. These Web sites are managed locally. Prices are shown and paid in the home currency of each country (credit card companies convert the currency according to exchange rates at the time of puchase), and most goods are shipped from the home country—making it possible for Amazon.com to handle 2.1 million orders (24 per second) and to ship more than 1 million packages in one day.

Now that you've read this chapter, you should better understand the complexity of the global business environment, the approach to taking a business global, the importance of entrepreneurship and intrapreneurship, differences in global business practices of MNCs and small international companies, and the need for developing global learning organizations that can adapt the management functions to fit the culture.

Take advantage of the companion Web site for *Management Fundamentals*, where you will find a broad array of resources to help you maximize what you learn in class:

- Try a quiz
- View chapter videos
- Download slides
- Boost your vocabulary
- Work through an Internet exercise
- Find related links

Take a look for yourself at *http://lussier.swlearning.com.*

Chapter Summary

1. Discuss the role of technology in the global village.
The global village refers to companies conducting business worldwide without boundaries. Technological advances, particularly in travel and communications, have made the global village possible. The Internet, e-commerce, and wireless communications will continue to play an important technological role in the global village.

2. State the difference between a domestic, an international, and a multinational business.
A domestic firm does business in only one country. An international firm is primarily based in one country but transacts business with other countries. MNCs have significant operations in more than one country.

3. List the six activities that make a business a global one, in order from lowest to highest cost and risk.
A business can become a global one by participating in global sourcing, importing and exporting, licensing, contracting, joint ventures, and direct investment. Global soucing is the least expensive and risky of these activities, and it can be a part of any of the others.

4. Describe some differences in the business practices of large multinational corporations and small international companies.
Global strategies of MNCs include joint ventures, strategic alliances, and direct investment; small international companies tend to use importing and exporting and global sourcing strategies to go global. MNCs tend to develop the latest technology and R&D, while small international companies tend to quickly copy MNCs.

5. Explain the difference between an entrepreneur and an intrapreneur.
Entrepreneurs commonly start a new small business venture. Intrapreneurs commonly start a new line of business within a

large organization, or they tend to run a small business within a large organization.

6. Describe how global diversity affects the management functions.
Global diversity means that management practices that work well in one country may not work in another country. Therefore, when performing the management functions of planning, organizing, leading, and controlling, managers must base their actions on the characteristics of the culture and the work-related values of the country where they are located.

7. Complete each of the following statements using one of this chapter's key terms.

_____ is regarding one's own group or culture as superior to others.

The _____ refers to companies conducting business worldwide without boundaries.

An _____ is primarily based in one country but transacts business in other countries.

A _____ has significant operations in more than one country.

_____ is the use of worldwide resources.

A _____ is created when firms share ownership of a new enterprise.

A _____ occurs when a company builds or purchases operating facilities (subsidiaries) in a foreign country.

_____ creation is the process of starting and operating a new business or a new line of business.

_____ commonly start new business ventures.

_____ commonly start a new line of business within a large organization.

A _____ is independently owned and operated, is not dominant in its field, and has annual receipts not in excess of $500,000.

_____ specifies how the organization offers unique customer value.

The _____ is offering a unique customer value before competitors do so.

A _____ is a written description of the new venture—its objectives and the steps for achieving them.

Key Terms

business plan, 94

competitive advantage, 94

direct investment, 86

entrepreneurs, 91

ethnocentrism, 78

first-mover advantage, 94

global sourcing, 85

global village, 79

international business, 84

intrapreneurs, 91

joint venture, 86

multinational corporation (MNC), 84

new venture, 91

small business, 91

Review and Discussion Questions

1. Should people in the United States make an effort to buy products made in America? If yes, how should "made in America" be defined?
2. As a business owner in the United States exporting goods to Japan, which currency do you prefer to be strong, the dollar or the yen? Why?
3. Is NAFTA of more benefit or harm to the United States? Why?
4. Can you name any international and global companies operating in your geographical area?
5. For any of the companies you listed in question 4, can you identify their method(s) of going global?
6. Are you interested in being an entrepreneur or an intrapreneur? Explain.
7. What is the difference between a small business and a large business?
8. What is a competitive advantage, and does a new venture need one?
9. What is a business plan, and does a new venture need one?
10. What is the major reason for differences in global business practices of large MNCs and small international businesses? Which group seems to be benefiting more from the Internet?
11. The United States is the most powerful country in the world, so why should its MNCs be concerned about cultural diversity?
12. How can the United States be classified on each of Hofstede's four work-related values?

Objective Case

CLAIMPOWER, INC.

Global giants are not the only companies cutting costs by shifting jobs overseas. Increasingly, small businesses are finding "offshore" jobs to be a boon for increasing their revenues while holding their bottom lines steady. Some smaller businesses are creating new jobs at home when routine jobs are shipped overseas.

A case in point: Rajeev Thadani wanted to expand his business, Claimpower, Inc., which is a medical billing service headquartered in Fairlawn, New Jersey. Thadani, a computer programmer by trade, started Claimpower after he developed a software program specifically for medical claims processing. Claimpower, Inc. is not a large company; it has only five U.S. employees. Thadani runs the company with his wife. In 2001, he was in Bombay, his native city, where he hired four Indian employees to help process insurance claims on behalf of his clients, New Jersey doctors.

Today, Thadani employs 35 people, 30 of whom work in India. Since he pays his Indian employees the U.S. equivalent of between $133 to $663 a month, he can charge his customers less than most of his New Jersey competitors. In less than three years, Claimpower's client list has grown from 10 doctors to 41, and his annual revenue has jumped from $100,000 to $700,000.

Claimpower's business plan calls for expansion of the client base to 500 physicians. To reach his goals, Thadani is adding a sales team and will hire new managers in the United States to work directly with doctors. He hopes to add as many as a dozen U.S. employees, plus 30 or more additional personnel in India.

Recent statistics indicate that the United States has lost 2.3 million jobs over the past three years, particularly to India, as outsourcing of work to foreign countries has increased. Is there any upside to this trend? Some believe that outsourcing can trigger the creation of new U.S. jobs and be a catalyst for lowering costs and driving innovation.

Medical billing seems to be an industry particularly well suited for outsourcing, and many larger medical billing companies, as well as some smaller ones, have hired workers abroad to cut costs at a time when insurance companies are paying doctors less per claim.

Many characterize the type of work outsourced to India and elsewhere as high volume, fairly predictable, and fairly repetitive work, such as data entry. Since Thadani is not preoccupied with the daily operations of the data-entry work that is done overseas, he can focus on client relations and sales. Although Thadani now has only five full-time U.S. employees, he maintains that his company is a "net positive" for the United States in terms of job growth. He has no apologies for creating offshore jobs. His business would never have been launched were it not for the possibility of hiring workers in India. It would never have shown a seven-fold increase in revenue without outsourcing. Being able to pay lower wages to his Indian employees cut Thadani's operating expenses, allowing him to increase his client base by offering attractive prices to physicians.

Thadani agrees with many economists who believe that outsourcing will put an even greater premium on innovation in the United States. The Information Technology Association of America (ITTA) and the American Electronics Association (AET) have pointed out that offshore outsourcing saves U.S. companies billions of dollars in labor costs and brings lower prices to consumers. Those savings, reinvested in the economy, ultimately create more jobs back in the United States. (Note that neither of these organizations is an impartial observer when it comes to outsourcing. Both represent some of the nation's biggest users of offshore workers.)

Reports from the ITTA and the AET point out that although the pain and suffering of people who lose their jobs in the transition should not be discounted, outsourcing has created more information technology jobs in the United States than it has displaced. Analysts from these two organizations calculated, for example, that, by 2003, 104,000 U.S. information technology jobs had been lost because of outsourcing to such places as India and Russia. But they calculated that the economic benefits of outsourcing, including savings on labor, increased productivity, and lowered prices, created 193,000 new jobs in the United States, for a net gain of nearly 90,000 jobs. But do these new jobs pay lower wages? Is it ethical to compare net job gains without taking up the issue of wage losses?

To learn more about Claimpower, Inc., log on to InfoTrac® College Edition at *http://infotrac. thomsonlearning.com* and use the advanced search function.

_____ 1. Most patients of doctors using Claimpower don't realize that the payment process is not "made in America."

a. True
b. False

_____ 2. Claimpower is a global village business.

a. True
b. False

_____ 3. Claimpower conducts business using e-commerce, e-business, and b2b.

a. True
b. False

_____ 4. Claimpower is classified as a

a. domestic business
b. international business
c. multinational corporation

_____ 5. Claimpower is using which method? (You may select more than one.)

a. global sourcing   d. contracting
b. importing and exporting   e. joint venture
c. licensing   f. direct investment

_____ 6. Adding employees in India was a new venture.

a. True
b. False

_____ 7. Rajeev Thadani is an

a. entrepreneur
b. intrapreneur

_____ 8. Today Claimpower is classified as a _____ business.

a. small
b. large

_____ 9. Claimpower has a competitive advantage. If true, what is it?

a. True
b. False

_____10. Claimpower has a first-mover advantage. If true, what is it?

    a. True

    b. False

11. Why is an industry, such as medical billing, considered advantageous of outsourcing?

12. Explain how the statement "outsourcing teaches the importance of keeping one's skills ahead of the curve in the job market" is relevant to you.

13. Is the U.S. economy, as a whole, helped or hurt through outsourcing?

Cumulative Case Questions

14. Which manager resources are relevant to Claimpower? (Chapter 1)

15. The importance of which internal environmental factor is best illustrated in this case? (Chapter 2)

16. Is Claimpower being ethical and socially responsible in using Indian workers, rather than U.S. workers, to process claims? (Chapter 2)

Skill Builder 1

SELECTING A NEW VENTURE

Would you like to be your own boss? Have you given any thought to running your own business someday? For this exercise you will think of a new venture you would like to start someday. The new venture can be entrepreneurial, if you are interested in running your own business, or intrapreneurial, if you want to start a new line of business for an existing company. With either approach, don't be concerned about financing the business. At this stage, you are only selecting a new venture. If you select intrapreneurship, you don't have to be working for the organization for which you would like to start a new venture. Provide information about your potential business in the following list. Give all of the topics some thought before writing down your final answers.

Company name (or line of business) _____

Products (goods and/or services)

Target market (potential customer profile)

Major competitors

Competitive advantage (will you have a first-mover advantage?)

Possible location of business (home, mall, downtown, near college/business/customers/suppliers, etc.)

Apply It

What did I learn from this experience? How will I use this knowledge in the future?

_____

_____

Your instructor may ask you to do this Skill Builder in class in a group. If so, the instructor will provide you with any necessary information or additional instructions.

Skill Builder 2

CULTURAL DIVERSITY AWARENESS

Objective

To develop your awareness of cultural diversity.

Procedure 1 (4–6 minutes)

You and your classmates will share your international experience and nationalities. Start with people who have lived in another country, then move to those who have visited another country, and follow with discussion of nationality (e.g., I am half French and Irish but have never been to either country). The instructor or a recorder will write the countries on the board until several countries/nationalities are listed or the time is up.

Procedure 2 (10–30 minutes)

You and your classmates will share your knowledge of cultural differences between the country in which the course is being taught and those listed on the board. This is a good opportunity for international students and those who have visited other countries to share their experiences. For example, in Spain most people have a two-hour lunch break and go home for a big meal and may take a nap. In Japan, people expect to receive and give gifts. You may also discuss cultural differences within the country.

Apply It

What did I learn from this experience? How will I use this knowledge in the future?

_____

_____

Learning Outcomes
After studying this chapter, you should be able to:

1. Explain the relationship among objectives, problem solving, and decision making. **PAGE 110**

2. Explain the relationship among the management functions, decision making, and problem solving. **PAGE 110**

3. List the six steps in the decision-making model. **PAGE 111**

4. Describe the differences between programmed and nonprogrammed decisions and among the conditions of certainty, uncertainty, and risk. **PAGE 114**

5. Describe when to use the rational decision-making model versus the bounded rationality model and group versus individual decision making. **PAGE 115**

4: Creative Problem Solving and Decision Making

6. State the difference between an objective and "must" and "want" criteria. **PAGE 120**

7. State the difference between innovation and creativity. **PAGE 122**

8. List and explain the three stages in the creative process. **PAGE 122**

9. Describe the differences among quantitative techniques, the Kepner-Tregoe method, and cost-benefit analysis for analyzing and selecting an alternative. **PAGE 127**

10. Define the following **key terms:**

   problem
   problem solving
   decision making
   decision-making model
   programmed decisions
   nonprogrammed decisions
   decision-making conditions
   criteria

   innovation
   creativity
   creative process
   devil's advocate
   brainstorming
   synectics
   nominal grouping
   consensus mapping
   participative decision-making model

Ideas on Management

at Nike

Phil Knight ran track for coach Bill Bowerman at the University of Oregon in the 1960s. From that athletic alliance, they went on together to start the Nike Corporation, in 1972. Initially the company imported track shoes from Japan, and Knight sold them out of his car at track meets. But the company soon began to design and market its own running shoes. The Nike mission is to bring inspiration and innovation to every athlete in the world, reflecting a key insight that Bill Bowerman had early in the company's history—that *everyone* is an athlete. This idea continues to drive Nike's business decisions and inform its marketing strategies.

Nike's aggressive retailing has led many to define it as the world's most competitive shoe and sportswear company. Today Nike employs around 23,000 people, operating on six continents; its partners—suppliers, shippers, retailers, and service providers—employ close to an additional 1 million people. In 2003, Nike surpassed $10 billion in sales for the first time.

© Miguel Villafan/Landov

I O M

1. **Which young NBA athlete did Nike sign to a large endorsement contract? What was the contract's price tag? How did Nike classify and define the problem or opportunity in making the decision to sign this player?**

2. **What objectives does Nike meet through its star endorsements?**

3. **What product is Nike currently marketing under this athlete's name? How does Nike demonstrate creativity and innovation?**

4. **Which techniques could Nike use to analyze the alternatives in the contract decision? Does the amount of the contract given to the young athlete pose a serious financial risk to Nike?**

5. **What unethical and socially irresponsible labor practices have critics accused Nike of in recent years?**

6. **Which decision style from the Vroom's participative decision-making model should Nike have used to make the decision to sign the athlete to a contract?**

To learn more about Nike, visit the company's Web site at *http://www.nike.com*, or log on to InfoTrac® College Edition at *http://infotrac. thomsonlearning.com*, where you can read articles on Nike. For example, use the advance search option to key in record numbers A97119293 and A93716529 to read about Nike's battle with critics of its labor practices and about the firm's latest marketing campaigns.

Source: Case information and answers to questions within the chapter were taken from the Nike Web site at *http://www.nike.com*, accessed May 14, 2004.

PROBLEM SOLVING AND DECISION MAKING: AN OVERVIEW

The ability to solve problems in innovative ways is one of the top qualities employers are seeking when hiring new managers.[1] Two major reasons managers are hired is to solve problems and make decisions.[2] Bad decisions can destroy careers and companies.[3] No one can say for sure how many decisions you will make as a manager, but you should realize that your problem-solving and decision-making skills will affect your career success.[4] Like all management skills, problem solving and decision making can be developed.[5]

In this section, we will discuss what a problem is and the relationship among objectives, problem solving, and decision making. This section also addresses the relationship among the management functions, decision making, and problem solving, as well as the problem-solving and decision-making models. The section concludes with an exploration of your preferred decision-making style.

Learning Outcome 1

Explain the relationship among objectives, problem solving, and decision making.

The Relationship among Objectives, Problem Solving, and Decision Making

WorkApplication1

Describe a situation in which a job objective was not met. Identify the problem created and the decision made in regard to this problem.

_____

_____

_____

_____

_____

When you do not meet your objectives, you have a problem. When you have a problem, you must make decisions.[6] The better you can develop plans that prevent problems before they occur, the fewer problems you will have and the more time you will have to take advantage of opportunities.

A **problem** *exists whenever objectives are not being met.* In other words, you have a problem whenever there is a difference between what is actually happening and what you and your boss want to happen. If the objective is to produce 1,500 units per day but the department produces only 1,490, a problem exists. **Problem solving** *is the process of taking corrective action to meet objectives.* **Decision making** *is the process of selecting a course of action that will solve a problem.* Decisions must be made when you are faced with a problem.[7]

The first decision faced by any manager who confronts a problem is whether or not to take corrective action. Some problems cannot be solved, and others do not deserve the time and effort it would take to solve them. However, your job requires you to achieve organizational objectives. Therefore, you will have to attempt to solve most problems.

Learning Outcome 2

Explain the relationship among the management functions, decision making, and problem solving.

The Relationship among the Management Functions, Decision Making, and Problem Solving

All managers perform the same four functions: planning, organizing, leading, and controlling. While performing these functions, managers must make decisions. Recall that conceptual and decision-making skills are one of the three types of skills needed for success in management. In fact, making decisions precedes taking action.[8] For example, when planning, managers must make decisions about objectives and when, where, and how they will be met. When organizing, managers must make decisions about what to delegate and how to coordinate the department's resources. When staffing, managers must decide whom to hire and how to train and evaluate employees. To lead, managers must decide how to influence employees. To control, managers must select methods to ensure that objectives are met. Managers who exhibit skilled decision making and systems thinking have fewer problems to solve.[9]

WorkApplication2

Give an example of a poor decision made by a manager performing a management function. Explain the management function and the problem created by the poor decision.

—————————— Learning Outcome 3 ——————————
List the six steps in the decision-making model.

The Decision-Making Model

The **decision-making model** *is a six-step process for arriving at a decision and involves (1) classifying and defining the problem or opportunity, (2) setting objectives and criteria, (3) generating creative and innovative alternatives, (4) analyzing alternatives and selecting the most feasible, (5) planning and implementing the decision, and (6) controlling the decision.* Exhibit 4-1 lists these steps. Notice that the steps do not simply go from start to finish. At any step, you may have to return to a prior step to make changes. For example, if you are at step 6, controlling, and the implementation is not going as planned (step 5), you may have to backtrack to prior steps to take corrective action by generating and selecting a new alternative or changing the objective. If you have not defined the problem accurately, you may have to go back to the beginning. Using the model develops critical thinking skills.[10]

Following the steps in the model will not guarantee that you will make good decisions. However, using the model will increase your chances of success in problem solving and decision making.[11] Consciously use the model in

---

ApplyingTheConcept 1

Steps in Decision Making

Identify the step in the decision-making model represented by each statement:

a. step 1   d. step 4
b. step 2   e. step 5
c. step 3   f. step 6

_____ 1. "We will use the brainstorming technique to solve the problem."

_____ 2. "Betty, is the machine still jumping out of sequence, or has it stopped?"

_____ 3. "I don't understand what we are trying to accomplish."

_____ 4. "What symptoms have you observed to indicate that a problem even exists?"

_____ 5. "Linear programming should be used to help us in this situation."

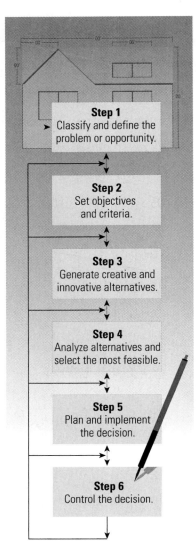

Step 1
Classify and define the problem or opportunity.

Step 2
Set objectives and criteria.

Step 3
Generate creative and innovative alternatives.

Step 4
Analyze alternatives and select the most feasible.

Step 5
Plan and implement the decision.

Step 6
Control the decision.

Exhibit 4-1
The Decision-Making Model

your daily life, and you will improve your ability to make decisions. The remainder of this chapter discusses the details of the model so that you can develop your creative problem-solving and decision-making skills.

Decision-Making Styles

Before learning about the three decision-making styles, determine your preferred style by completing the Self-Assessment.

REFLEXIVE STYLE

A reflexive decision maker likes to make quick decisions ("shooting from the hip") without taking the time to get all the information that may be needed and without considering alternatives. On the positive side, reflexive decision makers are decisive; they do not procrastinate. On the negative side, making quick decisions can lead to waste and duplication if the best possible alternative is overlooked. Failure is four times more likely when a decision maker implements the first possible solution without analyzing alternatives.[12] Employees view a reflexive decision maker as a poor manager if the decisions are consistently bad ones. If you use a reflexive style for important

Self-Assessment

Decision-Making Styles

Individuals differ in the way they approach decisions. To determine whether your decision-making style is reflexive, reflective, or consistent, evaluate each of the following eight statements, using the scale below. Place a number between 1 (indicating "This behavior is common for me") and 5 (indicating "This behavior is not common for me") on the line preceding each statement.

This behavior is common for me.   This behavior is not common for me.

1————————2————————3————————4————————5

_____ 1. Overall, I make decisions quickly.

_____ 2. When making decisions, I go with my first thought or hunch.

_____ 3. When making decisions, I don't bother to recheck my work.

_____ 4. When making decisions, I gather little or no information.

_____ 5. When making decisions, I consider very few alternative options.

_____ 6. When making decisions, I usually decide well before any deadline.

_____ 7. When making decisions, I don't ask others for advice.

_____ 8. After making decisions, I don't look for other alternatives or wish I had waited longer.

_____ Total score

To determine your style, add up the numbers you assigned to the statements; the total will be between 8 and 40. Note where you fall on the decision-style continuum:

          Reflexive   Consistent   Reflective

     8————————20————————30————————40

decisions, you may want to slow down and spend more time gathering information and analyzing alternatives.

REFLECTIVE STYLE

A reflective decision maker likes to take plenty of time to make decisions, gathering considerable information and analyzing several alternatives. On the positive side, the reflective type does not make hasty decisions. On the negative side, the reflective type may procrastinate and waste valuable time and other resources. The reflective decision maker may be viewed as wishy-washy and indecisive. If you constantly use a reflective style, you may want to speed up your decision making. As Andrew Jackson once said, "Take time to deliberate; but when the time for action arrives, stop thinking and go on."

CONSISTENT STYLE

Consistent decision makers tend to make decisions without either rushing or wasting time.[13] They know when they have enough information and alternatives to make a sound decision. Consistent decision makers tend to have the best record for making good decisions.[14] They tend to follow the decision-making steps in Exhibit 4-1 when appropriate. The next section will discuss when to make quick decisions without the model and when to take your time and use the model.

Managers in today's companies realize that speed in decision making is critical to success.[15] However, the quality of decisions must be considered along with speed.[16] Rapid sharing of knowledge has been found to make people more productive and able to solve problems more quickly.[17] Former CEO of **Alteon WebSystems** Dominic Orr noted that in the e-business world, companies need to make important strategic decisions, but fast decision making is hard. He pointed out that managers at Alteon focused on collecting as many facts as quickly as possible and then making the best—not necessarily the most perfect—decision. For Alteon managers, the goal was to make important decisions in a single meeting.[18]

Decision Making in the Global Village

Decision-making styles and the decision-making model are based on the approach to decision making typically used in U.S. companies. However, people from different cultures don't necessarily make decisions the same way.[19] Decision-making styles often vary based on time orientation. In some countries, decisions are made more quickly than in others. In countries that are less time-conscious, such as in Egypt, decision styles are more reflective than in time-conscious countries like the United States, where decision styles are more reflexive. In countries where managers use participative decision making, decisions take longer than in countries where managers use autocratic decision making. The Japanese, for whom decision making involves high levels of participation, often take longer to make decisions than U.S. managers do.

Managers in some countries (such as the United States) are more oriented to problem solving, whereas those in others (such as Thailand and Indonesia) tend to accept things the way they are. Culture influences the selection of problems to solve, the depth of analysis, the importance placed on logic and rationality, and the level of participation in decision making. Thus, in high power distance cultures (most Latin American countries and the Philippines and Yugoslavia), where decisions are more autocratic, participation is not acceptable. In lower power distance cultures (the United States, Ireland, Australia, New Zealand, Denmark, Israel, the Netherlands, and especially Japan), there is greater use of participation in decision making.

CLASSIFY AND DEFINE THE PROBLEM

Although it may seem surprising, it's true: Half the decisions made by managers fail to solve the problems they are aimed at, as they are not fully implemented within two years.[20] To improve your odds of successful problem solving, follow the steps in the decision-making model. The first step in the model is to classify and define the problem, which may sometimes take the form of an opportunity. In this section, we will discuss how to classify problems, select the appropriate level of participation, and determine the cause of problems.

Learning Outcome 4
Describe the differences between programmed and nonprogrammed decisions and among the conditions of certainty, uncertainty, and risk.

Classify the Problem

Problems may be classified in terms of the decision structure involved, the conditions under which a decision will be made, and the decision-making model used. Problems become clear, or make sense, when they are classified.[21]

DECISION STRUCTURE

For **programmed decisions**, *those that arise in recurring or routine situations, the decision maker should use decision rules or organizational policies and procedures to make the decision.* For example, a specified amount of inventory will be reordered every time stock reaches a specified level. *For* **nonprogrammed decisions**, *significant decisions that arise in nonrecurring and nonroutine situations, the decision maker should use the decision-making model.* To be significant, a decision must be expensive (such as purchasing major assets) and/or have major consequences (new product or reduction of employees) for the department or organization. Nonprogrammed decisions take longer to make than programmed decisions. The decision structure continuum is illustrated in Exhibit 4-2.

You must be able to differentiate between the two types of decision structures, because they provide a guideline as to how much time and effort you should spend to make effective decisions. Upper-level managers tend to make more nonprogrammed decisions than lower-level managers do.

DECISION-MAKING CONDITIONS

The three **decision-making conditions** *are certainty, risk, and uncertainty.* When making a decision under the conditions of *certainty,* you know the outcome of

Exhibit 4-2 *Decision Structure Continuum*

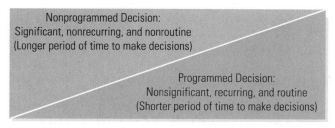

Nonprogrammed Decision:
Significant, nonrecurring, and nonroutine
(Longer period of time to make decisions)

Programmed Decision:
Nonsignificant, recurring, and routine
(Shorter period of time to make decisions)

each alternative in advance. When making a decision under conditions of *risk*, you do not know the outcome of each alternative in advance but can assign probabilities to each outcome. Under conditions of *uncertainty*, lack of information or knowledge makes the outcome of each alternative unpredictable so you cannot determine probabilities.

Most management decisions are made under conditions of risk. However, upper-level managers tend to make more uncertain decisions than lower-level managers do. When making decisions under uncertainty, it is difficult to determine what resources are needed to solve the problem. Although risk and uncertainty cannot be eliminated, they can be reduced with information.[22] Exhibit 4-3 illustrates the continuum of decision-making conditions.

―――――――――――― **Learning** Outcome 5 ――――――――――――

Describe when to use the rational decision-making model versus
the bounded rationality model and group versus individual
decision making.

DECISION-MAKING MODELS

There are two primary decision-making models: the rational model and the bounded rationality model. With the *rational model* (also called the *classical model*), the decision maker attempts to use optimizing, selecting the best possible alternative. With the *bounded rationality model* (also called the *administrative model*), the decision maker uses *satisficing*, selecting the first alternative that meets the minimal criteria. The decision-making model presented as Exhibit 4-1 is the rational model. With satisficing, only parts, or none, of the model would be used.

Exhibit 4-3 *Continuum of Decision-Making Conditions*

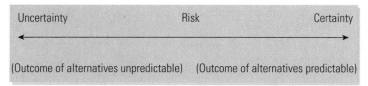

| Uncertainty | Risk | Certainty |

(Outcome of alternatives unpredictable)   (Outcome of alternatives predictable)

WorkApplication3

Give an example of a programmed and a nonprogrammed decision faced by an organization you work for or have worked for, and describe the decision condition in each case.

_____

_____

_____

_____

_____

You need to remember which model to use and when. The more complex and unstructured the decision and the higher the degree of risk and uncertainty, the greater the need to spend time conducting research with the aid of the decision-making model.[23] *Optimize* (select the best possible alternative) when you are making nonprogrammed, high-risk, or uncertain decisions. *Satisfice* (select the first alternative that meets the minimum criteria) when you are making programmed, low-risk, or certain decisions.

Select the Appropriate Level of Participation

When a problem exists, you must decide who should participate in solving it. As a rule of thumb, the key people involved with the problem should participate.[24] However, the current trend in management favors increased employee participation.[25] Thus, the major question is not whether managers should allow employees to participate in problem solving and decision making, but when and how this should be done. When making decisions, you should use the management style appropriate to the situation. In the last section of this chapter, you will learn about Vroom's participative decision-making model, and you will have a chance to practice using this model in Skill Builder 2. For now, you will learn about two levels of participation: individual and group decision making. However, realize that even though the trend is toward group decision making, some people want to be involved in decision making and others do not.[26]

Exhibit 4-4 lists the potential advantages and disadvantages of involving groups in decision making. The key to success when using groups is to maximize the advantages while minimizing the disadvantages.

ApplyingTheConcept 2

Classify the Problem

Classify the problem in each statement according to the structure and condition under which the decision must be made.

a. programmed, certainty
b. programmed, uncertainty
c. programmed, risk
d. nonprogrammed, certainty
e. nonprogrammed, uncertainty
f. nonprogrammed, risk

____ 6. "When I graduate from college I will buy an existing business rather than work for someone else."

____ 7. Sondra, a small business owner, has had a turnaround in business; it's now profitable. She wants to keep the excess cash liquid so that she can get it quickly if she needs it. How should she invest it?

____ 8. A purchasing agent must select new cars for the business. This is the sixth time in six years he has made this decision.

____ 9. In the early 1970s, investors had to decide whether to start the World Football League.

____ 10. A manager in a department with high turnover must hire a new employee.

Exhibit 4-4 *Potential Advantages and Disadvantages of Using Group Decision Making*

Potential Advantages	Potential Disadvantages
1. Better-quality decisions	1. Wasted time and slower decision making
2. More information, alternatives, creativity, and innovation	2. Satisficing
3. Better understanding of the decision	3. Domination and goal displacement
4. Greater commitment to the decision	4. Conformity and groupthink
5. Improved morale and motivation	
6. Good training	

POTENTIAL ADVANTAGES OF GROUP DECISION MAKING

When group members have something to contribute to the decision-making process, six potential advantages accrue:

1. *Better-quality decisions.* Groups usually do a better job of solving complex problems than the best individual in the group. Using groups to solve problems and make decisions is appropriate when an organization faces significant nonprogrammed decisions and conditions of risk or uncertainty.
2. *More information, alternatives, creativity, and innovation.* A group of people usually has more information than an individual. Creative or innovative ideas (or products) often arise from the combined input of members building on each others' ideas.
3. *Better understanding of the decision.* When people participate in decision making, they usually understand the alternatives presented and why the one selected was the best alternative. This allows easier implementation of the decision.
4. *Greater commitment to the decision.* Researchers have shown that people involved in making a decision have increased commitment to implementing the decision.
5. *Improved morale and motivation.* Participation in problem solving and decision making is rewarding and personally satisfying to the people involved.
6. *Good training.* Allowing participation in decision making trains people to work in groups by developing group process skills.

POTENTIAL DISADVANTAGES OF GROUP DECISION MAKING

Groups need to be careful to minimize the following disadvantages of group decision making:

1. *Wasted time and slower decision making.* It takes longer for a group to make a decision. Also, employees involved in decision making are not on the job producing. Thus, group involvement costs the organization time and money. With programmed decisions and conditions of certainty or low risk, individual decision making is generally more cost-effective than group decision making.
2. *Satisficing.* Groups are more likely to satisfice than an individual, especially when group meetings are not run effectively. When one person is responsible, that person stands out if a good or poor decision is made. But with a group, usually no one person gets the blame or credit for the decision.

3. *Domination and goal displacement.* One group member or a subgroup may dominate the group decision. *Goal displacement* occurs when an individual or subgroup tries to get the group to accept a particular alternative or dominates the group for personal reasons, rather than pursuing the original goal of finding the best solution.
4. *Conformity and groupthink.* Group members may feel pressured to go along with the group's decision without questioning it out of fear of not being accepted or because they do not want to cause conflict. *Groupthink* occurs when members withhold different views to appear as though they are in agreement. This nullifies the advantage of diversity.

In general, for a significant nonprogrammed decision with high risk or uncertainty, use group decision making. For a programmed decision with low risk or certainty, use individual decision making.

To be successful at decision making, you need to identify the type of problem to be solved and the level of participation to use. Exhibit 4-5 puts together the concepts from this section to help you better understand how to classify problems.

Exhibit 4-5 *Continua for Classifying a Problem*

Decision Structure

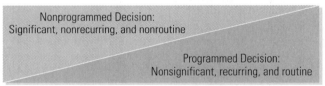

Decision-Making Conditions

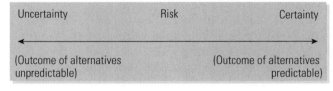

Which Decision Model to Use

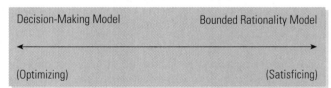

When to Use Group or Individual Decision Making

Define the Problem

After you have classified the problem, you or the group must define it clearly and accurately. Defining the problem accurately requires conceptual skills.

Because of time pressures, managers often hurry to solve problems and make decisions. Rushing to solve a problem that is not correctly defined often leads to a decision that does not solve the problem—haste makes waste. An important part of defining the problem is to distinguish symptoms from cause; it's an effective way to look at a problem.[27]

DISTINGUISH SYMPTOMS FROM THE CAUSE OF THE PROBLEM

Begin by listing the observable and describable occurrences (symptoms) that indicate that a problem exists. Only after doing this can you determine the cause of the problem. If you eliminate the cause, the symptoms should disappear. For example, Sam, an employee with six years on the job, has been an excellent producer. However, in the last month, Sam has been out sick or late more times than he was in the past two years. What is the problem? If you say "absenteeism" or "lateness," you are confusing symptoms and causes. They are symptoms of the problem, but they don't tell you why the problem has occurred. If you don't eliminate the cause of the problem, the symptoms will reappear.

Sun Microsystems is "a leading provider of industrial-strength hardware, software, and services that make the Net work." Its mission is "to solve complex network computing problems for governments, enterprises, and service providers." Sun is helping firms take advantage of the power of the Internet by offering proven products and comprehensive services to create competitive advantage. Sun has more than 35,000 employees in 100 countries dedicated to making organizations successful.[28]

eBay was a client user of Sun Microsystems. eBay had a few small computer crashes, and Sun was not sure what the problem was, as it focused primarily on the hardware. But when eBay's Web site went down for 22 hours, a permanent solution was needed. The *symptom* of the problem was the server's being down, but the cause was not the hardware. The actual *cause* of the problem was the fact that Sun systems are sophisticated and that eBay server users needed more help and training on how to use them. The solution was to have Sun consultants go beyond the sale of hardware and to help and train clients in the use of the hardware.[29] If Sun had merely continued to focus on the crashing hardware symptoms, rather than focusing on the cause (the lack of help and training), the problem would not have been solved.

Note that the same decision-making model is used to pursue opportunities and to solve problems. In fact, success is obtained by focusing on exploiting opportunities, not simply by focusing on solving problems.[30] Managers need to define the opportunities and determine their potential worth.[31] This is what Nike did when it signed LeBron James (6 foot 8 inch guard for the NBA Cleveland Cavaliers) to a massive, $90 million advertising deal.

Nike faced a problem—Michael Jordan was retiring from basketball and thus would no longer be an appropriate spokesman for Nike—and the company looked to LeBron James as an opportunity to replace Jordan. The decision to contract with James was a nonprogrammed decision characterized by high risk and uncertainty. When signed, James was a high school star going directly into the NBA, so there was no certainty that he would become a star. Nike was betting on him to take Jordan's place, but even

IOM

WorkApplication5

Define a problem in an organization you work for or have worked for. Be sure to clearly distinguish the symptoms from the causes of the problem.

IOM

if James became a star player, there was no certainty that he would have Jordan's personality, which is what helps sell Nike products. Therefore, the rational decision-making model was appropriate for this decision.

——————————— Learning Outcome 6 ———————————
State the difference between an objective and "must"
and "want" criteria.

SET OBJECTIVES AND CRITERIA

Generally, with simple programmed decisions, the objectives and the criteria have been set. Therefore, you need not complete steps 2–4 of the decision-making model. However, with nonprogrammed decisions, you should follow all the steps in the decision-making model. Therefore, the second step for the individual or group facing such a decision requires setting objectives and developing criteria.

Setting clear objectives helps managers to make better decisions.[32] Objectives drive decisions, and they must state what the decisions should accomplish—whether they will solve a problem or take advantage of an opportunity.[33] You'll learn how to set effective objectives in Chapter 5.

You should also specify the criteria for choosing an alternative solution to a problem. **Criteria** *are the standards that an alternative must meet to be selected as the decision that will accomplish the objective.* Having multiple criteria helps to optimize the decision. You should distinguish "must" and "want" criteria. "Must" criteria have to be met in order for an alternative to be acceptable, whereas "want" criteria are desirable but not necessary for the alternative to be acceptable. With satisficing, you stop with the first acceptable alternative; with optimizing, you seek to select the best possible option.

Suppose a regional manager faces the problem that a store manager has quit and a new manager must be hired. The objective is to hire a store manager by

WorkApplication6

Identify some of the qualification criteria (college degree, years of experience, etc.) for jobs at an organization you work for or have worked for. Distinguish any "must" and "want" criteria.

Join the Discussion   Ethics & Social Responsibility

Stem-Cell Research

1. Can Advanced Cell and other companies that are pursuing stem-cell research behave ethically with so much at stake financially? What can such companies do to help maintain their ethical standards?
2. Is the decision to use stem-cell research to treat diseases an ethical one? Is the objective of reproductive stem-cell research ethical?
3. Should the federal government even be considering funding stem-cell research? What criteria for funding stem-cell research should funding sources (either the government or private funding sources) set?

Advanced Cell Technology, Inc. is the leading biotechnology company in the emerging field of regenerative medicine. The company's focus is on the production of young cells for the treatment of cell degenerative disease. The company uses nuclear transfer (cloning) technology to produce healthy cells or tissue of any type that genetically matches a patient's own DNA. This eliminates the risk of the cells being rejected by the patient's immune system. The company can also create precise genetic modifications at the cellular level to cure genetic disorders as part of the treatment.

Join the Discussion Ethics & Social Responsibility

(*Continued*)

A stem cell, simply put, is a cell that can branch out like the branches or *stems* of a tree and change into two or more different cell types. The classic stem cells are the cells in bone marrow that can develop into many, but not all, of the cell types of the blood. Because bone marrow stem cells exist in all fully developed humans, they are called *adult stem cells*. In contrast, embryos in the first two weeks of human development have all-powerful stem cells that can develop into any cell type in the body. These stem cells are usually referred to as *human embryonic stem cells*.

Therapeutic cloning should be contrasted with reproductive cloning. Reproductive cloning is the cloning of a human embryo and the transfer of that embryo into a uterus to produce a pregnancy. Advocates of therapeutic cloning technology say that stem-cell research could lead to the elimination of diseases such as Parkinson's disease and muscular dystrophy—not to mention the potential profits that Advanced Cell and other biotechnology firms stand to gain. Advanced Cell Technology is not engaged in and does not support the cloning of human beings. However, critics of stem-cell research say that the kind of work done by Advanced Cell is a stepping-stone to cloning humans. And in 2003, the Bush Administration set specific restrictions on the kinds of stem-cell research that may be funded by the government.

Source: Taken from Advanced Cell Technology's Web site at *http://www.advancedcell.com*, accessed January 29, 2004.

June 30, 2007. The "must" criteria are that the person have a college degree and a minimum of five years' experience as a store manager. The "want" criterion is that the person should be a minority group member. The regional manager wants to hire a minority employee but will not hire one who does not meet the "must" criteria. In this situation, the manager would optimize the decision rather than satisfice. We will discuss criteria again later in this chapter.

Nike's objective in signing athletes to endorse its products is to make a profit. A necessary criterion for deciding to sign a contract with an athlete is that the athlete must have the potential to sell more products for Nike than the company would sell without the endorsement. In addition, Nike wants to be able to recoup the cost of the contract. Thus, LeBron James's endorsements must generate much more than $90 million in sales so that Nike also benefits from the contract.

IOM

GENERATE CREATIVE ALTERNATIVES

After the problem is defined and objectives and criteria are set, you generate possible alternatives for solving the problem or exploiting the opportunity (step 3 of the decision-making model). Usually many possible ways exist to solve a problem; in fact, if you don't have two or more alternatives, you don't have to make a decision.

With programmed decision making, the alternative is usually predetermined. However, with nonprogrammed decision making, time, effort, and resources are needed to come up with new creative and innovative ideas.[34] In this section, you will read about innovation and creativity, using information and technology to generate alternatives, and group methods for generating creative alternatives.

—————————————————— Learning Outcome 7 ——————————————————
State the difference between innovation and creativity.

Innovation and Creativity

INNOVATION

Innovation *is the implementation of a new idea.* Two important types of innovation are product innovation (new things) and process innovation (new ways of doing things).[35] *Product innovations* are changes in outputs (goods or services) to increase consumer value. *Process innovations* are changes in the transformation of inputs into outputs. Major companies are continually working on processes to cut costs. Successful innovation comes from clear communication, knowledge sharing, and creative problem solving.[36]

CREATIVITY

Creativity *is a way of thinking that generates new ideas.* **Adelphi University** provides an example of a creative solution that became an innovation. The university wanted to expand its graduate business program. However, many potential students felt that they did not have the time to further their education. The alternative that Adelphi developed was the "classroom on wheels," which offers classes four days a week on commuter trains into and out of New York City. Although many researchers have stated that creativity is important to the long-term survival of organizations, many managers do not encourage it.[37]

—————————————————— Learning Outcome 8 ——————————————————
List and explain the three stages in the creative process.

THE CREATIVE PROCESS

There is no definite relationship between intelligence and creativity; everyone has creative capability.[38] *The three stages in the* **creative process** *are (1) preparation, (2) incubation and illumination, and (3) evaluation* (see Exhibit 4-6). As with the decision-making model, you may have to return to prior stages as you work through the creative process.

1. *Preparation.* As a manager, you must become familiar with the problem by getting others' opinions, feelings, and ideas, as well as the facts.[39] When solving a problem or seeking opportunities, look for new angles, use imagination and invention, and don't limit yourself to the boundaries of past thinking. Generate as many possible solutions as you can think of without making a judgment.

2. *Incubation.* After generating alternatives, take a break; sleep on the problem. Take some time before working on the problem again. During the incubation stage, as your subconscious works on the problem, you may gain an insight into the solution—*illumination.*[40] Have you ever worked hard on something and become discouraged but found that when you gave up or took a break, the solution came to you? Illumination can also

Exhibit 4-6 *Stages in the Creative Process*

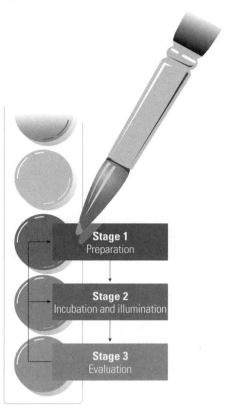

Stage 1
Preparation

Stage 2
Incubation and illumination

Stage 3
Evaluation

happen while working on the problem; it is sometimes referred to as the "Aha, now I get it" phenomenon.

3. *Evaluation.* Before implementing a solution, you should evaluate the alternative to make sure the idea is practical.[41] A good approach to use when evaluating a solution or alternative is to become the devil's advocate. *With the* **devil's advocate** *approach, group members focus on defending a solution while others try to come up with reasons the solution will not work.* Devil's advocate evaluation usually leads to more creativity as the idea is improved upon.[42]

Many organizations like to encourage creativity; **Coca-Cola, Fuji, Omron, Pitney Bowes, Shimizu,** and **Shiseido**, for example, have developed training programs that emphasize creativity.

Using Information and Technology to Generate Alternatives

The ideal managers of the 21st century use facts, information, and knowledge to make decisions.[43] Decisions should be based on solid information rather than simply intuition. However, when generating alternatives, the question for many managers is, "How much information and how many alternatives do I need, and where should I get them?" There is no simple answer. The more

WorkApplication7

Give an example of how you, or someone else, solved a problem using the stages in the creative process. Be sure to list the steps and note whether illumination came during incubation or while working on the problem.

_____

_____

_____

_____

_____

important the decision, generally, the more information and/or alternatives you need. However, if you get too much information or too many alternatives, the decision becomes too complex, and the best alternative may not be selected.[44]

Technology, especially telecommunications and computers, has shown considerable potential for assisting with problem solving and decision making. Idea-generating computer software helps individuals develop alternative solutions more creatively.[45]

Using Groups to Generate Creative Alternatives

Groups may face the potential difficulties of satisficing, dominance, and group-think, especially when they are well-established work groups. To avoid these difficulties, you need to be careful that the group does not just list a limited number of alternative solutions to a problem and quickly move to accept one.[46]

When the problem has been classified as one a group should solve, a variety of methods are available for generating creative alternative solutions.[47] Five of the more popular techniques, illustrated in Exhibit 4-7, are brainstorming, synectics, nominal grouping, consensus mapping, and the Delphi technique.

BRAINSTORMING

Brainstorming *is the process of suggesting many possible alternatives without evaluation.* The group is presented with a problem and asked to develop as many solutions as possible. Members should be encouraged to make wild, extreme suggestions.[48] They should also build on suggestions made by others. However, members should not react in any way, favorably or unfavorably, to any of the members' contributions, including their own. When selecting members for a brainstorming group, try to include diverse people;[49] 5 to 12 people make up a good-sized group. Status differences should be ignored. Everyone should have an equal voice. None of the alternatives should be evaluated until all possible alternatives have been presented. Brainstorming is commonly used, and companies are training employees to use it for tasks requiring creative ideas, such as naming new products or services.

With electronic brainstorming, people use computers to generate alternatives. Participants synchronously send ideas without getting together. People who are far apart geographically can brainstorm this way, and the number of participants does not have to be limited.[50]

Exhibit 4-7 *Group Decision-Making Techniques That Foster Creativity and Innovation*

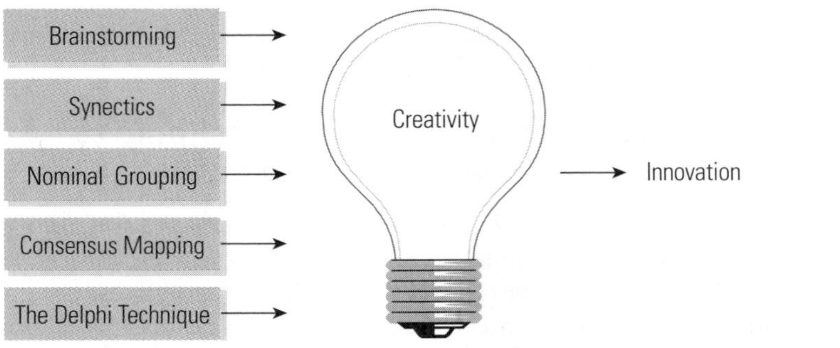

SYNECTICS

Synectics *is the process of generating novel alternatives through role playing and fantasizing.* Synectics focuses on generating novel ideas rather than a large quantity of ideas.[51] At first, the group leader does not even state the exact nature of the problem so that group members avoid preconceptions.

Nolan Bushnell wanted to develop a new concept in family dining, so he began by discussing leisure activities generally. Bushnell then moved to leisure activities having to do with eating out. The idea that came out of this synectic process was a restaurant–electronic game complex where families could entertain themselves while eating pizza and hamburgers. The complex is called ***Chuck E. Cheese ShowBiz Pizza Time.***

NOMINAL GROUPING

Nominal grouping *is the process of generating and evaluating alternatives using a structured voting method.* This process usually involves six steps:

1. *Listing.* Each participant generates ideas in writing.
2. *Recording.* Each member presents one idea at a time and the leader records them where everyone can see them. This continues until all ideas are posted.
3. *Clarification.* Alternatives are clarified through a guided discussion, and any additional ideas are listed.
4. *Ranking.* Each employee rank-orders the ideas and identifies what he or she sees as the top three; low-ranked alternatives are eliminated.
5. *Discussion.* Rankings are discussed for clarification, not persuasion. During this time, participants should explain their choices and their reasons for making them.
6. *Vote.* A secret vote is taken to select the alternative.

Nominal grouping is appropriate to use in situations in which groups may be affected by domination, goal displacement, conformity, and groupthink, because it minimizes these effects.[52]

CONSENSUS MAPPING

Consensus mapping *is the process of developing group agreement on a solution to a problem.* If a consensus cannot be reached, the group does not make a decision. Consensus mapping differs from nominal grouping because there can be no competitive struggle ending in a vote that may force a solution on some members of the group. The Japanese call this approach *Ringi.* Consensus mapping can be used after brainstorming. In consensus mapping, the group categorizes or clusters ideas in the process of trying to agree on a single solution. A major benefit of consensus mapping is that because any solution chosen is the group's, members generally are more committed to implementing it.[53]

THE DELPHI TECHNIQUE

The *Delphi technique* involves using a series of confidential questionnaires to refine a solution. Responses on the first questionnaire are analyzed and resubmitted to participants on a second questionnaire. This process may continue for five or more rounds before a consensus emerges.[54] Managers commonly use the Delphi technique for technological forecasting, such as projecting the next computer or Internet breakthrough and its effect on a specific industry. By knowing what is to come, managers can make creative decisions to plan for the future.[55]

WorkApplication8

Give examples of organizational problems for which brainstorming, nominal grouping, or consensus mapping would be appropriate techniques.

_____

_____

_____

_____

Upper-level managers commonly use synectics and the Delphi technique for a specific decision. Brainstorming, nominal grouping, and consensus mapping techniques are frequently used at the departmental level with work groups. As a manager working with a group to come up with a decision, you'll want to be on guard against the kinds of responses that can stifle creativity:

- "It can't be done."
- "We've never done it."
- "Has anyone else tried it?"
- "It won't work in our department (company/industry)."
- "It costs too much."
- "It isn't in the budget."
- "Let's form a committee."

If group members make such statements, your job is to remind the group to focus on generating ideas, the more offbeat the better, and to steer the discussion away from critiques of specific ideas, which are unproductive."[56]

IOM

The first LeBron James AirZoom Generation shoes went on sale for $110 at Niketown.com and other retailers on February 4, 2004. To cover its $90 million contract with James and make a profit, Nike will have to continue to come up with new creative and innovative products with the James name. James will also have to play well and be popular with fans so that they are motivated to pay a premium price for sportswear with his name on it.

Decision Trees

After you come up with alternative problem solutions, you may want to make a decision tree. A *decision tree* is a diagram of alternatives. The diagram gives a visual picture of the alternatives, which makes it easier for some people to analyze them.

Applying The Concept 3

Using Groups to Generate Alternatives

Identify the most appropriate group technique for generating alternatives in each situation.

a. brainstorming   d. consensus mapping

b. synectics   e. Delphi technique

c. nominal grouping

_____ 11. Upper-level managers at a toy manufacturer want to develop some new toys. They call in a consultant who is leading groups of employees and children to come up with ideas together.

_____ 12. A department is suffering from morale problems, and the manager doesn't know what to do about it.

_____ 13. A manager must choose new matching desks for the ten employees in the office.

_____ 14. A manager wants to reduce waste in the production department to cut costs and increase productivity.

_____ 15. Top managers want to project future trends in the banking industry, as part of their long-range planning.

Exhibit 4-8 *Decision Tree*

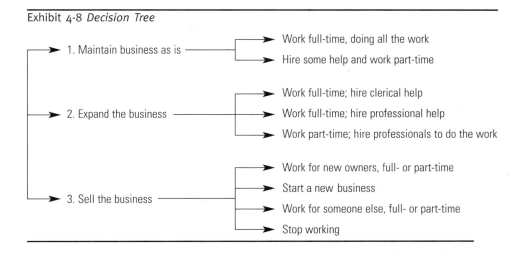

1. Maintain business as is
→ Work full-time, doing all the work
→ Hire some help and work part-time

2. Expand the business
→ Work full-time; hire clerical help
→ Work full-time; hire professional help
→ Work part-time; hire professionals to do the work

3. Sell the business
→ Work for new owners, full- or part-time
→ Start a new business
→ Work for someone else, full- or part-time
→ Stop working

Carolyn Blakeslee started **Art Calendar** (a business magazine for visual artists) in 1986. She was a first-mover, and the business's competitive advantage was that Art Calendar was the only publication dedicated to helping visual artists make a living doing what they love. Art Calendar's mission is to connect artists with opportunities for income and exhibition. Each issue features hundreds of listings of juried shows, residencies, grants, galleries reviewing portfolios, publishing opportunities, positions open, and much more.

Blakeslee started Art Calendar as a part-time business in a room in her house. She ran the business alone and read the mail and attended to other tasks during her daily five-mile ride on a stationary bike. But as the business grew, it became more than a full-time job for Blakeslee. She wanted to have it all—to meet financial goals and devote time to her family, to create her own artwork, and to relax with her hobbies. Like many small business owners, she had to make a decision. Her choices are diagrammed in a decision tree in Exhibit 4-8.

As Exhibit 4-8 shows, when creating a decision tree, you write down all the alternative solutions to a problem. Can you think of other alternatives not listed here? After listing alternatives, you analyze them and make a decision. Blakeslee decided to expand her business—to work full-time and hire professional help. Her husband, Dave Proeber, is now Director of Operations.[57]

—————————————— Learning Outcome 9 ——————————————
Describe the differences among quantitative techniques,
the Kepner-Tregoe method, and cost-benefit analysis for analyzing
and selecting an alternative.

ANALYZE ALTERNATIVES AND SELECT THE MOST FEASIBLE

Notice that in the decision-making model in Exhibit 4-1, generating alternatives and analyzing alternatives and selecting the most feasible are two different steps (steps 3 and 4). This is because generating and evaluating alternatives at the same time tend to lead to satisficing and wasting time discussing poor alternatives rather than optimizing.[58]

In evaluating alternatives, you should think forward and try to predict the possible outcome of each. Be sure to compare alternatives to the objectives and criteria set in step 2 of the decision-making process. In addition, compare each alternative to the others. This section presents three approaches that are commonly used to analyze alternative solutions: quantitative techniques (a general class of approaches, of which we will discuss five), the Kepner-Tregoe method, and cost-benefit analysis.

Quantitative Techniques

As you read in the Appendix to Chapter 1, one of the five approaches to management is management science, which uses math to aid in problem solving and decision making. Quantitative techniques use math in the objective analysis of alternative solutions. The discussion that follows will make you aware of five quantitative techniques; it will not make you a mathematician. If you are interested in the actual calculations, you should take courses in quantitative analysis.

Managers may not be expected to compute the math for all types of quantitative techniques. However, if you know when to use these techniques, you can seek help from specialists within or outside the organization.

BREAK-EVEN ANALYSIS

Break-even analysis allows calculation of the volume of sales or revenue that will result in a profit. It involves forecasting the volume of sales and the cost of production. The break-even point occurs at the level where no profit or loss results.

CAPITAL BUDGETING

This technique is used to analyze alternative investments in assets, such as machines. The payback approach allows the calculation of the number of years it will take to recover the initial cash invested. Another approach computes the average rate of return. It is appropriate when the yearly returns differ. A more sophisticated approach, *discounted cash flow*, takes into account the time value of money. It assumes that a dollar today is worth more than a dollar in the future. Organizations including **AMF, Kellogg, Procter & Gamble,** and **3M** use discounted cash flow analysis.

LINEAR PROGRAMMING

Optimum allocation of resources is determined using linear programming (LP). The resources that managers typically allocate are time, money, space, material, equipment, and employees. Companies primarily use LP for programmed decisions under conditions of certainty or low risk, but LP is also widely applied to product-mix decisions. **Lear Siegler, Inc.,** uses LP when determining work flow, to optimize the use of its equipment. **Bendix Corporation** uses LP to minimize transportation (shipping) costs for its truck fleet.

QUEUING THEORY

Queuing theory focuses on waiting time. An organization can have any number of employees providing service to customers. If the organization has too many employees working at one time, not all of them will be waiting on customers and money paid to them is lost. If the organization has too few employees working at one time, it can lose customers who don't want to wait for service, which results in lost revenue. Queuing theory, which helps the organization balance these two costs, is used by retail stores to determine the optimum number of checkout clerks, by airports to determine the optimum number of takeoffs and landings on runways, and by production departments to schedule preventive maintenance on equipment.

PROBABILITY THEORY

Probability theory enables the user to make decisions that take into consideration conditions of risk. The user assigns a probability of success or failure to each alternative. The user then calculates the expected value, which is the payoff or profit from each combination of alternatives and outcomes. The calculations are usually done on a payoff matrix by multiplying the probability of the outcome by the benefit or cost. Probability theory is used to determine whether to expand facilities and to what size, to select the most profitable investment portfolio, and to determine the amount of inventory to stock. You could use it to choose a job.

The Kepner-Tregoe Method

The Kepner-Tregoe method combines the objective quantitative approach with some subjectivity. The subjectivity comes from determining "must" and "want" criteria and assigning weighted values to them. As you read earlier in the chapter, "must" criteria are those attributes that an alternative solution must have if it is to be considered. "Want" criteria are attributes that make an alternative solution more attractive; they are desirable but not essential. Absence of certain "want" criteria does not cause an alternative to be eliminated.

The Kepner-Tregoe method is a technique for comparing alternatives using the criteria selected in step 2 of the decision-making model. It is helpful when

WorkApplication9

Give examples from an organization you work for or have worked for of decisions that might appropriately be analyzed using the quantitative techniques of break-even analysis, capital budgeting, linear programming, queuing theory, and probability theory.

_____

_____

_____

_____

_____

Applying The Concept 4

Selecting Quantitative Methods

Select the appropriate quantitative method to use in each situation.

a. break-even analysis

b. capital budgeting

c. linear programming

d. queuing theory

e. probability theory

_____16. The manager of a small clothing store wants to determine the quantity of items to purchase from wholesalers for resale in the store.

_____17. Claude must decide whether to repair his oldest machine or to replace it with a new one.

_____18. Bentley wants to invest money to make a profit.

_____19. The manager of a fast-food restaurant wants to even the workload in the store. At times, employees hang around with nothing to do; at other times, they work for hours without stopping.

_____20. A video store owner wants to know how many times a DVD will have to be rented out to recoup the expense of adding it to the rental list.

Exhibit 4-9 *The Kepner-Tregoe Method for Analyzing Alternatives*

"Must" Criteria	Car 1	Car 2	Car 3	Car 4
Cost under $12,000	Yes	Yes	Yes	Yes
Available within one week	Yes	Yes	Yes	No

		Car 1		Car 2		Car 3	
"Want" Criteria	Importance*	Criterion rating	Weighted score	Criterion rating	Weighted score	Criterion rating	Weighted score
Good gas mileage	7	5	$7 \times 5 = 35$	6	$7 \times 6 = 42$	8	$7 \times 8 = 56$
Sporty	8	5	$8 \times 5 = 40$	7	$8 \times 7 = 56$	4	$8 \times 4 = 32$
Color (blue)	3	10	$3 \times 10 = 30$	0	$3 \times 0 = 0$	0	$3 \times 0 = 0$
AM/FM stereo	5	7	$5 \times 7 = 35$	8	$5 \times 8 = 40$	3	$5 \times 3 = 15$
Good condition	10	5	$10 \times 5 = 50$	6	$10 \times 6 = 60$	8	$10 \times 8 = 80$
Low mileage	6	6	$6 \times 6 = 36$	4	$6 \times 4 = 24$	5	$6 \times 5 = 30$
Relatively new	7	3	$7 \times 3 = 21$	5	$7 \times 5 = 35$	5	$7 \times 5 = 35$
TOTAL WEIGHTED SCORE (WS)			247		257		248

*Indicates importance [on a scale of 10 (high) to 1 (low)] assigned to each criterion as a weight.

comparing purchase options (such as when a business is considering acquiring machines, computers, or trucks) and when selecting people to be hired and promoted. Exhibit 4-9 shows an example of its use. Refer to the exhibit as you read the discussion.

Step 1. Assess each alternative with regard to the "must" criteria. Eliminate any alternative that does not meet all "must" criteria. To illustrate, suppose that your objective is to buy a car within two weeks. The choice of car is a nonprogrammed decision, which you will make by yourself. Exhibit 4-9 lists the "must" and "want" criteria for each alternative. (Determination of "must" and "want" criteria corresponds to step 2 in the decision-making model in Exhibit 4-1, p. 112. The choice of alternative cars in this example corresponds to step 3 in the decision-making model.) As you can see, alternative car 4 does not meet all the "must" criteria and is eliminated.

Step 2. Rate the importance of each "want" criterion on a scale from 1 to 10 (10 being most important). Exhibit 4-9 lists these ratings in the Importance column. They range from 3 to 10. (Note that they are not ranked from 1 to 8. The same number, e.g., 7, may be used more than once.)

Step 3. Determine how well each alternative meets each "want" criterion. Assign a value of 1 to 10 (10 being the highest) to each alternative for each criterion. (Again, some "want" criteria may be assigned the same value.) This step involves not only assessing each alternative individually on each criterion, but also comparing the alternatives to each other on each criterion. For our example, Exhibit 4-9 shows that Car 1 meets the "color" criterion quite well. You can see how well Car 1 met each "want" criterion by reading down is column vertically. In addition, the Kepner-Tregoe method allows you to compare alternatives to each other. For example, of the three alternatives, Car 3 meets the "good gas mileage" criterion best, Car 2 meets the "sporty" criterion best, and Car 1 meets the "color" criterion best. You can see these comparisons by reading horizontally across from each "want" criterion.

Step 4. Compute the weighted score (WS) for each alternative on each criterion. Working horizontally, multiply the number that indicates the importance of each criterion by the number indicating how well the alternative meets the criterion. For example, Exhibit 4-9 shows that the criterion of "good gas mileage" was ranked 7 for importance. Car 1 was assigned a 5 to indicate how well it meets the "good gas mileage" criterion. Thus, Car 1's weighted score for "good gas mileage" is 35 (7×5). Exhibit 4-9 shows a weighted score for each criterion for Car 1 (as well as for Car 2 and Car 3). For each alternative, the eight individual weighted scores are added together to create a Total Weighted Score, shown at the bottom of each column.

Step 5. Select the alternative with the highest total weighted score as the solution to the problem. Car 2 should be selected because it has a total weighted score of 257 versus 248 and 247 for the other cars. By selecting Car 2, you rely entirely on your decision model and do not allow instinct, intuition, or judgment to influence your decision.

Cost-Benefit (Pros and Cons) Analysis

Quantitative techniques and the Kepner-Tregoe method are objective mathematical approaches to comparing alternatives. However, there are times when it is unclear whether the benefit to be gained from an alternative is worth its cost; in

Exhibit 4-10 *Continuum of Analysis Techniques*

Quantitative Techniques	Kepner-Tregoe Method	Cost-Benefit
←		→
(Objective)		(Subjective)
(Maximal use of math to make the decision)		(Minimal use of math to make the decision)

WorkApplication10

Give examples from an organization where you work or have worked of decisions that might appropriately be analyzed using the Kepner-Tregoe method and cost-benefit analysis.

such cases, management science approaches are unusable. *Cost-benefit analysis* is a technique for comparing the cost and benefit of each alternative course of action using subjective intuition and judgment along with math.[59] With pros and cons analysis, you identify the advantages, which can be considered the benefits, and the disadvantages, which can be considered the costs, of each alternative. Exhibit 4-10 compares the three approaches to analyzing and selecting alternatives.

Ben Franklin is said to have used pros and cons analysis. Franklin would draw a line down the middle of a piece of paper. On one side, he would list the pros and on the other the cons of whatever he was considering; seeing these in writing helped him select the best alternative. Many people think about costs and benefits, or pros and cons, without writing them down. You should write them down, however, when using this technique for important nonprogrammed decisions.

Cost-benefit analysis is more subjective than management science techniques. Therefore, when using this approach with a group, the group should do a critical evaluation of all alternatives.[60] Using a method such as the devil's advocate approach can help the group avoid the potential problems of satisficing, dominance, and groupthink. The group should also be careful of the way alternatives are presented for evaluation, as the order of presentation can affect the decision. People tend to remember best what they hear first and last.

Regardless of the method used to analyze alternatives, ideally the one selected is the optimal alternative that meets the criteria established in step 2 of the decision-making model.[61] If none of the alternatives meet the criteria, you have two options: (1) return to step 2 and change the criteria for the best alternative, or (2) return to step 3 and generate more alternatives.

IOM

$90 million is a lot of money to spend on an endorsement contract with LeBron James. However, this amount will be paid over several years, and Nike does $10 billion worth of business yearly. The contract also includes clauses that specify how it may be ended if things don't work out. So, relatively speaking, the contract was not a great financial risk for Nike. Nike could have used quantitative break-even analysis in making the decision to sign James, as Nike managers knew the cost and could figure the sales needed to break even on the contract. Probability theory might be used to analyze the decision, but capital budgeting, linear programming, and queuing theory are not relevant to this decision. The Kepner-Tregoe method also is not very applicable to this decision. Cost-benefit analysis was no doubt also applied in making the decision, as there was a cost to having a competitor contract with James, thereby causing Nike to lose sales and market share. Nike did not want anyone else to sign with James.

Ethics and Social Responsibility in Decision Making

One of the seven reasons that half of all decisions taken by managers do not solve the problems they are supposed to address is that decision makers ignore

Join the Discussion Ethics & Social Responsibility

Importing Medicines

1. Is it ethical to break the law? Are cities and states being ethical and socially responsible in making the decision to purchase medicines illegally from Canada?
2. Is the federal government (HHS) being ethical and social responsible in making it illegal to buy medicines from Canada?
3. Are Canadian companies being ethical and socially responsible by selling medicines to American customers, thus helping others to break U.S. law?

The American people and politicians and bureaucrats at different branches and levels of government are concerned about the high cost of medicines. The city of Springfield, Massachusetts, gained national media attention for buying prescription drugs for city employees from Canada. **The U.S. Department of Health and Human Services (HHS)** stated that it is illegal to buy these drugs from Canada, citing safety issues, and it will most likely turn down a request from the state of Illinois asking for federal clearance to import medications from Canada. However, officials in about a dozen states have said they are exploring ways to purchase cheaper drugs from Canada, even though importing them is illegal. Although it is not illegal in Canada to sell medicine to customers in the United States, some Canadian pharmacies are refusing to fill big orders from the United States.

Sources: "Illinois Asks Federal Clearance to Import," *Wall Street Journal* (December 23, 2003), p. A1; "About a Dozen States," *Wall Street Journal* (December 12, 2003), p. A1; "Some Canadian Pharmacies," *Wall Street Journal* (December 26, 2003), pp. A1, A9.

ethical questions.[62] When performing the management functions, you need to maintain high ethical standards and follow ethical guidelines, such as the stakeholders' approach to ethics.[63] Even when making unpopular decisions that don't benefit all stakeholders, such as lay-offs, you can still be ethical—for example, by giving advance notice and helping people who lose their jobs find new ones within the company or elsewhere.[64]

Although Nike has been criticized as a *sweatshop* (employing workers for very low wages and providing poor working conditions), it is the company's contract manufacturers that actually hire and pay the workers who make Nike products. However, in an effort to counter the criticisms, Nike continues to try to improve working conditions of its partner manufacturers.

PLAN, IMPLEMENT THE DECISION, AND CONTROL

The final two steps in the decision-making model involve planning and implementing the decision (step 5), and controlling (step 6).

After making a decision, you develop a plan of action with a schedule for implementation. You will learn the details of the planning process in the next chapter.

After a decision has been made and plans developed, the plans must be implemented. This seems obvious, but one in three decisions is not implemented.[65]

Communicating the plan to all employees is critical to successful implementation.[66] You will learn about communication in Chapter 11. In implementing a decision, it is likely to be necessary to delegate assignments to others. You will learn about delegating in Chapter 6.

Control methods should be developed while planning. Checkpoints should be established to determine whether the chosen alternative is solving the problem.[67] If not, corrective action may be needed. When managers will not admit that they made a bad decision, they are in the process known as *escalation of commitment.*[68] When you make a poor decision, you should admit the mistake and try to rectify it by going back over the steps in the decision-making model.

VROOM'S PARTICIPATIVE DECISION-MAKING MODEL

Earlier in the chapter, we discussed some of the advantages of group decision making. Today's managers need a way of determining not only when to use groups to arrive at decisions and when to make decisions alone, but also, when a group is used, what level of participation to use. The model developed by Victor Vroom and discussed in this section and in Skill Builder 2 is a tool that managers can use to answer these questions while improving decision-making effectiveness. (Note that Vroom's participative model does not take the place of the decision-making model; it tells you when to use a group and what level of participation you should use with the decision-making model.)

In 1973, Victor Vroom and Philip Yetton published a decision-making model, which Vroom and Arthur Jago refined and expanded to four models in 1988.[69] The models incorporate two factors: individual versus group decisions, and time-driven versus development-driven decisions.

In 2000, Vroom published a revised version of his model in an article entitled "Leadership and the Decision-Making Process." The current model is based on research by Vroom and his colleagues at Yale University on leadership and decision-making processes, involving more than 100,000 managers.[70]

The **participative decision-making model** *is a time-driven or development-driven decision tree that assists a user in selecting one of five leadership styles (decide, consult individuals, consult group, facilitate, and delegate) to use in a given situation (based on seven questions/variables) to maximize a decision.* Vroom's model is called a *normative model* because it provides a sequential set of questions that are rules (*norms*) to follow to determine the best decision style for the given situation. To use the participative model, you must have a specific decision to make, have the authority to make the decision, and have specific group members who may participate in the decision.

Participation Decision Styles

Vroom identified five leadership styles based on the level of participation of group members in the decision.

- **Decide.** The leader makes the decision alone and announces it, or sells it, to the group. The leader may get information from others outside the group and within the group without specifying the problem.
- **Consult Individuals.** The leader describes the problem to individual group members, gets information and suggestions, and then makes the decision.

- **Consult Group.** The leader holds a group meeting and describes the problem to the group, gets information and suggestions, and then makes the decision.
- **Facilitate.** The leader holds a group meeting and acts as a facilitator as the group works to define the problem and the limits within which a decision must be made. The leader seeks participation, debate, and concurrence on the decision without pushing his or her ideas. However, the leader has the final say on the decision.
- **Delegate.** The leader lets the group diagnose the problem and make the decision within stated limits. The role of the leader is to answer questions and provide encouragement and resources.

Questions That Determine the Appropriate Participative Decision Style

To determine which of the five leadership styles is the most appropriate for a given situation, you answer a series of diagnostic questions based on seven variables. The seven variables are listed in Exhibit 4-11 and explained below.

1. *Decision Significance: How important is the decision to the success of the project or organization? Is the decision of high (H) or low (L) importance?* When decisions are highly important, leaders need to be involved.

2. *Importance of Commitment: How important is group commitment to implementing the decision?* If group acceptance of the decision is critical to effective implementation, importance is high (H); if group commitment is not important, importance is low (L). When group commitment to implementing a decision is vital, the group generally needs to be involved in making the decision.

3. *Leader Expertise: How much knowledge and expertise does the leader have with respect to this decision? Is expertise high (H) or low (L)?* The more expertise the leader has, the less need there is for group participation.

4. *Likelihood of Commitment: If the leader were to make the decision alone, is the certainty that the group would be committed to the decision high (H) or low (L)?* When the decision is one that the group will like and want to implement, there is less need to involve them in the decision.

5. *Group Support for Objectives: Does the group show high (H) or low (L) support for the team or organizational goals to be attained?* Higher levels of group participation are acceptable with high levels of support.

6. *Group Expertise: How much knowledge and expertise do individual group members have with respect to this decision? Is expertise high (H) or low (L)?* The more expertise group members have, the greater the group participation can be.

7. *Team Competence: Is group members' competence in working together as a team to solve the problem high (H) or low (L)?* With high team competence, more participation can be used.

Not all seven questions are relevant to all decisions. In some situations, as few as two questions are needed to select the most appropriate leadership style. As questions 3 and 6 imply, for important decisions, it is critical to include the leader and/or group members with the expertise to solve the problem. The issue of commitment (questions 2 and 4) is also important. And as questions 5–7 imply, a leader should not delegate decisions to groups with low support for objectives, low group expertise, and low team competence.

Exhibit 4-11 *Participative Decision-Making Model*

The model is a decision tree that works like a funnel. Define the problem statement; then move from left to right and answer each question by responding either high (H) or low (L), skipping decisions that are not appropriate to the situation and avoiding crossing any horizontal lines. The last column indicates the appropriate leadership decision-making style for that situation. Select either the time-driven or development-driven version based on focus, value, and orientation.

Time-Driven (Problem Statement)

1 Decision Significance?	2 Importance of Commitment?	3 Leader Expertise?	4 Likelihood Commitment?	5 Group Supports?	6 Group Expertise?	7 Team Competence?	Decision Style
H	H	H	H	—	—	—	Decide
H	H	H	L	H	H	H	Delegate
H	H	H	L	H	H	L	Consult (Group)
H	H	H	L	H	L	—	Consult (Group)
H	H	H	L	L	—	—	Consult (Group)
H	H	L	H	H	H	H	Facilitate
H	H	L	H	H	H	L	Consult (Individuals)
H	H	L	H	H	L	—	Consult (Individuals)
H	H	L	H	L	—	—	Consult (Individuals)
H	H	L	L	H	H	H	Facilitate
H	H	L	L	H	H	L	Consult (Group)
H	H	L	L	H	L	—	Consult (Group)
H	H	L	L	L	—	—	Consult (Group)
H	L	H	—	—	—	—	Decide
H	L	L	—	H	H	H	Facilitate
H	L	L	—	H	H	L	Consult (Individuals)
H	L	L	—	H	L	—	Consult (Individuals)
H	L	L	—	L	—	—	Consult (Individuals)
L	H	—	H	—	—	—	Decide
L	H	—	L	H	—	—	Delegate
L	H	—	L	L	—	—	Facilitate
L	L	—	—	—	—	—	Decide

Development-Driven (Problem Statement)

1 Decision Significance?	2 Importance of Commitment?	3 Leader Expertise?	4 Likelihood of Commitment?	5 Group Support?	6 Group Expertise?	7 Team Competence?	Decision Style
H	H	—	H	H	H	H	Delegate
H	H	—	H	H	H	L	Facilitate
H	H	—	H	H	L	—	Consult (Group)
H	H	—	H	L	—	—	Consult (Group)
H	H	—	L	H	H	H	Delegate
H	H	—	L	H	H	L	Facilitate
H	H	—	L	H	L	—	Consult (Group)
H	H	—	L	L	—	—	Consult (Group)
H	L	—	—	H	H	H	Delegate
H	L	—	—	H	H	L	Facilitate
H	L	—	—	H	L	—	Consult (Group)
H	L	—	—	L	—	—	Consult (Group)
L	H	—	H	—	—	—	Decide
L	H	—	L	—	—	—	Delegate
L	L	—	—	—	—	—	Decide

Source: Adapted from Victor H. Vroom, "Leadership and the Decision-Making Process," *Organizational Dynamics* 28 (4), p. 87. Copyright © 2000 with permission from Elsevier.

Time-Driven versus Development-Driven Model

Having decided to use the Vroom model to determine whether to involve a group in a decision, the manager must choose either the time-driven version or the development-driven version of the model. The choice is determined by whether timeliness or group development is more important in the given situation. In other words, is it more important to make a decision relatively quickly, or more important to gain group commitment and support by giving group members decision-making practice? The two versions differ in their focus, in what they value, and in their time orientation.

- **Focus.** The time-driven version of the model focuses on making effective decisions with minimum cost. Time is costly, and it takes longer for groups to make decisions than it does for a manager alone. The development-driven version of the model focuses on making effective decisions through maximum development of group members; this version assumes that group development is worth the cost.
- **Value.** The time-driven version of the model emphasizes timely decision making; the development-driven version emphasizes group development.
- **Orientation.** The time-driven version of the model has a short-term time horizon; the development-driven version of the model has a long-term horizon, as group development takes time.

Vroom has developed a computerized version of his model that is more complex and more precise, yet easier to use than the versions just described. It combines the time-driven and development-driven versions into one model, includes 11 variables/questions (rather than 7), and has five possible levels for each variable (not simply H or L). In addition, the computerized version guides the user through the process of analyzing the situation with definitions, examples, and other forms of help. Although the computerized model is

WorkApplication11

Give an example of a specific decision that you or your boss have had to make. Was the decision time-driven or development-driven? Using Exhibit 4-11, select the appropriate decision style for the situation. Be sure to state the questions you answered and how (H or L) you answered each.

Applying The Concept 5

The Participative Decision Model

Refer to the time-driven model in Exhibit 4-11 and select the appropriate decision style for each situation.

a. decide
b. consult individually
c. consult group
d. facilitate
e. delegate

_____ 21. You are a new manager, and you find that someone in your department has been making lots of personal photocopies. The extra expense is affecting your budget. You want the copying to stop. You are pretty sure you know who is doing it.

_____ 22. Things are going okay in your department, but you know that performance could be better. The workers are knowledgeable, have positive work norms, and work well together. You are thinking about having a one-time brainstorming session. You've never led one.

Refer to the development-driven model in Exhibit 4-11 and select the appropriate decision style for each situation.

a. decide
b. consult individually
c. consult group
d. facilitate
e. delegate

_____ 23. You work in purchasing and have to buy five new cars for the sales staff, within a set budget.

_____ 24. You oversee a self-directed team, which requires very little supervision. One of the seven team members has retired and needs to be replaced.

_____ 25. You supervise five part-time employees who are high-school students. You know that your store has been losing customers, but you don't know why. You want to find out and improve the situation.

beyond the scope of this course, you will have a chance to practice using the time-driven and development-driven models in Skill Builder 2.

I O M

Suppose that in contemplating signing LeBron James to a $90 million advertising contract, managers at Nike had wanted to determine whether to leave the decision to a single person or have a group make the decision. Managers could have used one of the two versions of Vroom's decision model to answer this question. The first step would have been to decide which version to use. Since the company was contemplating spending $90 million, it was probably not important to the company to save time by making the decision quickly. Also, the decision had a long-term orientation, both because this particular contract would likely last several years and because advertising in general is an ongoing activity for Nike. Thus, managers would have wanted to use the development-driven version of Vroom's model.

Having read this chapter, you should understand the importance of problem solving and decision making, how to use the decision-making model (and when not to use it), the importance of creativity and quantitative techniques in analyzing alternatives, and the need to plan, implement the decision, and control it. Finally, it is important to be ethical and socially responsible in your decision making, and make sure that the employees you supervise are too.

Take advantage of the companion Web site for *Management Fundamentals*, where you will find a broad array of resources to help you maximize what you learn in class:

- Try a quiz
- View chapter videos
- Download slides
- Boost your vocabulary
- Work through an Internet exercise
- Find related links

Take a look for yourself at *http://lussier.swlearning.com.*

Chapter Summary

1. Explain the relationship among objectives, problem solving, and decision making.

Managers are responsible for setting and achieving organizational objectives. When managers do not meet objectives, a problem results. When a problem exists, decisions must be made about what, if any, action must be taken.

2. Explain the relationship among the management functions, decision making, and problem solving.

When managers perform the functions of planning, organizing, leading, and controlling, they make decisions. Managers who are skilled decision makers will have fewer problems to solve.

3. List the six steps in the decision-making model.

The steps in the decision-making model are (1) classifying and defining the problem, (2) setting objectives and criteria,

(3) generating alternatives, (4) analyzing alternatives and selecting the most feasible, (5) planning and implementing the decision, and (6) controlling the decision.

4. Describe the differences between programmed and nonprogrammed decisions and among the conditions of certainty, uncertainty, and risk.

Programmed decisions are recurrent, routine, and nonsignificant. Nonprogrammed decisions are nonrecurring, nonroutine, and significant.

The difference in decision-making conditions is based on the degree of certainty of the outcome of the decision. Under conditions of certainty, you know the outcome of alternatives. Under conditions of risk, you can assign probabilities to the outcomes, but you do not know the outcomes of alternatives.

5. Describe when to use the rational decision-making model versus the bounded rationality model and group versus individual decision making.

Use the rational decision-making model with a group when faced with a nonprogrammed decision with high risk or uncertainty. Use the bounded rationality model and make an individual decision when faced with a programmed decision with low risk or certainty. However, this is a general guide; there may be exceptions to the rule.

6. State the difference between an objective and "must" and "want" criteria.

An objective is the end result you want to achieve when making the decision. "Must" criteria are the requirements that an alternative must meet to be selected. "Want" criteria are desirable but are not necessary for an alternative to be selected.

7. State the difference between innovation and creativity.

Innovation is the implementation of new ideas for products and processes. Creativity is a way of thinking that generates new ideas.

8. List and explain the three stages in the creative process.

The three stages are (1) preparation—developing familiarity with the problem; (2) incubation and illumination—taking a break from the problem and perhaps getting an idea for the solution; and (3) evaluation—making sure the idea will work.

9. Describe the differences among quantitative techniques, the Kepner-Tregoe method, and cost-benefit analysis for analyzing and selecting an alternative.

Quantitative techniques and the Kepner-Tregoe method are management science approaches; cost-benefit analysis is not. Quantitative methods use math to objectively select the alternative with the highest value. The Kepner-Tregoe method uses math, with some subjectivity in selecting and weighting criteria, to select the alternative with the highest value. Cost-benefit analysis is primarily based on subjective analysis; it can use some math, but alternatives do not have a final number value to compare.

10. Complete each of the following statements using one of this chapter's key terms.

A _____ exists whenever objectives are not being met.

_____ is the process of taking corrective action to meet objectives.

_____ is the process of selecting an alternative course of action that will solve a problem.

The steps of the _____ include (1) classifying and defining the problem or opportunity, (2) setting objectives and criteria, (3) generating alternatives, (4) analyzing alternatives and selecting the most feasible, (5) planning and implementing the decision, and (6) controlling.

For _____, which are recurring or routine, the decision maker should use decision rules or organizational policies and procedures.

For _____, which are significant, nonrecurring, and nonroutine situations, the decision maker should use the decision-making model.

The three _____ are certainty, risk, and uncertainty.

_____ are the standards that an alternative must meet to be selected to accomplish the objective.

_____ is the implementation of a new idea.

_____ is a way of thinking that generates new ideas.

The three stages in the _____ are (1) preparation, (2) incubation, and (3) evaluation.

With the _____ _____ approach, group members focus on defending a proposed solution to a problem while others try to come up with criticisms of why the solution will not work.

_____ is the process of suggesting many possible alternative solutions to a problem without evaluation.

_____ is the process of generating novel alternative solutions to a problem through role playing and fantasizing.

_____ is the process of generating and evaluating alternative solutions to a problem using a structured voting method.

_____ is the process of developing group agreement on a solution to a problem.

The _____ is a time-driven or development-driven decision tree that enables the user to select one of five leadership styles as appropriate for the situation to maximize decisions.

Key Terms

brainstorming, 124
consensus mapping, 125
creative process, 122
creativity, 122
criteria, 120
decision making, 110

decision-making conditions, 114
decision-making model, 111
devil's advocate, 123
innovation, 122
nominal grouping, 125
nonprogrammed decisions, 114

participative decision-making
   model, 134
problem, 110
problem solving, 110
programmed decisions, 114
synectics, 125

Review and Discussion Questions

1. Are problem solving and decision making really important? Explain.
2. Why is it necessary to determine the decision structure and decision-making conditions?
3. What is the current trend concerning the use of groups to solve problems and make decisions?
4. Which potential disadvantage of group problem solving and decision making do you think arises most frequently?
5. Is a decrease in sales or profits a symptom or a cause of a problem?
6. Would a maximum price of $1,000 to spend on a stereo be an objective or a criterion?
7. Are creativity and innovation really important to all types of businesses? Is it important to evaluate a creative idea before it becomes an innovation?
8. Have you ever made a decision with information that was not timely, of good quality, complete, and/or relevant? If so, was the decision a good one? Why or why not?
9. What is the major difference between nominal grouping and consensus mapping?
10. Why are generating and analyzing alternatives separate steps in the decision-making model?
11. Have you ever used any of the techniques for analyzing and selecting an alternative? If yes, which one?
12. Do you know anyone who has experienced escalation of commitment? If yes, explain.

Objective Case

KMART ACQUIRES SEARS

Sears started as a catalogue company in 1886. Back then, 70 percent of the people lived on farms without cars and had difficulty getting to stores. Sears became a huge success through its mail-order shopping and money-back guarantee. As people began to move to the city, Sears opened stores in downtown areas. In time, people lost interest in downtown shopping, preferring malls with more convenient parking. So Sears moved its stores to suburban malls. After decades of success, Sears missed the trend to discounting and lost the title of the number one retailer in the U.S. to Kmart in 1986. But shortly thereafter, Kmart lost the title to Wal-Mart in 1992. In November 2004, Kmart announced plans to acquire its larger competitor, Sears. At the time, Sears had 2,000 stores (900 full-line and 1,100 specialty stores) and Kmart had 1,504 stores. Combined, Kmart and Sears would be the third-largest retailer.

Kmart has actually been in business for almost as long as Sears. The S.S. Kresge Company started in 1899 with downtown retail stores, and later changed its name to Kmart. Kmart used a different business model than Sears. Rather than paying high rent at malls, it developed stand-alone stores in lower-rent areas and offered discount prices. The discount model worked, but Kmart eventually ran into trouble. Managers made bad decisions, such as choosing poor store locations and not keeping stores up-to-date. They encountered inventory problems as they consistently did not have the right product on the shelves at the right time; this was largely due to outdated inventory methods. These problems led from profits to losses, resulting in Kmart filing for Chapter 11 bankruptcy protection and closing 283 stores. In May 2003, it emerged from Chapter 11 restructuring.

A major reason that Wal-Mart surpassed Kmart and Sears as the number one retailer was its use of technology, particularly for managing inventory. Wal-Mart perfected the discount business model, but it got off to a bad start the weekend after Thanksgiving 2004 as competitors took away some of its business by offering deep-discount specials for selected items. Competitors intended to attract customers to their stores in hopes that they would also buy additional, more profitable items—which they did. Wal-Mart had to rethink its "everyday low prices" strategy.

The question now is, how can the combined Kmart/Sears company compete against the superstar low-price Wal-Mart and its closest rival, Target, with its special discounts and strong positioning as a cachet brand?

To learn more about Kmart's acquisition of Sears and how the combined company is doing, log on to InfoTrac® College Edition at *http://infotrac.thomsonlearning.com* and use the advanced search function.

_____ 1. Kmart faced

    a. problems   c. decision making

    b. problem solving   d. all of these

_____ 2. The use of the decision-making model _____ appropriate for the Kmart decision to acquire Sears.

    a. was

    b. was not

_____ 3. The _____ decision-making style is most appropriate for the Kmart decision to acquire Sears.

    a. reflexive

    b. reflective

    c. consistent

_____ 4. The decision structure to acquire Sears is

    a. programmed

    b. nonprogrammed

_____ 5. The decision-making condition to acquire Sears is

    a. certainty

    b. uncertainty

    c. risk

_____ 6. The decision-making style used to make the acquisition is

    a. autocratic (by the CEO)

    b. participative (CEO uses input from others)

_____ 7. Setting specific objectives and criteria are important in the acquisition decision. Explain why or why not, and if they are important, explain what types of objectives and criteria are needed.

    a. true

    b. false

_____ 8. The use of group decision-making techniques that foster creativity and innovation should be used in the decision to acquire Sears.

    a. true

    b. false

_____ 9. The most appropriate quantitative technique to use in the acquisition decision is

    a. break-even   d. queuing theory

    b. capital budgeting   e. probability theory

    c. linear programming

_____ 10. Using the Kepner-Tregoe decision-making method to compare Sears with other retailers to possibly acquire is appropriate.

    a. true

    b. false

11. Was Kmart's acquisition of Sears a good decision?

12. Both Sears and Kmart were highly successful and became the number one retailer. What happened that led each of them to lose its position?

13. Do you shop more at Wal-Mart, Target, or Kmart/Sears? Why?

Cumulative Case Questions

14. Discuss how the misuse of managers' resources led to Kmart filing for bankruptcy protection. (Chapter 1)

15. Which internal and external environmental factors were most instrumental in Kmart's problems? (Chapter 2)

16. Discuss how the global borderless Internet environment has changed retailing, and classify Wal-Mart in the global village. (Chapter 3)

Video Case

GENERAL MOTORS

About the GMC TerraCross

This video explores the creation of the GMC TerraCross, a concept car unveiled at the 2001 Detroit Auto Show. The TerraCross, which is aimed at a new target market, the Millennials (kids aged 11 to 22), offers some important cues about the importance of exploring new design trends and provides a useful starting point for class discussion about decision making.

View the Video (12 minutes)

View the video on the GMC TerraCross in class or at *http://lussier.swlearning.com*.

Read the Case

At the 2001 North American International Auto Show in Detroit, the big splash was made by "Kiddie Cars" aimed at a new target market, the Millennials (kids aged 11 to 22). Looking to catch youngsters in anticipation of their first car purchases down the road, automakers rolled out various models priced between $12,500 and $20,000. The GMC TerraCross is a concept car par excellence. Designers have loaded the crossover SUV with lots of features.

True concept cars rarely make it to production without serious modification, so what is the motivation behind the creation of the concept car? First, companies like to explore new design trends. Second, concept cars may address particular social concerns, like gas mileage, emissions, roadway congestion, and so forth. Concept cars also serve as a beacon for the designs of future products and help automakers explore creative possibilities within their current product offerings. Although an entire concept car may not make it to dealer showrooms, elements of concept cars definitely show up in models that people drive every day. Think about it: Cup holders, sun roofs, and on-board global-positioning systems all started out as concepts.

Still, designers admit that one of their reasons for creating concept cars is to have fun. After all, who could deny the amusement of creating a rolling dorm room that can be hosed out?

Sources: "Here Come the Kiddie Cars," *Business Week*, January 21, 2002, 8; G. Vasilash, "Consider the Concepts in Terms of Capabilities and Competencies," *Automotive Manufacturing and Production*, April 1997, 46; Lyndon Conrad Bell, "A Sneak Drive of GM's Concept Cars," *http://www.forbes.com/2001/06/04/0604feat.html*, accessed February 9, 2004.

Answer the Questions

1. What are some of the problems GM expects its concept cars to solve?
2. How is development of the GM TerraCross concept car characteristic of nonprogrammed decisions?

Behavior **Modeling**
DECISION-MAKING STYLES

The scenario for this chapter features Richard, a human resources director, meeting with a supervisor, Denise, to discuss training changes. The video illustrates four management styles.

Objective

To better understand four management decision-making styles.

View the Video (13 minutes)

View the accompanying video in class or at *http://lussier.swlearning.com*. As you view each of the four scenes, identify the management decision-making style being used by the manager in each scene (autocratic, consultative, participative, or empowerment).

Scene 1. _____

Scene 2. _____

Scene 3. _____

Scene 4. _____

Apply It

What did I learn from this exercise? How will I use this knowledge in the future?

_____

_____

Skill Builder 1

MAKING A DECISION USING THE DECISION-MAKING MODEL

Select a problem or opportunity that you now face. Remember, a problem exists when objectives are not being met—when there is a difference between what is happening and what you want to happen. The problem or opportunity may be from any facet of your life—work, college, sports, a relationship, a purchase to be made in the near future, where to go on a date, and so on. Use the decision-making model outline that follows to solve your problem or take advantage of the opportunity.

Step 1. Classify and Define the Problem or Opportunity

Decision structure. Do you need to make a programmed or a nonprogrammed decision?

Decision condition. Are you facing a condition of uncertainty, of risk, or of certainty?

Decision-making model. Is the rational or the bounded rationality model appropriate? (Continue to follow all steps in the decision-making model even if bounded rationality is appropriate.)

Select the appropriate level of participation. Should the decision be made by an individual or a group? (If a group decision is appropriate, use a group for the following steps in the model. But remember to maximize the advantages and minimize the disadvantages of group decision making.)

Define the problem. List the symptoms and causes of the problem (or opportunity); then write a clear statement of it.

_____

_____

_____

_____

Step 2. Set Objectives and Criteria

Write down what is to be accomplished by the decision and the standards that any alternative must meet to be selected as the decision that will accomplish the objective. (Specify "must" and "want" criteria if appropriate for the decision.)

Objective: _____

_____

Criteria: (must) _____

(want) _____

Step 3. Generate Creative Alternatives

What information do you need? (Remember that information must be timely, of good quality, complete, and relevant to be useful.) Will you use any technology?

If you are working with a group, will brainstorming, nominal grouping, or consensus mapping be used?

List your alternatives (at least three) below; number them. If a decision tree will be helpful, make one.

_____

_____

_____

Step 4. Analyze Alternatives and Select the Most Feasible

Is a quantitative, Kepner-Tregoe, or cost-benefit (pros and cons) analysis appropriate? Choose a method and complete your analysis.

Step 5. Plan and Implement the Decision

Write out your plan for implementing the decision. Be sure to state the controls you will use to make sure you know if the decision is working. How can you avoid escalation of commitment?

_____

_____

_____

_____

_____

_____

_____

Step 6. Controlling

After implementing the decision, make notes about progress in solving the problem or taking advantage of the opportunity. Indicate any need for corrective action, and if you need to, return to prior steps in the decision-making model.

_____

_____

_____

Apply It

What did I learn from this experience? How will I use this knowledge in the future?

_____

_____

Your instructor may ask you to do this Skill Builder in class in a group. If so, the instructor will provide you with any necessary information or additional instructions.

Skill **Builder** 2
USING THE VROOM MODEL

You read about the Vroom participative decision-making model in this chapter. Using the appropriate version of the model (time-driven or development-driven), determine which leadership to use for each situation below.

Situation 1

You are the manager of the production department for a company that manufactures a mass-produced product. You have two production machines in your department with

10 people working on each. You have an important order that needs to be shipped first thing tomorrow. Your boss has made it very clear that you must meet this deadline. It's 2:00 p.m., and you are right on schedule to meet the order deadline. At 2:15, an employee tells you that one of the machines is smoking a little and making a noise. If you keep running the machine, it may make it until the end of the day and you will deliver the important shipment on time. If you shut down the machine, the manufacturer will not be able to check it until tomorrow and you will miss the deadline. You call your boss, but there is no answer; there is no telling how long it will take for the boss to get back to you if you leave a message. There are no higher-level managers to consult, and no one with more knowledge of the machine than you. Which leadership style should you use?

Step 1. Which version of the model should you use? (_____ time-driven _____ development-driven)
Step 2. How did you answer the model's questions? Did you skip any questions?
Step 3. Which leadership style is the most appropriate?
_____ Decide _____ Consult individuals _____ Consult group
_____ Facilitate _____ Delegate

Situation 2

You are the leader of your church, with 125 families (200 members). You have a doctor of religious studies degree with just two years' experience as the head of a church; you have not taken any business courses. The church has one paid secretary, three part-time program directors for religious instruction, music, and social activities, plus many volunteers. The paid staff members serve on your advisory board with 10 other church members who are primarily business leaders in the community. You develop a yearly budget, which is approved by the advisory board. The church's source of income is weekly member donations. The advisory board doesn't want the church to operate in the red, and the church has very modest surplus funds. Your volunteer accountant, who is a board members, asks to meet with you. During the meeting, she informs you that weekly collections are down 20 percent below budget, and that the cost of utilities has increased 25 percent over the yearly budget figure. You are running a large deficit, and at this rate your surplus will be gone in two months. Which leadership style will you use to address these problems?

Step 1: Which version of the model should you use? (_____ time-driven _____ development-driven)
Step 2: How did you answer the model's questions? Did you skip any questions?
Step 3: Which leadership style is most appropriate?
_____ Decide _____ Consult individuals _____ Consult group
_____ Facilitate _____ Delegate

Situation 3

You are the new dean of the school of business at a small private university. The faculty consists of 20 professors, only two of whom are nontenured; on average, these faculty members have been at the university for 12 years. You expect to leave this job for one at a larger school in three years. Your primary goal is to start an advisory board for the business school to improve community relations and alumni relations and to raise money for financial aid. As you are new to the area and have no business contacts, you need help to develop a network of alumni and other community leaders fairly quickly if you are to show results at the end of your three years on the job. Members of the faculty get along well and are generally talkative, but when you approach small groups of them, they tend to become quiet and disperse. Which leadership style would you use to achieve your objective?

Step 1: Which version of the model should you use? (_____ time-driven _____ development-driven)
Step 2: How did you answer the model's questions? Did you skip any questions?
Step 3: Which leadership style is most appropriate?
_____ Decide _____ Consult individuals _____ Consult group
_____ Facilitate _____ Delegate

Situation 4

You are the president of a dot.com company that has been having financial problems for a few years. As a result, your top two managers left for other jobs, one four months ago and the other two months ago. With your networking contacts, you replaced both within a month, but the new managers don't have a lot of time on the job and haven't worked together for very long. They currently have their own individual approaches to getting their jobs done. However, they are both very bright, hardworking, and dedicated to your vision of what the company can be. To turn the company around, you and your two managers will have to work together, with the help of all your employees. Virtually all the employees are high-tech specialists who want to be included in decision making. Your business partners have no more money to invest. If you cannot turn a profit in four to five months, you will most likely go bankrupt. Which primary leadership style would you use to achieve your objective?

Step 1: Which version of the model should you use? (_____ time-driven _____ development-driven)
Step 2: How did you answer the model's questions? Did you skip any questions?
Step 3: Which leadership style is most appropriate?
_____ Decide _____ Consult individuals _____ Consult group
_____ Facilitate _____ Delegate

Apply It

What did I learn from this experience? How will I use this knowledge in the future?

_____

_____

Your instructor may ask you to do this Skill Builder in class in a group. If so, the instructor will provide you with any necessary information or additional instructions.

Learning Outcomes

After studying this chapter, you should be able to:

1. Describe how strategic planning differs from operational planning. PAGE 149

2. State the differences among the three strategic levels: corporate, business, and functional. PAGE 151

3. Explain the reason for conducting an industry and competitive situation analysis. PAGE 152

5: The Strategic and Operational Planning Process

4. Explain the reason for conducting a company situation analysis. PAGE 153

5. List the parts of an effective written objective. PAGE 157

6. Describe the four grand strategies: growth, stability, turnaround and retrenchment, and a combination of these. PAGE 161

7. Describe the three corporate growth strategies: concentration, integration, and diversification. PAGE 162

8. Describe the three business-level adaptive strategies: prospecting, defending, and analyzing. PAGE 168

9. State the difference between standing plans and single-use plans. PAGE 175

10. Define the following **key terms:**

strategic planning	corporate growth strategies
operational planning	merger
strategy	acquisition
strategic levels	business portfolio analysis
corporate-level strategy	adaptive strategies
business-level strategy	functional strategies
functional-level strategy	standing plans
situation analysis	policies
SWOT analysis	procedure
benchmarking	rules
objectives	single-use plans
management by objectives (MBO)	contingency plans
grand strategy	

Ideas on Management

at Starbucks

Do you know who Starbucks is named after? Starbuck is the name of a quiet and right-minded character from Herman Melville's *Moby Dick* who longs for home. On a whaling ship far from home amidst a crew of renegades, castoffs, and cannibals, Starbuck is often characterized as the direct opposite of the ship's disturbed captain Ahab.

Starting from a single store selling freshly roasted coffee beans in Seattle's Pike Place Market in 1971, Starbucks has grown into a global chain of upscale coffee bars with more than 7,500 locations around the world. Around 25 million customers worldwide visit Starbucks each week. The idea that transformed the local coffee retailer into a global brand came to Howard Schultz, hired in 1982 and currently chairman and chief global strategist, on a visit to Italy. Observing the popularity of espresso bars there, Schultz thought of introducing the coffee bar concept back in the United States. In 1990, Orin Smith joined Starbucks as chief financial officer, when there were just 45 stores concentrated in the Pacific Northwest, becoming chief operating officer in 1994 and taking over as CEO in 2000. Smith was responsible for overseas operations until Schultz assumed responsibility for global strategy.

© Adam Berry/Bloomberg News/Landov

In an interview with the *Wall Street Journal*, CEO Orin Smith shared five lessons on expanding overseas: (1) Do not assume the market is like the United States, even if it is an English-speaking country; (2) partner with local firms abroad to grow faster; (3) never become better at opening stores than operating them; (4) hire local managers and employees; and (5) adapt to local cultures and tastes.

IOM

1. **What are some of Starbucks's strategic and operational plans?**
2. **What is Starbucks's mission? What are its six guiding principles?**
3. **What does five-force competitive analysis reveal about the growth potential of Starbucks? Identify the company's strengths, weaknesses, opportunities, and threats.**
4. **What long-range goals has Starbucks established?**
5. **What is the corporate grand strategy and primary growth strategy at Starbucks? Name some of the company's failed growth strategies.**
6. **What types of adaptive and competitive strategies does Starbucks currently employ? Which stage in the product life cycle has coffee reached in the U.S. market?**
7. **What type of functional and operational plans does Starbucks have?**

To learn more about Starbucks, visit the company's Web site at *http://www.starbucks.com* or log on to InfoTrac® College Edition at *http://www.infotrac.college.com*, where you can read an in-depth analysis of the competitive rivalry between Starbucks and Dunkin' Donuts, originally published in the *Boston Globe*. Use the advanced search option to key in record number CJ115285144 and discover why the New England market has been a difficult one for Starbucks to enter.

Sources: Information for the case was taken from "It's a Grande-Latte World," *Wall Street Journal*, December 15, 2003, p. B1; Starbucks's Web site at *http://www.starbucks.com*, accessed May 14, 2004; Joshua Kurlantzick, "There's Something to Be Said for Doing Things Your Way," *Entrepreneur*, November 2003, pp. 87–89.

Planning Dimensions

Strategic Planning
The Strategic Planning Process
Strategic Levels
Developing the Mission

Analyzing the Environment
Industry and Competitive Situation Analysis
Company Situation Analysis
Competitive Advantage

Setting Objectives
Goals and Objectives
Writing Effective Objectives
Criteria for Objectives
Management by Objectives (MBO)

Corporate-Level Strategy
Grand Strategy
Corporate Growth Strategies
Portfolio Analysis

Business-Level Strategy
Adaptive Strategies
Competitive Strategies
Product Life Cycle

Functional-Level (Operational) Strategies
Marketing Strategy
Operations Strategy
Human Resources Strategy
Finance Strategy
Other Functional-Level Strategies

Operational Planning
Standing Plans versus Single-Use Plans
Contingency Plans

Implementing and Controlling Strategies

PLANNING DIMENSIONS

Success in both the for-profit and the not-for-profit sectors is based on effective planning.[1] Bill Gates and other successful business leaders have a clear vision of what they want their businesses to be, and they develop plans to make the vision a reality.[2] However, planning is a continuing process; plans need to change as companies continually reinvent themselves.[3] Planning is determining what you want to accomplish and developing approaches to achieving your objectives.[4] To be successful, you should set both personal and business goals and develop plans for achieving them, with the help of your network of personal and professional contacts.[5]

Planning has several dimensions.[6] Exhibit 5-1 summarizes the five planning dimensions: management level, type of plan, scope, time, and repetitiveness. Note that upper-level and some middle-level managers spend more time developing strategic, broad/directional, long-range, single-use plans for the organization. Other middle-level and all lower-level managers, in contrast, spend more time specifying how the strategic plans will be accomplished by developing operational, narrow/specific, short-range plans and implementing standing plans (policies, procedures, and rules). Throughout this chapter, we will explore these five planning dimensions. Before we begin, complete the Self-Assessment to determine how well you plan.

Exhibit 5-1 *Planning Dimensions*

Management Level	Type of Plan	Scope	Time	Repetitiveness
Upper and Middle	Strategic	Broad/directional	Long-Range	Single-Use Plan
Middle and Lower	Operational	Narrow/specific	Short-Range	Standing Plan

Self-Assessment

Effective Planning

Indicate how well each statement describes your behavior by placing a number from 1 to 5 on the line before the statement.

Describes me   Does not describe me
5 —————————— 4 —————————— 3 —————————— 2 —————————— 1

_____ 1. I have a specific end result to accomplish whenever I start a project of any kind.

_____ 2. When setting objectives, I state only the end result to be accomplished; I don't specify how the result will be accomplished.

_____ 3. I have specific and measurable objectives; for example, I know the specific grade I want to earn in this course.

_____ 4. I set objectives that are difficult but achievable.

_____ 5. I set deadlines when I have something I need to accomplish, and I meet the deadlines.

Self-Assessment

Effective Planning   *(Continued)*

_____ 6. I have a long-term goal (what I will be doing in 3–5 years) and short-term objectives to get me there.

_____ 7. I have written objectives stating what I want to accomplish.

_____ 8. I know my strengths and weaknesses, am aware of threats, and seek opportunities.

_____ 9. I analyze a problem and alternative actions, rather than immediately jumping right in with a solution.

_____10. I spend most of my day doing what I plan to do, rather than dealing with emergencies and trying to get organized.

_____11. I use a calendar, appointment book, or some form of "to do" list.

_____12. I ask others for advice.

_____13. I follow appropriate policies, procedures, and rules.

_____14. I develop contingency plans in case my plans do not work out as I expect them to.

_____15. I implement my plans and determine if I have met my objectives.

Add up the numbers you assigned to the statements to see where you fall on the continuum below.

Effective planner   Ineffective planner

75————— 65————— 55————— 45————— 35————— 25————— 15

Don't be too disappointed if your score isn't as high as you would like. All of these items are characteristics of effective planning. Review the items that did not describe you. After studying this chapter and doing the exercises, you can improve your planning skills.

Learning Outcome 1
Describe how strategic planning differs from
operational planning.

STRATEGIC PLANNING

In this section, we'll discuss the strategic planning process and the levels of strategic planning. Simply having a great idea does not guarantee success, nor do hope and luck. Success takes planning.[7] There is an old saying: "When you fail to plan, you plan to fail."

The Strategic Planning Process

Strategic planning *is the process of developing a mission and long-range objectives and determining in advance how they will be accomplished.* **Operational planning** *is the process of setting short-range objectives and*

determining in advance how they will be accomplished. The differences between strategic planning and operational planning are primarily the time frame and management level involved. Strategic planning includes developing a mission statement and long-term objectives. *Long-term* generally means that it will take longer than one year to achieve the objective. Strategic plans are commonly developed for five years and reviewed and revised every year so that a five-year plan is always in place. Top-level managers develop strategic plans. Operational plans have *short-term* objectives that will be met in one year or less. Middle and first-line managers develop operational plans.

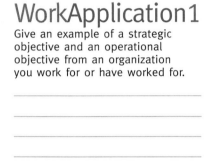

At Starbucks, the decision to expand into overseas markets, to develop Internet businesses, and even to build new store locations within the United States are all examples of strategic, long-term planning. Operational plans at Starbucks include short-term objectives developed for individual stores, such as an annual sales forecast or marketing plan for a specific location developed by a store or regional manager.

As noted above, upper-level managers (and some middle-level managers) develop long-range plans and middle- and lower-level managers develop operational plans to accomplish the long-range objectives. In other words, top managers determine the ends and middle- and lower-level managers determine the means to accomplish the ends.[8] The key to successful planning is the coordination of the strategic and operational plans—bridging the gap between levels.[9]

The steps in the *strategic planning process* are (1) developing the mission, (2) analyzing the environment, (3) setting objectives, (4) developing strategies, and (5) implementing and controlling strategies. Developing strategies takes place at all three levels. This section discusses developing strategies and developing the mission. Later sections of this chapter cover the other steps. Exhibit 5-2 illustrates the strategic planning process. Notice that the process is not simply linear; it does not proceed through steps 1–5 and then end. As the arrows indicate, managers may need to return to prior steps and make changes as part of an ongoing process.

WorkApplication1

Give an example of a strategic objective and an operational objective from an organization you work for or have worked for.

Exhibit 5-2 *The Strategic Planning Process*

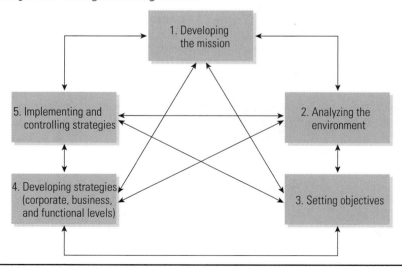

State the differences among the three strategic levels:
corporate, business, and functional.

Strategic Levels

A **strategy** is a plan for pursuing a mission and achieving objectives. The three **strategic levels** are corporate, business, and functional. You will learn more about these three levels in separate sections later in this chapter. For now, we will simply define each level.

The **corporate-level strategy** is the plan for managing multiple lines of business. Many large companies consist of several businesses. **Altria** has a **Philip Morris** tobacco line, **Kraft Foods** (with **General Foods, Oscar Meyer,** and **Post** cereals), and also owns 36 percent of **SABMiller**, a brewer. General Motors has GM Automobiles, **Electronic Data Systems,** and **Hughes Electronics. Jiffy Lube** is one of Pennzoil's lines of business. However, most companies are involved in only one line of business; therefore, they do not require a corporate strategy. **Kellogg Company,** for example, has continued to focus on cereal as a single line of business since 1906.

The **business-level strategy** is the plan for managing one line of business. Each of Altria's and General Motors' lines of business has its own strategy for competing in its industry environment.

The **functional-level strategy** is the plan for managing one area of a business. The functional areas are marketing, finance and accounting, operations/production, human resources, and others, depending on the line of business. Exhibit 5-3 illustrates strategic and operational levels.

DEVELOPING THE MISSION

Developing the mission is the first step in the strategic planning process.[10] However, after analyzing the environment, managers should reexamine the mission to see if it needs to be changed. The mission is the foundation of the other four steps in the strategic planning process. The organization's mission is its purpose or reason for being.[11] The mission states what business the company is in now and will be in the future.[12] A mission creates a vision of where the company is headed and why.[13] It contains the expectations the organization strives to achieve.[14]

WorkApplication2
Does a business you work for or have worked for have multiple lines of business? If yes, list them.

_____

_____

_____

_____

Exhibit 5-3 *Strategic and Operational Levels*

Management Level	Strategic Level	Planning Level/Time Range
Upper	Corporate Strategy	Strategic/Long
Upper and Middle	Business Strategy	Strategic/Long
Middle and Lower	Functional Strategies	Operational/Short

Operations   Marketing   Finance   Human Resources   Others

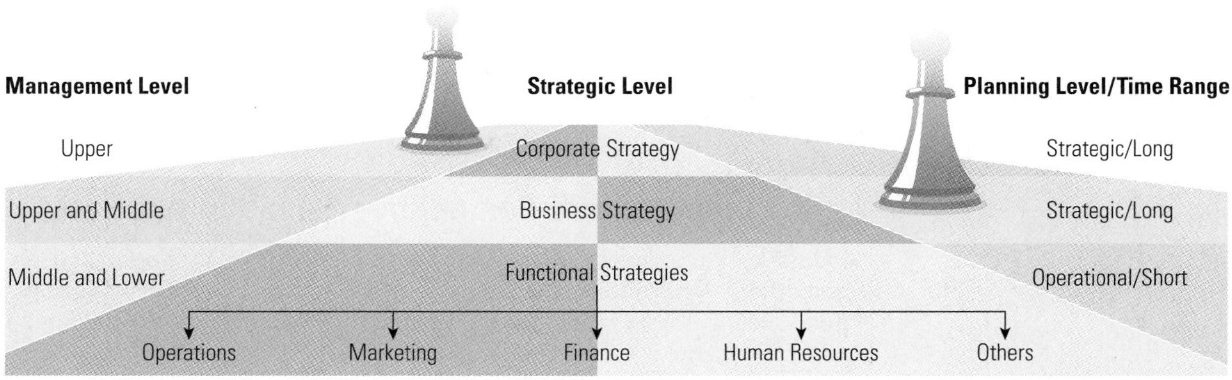

IOM

Starbucks's mission is to "establish Starbucks as the premier purveyor of the finest coffee in the world while maintaining our uncompromising principles while we grow." The company's mission statement goes on to specify "six guiding principles" as follows:

1. **Provide a great work environment and treat each other with respect and dignity.**
2. **Embrace diversity as an essential component in the way we do business.**
3. **Apply the highest standards of excellence to the purchasing, roasting, and fresh delivery of our coffee.**
4. **Develop enthusiastically satisfied customers all of the time.**
5. **Contribute positively to our communities and our environment.**
6. **Recognize that profitability is essential to our future success.**

YTL Corporation Berhad is one of Malaysia's leading integrated infrastructure conglomerates. Among the corporation's key businesses are utilities, high-speed rail, cement manufacturing, construction contracting, property development, hotels and resorts, and technology incubation.

YTL's mission (which it calls a philosophy or strategy) of providing "world-class products at third-world prices" has been the foundation for a compounded annual growth rate in pretax profits of 55 percent over the last 15 years. For example, YTL is able to make a profit selling power at the most competitive prices in the world (3.8 U.S. cents per kilowatt-hour, a lower average rate than anywhere in the United States). YTL constructed the Ritz-Carlton Kuala Lumpur hotel for about a third of the per room costs of other hotels.

Although YTL is profitable, its CEO Francis Yeoh says that the corporation's greatest contribution is improving the standard of living and quality of life of millions of people throughout the world. YTL's work on schools, hospitals, transport links, and power stations exhibits the corporation's sense of social responsibility.[15]

ANALYZING THE ENVIRONMENT

A business strategy must be congruent with the capabilities of the firm and its external environment.[16] Analysis of internal and external environmental factors, the second step of the strategic planning process, determines such congruence.[17] Analyzing the environment is also known as situation analysis.[18] *A* **situation analysis** *focuses on those features in a company's environment that most directly affect its options and opportunities.* This analysis has three parts: industry and competitive situation analysis, company situation analysis, and identification of a competitive advantage. Keep in mind that companies with multiple lines of business must conduct an environmental analysis for each line of business.[19]

––––––––––––––––––––––––––––– Learning Outcome 3 –––––––––––––––––––––––––––––
Explain the reason for conducting an industry and competitive
situation analysis.

Industry and Competitive Situation Analysis

Industries vary widely in their makeup, competitive situation, and growth potential.[20] Determining the position of an industry requires answering questions such as these: How large is the market? What is the growth rate? How many competitors are there?

According to Michael Porter, competition in an industry is a composite of five competitive forces that should be considered in analyzing the competitive situation.[21]

1. *Rivalry among competing sellers in the industry.* Porter calls this rivalry scrambling and jockeying for position. How do businesses compete for customers (for example, on the basis of price, quality, or speed)?[22] How competitive is the industry?[23] A company needs to anticipate the moves of its competitors.[24]

2. *Threat of substitute products and services.* Companies in other industries may try to take customers away. **Very Fine Juice, Snapple, Gatorade**, and others have targeted soda drinkers in an effort to get them to switch to juice drinks.

3. *Potential new entrants.* How difficult and costly is it for new businesses to enter the industry as competitors? Does the company need to plan for new competition? **Coke** and **Pepsi** don't have to be too concerned about new competition, but a local video store may have to compete with cable and online rentals.

4. *Power of suppliers.* How much does the business depend on the supplier? If the business has only one major supplier, without alternatives available, the supplier has great bargaining power over the business. Coca-Cola has great power over independently owned Coca-Cola bottlers because it is the sole supplier of the product they deal in. However, a small video store can buy its videos from any number of suppliers, who have little power over it.

5. *Power of buyers.* How much does the business depend on the buyer? If the business has only one major buyer, or a few, without alternatives available, the buyer has great bargaining power over the business. **GM** told its suppliers that they would have to cut their prices or lose its business. Many of these businesses sold mainly or solely to GM and therefore had no bargaining power.

Companies use industry and competitive situation analysis primarily at the corporate strategy level to make decisions regarding which lines of business to enter and exit and how to allocate resources among existing lines of business.[25] This process will be explained in more detail later in this chapter.

Although Starbucks does have some direct competitors in the United States, including Dunkin' Donuts, Tully's Coffee Corporation, and Diedrich Coffee, most of these competitors have much smaller operations. Other forces exerting pressure on Starbucks's growth potential are shown in Exhibit 5-4.

WorkApplication3

Conduct a simple five-force competitive analysis for a company you work for or have worked for. Use Exhibit 5-4 as an example.

_____

_____

_____

_____

_____

——————— Learning Outcome 4 ———————
Explain the reason for conducting a company situation analysis.

Company Situation Analysis

A company situation analysis is used at the business strategy level to determine the strategic issues and problems that need to be addressed through the next three steps of the strategic planning process. A complete company situation analysis has five key parts, listed in Exhibit 5-5.

1. *Assessment of the present strategy based on performance.* This assessment can be a simple statement or a more complex comparison of performance indicators (market share, sales, net profit, return on assets, and so on) over the last five years.[26]

Exhibit 5-4 *Starbucks's Five-Force Competitive Analysis*

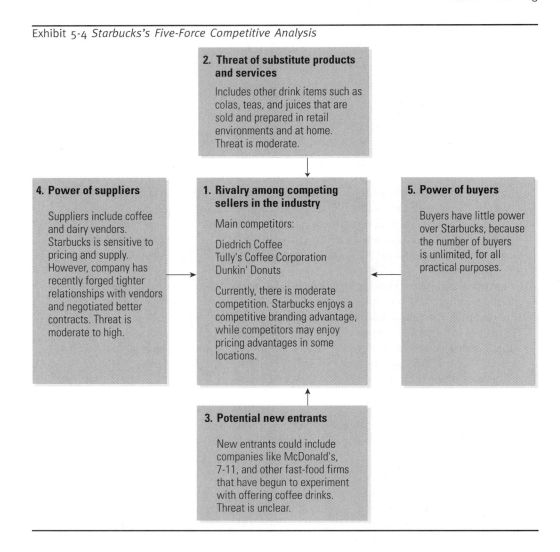

2. Threat of substitute products and services

Includes other drink items such as colas, teas, and juices that are sold and prepared in retail environments and at home. Threat is moderate.

4. Power of suppliers

Suppliers include coffee and dairy vendors. Starbucks is sensitive to pricing and supply. However, company has recently forged tighter relationships with vendors and negotiated better contracts. Threat is moderate to high.

1. Rivalry among competing sellers in the industry

Main competitors:

Diedrich Coffee
Tully's Coffee Corporation
Dunkin' Donuts

Currently, there is moderate competition. Starbucks enjoys a competitive branding advantage, while competitors may enjoy pricing advantages in some locations.

5. Power of buyers

Buyers have little power over Starbucks, because the number of buyers is unlimited, for all practical purposes.

3. Potential new entrants

New entrants could include companies like McDonald's, 7-11, and other fast-food firms that have begun to experiment with offering coffee drinks. Threat is unclear.

2. *SWOT analysis. An organization's internal environmental strengths and weaknesses and external environmental opportunities and threats are determined through a* **SWOT analysis.** (SWOT stands for strengths, weaknesses, opportunities, and threats.) In a SWOT analysis, the internal environmental factors analyzed for *strengths* and *weaknesses* are management, mission, resources, systems process, and structure. The external environmental

Exhibit 5-5 *Parts of a Company Situation Analysis*

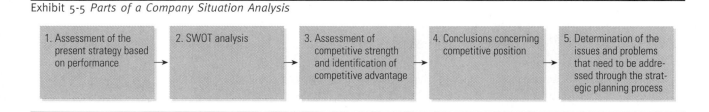

1. Assessment of the present strategy based on performance → 2. SWOT analysis → 3. Assessment of competitive strength and identification of competitive advantage → 4. Conclusions concerning competitive position → 5. Determination of the issues and problems that need to be addressed through the strategic planning process

Exhibit 5-6 *SWOT Analysis for Starbucks Coffee*

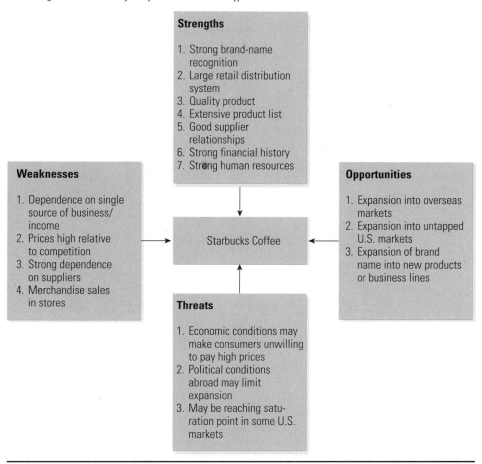

Strengths

1. Strong brand-name recognition
2. Large retail distribution system
3. Quality product
4. Extensive product list
5. Good supplier relationships
6. Strong financial history
7. Strong human resources

Weaknesses

1. Dependence on single source of business/income
2. Prices high relative to competition
3. Strong dependence on suppliers
4. Merchandise sales in stores

Starbucks Coffee

Opportunities

1. Expansion into overseas markets
2. Expansion into untapped U.S. markets
3. Expansion of brand name into new products or business lines

Threats

1. Economic conditions may make consumers unwilling to pay high prices
2. Political conditions abroad may limit expansion
3. May be reaching saturation point in some U.S. markets

factors analyzed for *opportunities* and *threats* are customers, competitors, suppliers, labor force, shareholders, society, technology, the economy, and governments. Exhibit 5-6 outlines a SWOT analysis for Starbucks Coffee.

3. *Assessment of competitive strength and identification of competitive advantage.* If a strategy is to be effective, it must be based on a clear understanding of the competition.[27] In assessing competitive strength, managers compare the *critical success factors* for their business to those of each major competitor. Critical success factors are the few major things that the business must do well to be successful. In conducting an assessment of competitive strength, managers may identify a competitive advantage that they elect to develop.[28]

There are two common approaches to assessing competitive strength. In the first approach, managers assign each critical success factor a rating of 1 (weak) to 10 (strong) and then add the ratings; they compare their own company's rating to those of their competitors. In the second approach, managers use the same rating system but weight each critical success factor, based on its importance; the total of the weights is 1.00.

WorkApplication4

List a couple of the major strengths and weaknesses of an organization you work for or have worked for.

_____

_____

_____

_____

_____

Exhibit 5-7 *Competitive Strength Assessment for Starbucks Coffee*

Critical Success Factor	Weight	Starbucks	Diedrich	Tully's	Dunkin' Donuts
Brand recognition	.50	8 × .50 = 4.00	5 × .50 = 2.50	3 × .50 = 1.50	8 × .50 = 4.00
Quality product	.25	9 × .25 = 2.25	8 × .25 = 2.25	7 × .25 = 1.75	8 × .25 = 2.00
Distribution	.25	7 × .25 = 1.75	4 × .25 = 1.00	3 × .25 = .75	8 × .25 = 2.00
Total	1.00	8.00	5.50	4.00	8.00

The rating of a given critical success factor (a number from 1 to 10) is multiplied by that factor's weight; the resulting scores are totaled to give a ranking that can be compared to the rankings of competitors. Exhibit 5-7 shows how Starbucks might compare to three of its competitors on three critical success factors.

4. *Conclusions concerning competitive position.* How is the business doing compared to its competition?[29] Are things improving or slipping?

5. *Determination of the issues and problems that need to be addressed through the strategic planning process.* Based on the results of the first four parts of the company situation analysis, what needs to be done in the future to improve the business's competitive position?

Competitive Advantage

We discussed competitive advantage in Chapter 3. As noted above, a firm may identify a competitive advantage in the process of assessing its competitive strength. Two aspects of a company's competitive advantage are core competency and benchmarking. A *core competency* is what a firm does well.[30] Starbucks Coffee's core competency is retail management and distribution. By identifying core competencies, managers can oversee the creation of new products and services that take advantage of the company's strengths.[31] For example, **Honda** has a core competency in engines. Honda went from producing only cars and motorcycles to also producing garden tillers, lawn mowers, snow blowers, snowmobiles, power generators, and outboard motors.

Benchmarking *is the process of comparing an organization's products or services and processes with those of other companies.* In benchmarking, managers try to find out about other products and processes, through *competitive intelligence,* and copy them or improve upon them legally and ethically. Most benchmarking takes place within an industry.

The Internet is an excellent source of information for benchmarking.[32] For example, Ready Lube and Oil Doctor basically resemble **Jiffy Lube. Pizza Hut** and **Little Caesars** copied **Domino's** delivery. However, looking at noncompetitors can provide good ideas that create a competitive advantage. **McDonald's** in mid-Manhattan copied its local competitors and began offering free delivery.

After managers have evaluated the organization and the competition by completing the situation analysis, they should go back and review the mission to see if it needs to be changed. Remember that situation analysis is an ongoing process, referred to as *scanning the environment.* It tells what is going on in the external environment that may require change to continually improve customer value.

Join the Discussion Ethics & Social Responsibility

Crop Genetic Structure

1. How do you feel about eating food that has been genetically altered?
2. Is it ethical and socially responsible to genetically alter food crops?

Monsanto is a leading provider of agricultural products and solutions. Monsanto uses innovations in plant biotechnology, genomics, and breeding to improve productivity and to reduce the costs of farming. It produces leading seed brands DEKALB and Asgrow and uses biotechnology to develop seeds that have integrated traits for insect and weed control. Monsanto also makes Roundup, the world's best-selling herbicide. Through its Holden's/Corn States business, Monsanto provides other seed companies with genetic material and biotechnologically developed traits for their seed brands. So you probably have eaten food that has been grown with the help of Monsanto products.

Using biochemistry and genomics to change the characteristics of crop plants seemed like a good *opportunity* to create beneficial new food products, such as foods that can lower cholesterol. However, genetically altered products are very controversial. They have been banned in much of Europe, and many U.S. farmers have refused to use them. In terms of SWOT analysis, this opposition to its products represents a *threat* to Monsanto.

Source: Information taken from the Monsanto Web site at *http://www.monsanto.com*, accessed February 16, 2004.

SETTING OBJECTIVES

Successful strategic management requires a commitment on the part of managers to a defined set of objectives.[33] After developing a mission and completing a situation analysis, managers are ready for the third step in the strategic planning process: setting objectives that flow from the mission to address strategic issues and problems identified through the situation analysis.[34] Objectives are end results; they do not state how they will be accomplished. In this section you will learn about goals and objectives, writing objectives, criteria for effective objectives, and management by objectives (MBO).

WorkApplication5

State one or more goals of an organization you work for or have worked for.

_____

_____

_____

_____

_____

Goals and Objectives

You should be able to distinguish between goals and objectives. *Goals* state general targets to be accomplished. **Objectives** *state what is to be accomplished in singular, specific, and measurable terms with a target date.* Goals should be translated into objectives.[35]

—————— Learning Outcome 5 ——————
List the parts of an effective written objective.

Writing Effective Objectives

All successful organizations and people set objectives for themselves.[36] What are yours? To help ensure that you will meet your objectives, it is a good idea to write them down and keep them someplace where they are constantly visible. You will practice setting objectives in Skill Builder 1.

Max E. Douglas developed a model that is helpful in writing effective objectives.[37] One variation on Douglas's model includes (1) the word *to*, followed by (2) an action verb, (3) a statement of the single, specific, and measurable result to be achieved, and (4) a target date. For example, a manager at Ford Motor Company might write the following objective:

(1) *To* +	(2) action verb +	(3) single, specific, measurable result +	(4) target date
(1) To	(2) earn	(3) $7 billion in pretax profits	(4) in 2005

Criteria for Objectives

As the model for writing objectives implies, an effective objective conforms to four "must" criteria: It expresses a *single result* that is *specific* and *measurable*, and it sets a *date* for achieving that result.

SINGLE RESULT

To avoid confusion, each objective should contain only one end result. If multiple objectives are listed together, one may be met while the others are not.

Ineffective Objectives	To increase pet food sales by 25 percent and to achieve a 5.4 percent market share
Effective Objectives	To increase pet food sales by 25 percent by December 2005
	To achieve a 5.4 percent market share in pet foods during 2005

SPECIFIC

The objective should state the exact level of performance expected. Research has shown that people with specific goals achieve higher levels of performance than those with general goals.[38]

Ineffective Objectives	To maximize profits in 2006 (How much is "maximize"?)
	To recycle 40 percent by the end of 2006 (40 percent of what—glass or paper? Type of paper?)
Effective Objectives	To earn a net profit of $1 million in 2006
	To recycle 40 percent of all office paper by the end of 2006

MEASURABLE

If people are to achieve objectives, they must be able to observe and measure their progress regularly to determine if the objectives have been met.[39]

Ineffective Objective	Perfect service for every customer (How is "perfect service" measured?)
Effective Objective	To attain an "excellent" satisfaction rating from 90 percent of customers surveyed in 2007

TARGET DATE

A specific date should be set for accomplishing the objective. When people have a deadline, they usually try harder to get a task done on time than when they are simply told to do it when they can.[40]

Ineffective Objective	To become a multimillionaire (By when?)
Effective Objective	To become a multimillionaire by December 2007

It is also more effective to set a specific date than to give a time span, because it's too easy to forget when a time period began and should end.

Somewhat Effective	To double international business to $5 billion annually within five years
Effective Objective	To double international business to $5 billion annually by the end of 2006

Note, however, that some objectives are ongoing and do not require a stated date. The target date is indefinite until it is changed.

Effective Objectives	To have 25 percent of sales coming from products that did not exist five years ago
	To be number one or two in world sales in all lines of business

Two of Starbucks Coffee's objectives are to have 10,000 stores in North America and to have 15,000 stores outside of North America. Recall that Starbucks had more than 7,500 stores globally at the end of 2003. Thus, Starbucks plans to triple its size. Note that this is an objective without a target date. However, Starbucks did set a dated objective that will help it proceed toward the 25,000 total: to open 1,300 new stores worldwide in fiscal year 2004.[41]

In addition to the four "must" criteria, objectives may conform to three "want" criteria.

Applying The Concept 1

Objectives

For each objective, state which "must" criteria is not met.

a. single result   c. measurable

b. specific   d. target date

_____ 1. To triple the sales of Lexus cars in Europe

_____ 2. To sell 2 percent more mufflers and 7 percent more tires in 2006

_____ 3. To increase revenue in 2006

_____ 4. To be perceived as the best restaurant in the Springfield area by the end of 2007

_____ 5. To write objectives within two weeks

WorkApplication6

Using the model for writing objectives, write one or more objectives for an organization you work for or have worked for, making sure they meet the "must" criteria.

DIFFICULT BUT ACHIEVABLE (REALISTIC)

A number of studies show that individuals perform better when given difficult but achievable objectives—what **GE**'s former CEO Jack Welch calls "stretch goals"—rather than objectives that are too difficult or too easy.[42] *Realistic* is a subjective concept; therefore, realism is a "want" rather than a "must" criterion for objectives.

PARTICIPATIVELY SET

Groups that participate in setting their objectives generally outperform groups with assigned objectives; participation helps members feel they have a shared destiny.[43] Managers should use the appropriate level of participation for the employees' capabilities. Because it is not always appropriate to have a group set its objectives, this is a "want" rather than a "must" criterion.

ACCEPTANCE AND COMMITMENT

If objectives are to be met, employees must accept them.[44] If employees do not commit to an objective, then even if it meets all the other "must" and "want" criteria, it may not be accomplished.[45] Participation helps employees to accept objectives. Because acceptance and commitment vary from individual to individual and because there are times when managers must set objectives that employees will not like, acceptance and commitment are "want" criteria.

For a review of the criteria that objectives should meet, see Exhibit 5-8.

Management by Objectives (MBO)

Management by objectives (MBO) *is the process in which managers and their employees jointly set objectives for the employees, periodically evaluate performance, and reward according to the results.* MBO is also referred to as work planning and review, goals management, goals and controls, or management by results.

MBO has met with both success and failure. A common reason for its failure is lack of commitment and follow-through on management's part. MBO often fails because employees believe that management is insincere in its efforts

Exhibit 5-8 *Criteria That Objectives should Meet*

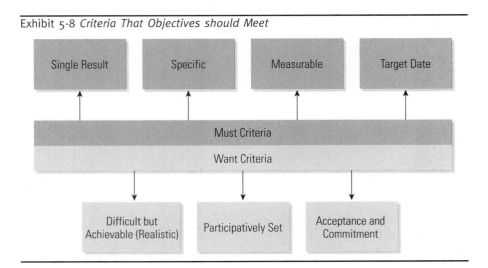

to include employees in the decision-making process. Employees feel that managers have already set the objectives and made the plans for implementation before talking to them.[46] You can use the MBO process successfully with your subordinates if you commit to the process and truly involve employees rather than trying to make them believe that your objectives are theirs.

MBO has three steps:

Step 1. Set individual objectives and plans. The manager sets objectives with each individual employee. The objectives are the heart of the MBO process and should meet the "must" and "want' criteria.

Step 2. Give feedback and evaluate performance. Communication is the key factor in determining MBO's success or failure.[47] Thus, the manager and employee must meet frequently to review progress. The frequency of evaluations depends on the individual and the job performed. However, most managers do not conduct enough review sessions.

Step 3. Reward according to performance. Employees' performance should be measured against their objectives. Employees who meet their objectives should be rewarded through recognition, praise, pay raises, promotions, and so on.[48]

CORPORATE-LEVEL STRATEGY

After the mission has been developed, the situation analysis has been completed, and objectives have been set, managers move on to the fourth step of the strategic planning process: developing strategies at the corporate, business, and functional levels. In this section, we will discuss corporate-level strategy, which includes grand strategy, corporate growth strategies, and portfolio analysis.[49]

—————————— Learning Outcome 6 ——————————
Describe the four grand strategies: growth, stability, turnaround
and retrenchment, and a combination of these.

Grand Strategy

Grand strategy *is an overall corporate-level strategy for growth, stability, or turnaround and retrenchment or for some combination of these.* Each grand strategy reflects a different objective. Let's discuss each separately.

GROWTH
With a *growth strategy*, the company makes aggressive attempts to increase its size through increased sales.[50] Starbucks is pursuing a growth strategy.

STABILITY
With a *stability strategy*, the company attempts to hold and maintain its present size or to grow slowly. Many companies are satisfied with the status quo, for example, the **WD-40 Company** produces a well-known petroleum-based lubricant, a product found in 75 percent of U.S. homes. The company can thus pursue a strategy of stability.

TURNAROUND AND RETRENCHMENT

A *turnaround strategy* is an attempt to reverse a declining business as quickly as possible. A *retrenchment strategy* is the divestiture or liquidation of assets. These strategies are listed together because most turnarounds include retrenchment. Turnaround strategies generally attempt to improve cash flow by increasing revenues, decreasing costs, reducing assets, or combining these strategies. **Texaco** made one of the most successful U.S. turnarounds by selling $7 billion in assets. A *spinoff* is a form of retrenchment in which a corporation sets up one of its business units as a separate company. **ITT** and **AT&T** both divided into three publicly traded companies in two of the largest-ever U.S. corporate breakups. **James River** had a spinoff of most of its nonconsumer paper and packaging operations.

COMBINATION

A corporation may pursue growth, stability, and turnaround and retrenchment for its different lines of business. Pennzoil, like many other companies, has had the grand strategy of buying and selling business lines. You will learn more about this combination in a later section.

McDonald's is the world's leading food retailer, with over 30,000 restaurants in 119 countries; it serves 47 million people each day. McDonald's is one of the world's most well-known brands. The corporation adopted a different strategy in 2003.

For years, McDonald's followed a growth strategy, as it continued to open new restaurants all over the globe. However, sales in the saturated U.S. market stumbled for years, and in 2003 McDonald's had is first ever quarterly loss. So Jim Cantalupo came out of retirement and took over as CEO to develop and implement a turnaround strategy to get the company back in the black. The primary goal was to change the focus away from opening new restaurants and toward bringing more customers into existing restaurants. Cantalupo gave top priority to speeding up service, offering friendly service, making the food taste better, and offering healthier and more varied menu items.

In line with the turnaround strategy, McDonald's also underwent a retrenchment, as it sold its 182-unit **Donatos Pizzeria** chain back to the founder, Jim Grote. McDonald's also ended its domestic joint venture with the Italian chain **Fazoli's**. As expected, McDonald's kept its majority interest in the 285-unit **Chipotle Mexican Grill** and its 33 percent stake in upscale British sandwich chain **Pret à Manger**, but it did close all 14 Pret à Manger units in Japan. It also unexpectedly kept its 652 **Boston Market** restaurants.

The turnaround and retrenchment strategy worked, as McDonald's posted a profit for the 4th quarter of 2003. McDonald's now accepts the fact that it may not always see annual growth of 15 percent. But it will continue to have respectable growth and high sales volume per unit.[51]

WorkApplication7
State the grand strategy for an organization you work for or have worked for.

───────────────── Learning Outcome 7 ─────────────────

Describe the three corporate growth strategies: concentration, integration, and diversification.

Corporate Growth Strategies

A company that wants to grow has three major options. *These* **corporate growth strategies** *are concentration, backward and forward integration, and related and unrelated diversification.*

CONCENTRATION

With a *concentration strategy*, the organization grows aggressively in its existing line(s) of business. **Wal-Mart** continues to open new stores.

INTEGRATION

With an *integration strategy*, the organization enters a new line or lines of business related to its existing one(s). *Forward integration* occurs when the organization enters a line of business closer to the final customer. *Backward integration* occurs when the organization enters a line of business farther away from the final customer. If Starbucks purchased a coffee plantation in order to produce its own coffee beans, that would be an example of backward integration. Some manufacturers, including **G. H. Bass** (Bass shoes) and **Apple Computer**, have engaged in forward integration by opening factory outlet stores, thus bypassing traditional retailers and selling their products directly to the customer.[52]

DIVERSIFICATION

With a *diversification strategy*, the organization goes into a related or unrelated line of products.[53] **Nike** used *related (concentric) diversification* when it diversified from sports shoes to sports clothing. **Sears** used *unrelated (conglomerate) diversification* when it went from selling retail goods to selling insurance through its **Allstate Insurance** line of business.[54]

Exhibit 5-9 summarizes strategies at the corporate level.

COMMON METHODS FOR PURSUING A GROWTH STRATEGY

Companies can pursue a growth strategy by means of mergers, acquisitions, takeovers, joint ventures, or strategic alliances.[55] A **merger** *occurs when two companies form one corporation. An* **acquisition** *occurs when one business buys all or part of another business.* One business becomes a part of an existing business. Companies engage in mergers and acquisitions to decrease competition, to compete more effectively with larger companies, to realize economies of size, to consolidate expenses, and to achieve access to markets, products, technology, resources, and management talent.[56] Companies often use an acquisition to enter a new line of business by buying an existing business rather than starting a new one.

WorkApplication8

Identify any growth strategies used by an organization you work for or have worked for. Be sure to identify the type of growth strategy and note if any mergers, acquisitions, takeovers, joint ventures, or strategic alliances were used.

Exhibit 5-9 *Corporate Grand and Growth Strategies*

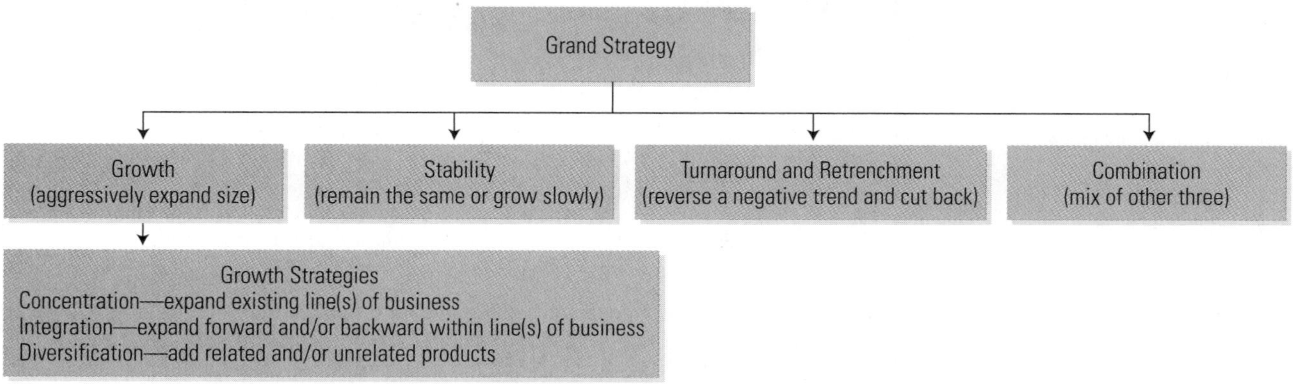

Grand Strategy

| Growth (aggressively expand size) | Stability (remain the same or grow slowly) | Turnaround and Retrenchment (reverse a negative trend and cut back) | Combination (mix of other three) |

Growth Strategies
Concentration—expand existing line(s) of business
Integration—expand forward and/or backward within line(s) of business
Diversification—add related and/or unrelated products

Corporate Growth Strategies

Identify the type of growth strategy described by each statement.

a. concentration
d. related diversification
b. forward integration
e. unrelated diversification
c. backward integration

_____ 6. Sears buys a tool manufacturer to make its Craftsman tools.

_____ 7. General Motors buys the Sea World theme park.

_____ 8. The Gap opens a new retail store in a mall.

_____ 9. Lee opens stores to sell its clothes.

_____10. Gateway, a computer manufacturer, produces printers.

When management of the target company rejects the purchasing company's offer, the purchasing company can make a bid to the shareholders of the target company to acquire the company through a *takeover*. For example, **Union Pacific Resources** tried to acquire **Pennzoil**. Pennzoil's board rejected the offer and urged shareholders to reject a hostile takeover bid, which they did. **Time** and **Warner** merged years ago, and more recently, **Time Warner** merged with America Online **(AOL)** to become **AOL Time Warner**, in one of the largest mergers in history.[57] **Price** and **Costco** warehouse membership clubs merged to become **PriceCostco**. **Bank of America** acquired **FleetBoston** to become the second-largest bank in the United States. However, less than a year later, **J. P. Morgan Chase** acquired **Bank One** and took over the number two spot.[58] Cross-national acquisitions, commonly used to establish a global presence, are also on the increase.[59]

IOM

Starbucks's grand strategy is a growth strategy: to expand to 25,000 locations. Its primary growth strategy is concentration, as it wants to continue to open more stores just like its current ones. Starbucks is using the company-owned business model,

Join the Discussion Ethics & Social Responsibility

Insider Trading

1. Insider trading is illegal, but is it unethical?
2. If you received information from an insider, would you buy the stock?
3. What are the implications of using insider information? Is anyone hurt by the practice? If yes, who is hurt and how are they hurt?
4. Without using insider information, some speculators try to predict which companies are likely to merge or be acquired and buy stock options. This is a legal way of making money, but is it ethical?

Insiders are people who have confidential information about upcoming events that will affect the price of a stock. Insiders are not supposed to buy or sell any stock they have confidential information about or to tell anyone this information so that that person can profit from stock dealing.

Join the Discussion Ethics & Social Responsibility

(Continued)

It is common for the price of a stock to go up when investors learn that the company is negotiating a deal to merge with, or be acquired by, another company. For example, **Sears** made the decision to acquire **Lands' End** to improve its retail performance. Top managers at Sears and Lands' End knew before the media covered the story that a deal would be made. Therefore, these top managers could have bought Lands' End stock and/or told others to buy it in order to profit from the pending acquisition through insider training.

Martha Stewart was not charged with criminal insider trading for selling her ImClone stock before it dropped sharply in price. She was charged with defrauding investors in her own company, **Martha Stewart Living Omnimedia**, by repeating the false reasons for her sale of **ImClone** stock.

rather than growing through franchising like McDonald's (with 30,000 stores) and Subway (19,500 stores now, with the objective of 30,000 stores by 2010).

All successful companies have some failures. Starbucks did try to diversify by going into cyberspace but did not succeed. Starbucks X, a separate division that would have been an Internet retail site selling everything from pots to clothing and furniture, failed. Starbucks also invested millions in other online ventures, including living.com (a furniture retailer), Talk City, (a chat service), and Kozmo.com (a home-delivery company for Web shoppers). All three investments failed. Starbucks offers high-speed, wireless Internet connections as a service in its current stores, not as a separate line of business. Starbucks closed all six of its stores in Israel, and it was not successful in selling premade sandwiches; customers prefer fresh sandwiches, which Starbucks stores are not set up to make.

Portfolio Analysis

Business portfolio analysis *is the corporate process of determining which lines of business the corporation will be in and how it will allocate resources among them. A business line*, also called a *strategic business unit (SBU)*, is a distinct business having its own customers that is managed independently of other businesses within the corporation. What constitutes an SBU varies from company to company, but it can be a division, a subsidiary, or a single product line. **Pennzoil** has several primary businesses: oil and natural gas, motor oil and refined products, and franchise operations (**Jiffy Lube**). An industry and competitive situation analysis can be used to analyze a business portfolio. Another method is the BCG Growth-Share Matrix.

BCG GROWTH-SHARE MATRIX

A popular approach to analyzing a business portfolio is to create a Boston Consulting Group (BCG) Growth-Share Matrix for each line of business. The four cells of the matrix are as illustrated in Exhibit 5-10.

- *Cash cows* generate more resources than they need; they often have low growth but high market share. Examples of cash cows include Coca-Cola

Exhibit 5-10 *BCG Growth-Share Matrix*

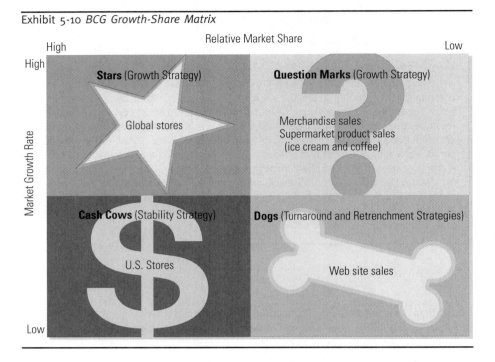

Classic, Crest toothpaste, and Toyota cars.[60] Cash cows tend to have stability strategies.

- *Stars* are emerging businesses with high growth and market share. Stars require continuing investment of profits into the product if they are to become cash cows. The minivan was a star for **Chrysler**, and Diet Coke was one for **Coca-Cola**. Stars tend to have growth strategies.
- *Question marks* are entries into new businesses in high-growth markets; such entries start out with negative returns and low market share. Question marks need investments from other lines of business to develop into stars.[61] But they can become dogs. **Maytag** acquired **Hoover's** European unit in hopes of making it a star. However, about five years later, it sold Hoover for a $170-million loss. Question marks tend to have growth strategies.
- *Dogs* have low returns in a low-growth market and have low relative market share. Dogs are often divested or liquidated when they no longer provide acceptable profits. Black-and-white televisions, record turntables, and audio tape-players have become dogs. Dogs tend to have turnaround and retrenchment strategies.

Portfolio analysis provides managers with ideas about how to allocate cash and other resources among business lines (as well as which corporate strategies to use). Generally, managers take resources from the cash cows (stability strategy) and allocate them to the question marks and possibly the stars (growth strategies). Any cash from dogs, as well as any resources from their sale (retrenchment strategy), is also given to question marks and stars. **Seagram** sold its **Tropicana** juice unit to help pay for the acquisition of music powerhouse **PolyGram. Entertainment**, not liquor, is now Seagram's main focus.

A company in a single line of business cannot conduct a business portfolio analysis. However, it should perform a *product portfolio analysis*. The BCG business portfolio matrix can also be used to analyze a product line. For example, **McDonald's** started by offering a simple hamburger and fries. Over the years, the company introduced new products, such as the Big Mac. The Big Mac started as a question mark, became a star, and then joined the hamburger and fries as a cash cow. McDonald's introduced pizza as a question mark, but rather than becoming a star, it became a dog and was dropped from most restaurants. It remains to be seen what will happen to McDonald's latest low-carb item.

THE ENTREPRENEURIAL STRATEGY MATRIX

The BCG matrix was designed for large companies with multiple lines of business; as noted earlier, it can also be used to analyze a single product line. Sonfield and Lussier developed the Entrepreneurial Strategy Matrix (ESM) for small businesses.[62] The ESM suggests strategies for new and ongoing entrepreneurial ventures that will lead to optimal performance based on the identification of different combinations of innovation and risk. The matrix answers these questions: What venture situation are you in? What are the best strategic alternatives for a given venture?

Innovation is defined as the creation of something new and different. The newer and more different a product or service is, the higher the level of innovation. *Risk* is defined as the probability of a major financial loss. The entrepreneur determines the chances of the venture failing and how serious the financial loss would be. The same dollar amount of possible loss might be more serious to one entrepreneur than to another. Combining levels of innovation and risk creates a four-cell matrix, as shown in Exhibit 5-11.

The ESM also suggests appropriate strategies in each cell, which are also presented in Exhibit 5-11. An entrepreneur first evaluates the levels of innovation and risk for the venture and identifies which of the four cells it is in. Then, the entrepreneur decides which of the strategies suggested in that cell to utilize. Empirical testing of the EMS has supported its validity.[63]

BUSINESS-LEVEL STRATEGY

Each line of business must develop its own mission, analyze its own environment, set its own objectives, and develop its own strategies. For the organization with a single line of products, corporate- and business-level strategies are the same. For the organization involved in multiple lines of business, linking corporate strategy with operations at the business unit level determines success. In this section, we'll discuss adaptive and competitive strategies and how to change strategies during the product life cycle.

Exhibit 5-11 *The Entrepreneurial Strategy Matrix*

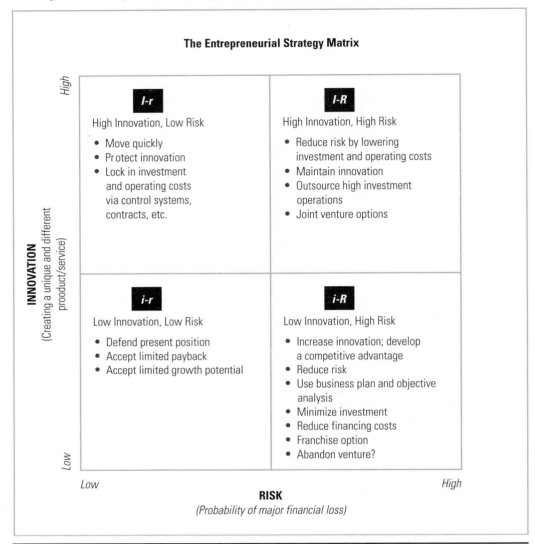

The Entrepreneurial Strategy Matrix

INNOVATION
(Creating a unique and different product/service)

High

I-r

High Innovation, Low Risk

• Move quickly
• Protect innovation
• Lock in investment
  and operating costs
  via control systems,
  contracts, etc.

I-R

High Innovation, High Risk

• Reduce risk by lowering
  investment and operating costs
• Maintain innovation
• Outsource high investment
  operations
• Joint venture options

i-r

Low Innovation, Low Risk

• Defend present position
• Accept limited payback
• Accept limited growth potential

i-R

Low Innovation, High Risk

• Increase innovation; develop
  a competitive advantage
• Reduce risk
• Use business plan and objective
  analysis
• Minimize investment
• Reduce financing costs
• Franchise option
• Abandon venture?

Low

Low   High

RISK
(Probability of major financial loss)

Adapted with permission from *Business Horizons* 40 (May–June), pp. 73–77. Sonfield, M. C., and Lussier, R. N. (1997). "The Entrepreneurial Strategy Matrix. A Model for New and Ongoing Ventures." ©1997 by Indiana University Kelley School of Business.

—————————————— Learning Outcome **8** ——————————————

Describe the three business-level adaptive strategies: prospecting, defending, and analyzing.

Adaptive Strategies

The overall strategy for a line of business, which corresponds to the grand strategy for a corporation, is called the *adaptive strategy*.[64] Adaptive strategies emphasize adapting to changes in the external environment and entering new markets as means of increasing sales.[65] The business-level **adaptive strategies** are *prospecting*,

Exhibit 5-12 *Business-Level Adaptive Strategies*

Adaptive Strategy	Rate of Environmental Change	Potential Growth Rate	Corresponding Grand Strategy
Prospecting	Fast	High	Growth
Analyzing	Moderate	Moderate	Combination
Defending	Slow	Low	Stability

defending, and *analyzing*; these correspond to the corporate grand strategies of growth, stability, and combination, respectively. Each adaptive strategy reflects a different objective. Exhibit 5-12 indicates which adaptive strategies are suitable for different rates of environmental change and potential growth rates.

PROSPECTING STRATEGY

The *prospecting strategy* calls for aggressively offering new products and/or entering new markets. **Wal-Mart** continues to open new stores to enter new markets. However, for a line of business, this growth strategy has to be concentration or related diversification. If it's integration or unrelated diversification, new lines of business will be acquired, and there will no longer be a single line of business. The prospecting strategy resembles the grand strategy of growth.

DEFENDING STRATEGY

The *defending strategy* calls for staying with the present product line and markets and maintaining or increasing customers. Defending resembles the stability grand strategy.

Yahoo! was once the search engine most people used to navigate the Internet. However, **Google** had the largest market share of search sites in 2003, 35 percent compared to Yahoo! (26 percent), **AOL** (16 percent), **MSN** (15 percent), and **Ask Jeeves** (3 percent).[66] In fact, Yahoo! was using Google's technology on its site, but it planned to replace it with its own technology in the first quarter of 2004. The Internet is still growing. Yahoo! is using the prospecting strategy to continue to grow and to take back its market leadership. Google, on the other hand, made an initial public offering of its stock in 2004, in order to raise needed capital to continue its prospecting strategy of expansion; simultaneously, it must use the defending strategy to maintain its market share leadership.

Yahoo!'s strategy was not simply to copy Google; it planned to create a competitive advantage by differentiating its site with features that competitors can't easily match. Yahoo! planned to combine personalization and customization features to extend the usefulness of Web searches. It also planned to expand the use of "paid inclusion." Merchants contract with Yahoo! to ensure that their Web sites are always listed when they are relevant to the search a user has submitted to Yahoo!. The merchant pays Yahoo! anywhere from 15 cents to more than $1 when a user clicks on a link for that merchant's site. Yahoo! frequently surveys participating merchants' sites for the most up-to-date information and includes the findings in its users' search results to get visitors to click merchant links. If Yahoo! gets a million people to use its search functions, and each user clicks on one link at an average fee of 50 cents, Yahoo! gains $500,000 in revenues.

WorkApplication9

Identify the adaptive strategy used by an organization you work for or have worked for. Be sure to describe how it used the strategy.

ANALYZING STRATEGY

The *analyzing strategy* calls for a midrange approach between prospecting and defending. Analyzing involves moving into new market areas at a cautious, deliberate pace and/or offering a core product group and seeking new opportunities.[67] **Procter & Gamble** has several established consumer products, including Pampers diapers and Crest toothpaste, and occasionally offers innovations such as Aleve, which competes with other pain relievers (Bayer, Tylenol, and Advil). Analyzing resembles the combination grand strategy.

Competitive Strategies

Michael Porter identified three effective business-level *competitive strategies:* differentiation, cost leadership, and focus.[68]

DIFFERENTIATION STRATEGY

With a differentiation strategy, a company stresses its advantage over its competitors.[69] **Nike, Ralph Lauren, Calvin Klein,** and others place their names on the outside of their products to differentiate them from those of the competition. Differentiation strategy somewhat resembles the prospecting strategy. According to **Coca-Cola**, the three keys to selling consumer products are differentiation, differentiation, differentiation, which it achieves with its scripted name logo and contour bottle.

COST LEADERSHIP

With a cost leadership strategy, the company stresses lower prices to attract customers.[70] To keep its prices down, it must have tight cost control and an efficient systems process. Growth demands high volume and high volume demands low prices. **Wal-Mart** and **Target** have had success with this strategy. Cost leadership somewhat resembles the defending strategy.

Applying The Concept 3

Adaptive Strategies

Identify the type of strategy represented in each statement.

a. prospecting

b. defending

c. analyzing

_____ 11. This is the primary strategy of industry leader Coca-Cola in the saturated U.S. cola market.

_____ 12. Nabisco comes out with a new cookie to compete with Keebler's cookies.

_____ 13. Friendly Ice Cream opens restaurants in the state of Washington.

_____ 14. IBM pioneers a computer that can be folded up and put in your pocket.

_____ 15. This is the strategy used by Domino's when Pizza Hut started to copy delivering pizza.

FOCUS

With a focus strategy, the company focuses on a specific regional market, product line, or buyer group.[71] Within a particular target segment, or market niche, the firm may use a differentiation or cost leadership strategy. Ed Boyd was hired by **PepsiCo** to direct what is believed to have been the first target marketing campaign for a major product. More than 50 years ago, Boyd developed an African American sales team to market Pepsi soft drinks to the African American community. Focus strategies are commonplace in the business world: *Ebony* and *Jet* magazines target African Americans, MTV focuses on young people, and Rolex watches have a market niche of upper-income people. Right Guard deodorant is aimed at men, and Secret at women.

Product Life Cycle

The *product life cycle* refers to a series of stages that a product goes through over time. The four stages of the product life cycle are introduction, growth, maturity, and decline. The speed at which products go through the life cycle varies.[72] Many products, like Tide detergent, stay around for years; in contrast, fad products, like pet rocks and pogs, may last only months. Exhibit 5-13 illustrates the appropriate portfolio analysis, corporate grand strategy, and business-level adaptive strategy for each stage of the product life cycle for Starbucks.

Exhibit 5-13 *Strategies for Starbucks over the Product Life Cycle*

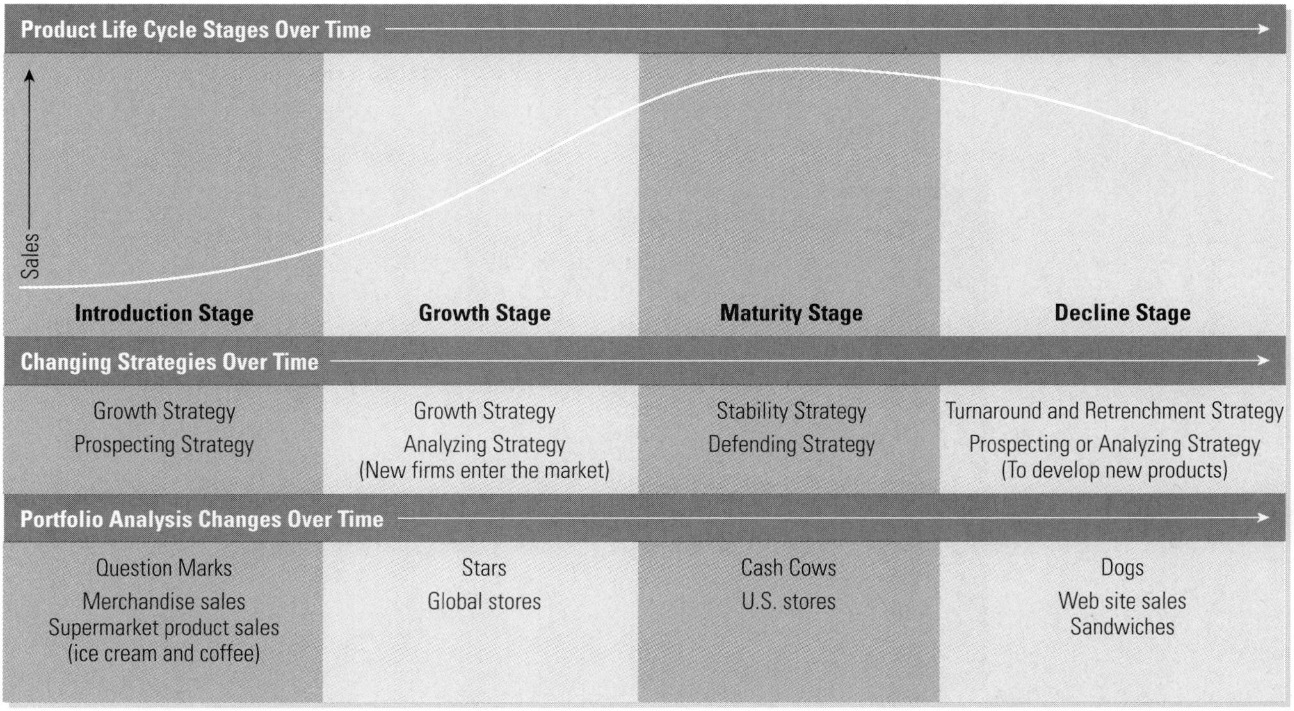

Product Life Cycle Stages Over Time			
Introduction Stage	**Growth Stage**	**Maturity Stage**	**Decline Stage**
Changing Strategies Over Time			
Growth Strategy Prospecting Strategy	Growth Strategy Analyzing Strategy (New firms enter the market)	Stability Strategy Defending Strategy	Turnaround and Retrenchment Strategy Prospecting or Analyzing Strategy (To develop new products)
Portfolio Analysis Changes Over Time			
Question Marks Merchandise sales Supermarket product sales (ice cream and coffee)	Stars Global stores	Cash Cows U.S. stores	Dogs Web site sales Sandwiches

Pricing strategies tend to change over the product life cycle. Prices tend to be higher in the introduction stage because there is little if any competition. Prices decline with product age, but this is offset if the number of units sold sustains a steady growth.

INTRODUCTION STAGE

As a growth strategy, the business introduces a product that has a differentiation strategy because it is new. In 2003, **Brother, Canon**, and **HP** introduced portable printers to use with laptops.[73]

GROWTH STAGE

Rapid sales growth takes place in this stage. When analyzers see that the product is doing well, they copy it through benchmarking. Analyzers may use a differentiation, focus, or cost leadership strategy to gain sales during the growth stage. A focus strategy often emphasizes quality and systems process improvements to gain economies of scale.[74] Portfolio stars, like Starbucks's global operation, are usually in the growth stage.

MATURITY STAGE

At the maturity stage, sales growth continues slowly, levels off, and begins to decline. In a saturated market, the growth strategy changes to one of stability (defending). Low cost becomes more important, and cost-cutting efforts are emphasized. Mature products, such as Starbucks's domestic retail operations, are usually analyzed as cash cows in the business portfolio.

DECLINE STAGE

In the decline stage, sales drop. The strategy changes from stability or defending to turnaround and retrenchment and prospecting or analyzing. **Procter & Gamble** used a turnaround strategy with some of its products, including Tide, calling them new and improved to revitalize sales and prevent decline to the point of retrenchment.

WorkApplication10

Identify the stage in the product life cycle of one of the products of an organization you work for or have worked for. Is the strategy you identified in Work Application 7 the appropriate strategy for this product at this stage of the product life cycle? Explain your answers.

Applying The Concept 4

Product Life Cycle

Select the most accurate product life cycle stage for each product.

a. introduction
b. growth
c. maturity
d. decline

_____16. Gasoline

_____17. Cassette tapes

_____18. Home carpeting (rugs)

_____19. Cellular phones

_____20. The fold-up computer that fits in your pocket

Remember that the various grand and adaptive strategies complement one another. Managers select the appropriate strategy based on the mission, situation analysis, and objectives.

Starbucks Coffee has an adaptive strategy of prospecting; it plans to grow to 25,000 stores by aggressively entering new markets worldwide. Its competitive strategy is differentiation, as it focuses on upscale buyers willing to pay higher prices than at Dunkin' Donuts. Until Starbucks saturates the U.S. and global markets, it will continue to be in the growth stage, as it opens more stores. However, in the United States, coffee shops are in the maturity stage as sales are not growing much. Starbucks must get people to buy its differentiated coffee rather than that of competitors, because it is not getting many new customers who don't already drink coffee.

FUNCTIONAL-LEVEL (OPERATIONAL) STRATEGIES

Earlier in this chapter, you learned about long-range, external, competitive strategic planning. In this section, we'll discuss operational-level planning. The functional departments of a company must develop internal strategies for achieving the business-level mission and objectives.[75] **Functional strategies** *are strategies developed and implemented by managers in the marketing, operations, human resources, finance, and other departments of a company.* Situation analysis also takes place at the functional levels to determine strengths and weaknesses. The functional departments also develop objectives and strategies for achieving them.[76]

The implementation stage of the strategic process has remained a stumbling block as organizations have difficulty translating business strategies into cohesive functional strategies. The need for greater integration of corporate, business, and functional strategies within the organization has long been recognized. One of the foremost difficulties is achieving greater cooperation across functional departments.[77]

Marketing Strategy

The marketing department has the primary responsibility for knowing what the customer wants, or how to add customer value, and for defining the target market. Marketing focuses on the four Ps: product, promotion, place, and price. In other words, the marketing department makes decisions about which products to provide, how they will be packaged, how they will be advertised, where they will be sold and how they get will there, and how much they will be sold for.

You may know that **Puma** makes athletic shoes and clothes. In the mid-1990s, Puma was having problems and was close to bankruptcy. A new management team led Puma through a turnaround based on a marketing strategy.

In 1998, the company began to focus on developing new products that combined sports and lifestyle. To be exclusive, it cut back the number of stores in which Puma products were sold; if you can buy Puma products in almost any store, what's so unusual about them? It also started selling Puma products in its own retail stores; it now has 20 around the world. As customers would expect with an exclusive product line, Puma prices are on the high end, and the company has increased promotional efforts to influence people to buy the Puma brand.[78]

Operations Strategy

The operations (or production) department is responsible for systems processes that convert inputs into outputs. Operations focuses on quality and efficiency in producing the products that marketing determines will provide customer value. (You will learn more about operations in Chapter 15.)

DuPont was founded over 200 years ago, in 1802. Today, DuPont puts science to work around the world solving problems in the areas of food and nutrition, health care, apparel, safety and security, construction, electronics, and transportation. You may not be aware of them, but you're likely to find dozens of items made with DuPont materials at work and home. Do you recognize any of these DuPont brands: Teflon® resins, Lycra® spandex fiber, Stainmaster® stain-resistant carpet, Antron® carpet fiber, Dacron® polyester fiber, Kevlar® fiber, Nomex® fire-retardant material, Corian® solid surface material, Tyvek® protective material, or Coolmax® and Cordura® textile fibers?

In 2003, DuPont employed 78,000 people globally, operated in more than 70 countries with 135 manufacturing and processing facilities. For 2004 and beyond, DuPont developed a retrenchment strategy that focuses on cutting operations costs by $900 million to become smaller and more profitable.[79]

Human Resources Strategy

The human resources department is responsible for working with all the other functional departments in the areas of recruiting, selecting, training, evaluating, and compensating employees. (You will learn more about human resources in Chapter 8.)

Finance Strategy

The finance department has at least two functions: (1) financing the business activities by raising money through the sale of stock (equity) or bonds or through loans (debt), deciding on the debt-to-equity ratio, and paying off the debt and dividends (if any) to shareholders; and (2) keeping records of trans-actions, developing budgets, and reporting financial results (income statement and balance sheet). A third function of the finance department in many organizations is making the optimum use of cash reserves, in particular, investing as a means of making money.[80]

Other Functional-Level Strategies

Based on the type of business, any number of other departments will also need to develop a strategy. One area that varies in importance is research and development (R&D). Businesses that sell a product usually allocate greater resources (budgets) for R&D than do businesses that provide a service.

WorkApplication11

Identify one functional area of an organization you work for or have worked for. What was its operational strategy?

OPERATIONAL PLANNING

Recall from Exhibit 5-1 that one dimension of planning is the repetitiveness of the plans—whether they are standing plans or single-use plans. Most strategic plans are single-use, whereas operational plans are more often standing plans. We'll explore the difference between these types of plans and also discuss contingency plans in this section.

————————— Learning Outcome 9 —————————
State the difference between standing plans and single-use plans.

Standing Plans versus Single-Use Plans

Depending on how repetitive they are, plans may be either *standing plans*, which are made to be used over and over again (repeated), or *single-use plans*, which are made to be used only once (nonrepetitive). Exhibit 5-14 illustrates the different types of standing and single-use plans.

STANDING PLANS

Operational objectives may be accomplished by following standing plans, which save planning and decision-making time.[81] **Standing plans** *are policies, procedures, and rules developed for handling repetitive situations.* Their purpose is to guide employees' actions in decision making. Union contract agreements, for example, are one type of standing plan.

Policies *provide general guidelines to be followed when making decisions.* Here are a few examples of policy statements: "The customer is always right." "We produce high-quality goods and services." "We promote qualified employees from within." "Employees will receive due process in grievances." Notice that policy statements are intentionally general guides; the manager uses his or her discretion in implementing them. As a manager, your daily decisions will be guided by policies. It will be your job to interpret, apply, and explain company policies to employees.

A **procedure** *is a sequence of actions to be followed in order to achieve an objective.* Procedures may also be called *standard operating procedures* (SOPs) or *methods*. Procedures are more specific than policies; they entail a series of decisions rather than a single decision and may involve more than one functional area. Procedures ensure that all recurring, routine situations are handled in a consistent, predetermined manner. Many organizations have procedures for purchasing, taking inventory, settling grievances, and so forth.

Rules *state exactly what should or should not be done.* Employees have no discretion on how to implement rules and regulations.[82] These are examples of rules: "No smoking or eating in the work area." "Everyone must wear a hard hat on the construction site." "Stop at a red light." Violating rules usually subjects a person to penalties that vary in severity according to the seriousness of the violation and the number of offenses. Managers are responsible for establishing and enforcing rules in a uniform manner.[83]

WorkApplication12
Give an example of a policy, a procedure, and a rule from an organization you work for or have worked for.

_____

_____

_____

_____

Exhibit 5-14 *Standing Plans versus Single-Use Plans*

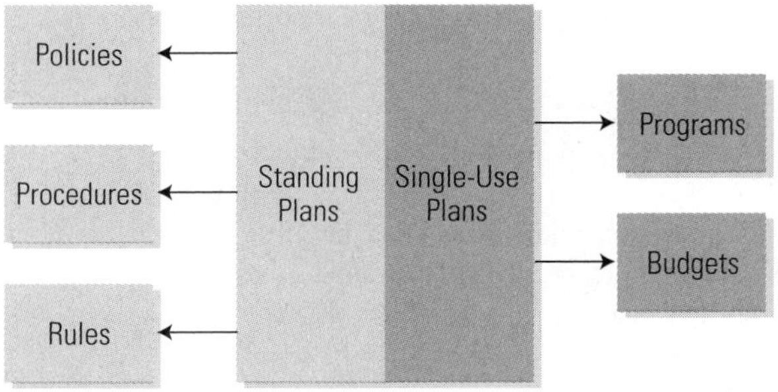

WorkApplication13

Give an example of a program you were involved in at work.

_____

_____

_____

_____

_____

SINGLE-USE PLANS

Single-use plans *are programs and budgets developed for handling nonrepetitive situations.* Single-use plans, unlike standing plans, are developed for a specific purpose and probably will not be used again in the same form. However, a single-use plan may be used as a model for a future version of the program or budget. A growth strategy is a single-use plan.

A *program* describes a set of activities and is designed to accomplish an objective over a specified time period. Programs are not meant to exist over the life of the organization. A program may have its own policies, procedures, budget, and so forth. It might take several years or less than a day to complete a given program. Examples include the development of a new product, expansion of facilities, or research and development to find a cure for a disease.

When developing a program, managers typically (1) set project objectives, (2) break the project down into a sequence of steps, (3) assign responsibility for each step, (4) establish starting and ending times for each step, and (5) determine the resources needed for each step.

A *budget* is the funds allocated to operate a unit for a fixed period of time. When that time has passed, a new budget is needed. Developing a budget requires planning skills rather than mathematical skills. When developed, a budget is a planning tool, and when implemented, it is a control tool.

Contingency Plans

WorkApplication14

Describe a situation in which a contingency plan is appropriate. Explain the plan.

....

....

....

....

....

No matter how effectively you plan, there will be times when events prevent you from achieving your objectives. Things that go wrong are often beyond your control. For example, a machine may break down or an employee may call in sick. When the uncontrollable occurs, you should be prepared with a backup, or contingency, plan.[84] **Contingency plans** *are alternative plans to be implemented if uncontrollable events occur.* If a key employee calls in sick, another employee fills in to do the job. Construction work is usually contingent

---

ApplyingTheConcept 5

Identifying Plans

Identify the type of plan exemplified by each statement.

a. policy   d. program

b. procedure   e. budget

c. rule

_____ 21. "Quality is job one."

_____ 22. President John F. Kennedy's plan to land someone on the moon

_____ 23. How much will it cost to operate your department next month?

_____ 24. Everyone should wear safety glasses while touring the factory.

_____ 25. Forms for leaves of absence must be approved by the manager and submitted to the personnel office one month in advance of the planned leave.

on the weather. If it's nice, employees work outside; if it is not, they work indoors. Shippers have contingency plans to use in case of a strike by union workers.

To develop a contingency plan, you should answer three questions:

1. What might go wrong?
2. How can I prevent it from happening?
3. If it does occur, what can I do to minimize its effect?

The answer to question 3 is your contingency plan. When developing contingency plans, ask everyone involved what can go wrong and what should be done if it does go wrong. Also ask others within and outside the organization who have implemented similar plans. They may have encountered problems you haven't thought of, and they may have good contingency plans to suggest.

Functional-level strategies are critical to the success of Starbucks. The marketing department works on improving and developing new products and promoting the Starbucks brand. To increase the number of stores from 7,500 to 25,000, marketing will have a lot to do in determining locations throughout the globe. The operations department has two primary functions: to create new stores and to operate existing stores effectively. President and CEO Orin Smith says that Starbucks will never lose its focus and become better at opening stores than operating them. The human resources department will have to recruit, select, train, evaluate, and compensate a lot more employees as Starbucks grows. In addition, growth requires an effective finance strategy to raise money and keep track of accounting and budgeting.

Opening each new Starbucks store requires a single-use plan; each store is somewhat different. However, standing plans for the store-opening process, which take advantage of organizational learning, are also in place. Starbucks also has extensive policies, procedures, and rules to operate each store in a consistent manner. Finally, opening stores and operating them require contingency plans.

I
O
M

IMPLEMENTING AND CONTROLLING STRATEGIES

The first four steps in the strategic planning process are directly concerned with planning. The fifth and final step involves implementing and controlling strategies to ensure that the mission and objectives, at all three levels, are achieved. Top and middle managers are more involved with the planning, whereas the lower-level functional managers and employees implement the strategies on a day-to-day basis. Successful implementation of strategies requires effective and efficient support systems throughout the organization. Although strategic planning usually goes well, implementation is often a problem.[85] One reason is that strategic plans often end up buried in bottom drawers; no action is taken to implement the strategy. Throughout Chapters 6 through 13, you will learn how to organize and lead so as to implement strategies.

As strategies are being implemented, they must also be controlled. *Controlling* is the process of establishing and implementing mechanisms to ensure that objectives are achieved. An important part of controlling is measuring progress toward the achievement of the objective and taking corrective action when needed. Another important part of controlling is staying within the budget when appropriate or changing it when necessary to meet changes in the environment. You will develop your controlling skills in Chapters 14 and 15.

Having read this chapter, you should understand the importance of effective planning and recognize the five planning dimensions and the differences between standing plans and single-use plans and between strategic and operational plans. You should be able to analyze the environment and set effective objectives using a model. You should also understand the difference between the three levels of strategy, the need to coordinate all three levels, and the importance of implementing and controlling strategies.

Take advantage of the companion Web site for *Management Fundamentals*, where you will find a broad array of resources to help you maximize what you learn in class:

- Try a quiz
- View chapter videos
- Download slides
- Boost your vocabulary
- Work through an Internet exercise
- Find related links

Take a look for yourself at *http://lussier.swlearning.com.*

Chapter Summary

1. Describe how strategic planning differs from operational planning.
The primary differences concern the time frame and the level of management involved. Strategic planning involves developing a mission and long-range objectives and plans; operational planning involves short-range objectives and plans. Upper-level managers develop strategic plans, and lower-level managers develop operational plans.

2. State the differences among the three strategic levels: corporate, business, and functional.
The strategic levels differ primarily in their focus, which becomes narrower in lower levels of the organization, and in the management level involved in developing the strategy. Corporate-level strategy focuses on managing multiple lines of business. Business-level strategy focuses on managing one line of business. Functional-level strategy focuses on managing an area of a business. Upper-level managers develop corporate- and business-level strategy, and lower-level managers develop functional-level strategy.

3. Explain the reason for conducting an industry and competitive situation analysis.
The industry and competitive situation analysis is used to determine the attractiveness of an industry. It is primarily used at the corporate strategy level to make decisions regarding which lines of business to enter and exit, and how to allocate resources among lines of business.

4. Explain the reason for conducting a company situation analysis.
The company situation analysis is used at the business strategy level to determine the issues and problems that need to be addressed through the strategic planning process.

5. List the parts of an effective written objective.
The parts of the objective are (1) *to* + (2) action verb + (3) singular, specific, and measurable result to be achieved + (4) target date.

6. Describe the four grand strategies: growth, stability, turnaround, and retrenchment, and a combination of these.
With a growth strategy, the firm aggressively pursues increasing its size. With a stability strategy, the firm maintains the same size or grows slowly. With a turnaround strategy, the firm attempts a comeback; with retrenchment, it decreases in size. With a combination strategy, two or more of the three strategies are used for different lines of business.

7. Describe the three corporate growth strategies: concentration, integration, and diversification.
With a concentration strategy, the firm grows aggressively in its existing line(s) of business. With integration, the firm grows by entering forward or backward line(s) of business. With diversification, the firm grows by adding related or unrelated products.

8. Discuss the three business-level adaptive strategies: prospecting, defending, and analyzing.

With the prospecting strategy, the firm aggressively offers new products or services and/or enters new markets. With the defending strategy, the firm stays with its product or line and markets. With the analyzing strategy, the firm moves into new markets cautiously and/or offers a core product group and seeks new opportunities.

9. State the difference between standing plans and single-use plans.

The major difference is the repetitiveness of the situation the plan is intended to address. Standing plans are policies, procedures, and rules developed for handling repetitive situations. Single-use plans are programs and budgets developed for handling nonrepetitive situations.

10. Complete each of the following statements using one of this chapter's key terms.

_____ is the process of developing a mission and long-range objectives and determining in advance how they will be accomplished.

_____ is the process of setting short-range objectives and determining in advance how they will be accomplished.

A _____ is a plan for pursuing the mission and achieving objectives.

The _____ are corporate, business, and functional.

The _____ is the plan for managing multiple lines of business.

The _____ is the plan for managing one line of business.

The _____ is the plan for managing one area of the business.

A _____ reveals those features in a company's environment that most directly affect its options and opportunities.

Through a _____, the organization's internal environmental strengths and weaknesses and external environmental opportunities and threats are determined.

_____ is the process of comparing the organization's products or services and processes with those of other companies.

An _____ states what is to be accomplished in singular, specific, and measurable terms with a target date.

_____ is the process in which managers and their employees jointly set objectives for the employee, periodically evaluate performance, and reward according to the results.

The _____ is the overall corporate-level strategy of growth, stability, turnaround, and retrenchment, or a combination thereof.

_____ include concentration, backward and forward integration, and related and unrelated diversification.

A _____ occurs when two companies form one corporation.

An _____ occurs when one business buys all or part of another business.

_____ is the corporate process of determining which lines of business the corporation will be in and how it will allocate resources among them.

Business-level _____ include prospecting, defending, and analyzing.

_____ are developed by managers in marketing, operations, human resources, finance, and other departments.

_____ are policies, procedures, and rules developed for handling repetitive situations.

_____ provide general guidelines to be followed when making decisions.

A _____ is a sequence of actions to be followed in order to achieve an objective.

_____ state exactly what should or should not be done.

_____ are programs and budgets developed for handling nonrepetitive situations.

_____ are alternative plans to be implemented if uncontrollable events occur.

Key Terms

acquisition, 163

adaptive strategies, 168

benchmarking, 156

business portfolio analysis, 165

business-level strategy, 151

contingency plans, 177

corporate growth strategies, 162

corporate-level strategy, 151

functional strategies, 173

functional-level strategy, 151

grand strategy, 161

management by objectives (MBO), 160

merger, 163

objectives, 157

operational planning, 149

policies, 175

procedure, 175

rules, 176

single-use plans, 176

situation analysis, 152

standing plans, 175

strategic levels, 151

strategic planning, 149

strategy, 151

SWOT analysis, 154

Review and Discussion Questions

1. What are the five planning dimensions?
2. How does planning differ at each level of management?
3. Why are strategic and operational planning important?
4. Is there a difference between a plan and a strategy?
5. Should all businesses have corporate-, business-, and functional-level strategies?
6. Should a mission statement be customer-focused?
7. Why is a company situation analysis part of the strategic planning process?
8. Should all businesses have a competitive advantage?
9. Is it ethical to copy other companies' ideas through benchmarking?
10. Are both goals and objectives necessary for a business?
11. Is it important to write objectives?
12. As a manager, would you use MBO?
13. Which growth strategy would you say is the most successful?
14. What is the difference between a merger and an acquisition?
15. Is there a difference between grand strategies and adaptive strategies?
16. Why would a business use a focus strategy rather than trying to appeal to all customers?
17. Give examples of functional departments other than those mentioned in the text.

Objective Case

KRISPY KREME

Krispy Kreme's mission is to strive to provide the highest quality product and the best service to customers. Vernon Rudolph, the founder of Krispy Kreme, always believed in top quality and top service, as well as focusing on people, both customers and employees. These values have helped Krispy Kreme grow from a small donut shop in Winston-Salem, North Carolina, in 1937 to a national phenomenon in the 1990s.

The company is now a major corporation, with 366 stores in more than 44 states. Two-thirds of Krispy Kreme shops are owned by franchisees. Other stores are corporate-owned stand-alone units, which include drive-throughs.

Despite being seen by some analysts as a fad, Krispy Kreme's business had been expanding through the years. However, the company did not earn as much as it had projected in the first quarter of 2004, which ended May 2. Therefore, in May 2004, the corporation announced it would sell Montana Mills Bread a mere 13 months after purchasing the company, and take a loss of nearly $40 million.

Krispy Kreme's business has been split about evenly between off-premise sites (grocery stores, convenience stores, and the like that stock the donuts) and retail operations. However, off-premise sales have slowed, leaving boxes of unsold donuts piled up on display tables.

The low-carb diet trend that began gaining popularity in 2003 affected Krispy Kreme sales. The company's earnings dropped, and in early 2004 its stock price plunged to less than half of its August 2003 level. In May 2004, Krispy Kreme, the donut icon of the last decade, issued its first profit warning since going public in April 2000. For the first time in recent memory, retail customer counts declined, according to John Tate, the company's chief operating officer.

But analysts have commented that the many issues affecting Krispy Kreme internally are not solely caused by the low-carb diet consumers are eating. Krispy Kreme stores are also experiencing declining sales as the chain opens more outlets. Among the key factors that may be adversely affecting Krispy Kreme's operating performance is its dependence on new franchisees to execute its store expansion strategy. Potential franchisees have been holding back from commitments to open new stores. As a result, the company is growing too reliant on sales in off-site locations that are less profitable.

For half a century Krispy Kreme and Dunkin' Donuts have been competitors. Each chain has built its own following: Krispy Kreme has traditionally offered only its very sweet glazed donuts; Dunkin' Donuts has been a stopping point for many coffee customers, including those who do not want to pay the higher prices at Starbucks. Although Krispy Kreme has added some special items, Dunkin' Donuts has focused much of its growth on its coffee and other food businesses, including bagels, sandwiches, and pastries. Donuts are just a quarter of its sales, and beverages are more than half.

The competitive situation between Dunkin' Donuts and Krispy Kreme is interesting. Dunkin' Donuts is not reporting carbohydrate difficulties, as Krispy Kreme has recently done. Instead, it is focusing on opening shops inside Wal-Mart stores. Management hopes to expand to 100 stores within the next couple of years or earlier. Dunkin' Donuts going into Wal-Mart stores could be a major boost for the corporation, which is part of the British spirits company Allied Domecq PLC. The strategy to set up shop inside Wal-Mart will help Dunkin' Donuts come closer to the goal of moving beyond its northeast United States location to promote its products in a national market. Wal-Mart also sells boxed Krispy Kreme donuts, placed in the main area of more than 500 of its stores. Some analysts believe that selling Krispy Kreme within other stores, such as in Wal-Mart, has been detrimental to the sales at Krispy Kreme stand-alone stores.

Both Krispy Kreme and Dunkin' Donuts have been seeking to expand, even though Krispy Kreme saw its stock value plunge in May 2004. Both companies are now trying to enter new markets. Krispy Kreme already has an agreement to test placement of its outlets inside two Wal-Mart stores. Dunkin' Donuts and Krispy Kreme would not clash, even if both happened to be located within the same Wal-Mart store, as they would be in separate locations.

Krispy Kreme had planned to open 120 retail stores in 2004, as part of its strategic plans. Opening new stores as quickly as possible has been crucial to Krispy Kreme's growth strategy. But given that its average weekly sales declined in fiscal year 2003 for the first time since the company went public, Krispy Kreme is presently closing a handful of company-owned stores and reducing plans to open new ones.

As Dunkin' Donuts' CEO stated, "competitors do create opportunities." Is it possible for Krispy Kreme to "reengineer" its donut into a form that consumers will still enjoy? Dunkin' Donuts, Starbucks, and Krispy Kreme all sell pastries and caffeinated beverages. Customers visit Krispy Kreme retail outlets occasionally and may buy donuts by the dozen to take home or to work. Starbucks and Dunkin' Donuts want customers to make their stores the consumers' morning, lunch, evening, and "in-between" eateries. Is there a market niche for each of these companies?

 To learn more about Krispy Kreme, log on to InfoTrac® College Edition at *http://infotrac. thomsonlearning.com* and use the advanced search function.

_____ 1. The planning dimension focus of the Krispy Kreme case is

    a. upper-level management, strategic, broad, long-range single use

    b. lower-level management, operational, narrow, short-range, standing plans

_____ 2. The strategic level focus of the Krispy Kreme case is

    a. corporate-level

    b. business-level

    c. functional-level

_____ 3. Krispy Kreme can benefit from conducting industry and company (SWOT) situational analysis.

    a. true

    b. false

_____ 4. Krispy Kreme's objective "to open 120 retail stores in 2004" is missing which part of the criteria for writing objectives?

    a. singular   d. target date

    b. specific   e. the objective meets

    c. measurable   all these criteria

_____ 5. In terms of Krispy Kreme's grand strategy, selling Montana Mills Bread Company to focus on donuts is known as a _____ strategy.

    a. growth   c. turnaround

    b. stability   d. retrenchment

_____ 6. The purchase and sale of Montana Mills Bread is known as

    a. merger   c. MBO

    b. acquisition   d. benchmarking

_____ 7. Krispy Kreme's strategy of opening more stand-alone stores is a _____ strategy.

    a. concentration

    b. forward integration

    c. backward integration

    d. related diversification

    e. unrelated diversification

_____ 8. Dunkin' Donuts' strategy of offering bagels, sandwiches, soup, and a variety of drinks is a _____ strategy.

    a. concentration

    b. forward integration

    c. backward integration

    d. related diversification

    e. unrelated diversification

_____ 9. Krispy Kreme can benefit from conducting a portfolio analysis.

    a. true

    b. false

_____ 10. Krispy Kreme's primary adaptive strategy of past years has been

    a. prospecting

    b. defending

    c. analyzing

11. Krispy Kreme's primary competitive strategy of past years has been

    a. differentiation
    b. cost leadership
    c. focus

_____ 12. Donuts are in the _____ stage of the product life cycle.

    a. introduction   c. maturity
    b. growth   d. decline

_____ 13. Growth through attracting more franchisees is primarily the _____ functional-level operational strategy responsibility.

    a. marketing   c. human resources
    b. operation   d. finance

_____ 14. Opening 120 new stores in 2004 is a _____ operational plan.

    a. single-use
    b. standing plan

_____ 15. The major function of the operations department is to develop _____ for franchises to follow.

    a. policies
    b. procedures
    c. rules

16. Explain Krispy Kreme's strategic and operational plans.

17. Why is Krispy Kreme facing the need to revamp its strategic plans?

18. Is Krispy Kreme's performance being affected by the low-carb diets that are currently popular? Explain.

Cumulative Case Questions

19. Which management function is the focus of this case? (Chapter 1)

20. To which environmental factor does Krispy Kreme attribute its problems, and to which environmental factor do analysts attribute the problems? (Chapter 2)

21. Follow the six steps in the decision-making model to determine what Krispy Kreme should do in the future. (Chapter 4)

Skill Builder 1

WRITING OBJECTIVES

For this exercise, you will first work at improving ineffective objectives. Then you will write nine objectives for yourself.

Part 1

Indicate which of the "must" criteria each of the following objectives fails to meet and rewrite the objective so that it meets all those criteria. When writing objectives, use the following model:

to + action verb + single, specific, and measurable result + target date

1. To improve our company image by the end of 2006.

    Criteria not met: _____

    Improved objective: _____

2. To increase the number of customers by 10 percent.

    Criteria not met: _____

    Improved objective: _____

3. To increase profits during 2006.

    Criteria not met: _____

    Improved objective: _____

4. To sell 5 percent more hot dogs and soda at the baseball game on Sunday, June 13, 2006.

    Criteria not met: _____

    Improved objective: _____

Part 2

Write three educational, three personal, and three career objectives you want to accomplish. Your objectives can be short-term (something you want to accomplish today) or long-term (something you want to have accomplished 20 years from now) or in between those extremes. Be sure your objectives meet the criteria for effective objectives.

Educational Objectives

1. _____

    _____

    _____

2. _____

    _____

    _____

3. _____
   _____
   _____

Personal Objectives

1. _____
   _____
   _____

2. _____
   _____
   _____

3. _____
   _____
   _____

Career Objectives

1. _____
   _____
   _____

2. _____
   _____
   _____

3. _____
   _____
   _____

Apply It

What did I learn from this experience? How will I use this knowledge in the future?

_____
_____

Your instructor may ask you to do this Skill Builder in class in a group. If so, the instructor will provide you with any necessary information or additional instructions.

Skill **Builder** 2
ENTREPRENEURIAL STRATEGIC PLANNING

This exercise is an extension of Skill Builder 1 in Chapter 3; if you have not completed that Skill Builder, do so now. You are now going to develop a strategic plan for your new venture by completing the strategic planning steps that follow.

Step 1. Developing a Mission

Write a mission statement for your new venture.

_____
_____

Step 2. Analyzing the Environment

A. Develop a five-force competitive analysis, like that in Exhibit 5-4 (page 54).
B. Complete a company situation analysis.

1. SWOT analysis.

Strengths	*Weaknesses*
_____	_____
_____	_____
_____	_____

Opportunities	*Threats*
_____	_____
_____	_____
_____	_____

2. Determine your company's competitive advantage (if any). You may wish to do a competitive strength assessment.

_____
_____
_____

3. What conclusions did you come to concerning competitive position?

_____
_____
_____

4. Determine the issues and problems that need to be addressed through the strategic planning process.

_____
_____
_____

Step 3. Setting Objectives

List three objectives for your new venture.

_____
_____

Step 4. Developing Strategies

Being in a single line of business, you do not need to develop a grand strategy or conduct a portfolio analysis. However, you should have an adaptive and competitive strategy based on the product life cycle.

Stage of the product life cycle: _____

Adaptive and competitive strategies (explain each briefly):

_____

_____

Step 5. Implementing and Controlling Strategies

List a few major controls you will use after implementing each strategy.

_____

_____

Apply It

What did I learn from this experience? How will I use this knowledge in the future?

_____

_____

Your instructor may ask you to do this Skill Builder in class in a group. If so, the instructor will provide you with any necessary information or additional instructions.

APPENDIX B
Time Management

Learning Outcomes

After studying this appendix, you should be able to:

1. Explain the use of a time log. PAGE 185

2. List and briefly describe the three steps in the time management system. PAGE 187

3. Define the following **key terms:**

time management
time management system

Time management is an important aspect of any company's competitive advantage.[1] Fast delivery of products and services creates customer value.[2] Companies such as Motorola, Cadillac, and Texas Instruments now focus on time, whereas FedEx, Domino's, and Jiffy Lube based their business on time-based competition from the start. Companies have discovered that poor productivity and inadequate customer service are related to poor time management. Time management skills will have a direct effect on your productivity and career success.[3]

Time management *refers to techniques that enable people to get more done in less time with better results.* Time is one of a manager's most valuable resources. However, many managers do not use their time effectively because they have never been taught the importance of prioritizing activities and using a time management system. Some companies do offer training in time management. Unfortunately, many managers don't actually put the time management skills they learn into practice on the job on a regular basis—but you can.

───────────── Learning Outcome 1 ─────────────
Explain the use of a time log.

ANALYZING TIME USE

The first step to successful time management requires determining how your time is spent and how much is wasted. People often do not realize how they waste their time until they analyze time use. An analysis of how you use your time will indicate areas for improvement. You need to break habits that waste time.[4]

The Time Log

A *time log* is a daily diary that tracks your activities and enables you to determine how you spend your time each day. Exhibit A gives an example you can use as a template to develop your own time logs. You should keep track of your time every day over a period of one or two typical weeks. Try to keep the time log with you throughout the day. Fill in the Description column for each 15-minute time slot, if possible, describing what you did.

Analyzing Time Logs

After keeping time logs for five to ten working days, analyze the information. Write notes in the evaluation column of the log, using the following abbreviations:

- Determine how much time you are spending on your high-priority (HP) and low-priority (LP) responsibilities. How do you spend most of your time?
- Identify areas where you spend too much time (TT).
- Identify areas where you do not spend enough time (NT).
- Identify major interruptions (I) that keep you from doing what you want to get done. How can you eliminate them?[5]
- Identify tasks you are performing that you could delegate to someone else (D). To whom can you delegate these tasks?

Exhibit A *Daily Time Log*

Daily Time Log for: Day _____		Date _____
Starting Time	Description	Evaluation of Time Use
8:00 8:15 8:30 8:45		
9:00 9:15 9:30 9:45		
10:00 (etc., to ending time)		

- How much time does your boss control (B)? How much time do your employees control (E)? How much time do others outside your department control (O)? How much time do you actually control (M)? How can you gain control of more of your time?
- Look for crisis situations (C). Were they caused by something you did or did not do? Do you experience recurring crises? How can you plan to help eliminate recurring crises?[6] Do you have effective contingency plans?
- Look for habits, patterns, and tendencies. Do they help or prevent you from getting the job done? How can you change them to your advantage?

WorkApplication1
Review your time log to identify your three biggest time wasters. How can you cut down or eliminate these time wasters?

———— Learning Outcome 2 ————
List and briefly describe the three steps in the time management system.

A TIME MANAGEMENT SYSTEM

Time management remains one of the most daunting challenges confronting many people.[7] The time management system you will read about in this section has a proven record of success and is used by thousands of managers. Try it for three weeks; after that, you can adjust it to meet your own needs.

The problem we face is not a shortage of time, but ineffective use of our time.[8] Could you use an extra two hours every day? Experts say that people waste at least this much time every day. The average manager could improve time use by 20 percent.

There are four key components of the time management system:

- *Priorities*. Seldom, if ever, do we have enough time to do everything we want to do. However, there is always time to do what is really important. Setting priorities involves determining which of your major responsibilities is most important.
- *Objectives*. You should set weekly objectives, following the guidelines described in Chapter 4.
- *Plans*. You should develop operational plans to meet your objectives.
- *Schedules*. You should schedule each week and workday.[9]

Time management systems all boil down to developing a plan and sticking to it as much as possible. *The* **time management system** *involves planning each week, scheduling each week, and scheduling each day.*

Step 1. Plan each week. On the last day of each week, plan the upcoming week. (You can develop your plan on the first day of the week if you prefer.) Using your previous week's plan and departmental objectives, fill in a plan for the upcoming week on a weekly planner sheet; you can use Exhibit B as template. Start by listing the objectives you want to accomplish during the week. These should be nonroutine things, not routine tasks you perform weekly or daily.[10] For example, if an employee's annual performance review is coming up, set conducting it as one of your objectives.

After setting a few major objectives, list major activities necessary to accomplish each objective.[11] Indicate the priority level of each activity: high, medium, or low. All high-priority activities must be done that week; others can be pushed into the next week if necessary. For example, suppose that for the employee's annual review, you need to complete the appraisal

Exhibit B *Weekly Planner*

Plan for the week of: _____			
Objectives:			
Activities	Priority	Time Needed	Day to Schedule
Total time for the week			

form, make an appointment with the employee, and conduct the performance review. Of these, completing the performance appraisal form is a high (H) priority.

The last two columns to fill in are "Time Needed" and "Day to Schedule." Suppose it will take you 20 minutes to prepare for the performance appraisal and about 30 minutes to complete it. The best day to schedule it might be your relatively quiet day. Total the time it will take to achieve your objectives for the week. Is the total time realistic, considering you still need time for routine tasks and unexpected events? With experience, you will learn whether you tend to be too optimistic about how much you can plan for and accomplish in one week. Planning too much is frustrating and causes stress when you cannot get everything done. On the other day, if you do not plan enough activities, you will end up wasting time.

Step 2. Schedule each week. Scheduling your work gets you organized to achieve your objectives for the week.[12] You may make a schedule for the week while you plan it or afterward, whichever you prefer. Planning and scheduling the week should take about 30 minutes. Exhibit C shows a template for a weekly schedule. Start scheduling by filling in already committed time slots, such as regular weekly meetings. Then schedule controllable events like performance appraisals. Most managers should leave about 50 percent of the week unscheduled to accommodate unexpected events. Your job may require more or less unscheduled time. With practice, you will perfect weekly planning and scheduling.

Step 3. Schedule each day. At the end of each day, you should schedule the following day. (Or, you can schedule your day first thing each morning.) This should take 15 minutes or less. Base the day's schedule on your plan and schedule for the week, using the template in Exhibit D. Basing your daily schedule on the weekly schedule you've already created allows for adjustment for unplanned events. Begin by scheduling the activities over which

Exhibit C *Weekly Schedule*

Schedule for the week of: _____					
Time	Mon.	Tues.	Wed.	Th.	Fri.
8:00 8:15 8:30 8:45					
9:00 (etc., to ending time)					

you have no control, such as meetings you must attend. Leave your daily schedule flexible. Here are some scheduling tips:

- Don't be too optimistic; schedule enough time to do each task. Many managers find it useful to estimate the time they think something will take, and then double it. With practice, you should get better at estimating time for certain tasks.[13]
- Once you have prioritized and scheduled tasks, focus on only one at a time.[14] There are people who seem able to accomplish an incredible number of things each day. However, their impressive productivity is based mainly on doing one thing at a time.
- Schedule high-priority items during your "prime time," when you perform at your best. For most people, this is early in the morning. However, some people are slow starters and perform better later in the day. Determine your

Exhibit D *Daily Schedule*

Schedule for the day of: _____
Time
8:00 8:15 8:30 8:45
9:00 (etc., to ending time)

prime time and schedule the tasks that need your full attention during that time. Do routine things, such as checking your mail, at other times.

- Try to set aside a regular time-slot for activities or events that you cannot anticipate. For example, employees occasionally have issues or concerns they want to discuss. You may decide to set aside a half-hour at the same time each afternoon for such events. You can have people call you at this time as well.

- Do not perform an unscheduled task before determining its priority. If you are working on a high-priority item and you find yourself facing a medium-priority task, let it wait. Even the so-called urgent matters can often wait.

The time management system described here works well for managers who have to plan for a variety of nonrecurring tasks. For managers and employees who deal primarily with routine tasks, the time management system may not be necessary. For people in routine situations, a "to-do" list that prioritizes items may work quite well. The Skill Builder gives you the opportunity to assess your time management skills by using the time management system. Forms similar to those in Exhibits B through D can be purchased in any number of formats, including in electronic form. Or you can make your own forms.

TIME MANAGEMENT TECHNIQUES

The Self-Assessment contains 49 time management techniques arranged by management function. Planning and controlling are placed together because they are so closely related. Organizing and leading are separated.

After you have completed the Self-Assessment, implement the items you checked as "should do." Once you are using all the "should do" items, work on your "could do" items. After implementing all the "should do" and "could do" items, reread the "does not apply" column to see if any of the items apply now. In this manner, you can continually improve your time management skills.

WorkApplication2

From the time management techniques listed in the Self-Assessment, choose the three most important ones you "should" be using. Explain how you will implement each technique.

_____

_____

_____

_____

_____

Self-Assessment

Time Management Techniques

Following is a list of 49 ideas that can be used to improve your time management skills. Place a checkmark in the appropriate box for each item.

Planning and Controlling Management Functions	Should Do	Could Do	Already Doing	Does Not Apply To Me
1. Use a time management system.	☐	☐	☐	☐
2. Use a to-do list and prioritize the items on it. Do the important things rather than the seemingly urgent things.	☐	☐	☐	☐
3. Get an early start on top-priority items.	☐	☐	☐	☐
4. Do only high priority items during your best working hours (prime time); schedule unpleasant or difficult tasks during prime time.	☐	☐	☐	☐

Time Management Techniques   (*Continued*)

5. Don't spend time performing unproductive activities to avoid or escape job-related anxiety. It doesn't really work; get the job done.	☐	☐	☐	☐
6. Throughout the day ask yourself, "Should I be doing this now?"	☐	☐	☐	☐
7. Plan before you act.	☐	☐	☐	☐
8. Plan for recurring crises to eliminate crises (contingency planning).	☐	☐	☐	☐
9. Make decisions. It is better to make a wrong decision than to make none at all.	☐	☐	☐	☐
10. Schedule enough time to do the job right the first time. Don't be too optimistic about the amount of time it takes to do a job.	☐	☐	☐	☐
11. Schedule a quiet hour to be interrupted only by true emergencies. Have someone take messages or ask people who call then to call you back.	☐	☐	☐	☐
12. Establish a quiet time for the entire organization or department. The first hour of the day is usually the best time.	☐	☐	☐	☐
13. Schedule large blocks of uninterrupted (emergencies-only) time for projects and so forth. If this doesn't work, hide somewhere.	☐	☐	☐	☐
14. Break large (long) projects into parts (time periods).	☐	☐	☐	☐
15. Before abandoning a scheduled item to do something unscheduled, ask yourself, "Is the unscheduled event more important than the scheduled event?" If not, stay on schedule.	☐	☐	☐	☐
16. Do related activities (for example, making and returning calls, writing letters and memos) in the same time slot.	☐	☐	☐	☐

Organizing Management Function

17. Schedule time for unanticipated events and let people know the time. Ask people to see or call you only during this time, unless it's an emergency. Answer mail and do routine things while waiting for people to contact you. If people ask to see you—"Got a minute?"—ask whether it can wait until your scheduled time.	☐	☐	☐	☐
18. Set a scheduled time, agenda, and time limit for all visitors, and keep on topic.	☐	☐	☐	☐
19. Keep a clean, well-organized work area/desk.	☐	☐	☐	☐
20. Remove all non–work-related or distracting objects from your work area/desk.	☐	☐	☐	☐
21. Do one task at a time.	☐	☐	☐	☐
22. When paperwork requires a decision, make it at once; don't read through the paperwork again later and decide.	☐	☐	☐	☐
23. Keep files well arranged and labeled with an active and inactive file section. When you file an item, put a throwaway date on it.	☐	☐	☐	☐
24. Call rather than write or visit, when appropriate.	☐	☐	☐	☐
25. Delegate someone else to write letters, memos, and so forth.	☐	☐	☐	☐
26. Use form letters and form paragraphs in a word processor.	☐	☐	☐	☐
27. Answer letters (memos) on the letter itself.	☐	☐	☐	☐
28. Have someone read and summarize things for you.	☐	☐	☐	☐
29. Divide reading requirements with others and share summaries.	☐	☐	☐	☐
30. Have calls screened to be sure the right person handles each call.	☐	☐	☐	☐

(*Continued*)

Time Management Techniques   (Continued)

31. Plan before calling. Have an agenda and all necessary information ready; take notes on the agenda. ☐ ☐ ☐ ☐

32. Ask people to call you back during your scheduled unexpected time. Ask about the best time to call them. ☐ ☐ ☐ ☐

33. Have a specific objective or purpose for every meeting you conduct. If you cannot think of an objective, don't have the meeting. ☐ ☐ ☐ ☐

34. Invite to meetings only the necessary participants and keep them only as long as needed. ☐ ☐ ☐ ☐

35. Always have an agenda for a meeting and stick to it. Start and end as scheduled. ☐ ☐ ☐ ☐

36. Set objectives for travel. List everyone you will meet with. Call or send them agendas, and have a file folder for each with all necessary data for your meeting. ☐ ☐ ☐ ☐

37. Combine and modify activities to save time. ☐ ☐ ☐ ☐

Leading Management Function

38. Set clear objectives for subordinates and make sure they know what they are accountable for; give them feedback and evaluate results often. ☐ ☐ ☐ ☐

39. Don't waste others' time. Don't make subordinates wait idly for decisions, instructions, or materials, at meetings, and so on. Conversely, wait for a convenient time to speak to subordinates or others, rather than interrupting them and wasting their time. ☐ ☐ ☐ ☐

40. Train your subordinates. Don't do their work for them. ☐ ☐ ☐ ☐

41. Delegate activities in which you do not need to be personally involved, especially non-management functions. ☐ ☐ ☐ ☐

42. Set deadlines earlier than the actual deadline. ☐ ☐ ☐ ☐

43. Use the input of your staff. Don't reinvent the wheel. ☐ ☐ ☐ ☐

44. Teach time management skills to your subordinates. ☐ ☐ ☐ ☐

45. Don't procrastinate; do it. ☐ ☐ ☐ ☐

46. Don't be a perfectionist—define "acceptable" and stop there. ☐ ☐ ☐ ☐

47. Learn to stay calm. Getting emotional only causes more problems. ☐ ☐ ☐ ☐

48. Reduce socializing, but don't become antisocial. ☐ ☐ ☐ ☐

49. Communicate well. Don't confuse employees. ☐ ☐ ☐ ☐

Appendix Summary

1. Explain the use of a time log.
A time log is a daily diary used to analyze how time is spent and wasted. Time log analysis can reveal ways to improve time use.

2. List and briefly describe the three steps in the time management system.
The steps in the time management system are (1) Plan each week by determining the objectives to be achieved that week and activities necessary to achieve the objectives. (2) Schedule each week by selecting days and times to perform the activities necessary to achieve the week's objectives. (3) Schedule each day by selecting the times to perform the activities to achieve the week's objectives. Going from a weekly to a daily schedule allows for adjustment for unplanned events.

3. Complete each of the following statements using one of this appendix's key terms.

_____ refers to techniques that enable people to get more done in less time with better results.

The _____ involves planning each week, scheduling each week, and scheduling each day.

Key **Terms**

time management, 185

time management system, 187

Skill Builder

TIME MANAGEMENT

For this exercise you will need to make copies of Exhibits B through D to serve as templates. Before using the time management system, it is helpful, but not necessary, to keep a time log (Exhibit A) for one or two typical weeks to determine areas where you might improve your time management.

Step 1. Planning Your Week
Using Exhibit B, develop a plan for the rest of this week. Begin with today.

Step 2. Scheduling Your Week
Using Exhibit C, schedule the rest of this week. Be sure to schedule a 30-minute period to plan and schedule next week, preferably on the last day of this week.

Step 3. Scheduling Your Day
Using Exhibit D, schedule each day. Be sure to bring your plans and schedules to class.

Apply It
What did I learn from this experience? How will I use this knowledge in the future?

_____

_____

Your instructor may ask you to do this Skill Builder in class in a group. If so, the instructor will provide you with any necessary information or additional instructions.

Learning Outcomes
After studying this chapter, you should be able to:

1. Explain the difference between a flat organization and a tall organization. **PAGE 197**

2. Describe the similarities and differences among liaisons, integrators, and people in boundary roles. **PAGE 197**

3. Discuss the difference between formal and informal authority and centralized and decentralized authority. **PAGE 200**

4. List and briefly explain the four levels of authority. **PAGE 200**

5. Describe the relationship between line authority and staff authority. **PAGE 201**

6. Explain what an organization chart is and list the four aspects of a firm that it shows. **PAGE 204**

6: Organizing and Delegating Work

7. Discuss the difference between internal and external departmentalization. **PAGE 205**

8. State the similarities and differences between matrix and divisional departmentalization. **PAGE 207**

9. Explain the difference between job simplification and job expansion. **PAGE 210**

10. Describe the job characteristics model. **PAGE 212**

11. Explain how to set priorities by answering three priority questions and determining whether activities have high, medium, or low priority. **PAGE 215**

12. List the four steps in the delegation process. **PAGE 218**

13. Define the following **key terms:**

span of management	organization chart
responsibility	departmentalization
authority	divisional structure
delegation	job design
levels of authority	job enrichment
line authority	job characteristics model
staff authority	priority-determination questions
centralized authority	
decentralized authority	

Ideas on Management

at Post & Schell

Post & Schell began life as a two-person law firm in Philadelphia in 1968. With success came more clients, and over time, the partnership hired additional attorneys, paralegals, and clerical staff and expanded its services to meet aggressive growth targets. The firm's cases are grouped into five practice areas: business law, casualty law, contract law, workers' compensation cases, and professional liability cases.

Today the Post & Schell law firm employs 160 lawyers based in offices in Philadelphia, Pittsburgh, Harrisburg, Lancaster, and Allentown, Pennsylvania, and Princeton, New Jersey. Specializing in high-end litigation and consulting, Post & Schell provides litigation, transaction, compliance, consulting, and educational services to a broad spectrum of industries.

Until recently, a five-member management committee oversaw all strategic and administrative decisions at Post & Schell. Each committee member was a senior partner who was responsible for the day-to-day operations of one of the individual practice areas as well as for managing the ongoing needs of clients. Although Post & Schell used this structure for a number of years, it was far from ideal. With each senior partner free to set standards, there was little uniformity in how administrative functions were handled. As a result, different divisions charged clients different fees, costly purchasing overlaps were common, and there were few companywide standards for measuring and rewarding employee performance. In addition, decisions affecting the entire firm required

© Grantpix/Index Stock Imagery

the consensus of the entire management committee, whose rather slow and ponderous deliberations often led to potentially costly delays. The Post & Schell management committee eventually realized that the firm needed to reorganize to become more efficient if it were to continue to expand.

I O M

1. **What key organizational principles guided Post & Schell in its reorganization?**
2. **How has authority changed at Post & Schell?**
3. **What organizational design did Post & Schell adopt?**
4. **What type of job design does Post & Schell use?**
5. **What prioritization and delegating issues does Post & Schell face?**

You'll find answers to these questions about management practices at Post & Schell throughout the chapter, which will help you understand what it takes to succeed in managing a professional services firm, such as a law office.

To learn more about Post & Schell, visit the company's Web site at *http://www.postschell.com* or log on to InfoTrac® College Edition at *http://infotrac.thomsonlearning.com*, where you can read more about Post & Schell and other law firms that have adopted new organizational structures. Use the advanced search option to key in record numbers A70203418, A112542038, and A98645245 and discover why management by committee ceased to be effective at Post & Schell.

Sources: Information for the case was taken from the Post & Schell Web site at *http://www.postschell.com*, accessed June 28, 2004.

PRINCIPLES OF ORGANIZATION

Organizing, the second function of management, is defined as the process of delegating and coordinating tasks and resources to achieve objectives. The four resources managers organize are human, physical, financial, and information. Within an organization, organizing involves grouping activities and resources.[1]

As discussed in the last chapter, firms develop strategic plans that must be implemented somehow. In this chapter, we focus on organizing to implement strategies, as structure follows strategy.[2] Ineffective organization is costly; therefore, resources and activities need to be organized to yield the greatest value for the enterprise.[3] New technology and information are also affecting how firms organize.[4] To stay successful in a changing environment, many companies need to reorganize.[5] Consider these examples of reorganizations:

- *HP* reorganized the way it sells computers and services to corporate customers by merging its consulting and hardware units so that they could work together to better coordinate sales and service.[6]
- When *GE* hit a period of little or no growth, it decided to reorganize to bring similar lines of business together, resulting in fewer but larger business units.[7]

There are at least six questions that managers need to answer when organizing. The questions are listed in Exhibit 6-1. The answers are discussed in more detail in the indicated sections of this chapter.

As a manager, you must organize your departmental resources to achieve objectives.[8] Exhibit 6-2 lists the organizational principles we discuss in this section.

Unity of Command and Direction

The principle of *unity of command* requires that each employee report to only one boss. The principle of *unity of direction* requires that all activities be directed toward the same objectives. Although Post & Schell's existing structure provided unity of command, there was no unity of direction. Senior partners set standards for their division as they saw fit, resulting in differences in the way strategies were implemented and tasks were accomplished throughout the organization.

WorkApplication1

Follow the chain of command from your present position (or one you held in the past) to the top of the organization. Start by identifying anyone who reported to you, then list your boss's title, your boss's boss's title, and on up to the top manager's title.

Exhibit 6-1 *Organizing Questions*

Questions for Managers	Chapter Topic
Who should departments and individuals report to?	Chain of command; organization chart
How many individuals should report to each manager?	Span of management
How should we subdivide the work?	Division of labor; departmentalization
How do we get everyone to work together as a system?	Coordination
At what level should decisions be made?	Centralization vs. decentralization of authority
How do we organize to meet our mission and strategy?	Departmentalization

Exhibit 6-2 *Principles of Organization*

- Unity of command and direction
- Chain of command
- Span of management (flat and tall organizations)
- Division of labor (specialization, departmentalization, integration)
- Coordination
- Balanced responsibility and authority
- Delegation
- Flexibility

Chain of Command

Chain of command, also known as the Scalar Principle, is the clear line of authority from the top to the bottom of an organization. All members of the firm should know to whom they report and who, if anyone, reports to them. The chain of command forms a hierarchy, which is illustrated in the organization chart.

—————————— Learning Outcome 1 ——————————
Explain the difference between a flat organization and a tall organization.

Span of Management

The **span of management** *(or span of control) refers to the number of employees reporting to a manager*. The fewer employees supervised, the smaller or narrower the span of management. The more employees supervised, the greater or wider the span. There is no best number of employees to manage, but the average number of employees reporting to a manager is eleven.[9]

The span of management in an organization is related to the number of its organizational levels, which determines its organizational height. In a *tall organization*, there are many levels with narrow spans of management. In a *flat organization*, which tends to result after downsizing, there are few levels with wide spans of management.[10] In recent years, many organizations have cut management levels and have restructured so as to have flatter management hierarchies.[11]

Division of Labor

With *division of labor*, employees have specialized jobs. Related functions are grouped together under a single boss. Employees generally have specialized jobs in a functional area such as accounting, production, or sales.

Paul Lawrence and Jay Lorsch coined the terms *differentiation* and *integration*.[12] Differentiation refers to the need to break the organization into departments, and integration refers to the need to coordinate the departmental activities.[13]

—————————— Learning Outcome 2 ——————————
Describe the similarities and differences among liaisons, integrators, and people in boundary roles.

Coordination

Coordination ensures that all departments and individuals within an organization work together to accomplish strategic and operational objectives. Coordination is

WorkApplication2

Identify your boss's span of management, or your own if you are or were a manager. How many levels of management are there in your organization? Is it a flat or a tall organization?

_____

_____

_____

_____

_____

the process of integrating tasks and resources to meet objectives.[14] It is important that organization resources be coordinated through cooperative relationships.[15]

All of the organizational principles discussed above are used as coordination techniques. In addition, there are other means of coordination:

- Through *direct contact* between people within and among departments
- Through *liaisons*, who work in one department and coordinate information and activities with one or more other departments
- Through *committees* made up of people from different departments
- Through *integrators*, such as product or project managers, who do not work for any department but coordinate departmental activities to reach an objective[16]
- Through employees in *boundary roles*, including employees in sales, customer service, purchasing, and public relations, who coordinate efforts with people in the external environment[17]

Balanced Responsibility and Authority

With balanced responsibility and authority, the responsibilities of each individual in the organization are clearly defined. Each individual is also given the authority necessary to meet these responsibilities and is held accountable for meeting them. When you delegate, you do not give responsibility and authority away; you share them.

Responsibility *is the obligation to achieve objectives by performing required activities.* When strategic and operational objectives are set, the people responsible

---

Applying The Concept 1

Principles of Organization

Identify which organizational principle(s) is (are) represented by each statement.

a. unity of command and direction
b. chain of command
c. span of management
d. division of labor
e. coordination
f. balanced responsibility and authority
g. delegation
h. flexibility

_____1. "Karl told me to pick up the mail. When I got to the post office, I did not have a key to the box, so the postal worker wouldn't give me the mail."

_____2. Players on a football team are on either the offensive or the defensive squad.

_____3. "My job is frustrating at times because I work in a matrix structure. Sometimes my department manager tells me to do one thing but my project manager tells me to do something else at the same time."

_____4. Middle manager: "I want an employee to deliver this package but I can't give anyone a direct order to do it. I have to have one of my supervisors give the order."

_____5. "There has been an accident, and the ambulance is on the way. Juan, call Doctor Rodriguez and have her get to emergency room C in 10 minutes. Pat, get the paperwork ready. Karen, prepare emergency room C."

for achieving them should be clearly identified. Managers are responsible for the performance of their units.

Authority is the right to make decisions, issue orders, and use resources. As a manager, you will be given responsibility for achieving unit objectives. You must also have the authority to get the job done. Authority is delegated. The CEO is responsible for the results of the entire organization and delegates authority down the chain of command to the lower-level managers, who are responsible for meeting operational objectives.

Accountability is the evaluation of how well individuals meet their responsibilities. All members of an organization should be evaluated periodically and held accountable for achieving their objectives.[18]

Managers are accountable for everything that happens in their departments. As a manager, you delegate responsibility and authority to perform tasks, but you should realize that you can never delegate your accountability.

Delegation

Delegation *is the process of assigning responsibility and authority for accomplishing objectives.* Responsibility and authority are delegated down the chain of command.[19] Delegation is an important skill for managers that will be covered in detail later in this chapter.[20]

Flexibility

Flexibility in employees is vital, because there will always be exceptions to the rule.[21] Many employees focus on company rules rather than on creating customer satisfaction; they fear getting into trouble for breaking or bending the rules.[22] Today's successful organizations realize that flexibility is important to customer satisfaction.[23] For example, suppose a rule is "No sales slip with

WorkApplication3

Does an organization you work for or have worked for emphasize following the standing procedures or being flexible? Explain your answer.

Join the Discussion — Ethics & Social Responsibility

Breaking the Rules

1. Is it unethical to be flexible and break the law against kickbacks?
2. Why are kickbacks illegal? Who benefits from kickbacks, who gets hurt by them, and how?
3. What would you do in this situation? (Would you start giving kickbacks yourself? Blow the whistle on sales reps to their managers? Blow the whistle to an outside source like the government or the media? Do nothing?)

Suppose you are a sales rep for a major pharmaceutical company. You get paid by commission, so the more drugs you sell to doctors, the more money you make. You know that sales reps in your company have been visiting doctors and telling them that if they prescribe your company's medication, they will receive 5 percent of the sales revenues. This arrangement can bring in thousands of dollars each year for both the sales reps and the doctors. You know the names of a few sales reps who are allegedly giving these kickbacks, but you are not sure how many sales reps are involved. You also don't know if sales managers know about the kickbacks or are receiving payments from the reps.

returned merchandise, no cash refund." This rule helps to protect the store from people who steal merchandise and then return it for cash. What happens when a well-known, excellent customer comes into the store and demands a cash refund without a sales slip? In analyzing the situation, the employee realizes that the store could lose a good customer. Should the employee follow the rules and lose a good customer, or be flexible and keep the good customer?

IOM

Unity of direction was a problem as Post & Schell expanded. Senior partners set standards for their own divisions as they saw fit, resulting in differences in the way strategies were implemented and tasks were performed throughout the law firm. Thus, all five divisions "did their own thing." Not only was there too much flexibility and a need for better coordination, but the division of labor lacked differentiation and integration. The division of labor into five groups by types of legal practice was fine, but there was no division of labor with regard to the partners' jobs. This created a problem because each of the five partners was managing a practice division, serving on the management committee, and running a practice dealing with clients every day.

Learning Outcome 3

Discuss the difference between formal and informal authority
and centralized and decentralized authority.

AUTHORITY

In this section, you will learn about formal and informal authority, levels of authority, line and staff authority, and centralized and decentralized authority.

Formal and Informal Authority

FORMAL AUTHORITY

Formal authority (or structure) is based on the specified relationships among employees. It is the sanctioned way of getting the job done. The organization chart illustrates formal authority and shows the lines of authority.[24]

INFORMAL AUTHORITY

Informal authority (or structure) arises from the patterns of relationships and communication that evolve as employees interact and communicate. It is the unsanctioned way of getting the job done.

SCOPE OF AUTHORITY

The *scope of authority* is a hierarchy that narrows as it flows down the organization.[25] The president has more authority than a vice president, who has more authority than a manager. Responsibility and authority are delegated and flow down the organization, whereas accountability flows up the organization, as Exhibit 6-3 illustrates.

Exhibit 6-3
Scope of Authority

Learning Outcome 4

List and briefly explain the four levels of authority.

Levels of Authority

In any work situation, you should be aware of your formal authority. Levels of authority can vary from task to task.

The **levels of authority** *are the authority to inform, the authority to recommend, the authority to report, and full authority.*

1. *The authority to inform.* You inform your supervisor of possible alternative actions. The supervisor has the authority to make the decision.
2. *The authority to recommend.* You list alternative decisions/actions, analyze them, and recommend one action. However, you may not implement the recommendation without the boss's okay. The boss may require a different alternative if he or she does not agree with the recommendation. Committees are often given authority to recommend.
3. *The authority to report.* You may freely select a course of action and carry it out. However, afterward you must report the action taken to the boss. Nurses have the authority to alter medical records when the situation calls for it; however, they are obligated to inform the doctor who wrote the original entry of the alteration.
4. *Full authority.* You may freely make decisions and act without the boss's knowledge. However, even people with full authority may consult their bosses for advice.

To illustrate: Suppose a new machine is needed in a certain company's manufacturing department. If Tania, the department manager, has no authority at all, it is up to someone else to choose and purchase the machine. If Tania has the authority to inform, she can give her supervisor a list of suitable machines and descriptions of their features, prices, and so forth. If Tania has authority to recommend, she can analyze the machines' features and suggest which one to purchase. If Tania has the authority to report, she can actually purchase the machine, but must tell her boss about the purchase, possibly by sending him or her a copy of the purchase order. With full authority, Tania can purchase the machine without telling her boss about it.

WorkApplication4

Identify and explain your level of authority for a specific task in an organization.

_____

_____

_____

_____

Learning Outcome 5

Describe the relationship between line authority
and staff authority.

Line and Staff Authority

Line authority *is the responsibility to make decisions and issue orders down the chain of command.* Line managers are primarily responsible for achieving the organization's objectives, and staff people provide them with services that help them do that. Since the reorganization, the senior partners at Post & Schell have line authority for achieving the law firm's strategic objectives in its five practice areas.

Staff authority *is the responsibility to advise and assist other personnel.* Operations and marketing are usually line departments (as is finance, in some organizations). Human resources management, public relations, and data processing are almost always staff departments. The line departments are internal "customers" of the staff departments. The reorganization at Post & Schell clearly established staff authority for administrative operations such as hiring, financial reporting, and information technology. These are now handled by departments whose managers report directly to the CEO.

FUNCTIONAL AUTHORITY

A staff department's primary role is to advise and assist, but there are certain situations in which staff personnel can give orders to line personnel. *Functional authority* is the right of staff personnel to issue orders to line personnel in established areas of responsibility.[26] For example, the maintenance department assists production by keeping machines operating. If maintenance employees determine that a machine is unsafe, the maintenance department manager may issue an order to a line manager not to use the machine.

DUAL LINE AND STAFF AUTHORITY

Staff managers may have both staff and line authority. For example, Ted, a public relations (staff) manager, advises and assists all departments in the organization. However, Ted also has line authority within his own department and issues orders (a line function) to the employees in that department.

GENERAL AND SPECIALIST STAFF

General staff work for only one manager and help the manager in any way needed. *Specialist staff* help anyone in the organization who needs it. Human resources, finance, accounting, public relations, and maintenance offer specialized advice and assistance. Line managers and division managers use the services of staff departments such as printing, finance, and human resources.

Centralized and Decentralized Authority

The major distinction between centralized and decentralized authority lies in who makes the important decisions.[27] With **centralized authority**, *important decisions are made by top managers.* With **decentralized authority**, *important decisions are made by middle and first-line managers.*

The major advantages of centralization are control and reduced duplication of work. The major advantages of decentralization are efficiency and flexibility. Which type of authority works best? There is no simple answer. **Sears**, **General Electric**, and **General Motors** have successfully used decentralized authority, and **General Dynamics** and **McDonald's** have successfully used centralized authority.

Authority is a continuum, with centralized authority at one end and decentralized authority at the other. With the exception of very small companies, which tend to be centralized, most organizations lie somewhere between the two extremes, but can be classified overall. The key to success seems to be having the right balance between the two extremes.[28] One of the key reasons CEO Steve Ballmer reorganized **Microsoft** into seven business units was to decentralize authority.[29] Exhibit 6-4 reviews types and levels of authority.

Many organizations find that there is a need to change or adapt their authority structure over time. As you saw in the opening case, Post & Schell originally had

WorkApplication5

Identify one or more line and staff positions in an organization you work for or have worked for. Also, indicate whether the staff positions are general staff or specialist staff.

_____

_____

_____

_____

_____

WorkApplication6

Describe the type of authority (centralized or decentralized) used in an organization you work for or have worked for.

_____

_____

_____

_____

_____

Exhibit 6-4 *Authority*

Authority			
Formal (sanctioned) Informal (unsanctioned)	Line (issue orders) Staff (assist line)	Inform (present alternatives) Recommend (present alternatives and suggest one) Report (do and tell) Full (do and don't tell)	Centralized (top managers) Decentralized (middle and first-line managers)

a highly centralized authority structure in which the two founding partners managed day-to-day operations and made key decisions. As the firm grew and expanded into new practice areas, however, it became too time-consuming and difficult for the two original partners to make all of the decisions. Therefore, the firm developed a more decentralized authority structure, whereby senior partners assumed individual authority over independent practice areas and overall corporate strategy was made by consensus. While this structure worked to a point, it hindered Post & Schell's ability to branch out into new practice areas and devise and implement clear overall strategy.

To address this structural problem, the management committee at Post & Schell appointed partner Brian Peters as CEO. The CEO has the final say on many decisions, thus establishing a more centralized form of authority. The CEO hired a chief operations officer and created the specialist staff positions of chief development officer, chief technical officer, chief human resources officer, and controller. These actions created a professional management team, which relieved partners of management committee work and other management tasks, allowing them to focus on their legal practices with clients.

Post & Schell has addressed the classic dilemma of how to create value from centralized and decentralized forms of organization simultaneously.[30] Today, authority is centralized in a team of management experts who take care of management functions for all five legal divisions, instead of having the five divisions duplicate these functions. However, the firm's lawyers are organized in a decentralized way, so that they have the authority to make decisions on how to best represent their clients. Since the reorganization, Post & Schell has successfully expanded the legal services it offers and has hired additional lawyers.

MTV has implemented a global diversity strategy by allowing programming to be decentralized, or specialized for each country. Seventy percent of MTV programming is local content. For example, MTV plays lots of "Bollywood" music in India, and it airs *MTV Kitchen* in Italy, a program on which singers and songwriters chat while cooking. But MTV's decentralization has also encountered problems; for example, management had to pull a nude wrestling program off the air in Taiwan.

Applying The Concept 2

Authority

Identify the type of authority referred to in each statement.

a. formal
b. informal
c. to recommend
d. line
e. staff
f. centralized
g. decentralized

_____ 6. "My job is interesting, but it is frustrating when I recommend employees to the production and marketing managers and they do not hire them."

_____ 7. "It is great working for an organization that encourages everyone to share information with everyone else."

_____ 8. "Managers here have the autonomy to run their departments in the way they want to."

_____ 9. "Wendy asked me to put together a list of company cars and recommend which ones to replace."

_____10. "That is a great idea. I'll talk to the boss, and if he likes it, he'll let us present the idea to his boss."

———————————— Learning Outcome 6 ————————————
Explain what an organization chart is and list the four aspects
of a firm that it shows.

ORGANIZATIONAL DESIGN

Organizational design refers to the internal structure of an organization, or the arrangement of positions in the organization into work units or departments and the interrelationships among these units or departments. You'll recall from the appendix to Chapter 1 that contingency theorists look at how the environment and production technology affect organizational structure. Strategy, the means by which management achieves its objectives, also affects structure. As Alfred Chandler stated, strategy precedes and leads to changes in structure. Size also affects structure, as large businesses tend to have a more formal division of labor and many more standing plans than small businesses do.[31]

As you'll learn in this section, organizational design is illustrated in the organization chart and is determined by the type of departmentalization.

Organization Chart

The formal authority or structure within an organization defines the working relationships between the organization's members and their jobs and is illustrated by an organization chart.[32] *An* **organization chart** *is a graphic illustration of the organization's management hierarchy and departments and their working relationships.* Each box represents a position within the organization, and each line indicates the reporting relationships and lines of communication. (An organization chart does not show the day-to-day activities performed or the structure of the informal organization.)

Exhibit 6-5, an adaptation of **General Motors'** organization chart, illustrates four major aspects of such a chart:

- *The level of management hierarchy.* The CEO and division presidents are top management, the vice presidents and managers are middle management, and the supervisors are first-line management.
- *Chain of command.* By following the vertical lines, you can see that the division presidents report to the CEO. Within each division, vice presidents report to the president. The managers report to a vice president, and supervisors report to a manager. The assistant to the CEO is a general staff person, and the finance and human resources departments include specialist staff.[33]
- *The division and type of work.* GM divides work by type of automobile: for example, Buick, Cadillac, Chevrolet, and Pontiac. Each vice president within a division is responsible for a function.
- *Departmentalization.* An organization chart shows how the firm is divided into permanent work units. GM is organized primarily by product, but other types of departmentalization are common.

To better focus on the customer, some organizations, including **Dana Corporation**, **FedEx**, **Nordstrom**, and **Wal-Mart**, have developed an upside-down organization chart with the customer at the top of the chart and management at the bottom. The upside-down chart reminds everyone in the organization that the ultimate goal is to provide customer value and emphasizes to managers that their role is to support employees in providing customer value.

Exhibit 6-5 *Organization Chart*

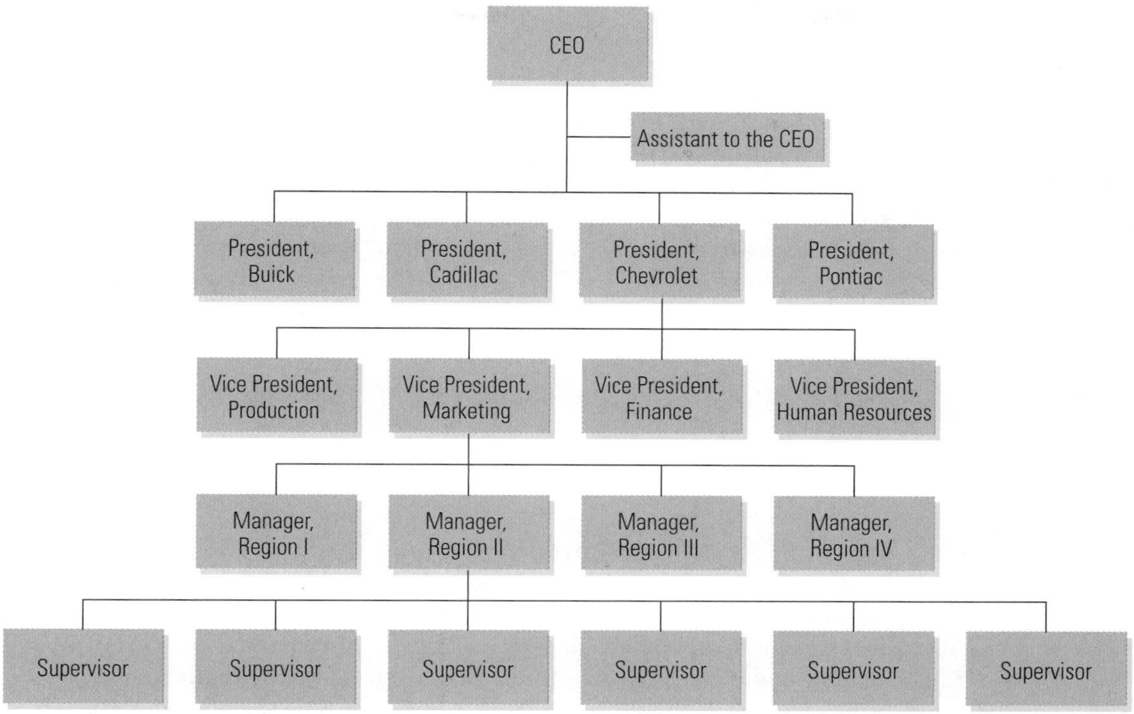

```
                            ┌──────────┐
                            │   CEO    │
                            └────┬─────┘
                                 │    ┌────────────────────┐
                                 ├────│ Assistant to the CEO│
                                 │    └────────────────────┘
        ┌───────────────┬────────┴──────────┬───────────────┐
  ┌───────────┐   ┌───────────┐      ┌───────────┐    ┌───────────┐
  │ President, │   │ President, │      │ President, │    │ President, │
  │   Buick    │   │  Cadillac  │      │ Chevrolet  │    │  Pontiac   │
  └───────────┘   └───────────┘      └─────┬─────┘    └───────────┘
            ┌──────────────┬───────────────┴──┬──────────────┐
     ┌────────────┐  ┌────────────┐    ┌────────────┐  ┌──────────────┐
     │Vice President,│ │Vice President,│  │Vice President,│ │Vice President,│
     │  Production  │  │  Marketing  │    │   Finance   │  │Human Resources│
     └────────────┘  └────────────┘    └────────────┘  └──────────────┘
          ┌──────────────┬───────────────┴──┬──────────────┐
   ┌────────────┐  ┌────────────┐    ┌────────────┐  ┌────────────┐
   │  Manager,  │  │  Manager,  │    │  Manager,  │  │  Manager,  │
   │  Region I  │  │ Region II  │    │ Region III │  │ Region IV  │
   └────────────┘  └────────────┘    └────────────┘  └────────────┘
```

| Supervisor | Supervisor | Supervisor | Supervisor | Supervisor | Supervisor |

Learning Outcome 7
Discuss the difference between internal and external
departmentalization.

Departmentalization

Departmentalization *is the grouping of related activities into units.* Departments may have either an internal or an external focus. Departmentalization based on the internal operations or functions that the employees perform and the resources needed to accomplish that work is called *functional departmentalization.*[34] External, or output, departmentalization is based on activities or factors outside the organization; it is referred to more specifically as *product, customer, or territory departmentalization.*

FUNCTIONAL DEPARTMENTALIZATION
Functional departmentalization involves organizing departments around essential input activities, such as production, sales, and finance, that are managerial or technological functions.[35] Functional departmentalization is illustrated in the top left portion of Exhibit 6-6.

The functional approach is the form most widely used by small organizations. Large organizations that have a diversity of products or types of customers or that cover a wide territory cannot departmentalize effectively around functions. Instead, they focus on factors external to the company.[36]

Exhibit 6-6 *Types of Departmentalization*

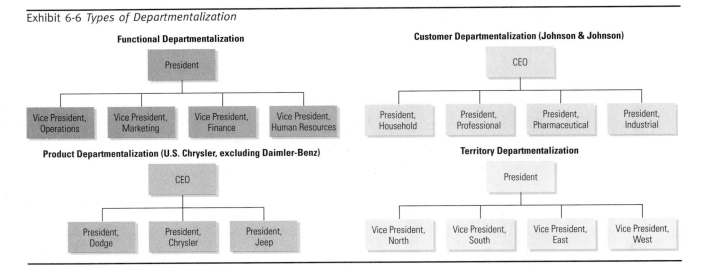

PRODUCT (SERVICE) DEPARTMENTALIZATION

Product (service) departmentalization involves organizing departments around goods (or services). Companies with multiple products commonly use product departmentalization. Each department may become a self-contained company, making and selling its own goods (or service). Retail chains like **Sears** use product departmentalization. The organization chart at the bottom left in Exhibit 6-6 illustrates product departmentalization.

CUSTOMER DEPARTMENTALIZATION

Customer departmentalization involves organizing departments around the needs of different types of customers. The product or service may be the same or slightly different, but the needs of the customer warrant different marketing approaches. **Motorola** restructured to merge about a half-dozen business units into two huge divisions—one geared to consumers and the other to industrial customers. Organizations that offer a wide diversity of products often use customer departmentalization, as do some not-for-profit organizations. For example, a counseling center may offer drug counseling, family counseling, and so on. However, these units usually are not self-contained. The organization chart at the top right in Exhibit 6-6 illustrates customer departmentalization.

TERRITORY (GEOGRAPHIC) DEPARTMENTALIZATION

Territory (geographic) departmentalization involves establishing separate units in each area in which the enterprise does business. The federal government uses this structure. For example, the **Federal Reserve System** is divided into 12 geographic areas, and each one has a similar central bank. The organization chart at the bottom right in Exhibit 6-6 illustrates departmentalization by territory.

Subway Restaurants, started in 1965 as a single sandwich shop called "Pete's Subs" in Bridgeport, Connecticut, had surpassed **McDonald's** as the largest restaurant chain in the United States by the close of 2003. Subway operated 13,247 stores in the United States, 148 more than McDonald's.

Subway is departmentalized primarily by territory. The company has more than 20,700 franchise locations in 72 countries; its goal is to have 30,000 locations by 2010. **TGI Friday's** is also organized by territory, with 723 restaurants in 56 countries.[37]

Learning Outcome **8**

State the similarities and differences between matrix and divisional departmentalization.

Multiple Departmentalization

Many organizations, particularly large, complex ones, use several types of departmentalization to create a hybrid structure. Any mixture of types can be used. For example, some organizations have functional departments within a manufacturing facility, but sales are departmentalized by territory with separate sales managers and salespeople in different areas.

MATRIX DEPARTMENTALIZATION

Matrix departmentalization combines functional and product departmentalization. With matrix departmentalization, an employee works for a functional department and is also assigned to one or more products or projects. The major advantage of matrix departmentalization is flexibility. It allows the enterprise to temporarily organize for a project. The major disadvantage is that each employee has two bosses—a functional boss and a project boss—which violates the unity of command principle.[38] Coordination can also be difficult.[39] **Xerox** and **Boeing** use matrix departmentalization. Exhibit 6-7 illustrates a matrix structure.

Exhibit 6-7 *Matrix Departmentalization*

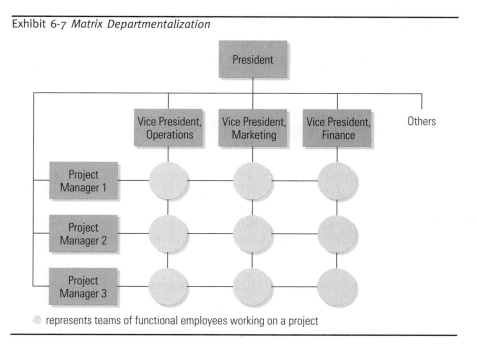

represents teams of functional employees working on a project

WorkApplication7

Draw a simple organization chart for an organization you work for or have worked for. Identify the type of departmentalization and staff positions, if any.

DIVISIONAL DEPARTMENTALIZATION

*A **divisional structure** is based on semiautonomous strategic business units.* In essence, this structure creates coordinated companies within a company. Within the divisional structure, any mixture of the other forms of departmentalization may also be used. Divisional structure is common for large, complex global businesses that offer related goods and services. **Westinghouse** uses divisional departmentalization to organize its dozens of divisions.

The *conglomerate* (holding company) *structure* is based on autonomous profit centers.[40] Companies with unrelated diversified business units use the conglomerate structure. Top management focuses on business portfolio management to buy and sell lines of business without great concern for coordinating divisions.[41] **YTL** uses the conglomerate structure.[41] **Johnson & Johnson** is a family of more than 100 companies that are encouraged to act independently.

New Approaches to Departmentalization

Firms are using teams and other new approaches to change the way work is organized and how it is managed.[42] These approaches are intended to bond employees together and to link them to the organizational culture.[43] Some of the new approaches to departmentalization are horizontal team organizations, network structures, virtual organizations, and learning organizations.

HORIZONTAL TEAM ORGANIZATION

Many companies are moving away from a hierarchical, top-down focus to a horizontal organization to increase speed of response, individual accountability, flexibility, knowledge sharing, and coordination throughout the organization.[44] Firms are breaking down barriers between departments and using work processes rather than departmental functions to organize units. Teams are commonly used to reengineer the organizational structure.[45] You will learn about work teams later in the chapter. **Cummins Engine, General Foods, Mead, Procter & Gamble, Sherwin-Williams**, and **TRW** have all developed team structures.

NETWORK STRUCTURE AND THE VIRTUAL ORGANIZATION

Networks are boundaryless interrelationships among different organizations.[46] Network firms focus on what they do best, outsource the rest to other companies, and coordinate their activities from a small headquarters organization. A network firm may be viewed as a central hub surrounded by a network of outside specialists that change as needed.[47] **Nike** and **Reebok** design and market their footwear and outsource manufacturing. Some companies, including **Dell, Gateway**, and **RCA**, either purchase products ready-made or buy all the parts and only assemble the product.

A further development of the network structure is the virtual organization. A *virtual organization* is a continually evolving group of companies that unite temporarily to exploit specific opportunities or to attain strategic advantages and then disband when objectives are met. The virtual organization has no central hub, as each independent company gives up some control to temporarily become part of a new larger organizational system. E-commerce is making the virtual organization an increasingly dominant model.[48] **IBM** uses network structures for outsourcing, and it has a continually changing virtual organization of partnered projects.

Applying The Concept 3

Departmentalization

Identify the type of departmentalization illustrated by each organization chart.

a. functional   d. territory
b. product (service)   e. matrix
c. customer   f. divisional

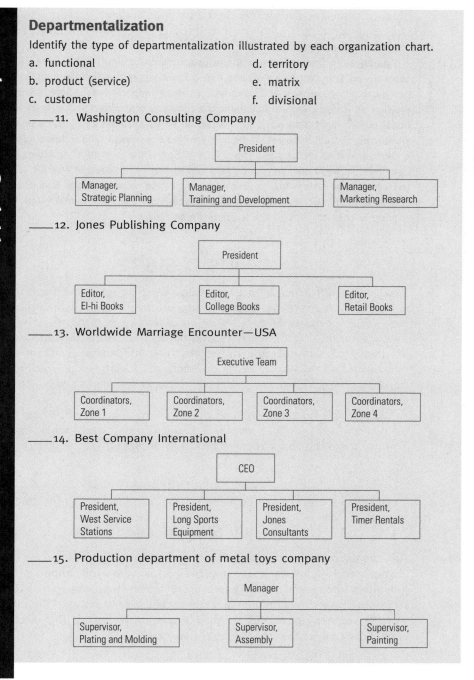

_____11. Washington Consulting Company

President
- Manager, Strategic Planning
- Manager, Training and Development
- Manager, Marketing Research

_____12. Jones Publishing Company

President
- Editor, El-hi Books
- Editor, College Books
- Editor, Retail Books

_____13. Worldwide Marriage Encounter—USA

Executive Team
- Coordinators, Zone 1
- Coordinators, Zone 2
- Coordinators, Zone 3
- Coordinators, Zone 4

_____14. Best Company International

CEO
- President, West Service Stations
- President, Long Sports Equipment
- President, Jones Consultants
- President, Timer Rentals

_____15. Production department of metal toys company

Manager
- Supervisor, Plating and Molding
- Supervisor, Assembly
- Supervisor, Painting

THE LEARNING ORGANIZATION

As discussed in Chapter 2, in a learning organization, everyone in the firm is engaged in identifying and solving problems to continuously improve and achieve the firm's objectives. There is no agreement about what the learning organization looks or operates like. However, it does use the horizontal team structure with open information and knowledge sharing.[49] Learning organizations are also characterized by decentralized decision making, participative strategy, empowered employees who share responsibility, and a strong adaptive nature.[50]

I O M

As noted, a firm can use multiple departmentalization. Post & Schell replaced its separate-division structure with one that acknowledges the divisions' similar product— five legal service groups—blended with customer departmentalization. Instead of each division performing its own functions, the company centralized authority by hiring functional professional managers. Post & Schell takes an industry focus to ensure that it knows the clients' business. It blends specific experience with a team approach and a commitment to technology. Thus, Post & Schell has a matrix structure, as lawyers from the five legal service groups team up to meet the needs of specific clients. Each lawyer can be using his or her legal expertise with multiple teams and clients simultaneously. Post & Schell's use of teams with open information and knowledge sharing is characteristic of the learning organization.

JOB DESIGN

Tasks to be performed by organizations are grouped into functional departments, and the tasks are further grouped into jobs for each employee.[51] **Job design** *is the process of identifying tasks that each employee is responsible for completing.* Job design is crucial because it affects job satisfaction and productivity.[52] Empowering employees to be involved in designing their own jobs motivates them to increase productivity.[53] Many organizations, including **GE** and **Pizza Hut**, are asking employees to suggest ways to redesign their work.

As we will discuss in this section, jobs may be simplified, so that they involve few tasks, or they may be expanded so that they involve many tasks. You can use a job characteristics model to design jobs.

Learning Outcome 9
Explain the difference between job simplification and job expansion.

Job Simplification

Job simplification is the process of eliminating or combining tasks, and/or changing the work sequence to improve performance. Job simplification makes jobs more specialized.[54] It is based on the organizing principle of division of labor and Taylor's scientific management. The idea behind job simplification is to work smarter, not harder. A job is broken down into steps (flowchart), and employees analyze the steps to see if they can

- *Eliminate.* Does the task have to be done at all? If not, don't waste time doing it.
- *Combine.* Doing similar things together often saves time. Make one trip to the mail room at the end of the day instead of several throughout the day.
- *Change sequence.* Often a change in the order of doing things results in a lower total time.

Intel, founded in 1968, today employs 78,000 people in 294 offices and facilities worldwide. Intel offers more than 450 products and services but is best known for its processor chips used in personal computers. You have most likely seen a computer with an "Intel Inside®" label, indicating that that computer is powered by Intel technology.[55] Intel managers decided that it was not necessary to fill out a voucher for expenses amounting to less than $100. Thus, fewer vouchers were filled out, saving time and paperwork. **GE** developed its Work Out Program to improve and eliminate work, and **Pizza Hut** credits up to a 40 percent increase in store sales to job simplification.

Job Expansion

Job expansion is the process of making jobs less specialized. Jobs can be expanded through rotation, enlargement, and enrichment.

JOB ROTATION

Job rotation involves performing different jobs in some sequence, each one for a set period of time. For example, employees making cars on a Ford assembly line might rotate so that they get to work on different parts of the production process for a set period of time. Many organizations develop conceptual skills in management trainees by rotating them through various departments. A few of the companies that have used job rotation are **Bethlehem Steel, Target Corporation, Ford, Motorola, National Steel**, and **Prudential Insurance**.

Related to job rotation is *cross-training*. With cross-training, employees learn to perform different jobs so they can fill in for those who are not on the job. As skills increase, employees become more valuable to the organization.

JOB ENLARGEMENT

Job enlargement involves adding tasks to broaden variety. For example, rather than rotate jobs, the car workers could combine tasks into one job. **AT&T, Chrysler, GM, IBM**, and **Maytag** are a few of the companies that have used job enlargement. Unfortunately, adding more tasks to an employee's job is often not a great motivator.

JOB ENRICHMENT

Job enrichment *is the process of building motivators into the job itself to make it more interesting and challenging.* Job enrichment works for jobs of low motivation potential and employees who are ready to be empowered.[56] A simple way to enrich jobs is for the manager to delegate more responsibility to employees to make a job satisfying.[57] **AT&T, General Motors, IBM, Maytag, Monsanto, Motorola**, and **Traveler's Insurance Company** have successfully used job enrichment.

Work Teams

The traditional approach to job design has been to focus on individual jobs. Recently, there has been a trend toward designing jobs for work teams—or, to be more accurate, teams are redesigning members' jobs.[58] The development of work teams is a form of job enrichment. Two common types of work teams are integrated teams and self-managed teams.

WorkApplication8

Describe how a job at an organization you work for or have worked for could be simplified. Be sure to specify if you are eliminating, combining, or changing the sequence of the job.

_____

_____

_____

_____

WorkApplication9

Describe how a job at an organization you work for or have worked for could be expanded. Be sure to specify if you are using job rotation, job enlargement, or job enrichment and to be explicit about how the job is changed.

_____

_____

_____

_____

Exhibit 6-8 *Job Design Options*

Job Simplification	Eliminate tasks
	Combine tasks
	Change task sequence
Job Expansion	Rotate jobs
	Add tasks
	Job enrichment (increase task variety and employee responsibility)
Work Teams	Integrated
	Self-managed

WorkApplication10

Describe how an organization you work for or have worked for uses, or could use, teams. Be sure to specify if the teams are integrated or self-managed.

_____

_____

_____

_____

INTEGRATED WORK TEAMS

Integrated work teams are assigned a number of tasks by a manager, and the team in turn gives specific assignments to members and is responsible for rotating jobs.

SELF-MANAGED WORK TEAMS

Self-managed work teams are assigned a goal, and the team plans, organizes, leads, and controls to achieve the goal. Usually, self-managed teams operate without a designated manager; the team is both manager and worker. Teams commonly elect their own members and evaluate each other's performance.[59]

Exhibit 6-8 reviews the job design options we have discussed so far. In designing jobs, managers can use the job characteristics model, to be discussed next.

———————————— Learning Outcome 10 ————————————
Describe the job characteristics model.

The Job Characteristics Model

The job characteristics model, developed by Richard Hackman and Greg Oldham, provides a conceptual framework for designing or enriching jobs.[60] The model can be used by individual managers or by members of a team. As Exhibit 6-9 illustrates, users of the **job characteristics model** *focus on core job dimensions, psychological states of employees, and the strength of employees' need for growth.* Use of the job characteristics model improves employees' motivation, performance, and job satisfaction and reduces their absenteeism and job turnover; research supports the idea that use of the model increases performance.[61]

Five core dimensions can be fine-tuned to improve the outcomes of a job in terms of employees' productivity and their quality of working life:[62]

1. *Skill variety* is the number of diverse tasks that make up a job and the number of skills used to perform the job.
2. *Task identity* is the degree to which an employee performs a whole identifiable task. For example, does the employee put together an entire television, or just place the screen in the set?

Exhibit 6-9 *The Job Characteristics Model*

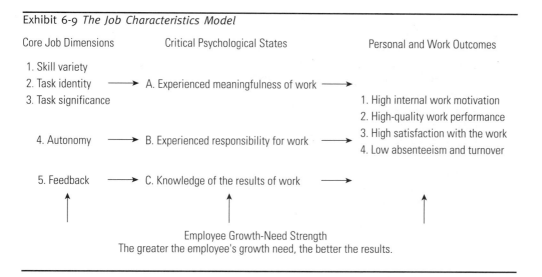

Core Job Dimensions

1. Skill variety
2. Task identity
3. Task significance

4. Autonomy

5. Feedback

Critical Psychological States

A. Experienced meaningfulness of work

B. Experienced responsibility for work

C. Knowledge of the results of work

Personal and Work Outcomes

1. High internal work motivation
2. High-quality work performance
3. High satisfaction with the work
4. Low absenteeism and turnover

Employee Growth-Need Strength
The greater the employee's growth need, the better the results.

3. *Task significance* is an employee's perception of the importance of the task to others—the organization, the department, coworkers, and/or customers.
4. *Autonomy* is the degree to which the employee has discretion to make decisions in planning, organizing, and controlling the task performed.
5. *Feedback* is the extent to which employees find out how well they perform their tasks.

Note that if employees are not interested in enriching their jobs, the job characteristics model will fail. You will learn more about needs and motivation in Chapter 12.

Applying The Concept 4

Job Designs

Identify which job design technique is exemplified in each statement.

a. job simplification
b. job rotation
c. job enlargement

d. job enrichment
e. work teams
f. job characteristics model

_____16. "Jill, I'm delegating a new task to you, which will give you more of a challenge."

_____17. "Sales reps who have business lunches that are under $20 no longer need to provide a sales receipt."

_____18. "We'd like to change your job so that you can develop new skills, complete entire jobs by yourself so that the job is more meaningful, do the job the way you want to, and know how you are doing."

_____19. "To make your job less repetitive, we are going to add three new tasks to your job responsibility."

_____20. "I'd like you to learn how to run the switchboard so that you can fill in for Ted while he is at lunch."

IOM

Jobs at Post & Schell are primarily professional-level legal jobs that are already quite enriched. Managers could use the job characteristics model (Exhibit 6-9) to analyze these jobs: (1) Skill variety is high, as each case has its own unique circumstances. (2) Task identity is high as jobs are team-based; all members of a team get to work on an entire legal case. (3) Task significance is high; in addition to doing conventional legal work, lawyers at Post & Schell specialize in high-end litigation and consulting. (A) Thus, the lawyers experience meaningful work. (4) Autonomy is high, as teams manage client cases. (B) Thus, the lawyers have responsibility for their work. (5) Feedback is given, (C) so lawyers have knowledge of the results of their work.

Based on analysis of the five core job dimensions and the three critical psychological states in the job characteristics model, personal and work outcomes at Post & Schell likely include high motivation, high-quality work, high satisfaction with work, and low absenteeism and turnover.

ORGANIZING YOURSELF AND DELEGATING

Successful managers are effective at setting priorities and delegating work.[63] Recall that planning entails setting objectives and that organizing is the process of delegating and coordinating resources to achieve objectives. Thus, prioritizing objectives is important, because some objectives are more important than others; as a manager, you get the work done by delegating it to employees.[64]

Now that you understand how organizations and jobs are designed, it's time to learn how to organize yourself by setting priorities and delegating work. Self-organization reduces stress and increases performance.[65] Start by completing the Self-Assessment, prioritizing to determine what is important to you personally (your values).

Self-Assessment

Personal Priorities

Rate how important each of the following is to you on a scale from 0 (not important) to 100 (very important). Write the number you choose on the line to the left of each item.

Not Important						Somewhat Important				Very Important
0	10	20	30	40	50	60	70	80	90	100

_____1. An enjoyable, satisfying job

_____2. A high-paying job

_____3. A good marriage

_____4. Meeting new people, attending social events

_____5. Involvement in community activities

_____6. My relationship with God, my religion

_____7. Exercising, playing sports

_____8. Intellectual development

_____9. A career with challenging opportunities

_____10. Nice cars, clothes, home, etc.

_____11. Spending time with family

_____12. Having several close friends

_____13. Volunteer work for not-for-profit organizations

_____14. Meditation, quiet time to think, pray, etc.

_____15. A healthy, balanced diet

_____16. Educational reading, self-improvement TV programs, etc.

(Continued)

Personal Priorities   (Continued)

Below, copy the number you assigned to each of the 16 items in the space next to the item number; then add the two numbers in each column.

Professional	Financial	Family	Social	Community	Spiritual	Physical	Intellectual
1. ___	2. ___	3. ___	4. ___	5. ___	6. ___	7. ___	8. ___
9. ___	10. ___	11. ___	12. ___	13. ___	14. ___	15. ___	16. ___
Totals ___	___	___	___	___	___	___	___

The higher the total in any area, the higher the value you place on that particular area. The closer the totals are in all eight areas, the more well-rounded you are.

Think about the time and effort you put into your top three values. Are you putting in enough time and effort to achieve the level of success you want in each area? If not, what can you do to change?

Learning Outcome 11

Explain how to set priorities by answering three priority questions and determining whether activities have high, medium, or low priority.

Setting Priorities[66]

As a manager, you'll be required to carry out several tasks at any given time. How you select the priority order in which these tasks will be completed will affect your success.[67] To prioritize successfully, list on a to-do list tasks that you must perform and then assign each task a priority.[68] After prioritizing tasks, focus on accomplishing only one task at a time.[69]

PRIORITY-DETERMINATION QUESTIONS

You should answer "yes" or "no" to the following three **priority-determination questions** about each task that needs to be completed:

1. *Do I need to be personally involved because of my unique knowledge or skills?* Often, you are the only one who can do the task; if so, then you must be involved.
2. *Is the task my responsibility, or will it affect the performance or finances of my department?* You must oversee the performance of your department and keep finances in line with the budget.
3. *When is the deadline—is quick action needed?* Should you work on this activity right now, or can it wait? The key is to start the task soon enough so that you will meet the deadline.

ASSIGNING PRIORITIES

After answering the three questions, you can assign a high, medium, or low priority to each activity:

- *Delegate (D) priority:* The task is delegated if the answer to question 1 is no. If the answer to question 1 is no, it is not necessary to answer questions 2 and 3. However, planning how to delegate the task now becomes a priority.

- *High (H) priority:* Assign the task a high priority if you answer yes to all three questions.
- *Medium (M) priority:* Assign the task a medium priority if you answer yes to question 1 but no to one of the remaining two questions.
- *Low (L) priority:* Assign the task a low priority if you answer yes to question 1 but no to both questions 2 and 3.

THE PRIORITIZED TO-DO LIST

Exhibit 6-10 is a prioritized to-do list that you can copy and use on the job. Follow these steps when using the prioritized to-do list:

1. *Write the task* that you must perform on the task line.
2. *Answer the three priority questions* by placing a Y (yes) or N (no) in the relevant column. Also place the deadline and time needed to complete the

Exhibit 6-10 *Prioritized To-Do List*

Assigning a Priority		Priority-Determination Questions				
		#1	#2	#3		
D Delegate priority	(N) No to question 1	1. Do I need to be personally involved?	2. Is it my responsibility, or will it affect the performance or finances of my department?	3. Is quick action needed?	Deadline/time needed	Priority
H High priority	(YYY) Yes to all three questions					
M Medium priority	(YNY or YYN) Yes to question 1 and No to question 2 or 3					
L Low priority	(YNN) Yes to question 1 and No to questions 2 and 3					
Task						

task in the relevant column. The deadline and time needed are used with lower-level priorities that change into high priorities as the deadline approaches. You may want to write in the deadline for starting the task rather than the completion deadline.

3. *Assign a priority* to the task by placing the letter D (delegate), H (high), M (medium), or L (low) in the priority column. The top left of the prioritized to-do list shows how to determine priority based on the answers to the priority-determination questions. If you write D, set a priority on when to delegate the task.

4. *Determine which task to complete now.* You may have more than one high-priority task, so select the most important one. When all high priorities are completed, go to medium-priority tasks followed by low-priority tasks.

Update the prioritized to-do list and add new tasks. As time passes, the medium- and low-priority tasks become high-priority tasks. There is no set rule for how often to update, but do it at least daily. As new tasks come up, be sure to add them to your to-do list and prioritize them. In doing so, you will avoid the tendency to put off a high-priority task to work on a lower-level task.[70]

If you have a management job with a large variety of changing tasks that require long-range planning, you may want to use the time management system described in the appendix to Chapter 5. You can use the prioritized to-do list with the time management system for daily scheduling. If you have a job with a small variety of changing tasks that require short-range planning, you may simply use the prioritized to-do list to keep yourself organized and focused on high-priority tasks. Complete Skill Builder 1 at the end of this chapter to develop your skill at setting priorities using a prioritized to-do list.

Delegation

Delegation is the process of assigning responsibility and authority for accomplishing objectives. Telling employees to perform tasks that are part of their job design is issuing orders, not delegating. Delegating refers to giving employees new tasks. The new task may become part of a redesigned job, or it may simply be a one-time task.

BENEFITS OF DELEGATION
When managers delegate, they have more time to perform high-priority tasks. Delegation trains employees and improves their self-esteem; it is a means of enriching jobs and can result in improved personal and work outcomes.[71]

OBSTACLES TO DELEGATION
Managers become used to doing things themselves. Managers fear that employees will fail to accomplish the task or will show them up. Managers believe that they can perform the task more efficiently than others. You should realize that delegating is an important management skill; don't let these or other obstacles stop you from delegating.[72]

WorkApplication11

List three to five tasks you must complete in the near future and prioritize them using Exhibit 6-10.

_____

_____

_____

_____

WorkApplication12

Describe an obstacle to delegation or sign of delegating too little that you have observed.

_____

_____

_____

_____

You'll recall from Chapters 1 and 2 that CEO Steve Ballmer changed **Microsoft's** organizational structure. He reorganized to set up a divisional structure with seven business units to be held accountable as profit centers. (See page 29 in Chapter 1 for a list of the seven units.) The seven units also reflect customer departmentalization, as each unit has customers with different needs for its products or services.

Steve Ballmer realized that he was making too many of the decisions and that he needed to delegate more. Thus, an important reason for restructuring was to allow Ballmer to delegate more decision-making authority down the chain of command to each of the seven division heads, who would further delegate some of the decision making.[73]

Delegation Decisions

Successful delegation is often based on selecting what to delegate and to whom to delegate it. Exhibit 6-11 suggests what to delegate and what not to delegate.

───────── Learning Outcome 12 ─────────
List the four steps in the delegation process.

The Delegation Process

After determining what to delegate and to whom, you must plan for and delegate the tasks. The steps in the delegation process are (1) explain the need for delegating and the reasons for selecting the employee; (2) set objectives

Join the Discussion Ethics & Social Responsibility

Delegating Destroying Documents

1. Is it ethical and socially responsible to delegate the task of destroying documents that may potentially be used as evidence of wrongdoing?
2. What would you do if your boss asked you to destroy documents and you thought the goal was to cover up evidence of wrongdoing by the firm? (Would you just do it? Say nothing but neglect to do it? Question your boss's motives? Look closely at what you were asked to destroy? Check with your boss's boss to make sure it's okay to do it? Tell the boss you will not do it? Tell the boss to do it himself or herself? Blow the whistle to an outside source?)
3. If you were charged with destroying evidence, do you believe it would be a good defense to say "I was only following orders"?

   Arthur Andersen, a consulting company, and **Global Crossing**, a multimedia communications company, were both taken to court for destroying evidence that could have been used in court to support allegations of illegal activities. Arthur Andersen destroyed evidence related to the auditing of Enron to protect both companies from being found guilty of engaging in illegal business practices. Arthur Andersen claimed that it was not trying to destroy incriminating evidence, that it was simply destroying records, which is done periodically. Destroying documents is, in fact, routine. The key question is this: What is being destroyed and why is it being destroyed?

Exhibit 6-11 *What to Delegate and What Not to Delegate*

What to Delegate	What Not to Delegate
• Paperwork	• Anything that you need to be involved with because of your unique knowledge or skill
• Routine tasks	• Personnel matters (evaluating, disciplining, firing)
• Technical matters	• Confidential matters
• Tasks that develop employees	• Projects or tasks in crisis
• Tasks associated with solving employee's problems	• Activities delegated to you personally

that define responsibility, the level of authority, and the deadline; (3) develop a plan; (4) establish control checkpoints and hold employees accountable. Following these four steps can increase your chances of delegating successfully. In this section, you will see how the delegation process is used with the job characteristics model, core job dimensions, and critical psychological states to influence performance and work outcomes.

Step 1. Explain the need for delegating and the reasons for selecting the employee. It is helpful for an employee to whom you delegate a task to understand why the assignment must be completed and to realize the importance of the task. Telling the employee why he or she was selected should make him or her feel valued.[74] Don't use the "it's a lousy job but someone has to do it" approach. Be positive; make the person aware of how he or she may benefit from the assignment. If step 1 is completed successfully, the employee should be motivated, or at least willing, to do the assignment.

Step 2. Set objectives that define responsibility, the level of authority, and the deadline. The objectives should clearly state the end result the employee is responsible for achieving by a specific deadline.[75] Define the level of authority the employee has.[76] (See the discussion on levels of authority earlier in this chapter.)

Step 3. Develop a plan. Once the objectives are set, a plan is needed to achieve them. The level of autonomy for developing the plan to accomplish the task should be based on the employee's capability level. (Refer back to Skill Builder 2 in Chapter 1 for details on selecting the management style appropriate for the employee's capability level.) Make sure instructions for completing the task are clear; writing them down helps.[77]

Step 4. Establish control checkpoints and hold employees accountable. For simple, short tasks, a deadline without control checkpoints is appropriate. However, when tasks have multiple steps and/or will take some time to complete, it is often advisable to check progress at predetermined times (control checkpoints). This approach builds information flow into the delegation system from the start.[78] You and the employee should agree on how (phone call, visit, memo, or detailed report) and when (daily, weekly, or after specific steps are completed but before going on to the next step) the employee will provide information regarding the assignment. When

WorkApplication13

Select a manager you work for or have worked for and analyze how well he or she implements the four steps of delegation. Which steps does the manager typically follow and not follow?

_____

_____

_____

_____

_____

establishing control, consider the employee's capability level. The lower the capability, the more frequent the checks; the higher the capability, the less frequent the checks. All parties involved should note the control checkpoints on their calendars.

In Skill Builder 2 at the end of this chapter, you will practice using the delegation process so you can develop your delegation skills.

IOM

Because Post & Schell is organized by type of legal practice, the company uses a matrix structure that has its lawyers working on multiple cases with multiple bosses. Thus, prioritization is an important issue, as lawyers must decide which case to work on at any given time. Delegation is also important, as the heads of the five legal groups must delegate cases to the lawyers who will work on them. The case teams also need to delegate their work between lawyers and legal assistants. Knowing how to set priorities and how to delegate increases the efficiency of Post & Schell.

Having completed this chapter, you should understand the principles of organization, authority, departmentalization, job design, and delegation.

Take advantage of the companion Web site for *Management Fundamentals*, where you will find a broad array of resources to help you maximize what you learn in class:

- Try a quiz
- View chapter videos
- Download slides
- Boost your vocabulary
- Work through an Internet exercise
- Find related links

Take a look for yourself at *http://lussier.swlearning.com.*

Chapter Summary

1. Explain the difference between a flat organization and a tall organization.

A flat organization has few levels of management with wide spans of management. A tall organization has many levels of management with narrow spans of management.

2. Describe the similarities and differences among liaisons, integrators, and people in boundary roles.

They are similar because they are all coordination techniques. Liaisons and integrators are similar because they coordinate internally, whereas people in boundary roles coordinate efforts with customers, suppliers, and other people in the external environment. Liaisons and integrators are different because liaisons work in one department and

coordinate with other departments, whereas integrators coordinate departmental activities but do not work for any department.

3. Discuss the difference between formal and informal authority and centralized and decentralized authority.

Formal authority involves sanctioned relationships and ways of getting the job done, whereas informal authority involves unsanctioned relationships and ways of getting the job done. With centralized authority, top managers make important decisions; with decentralized authority, middle and first-line managers make important decisions.

4. List and briefly explain the four levels of authority.
(1) *The authority to inform*—the person simply presents an alternative. (2) *The authority to recommend*—the person presents alternatives and suggests one. (3) *The authority to report*—the person takes action and then tells the boss. (4) *Full authority*—the person takes action and does not have to tell the boss about it.

5. Describe the relationship between line authority and staff authority.
The staff personnel advise and assist line personnel, who are responsible for making decisions and who issue orders down the chain of command.

6. Explain what an organization chart is and list the four aspects of a firm that it shows.
An organization chart is a graphic illustration of the organization's management hierarchy and departments and their working relationships. It shows the level of management hierarchy, chain of command, division and type of work, and departmentalization.

7. Discuss the difference between internal and external departmentalization.
Internal departmentalization focuses on functions performed within the organization and the resources needed to accomplish the work; this type is also known as functional departmentalization. External departmentalization can be based on the organization's product(s), its customers, or the territories in which the organization does business.

8. State the similarities and differences between matrix and divisional departmentalization.
They are similar because they are both multiple departmentalization methods. Matrix combines the functional and product departmental structures to focus on projects. Divisional structure is based on semiautonomous strategic business units.

9. Explain the difference between job simplification and job expansion.
Job simplification is used to make jobs more specialized by eliminating or combining tasks and/or changing the sequence of work. Job expansion is used to make jobs less specialized by rotating employees, enlarging the job, and/or enriching the job to make it more interesting and challenging.

10. Describe the job characteristics model.
The job characteristics model is a conceptual framework for designing enriched jobs. It addresses core job dimensions, critical psychological states, and employee growth needs. It is used to improve the quality of working life for employees and productivity for the organization.

11. Explain how to set priorities by answering three priority questions and determining whether activities have high, medium, or low priority.
A manager first answers "yes" or "no" to the three priority questions: (1) Do I need to be personally involved? (2) Is the task my responsibility, or will it affect the performance or finances of my department? (3) When is the deadline—is quick action needed? Depending on the answers to these questions, the manager delegates the task or assigns it a high, medium, or low level of priority.

12. List the four steps in the delegation process.
The steps in the delegation process are (1) explain the need for delegating and the reasons the employee was selected; (2) set objectives that define responsibility, the level of authority, and the deadline; and (3) develop a plan; (4) establish control checkpoints and hold employees accountable.

13. Complete each of the following statements using one of this chapter's key terms.
The _____ refers to the number of employees reporting to a manager.

_____ is the obligation to achieve objectives by performing required activities.

_____ is the right to make decisions, issue orders, and use resources.

_____ is the process of assigning responsibility and authority to achieve objectives.

The _____ are the authority to inform, the authority to recommend, the authority to report, and full authority.

_____ is the responsibility to make decisions and issue orders down the chain of command.

_____ is the responsibility to advise and assist other personnel.

With _____, important decisions are made by top managers.

With _____, important decisions are made by middle and first-line managers.

An _____ is a graphic illustration of an organization's management hierarchy and departments and their working relationships.

_____ is the grouping of related activities into units.

_____ departmentalizes based on semiautonomous strategic business units.

_____ is the process of identifying tasks that each employee is responsible for completing.

_____ is the process of building motivators into a job to make it more interesting and challenging.

The _____ is a conceptual framework for designing or enriching jobs that focuses on core job dimensions, psychological states of employees, and employees' need for growth.

_____ are questions that help determine the priority of tasks to be completed.

Key **Terms**

authority, 199
centralized authority, 202
decentralized authority, 202
delegation, 199
departmentalization, 205
divisional structure, 208

job characteristics model, 212
job design, 210
job enrichment, 211
levels of authority, 201
line authority, 201

organization chart, 204
priority-determination questions, 215
responsibility, 198
span of management, 197
staff authority, 201

Review and **Discussion** Questions

1. What is the difference between unity of command and unity of direction?
2. What is the relationship between the chain of command and the span of management?
3. What do the terms *differentiation* and *integration* mean?
4. What is the difference between responsibility and authority?
5. Can accountability be delegated?
6. How does the scope of authority change throughout an organization, and what is the flow of responsibility, authority, and accountability?
7. What is the difference between general staff and specialist staff?
8. What does an organization chart show? What doesn't it show?

9. What is the difference between product and customer departmentalization?
10. What is the difference between a network structure and a virtual organization?
11. What is job design, and why is it necessary?
12. What is the difference between an integrated work team and a self-managed work team?
13. Why is the strength of employees' need for growth important to the job characteristics model?
14. Why is it important to update priorities on a to-do list?
15. As a simple guide, what one question can a manager ask to determine what and what not to delegate?
16. Why is each of the four steps in the delegation process necessary?

Objective **Case**
HITACHI

Hitachi, headquartered in Japan, is one of the world's largest technology corporations. Hitachi products are used throughout the world in telecommunications, in energy and chemical industries, in plant engineering, and in consumer electronics. For Hitachi, manufacturing "high-tech" means being a responsible corporate citizen by developing environmentally sound solutions to customers' problems.

Since its founding in 1910, Hitachi has acted from a corporate philosophy of contributing to society through

technology. For more than 90 years, its motto has been "Where there is high-tech, there is Hitachi." Recognizing that survival in the 21st century demands responding to global change, Hitachi has adopted the phrase "Inspire the Next" as a declaration of its corporate vow that the Hitachi brand will meet the expectation of its customers and society in the 21st century and beyond.

Hitachi considers its employees its most valuable assets. Their talent, know-how, and expertise make it possible for Hitachi to manufacture high-quality products that meet certified international standards. To create and keep up with whatever comes next, Hitachi uses a team approach with self-managing work teams. Team members share the management functions. Everyone on a team works together to continually improve products and processes.

The Hitachi Group recently identified four key areas for harnessing the synergy of its technologies, knowledge, people, and other resources:

1. IT-based quality lifestyle solutions
2. Sustainable environmental solutions
3. Advanced health care solutions
4. Intelligent management solutions

Hitachi wished to realign its business portfolio to focus on businesses that will strengthen its capabilities in these domains. The company remains a corporate vertical umbrella encompassing more than 40 subsidiaries or business units, which operate horizontally—or independently of each other. However, some of these units are not performing well; so, to continue to expand, Hitachi is making some organizational changes.

In 2004, Hitachi began selling some lines of business and acquiring others. When Hitachi takes over another corporation its management is usually more formal than that of the existing company. In the Japanese tradition, Hitachi's structure is formal and its organization charts show the lines of authority for each business unit of the corporate body.

Hitachi is changing its go-it-alone strategy and creating joint ventures. One example is the establishment of Renesas Technology Corporation, a semiconductor joint venture with Mitsubishi Electric Corporation. Hitachi's electronic device division transferred its dynamic random-access memory business to Elpida Memory Inc., a joint venture with NEC, while consolidating most of its other semiconductor operations into Renesas Technology Corporation in April 2003.

All business units conduct their own research and development (R&D) to continually improve existing products and create new ones. However, Hitachi is working to get each business unit to share its knowledge with other units, and it is also creating R&D based on the four key areas. Using people in boundary roles as well as the Internet and the companies' intranets is helping.

 To learn more about Hitachi, log on to InfoTrac® College Edition at *http://infotrac. thomsonlearing.com* and use the advanced search function.

____ 1. Hitachi appears to follow the unity of command principle of organization.

    a. true
    b. false

____ 2. The organizational changes at Hitachi affect the chain of command by making it a flat organization.

    a. true
    b. false

____ 3. The R&D changes best reflect the ____ principle of organization.

    a. unity of command and direction
    b. chain of command
    c. span of management
    d. division of labor
    e. coordination
    f. balanced responsibility of authority
    g. delegation
    h. flexibility

____ 4. Hitachi's organizational structure reflects ____ authority.

    a. centralized
    b. decentralized

____ 5. Hitachi's four key areas best reflect ____ departmentalization.

    a. functional   c. customer
    b. product   d. territory

____ 6. Hitachi's overall departmentalization is

    a. functional   d. territory
    b. product   e. matrix
    c. customer   f. divisional

____ 7. Sharing R&D best reflects the ____ approach to departmentalization.

    a. horizontal team   c. virtual
    b. network   d. learning

____ 8. As discussed in the case, job design at Hitachi is accomplished primarily by

    a. job simplification
    b. job expansion
    c. work teams
    d. the job characteristics model

____ 9. Selecting four key areas and realigning its business portfolio best reflect Hitachi's

    a. unity of command   d. setting priorities
    b. division of labor   e. staff authority
    c. delegation

10. Based on Chandler's theory, how has strategy at Hitachi affected its structure?

11. How can Hitachi use the job characteristics model?

Cumulative Case Questions

12. Which environmental forces affected Hitachi's decision to change its strategy and structure? (Chapter 2)

13. Was the use of the decision-making model appropriate in deciding how to change Hitachi? (Chapter 4)

14. What process did Hitachi use to come up with its changes in strategies, at what level were these strategies implemented, and what are Hitachi's strategies? (Chapter 5)

Skill **Builder** 1
SETTING PRIORITIES

Preparing for Skill Builder 1

For this exercise, assume that you are the first-line manager of a production department in a large company. Read the to-do list of 10 tasks that accompanies this exercise and assign priorities to each task by following the steps below. (Note: The 10 tasks have been numbered for you. When you make a to-do list for your own tasks, we recommend that you not number them.)

1. Answer the three priority-determination questions by placing a Y for yes or N for no in the columns labeled 1, 2, and 3. Because you are not the top manager of this department, do not fill in the deadline/time needed column.

2. Assign a priority to the task by placing the letter D (delegate), H (high), M (medium), or L (low) in the priority column. Use the list at the top left to determine the priority based on the answers to the priority questions.

3. Determine which task to complete the first. You may have more than one high priority, so select the most important one to do first.

Apply It

What did I learn from this experience? How will I use this knowledge in the future?

_____

_____

Your instructor may ask you to do this Skill Builder in class in a group. If so, the instructor will provide you with any necessary information or additional instructions.

Prioritized To-Do List		Priority-Determination Questions				
		#1	#2	#3		
D Delegate priority	(N) No to question 1					
H High priority	(YYY) Yes to all three questions					
M Medium priority	(YNY or YYN) Yes to question 1 and No to question 2 or 3					
L Low priority	(YNN) Yes to question 1 and No to questions 2 and 3	1. Do I need to be personally involved?	2. Is it my responsibility, or will it affect the performance or finances of my department?	3. Is quick action needed?	Deadline/time needed	Priority
Task						
1. Tom, the sales manager, tells you that three customers stopped doing business with your company because your products have decreased in quality. As production manager, it is your job to meet with the production crew and determine how to solve this problem.						

2. Your secretary, Michele, tells you that there is a salesperson waiting to see you. He does not have an appointment. You don't do any purchasing.					
3. Molly, a vice president, wants to see you to discuss a new product to be introduced in one month.					
4. Tom, the sales manager, sent you a memo stating that the sales forecast was incorrect. Sales are expected to increase by 20 percent starting next month. Inventory must be increased to meet the unexpected sales forecast.					
5. Dan, the personnel director, sent you a memo informing you that one of your employees has resigned. Your turnover rate is one of the highest in the company.					
6. Michele tells you that someone named Bob Furry called while you were out. He asked you to return his call, but wouldn't state why he was calling. You don't know who he is or what he wants.					
7. Phil, one of your best workers, wants an appointment to tell you about an incident that happened in the shop.					
8. Tom calls and asks you to meet with him and a prospective customer for your product. The customer wants to meet you.					
9. John, your boss, calls and asks to see you about the decrease in the quality of your product.					
10. In the mail you got a note from Randolf, the president of your company, and an article from the *Wall Street Journal*. The note says FYI (for your information).					

Behavior Modeling

DELEGATING

The scenario for this chapter shows Steve, production manager, delegating the completion of production output forms to Dale, following the steps discussed in the chapter.

Objective

To better understand the delegation process.

View the Video

View the accompanying video in class or at *http://lussier.swlearning.com*. This video can be used prior to conducting Skill Builder 2.

Skill Builder 2

DELEGATING AUTHORITY

Preparing for Skill Builder 2

Before beginning this exercise, review the text material on delegating.

Objective

To develop delegating skills. (Your instructor may have you watch the Behavior Modeling video before completing this exercise.)

Procedure

Work in groups of three. Each person in the group will role-play delegating one of the following three tasks to another member of the group, following the steps described in the text (explaining, setting objectives, and developing a plan). The third group member will observe and evaluate the delegation of the task; an evaluation form appears at the end of this exercise. Members then switch roles for the second task and again for the third. By the end of the exercise, each person in the group will have delegated a task, received an assignment, and observed the delegation of a task. (Note that in the real world, the process would not end with the delegation of the task. As a manager, you would establish control checkpoints to ensure that the task was completed as required.) After each person in the group has delegated a task, the group should discuss how effectively he or she delegated.

Delegation Task 1

Delegator: You are a college student with a paper due in three days. It must be typed. You don't type well, so you have decided to hire someone to do it for you. The going rate is $1.50 per page. Be sure to include the course name, paper title, special typing instructions, and so on. Assume that you are meeting the typist for the first time and that he or she doesn't know you.

    Receiver of assignment: Assume that you are willing to do the job.

Delegation Task 2

Delegator: You are the manager of a fast-food restaurant. In the past, you have set workers' schedules, and your policy has been to continually vary them. You have decided to delegate the scheduling to your assistant manager. This person has never done any scheduling but appears to be very willing and confident about taking on new responsibility.

    Receiver of the assignment: Assume that you are interested in doing the scheduling if the manager delegates the task.

Delegation Task 3

Delegator: You own and manage your own business. You have eight employees, one of whom is the organization's secretary. The secretary presently uses an old memory typewriter, which needs to be replaced. You are not sure whether it should be replaced with a word processor or a computer with word-processing software. You can afford to spend up to $2,500. Because the secretary will use the new machine, you believe that this employee should be involved in, or maybe even make, the decision. The secretary has never purchased equipment, and you believe the person will be somewhat insecure about the assignment.

    Receiver of the assignment: Assume that you are able to do the job but are somewhat insecure.

Evaluation Form

Each group should use three copies of this form: one for the observer, one for the person filling the role of delegator, and one for the person filling the role of receiver of the assignment. (The three forms should be labeled somehow, perhaps with O for observer, D for delegator, and R for receiver.) As one person in the group is delegating a task, the observer checks the steps that the delegator accomplishes. On another copy of the form, the delegator of the task checks those steps he or she believes are accomplished. On the third copy of this form, the receiver of the assignment checks those steps the delegator accomplishes. (When group members change roles for the next delegation task, they should exchange evaluation forms so that each person has the form appropriate to his or her role.) Discuss the questions below after each delegation situation. (The discussion should focus on any discrepancies between the evaluations of the three group members.)

Did the delegator follow these steps?	Task		
	1	2	3
Step 1. Explain the need for delegating and the reason for selecting the employee			
Step 2. Set an objective that defines responsibility and level of authority, and set a deadline			
Step 3. Develop a plan. Was the plan effective?			

Did the receiver of the assignment clearly understand what was expected of him or her and how to follow the plan?

_____

_____

How could the delegation be improved?

_____

_____

_____

_____

_____

Apply It

What did I learn from this experience? How will I use this knowledge in the future?

_____

_____

Learning Outcomes

After studying this chapter, you should be able to:

1. Identify the sources of forces for change. **PAGE 230**

2. List the four types of change. **PAGE 230**

3. List the reasons people resist change, and suggest ways of overcoming such resistance. **PAGE 235**

4. State the difference between a fact, a belief, and a value. **PAGE 237**

5. Explain intrapreneurship, and identify its three roles. **PAGE 240**

7: Managing Change: Innovation and Diversity

6. Discuss the relationship among diversity, innovation, and quality. **PAGE 243**

7. Explain the difference between team building and process consultation. **PAGE 249**

8. State the difference in the use of forcefield analysis and survey feedback. **PAGE 250**

9. Define the following **key terms:**

types of change	team building
information systems (IS)	process consultation
stages of the change process	forcefield analysis
organizational development (OD)	survey feedback
OD interventions	large-group intervention

Ideas on Management

at Hewlett-Packard

William Hewlett and David Packard started the Hewlett-Packard Company (HP) in a garage, back in 1939. Since then, HP has grown into a huge corporation of nearly 150,000 employees offering a wide portfolio of technology products and services for businesses and individual consumers. HP offers technology and services ranging from IT infrastructure, personal computing and access devices, and global services to imaging and printing for consumers and small and medium businesses.

In the late 1990s, HP was falling behind its competitors, and the company needed to counter threats from IBM and other technology companies, including Dell and Canon. To bring about the necessary changes, HP sought an outsider who could lead the corporation with fresh ideas. In 1999, HP's board of directors named 44-year-old Carly Fiorina as CEO. The board charged Fiorina with the task of reorganizing operations, developing new strategies, and undertaking acquisitions. Fiorina oversaw extensive restructuring of HP and the controversial acquisition of a personal computer manufacturer. In the process, she has become America's most recognizable female CEO. Critics, however, have accused her of pushing for too much change too fast. Fiorina argued that people should focus on results, not on executive shuffling.

© Reuters/Landov

I O M

1. How did Fiorina reorganize HP, and in what ways did she change its competitive strategy? What company did HP acquire in 2002?
2. How did Fiorina confront resistance to the acquisition?
3. How is HP committed to innovation?
4. What diversity initiatives has HP undertaken?
5. How does HP use organizational development (OD), and how does HP assist other firms with OD?

You'll find answers to these questions about HP and the management initiatives that Carly Fiorina implemented as you work your way through this chapter.

To learn more about HP, visit the company's Web site at *http://www.hp.com* or log on to InfoTrac® College Edition at *http://infotrac.thomsonlearning.com*, where you can research and read articles on HP and the latest developments in technology markets. For in-depth articles on HP's performance under Fiorina and its merger with Compaq, select the advanced search option and key in record number A114706478, A107123686, A105870432, or A117056244 to get started.

Sources: Information for the opening case and answers within the chapter are taken from "Carly Fiorina, Up Close," *Wall Street Journal*, January 13, 2003, pp. B1 & B6; Adam Lashinsky, "Wall Street to Carly: Prove It!" *Fortune*, January 12, 2004, p. 31; and the Hewlett Packard Web site at *http://www.hp.com*, accessed March 15, 2004.

CHANGE

Plato said, "Change takes place no matter what deters it." Today, change is the only constant, and an organization's long-term success is determined by its ability to manage change.[1] As you saw in the opening case, Hewlett-Packard was slow to respond to changes in the fast-paced technology marketplace and thus lost some opportunities that were captured by nimbler competitors.

Your ability to be flexible enough to change with the diversifying global environment will affect your career success.[2] In this section, we discuss the forces for change and types and forms of change.

Learning Outcome 1
Identify the sources of forces for change.

Forces for Change

THE ENVIRONMENT

WorkApplication1

Give an example of a force that resulted in a change in an organization you work for or have worked for.

_____

_____

_____

_____

_____

The changing business environment presents many challenges.[3] An organization interacts with its external and internal environments. As you saw in Chapter 2, these factors require change in an organization, and the organization needs to be proactive, rather than merely reacting to the environment.

THE MANAGEMENT FUNCTIONS AND CHANGE

Most plans that managers develop require changes. When managers organize and delegate tasks, they often require employees to make some changes in their regular routine. When managers hire, orient, train, and evaluate performance, change is required. Leadership calls for influencing employees, often to change in some way, and control may require the use of new methods or techniques.

Learning Outcome 2
List the four types of change.

Types of Change

Types of change refer to what actually changes within the organization. *The four **types of change** are changes in strategy, in structure, in technology, and in people.* Because of the systems effect, managers need to consider the repercussions of a change in one variable (type of change) on the other variables and plan accordingly.

Blockbuster Inc. is the U.S. movie rental leader, with more than 5,500 stores. **Netflix** took some of its business by offering mail-order rentals, and it also offered unlimited monthly rentals for a flat monthly rental charge, initially of $20. Blockbuster first followed Netflix by offering a flat monthly rental fee of $25. Then, in February 2004, Blockbuster decided to change its strategy and copy Netflix's mail-order service. However, Blockbuster will have the competitive advantage of offering both store and mail-order service. So customers can order movies online or in the store, pick them up or have them mailed, and return them to the store personally or by mail.[4]

Structure follows strategy, and so Blockbuster's change in strategy will also require a change in structure, as the company will need to add a mail-order unit. Online and mail-order business will also require technology changes at

Blockbuster. The company will also need to hire people with different skills to offer online mail-order rental services but will also need to retrain its current store employees to handle the dual option of in-store and online rentals.

CHANGES IN STRATEGY

You'll recall from Chapter 5 that an organization may change its strategy at the corporate, business, and/or functional level.[5] HP hired Carly Fiorina as CEO to make strategic changes.

CHANGES IN STRUCTURE

Structure commonly follows strategy. In other words, a change in strategy results in a change in structure.[6] HP collapsed its product-focused structure to establish one focused on customers. Over time, organizations often make changes in structure.[7] Exhibit 7-1 summarizes the types of organizational change in these areas.

CHANGES IN TECHNOLOGY

Technological changes, such as the introduction of computers, fax machines, e-mail, e-commerce, and the Internet, have increased the rate of speed at which change takes place.[8] Technology is a commonly used method of increasing productivity to gain competitive leverage.[9] **Wal-Mart**, for example, is committed to technology; its operating costs are less than those of its competitors as a result.

Technology often leads to a change in strategy or structure. There are several major areas of technology change:

- *Machines.* Companies regularly install new machinery or equipment. Computers are sophisticated machines that also are built into many other machines.
- *Systems process.* Systems process refers to how the organization transforms inputs into outputs. Changes in the systems process, such as the sequence of the work, are technology changes.

Exhibit 7-1 *Types of Organizational Change*

STRATEGY	STRUCTURE	TECHNOLOGY	PEOPLE
Corporate (growth, stability, and turnaround and retrenchment)	**Principles** (unity of command and direction, chain of command, span of management, division of labor, coordination, balanced responsibility and authority, delegation, and flexibility)	**Machines** **Systems Process** **Information Process** **Automation**	**Skills** **Performance** **Attitudes** **Behavior** **Culture**
Business Level (prospecting, defending, and analyzing)	**Authority** (formal and informal, levels of, line and staff, and centralized and decentralized)		
Functional (marketing, operations, finance, and human resources)	**Organizational Design** (departmentalization)		
	Job Design (job simplification, rotation, enlargement, enrichment, and work teams)		

- *Information process.* With the aid of computers, organizations have changed the way they process information. **Information systems (IS)** *are formal systems for collecting, processing, and disseminating information that aids in decision making.* Information systems centralize and integrate all or most of an organization's information, such as that on finance, production, inventory, and sales. In this way, the various departments can coordinate their efforts.[10]
- *Automation. Automation* is the simplification or reduction of human effort to do a job. Computers and other machines have replaced people for many tasks. If you want raises and promotions, be the first to master the use of new technologies.

WorkApplication2

Give one or more examples of a type of change (in strategy, structure, technology, or people) you experienced in an organization you work for or have worked for.

_____

_____

_____

_____

CHANGES IN PEOPLE

Organizations can't change without changes in people.[11] Tasks are the day-to-day things that employees do to perform their jobs, and tasks change with technology and structural changes. When tasks change, people's *skills* and *performance* must change. Organizations often attempt to change employees' *attitudes* and *behavior*.[12] A change in organizational *culture* is also considered a people change. You learned about culture in Chapter 2, and we will talk about the relationship between change and culture throughout this chapter.

People develop and implement strategy and structure. People also create, manage, and use technology; therefore, people are the most important resource. Change in other variables will not be effective without people.[13]

Forms of Change

Change also takes one of two broad forms: It is either incremental or radical.[14] Because HP did not do a good job of incremental change, it hired Carly Fiorina to make radical changes.

ApplyingTheConcept 1

Types of Change

Identify the type of change in each statement:

a. strategy
c. technology
b. structure
d. people

_____1. "We bought a new computer system to speed up the time it takes to bill customers."

_____2. "With the increasing number of competitors, we are going to have to spend more time and effort to keep our existing customers."

_____3. "Jamie, I'd like you to consider getting a college degree if you are serious about a career in management with us."

_____4. "We are switching suppliers so that we can get a higher-quality component to put into our product."

_____5. "We are laying off some managers to increase the number of people reporting to one boss."

Incremental change is continual improvement that takes place within already accepted frameworks, value systems, or organizational structure. Incremental change is necessary for survival and success.[15]

Radical change is rapid change in strategy, structure, technology, or people. Radical change alters accepted frameworks, value systems, or organizational structure.[16] Incremental and radical change are sometimes referred to as incremental and fundamental change, first-order and second-order change, alpha and beta change, or evolutionary and revolutionary change.[17] Adjusting to incremental change is like canoeing in calm water. By contrast, coping with a dynamic environment filled with uncertainty and requiring rapid change in order to react to unexpected events is like white-water rafting. Today's turbulent global environment is characterized by rapid change, ambiguity, and hyper-competition.[18]

John H. Patterson made the first mechanical cash register, and in 1884 he founded the National Cash Register Company. Over the years, NCR diversified into computers and electronics, and in 1974, it changed its name to **NCR Corporation** so that it would not be viewed as only a cash register business.

Today, NCR focuses on "transforming transactions into relationships." Whether these transactions and interactions take place across a counter, by telephone, at a kiosk or ATM machine, or over the Internet, NCR is there with hardware, software, and solutions that make these interactions easier, more convenient, and more relevant to customers, while giving companies the tools they need to gather critical data about their individual preferences, needs, and requirements.[19]

NCR is an excellent example of a company that has been able to make radical and incremental changes as it has moved from offering mechanical cash registers to electronic ones and now digital computing. In contrast, **Smith Corona**, which dominated the typewriter business, failed to change its product lines and offer computers and word-processing software and went bankrupt.[20]

Carly Fiorina changed HP's strategy—and thus the company's structure—with what she called "inventing at the intersection." Rather than have 83 independent business units, she reorganized the company into four core business groups. Thus, 83 products were sold together as a full line of products to four different groups of customers.

- **HP's Enterprise Systems Group (ESG) focuses on providing key information technology components, including storage equipment, servers, management software, and a variety of solutions to enhance business agility.**
- **The Imaging and Printing Group (IPG) focuses on printing and imaging solutions for both business and consumer use. IPG offers printer hardware, digital imaging devices such as cameras and scanners, and associated supplies and accessories. It also is expanding into the commercial printing market.**
- **HP Services (HPS) focuses on offering guidance, know-how, and a comprehensive portfolio of services to help business customers realize value from their IT investments globally.**
- **The Personal Systems Group (PSG) focuses on supplying simple, reliable, and affordable personal-computing solutions and devices for home and business use, including desktop PCs, notebooks, workstations, and personal devices.**

On May 3, 2002, HP completed its acquisition (which it called a "merger transaction") of its competitor Compaq Computer Corp., the largest tech merger in history. HP's acquisition was designed to help it compete against IBM.

MANAGING CHANGE

Today's successful firms are dynamic, adaptive, and evolving with the environment; they thrive on and welcome change.[22] Companies like Korean IT giant **Samsung Electronics** are not satisfied with past accomplishments; they constantly strive to develop new core competencies and profitable new business areas.[23] For companies like these, managing change is critical. In this section, we discuss stages in the change process and resistance to change and how to overcome it and present a model for identifying and overcoming resistance to change.

Stages in the Change Process

People go through four distinct stages when facing change. *The four **stages of the change process** are denial, resistance, exploration, and commitment.*

1. *Denial.* When people first hear that change is coming, they may deny that it will affect them. The Hewlett-Packard sales force, for example, initially thought that Carly Fiorina would focus her change efforts on HP's research and development and engineering departments. When Fiorina began changing sales responsibilities and commission structures, many sales representatives were surprised.
2. *Resistance.* Once people get over the initial shock and realize that change is going to be a reality, they often resist the change. When Fiorina revealed her plans for restructuring HP, the firm's executives and managers expressed doubt that the restructure was necessary. After Fiorina began to implement her plan, employee surveys showed widespread dissatisfaction with and even anger at the changes.
3. *Exploration.* When the change begins to be implemented, employees explore the change, often through training, and ideally, they begin to better understand how it will affect them. As the restructuring took place, HP employees began to explore the new partnerships developing between engineering and sales and, as a result, began working on new technologies for meeting customer needs. In the first year alone, HP patent applications tripled.

Exhibit 7-2 *Stages in the Change Process*

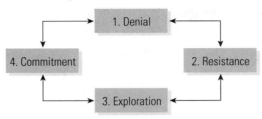

4. *Commitment.* Through exploration, employees determine their level of commitment to making the change a success. The level of commitment can change. HP lost about 5 percent of its workforce after Fiorina took command. Not all of the loss came from layoffs: a fair number of longtime HP employees left the company voluntarily, unwilling to adapt to the changes. Others, however, were excited about the changes.

Exhibit 7-2 illustrates the four-stage change process. Notice that the stages are in a circular formation because change is an ongoing process, not a linear one. People can regress, as the arrows show.

Resistance to Change

Most change programs fail because of employee resistance.[24] Why do people resist change, and how do managers overcome resistance to change?

———————————— **Learning** Outcome 3 ————————————
List the reasons people resist change, and suggest ways of overcoming such resistance.

As shown in Exhibit 7-3, employees resist change for five major reasons.

- *Uncertainty.* Fear of the unknown outcome of change is common. People often get anxious and nervous and resist change in order to cope with these feelings.
- *Learning anxiety.* The prospect of learning something new produces anxiety—*learning anxiety*.[25] We realize that new learning may make us temporarily incompetent and may expose us to rejection by valued groups. Learning anxiety makes us react defensively by denying the reality or validity of the data that triggered the anxiety and allows us to rationalize that we do not really need to change after all.
- *Self-interest.* People resist change that threatens their own self-interest. Employees are commonly more concerned about their best interests than about the interests of the organization.
- *Fear of loss.* With change, jobs may possibly be lost. Change may involve an economic loss as a result of a pay cut. A change in work assignments or schedules may create a loss of social relationships.
- *Fear of loss of control.* Change can also result in an actual or perceived loss of power, status, security, and especially control. People may resent the feeling that their destiny is being controlled by someone else.

WorkApplication3

Give an example of a situation when you resisted a change. Be sure to specify which of the five reasons fueled your resistance to change.

_____

_____

_____

_____

Exhibit 7-3 *Resistance to Change and Ways to Overcome Resistance*

Resistance to Change	Overcoming Resistance
Uncertainty	Develop trust climate for change
Learning anxiety	Plan
Self-interest	State why change is needed and how it will affect employees
Fear of loss	Create a win-win situation
Fear of loss of control	Involve employees
	Provide support
	Create urgency

How to Overcome Resistance to Change

Seven major steps you can take to overcome resistance to change are discussed below. Carly Fiorina used some of these techniques at HP.

1. *Develop a positive trust climate for change.* Develop and maintain good human relations. Make employees realize you have their best interests in mind and develop mutual trust. Constantly look for better ways to do things. Encouraging employees to suggest changes and implementing their ideas are important parts of continuous improvement.[26]
2. *Plan.* Implementing changes successfully requires good planning. You need to identify the possible resistance to change and plan how to overcome it. View change from the employees' position. Set clear objectives so employees know exactly what the change is and how it affects them. The next four steps should be part of your plan.
3. *Clearly state why the change is needed and how it will affect employees.* Communication is the key to change. Employees want and need to know why the change is necessary and how it will affect them, both positively and negatively.[27] Be open and honest with employees. Giving employees the facts as far in advance as possible helps them to overcome fear of the unknown. If the grapevine starts to spread incorrect information, correct it as quickly as possible. Fiorina attempted to communicate her change vision to HP workers in many ways. For example, she traveled to HP offices in 20 countries to hold personal meetings with employees to explain why the changes were necessary and how they would occur.
4. *Create a win-win situation.* The goal of human relations is to meet employee needs while achieving departmental and organizational objectives. To overcome resistance to change, be sure to answer the other parties' unasked question, "What's in it for me?" When people can see how they benefit, they are more willing to change. If the organization is going to benefit by the change, so should the employees. Fiorina adjusted HP's reward system as part of the restructuring. In the past, all employees had received bonuses of between 4 percent and 7 percent of their base salary every six months, regardless of how well their division performed. After the restructuring, employees received between 0 percent and

15 percent in bonuses, depending on their level of performance in reaching the goals that would help the division and company succeed.

5. *Involve employees*. To create a win-win situation, involve employees. A commitment to change is usually critical to its successful implementation. Employees who participate in developing changes are more committed to them than employees who have changes dictated to them.[28]

6. *Provide support*. To overcome resistance to change, employees need to know that managers are there to help them cope with the changes. Managers need to stay committed not only to the change objective, but also to making the learning process as painless as possible by providing training and other support. Managers must also give participatory power to the learners by soliciting feedback on how to meet the change goals. Employees need to realize that there will be a temporary drop in productivity that will be followed by an increase in productivity that will make the change worthwhile. It's the managers' job to get employees through this difficult period by providing support.[29]

7. *Create urgency*. Many people procrastinate making changes. A feeling of urgency is the primary driver toward taking action.[30] If something is perceived as urgent, it is given a high priority and is done immediately.[31] Fiorina made HP employees realize that the company was slipping and that it was urgent to turn things around.

Carly Fiorina ran into resistance to acquiring Compaq from a few members of the HP board of directors and some of the stockholders. They resisted the change because of uncertainty about whether the merger would work and fear of loss of value in their stock. Fiorina explained why the radical change was needed to get HP back on track and tried to get directors and stockholders to trust in her plan that the Compaq acquisition would be beneficial. Resistance to the acquisition led to a proxy battle, in which shareholders got to vote for or against the acquisition. Ultimately, Fiorina did overcome their resistance.

I
O
M

A Model for Identifying and Overcoming Resistance to Change

Before making changes, managers should anticipate how employees will react. Resistance to change varies in its intensity, source, and focus.[32]

INTENSITY

People have different attitudes toward change. Some thrive on it; some are upset by it; many resist it at first but gradually accept it. As a manager of change, you must anticipate whether resistance will be strong, weak, or somewhere in between. Intensity will be lower if you use the seven methods for overcoming resistance to change.

––––––––––– Learning Outcome 4 –––––––––––
State the difference between a fact, a belief, and a value.

SOURCE

There are three major sources of resistance to change:

1. *Facts*. The facts (provable statements) about an impending change are often circulated through the grapevine—but people tend to use facts selectively to prove their point. Facts used correctly help to overcome fear of the unknown.

2. *Beliefs.* Facts can be proven; beliefs cannot. Beliefs are subjective opinions that can be shaped by others. Our beliefs lead us to think that a change is correct or incorrect or good or bad. Differences in perception can cause resistance to change.
3. *Values.* Values are what people believe are worth pursuing or doing. What we value is important to us. Values pertain to right and wrong and help establish priorities.

FOCUS

There are three major focuses of resistance to change:

1. *Self.* People naturally want to know "What's in it for me? What will I gain or lose?" When the facts of change have a negative effect on employees, creating a perceived loss, employees resist the change.
2. *Others.* After considering what's in it for them and concluding that a change does not affect them, people tend to consider how the change will affect their friends, peers, and colleagues. If employees analyze the facts and believe that a change will affect others negatively, they may be resistant to the change.
3. *Work environment.* The work environment includes the physical setting, the work itself, and the climate. People like to be in control of their environment, and they resist changes that take away their control.

Exhibit 7-4 is a resistance matrix with examples of each area of resistance. Once you have identified the probable resistance to change, you can work at overcoming it. Note that the intensity of resistance can be strong, moderate, or weak for each of the nine matrix boxes. In Skill Builder 1 you will use the resistance matrix to identify the source and focus of change.

WorkApplication4

Describe the intensity, source, and focus of the resistance to change you identified in Work Application 3.

_____

_____

_____

_____

INNOVATION

Recall from Chapter 4 that *creativity* is a way of thinking that generates new ideas, and *innovation* is the implementation of new ideas. Two important types of innovation are product innovation (new things) and process innovation (new ways of doing things).[33] Innovation is the key to survival, growth, and performance.[34] In this section, we discuss organizational structures and cultures that stimulate creativity and innovative change.

Intel offers more than 450 products and services. Intel is very committed to innovation. In fact, on its Web site, the company has this to say about itself: "Intel believes in innovation. We're driven by it. We live by it. And it's this principle that led us to create the world's first microprocessor back in 1971. Today, Intel is behind everything from the fastest processor in the world to the cables that power high-speed Internet. We keep innovating because it's in our blood. Because it's part of our heritage. And because the technology we invent today will shape the world's future."[35]

Innovative Organizational Structures

Organizations that stimulate innovation are commonly structured as flat organizations with limited bureaucracy, have a generalist division of labor, coordinate with cross-functional teams, and are flexible. Use of informal

WorkApplication5

Give an example of an innovation from an organization you work for or have worked for. Be sure to specify whether it was a product or a process innovation.

_____

_____

_____

_____

Exhibit 7-4 *Resistance Matrix*

	Sources of Resistance (fact, belief, value)		
Focus of resistance (work, others, self)	**1. Facts about self** • I have never done the task before. • I failed the last time I tried.	**4. Beliefs about self** • I'm too busy to learn it. • I'll do it, but don't blame me if it's wrong.	**7. Values pertaining to self** • I like the way I do my job now. Why change? • I like working in a group.
	2. Facts about others • She has the best performance record in the department. • Others employees told me it's hard to do.	**5. Beliefs about others** • He just pretends to be busy to avoid extra work. • She's better at it than I am; let her do it.	**8. Values pertaining to others** • Let someone else do it; I do not want to work with her. • I like working with him. Don't cut him from our department.
	3. Facts about the work environment • We are only paid $7 an hour. • It's over 100 degrees.	**6. Beliefs about the work environment** • This is a lousy job. • The pay here is too low.	**9. Values pertaining to the work environment** • I don't care if we meet the goal or not. • The new task will make me work inside. I'd rather be outside.
	Intensity (high, medium, or low for each box)		

Source: Adapted from Ken Hultman, *Resistance Matrix: The Path of Least Resistance* (Austin, TX: Learning Concepts, 1979).

authority is common, and authority is decentralized. Job design includes job enrichment and work teams. [36]

Innovative organizations commonly create separate systems for innovative groups, such as new venture units.[37] To develop the Macintosh computer, Steve Jobs took a small group of engineers and programmers and set up operations apart from the remainder of the organization. **Colgate-Palmolive** created **Colgate Venture Company** as a separate unit.

Innovative companies recruit and train creative employees and set up a reward system that encourages creativity and innovation. Rewarding innovation leads to increased creativity. Many organizations provide financial and nonfinancial rewards to employees who develop innovations, as individuals or in groups.[38] Organizations commonly use cash, prizes (such as trips), praise, and recognition to encourage people to be creative. Many companies reward employees with a percentage of the savings or earnings generated by their innovations for the first year. **Monsanto** gives $50,000 each year to the individual or group that develops the biggest commercial breakthrough.

AT&T is one organization that has had problems innovating. In early 2004, the telecommunications company faced a key question: could it make its Voice over Internet Protocol (VoIP) a success? VoIP sends phone calls using the same processes as e-mail and works by essentially turning a phone into a little computer. VoIP calls—whether local or long distance—are much cheaper than traditional calls. AT&T advertised VoIP as its most significant advancement in decades, one that would benefit consumers and the telecom companies. AT&T needs this innovation to do well to ensure the company's future success.[39]

----------------------------------- Learning Outcome 5 -----------------------------------
Explain intrapreneurship, and identify its three roles.

Innovative Organizational Cultures

The most successful organizations encourage creativity and innovation.[40] Organizations known to have strong innovative cultures include Corning, **Hewlett-Packard, Intel, Johnson & Johnson, Merck, Monsanto, Procter & Gamble, Rubbermaid, Texas Instruments**, and **3M**. Such organizations develop structures that match, and become a part of, their innovative cultures.

Innovative organizations tend to have similar cultures that encourage experimentation. Innovative cultures commonly have the following six characteristics:

- *Encouragement of risk-taking*. Innovative cultures encourage employees to be creative without fear of punishment if they fail. Mistakes and failure are viewed as learning experiences. For example, about 60 percent of the innovations at 3M do not succeed in the marketplace.
- *Intrapreneurship*. As discussed in Chapter 3, intrapreneurship encourages the development of new ventures that might become separate business units. Intrapreneurship is commonly seen in three roles in large organizations. The *inventor* is the one who comes up with the creative idea. However, inventors often lack the skill to transform the idea into an innovation. The *champion* is the one responsible for transforming the idea into an innovation. The champion, usually a middle manager, believes in the idea and promotes it by finding a sponsor to provide the resources needed for the innovation. The *sponsor*, a top-level manager, supports the innovation by providing the resources and structure for the innovation. Sponsors deal with the politics necessary to get the resources. At Texas Instruments, only creative ideas with an acknowledged inventor, champion, and sponsor are formally transformed into products or services.
- *Open systems*. Organizational members constantly scan the environment for creative ideas. Benchmarking (Chapter 5) is commonly used.
- *Focus on ends rather than means*. Innovative cultures tell employees the objectives (ends), but the employees decide on the means to achieve them.
- *Acceptance of ambiguity and impractical ideas*. Requiring clear, practical ideas stifles creativity. Innovative cultures encourage employees to work on creative ideas even when it is not clear to managers what the employees are doing. The employees do not have to have an immediate practical value for the ideas. What seems ambiguous and impractical sometimes ends up as a great innovation.
- *Tolerance of conflict*. Innovative cultures encourage diversity of opinions as a means of coming up with creative ideas and improving on them.[41]

WorkApplication6
Does an organization you work for or have worked for have any of the six characteristics of innovative cultures? Overall, does the organization have a creative culture?

3M is generally recognized as a leader in innovation. 3M uses the six rules listed below to stimulate innovation. These six rules, which have been copied by other companies, are deeply woven into 3M's culture.

- *Set goals for innovation.* 3M's goal is to have 25 to 30 percent of annual sales come from products that are five years old or less. About one-third of 3M's revenues come from new products.
- *Commit to research and development.* 3M invests nearly twice as much in R&D as the average U.S. company. 3M's goal is to cut the time it takes to introduce new products in half.
- *Inspire intrapreneurship.* Champions are allowed to manage their products as if they were running their own businesses. 3M employees can spend 15 percent of their time on personal research interests unrelated to their current job.
- *Facilitate, don't obstruct.* Divisions are small and autonomous and have access to information and technical resources throughout the entire company. Researchers with good ideas receive $50,000 Genesis grants to develop their creative ideas into innovative products.
- *Focus on the customer.* Quality is defined by the customer.
- *Tolerate failure.* Managers know that mistakes will be made and that destructive criticism kills creativity. Employees know that if an idea fails, they will be encouraged to pursue other ideas.

HP is clearly committed to innovation. In fact, HP's motto is "HP Invent." Carly Fiorina was hired to get HP back on track as a leading high-tech innovator. Here is what HP says on its Web site about innovation: "Our $4 billion annual R&D investment fuels the invention of products, solutions and new technologies, so that we can better serve customers and enter new markets. We invent, engineer and deliver technology solutions that drive business value, create social value, and improve the lives of our customers."

I O M

Innovative and Noninnovative Cultures

Identify the type of organizational culture described in each statement.

a. innovative culture

b. noninnovative culture

_____ 6. "We have a very tall organization."

_____ 7. "I tried to develop a faster rotating blade, but it didn't work. However, my boss gave me a very sincere thank-you for trying."

_____ 8. "It drives me crazy when I'm delegated a task and the boss tells me the details of how to do the job. Why can't I meet the objective my way for a change?"

_____ 9. "This company makes heavy use of policies, procedures, and rules."

_____ 10. "We have jobs that are broad in scope and a lot of autonomy to do the jobs the way the team wants to do them."

Applying The Concept 2

Join the Discussion Ethics & Social Responsibility

Upgrading

1. Do you believe that software companies come out with upgrades just to make more money, or are these companies being honestly innovative?
2. As a sales rep, would you push a customer to purchase an unnecessary upgrade so that you could make a commission?
3. What would you do if your boss pressured you to sell unneeded upgrades?
4. Is it ethical and socially responsible to "require" companies to purchase upgrades if they wish to continue using the product or service?

SAP is the world's largest business software company, and the world's third-largest independent software supplier overall. SAP, headquartered in Germany, employs over 28,900 people in more than 50 countries.[42]

Fluor Corporation is one of the world's largest publicly owned engineering, procurement, construction, and maintenance services organizations. Fluor has more than 30,000 employees, and it maintains a network of offices in more than 25 countries across 6 continents.[43]

Fluor and other businesses have accused SAP of forcing them to upgrade their SAP software. Fluor claims that SAP upgrades are often minor and not needed, yet Fluor is required to purchase the upgrades. In fact, Fluor dropped parts of the products it had licensed from SAP and tried to take over its own software, hiring its own Chief Information Officer (CIO). However, SAP told Fluor that it would have to install new versions of its software or pay even higher annual fees to get upgrades, fixes for bugs, and access to SAP's technicians.[44]

DIVERSITY

Diversity programs have replaced most equal employment opportunity (EEO) and affirmative action programs. EEO stressed treating all employees equally, whereas affirmative action was created to correct the past exclusion of women and minorities from organizations. Affirmative action established percentages and quotas. Although quotas are being used less frequently, many organizations are actively recruiting a diverse workforce. They realize that a diverse workplace responds better to problems and change.[45] In this section, we'll define *diversity* and discuss the importance of diversity, how diversity relates to organizational culture, the difference between valuing and managing diversity, gender diversity, and how the learning organization embraces diversity.

What Is Diversity, and Is It Really Important?

When we talk about diversity, we are referring to characteristics of individuals that shape their identities and their experiences in the workplace. *Diversity* refers to the degree of differences among members of a group or an organization. People are diverse in many ways. Within the workforce, people differ in their race/ethnicity, religion, gender, age, and ability. They also differ in their military status, sexual preference, expectations and values, lifestyle, socioeconomic class, work style, and function and/or position within the organization. As an employee and manager, you should deal with all people in an ethical manner.

Is diversity really all that important? The answer is yes. For one thing, there is currently a shortage of skilled workers, so to exclude a qualified person because he or she is different in some way is counterproductive to business success.[46] The U.S. population is rapidly diversifying.[47] It has been estimated that by the year 2030, less than 50 percent of the U.S. population will be Caucasian. The state of California is already less than 50 percent Caucasian, as are some major cities. Today, 53 percent of college-age students are members of minority groups.[48] The percentage of immigrants in the United States continues to surge. One in five Americans doesn't speak English at home.[49] Hispanics have surpassed African Americans as the largest U.S. minority group. The traditional family has declined to 24 percent of homes; households with children headed by single women rose by 25 percent in the 1990s.[50] Hence, much of the new labor force will consist of minorities and women.

With these statistics, it should be clear that increasing cultural diversity in the workforce poses one of the most challenging human resource and organizational issues of our time.[51] Diversity provides both potential and challenges.[52]

-------------------------------- Learning Outcome 6 --------------------------------
Discuss the relationship among diversity, innovation, and quality.

Diversity and Organizational Culture

An organizational culture can value innovation, quality, and diversity. In fact, the same organizational structure supports all three values. According to the National Performance Review report, there is a relationship between quality and diversity. The report stated that before organizations can improve the quality of their products or services, they must first understand and address the requirements of all their employees.

Although organizations have different cultures, they can all develop cultures that value diversity.[53] The approach to developing a culture that values diversity is to recognize the realities of the new workforce and how these affect the efficiency and effectiveness of the organization as a system. Organizations need an inclusionary culture.[54]

Valuing Diversity versus Managing Diversity

Valuing diversity emphasizes training employees of different races and ethnicities, religions, genders, ages, and abilities to function together effectively. To be creative and innovative and to continuously improve customer value, employees must work together as a team in an atmosphere of dignity and trust. Diversity affects bottom-line profits. In other words, if people don't work well together, the organization does not work well.

Managing diversity emphasizes fully utilizing human resources through organizational actions that meet all employees' needs. Diversity can be managed successfully only in an organizational culture that values diversity.[55]

As Exhibit 7-5 illustrates, to manage diversity successfully requires top management support and commitment. Employees throughout an organization look to top management to set an example. If top management is

Exhibit 7-5 *Managing Diversity*

committed to maintaining a diverse workplace characterized by dignity, others at all levels of the organization will be as well. Managing diversity further requires leadership. Diversity leadership refers to having top-level managers responsible for managing diversity. The diversity leaders must also set procedures relating to maintaining diversity. Finally, and most important, employees must be provided with training so that they can work together as teams despite differences in race, gender, age, ability, and the like. Skill Builder 2 will give you a chance to understand differences among coworkers.

Gender Diversity

Before reading further, complete the Self-Assessment to determine your attitude toward women at work.

The "traditional" family, in which the husband worked and the wife was not employed, is no longer the norm. Two-income marriages are now the

---

Join the Discussion Ethics & Social Responsibility

Speaking English

1. Why are some organizations no longer requiring workers to speak English?
2. Should a worker be required to be able to speak English to get a job in the United States?
3. Is it ethical and socially responsible to hire people who can't speak English and to provide translators and policies written in multiple languages?

The United States was once known as the "melting pot," as people from all over the world came to the country and adjusted to its culture. In the past, generally, immigrants had to learn English to get a job. Today, however, many organizations hire people who can't speak English, and they use translators and have policies written in multiple languages for these employees. Government agencies at the federal, state, and local levels are also providing translators and written materials in other languages.

Self-Assessment

Women at Work

For each of the following 10 statements, select the response that best describes your belief about women at work. Place the number 1, 2, 3, 4, or 5 on the line before each statement.

5—Strongly agree   3—Not sure   1—Strongly disagree

4—Agree   2—Disagree

_____ 1. Women lack the education necessary to get ahead.

_____ 2. Women working has caused rising unemployment among men.

_____ 3. Women are not strong enough or emotionally stable enough to succeed in high-pressure jobs.

_____ 4. Women are too emotional to be effective managers.

_____ 5. Women managers have difficulty in situations calling for quick and precise decisions.

_____ 6. Women work to earn extra money rather than to support a family.

_____ 7. Women are out of work more often than men.

_____ 8. Women quit work or take long maternity leaves when they have children.

_____ 9. Women have a lower commitment to work than men.

_____ 10. Women lack motivation to get ahead.

_____ Total

To determine your attitude score, add up the total of your 10 answers and place it on the following continuum.

10_____ 20_____ 30_____ 40_____ 50

Positive attitude   Negative attitude

Each statement is a commonly held attitude about women at work. However, research has shown all of these statements to be false; they are considered myths about women at work. Such statements stereotype women unfairly and prevent women from gaining salary increases and promotions.

norm, and single mothers continue to incraase and may become the norm. Women now make up 46 percent of the U.S. workforce.[56] Organizations should realize that both males and females want a balance between work and family and prefer flexible work hours.[57]

Do women get equal treatment at work today? In spite of the Equal Pay Act, which requires equal pay for the same job, women's average hourly earnings are 72.2 percent of men's.[58] Although there has been progress in the promotion of minority group members and women, the glass ceiling—the invisible barrier that prevents minorities and women from advancing beyond a certain level in organizations—still exists.[59] Women are well represented in all domestic U.S. management positions. However, they hold only 6.2 percent of top management positions.[60] Women are also more likely than men are to be sexually harassed at work. *Sexual harassment* is any unwelcome behavior of a sexual nature.

Sexual Harassment

Indicate which kind of behavior is described in each statement.

a. sexual harassment

b. not sexual harassment

_____11. Ted, the supervisor of the production department, tells Claire, the department's current student intern, that he thinks she is sexy and that he'd like to take her out.

_____12. Sue tells her assistant Josh that he will have to go to a motel with her if he wants to be recommended for a promotion.

_____13. Joel and Kathy have each hung up pictures of nude men and women on the walls near their desks, in view of other employees who walk by.

_____14. George tells his coworker Sandra an explicitly sexual joke, even though twice before Sandra expressed her distaste for such humor.

_____15. Ray typically puts his hand on his secretary's shoulder as he talks to her, and she is perfectly comfortable with the way he treats her.

Mentoring

Mentors are higher-level managers who prepare high-potential employees for advancement. Mentoring is a process that enhances management skills, encourages diversity, and improves productivity.[61] Top-level managers should be mentors, and the employees they help should not be limited to managers. Mentoring programs have helped women and minorities to advance in organizations and break through the glass ceiling.[62] Having mentors who are willing to work with you to develop your knowledge, abilities, and skills can help you in both your professional and your personal life.[63] So, regardless of your gender or race, you would be wise to select a possible mentor and ask the person to mentor you.[64]

The Learning Organization and Diversity

You'll recall that the learning organization has a culture that values sharing knowledge to adapt to the changing environment and continuously improve.[65] The learning organization has decentralized decision making, participative strategy, empowered employees who share in responsibility, and a strong adaptive culture.[66] Learning organizations include all employees.[67] In other words, they value and manage diversity as part of their culture.[68]

With 142,000 employees in 170 countries doing business in more than 40 currencies and more than 10 languages, HP is clearly a diversified company. HP believes that a diverse workforce encourages creativity, innovation, and invention, and the company wants employees to reflect the diversity of the world in which it does business. HP has a Diversity and Inclusion Leadership Committee (DILC) that plays a critical role in helping to promote diversity and inclusion throughout the company. Managers are responsible for creating and maintaining diversity through development programs, recruitment opportunities, and training practices. The HP Web site includes a global citizenship report that includes a section on diversity.

HP has exhibited gender diversity in its top-level management. Its former CEO was a woman, and so are five of the 13 members of the executive team—almost 40 percent. HP is ranked 14th in the Fortune 1000, and Carly Fiorina was one of only 16 women CEOs in the ranking. Being the CEO of the largest company headed by a woman, she was at one time the most powerful woman in business, according to *Fortune*.[69]

ORGANIZATIONAL DEVELOPMENT

Organizational development is the commonly used method of managing change.[69] **Organizational development (OD)** *is the ongoing planned process of change used as a means of improving performance through interventions.* The human resources management department (discussed in Chapter 8) is usually responsible for OD throughout an organization. The *change agent* is the person selected by human resources management to be responsible for the OD program. The change agent may be a member of the organization or a hired consultant. In this section, we'll discuss change models and interventions.

Change Models

LEWIN'S CHANGE MODEL
In the early 1950s, Kurt Lewin developed a technique that is still used today for changing people's behavior, skills, and attitudes. Lewin's change model consists of the three steps listed in Exhibit 7-6.

1. *Unfreezing.* This step usually involves reducing the forces that are maintaining the status quo. Organizations sometimes accomplish unfreezing by introducing information that shows discrepancies between desired performance and actual performance.
2. *Moving.* This step is the change process in which employees learn new, desirable behaviors, values, and attitudes.
3. *Refreezing.* The desirable performance becomes the permanent way of doing things, or the new status quo. Refreezing often takes place through reinforcement and support for the new behavior.

A COMPREHENSIVE CHANGE MODEL
Lewin's general change model requires a more detailed reformulation for today's rapidly evolving business environment. The model consists of five steps, as shown in Exhibit 7-6:

1. *Recognize the need for change.* Clearly state the change needed—set objectives. Don't forget to consider how the change will affect other areas of the organization.
2. *Identify possible resistance to the change, and plan how to overcome it.*
3. *Plan the change interventions.* Based on the diagnosis of the problem, the appropriate intervention must be selected. The change agent may select one or more interventions.
4. *Implement the change interventions.* The change agent, or someone he or she selects, conducts the intervention to bring about the desired change.
5. *Control the change.* Follow up to ensure that the change is implemented and maintained. Make sure the objective is met. If not, take corrective action.

Exhibit 7-6 *Lewin's Change Model*

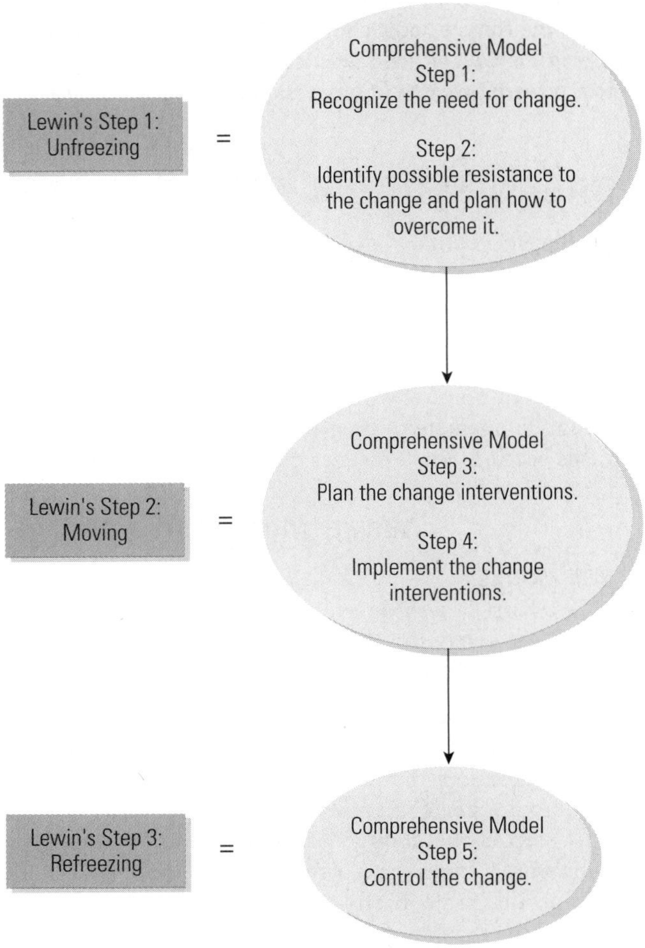

Organizational Development Interventions

OD interventions *are specific actions taken to implement specific changes.* Although there are many types, we will discuss the nine OD interventions listed in Exhibit 7-7.

TRAINING AND DEVELOPMENT
Training and development are listed first because these focus on the individual, and the other interventions often include some form of training. Training is the process of developing skills, behaviors, and attitudes to be used on the job. You will learn about training in the next chapter. Recall that training is an important part of valuing diversity. **Levi Strauss & Company** has a $5-million-a-year educational program designed to get employees to become more tolerant of personal differences. **IBM** is highly regarded as one of the top companies in commitment to and quality of its training and development programs.

Exhibit 7-7 *OD Interventions and Their Focus*

OD Intervention	Individual focus	Group focus	Organization focus
1. Training and Development	X		
2. Sensitivity Training	X		
3. Team Building		X	
4. Process Consultation		X	
5. Forcefield Analysis		X	
6. Survey Feedback			X
7. Large-Group Intervention			X
8. Work Design	X	X	X
9. Direct Feedback	X	X	X

SENSITIVITY TRAINING

Sensitivity training takes place in a group of 10 to 15 people. The training sessions have no agenda. People learn about how their behavior affects others and how others' behavior affects theirs. So the focus is on individual behavior in a group.

Learning Outcome 7

Explain the difference between team building and process consultation.

TEAM BUILDING

Team building is probably the most widely used OD technique today, and its popularity will continue as more companies use work teams. The effectiveness of each team and how the teams work together directly affect the entire organization.[70] **Team building** *is an OD intervention designed to help work groups increase structural and team dynamics performance.* Team building is widely used as a means of helping new or existing groups improve in their effectiveness.

The goals of team-building programs vary considerably, depending on the group's needs and the change agent's skills. Some typical goals are

- To clarify the objectives of the team and the responsibilities of each team member.
- To identify problems preventing the team from accomplishing its objectives.
- To develop team problem-solving, decision-making, objective-setting, and planning skills.
- To develop open, honest working relationships based on trust and an understanding of group members.

Team-building programs vary in terms of agenda and length, depending on team needs and the change agent's skills. Typical programs go through six stages:

1. *Climate building and goals*. The program begins with the change agent trying to develop a climate of trust, support, and openness. The change agent discusses the program's purpose and goals based on data gathered earlier. Team members learn more about each other and share what they would like to accomplish (goals) through team building.

2. *Evaluation of structure and team dynamics.* The team evaluates its strengths and weaknesses in areas of how the work is done (structure) and how team members work together as they do the work (team dynamics).
3. *Problem identification.* The team identifies its weaknesses or areas where it can improve. Problems may be identified in the change agent's interviews and/or the feedback survey. The team prioritizes the problems based on how solving them will help the team improve performance.
4. *Problem solving.* The team takes the top priority and develops a solution. It then moves to the other priorities on the list, in order.
5. *Training.* Team building often includes some form of training that addresses the problem(s) facing the group.
6. *Closure.* The program ends with a summary of what has been accomplished. Team members commit to specific improvements in performance. Follow-up responsibility is assigned, and a future meeting is set to evaluate results.

PROCESS CONSULTATION

Process consultation is often part of team building, but it is commonly used as a separate, more narrowly focused intervention. **Process consultation** *is an OD intervention designed to improve team dynamics.* Team building may focus on the process of getting a job itself done; process consultation focuses on how people interact as they get the job done. Team dynamics (or process) includes how the team communicates, allocates work, resolves conflict, handles leadership, solves problems, and makes decisions.[71] The change agent observes the group members as they work in order to give them feedback on team process. During process consultation, the team discusses its process and how to improve it. Training may also be conducted to improve group skills. The ultimate objective is to train the group so that process consultation becomes an ongoing team activity. You will learn more about team dynamics in Chapter 10.

—————————————— Learning Outcome 8 ——————————————
State the difference in the use of forcefield analysis
and survey feedback.

FORCEFIELD ANALYSIS

Forcefield analysis is particularly useful for small group (4 to 18 members) problem solving. **Forcefield analysis** *is an OD intervention that diagrams the current level of performance, the forces hindering change, and the driving forces toward change.* For example, Exhibit 7-8 represents a possible forcefield analysis for **HP's** corporate computing division, which has had difficulty gaining market share. The process begins with an appraisal of the current level of performance, which appears in the middle of the diagram. The hindering forces holding back performance are listed on the top or left part of the diagram. The driving forces keeping performance at this level are listed on the bottom or right of the diagram. After viewing the diagram, group members develop strategies for maintaining or increasing the driving forces and for decreasing the hindering forces. After group members agree on the diagram, the solution often becomes clear to them, and they can develop a plan to change the present situation.

Exhibit 7-8 *Forcefield Analysis*

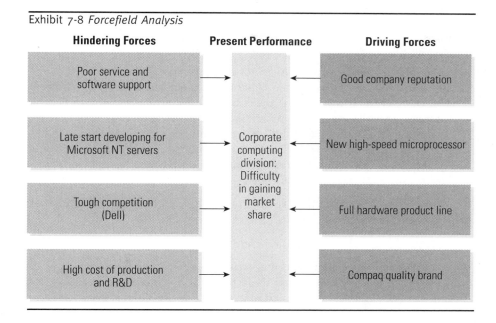

Hindering Forces	Present Performance	Driving Forces
Poor service and software support		Good company reputation
Late start developing for Microsoft NT servers	Corporate computing division: Difficulty in gaining market share	New high-speed microprocessor
Tough competition (Dell)		Full hardware product line
High cost of production and R&D		Compaq quality brand

SURVEY FEEDBACK

Collecting feedback is one of the oldest and most popular OD techniques at the department, division, and organizational levels. **Survey feedback** *is an OD intervention that uses a questionnaire to gather data to use as the basis for change.* Different change agents use slightly different approaches; however, a commonly used survey feedback process includes six steps:

1. Management and the change agent do some preliminary planning to develop an appropriate survey questionnaire.
2. The questionnaire is administered to all members of the organization/unit.
3. The survey data are analyzed to uncover problem areas for improvement.
4. The change agent reports the results to management.
5. Managers evaluate the feedback and discuss the results with their subordinates.
6. Corrective intervention action plans are developed and implemented.

LARGE-GROUP INTERVENTION

Large-group intervention *is an OD technique that brings together participants from all parts of the organization, and often key outside stakeholders, to solve problems or take advantage of opportunities.* Large-group interventions often include 50 to 500 people and may last for days. A major difference between large-group interventions and the other OD interventions is the focus on functional diversity and inclusion of key stakeholders.[72] For example, when developing a new product, a company might convene a large group of people in product development, engineering and R&D, marketing, production, and service from within the firm and also customers and suppliers, who would meet to analyze the new product in an effort to ensure its success.

GE uses large-group intervention sessions, which it calls GE Work Outs, in each of its business units. A Work Out is a process of focusing on how work is done and problems are solved. Work Outs usually follow these steps:

1. Select a work process or problem for improvement.
2. Select an appropriate cross-functional team with outside stakeholder members. The team includes top leaders and a human resources specialist to run the meetings. Outside consultants with relevant expertise may also be included.
3. Appoint a "champion" to follow through on recommendations.
4. Meet for several days to come up with recommendations for improvements.
5. Meet with leaders to get their immediate response to the recommendations.
6. Hold follow-up meetings, as needed, to implement the recommendations.

GE Work Outs have solved problems and increased productivity and have helped make GE a learning organization that continuously improves.[73]

WORK DESIGN
Work design refers to organizational structure. Work can be designed as an individual job, as a job for a group to perform, or by departmentalization. Job enrichment is commonly used to change jobs to make them more interesting and challenging.

DIRECT FEEDBACK
In certain situations, especially those involving technology changes, the most efficient intervention is to have a change agent make a direct recommendation about a specific change. Often such a change agent is an outside consultant.

WorkApplication7
Give an example of one or more OD interventions used in an organization that you work for or have worked for.

ApplyingTheConcept 4

OD Interventions
Identify the appropriate OD intervention for the change described in each statement.

a. training and development
b. sensitivity training
c. team building
d. process consultation
e. forcefield analysis
f. survey feedback
g. large group intervention
h. work design
i. direct feedback

_____ 16. "Things are going well, but I think we could benefit from an organizationwide intervention to solve our slow delivery problem."

_____ 17. "Morale and motivation have fallen throughout the division in recent months. We need an intervention that can identify the problems so we can change the situation."

_____ 18. "We have outgrown our present inventory system, which is also dated. What intervention should we use to develop a new one?"

_____ 19. "The new offset printing machine is installed. Who are we going to teach to run it and what intervention should we use?"

_____ 20. "What intervention should we use to prepare our employees to put the product together as a group rather than each person continuing to produce one part of it?"

From this chapter, you should understand the importance of managing change and how to manage change using OD interventions, as well as the importance of innovation and diversity, which need to be part of the organizational culture.

HP uses many of the OD interventions. Carly Fiorina used work design to change HP, as the organizational structure was trimmed from 83 business units down to 4. In 2003, HP began its Adaptive Enterprise strategy to help businesses manage change and get more from their IT investments.

I
O
M

Take advantage of the companion Web site for *Management Fundamentals*, where you will find a broad array of resources to help you maximize what you learn in class:

- Try a quiz
- View chapter videos
- Download slides
- Boost your vocabulary
- Work through an Internet exercise
- Find related links

Take a look for yourself at *http://lussier.swlearning.com.*

Chapter Summary

1. Identify the sources of forces for change.
The forces for change come from the organization's external and internal environment.

2. List the four types of change.
The four types of change are changes in strategy, in structure, in technology, and in people.

3. List the reasons people resist change, and suggest ways of overcoming such resistance.
People resist change because of fear of the unknown, learning anxiety, self-interest, and fear of economic loss or loss of power, status, or control. These forms of resistance can be overcome by establishing a positive climate for change, planning, clearly explaining the need for the change, pointing out how individual employees will benefit from the change, and involving and supporting employees during the change.

4. State the difference between a fact, a belief, and a value.
A fact is a provable statement. A belief cannot be proven because it is an opinion. A value is what is important to people; values help establish priorities.

5. Explain intrapreneurship, and identify its three roles.
Intrapreneurship is the development of new ventures that might become separate business units. The *inventor* comes up with the creative idea. The *champion* is responsible for the transformation of the idea into an innovation. The champion finds a *sponsor* who provides the resources needed for the innovation.

6. Discuss the relationship among diversity, innovation, and quality.
Diversity has a direct effect on innovation and quality. Before an organization can improve quality through innovation, it must address diversity.

7. Explain the difference between team building and process consultation.
Team building is broader in scope than process consultation. Team building is an OD intervention designed to improve both how the work is done and how team members work together as they do the work (team dynamics). Process consultation is designed to improve team dynamics.

8. State the difference in the use of forcefield analysis and survey feedback.
Forcefield analysis is used by a small group to diagnose and solve a specific problem. Survey feedback uses a questionnaire filled out by a large group to identify problems; the group does not work together to solve a problem. Forcefield analysis can be used to solve a problem identified through survey feedback.

9. Complete each of the following statements using one of this chapter's key terms.

The _____ are changes in strategy, in structure, in technology, and in people.

_____ are formal systems for collecting, processing, and disseminating information that aids in decision making.

The _____ are denial, resistance, exploration, and commitment.

_____ is the ongoing planned process of change used as a means of improving performance through interventions.

_____ are specific actions taken to implement specific changes.

_____ is an OD intervention designed to help work groups increase structural and team dynamics performance.

_____ is an OD intervention that is designed to improve team dynamics.

_____ is an OD intervention that diagrams the current level of performance, the forces hindering change, and the driving forces toward change.

_____ is an OD intervention that uses a questionnaire to gather data that are used as the basis for change.

_____ is an OD intervention that brings together participants from all parts of the organization, and often key outside stakeholders, to solve problems or take advantage of opportunities.

Key Terms

forcefield analysis, 250

information systems (IS), 232

large-group intervention, 251

OD interventions, 248

organizational development (OD), 247

process consultation, 258

stages of the change process, 234

survey feedback, 251

team building, 249 •

types of change, 230

Review and Discussion Questions

1. How do the management functions relate to change?
2. How does the systems effect relate to the four types of change?
3. List the four stages in the change process.
4. Which of the five reasons for resisting change do you believe is most common?
5. Which of the six ways to overcome resistance to change do you believe is the most important?
6. What are the two types of innovation?
7. List the six characteristics of an innovative culture.
8. What is the glass ceiling, and what can help people break through it?
9. What is sexual harassment?
10. Do you believe that it is acceptable for people who work together to date each other?
11. Which change model do you prefer? Why?

Objective Case

KRAFT FOODS

Obesity has become a major health problem in the United States. Public interest organizations are raising concerns about food companies' role in driving an epidemic of obesity through the marketing of junk food, while undermining measures to promote public health. Junk food is food with little nutritional value, including processed foods that contain white flour (white breads, pastries, cookies, crackers), white sugar (candy, soda, ice cream, cereal), and many fried or packaged foods (chips, pretzels, and other highly salted snacks, French fries). Most people do eat some junk food, but as with most things in life, eating junk food in moderation and making

sure one's diet primarily contains nutritional foods is the key to good health and weight control for most people.

People want to be healthy, and some people are reading the ingredients on labels before they buy products. In an effort to maintain or lose weight, more people are dieting by following the Atkins or South Beach low-carb diets, as well as many other diet plans. These diets have cut into the sales of processed snack food. Consumers want the benefits of less salt and sugar, fewer calories, reduced carbohydrates and fat, and zero trans-fatty acids—but they still want foods to taste good.

However, the reality is that only a small percentage of people are staying away from junk food for very long. The low-carb diet fad seems to have peaked and begun to decline. So, should the food industry change to offering more healthy foods? For Kraft Foods, the answer is yes. The company is working to increase the nutritional value of its foods.

Kraft Foods is a business unit of the former tobacco giant Philip Morris. Philip Morris changed its name to Altria Group, Inc. to better clarify its identity as the owner of both food and tobacco companies that manage some of the world's most successful brands. Altria acquired Kraft Foods and General Foods and combined them under the Kraft name to enter the processed food industry. Kraft owns a diverse portfolio of brands. Some of its U.S. brands include Oscar Mayer, Jell-O, Nabisco (Oreo, Chips-Ahoy, Ritz), Hearty Man's Frozen foods, Boca Burgers, Planters, Stove Top, Shake' n' Bake, Oven Fry, Post, Minute, Maxwell House, Kool-Aid, and Philadelphia. Kraft has international brands as well, and its products are sold in more than 150 countries. Some of these brands are actually separate business units.

In November 2004, Kraft agreed to sell its sugar confectionery/candy business to the Wm. Wrigley Jr. Company, a leading manufacturer and marketer of gum and candy. The sale included the Life Savers, Creme Savers, Altoids, Trolli, and Sugus brands, which had contributed about 1.5 percent of Kraft's global revenues.

As a leading food processor, Kraft is being proactive. In May 2004, Kraft unveiled more than 70 innovative foods and beverages during the Supermarket Industry convention, among them Crystal Light Sunrise, a new low-calorie beverage for breakfast; Boca Burgers, organically grown vegetarian burgers; and VeryFine flavored water. In addition, Kraft is doing several things to improve the nutritional value of its foods:

- Triscuits and Oreo no longer include trans-fatty acids.
- Jello-O and other products use low-cal sweeteners instead of sugar.
- Macaroni and cheese has less fat.
- Many of the single-serving sizes contain less fat, sugar, and salt per serving.

 To learn more about Kraft, log on to InfoTrac® College Edition at *http://infotrac. thomsonlearning.com* and use the advanced search function.

_____ 1. The pressure to change to more nutritious food is coming from the _____ environment.
   a. internal
   b. external

_____ 2. The change to more nutritious foods is primarily a change in
   a. strategy   c. technology
   b. structure   d. people

_____ 3. Removing trans-fatty acids from products such as Oreo cookies is primarily a change in
   a. strategy   c. technology
   b. structure   d. people

_____ 4. Kraft's sale of its sugar confectionery/candy business, which includes the business units that make the products, is primarily a change in
   a. strategy   c. technology
   b. structure   d. people

_____ 5. In offering more nutritious foods, Kraft is at what stage in the change process?
   a. denial   c. exploration
   b. resistance   d. commitment

_____ 6. People who don't believe they are overweight and who believe that Kraft processed foods are nutritious are at what stage in the change process?
   a. denial   c. exploration
   b. resistance   d. commitment

_____ 7. People who admit that processed foods are not as nutritious as less processed foods but who continue to buy them are at what stage in the change process?
   a. denial   c. exploration
   b. resistance   d. commitment

_____ 8. What is the primary reason that people resist changing to more nutritious foods?
   a. uncertainty   d. loss
   b. learning anxiety e. control
   c. self-interest

_____ 9. Which organizational development intervention is most appropriate for Kraft to use to find out if consumers like its new, more nutritious products?
   a. training and development
   b. sensitivity training
   c. team building
   d. process consultation
   e. forcefield analysis
   f. survey feedback
   g. large-group intervention
   h. work design
   i. direct feedback

10. If only a small percentage of people today are buying more nutritious foods, do you agree that Kraft should be introducing many new products?

11. Use the five steps of the comprehensive change model to explain how Kraft is changing to offer more nutritional foods.

Cumulative Case Questions

12. Discuss new ventures in this case. (Chapter 3)

13. Identify the strategy changes Kraft made with the introduction of more nutritional foods. Be sure to state Kraft's corporate and brand strategies. (Chapter 5)

14. What type of departmentalization does Kraft have? (Chapter 6)

Video Case

PETER PAN BUS LINES

About Peter Pan Bus Lines

This video looks at change at Peter Pan Bus Lines. Based in Springfield, Massachusetts, Peter Pan has been in business since 1933 and has no doubt experienced evolutionary and revolutionary change over its long history. But its attention to the details of safety and security since the terrorist attacks of September 11, 2001, which has been focused and intense, is the real subject of this segment.

View the Video (10–15 minutes)

View the accompanying video on Peter Pan Bus Lines in class or at *http://lussier.swlearning.com.*

Read the Case

Peter Pan Bus Lines has instituted a lot of changes to promote a safe and secure environment for all of its 850 employees, its 3.5 million passengers, and its 150 coaches. With destinations ranging from Concord, New Hampshire, to Washington, D.C., the entire Peter Pan Group, which includes the bus lines, Peter Pan World Travel, several hotels, and other affiliates, has a lot to protect. Some new safety practices involve technological change; others involve changing people's behavior and the corporate culture, for example, by creating a heightened alertness to safety issues. Of course, it is important that changes be supported by managers at the top of the organization; otherwise, they will not receive the attention and resources needed for implementation.

New policies and procedures for the company include requiring identification of all passengers when they buy tickets, issuing company ID badges to all employees, instituting a new security plan, adding interior mirrors to buses to give drivers greater visibility of passengers' activities, and improving luggage-hatch security so that no new items may be added after the hatches are shut. In addition, Peter Pan has worked with the local police to make sure that its emergency action plans are up-to-date and workable.

Change isn't easy. People need to be reeducated and motivated to implement changes on a daily basis, and sometimes it takes weeks or months for the changes to be complete. But when change begins at the top, it is likely to succeed.

Answer the Questions

1. How do Peter Pan's top managers show their support for change?
2. Why did one employee's resistance to the company's anti-profiling stipulations create such a strong reaction in Peter Pan's managers? How would you advise Peter Pan overcome this resistance?
3. Who are Peter Pan's change agents? What evidence can you cite from the video in support of their use of team building as an intervention method for driving organizational change?

Skill **Builder** 1

IDENTIFYING RESISTANCE TO CHANGE

Preparing for Skill Builder 1

Below are 10 statements made by employees who have been asked to make a change on the job. Identify the source and focus of their resistance using Exhibit 7-4. Because it is difficult to identify intensity of resistance on paper, skip the intensity factor. However, when you deal with people on the job, you need to identify the intensity. Place the number of the box (1–9) that best represents the resistance on the line in front of each statement.

_____ 1. "But we never did the job that way before. Can't we just do it the same way as always?"

_____ 2. The tennis coach asked Jill, the star player, to have Louise as her doubles partner. Jill said, "Come on, Louise is a lousy player. Betty is better; don't break us up." The coach disagreed and forced Jill to accept Louise.

_____ 3. The manager, Winny, told Mike to stop letting everyone in the department take advantage of him by sticking him with extra work. Mike said, "But I like my coworkers and I want them to like me, too. If I don't help people they may not like me."

____ 4. "I can't learn how to use the new computer. I'm not smart enough to use it."

____ 5. The police sergeant asked Chris, a patrol officer, to take a rookie cop as her partner. Chris said, "Do I have to? I broke in the last rookie. He and I are getting along well."

____ 6. An employee asked Chuck, the manager, if she could change the work-order form. Chuck said, "That would be a waste of time; the current form is fine."

____ 7. Diane, an employee, is busy at work. Her supervisor tells her to stop what she is doing and begin a new project. Diane says, "The job I'm working on now is more important."

____ 8. "I don't want to work with that work team. It has the lowest performance record in the department."

____ 9. A restaurant worker tells the restaurant manager, "Keep me in the kitchen. I can't work in the bar because drinking is against my religion."

____10. "But I don't see why I have to stop showing pictures of people burning in a fire to help get customers to buy our smoke detector system. I don't think it's unethical. Our competitors do it."

Apply It

What did I learn from this experience? How will I use this knowledge in the future?

_____

_____

Your instructor may ask you to do this Skill Builder in class in a group. If so, the instructor will provide you with any necessary information or additional instructions.

Skill Builder 2

DIVERSITY TRAINING

Answer the following questions.

Race and Ethnicity

1. My race (ethnicity) is _____.

2. My name, _____, is significant because it means _____. [or]

   My name, _____, is significant because I was named after _____.

3. One positive thing about my racial/ethnic background is _____.

4. One difficult thing about my racial/ethnic background is _____.

Religion

5. My religion is _____.

6. One positive thing about my religious background is _____.

7. One difficult thing about my religious background is _____.

Gender

8. I am _____ (male/female).

9. One positive thing about being (male/female) is _____.

10. One difficult thing about being (male/female) is _____.

Age

11. I am _____ years old.

12. One positive thing about being this age is _____.

13. One difficult thing about being this age is _____.

Other

14. One way in which I am different from other people is _____.

15. One positive thing about being different in this way is _____.

16. One negative thing about being different in this way is _____.

Prejudice, Stereotypes, Discrimination

17. If you have ever been prejudged, stereotyped, or discriminated against, describe what happened.

_____

_____

_____

_____

_____

_____

Apply It

What did I learn from this experience? How will I use this knowledge in the future?

_____

_____

Your instructor may ask you to do this Skill Builder in class in a group. If so, the instructor will provide you with any necessary information or additional instructions.

Learning Outcomes

After studying this chapter, you should be able to:

1. List the four parts of the human resources management process. **PAGE 260**

2. Distinguish between a job description and a job specification, and explain why job analysis is needed. **PAGE 265**

3. Describe recruiting sources for candidates for jobs and the selection process. **PAGE 267**

4. Describe hypothetical questions and probing questions. **PAGE 271**

5. Explain what orientation and training and development of employees involve. **PAGE 275**

6. List the steps in job instructional training. **PAGE 277**

8: Human Resources Management

7. Explain the two types of performance appraisal. **PAGE 279**

8. Explain the concept "You get what you reward." **PAGE 281**

9. Identify the major components of compensation. **PAGE 284**

10. Describe the difference between job analysis and job evaluation. **PAGE 285**

11. Explain why most organizations do not have to address labor relations. **PAGE 287**

12. Define the following **key terms:**

human resources management process	training
bona fide occupational qualification (BFOQ)	development
strategic human resources planning	vestibule training
job description	performance appraisal
job specifications	compensation
recruiting	job evaluation
selection	labor relations
assessment centers	collective bargaining
orientation	

Ideas on Management
at Scitor

Scitor is a Latin word meaning "to seek to know." Scitor Corporation of Sunnyvale, California, produces goods and services for program management, systems engineering, and customized computer information systems. Founder Roger Meade developed a unique organizational culture at Scitor based on his singular approach to human resources management. He believes that the key to productivity is taking care of employees' needs. Because of his strong belief in human capital, Meade sees Scitor's human resources programs as investments, not costs of doing business.

The human resources management process focuses on making life on the job as agreeable and as easy to handle as possible. Among Scitor's practices is providing benefits to all employees who work at least 17.5 hours per week. Scitor provides unlimited paid sick leave and does not track the number of sick days taken. The company's health care plan offers a $1,400 fund for each employee for dental and vision care and unreimbursed medical expenses. New mothers get 12 weeks of paid maternity leave and the option of full- or part-time work when they return.

© The Image Bank/Getty Images

Scitor organizes picnics, chili cook-offs, ski trips, fishing trips, and road rallies for employees. Scitor also hosts an annual fiscal-year kick-off meeting in a first-class resort that all employees attend. Scitor pays for transportation, food, and lodging for each employee and a guest for the three-day meeting.

Meade does not view his human resources policies as generous or liberal; it's simple economics. Everything Scitor does for employees is aimed at increasing the company's competitiveness and productivity. Employee benefits are offered because they support the objective of attracting and retaining employees. The money that would otherwise be spent on attracting and training new employees pays for the benefits.

IOM

1. **How does Scitor view its human resources management process?**
2. **What effect does Scitor's approach to human resources management have on attracting employees?**
3. **What types of training and appraisal does Scitor provide its employees?**
4. **What does Scitor do to retain employees?**

You'll find answers to these questions about human resources management at Scitor throughout the chapter.

To learn more about Scitor, visit the company's Web site at *http://www.scitor.com* or log on to InfoTrac® College Edition at *http://infotrac.thomson learning.com*. For recent articles on developments in human resources management, use the advanced search option to key in A111933408, A118542985, A117445522, A118446125, or A118446134.

Source: Information for the opening case was taken from the second edition of this book and the Scitor Web site at *http://www.scitor.com*, accessed March 19, 2004.

——————————— Learning Outcome 1 ———————————
List the four parts of the human resources management process.

THE HUMAN RESOURCES MANAGEMENT PROCESS

Management experts have conducted research on human resources management (HRM) for several years.[1] HRM practices in general, and compensation systems in particular, have been found to be highly related to organizational performance.[2] More specifically, effective HRM practices result in higher individual performance, organizational productivity, and steady financial performance.[3] HRM can be a source of competitive advantage in the knowledge economy.[4] However, research demonstrates that most organizations do not employ state-of-the-art HRM practices.[5] A key challenge today is to integrate global HRM practices.[6]

The **human resources management process** *involves planning for, attracting, developing, and retaining employees.* It is also known as the *staffing process.* Exhibit 8-1 illustrates the process; each of the four parts of the process is discussed this chapter. Notice the arrows used to illustrate the systems effect. For example, planning and compensation affect the kinds of employees an organization can attract; labor relations affects planning; job analysis affects training; and so on.

Managers at Scitor believe in taking care of employees. Roger Meade knew from the start that if employees were treated right, including being offered good pay and benefits and agreeable jobs, the company's HRM costs would easily be recouped. Meade knew that taking care of people makes it easier to attract and retain good employees. Satisfied employees are motivated to work hard and produce more, and the increased productivity more than exceeds the cost of attracting, training, and compensating new employees.

Exhibit 8-1 *The Human Resources Management Process*

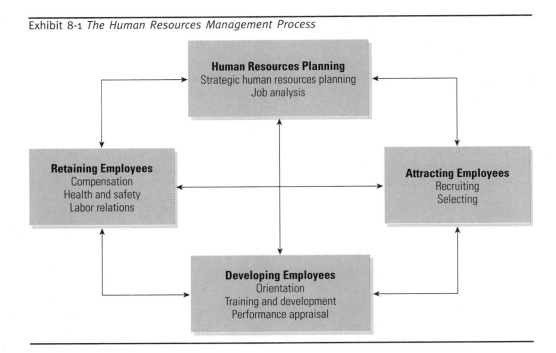

KnowledgePoint.com is a leading developer of human resource management software designed to help organizations attract, manage, and retain a workforce. KnowledgePoint.com offers solutions for HRM professionals and first-line managers in four areas: performance management, workforce management, job definition and hiring, and personnel policies and employment law. Among the company's products are online applications such as HRTools.com, PersonnelPolicies.com, JobDescriptions.com, PerformanceReviews.com, HRLegiState.com, and HRAnswersNow.com.[7]

HRLegiState.com provides up-to-the-minute online information about federal and state employment law, including new developments, complete law summaries of both federal and state laws, easy-to-use survey tools to research state law information, and comprehensive answers to common questions. **HRTools.com** provides online information about compliance with EEO/diversity, sexual harassment, ADA, and discipline and termination regulations.

We'll begin our examination of the HRM process with a discussion of the legal environment, as the law affects all four functions of the HRM process, and of the HRM department, which is responsible for carrying out the HRM process.

The Legal Environment

The external environment, especially the competitive and legal environment, has a major impact on human resources practices. Organizations are not completely free to hire whomever they want. The human resources department usually has the responsibility of seeing that the organization complies with the law.

FEDERAL LAWS RELATED TO HRM

Some of the major federal laws and regulations affecting employment in U.S. companies are presented in Exhibit 8-2 and discussed below.

Major laws affecting employment are the Equal Employment Opportunity Act of 1972 and executive orders on affirmative action. The Equal Employment Opportunity Act is an amendment to the Civil Rights Act of 1964 that prohibits employment discrimination on the basis of sex, religion, race or color, or national origin and applies to virtually all private and public organizations that employ 15 or more employees. The Equal Employment Opportunity Commission (EEOC) minority guidelines identify Hispanics, Asians, African Americans, Native Americans, and Alaskan natives as minorities protected under the act; the act also protects disadvantaged young people, disabled workers, and persons over 40 years of age. Although the law protects women from discrimination in employment, they are not considered to be a statistical minority because they make up half of the population; in some work situations, women are a majority.

The EEOC is responsible for enforcing equal opportunity laws. It has 47 field offices across the nation, and it operates a toll-free line (1-800-USA-EEOC) around the clock to provide information on employee rights.

Violation of the law can lead to being investigated by the EEOC or to becoming a defendant in a lawsuit. Courts find discrimination when employee selection criteria are vague, elusive, unstructured, undefined, or poorly conceived. As a manager, you should be familiar with your organization's EEO and affirmative action program guidelines.

Exhibit 8-2 *Federal Laws Related to HRM*

Law	Description
Equal Employment Opportunity	
Equal Employment Opportunity Act of 1972 (Title VII of the Civil Rights Act of 1964)	Prohibits discrimination on the basis of race, religion, color, sex, or national origin in all areas of the employment relationship
Civil Rights Act of 1991	Strengthened civil rights by providing for possible compensation and punitive damages for discrimination
Age Discrimination in Employment Act of 1967 (amended 1978, 1984)	Prohibits age discrimination against people older than 40 and restricts mandatory retirement
Vocational Rehabilitation Act of 1973	Prohibits discrimination based on physical or mental disability
Americans with Disabilities Act of 1990	Strengthened the Vocational Rehabilitation Act to require employers to provide "reasonable accommodations" to allow disabled employees to work
Compensation and Benefits	
Equal Pay Act of 1963	Requires that men and women be paid the same for equal work
Family and Medical Leave Act of 1993	Requires employers with 50 or more employees to provide up to 12 weeks unpaid leave for family (childbirth, adoption) or medical reasons
Health and Safety	
Occupational Safety and Health Act of 1970	Establishes mandatory safety and health standards in organizations; regulated by the Occupational Safety and Health Administration (OSHA)

PREEMPLOYMENT INQUIRIES

On a job application or during an interview, no member of an organization can ask discriminatory questions. However, one survey found that 21 percent of job applicants had been asked inappropriate questions at job interviews.[8] The two major rules of thumb to follow are (1) Every question asked should be job-related. When developing questions, you should have a purpose for using the information. Only ask questions you plan to use in the selection process. (2) Any general question that you ask should be asked of all candidates.

Exhibit 8-3 lists what can and cannot be asked during the selection process. In all cases, the assumption is that the information asked for must be related to a bona fide occupational qualification for the job. *A* **bona fide occupational qualification (BFOQ)** *is one that is reasonably necessary to normal operation of a particular organization.* For example, a BFOQ whose legality has been upheld by the Alabama Supreme Court is one that requires all guards in male maximum-security correctional facilities to be male. People who believed that this requirement was sexual discrimination took the corrections department to court. The Supreme Court upheld the male sex requirement on the grounds that 20 percent of the inmates were convicted of sex offenses, which created an excessive threat to the security of female guards.

WorkApplication1

Have you or has anyone you know been asked discriminatory questions during the preemployment process? If yes, please explain the situation in language acceptable to all.

_____

_____

_____

_____

Exhibit 8-3 *Preemployment Inquiries*

Topic	Can Ask ...	Cannot Ask ...
Name	Current legal name and whether the candidate has ever worked under a different name	Maiden name or whether the person has changed his or her name
Address	Current residence and length of residence there	Whether the candidate owns or rents his or her home, unless one or the other is a bona fide occupational qualification (BFOQ)
Age	Whether the candidate's age is within a certain range (if required for a particular job; for example, an employee must be 21 to serve alcoholic beverages); if hired, can ask for proof of age	How old are you? What is your date of birth? Can you provide a birth certificate? How much longer do you plan to work before retiring?
Sex	Can require candidate to indicate sex on an application if sex is a BFOQ	Candidate's sexual preference
Marital and Family Status	Whether candidate can adhere to the work schedule; whether the candidate has any activities, responsibilities, or commitments that may hinder him or her from coming to work	Specific questions about marital status or any question regarding children or other family issues
National Origin, Citizenship, or Race	Whether the candidate is legally eligible to work in the United States, and whether the candidate can provide proof of status if hired	Specific questions about national origin, citizenship, or race
Language	What languages the candidate speaks and/or writes; can ask candidate to identify specific language(s) if these are BFOQ	What language the candidate speaks when not on the job or how the candidate learned the language
Criminal Record	Whether the candidate has been convicted of a felony; if the answer is yes, can ask other information about the conviction if the conviction is job-related	Whether the candidate has ever been arrested (an arrest does not prove guilt); for information regarding a conviction that is not job-related
Height and Weight	Whether the candidate meets BFOQ height and/or weight requirements and whether the candidate can provide proof of height and weight if hired	Candidate's height or weight if these are not BFOQ
Religion	If candidate is of a specific religion, if religious preference is a BFOQ	Candidate's religious preference, affiliation, or denomination
Credit Rating	Can request information if a particular credit rating is a BFOQ	Unless a particular credit rating is a BFOQ
Education and Work Experience	For information that is job-related	For information that is not job-related
References	For names of people willing to provide references or who suggested the candidate apply for the job	For a reference from a religious leader
Military Record	For information about candidate's military service that is job-related	Dates and conditions of discharge from the military; draft classification; National Guard or reserve unit of candidate
Organizations	About membership in job-related organizations, such as unions or professional or trade associations	About membership in any non-job-related organization that would indicate candidate's race, religion, or the like
Disabilities	Whether candidate has any disabilities that would prevent him or her from performing the job being applied for	General questions about diabilities

ApplyingTheConcept 1

Legal or Illegal Questions

Using Exhibit 8-3, identify whether each question can or cannot be asked during a job interview.

a. legal (can ask)

b. illegal (cannot ask during preemployment)

_____ 1. What languages do you speak?

_____ 2. Are you married or single?

_____ 3. How many dependents do you have?

_____ 4. So you want to be a truck driver. Are you a member of the Teamsters Union?

_____ 5. How old are you?

_____ 6. Have you been arrested for stealing on the job?

_____ 7. Do you own your own car?

_____ 8. Do you have any form of handicap?

_____ 9. What type of discharge did you get from the military?

_____ 10. Can you prove you are legally eligible to work?

The Human Resources Department

WorkApplication2

Describe the kinds of interactions you have had with the human resources department of an organization you work for or have worked for.

Human resources is one of the four major functional departments in an organization. It is a staff department that advises and assists all the other departments in the organization. Unfortunately, one survey revealed that only 34 percent of respondents thought that the HRM department at their organization was competent.[9]

In organizations large enough (usually about 100 or more employees) to have a separate human resources department, the department develops the human resources plans for the entire organization:

- It recruits employees so that the line managers can select which employees to hire.
- It orients employees and trains many of them to do their jobs.
- It usually develops the performance appraisal system and forms used by managers throughout the organization.
- It determines compensation for employees.
- It is usually responsible for employee health and safety programs, labor relations, and the termination of employees. Employment records are kept in and by the human resources department, and it is often involved with legal matters.

As discussed in Chapter 3, outsourcing is becoming more common in business. Many firms are outsourcing most, or parts of, their HRM functions, and the trend is expected to continue. Over 50 percent of large firms are expected to outsource at least some of their HRM functions by the year 2010.[10]

Since 1920, **Young Electric Sign Company (YESCO)** of Las Vegas has produced custom signs and other display systems for businesses of all types and sizes, from the smallest retail store to the largest multinational organization. YESCO designs, manufactures, installs, and maintains signs and displays tailored to any business's specific needs.[11] HRM chief Paul Bradley couldn't keep up with the paperwork for 1,200 employees, and his other important HRM functions were suffering. In desperation, Bradley outsourced the work to **Ceridian,** an HRM firm, and was able to get back to helping YESCO meet customer needs. Ceridian performs HRM functions in the United States, Canada, and the United Kingdom. Ceridian enables companies to be free to succeed in their core business through outsourcing of human resources services for payroll, tax filing, time and attendance records, benefits administration, and employee effectiveness. Ceridian serves more than 20 million employees and deposits more than $125 billion in federal taxes annually for employers.[12]

HUMAN RESOURCES PLANNING

In this section, we discuss strategic human resources planning and job analysis.

Strategic Human Resources Planning

Strategic human resources planning *is the process of staffing the organization to meet its objectives.* The job of the human resources department is to provide the right kinds of people, in the right quantity, with the right skills, at the right time. HRM planning should be based on the mission, goals, and strategy of the organization.[13] Effective strategic HRM practices can lead to higher levels of performance and sustained competitive advantage.[14] Unfortunately, in one survey, only 20 percent of respondents agreed that their HRM department had a clear strategy guiding its activities.[15] But there is a direct link between the HRM function and company strategy.[16] If the strategy is growth, then employees will need to be hired. If the strategy is retrenchment, then there will be a layoff.

Human resources managers analyze the organization's strategy and its current human resources in light of the environment and sales forecast. The next step is to forecast specific human resources needs. The final step is to develop a plan to provide the employees necessary to meet the organization's objectives.

At **Lands' End,** a mail-order business, the staffing needs increase during the Christmas holiday season. More than 2,000 seasonal and temporary workers are required to fill these jobs. Staffing is done according to a plan formulated as early as January of that year.

—————————————— Learning Outcome 2 ——————————————

Distinguish between a job description and a job specification, and explain why job analysis is needed.

Job Analysis

Strategic human resources planning determines the number of people and skills needed, but it does not specify how each job is performed. An important part of human resources planning is the review of information about

---

Exhibit 8-4 *Job Description*

DEPARTMENT: Plant Engineering

JOB TITLE: Lead Sheet Metal Specialist

JOB DESCRIPTION:

Responsible for the detailed direction, instruction, and leading of sheet metal department personnel in the construction and repair of a wide variety of sheet metal equipment. Receives verbal or written instructions from foreperson as to sequence and type of jobs or special methods to be used. Allocates work to members of the group. Directs the layout, fabrication, assembly, and removal of sheet metal units according to drawings or sketches and generally accepted trade procedures. Obtains materials or supplies needed for specific jobs according to standard procedures. Trains new employees, as directed, regarding metal-working procedures and safe working practices. Checks all work performed by the group. Usually makes necessary contacts for the group with supervision or engineering personnel. May report irregularities to higher supervision but has no authority to hire, fire, or discipline other employees.

WorkApplication3

Complete a job analysis for a job you hold or held; write a simple job description and job specifications.

WorkApplication4

For the job considered in Work Application 3, were you given a realistic job preview? Explain.

jobs.[17] Job design is the process of selecting the tasks that each employee is responsible for completing. In order for jobs to be designed, they must be analyzed. Job analysis is the process of determining what the position entails and the qualifications needed to staff the position. As the definition implies, job analysis is the basis for the job description and the job specifications.

The **job description** *identifies the tasks and responsibilities of a position.* The trend is to describe jobs more broadly in order to design enriched jobs. Exhibit 8-4 shows a sample job description.

At **JobDescription.com**, you can create individual, customized job descriptions that meet legal requirements. You work completely online, and it's fast and easy. The job library has more than 3,700 job descriptions that include competencies that you can customize to help define the job. The Web site also helps you create and place job advertisements on the Web and generate job-specific behavioral-based interview questions; it provides expert advice for each step.[18]

Part of the job analysis should be to develop a *realistic job preview (RJP).* The RJP provides the candidate with an accurate, objective understanding of the job.[19] Research indicates that employees who feel that they were given accurate descriptions are more satisfied with the organization, believe the employer stands behind them and is trustworthy, and express a lower desire to change jobs than do those who feel that they were not given an accurate job description.[20]

Based on the job description, the second part of job analysis is to determine job specifications. **Job specifications** *identify the qualifications needed in the person who is to fill a position.* The job specifications identify the types of people needed.

Job analysis is an important part of human resources planning because it serves as a basis for attracting, developing, and retaining employees. If you don't understand the job, how can you select employees to do the job? How can you train them to do the job? How can you evaluate their performance? How do you know how much to pay employees?

Learning Outcome 3

Describe recruiting sources for candidates for jobs and the
selection process.

ATTRACTING EMPLOYEES

After hiring needs have been determined and jobs analyzed, the human
resources department generally recruits people to fill positions and presents
potential employees for line managers to select from. In this section, you will
learn about recruiting, the selection process, and how to conduct an interview.

Recruiting

Recruiting *is the process of attracting qualified candidates to apply for job
openings.* To fill an opening, possible candidates must first be made aware that
the organization is seeking employees.[21] They must then be persuaded to
apply for the jobs.[22] Recruiting can be conducted internally and externally;
Exhibit 8-5 lists possible recruiting sources.

INTERNAL RECRUITING
Internal recruiting involves filling job openings with current employees or people they know. There are two common types of internal recruiting:

* *Promotions from within.* Many organizations post job openings on bulletin boards, in company newsletters, and so on. Current employees may
  apply or bid for the open positions.
* *Employee referrals.* Employees may be encouraged to refer friends and relatives for positions.

EXTERNAL RECRUITING
The following are *external recruiting* sources:

* *Walk-ins.* Without actually being recruited, good candidates may come to an
  organization "cold" and ask for a job. Those seeking management-level positions generally tend to send a résumé and cover letter asking for an interview.

WorkApplication5
Identify the recruiting source used
to hire you for your current job
or one of your previous jobs.

Exhibit 8-5 *Recruiting Sources*

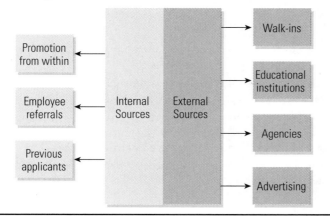

- *Educational institutions.* Recruiting takes place at high schools, vocational/technical schools, and colleges. Many schools offer career planning and placement services to aid the students and potential employers. Educational institutions are good places to recruit people who have no prior experience.
- *Agencies.* There are three major types of agencies: (1) *Temporary agencies*, like **Kelly Services**, provide part- or full-time help for limited periods. They are useful for replacing employees who will be out for a short period of time or for supplementing the regular workforce during busy periods. (2) *Public agencies* are nationwide state employment services. They generally provide job candidates to employers at no cost or very low cost. (3) *Private employment agencies* are privately owned and charge a fee for their services. Agencies are good for recruiting people with prior experience. *Executive recruiters* work for a particular type of private agency and are often referred to as "headhunters." They specialize in recruiting managers and/or those with specific high-level technical skills, like engineers and computer experts. They tend to charge the employer a large fee.
- *Advertising.* It is important to use the appropriate source to reach qualified candidates. A simple help-wanted sign in the window is an advertisement. Newspapers are good places to advertise most positions, but professional and trade magazines may be more suitable for specific professional recruiting.

The U.S. Bureau of Labor Statistics is forecasting a shortage of 4 million workers by 2006 and 10 million by 2010, based on demographics and a shrinking pool of skilled labor, which will make attracting and retaining employees more difficult.[23] Technology is changing how organizations recruit and select employees. A new form of advertising is available on the World Wide Web. Twice as many people now look for work online as use private employment agencies.[24] Several Web sites provide job opportunities. An

---

Applying The Concept 2

Recruiting Sources

Select the major recruiting source(s) that should be used for each of the job openings described.

Internal Sources
a. promotion from within
b. employee referrals
c. walk-ins
d. educational institutions

External Sources
e. advertising
f. agencies
g. executive recruiters

_____ 11. One of your workers was hurt on the job and will be out for one month. The person must be replaced.

_____ 12. One of the first-line supervisors is retiring in two months.

_____ 13. You need an engineer who has very specific qualifications. There are very few people who can do the job.

_____ 14. Your sales manager likes to hire young people without experience in order to train them to sell using a unique approach.

_____ 15. Your maintenance department needs a person to perform routine cleaning services.

example is **Monster.com**, which introduced job fairs intended for particular localities and industries.

The Selection Process

Selection *is the process of choosing the most qualified applicant recruited for a job.* No set sequence of steps is universally followed. Organizations may even use different selection methods for different jobs.[25] Selection is important because bad hiring decisions can haunt an organization for quite a while. We will discuss the application form, screening interviews, testing, background and reference checks, interviewing, and hiring.

APPLICATION FORM

As part of the selection process, the recruited candidates are typically asked to complete an application. Organizations may use different application forms for different jobs. For professional jobs, a résumé may replace the application form.[26]

SCREENING INTERVIEWS

Specialists in the human resources department often conduct screening interviews to select the top candidates who will continue on in the selection process. This step helps save line managers' time when there are large numbers of job applicants. Organizations including **Nike** and **PricewaterhouseCoopers** are using computers to conduct screening interviews. For example, at **Great Western Bank**, job candidates for a teller job sit before a computer, which asks them to make change, respond to tough customers, and sell products that customers don't ask for.

TESTING

Tests can be used to predict job success, as long as the tests meet EEOC guidelines for validity (people who score high on the test do well on the job and those who score low do not do well on the job) and reliability (if people take the same test on different days, they will get approximately the same score each time).[27] Illegal tests can result in lawsuits. Some of the major types of tests include achievement tests, aptitude tests, personality tests, interest tests, and physical exams.

Internal and external candidates for management positions are tested through assessment centers. **Assessment centers** *are places where job applicants undergo a series of tests, interviews, and simulated experiences to determine their managerial potential.* Candidates who perform well are selected for management positions.

BACKGROUND AND REFERENCE CHECKS

Organizations should prevent poor hiring decisions and the negative effects of negligent hiring by instituting a reference-checking system to verify the information on a candidate's application form and/or résumé. Many applications contain false or erroneous material. For example, people have stated that they have earned college degrees when they have never even attended college.

WorkApplication6

Identify which selection methods were used in the process of selecting you for a job you have now or one you held in the past. If a test was used, specify the type of test.

_____

_____

_____

_____

_____

INTERVIEWING

The interview is usually the most heavily weighted and the last of the steps in the selection process. One human resources manager for **Xerox** gives the résumé about 30 percent and the interview about 60 percent of the weight in the selection process. The interview gives the candidate a chance to learn about the job and organization. The interview also gives a manager a chance to assess things about a candidate that can't be obtained from an application, test, or references, such as the candidate's ability to communicate and his or her personality, appearance, and motivation.[28] Because job interviewing is so important, you will learn how to prepare for and conduct a job interview in this section.

HIRING

After obtaining information using the selection methods discussed, the manager compares the candidates, and decides who is best suited for the job.[29] Diversity should be considered when selecting a candidate. The candidate is contacted and offered the job. If the candidate does not accept the job, or accepts but leaves after a short period of time, the next best candidate is offered the job.

IOM

Scitor has a growth strategy; therefore, it is continually seeking employees. However, because of its reputation as an excellent company to work for, which was developed through its human resources practices, it does not have problems attracting well-qualified employees.

HRTools.com offers online help with the selection process. The company's Web site can help managers screen applicants and assess their skills, create interview scripts and improve interviewing skills, provide salary information for jobs offered by other organizations, conduct a background check, and make the final selection.

The focus of this chapter is on hiring others. But take a few minutes to determine how ready you are to progress in your own career by completing the Career Development Self-Assessment.

Self-Assessment

Career Development

Indicate how accurately each statement describes you by placing a number from 1 to 5 on the line before the statement.

Describes me		Does not describe me		
5	4	3	2	1

_____1. I know my strengths, and I can list several of them.

_____2. I can list several skills that I have to offer an employer.

_____3. I have career objectives.

_____4. I know the type of full-time job that I want next.

_____5. My written job objective clearly states the type of job I want and the skills I will use on the job.

_____6. I have analyzed help-wanted ads or job descriptions and determined the most important skills I will need to get the type of full-time job I want.

Self-Assessment

Career Development   (*Continued*)

_____ 7. I have, or plan to get, a part-time job, summer job, or internship related to my career objectives.

_____ 8. I know the proper terms to use on my résumé to help me get the full-time job, part-time job, or summer internship I want.

_____ 9. I understand how my strengths and skills are transferable, or how they can be used on jobs I apply for, and I can give examples on a résumé and in an interview.

_____10. I can give examples (on a résumé and in an interview) of suggestions or direct contributions I made that increased performance for my employer.

_____11. My résumé focuses on the skills I have developed and on how they relate to the job I am applying for rather than on job titles.

_____12. My résumé gives details of how my college education and the skills developed in college relate to the job I am applying for.

_____13. I have a résumé that is customized to each part-time job, summer job, or internship I apply for, rather than one generic résumé.

Add up the numbers you assigned to the statements and place the total on the continuum below.

65————55———— 45———— 35———— 25————15 or less
Career-ready   In need of career development

Career planning and networking to get jobs are discussed in the appendix to the chapter.

——————————— Learning Outcome 4 ———————————
Describe hypothetical questions and probing questions.

Selection Interviewing

As a manager, you will need to know how to conduct a job interview. You can practice this skill in Skill Builder 1.

TYPES OF INTERVIEWS AND QUESTIONS

Exhibit 8-6 shows the types of interviews and questions.

INTERVIEWS

Three basic types of interviews are based on structure: (1) In a *structured interview*, all candidates are asked the same list of prepared questions. (2) An *unstructured interview* has no preplanned questions or sequence of topics. (3) In a *semistructured interview*, the interviewer has a list of questions, but also asks unplanned questions. The semistructured interview is generally preferred: It helps avoid discrimination (because the interviewer has a list of prepared questions to ask all candidates), but it also allows the interviewer to

WorkApplication7

What types of job interviews have you experienced?

_____

_____

_____

_____

_____

Exhibit 8-6 *Types of Interviews and Questions*

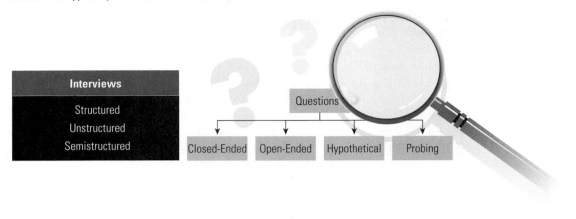

QUESTIONS

The questions you ask give you control over the interview; they allow you to get the information you need to make your decision.[30] All questions should have a purpose and should be job-related. You may use four types of questions during an interview: (1) The *closed-ended question* requires a limited response, often a yes or no answer, and is appropriate for dealing with fixed aspects of the job. "Do you have a class-one license? Can you produce it if hired?" (2) The *open-ended question* requires a detailed response and is appropriate for determining abilities and motivation. "Why do you want to be a computer programmer for our company?" "What do you see as a major strength you can bring to our company?" (3) The *hypothetical question* requires the candidate to describe what he or she would do and say in a given situation; it is appropriate in assessing capabilities.[31] "What would the problem be if the machine made a ringing sound?" (4) The *probing question* requires a clarification response and is appropriate for improving the interviewer's understanding. The probing question is not planned. It is used to clarify the candidate's response to an open-ended or hypothetical question. "What do you mean by 'it was tough'?" "What was the dollar increase in sales you achieved?"

WorkApplication8

Identify the types of questions you were asked during a job interview.

_____

_____

_____

_____

_____

ask each candidate questions relating to his or her own situation. The interviewer departs from the structure when appropriate. At the same time, using a standard set of questions makes it easier to compare candidates. The amount of structure you should use depends on your experience as an interviewer. The less experience you have, the more structure you need.

PREPARING FOR THE INTERVIEW

Completing the interview preparation steps shown in Exhibit 8-7 will help you improve your interviewing skills.

Step 1. Review the job description and specifications. You cannot effectively match a candidate to a job if you do not thoroughly understand the job.

Exhibit 8-7 *Interview Preparation Steps*

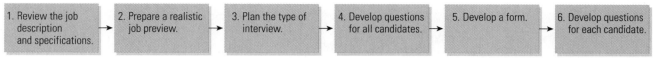

| 1. Review the job description and specifications. | → | 2. Prepare a realistic job preview. | → | 3. Plan the type of interview. | → | 4. Develop questions for all candidates. | → | 5. Develop a form. | → | 6. Develop questions for each candidate. |

Read and become familiar with the job description and job specifications. If they are outdated, or do not exist, conduct a job analysis.

Step 2. Prepare a realistic job preview. Candidates should understand what the job is and what they are expected to do. They should know the good and bad points of the job. Plan how you will present a realistic preview of the job, based on the job description. It often helps to give candidates a tour of the work area.

Step 3. Plan the type of interview. What level of structure will you use? The interview should take place in a private, quiet place, without interruptions. It may be appropriate to begin the interview in an office and then tour the facilities while asking questions. Decide when the tour will take place and what questions will be asked. Take a list with you if you intend to ask questions during the tour.

Step 4. Develop questions for all candidates. Your questions should be job-related, nondiscriminatory, and asked of all candidates. Use the job description and specifications to develop questions that relate to each job task and responsibility. Use a mixture of closed-ended, open-ended, and hypothetical questions. Don't be concerned about the order of questions; just write them out at this point.

Step 5. Develop a form. Once you have created a list of questions, determine the sequence. Start with the easy questions. One approach starts with closed-ended questions, moves on to open-ended questions and then to hypothetical questions, and uses probing questions as needed. Another approach structures the interview around the job description and specifications; each responsibility is explained and then questions relating to each are asked.

Write out the questions in sequence, leaving space for checking off closed-ended responses, for making notes on the responses to open-ended and hypothetical questions, and for follow-up questions. Add information gained from probing questions where appropriate. Make a copy of the form to use with each candidate you will be interviewing and a few extras for future use when filling the same job or for a reference when developing forms for other jobs.

Step 6. Develop questions for each candidate. Review each candidate's application and or résumé. You will most likely want to add specific questions to a copy of the form to verify or clarify some of the information provided; for example: "I noticed that you did not list any employment during 1995; were you unemployed?" "On the application you stated you had computer training; what computer were you trained to operate?" Be sure the individual questions are not discriminatory. For example, do not ask only women whether they can lift 50 pounds; ask all candidates, men or women, this question.

Exhibit 8-8 *Interviewing Steps*

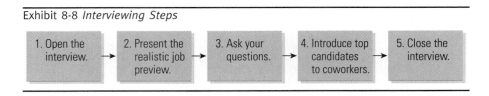

CONDUCTING THE INTERVIEW

Following the steps listed in Exhibit 8-8 will help you do a better job of interviewing candidates.[32]

Step 1. Open the interview. Develop rapport. Put the candidate at ease by talking about some topic not related to the job. Maintain eye contact in a way that is comfortable for you and the candidate.

Step 2. Present the realistic job preview. Be sure the candidate understands the job requirements. Answer any questions the candidate has about the job and the organization. If the job is not what the candidate expected, or wants to do, allow the candidate to disqualify himself or herself and close the interview at that point.

Step 3. Ask your questions. Steps 2 and 3 can be combined if you like. To get the most out of a job interview, you must take notes on responses to your questions. Tell the candidate that you have prepared a list of questions you will be asking, and that you plan to take notes.

During the interview, the candidate should do most of the talking. Give the candidate a chance to think and respond. If the candidate did not give you all the information you wanted, ask a probing question. However, if it is obvious that the candidate does not want to answer a question, don't force it. Go on to the next question or close the interview. End with a closing question, for example: "I'm finished with my questions. Is there anything else you want to tell me about, or ask me?"

Step 4. Introduce top candidates to coworkers. Introduce top candidates to people with whom they will be working to get a sense of the candidates' interpersonal skills and overall attitude. Introductions can also give you a sense of whether the person is a team player.

Step 5. Close the interview. Do not lead candidates on. Be honest without making a decision during the interview. Thank candidates for their time, and tell them what the next step in the selection process is, if any. Tell candidates when you will contact them. For example, say, "Thank you for coming in for this interview. I will be interviewing over the next two days and will call you with my decision by Friday of this week." After the interview, be sure to jot down general impressions not covered by specific questions.

WorkApplication9

Identify the steps that were used when you were interviewed for a job.

_____

_____

_____

_____

SELECTING THE CANDIDATE

After all interviews are completed, compare each candidate's qualifications to the job specifications to determine who would be best for the job. Be sure to get coworkers' impressions of each candidate.

Join the Discussion Ethics & Social Responsibility

Homeless Workers

1. Is Andre Jehan exploiting the homeless?
2. Is it ethical and socially responsible to give homeless people food for carrying signs?

Entrepreneur Andre Jehan owns and manages **Pizza Schmizza** in Portland, Oregon. He gives homeless people pizza slices and soda and sometimes a couple of dollars to carry a sign that reads "Pizza Schmizza paid me to hold this sign instead of asking for money." Jehan believes he is helping the homeless. However, Donald Whitehead, executive director of the National Coalition for the Homeless, says Jehan is exploiting the homeless and that any employee should be paid at least minimum wage. Jehan has hired homeless employees to work in the pizza shop, but has not retained anyone for an extended period. Many people are homeless because of mental illness or other problems that keep them from being able to hold a job. Jehan says carrying the signs has been a win-win situation, as the homeless don't feel embarrassed or exploited; they look forward to the work and food.[33]

PROBLEMS TO AVOID

Avoid the following problems during the selection process:

- *Rushing.* Try not to be pressured into hiring just any candidate. Find the best person available.
- *Stereotyping.* Don't prejudge or leap to conclusions. Match the candidate to the job based on analysis rather than instinct.
- *"Like me" syndrome.* Don't look for a candidate who is your clone. People who are not like you may do an excellent job. Remember the benefits of diversity.[34]
- *Halo and horn effect.* Do not judge a candidate on the basis of one or two favorable characteristics (the "halo effect") or one or two unfavorable characteristics (the "horn effect"). Make the selection on the basis of the total qualifications of all candidates.
- *Premature selection.* Don't make your selection based only on a candidate's application or résumé or after interviewing a candidate who impressed you. Do not compare candidates after each interview. The order in which you interview applicants can influence you. Be open-minded during all interviews, and make a choice only after you have finished all interviews. Compare each candidate on each job specification.

—————————— Learning Outcome 5 ——————————
Explain what orientation and training and development
of employees involve.

DEVELOPING EMPLOYEES

After employees have been recruited and selected, they must be oriented, trained, and evaluated—all of which are part of developing employees.

Orientation

Orientation *is the process of introducing new employees to the organization and their jobs.* Orientation gives new employees a chance to "learn the ropes" or the "rules of the game." Some of the benefits of effective orientation include a reduction in the time it takes a new employee to perform to standard levels, reduced anxiety about doing a good job and getting along with peers, as well as accurate perceptions of what is expected of the employee. Employees tend to stay on the job longer (reduced turnover) and have improved attitudes and performance when they go through orientation.

ORIENTATION PROGRAMS

Although orientation programs vary in formality and content, five important elements should be included: (1) description of organization and department functions, (2) specification of job tasks and responsibilities, (3) explanation of standing plans, (4) a tour, and (5) introduction to coworkers. Organizations that have developed innovative orientation programs include **Ernst & Young, Quad/Graphics, Southwest Airlines**, and **System One**.

During the orientation and training period, organizations tell employees the firm's personnel policies, such as how many sick days are allowed. Many organizations have some form of personnel policy handbook, which they give to employees. At **PersonnelPolicies.com**, you can create customized personnel policies or write a complete handbook online. The Web site includes an extensive list of policy topics to select from, any of which can be customized to meet an organization's unique requirements. The Web site also offers expert advice.

WorkApplication10

Recall an orientation you experienced. Which elements did it include and exclude? Briefly describe the orientation.

_____

_____

_____

_____

_____

Training and Development

Employees have to be taught how to perform a new job. Orientation and training may, and often do, take place simultaneously. **Training** *is the process of teaching employees the skills necessary to perform a job.* Training typically addresses the technical skills of nonmanagers.[35] **Development** *is ongoing education to improve skills for present and future jobs.* Development is less technical and is aimed at improving human, communication, conceptual, and decision-making skills in managerial and professional employees.[36]

Training and development constitute a good investment because they benefit individuals, their organizations, and the economy as a whole.[37] **IBM, General Motors, Motorola, Texas Instruments**, and **Xerox** invest heavily in training and development. In fact, in the United States, total corporate spending on training and development exceeds by a third the total spending by colleges and universities.[38]

OFF-THE-JOB AND ON-THE-JOB TRAINING

Employees can learn to perform their assigned tasks both off the job and on the job.

As the name implies, *off-the-job training* is conducted away from the work site, often in some sort of classroom setting. A common method is vestibule training. **Vestibule training** *develops skills in a simulated setting.* It is used when teaching job skills at the work site is impractical. For example, many large retail stores have training rooms where new employees learn how to run cash registers and other equipment. The training is usually conducted by a training specialist. Most organizations conduct development programs off the job.

On-the-job training (OJT) is done at the work site with the resources the employee uses to perform the job. The manager, or an employee selected by the manager, usually conducts the training. Because of its proven record of success, job instructional training (JIT) is a popular training method used worldwide.

Learning Outcome 6
List the steps in job instructional training.

JOB INSTRUCTIONAL TRAINING

JIT has four steps, presented in Exhibit 8-9 and described here.

Step 1. Preparation of the trainee. Put the trainee at ease as you create interest in the job and encourage questions. Explain the task objectives and quantity and quality requirements, and discuss their importance.

Step 2. Presentation of the task by trainer. Perform the task yourself slowly, explaining each step several times. Once the trainee seems to have the steps memorized, have him or her explain each step as you perform the task. Prepare a written list of the steps in complex tasks and give a copy to the trainee.

Step 3. Performance of the task by the trainee. Have the trainee perform the task slowly while explaining each step. Correct any errors and be willing to help the trainee perform any difficult steps. Continue until the employee can perform the task proficiently.

Step 4. Follow-up. Tell the trainee who is available to provide help with any questions or problems. Gradually leave the trainee alone. Begin by checking quality and quantity frequently, then decrease the amount of checking based on the trainee's skill level. Watch the trainee perform the task and be sure to correct any errors or faulty work procedures before they become habits. Be patient and encouraging.

Training Methods

Exhibit 8-10 lists various commonly used training methods, many of which can be used as part of JIT. The training methods are grouped on the basis of the primary skills developed. However, some of the technical methods can be combined.

When selecting a training method, keep the following statistics in mind: People learn 10 percent of what they read, 20 percent of what they hear, and 30 percent of what they see. People learn 50 percent of what they see and hear. They learn 70 percent of what they talk over with others. People learn 80 percent

WorkApplication11

Identify which steps of JIT your trainer used to train you for a present or past job. Was the training conducted on or off the job?

_____

_____

_____

_____

WorkApplication12

Explain the training methods used to teach you how to perform your present job or a past job.

_____

_____

_____

_____

_____

Exhibit 8-9 *Job Instructional Training Steps*

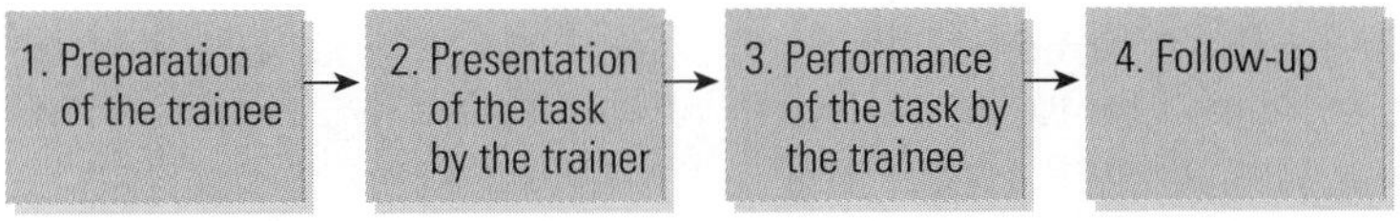

1. Preparation of the trainee → 2. Presentation of the task by the trainer → 3. Performance of the task by the trainee → 4. Follow-up

Exhibit 8-10 *Training Methods*

Skills Developed	Methods	Description
Technical skills	Written material, lectures, videotapes, question-and-answer sessions, discussions, demonstrations	
	Programmed learning	Questions or problems related to previously presented material are presented to the trainee in a booklet or on a computer screen. The trainee is asked to select a response to each question or problem and is given feedback on the response. Depending on the material presented, programmed learning may also develop interpersonal and communication skills.
	Job rotation	Employees are trained to perform different jobs. Job rotation also develops trainees' conceptual skills.
	Projects	Trainees are given special assignments, such as developing a new product or preparing a report. Certain projects may also develop trainees' interpersonal skills and conceptual skills.
Interpersonal and communication skills	Role playing	Trainees act out situations that might occur on the job, such as handling a customer complaint, to develop skill at handling such situations on the job.
	Behavior modeling	Trainees observe how to perform a task correctly (by watching either a live demonstration or a videotape). Trainees role play the observed skills and receive feedback on their performance. Trainees develop plans for using the observed skills on the job.
Conceptual and decision-making skills	Cases	The trainee is presented with a simulated situation and asked to diagnose and solve the problems involved. The trainee usually must also answer questions about his or her diagnosis and solution.
	In-basket exercises	The trainee is given actual or simulated letters, memos, reports, and so forth that would typically come to the person holding the job. The trainee must determine what action each item would require and must assign priorities to the actions.
	Management games	Trainees work as part of a team to "manage" a simulated company over a period of several game "quarters" or "years."
	Interactive videos	Trainees can view videotapes that present situations requiring conceptual skills or decision making.

of what they use and do in real life, and they learn 95 percent of what they teach someone else. People learn by doing, so this is the approach this book takes.[39] And the level of skill needed to succeed in the global village continues to increase.[40]

MANAGERIAL USE OF TRAINING METHODS

All of the methods listed in Exhibit 8-10 under technical skills are commonly used in training employees to perform their jobs. Managers do not commonly use role playing and behavior modeling. However, these methods are appropriate for managers who need to train employees how to handle

Applying The Concept 3

Training Methods

Select the appropriate training method(s) for each situation.

a. written material
b. lecture
c. videotape
d. question-and-answer session
e. discussion
f. programmed learning
g. demonstration

h. job rotation
i. projects
j. role playing
k. behavior modeling
l. management games
m. in-basket exercise
n. cases

_____16. You have a large department with a high turnover rate. Employees must learn several rules and regulations in order to perform their jobs.

_____7. You occasionally have new employees whom you must train to handle the typical daily problems they will face on the job.

_____18. Your employees will be preparing a special report.

_____19. You want to be sure that employees can cover for each other if one or more of them is absent.

_____20. You need to teach employees how to handle customer complaints.

human relations problems such as customer complaints.[41] Managers can also teach human relations skills to employees by example.

Management games, in-basket exercises, and cases are commonly used to train managers. In other words, managers may be trained with these methods but may not use these training methods with their employees. Only 36 percent of respondents to one survey agreed that employees received the training they needed to do a good job.[42] So, be sure to do a good job of training others.

— Learning Outcome 7 —

Explain the two types of performance appraisal.

Performance Appraisal

After managers have hired and trained employees, they must evaluate how well employees perform their jobs. **Performance appraisal** *is the ongoing process of evaluating employee performance.*

TYPES OF PERFORMANCE APPRAISAL

The two types of performance appraisal (PA) are developmental and evaluative. A *developmental performance appraisal* is used to make decisions and plans for performance improvements. An *evaluative performance appraisal* is used to make administrative decisions about such issues as pay raises, transfers and promotions, and demotions and terminations. The evaluative PA focuses on the past, whereas the developmental PA focuses on the future. They are related because a developmental PA is always based on an evaluative PA. However, the primary purpose of performance appraisal should be to help employees to continuously improve their performance, as performance influences employee productivity and job satisfaction.[43] Unfortunately, only 35 percent of respondents in one survey said that appraisal systems accurately assess people's strengths and weaknesses.[44]

When a developmental and an evaluative PA are conducted together (which they commonly are), the appraisal is often less effective, especially when the employee disagrees with the evaluation. Most managers are not good at being a judge and a coach at the same time. Therefore, separate meetings make the two uses clear and can help the manager be both a judge and a coach.

THE PERFORMANCE APPRAISAL PROCESS

Exhibit 8-11 illustrates the performance appraisal process. Note the connection between the organization's mission and objectives and the performance appraisal process. Performance should be measured in terms of the mission and objectives.

A performance appraisal should not be simply a once-a-year formal interview.[45] As its definition states, performance appraisal is an ongoing process. Employees need regular informal feedback on their performance.[46] Coaching involves giving praise for a job well done to maintain performance or taking corrective action when standards are not met. The employee performing below standards may need daily or weekly coaching or discipline to meet standards. In Chapter 14, we will discuss coaching and discipline.

As a manager, part of your job is to make sure that employees know what the standards are. If you give an employee an average rather than a good rating, you should be able to clearly explain why. The employee should understand what needs to be done during the next performance period to get the higher rating. With clear standards and coaching, you can minimize disagreements over performance during the formal performance appraisal. In Chapter 14, you will learn how to set standards for quantity, quality, time, cost, and behavior.

Exhibit 8-11 *The Performance Appraisal Process*

Learning Outcome **8** ---

Explain the concept "You get what you reward."

YOU GET WHAT YOU REWARD

One of the important things you should learn in in your study of the management process is that people will do what they are rewarded for doing. People seek information concerning what activities are rewarded, and then seek to do those things, often to the exclusion of activities not rewarded. The extent to which this occurs depends on the attractiveness of the rewards offered.[47]

For example, if a professor gives a class a reading list of several resources, but students realize they will not discuss them in class or be tested on them, how many students will read what's on the list? Or, "A, B, and C from this chapter are important and I'll test you on them, but X, Y, and Z are not." Will students spend equal time studying both?

MEASUREMENT METHODS

The formal performance appraisal often involves the use of a standard form, usually a rating scale or a behaviorally anchored rating scale (BARS) developed by the human resources department to measure employee performance.[48] Exhibit 8-12 explains the commonly used performance appraisal measurement methods and displays them on a continuum based on their use in administrative and developmental decisions.

Determining the best appraisal method to use depends on the objectives of the organization. A combination of the methods is usually superior to any one method used by itself. For developmental objectives, the critical incidents file and MBO work well. For administrative decisions, a ranking method based on

---

Applying The **Concept** **4**

Selecting Performance Appraisal Methods

Select the performance appraisal method that is most appropriate for the given situation.

a. critical incidents file	d. ranking
b. rating scale	e. MBO
c. BARS	f. narrative method

_____ 21. You started a small company with 10 employees. You are overworked, so you want to develop one performance appraisal form you can use with all employees.

_____ 22. You have been promoted from a supervisory position to a middle management position. You have been asked to select your replacement.

_____ 23. Winnie is not performing up to standard. You decided to talk to her in order to improve her performance.

_____ 24. You want to create a system for developing each employee.

_____ 25. Your small business has grown to 50 employees. Employees have complained that the one existing appraisal form does not work well for different types of employee jobs. You have decided to hire a professional to develop a performance appraisal system that is more objective and job-specific, with forms for various employee groups.

Exhibit 8-12 *Performance Appraisal Measurement Methods*

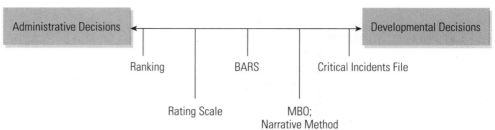

The Critical Incidents File is a performance appraisal method in which a manager keeps a written record of positive and negative performance of employees throughout the performance period.

The Rating Scale is a performance appraisal checklist on which a manager simply rates the employee's quantity of work, quality of work, dependability, judgment, attitude, cooperation, and initiative.

Behaviorally Anchored Rating Scale (BARS) is a performance appraisal method combining the rating scale and the critical incidents file. It is more objective and accurate than either method used separately. Rather than having ratings of excellent, good, average, and so forth, the form has several statements that describe the employee's performance, from which the manager selects the best one. Standards are clear when a good BARS is developed.

Ranking is a performance appraisal method that is used to evaluate employee performance from best to worst. Under the ranking method, the manager compares an employee to other employees, rather than to a standard measurement. An offshoot of ranking is the forced distribution method, which is similar to grading on a curve. Predetermined percentages of employees are placed in various performance categories, for example: excellent, 5%; above average, 15%; average, 60%; below average, 15%; and poor, 5%.

Management by Objectives (MBO) is a process in which managers and employees jointly set objectives for the employees, periodically evaluate performance, and reward according to the results.

The narrative method requires a manager to write a statement about the employee's performance. The system can vary. Managers may be allowed to write whatever they want, or they may be required to answer questions about the employee's performance. The Narrative Method is often combined with another method.

rating scales or BARS works well. The success of performance appraisal does not lie in the method or form used; it depends on the manager's human relations skills.

PerformanceReviews.com is a Web site that has been designed to help managers write complete and effective performance appraisals online. The site offers practical advice to guide managers through the appraisal.[49]

The Evaluative Performance Appraisal Interview

Planning ahead is critical when it comes to performance appraisal interviews. Therefore, this section is separated into preparing for and conducting the PA interview. Because the evaluative interview is the basis for the developmental interview, it should be conducted first.

PREPARING FOR AN EVALUATIVE INTERVIEW

When preparing for an evaluative interview, follow the steps outlined in Exhibit 8-13.

Exhibit 8-13 *The Evaluative Performance Appraisal Interview*

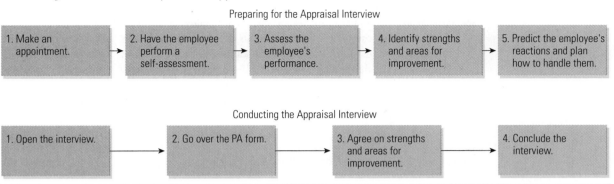

Preparing for the Appraisal Interview

| 1. Make an appointment. | 2. Have the employee perform a self-assessment. | 3. Assess the employee's performance. | 4. Identify strengths and areas for improvement. | 5. Predict the employee's reactions and plan how to handle them. |

Conducting the Appraisal Interview

| 1. Open the interview. | 2. Go over the PA form. | 3. Agree on strengths and areas for improvement. | 4. Conclude the interview. |

CONDUCTING AN EVALUATIVE INTERVIEW

Encourage the employee to talk. The appraisal should be a give-and-take interview with both parties contributing equally.

The Developmental Performance Appraisal Interview

PREPARING FOR A DEVELOPMENTAL INTERVIEW

After the employee's performance evaluation is completed, you should prepare for the developmental interview. To do this, follow the steps in Exhibit 8-14.

CONDUCTING A DEVELOPMENTAL INTERVIEW

The steps to follow when conducting a developmental performance appraisal interview are listed in Exhibit 8-14.

Today, one of the most popular management development tools is the *360-degree assessment*.[50] This approach can use any of the measurement methods discussed in Exhibit 8-12. The term "360-degree assessment" refers to the fact that all of the people who have working relationships with the person being evaluated complete whatever evaluation form is being used. These include subordinates, peers, supervisors, and, in certain situations, even customers and

Exhibit 8-14 *The Developmental Performance Appraisal Interview*

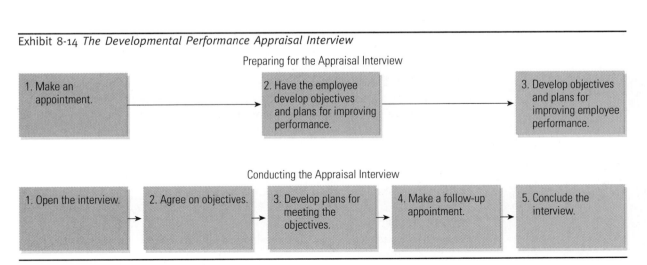

Preparing for the Appraisal Interview

| 1. Make an appointment. | 2. Have the employee develop objectives and plans for improving performance. | 3. Develop objectives and plans for improving employee performance. |

Conducting the Appraisal Interview

| 1. Open the interview. | 2. Agree on objectives. | 3. Develop plans for meeting the objectives. | 4. Make a follow-up appointment. | 5. Conclude the interview. |

suppliers. Those who fill out the appraisal form do so confidentially. The feed-back from all these people is used to evaluate and develop the employee.

Scitor has a formal orientation program. Employees are well trained to perform their jobs, and the company is committed to developing employees for future jobs as the industry changes quickly and the firm continues to grow. Scitor offers internal training seminars, outside training selected by the employee, and monitoring by senior personnel. Given Scitor's growth strategy, ongoing training is a necessity to achieve organizational objectives. Performance appraisal is also very important at Scitor because it serves as the basis for evaluating the effectiveness of the training.

RETAINING EMPLOYEES

After attracting and developing employees, an organization must have human resources systems to retain employees.[51] Employee turnover can reduce overall efficiency, profitability, and morale.[52] The cost of replacing a good employee varies, depending on the job. Half of job replacements costs $10,000 and 20 percent cost $30,000.[53] Thus, rather than focus on recruiting new workers, organizations need to try to keep the ones they have.[54] Employees who believe that they are being justly rewarded tend to stay (but pay is not the only factor). Challenging work and good feedback also help retain people.[55] The Society of Human Resources Management has said that retention is its hottest topic.[56] In this section, we discuss compensation, health and safety, labor relations, and termination and outplacement.

Learning Outcome **9**

Identify the major components of compensation.

Compensation

Compensation *is the total of an employee's pay and benefits.* Compensation affects both attracting and retaining employees.[57] An important overall compensation decision is pay level.[58] *Pay level* reflects top management's choice to be a high-, medium-, or low-paying organization. Low-paying firms may save money on pay, but the savings can be lost to the high cost of turnover. We will cover pay and benefits separately.

Wal-Mart, the number-one global retailer and one of the world's largest employers, is known as a low-paying firm. Its annual turnover rate is 50 percent; some 400,000 employees leave and must be replaced every year. To help retain employees, Wal-Mart is being more selective in hiring and training and is offering recognition and pay for performance. It also continues to promote heavily from within.[59] **Costco Wholesale Corporation**, which requires customers to pay a membership fee to shop, competes head-to-head with Wal-Mart's **Sam's Club**. However, some analysts think that Costco pays its employees too much and is too generous with benefits; 82 percent of its employees receive health insurance, and Costco pays for 92 percent of the cost. Thus, its annual turnover rate is only half that of Wal-Mart, at 24 percent.[60]

PAY SYSTEMS
There are three general pay methods, and an organization can use all three. (1) *Wages* are paid on an hourly basis. (2) *Salary* is based on time—a week,

Join the Discussion Ethics & Social Responsibility

Commissions

1. Offering higher commissions for different funds is not illegal. What is the ethical issue?
2. As a broker, would you intentionally sell more of the products that gave you a higher commission?

Putnam Investments manages money for individual and institutional investors around the world. It offers all types of investment advice, including retirement planning, and conducts financial transactions for its clients. Like many other financial companies, Putnam offered its brokers a higher commission for selling certain investments. However, in November 2003, Putnam publicly announced that it was dropping its practice of rewarding with direct commissions brokers who sell more of Putnam's own products.[61]

a month, or a year. A salary is paid regardless of the number of hours worked. (3) *Incentives* are pay for performance. Incentives include piece rate (pay based on production), commissions (pay based on sales), merit raises (the more productive workers get paid more), and bonuses. Two common types of bonuses are a specific reward for reaching an objective and profit sharing, in which employees get a part of the profits. The use of bonuses is on the increase.[62] Organizations including **Hewlett-Packard, Polaroid**, and **West Bend** are creating innovative incentive pay systems. The trend is toward replacing wages with salaries and offering incentives to all employees.[63] Pay for performance is also commonly used.[64]

————————————— Learning Outcome 10 —————————————
Describe the difference between job analysis and job evaluation.

PAY DETERMINATION

A difficult decision is how much to pay each employee. An external approach is to find out what other organizations pay for the same or similar jobs and set pay levels that are comparable. An internal approach is to use job evaluation. **Job evaluation** *is the process of determining the worth of each job relative to the other jobs within the organization.* Organizations commonly group jobs into pay grades. The higher the grade of the job, the higher the pay. The external and internal approaches are often used together.

A controversial issue related to job evaluation is comparable worth. *Comparable worth* is the principle that jobs that are distinctly different but that entail similar levels of ability, responsibility, skills, working conditions, and so on are of equal value and should have the same pay scale.

BENEFITS

Benefits are the part of compensation offered by an employer that are commonly noncash and not merit-based.[65] Legally required benefits include *workers' compensation* to cover job-related injuries, *unemployment compensation* to provide for employees who are laid off or terminated, and *Social Security* for retirement.

The employer matches the amount the government takes out of each employee's pay for Social Security.

Commonly offered optional benefits include health insurance; paid sick days, holidays, and vacations; and pension plans. Optional benefits can be paid in full by employers or split between employee and employer. Other benefits less commonly offered include dental and life insurance, membership in fitness centers, membership in credit unions, and tuition reimbursement for education.[66]

The percentage of compensation made up of benefits has been increasing over the years, primarily because of the high cost of health insurance.[67] (The increase in health care costs has been as high as seven times the rate of inflation.[68]) The percentage varies with the level of job from one-third to two-thirds of compensation, but it has been estimated that the average employee receives slightly over 40 percent of compensation from benefits. Work-family benefits, such as elder care and child care, are on the increase, as organizations focus on employees' family life issues.[69] Employees want more family-friendly workplace benefits, so that they can better balance work and family responsibilities.[70] Employees also want "cafeteria-style," or flexible, benefit plans that let them select the benefits that best meet their needs, up to a preset dollar value.[71]

Health and Safety

The Occupational Safety and Health Act (OSHA) of 1970 requires employers to pursue workplace safety. Employers must meet OSHA safety standards, maintain records of injuries and deaths due to workplace accidents, and submit

WorkApplication13

Describe the compensation package offered by your present or past employer.

_____

_____

_____

_____

_____

Join the Discussion   Ethics & Social Responsibility

Sweatshops

1. In your opinion, are companies that hire sweatshop workers helping these workers or exploiting them?
2. Should a global company compensate all employees at the same rates, or should compensation be based on the cost of doing business and the cost of living in a given country?
3. Is it possible for a company to apply the same health and safety standards that it follows in the United States to its operations in other countries and still compete globally with companies that don't apply such standards?
4. Is it ethical and socially responsible to operate sweatshops?
5. What, if anything, should be done about sweatshops?

Nike and many other companies have been criticized for operating sweatshops. Sweatshops employ workers for very low wages and in poor working conditions. In the United States, OSHA protects the health and safety of workers. However, in many countries where much of today's manufacturing takes place, there are no health and safety regulations. Some employees get hurt on the job. People complain that the United States is losing jobs overseas to companies that are exploiting people. However, others argue that most people in the United States don't want these jobs and that U.S. companies are helping people in other countries by giving them jobs. Thus, these companies are raising the standard of living in other countries.

to on-site inspections. The human resources department commonly has responsibility for ensuring the health and safety of employees. It works closely with the other departments and maintains health and safety records.[72] A growing area of safety concern is workplace violence.[73] As a manager, you should know the safety rules, be sure your employees know them, and enforce them to prevent accidents.

─────────── Learning Outcome 11 ───────────
Explain why most organizations do not have to address labor relations.

Labor Relations

Labor relations *are the interactions between management and unionized employees.* Labor relations are also called *union-management relations* and *industrial relations.*[74] There are many more nonunionized than unionized employees. Therefore, not all organizations have to deal with labor relations as part of their human resources systems. A *union* is an organization that represents employees in collective bargaining with the employer. Unions are also a source of recruitment. The National Labor Relations Act (also known as the Wagner Act, after its sponsor) established the National Labor Relations Board (NLRB), which oversees labor relations in the United States by conducting unionization elections, hearing unfair labor practice complaints, and issuing injunctions against offending employers.

THE UNION-ORGANIZING PROCESS
There are typically five stages in forming a union, as shown in Exhibit 8-15.

Exhibit 8-15 *The Union-Organizing Process*

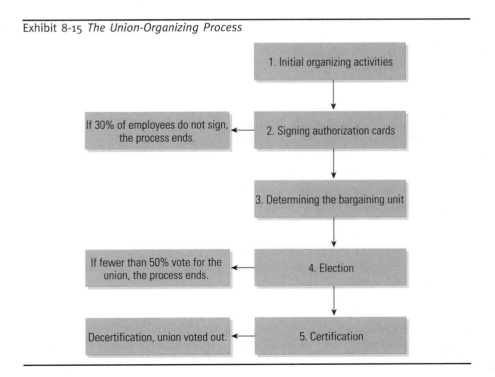

COLLECTIVE BARGAINING

Collective bargaining *is the negotiation process resulting in a contract between employees and management that covers employment conditions.* The most common employment conditions covered in contracts are compensation, hours, and working conditions, but a contract can include any condition that both sides agree to. Job security is a major bargaining issue for unions today.

To avoid a strike or a lockout (a refusal by management to let employees work) and to handle *grievances* by either side, collective bargainers sometimes agree to use neutral third parties, called mediators, from the Federal Mediation and Conciliation Service (FMCS). A *mediator* is a neutral party who helps management and labor settle their disagreements. In cases where management and employees are not willing to compromise but do not want to call a strike or a lockout, they may call in an arbitrator. An *arbitrator* is different from a mediator in that the arbitrator makes a binding decision, one to which management and labor must adhere. The services of an arbitrator are more commonly used to settle grievances than to deal with impasses in collective bargaining.

LOSS OF EMPLOYEES

Organizations lose employees for three primary reasons: (1) Through attrition, employees leave for other jobs, elect to stop working for a period of time, or retire. Employees lost through attrition need to be replaced. Employees who leave voluntarily are often interviewed so that managers can find their reasons for leaving. The *exit interview*, usually conducted by someone from the human resources department, can help identify problem areas that lead to turnover. (2) Employees who break the rules or do not perform to standards are fired. (3) Employees are laid off. Layoffs usually occur because of poor economic conditions, organizational problems, or mergers and acquisitions.[75] For example, **Apple, Boeing, General Dynamics, GM, IBM, McDonnell Douglas**, and **Sears** laid off tens of thousands of employees during the 1990s to cut costs.

When companies lay off workers, they may offer outplacement services. *Outplacement services* help employees find new jobs. For example, when General Electric laid off 900 employees, it set up a reemployment center to help employees find new jobs or to learn new skills.

IOM

All of Scitor's HRM practices help it retain employees. Scitor has a turnover rate of around 2 percent, compared to an industry average of around 17 percent. The company pays people well and offers good benefits. Scitor provides unlimited paid sick leave with no tracking of how many sick days have been taken, good medical insurance coverage, and educational reimbursement. It gives employees tickets to sports events and schedules company picnics, chili cook-offs, ski trips, fishing trips, wine-tastings, and road rallies. Scitor also has an annual all-expenses-paid fiscal-year kick-off meeting in a first-class resort, attended by all employees. Scitor does not have to address labor relations, and because it has low turnover and seldom terminates employees, it has had no need for outplacement services.

HRTools.com can help managers select compensation plans, including benefits packages. HRTools.com can also help with safety. The safety section of the Web site offers help with emergency planning, workers' compensation, workplace violence, drug and alcohol testing, and ergonomics. Finally, HRTools.com can help with employment termination.[76]

Having read this chapter, you should understand the human resources management process of (1) planning for, (2) attracting, (3) developing, and (4) retaining employees.

Take advantage of the companion Web site for *Management Fundamentals*, where you will find a broad array of resources to help you maximize what you learn in class:

- Try a quiz
- View chapter videos
- Download slides
- Boost your vocabulary
- Work through an Internet exercise
- Find related links

Take a look for yourself at *http://lussier.swlearning.com.*

Chapter Summary

1. List the four parts of the human resources management process.

The four parts of the human resources management process are (1) planning for, (2) selecting, (3) developing, and (4) retaining employees.

2. Distinguish between a job description and a job specification, and explain why job analysis is needed.

The job description identifies the tasks and responsibilities of a position, whereas the job specification identifies the qualifications needed in the person who is to fill the position. Job analysis is necessary because it is the basis for attracting, developing, and retaining employees.

3. Describe recruiting sources of candidates for jobs and the selection process.

Recruiting can be either internal or external. Internal sources of job candidates are promotions and employee referrals. External sources include walk-ins, educational institutions, agencies, and advertising. The selection process can include having candidates complete application forms, be interviewed, take tests, and submit to background and reference checks.

4. Describe hypothetical questions and probing questions.

A hypothetical question requires the candidate to describe what he or she would do and say in a given situation. A probing question is an unplanned question used to clarify a response to an open-ended or a hypothetical question.

5. Explain what orientation and training and development of employees involve.

Orientation is the process of introducing new employees to the organizational culture and their jobs. Training and development is the process of teaching employees the skills necessary to perform present and future jobs.

6. List the steps in job instructional training.

The steps in job instructional training are (1) preparation of the trainee, (2) presentation of the task, (3) performance of the task by the trainee, and (4) follow-up.

7. Explain the two types of performance appraisal.

The two types of performance appraisal are the developmental performance appraisal and the evaluative performance appraisal. A developmental PA is used to make decisions and plan for performance improvements. An evaluative PA is used to make administrative decisions, including decisions about pay raises, transfers and promotions, and demotions and terminations.

8. Explain the concept "You get what you reward."

People seek information concerning what activities are rewarded, and then seek to do those things, often to the exclusion of activities not rewarded.

9. Identify the major components of compensation.

The two components of compensation are pay and benefits.

10. Describe the difference between job analysis and job evaluation.

A job analysis is used to determine what the job entails and the qualifications needed to staff the position. Job evaluation is used to determine how much to compensate employees for their jobs.

11. Explain why most organizations do not have to address labor relations.

Labor relations are the interactions between management and unionized employees. Because most organizations do not have unionized employees, they do not have to deal with labor relations.

12. Complete each of the following statements using one of this chapter's key terms.

The _____ consists of planning for, attracting, developing, and retaining employees.

A _____ allows discrimination where it is reasonably necessary to normal operation of a particular organization.

_____ is the process of staffing the organization to meet its objectives.

The _____ identifies the tasks and responsibilities of a position.

_____ identify the qualifications needed in a person who is to fill a position.

_____ is the process of attracting qualified candidates to apply for job openings.

_____ is the process of choosing the most qualified applicant recruited for a job.

_____ are places where job applicants undergo a series of tests, interviews, and simulated experiences to determine their managerial potential.

_____ is the process of introducing new employees to the organization and their jobs.

_____ is the process of teaching employees the skills necessary to perform a job.

_____ is ongoing education to improve skills for present and future jobs.

_____ develops skills in a simulated setting.

_____ is the ongoing process of evaluating employee performance.

_____ is the total of an employee's pay and benefits.

_____ is the process of determining the worth of each job relative to other jobs within the organization.

_____ are the interactions between management and unionized employees.

_____ is the negotiation process resulting in a contract between employees and management that covers employment conditions.

Key **Terms**

assessment centers, 269
bona fide occupational qualification (BFOQ), 262
collective bargaining, 288
compensation, 284
development, 276
human resources management process, 260

job description, 266
job evaluation, 285
job specifications, 266
labor relations, 287
orientation, 276
performance appraisal, 279
recruiting, 267

selection, 269
strategic human resources planning, 265
training, 276
vestibule training, 276

Review and **Discussion** Questions

1. What is your opinion of the use of bona fide occupational qualifications?
2. What are the components of a job analysis?
3. What is your opinion of using promotion from within as a recruiting source?
4. Do you agree that the job interview should be the primary criterion for selection?
5. What is the most common problem to avoid during interviewing?
6. If you as a manager work for a company with a human resources department, does this mean that you don't have to orient and train employees? Explain.

7. How does setting objectives affect the measurement and evaluation of training results?
8. How is compensation used to both attract and retain employees?
9. Why don't most employees realize how expensive benefits are and how much they contribute to compensation cost?
10. Are unions greedy because they expect workers to receive more than they are worth, or is management greedy because it takes excessive salaries and gives too large a share of the profits to the owners?
11. What is the difference between a mediator and an arbitrator?

Objective **Case**
AMERICAN AIRLINES

AMR Corporation is the parent of American Airlines (AA). AA has been on the brink of bankruptcy, as it lost more than $6.6 billion since the airline slump in 2001. The disclosure in a 2003 Securities and Exchange Commission filing of proposals to give executives huge financial incentives to stay on with the company and to shelter their pensions in the event of bankruptcy eroded the already strained relationship between management and labor. Let's discuss some of AA's problems and successes.

AA was competitive in the era when the government regulated the airline industry. In those days, ticket prices were the same no matter what airline you flew, so airlines had little incentive to keep costs down. Over the years, unions gained great wages and benefits. Things were going fine for airlines until the industry was deregulated and carriers could compete on ticket price.

Southwest Airlines and others began to compete using business models that focused on keeping costs and ticket prices low. Low-cost discount carriers hired nonunion workers for much lower wages and benefits than the other carriers. This gave discount carriers a great competitive advantage, as airlines are labor-intensive, with compensation representing around 40 percent of operating expenses.

Discount carriers took business away from the high-cost carriers, which began to lose money. Things went from bad to worse for AA when the travel industry plunged into its worst slump ever after the September 11, 2001, terrorist attacks on New York and Washington, D.C. In 2003, the outbreak of severe acute respiratory syndrome (SARS) made travelers wary of Asia, which hurt AA's Pacific operations, and in 2004, the high price of fuel delivered another blow.

AA appealed to its employees in order to avert bankruptcy filing. It sought deep wage concessions from its unions: the Allied Pilots Association, the Transport Workers Union, and the Association of Professional Flight Attendants. AA secured a total of $1.8 billion in wage cuts from its employees and it cut over 30,000 jobs. The company was also able to save another $2.2 billion with other cost cuts; for example, AA saves millions by flying the same number of flights but using fewer employees and planes.

Needless to say, many employees were not happy with pay cuts and lost jobs. But they realized that it was better than having AA go into bankruptcy and possibly everyone losing their jobs. As a concession, in 2003, employees were granted $38 million in options to buy AMR shares at $5 a share. Thus, if AA does well financially, employees can also benefit. However, morale went down at AA and performance and baggage handling suffered, as complaints increased for a while.

AA is a highly centralized organization, and it faced difficulties reaching out to its widely dispersed employees (more than 96,000 at year end 2003). Employees were wasting too much time dealing with human resources (HR) issues; the company's existing HR structure made accomplishing simple tasks—getting information about benefits, for example—overly complicated. So even though AA was losing money, it had Sapient Corporation engineer and design PeopleLink, which automated many HR functions. The PeopleLink HR system is a multichannel system that employees can access through the Internet, the AA intranet, or (if they wish to speak to an HR staff member) by phone. The changes freed HR personnel to focus on strategic and consultative services and reduced the amount of time they spent on transactional functions. Employees now have less paperwork, interactions with HR take up less of their time, and transaction turnaround time is quicker. The Internet- and intranet-based human resources systems are now boosting HR service levels while at the same time increasing employee satisfaction, and turnover is down.

AA's costs used to be among the highest in the industry, but it now has the lowest unit costs among higher-cost airlines. Amid the broad industry slump, it has cut costs and increased productivity. AA now flies as many average hours a day (11.4) as Southwest. In 2004, travelers came back to AA in record numbers. Today, American Airlines is working hard to compete with the low-cost carriers and climb back up the financial ladder.

To learn more about American Airlines, log on to InfoTrac® College Edition at *http://infotrac. thomsonlearning.com* and use the advanced search function.

_____ 1. Was human resources planning an important HR process in this case?

    a. yes

    b. no

_____ 2. Was attracting employees an important HR process in this case?

    a. yes

    b. no

_____ 3. Was developing employees an important HR process in this case?

    a. yes

    b. no

_____ 4. Was retaining employees an important HR process in this case?

    a. yes

    b. no

_____ 5. Were performance appraisals important in this case?

    a. yes

    b. no

_____ 6. Was compensation important in this case?

    a. yes

    b. no

_____ 7. Was health and safety an important HR issue in this case?

    a. yes

    b. no

_____ 8. Were labor relations important in this case?

    a. yes

    b. no

_____ 9. Were termination and outplacement important issues in this case?

    a. yes

    b. no

_____ 10. Which of the four human resources management processes is the major focus of this case?

    a. human resources (HR) planning

    b. attracting employees

    c. developing employees

    d. retaining employees

11. Discuss the role of the HR department in helping AA compete with low-cost carriers.

12. How has AA changed its human resources management process focus since the 1990s?

Cumulative Case Questions

13. Explain how changes in the external environment of the airline industry required changes in the internal environment at AA. (Chapter 2)

14. Which type of departmentalization does AA use, and did it change departmentalization to compete with low-cost carriers? (Chapter 6)

15. Which type of change did AA make to improve the efficiency and effectiveness of its HR processes? (Chapter 7)

Behavior Modeling 1

EMPLOYMENT INTERVIEWING

The first scenario for this chapter shows a manager conducting a job interview, following the steps in Exhibit 8-8.

Objective

To better understand the steps in the interviewing process.

View the Video (8 minutes)

View the accompanying video in class or at *http://lussier.swlearning.com*. Your instructor may ask you to watch the video prior to completing Skill Builder 1.

Skill Builder 1

SELECTING A TENNIS COACH

Objectives

To perform a job analysis and to develop skills in employment interviewing

You are in your first year as athletic director at a high school. The tennis coach position is open, and you must fill it. The compensation for the job is set in the budget; the coach is to be paid in one lump sum at the end of the season. The salary is competitive with the pay of other tennis coaches in the area.

Recruiting

Because you have no recruiting budget, you do some internal recruiting and contact some athletic directors in your area to spread the word about the opening. You recruit three candi-

dates for the coaching position. Following are descriptions of their qualifications.

Candidate A has been a history teacher at your school for ten years. This person was the tennis coach for two years. It's been five years since this person coached the team. You don't know why the candidate stopped coaching or how good a job was done. Candidate A never played competitive tennis. However, someone told you that the candidate plays regularly and is pretty good. You guess the teacher is about 35 years old.

Candidate B works as a supervisor on the 11 P.M. to 7 A.M. shift for a local business. This candidate has never coached before. However, the person was a star player in high school and college. Candidate B still plays in local tournaments, and you see the name in the paper now and then. You guess this candidate is about 25 years old.

Candidate C has been a basketball coach and physical education teacher at a nearby high school for the past five years. The person has a master's degree in physical education. You figure it will take the person 20 minutes to get to your school. Candidate C has never coached tennis, but did play on the high school team. The candidate plays tennis about once a week. You guess the person is about 45 years old.

Preparing for the Interviews

Follow the six interview preparation steps in Exhibit 8-7. (You can skip step 1, as there is no job description or specifications.) Because there are only three candidates, you have decided to interview them all.

Conducting the Interviews

During the in-class part of this exercise, you will conduct a job interview. Be sure to bring your written list of questions to class.

Procedure 1 (5–10 minutes). Break into groups of five or six, pass the lists of questions around to the other members, and discuss them. You may make changes to improve your list. For example, you may want to add some questions you had not thought of.

Procedure 2 (30–80 minutes). Each person elects to play the role of one of the three job candidates. While playing the role, you may use your real name but assume that you have the qualifications described earlier. Ad lib as necessary. Another member of the group plays the role of interviewer, and the third person is the observer. The interviewer uses the questions she or he devised earlier to conduct the interview. The observer gives feedback at the end of the interview, and the group members discuss how the interview could be improved.

After the discussion, group members switch roles: A different group member plays another job candidate, and another group member acts as interviewer. Again, discuss the interview once it is completed before switching roles for a third time.

Procedure 3. Each member of the group selects the candidate he or she would offer the job to; members of the other groups will do the same. The class can discuss the reasons for choosing a particular candidate.

Apply It

What did I learn from this experience? How will I use this knowledge in the future?

_____

_____

Behavior Modeling 2
JOB INSTRUCTIONAL TRAINING

The second scenario in this chapter shows a manager conducting a job instructional training session with a new employee, following the steps in Exhibit 8-9.

Objective

To better understand the job instructional training process.

View the Video (4 1/2 minutes)

View the accompanying video in class or at *http://lussier.swlearning.com*. This video can be shown prior to having students complete Skill Builder 2.

Skill Builder 2
JOB INSTRUCTIONAL TRAINING

Preparing for Skill Builder 2

For this Skill Builder, you will prepare to conduct a training session in which you will use the steps of the job instructional training (JIT) process outlined in the text and illustrated in Exhibit 8-9.

Select a task: Begin by selecting a task or a skill that you are familiar with but that other class members may not know how to do. It should be a task or a skill that you can teach someone else in about 10 minutes (for example, how to knit, an athletic technique, the basics of some computer software, the rules of a card game, how to perform a magic trick, or the like).

Set objectives: Write down your objectives for the training session.

Prepare for training: Write a description of your training session, making sure that it follows the steps in the JIT process. Your plan should include a description of how you will measure and evaluate your training results. The training itself will be conducted in class. Plan to bring to class anything you'll need for your training (knitting needles and yarn, a deck of cards, or whatever).

Apply It

What did I learn from this experience? How will I use this knowledge in the future?

_____

_____

Career Management and Networking

Learning Outcomes

After studying this appendix, you should be able to:

1. List the steps in career planning.

2. List the steps in the networking process.

3. Describe a one-minute self-sell.

4. Define the following **key terms**:

   career
   career planning
   career development
   networking
   one-minute self-sell

CAREER MANAGEMENT

A **career** *is a sequence of related job positions, involving increasing responsibility and increased compensation and held over a lifetime.* Career success depends on hard work and planning.[1] You must take the responsibility for managing your career; you can't simply rely on others to give you jobs, raises, and promotions.[2] This appendix will help you with your career by discussing career planning and development and getting a job. If you have not completed the Career Development Self-Assessment in Chapter 8, do so now.

Learning Outcome 1
List the steps in career planning.

Career Planning and Development

There is a difference between career planning and career development. **Career planning** *is the process of setting career objectives and determining how to accomplish them.* **Career development** *is the process of gaining skill, experience, and education to achieve career objectives.*

In order to be successful, you need a career plan.[3] Most colleges offer career planning services that can help you. The career-planning counselor's role is not to find people jobs but to help them set realistic career objectives and plans. The *career-planning model* can help you develop your own career plan. The steps in the career-planning model are completing a self-assessment, determining your career preferences, setting objectives, developing a plan, and controlling the plan. Skill Builder 1 will guide you in the use of these steps to develop your own career plan.

Step 1. Self-assessment. The starting point in career planning is the self-assessment inventory: Who are you? What are your interests, values, needs, skills, experience, and competencies?[4] What do you want to do during your career? The key to career success is to determine what you do well, what you enjoy doing, and how to find a job that combines your interests and skills.

Step 2. Career preferences. Others can help you get a job, but you are responsible for selecting your career. Based on your self-assessment, you must decide what you want from your job and career and prioritize these preferences. It is not enough simply to determine what you want to do. It is also important to determine why you want to do these things. What motivates you? How much do you want it? What is your commitment to your career? Without the appropriate level of motivation and commitment to your career objectives and plans, you will not be successful in attaining them.

Some of the things you should consider as you think about your career preferences are (1) what industry you want to work in, (2) what size organization you want to work for, (3) what type of job(s) you want in your career and which functional areas interest you (production/operations, marketing, finance, human resources, and so on), (4) what city, state, or country you want to work in, and (5) how much income you expect when you start your career and 5 years and 10 years after that.

Once you have thought about these preferences, read about the career areas that interest you.[5] Talk to people in your school's career-planning office and to people who hold the types of jobs you are interested in. (This is called *networking*, and we will discuss networking in more detail later in this appendix.) People in these positions can give you information that you can use in developing your career plan. Get their advice. Determine the requirements and qualifications you need to get a job in the career that interests you. Participating in an internship or fieldwork and taking on a part-time job and/or a summer job in your field of interest can help you land the job you want after graduation.

Step 3. Career objectives. Set short- and long-range objectives, using the planning guidelines discussed in Chapter 5.

Step 4. Plan. Develop a plan that will enable you to attain your objectives.[6] This is where career development fits in. You must determine what skills, experience, and education you need in order to progress from your current level to your career goal. You should write out your career plan—but just because it's written down doesn't mean it can't be changed. You should be open to unplanned opportunities and be willing to take advantage of them.

Step 5. Control. It is your responsibility to achieve your objectives. As you carry out the plan you develop for yourself, you may have to take corrective action. Review your objectives, check your progress at least once a year, and change and develop new objectives and plans. Update your résumé as necessary. Having good mentors can help you get a job, and mentors can help you advance through career stages.[7]

WorkApplication1

What career development efforts are you making?

_____

_____

_____

_____

Getting a Job

It has been said that getting a good job is a job in itself. If you want to land a good job, you need to develop a career plan before you begin your job search. Then you prepare a résumé and cover letter for each job, research the organization, and prepare for the interview.

RÉSUMÉ AND COVER LETTER

According to one recruiting executive at **Xerox**, the résumé is about 40 percent of getting a job. Your résumé and the cover letter you send with it are your introduction to the organization you wish to work for. If the résumé is messy or contains mistakes, you may not get an interview.[8] The cover letter should be short—one page or less. Its purpose is to introduce your résumé and to request an interview. The résumé should also be short; one page is recommended, unless you have extensive education and experience. The résumé's primary purpose is to get you invited for an interview.[9] Note that presenting a résumé when you are applying for part-time or summer employment or an internship can give a positive impression that makes you stand out from the competition.

When listing internships and other work experience on your résumé, be sure to focus on accomplishments and skills that can be used on the job you are applying for. Also, explain what value you added.[10] How did the organization benefit by having you as an employee? If you offered ideas on how to improve performance or developed a new way of doing things, say so. Skill Builder 2 will give you practice in preparing a résumé.

RESEARCH

In setting your career objectives, you may have done some research into particular organizations you might want to work for. In actually looking for a job, you'll find yourself doing more research. Many colleges offer seminars in job-search strategies. Help-wanted ads in newspapers and online job-search services (such as *http://www.monster.com*) are common places to research jobs.

Once you have been invited to an interview, but before you go to it, you should research the organization in more detail. You want to determine as much about the organization as you can. For example, you should know something about the products and/or services it offers, the industry and its trends, and the organization's profits and future plans. The organization's Web site is one place to find this information.

THE INTERVIEW

In most hiring decisions, the interview is given the most weight—usually about 60 percent. Your résumé and your references can get you an interview, but how you perform during the interview usually determines whether you get the job. It is vital to make a very positive first impression. This involves a relaxed appearance and an ability to convey accomplishments and pique the interviewer's interest quickly.

After the interview, evaluate your own performance; make some notes on what you did and did not do well. Send a thank-you letter to the interviewer, adding anything you forgot to say, stating your interest in the job, and closing by saying that you look forward to hearing from the interviewer. Enclose a copy of your résumé. If you already know that you did not get the job, ask the

WorkApplication2

Which specific ideas on getting
a job do you plan to use?

interviewer why. You may or may not be told, but an honest answer can be helpful in preparation for future interviews.

Many college career-planning services offer workshops on how to interview for a job. Some provide the chance to go through a mock interview that is videotaped so that you can evaluate yourself afterward. If your career-planning office offers this service, take advantage of it. For more information on job searching, résumé writing, and interviewing, visit Proven Resumes.

ProvenResumes.com has an excellent Web site to help you with career development. The company offers 60 free workshops to help you with job search strategies, writing cover letters and résumés, and interviewing. It provides career-specific résumé tips in more than 30 areas, including business management, and tips for people making career moves and college students. Proven Resumes even has a quiz that will help you rate your résumé so that you can improve it before sending it.[11]

NETWORKING

We'll begin by discussing the importance of networking, and then we'll outline the five steps of the networking process.

The Importance of Networking

Everybody has heard the statement "It's not what you know, it's who you know that's important." To a large extent this is true, particularly in business. Sending out résumés or posting them on the Web is not how most people are getting jobs today. Of the many ways to discover employment opportunities, networking is by far the most successful. **Networking** *is the process of building relationships for the purpose of politicking and socializing.* According to the U.S. Department of Labor, two-thirds of all jobs are located by word of mouth and informal referrals by relatives, friends, and acquaintances. Networking results in more jobs than all of the other job search methods combined.

The higher the level of management job you are seeking, the more important networking is.[12] Networking is particularly important if you take a job in a new location. It can be difficult for women to get into the right networks—especially the "old boy" network—which is one of the key reasons for the existence of the glass ceiling.[13] Research indicates that people without mentors, including women and members of minority groups, miss out on a key aid to career development, as one role of a mentor is to help the protégé connect to useful networks.[14]

Networking implies connecting with others and receiving (or giving) advice, industry information, contacts, or assistance. Networking is about building professional relationships and friendships through effective communication.[15] In other words, networking is marketing yourself; through networking you are being responsible for your career and the exposure of your talents and skills.[16] Think of networking as career insurance.[17]

There are many reasons to develop your networking skills:

- To get a job
- To learn how to perform better at your current job[18]
- To advance within an organization
- To stay current in your field

- To maintain mobility
- To get advice and resources to start a business[19]
- To develop professional relationships

─────────────── Learning Outcome 2 ───────────────
List the steps in the networking process.

The Networking Process

When you need any type of help, who do you turn to? Networking sounds easy, and people tend to think that it should come naturally. However, the reality is that networking is a learned skill that just about everyone struggles with at one time or another.[20] In this section, we'll discuss a process that will enhance your career development.[21] The *networking process* involves performing a self-assessment and setting objectives, creating a one-minute self-sell, developing a list of potential network contacts, conducting networking interviews, and maintaining the network. Although the same networking process is used for both job searches and broad career development, this discussion focuses more on the job search.[22]

Step 1. Perform a self-assessment and set objectives. You conduct the same kind of self-assessment for networking as you do when planning for career development. However, in networking, you set narrower objectives. For example, your own networking objectives might include "get a mentor," "determine the expertise, skills, and requirements needed for [a specific job]," and "get feedback on my résumé and job and/or career preparation so that I can be ready to move into [a specific job]." Again, focus on your skills and accomplishments and tie them to the job you want.[23]

WorkApplication3
Write a networking objective.

_____

_____

_____

_____

_____

─────────────── Learning Outcome 3 ───────────────
Describe a one-minute self-sell.

Step 2. Create your one-minute self-sell. The next step in the networking process is to create a brief statement about yourself to help you accomplish your goal. *A* **one-minute self-sell** *is an opening statement used in networking that quickly summarizes your history and career plan and asks a question.* If it is to take 60 seconds or less, your message must be concise, but it also needs to be clear and compelling. It gives the listener a sense of your background, identifies your career field and a key result you've achieved, and it tells the listener what you plan to do next and why. It also should stimulate conversation.

- *History.* Start with a summary of the highlights of your career to date. Briefly describe the jobs or internships you've held and relevant courses you have taken.
- *Plans.* Identify the career you are seeking, the industry you prefer, and a specific function or role. You can also mention names of organizations you are targeting and state why you are looking for work.
- *Question.* Finally, ask a question to encourage two-way communication. The question will vary, depending on the person you hope to network with and the goal of your one-minute self-sell. For example, you might ask, "What areas might offer opportunities for a person with my experience?"

"In what other fields can I use these skills or this degree?" "Are there other positions in your organization where my skills could be used?" "What do you think of my career goals? Are they realistic, given my education and skills?" "Do you know of any job openings in my field?"

In your one-minute self-sell, be sure to clearly separate your history, your plans, and your question, and customize your question based on the contact you are talking to. Consider the following example:

Hello. My name is Will Smith. I am a senior at Springfield College, graduating in May with a major in marketing, and I have completed an internship in the marketing department at the Big Y supermarket. I'm seeking a job in sales in the food industry. Can you give me some ideas of the types of sales positions available in the food industry?

Practice delivering your self-sell to family members and friends, and get feedback from them to improve it. The more opportunities you find to use this brief introduction, the easier it becomes. Skill Builder 3 will give you the opportunity to practice your one-minute self-sell.

Step 3. List your potential network contacts. You should build a network before you need it, so start today.[24] Begin with who you know, your primary contacts; look through your address book or your Rolodex. Your goal is to create a list of professional and personal contacts. Professional contacts include colleagues (past and present); members of trade or professional organizations and alumni associations; vendors, suppliers, or managers from current or past jobs; and mentors. On a personal level, your network includes relatives, neighbors, friends, and even personal service providers (your doctor, dentist, insurance agent, stock broker, accountant, or hairstylist).

Ask your primary contacts for secondary contacts you can network with.[25] You'll want to continually update and add to your list as you get referrals from others.[26] You will discover that your network grows exponentially.

Next, expand your list to include people you don't know. How do you do this? Make a point to go where people gather: meetings of the Chamber of Commerce or college alumni clubs, college reunions, trade shows and career fairs. There are e-groups and chat rooms for all types of interests; seek these out and participate. Get more involved with professional associations; many have special student memberships, and some even have college chapters. To develop your career reputation, become a leader, not just a member, in whatever civic/social/religious organizations you join. Volunteer to be on committees or boards, to give presentations, and so on.

Step 4. Conduct networking interviews. Consult your list of potential network contacts and set up a networking interview to begin meeting your objective. It may take many interviews to meet a goal, such as getting a job. You may have to begin with an informational interview—a phone call or (preferably) a meeting that you initiate to gain information from a contact who has hands-on experience in your field of interest. In such a situation (in contrast to a job interview), you are the interviewer, so you need to be prepared with specific questions to ask the contact regarding your targeted career or industry.

WorkApplication4

Write a one-minute self-sell to achieve the networking objective you wrote for Work Application 3.

You'll find that if you ask, many people will agree to talk to you for 15 or 20 minutes.[27] These meetings can be most helpful, especially if you can talk to someone within an organization you'd like to join or in an industry you are targeting. Leave a business card and résumé so that the person can contact you in case something comes up.

During the interview, be sure to do the following:

- Establish rapport—thank the person for talking with you.[28]
- Deliver your one-minute self-sell.
- Ask your prepared questions, such as "What do you think of my qualifications for this field?" "With your knowledge of the industry, what career opportunities do you see in the future?" "What advice do you have for me as I begin my career?"
- Get additional contacts for your network.[29] You might ask a question like "If you were exploring this field, who else would you talk with?" Most people can give you three names; if you are offered only one, ask for others. Add the new contacts to your network list and plan to interview them. (When contacting new people, be sure to mention who referred you to them.)
- Ask your contact how you might help him or her.

Follow up the interview with a thank-you note and a status report, and enclose your résumé.

Step 5. Maintain your network. It is important to keep members of your network informed of your career progress. Saying thank you to those who helped you along the way will strengthen your business relationships; providing updated information about yourself will increase the likelihood of getting help in the future. It is also a good idea to notify everyone in your network that you are in a new position and to provide contact information. Networking doesn't stop once you've made a career change. Make a personal commitment to continue networking in order to be in charge of your career development.[30] Go to trade shows, conventions, make business contacts and continue to update, correct, and add to your network list.[31] Always thank others for their time.

Networking is not only about getting help; it's also about helping others, especially those in your network. You will be amazed at how helping others can help you. Try to contact everyone on your network list at least once a year and find out what you can do for him or her. Send congratulations on recent achievements.

Appendix Summary

1. List the steps in career planning.
The steps in the career planning model are (1) completing a self-assessment, (2) determining your career preferences, (3) setting objectives, (4) developing a plan, and (5) controlling the plan.

2. List the steps in the networking process.
The steps in the networking process are (1) performing a self-assessment and setting objectives, (2) creating a one-minute self-sell, (3) developing a list of potential network contacts, (4) conducting networking interviews, and (5) maintaining the network.

3. Describe a one-minute self-sell.
A one-minute self-sell is an opening statement used in networking that quickly summarizes a person's history and career plan and asks a question.

4. Complete each of the following statements using one of this appendix's key terms.

A _____ is a sequence of related job positions, involving increasing responsibility and increased compensation and held over a lifetime.

_____ is the process of setting career objectives and determining how to accomplish them.

_____ is the process of gaining skill, experience, and education to achieve career objectives.

_____ is the process of building relationships for the purpose of politicking and socializing.

The _____ is an opening statement used in networking that quickly summarizes your history and career plan and asks a question.

Key **Terms**

career, 295

career development, 295

career planning, 295

networking, 298

one-minute self-sell, 299

Skill Builder **1**

CAREER PLANNING

Preparing for Skill Builder 1

Answering the following questions will help you develop a career plan. Use additional paper if needed. If your instructor asks you to do this exercise in class, do not reveal anything about yourself that you prefer not to share with classmates.

Step 1. Self-assessment
   a. Write two or three statements that answer the question "Who am I?"
   b. Write about two or three of your major accomplishments. (They can be in school, work, sports, or hobbies.) List the skills it took to accomplish each one.
   c. Identify skills and abilities you already possess that you can use in your career (for example, skills related to planning, organizing, communicating, or leading).

Step 2. Career preferences
   a. What type of industry would you like to work in? (List as many as interest you.)
   b. What type and size of organization do you want to work for?
   c. List in priority order, beginning with the most important, the five factors that will most influence your

job/career decisions (examples are opportunity for advancement, challenge, security, salary, hours, location of job, travel involved, educational opportunities, recognition, prestige, environment, coworkers, boss, responsibility, and variety of tasks).
   d. Describe the perfect job.
   e. What type of job(s) do you want during your career (marketing, finance, operations, personnel, and so forth)? After selecting a field, select a specific job (for example, salesperson, manager, or accountant).

Step 3. Career objectives
   a. What are your short-term objectives for the first year after graduation?
   b. What are your intermediate-term objectives (the second through fifth years after graduation)?
   c. What are your long-range objectives?

Step 4. Develop an action plan to help you achieve your objectives.
   Be sure to state deadlines for each action you plan to take.

Skill **Builder** 2

RÉSUMÉ

Preparing for Skill Builder 2

Now that you have a career plan, create a résumé that reflects your plan. For help, visit your college career center and/or the Proven Resume Web site at *http://www. provenresumes.com*. Before finalizing your résumé, improve it by using the following assessment procedure.

Résumé Assessment

1. Could a reader understand, within 10 seconds, what job you are applying for and that you are qualified for the position on the basis of skills, experience, and/or education?

2. Does the résumé include an objective that clearly states the position being applied for (such as sales rep)?

3. Does the résumé list skills or experience that support the claim that you can do the job? (For example, if you don't have sales experience, does the résumé list skills developed on other jobs, such as communication skills? Or, does it indicate that you have product knowledge, or point out that you enjoy meeting new people and that you are able to easily converse with people you don't know?)

4. If education is a major qualification for the job, does the résumé list courses you've taken that prepared you for the position applied for?

5. Does the résumé clearly list your accomplishments and contributions you made during your job experiences to date?

Skill Builder 3*

NETWORKING SKILLS

Preparing for Skill Builder 3

Review the appendix section on the networking process, and complete the following steps.

1. Perform a self-assessment and set objectives. List two or three of your accomplishments, and set an objective—for example, to learn more about career opportunities in your major or to get an internship or a part-time, summer, or full-time job.

2. Practice the one-minute self-sell that you wrote for Work Application 4.

3. Develop your network. List at least five people to be included in your network, preferably individuals who can help you achieve your objective.

4. Conduct a networking interview. To help meet your objective, select one person from your network list to interview (by phone if it is not possible to meet in person) for about 20 minutes. Write questions to ask during the interview.

*Source: This exercise was developed by Andra Gumbus, assistant professor, College of Business, Sacred Heart University. © Andra Gumbus, 2002. It is used with Dr. Gumbus's permission.

Learning Outcomes

After studying this chapter, you should be able to:

1. Describe each of the big five personality dimensions. PAGE 308

2. Explain the perception process, and identify the two factors that influence it. PAGE 310

3. Describe the interrelationship among personality, perception, and attitude, and explain the contribution of each to a manager's behavior. PAGE 312

4. Explain what job satisfaction is and why it is important. PAGE 313

5. Define *power*, and explain the difference between position and personal power. PAGE 315

6. Identify the differences among reward, legitimate, and referent power. PAGE 317

9: Organizational Behavior: Power, Politics, Conflict, and Stress

7. Discuss how power and politics are related. PAGE 319

8. Describe how money and politics have a similar use. PAGE 319

9. Explain what networking, reciprocity, and coalitions have in common. PAGE 320

10. List and define five conflict management styles. PAGE 324

11. List the steps in initiating and using the collaborative conflict resolution model. PAGE 332

12. Explain the stress tug-of-war analogy. PAGE 339

13. Define the following **key terms**:

organizational behavior	coalition
personality	conflict
perception	functional conflict
attribution	collaborative conflict
attitudes	resolution model
Pygmalion effect	BCF statement
citizenship behavior	mediator
power	arbitrator
politics	stress
networking	stressors
reciprocity	

Ideas on Management
at Black Entertainment Television

Robert L. Johnson is founder, chairman, and CEO of Black Entertainment Television (BET), a subsidiary of Viacom and the leading media and entertainment company in the United States owned and operated by African Americans. Founded in 1980, BET offers 24-hour programming targeted at African Americans in more than 65 million U.S. households and reaches 74 million cable subscribers.

Johnson did not start at the top. He spent time climbing the corporate ladder at the Corporation for Public Broadcasting and the Washington Urban League, and was also press secretary for a congressman. Prior to founding BET, he was the vice president of government relations for the National Cable and Telecommunications Association (NCTA), which is a trade association representing more than 1,500 cable television companies. Through the years, Johnson has served on several boards of for-profit and not-for-profit organizations.

Johnson is also the first African American to be a majority owner of a professional sports franchise in the United States. He is the majority owner of the National Basketball Association's (NBA) Charlotte Bobcats and the Women's National Basketball Association's (WNBA) Charlotte Sting.

© AP Photo/Diane Bondareff

1. **How would you describe Robert Johnson's personality?**
2. **How have perception and attitudes affected Robert Johnson's career? How did he deal with discrimination?**
3. **What types of power does Johnson have? How does he use his power?**
4. **How does Johnson effectively use organizational politics at BET?**
5. **What types of negotiating and collaborating does Johnson do?**

You'll find answers to these questions about Robert Johnson and power and politics at BET throughout this chapter.

To learn more about BET, visit the company's Web site at *http://www.bet.com* or log on to InfoTrac® College Edition at *http://infotrac.thomsonlearning.com* to read the latest news on BET and Robert Johnson. Use the advanced search option to key in record number A115759686 and learn about the premiere of Robert Johnson's new Charlotte-based regional sports network.

Source: Information for the opening case was taken from R. Lapchick's interview with Robert Johnson of Black Entertainment Television, *Academy of Management Executive* (2004), Vol. 18, No. 1, pp. 114–119.

ORGANIZATIONAL BEHAVIOR

Human and communication skills are among the most important management skills. Management requires getting jobs done through others. Thus, how well you relate to others determines your career success.[1] To climb the corporate ladder, you will have to understand organizational behavior and know how to gain power, engage in politics, and manage conflicts and stress. You will learn about these concepts in this chapter.

Have you ever wondered why people behave the way they do at work? **Organizational behavior** *is the study of actions that affect performance in the workplace.* The *goal of organizational behavior theorists* is to explain and predict actions and how they will affect performance.[2] The field of organizational behavior has three levels of focus: the individual, the group, and the organization. In this chapter, you will learn about individual behavior; the next chapter will focus on group behavior. You learned about the organizational level in Chapter 7's discussion of organizational development.

Generally, the better you understand organizational behavior, the more effective you will be at working with others as a manager.[3] The foundations of individual behavior include personality, perception, and attitudes. However, these foundations are not observable. You can only observe individuals' actions and try to explain their behavior based on your understanding of the foundations. At the next level, you can try to predict people's actions in a given situation based on an understanding of their personalities, perceptions, and attitudes. The next three sections focus on these foundations of individual behavior.

PERSONALITY

Why are some people outgoing and others shy, some loud and others quiet, some warm and others cold, some aggressive and others passive? **Personality** *is a combination of behavioral, mental, and emotional traits that define an individual.* Personality is based on genetics and environmental factors. Your personality dimensions are influenced by genes you received before you were born. Your basic personality is developed by age five, thus making parents and child care providers important in the early years of life, but your personality can change.[4] Your family, friends, school, and work relationships influence your personality.

People who have personalities similar to that of an interviewer have a better chance of getting the job they interview for, and once on the job, they tend to get higher performance assessments. In addition, coworkers with similar personalities tend to get along better.[5] However, you'll recall that diversity generally leads to higher levels of performance. To be successful, you must be prepared to work well with people with a variety of personality types.[6] You'll do your best on the job if you can understand your boss's and coworkers' personalities and preferences.[7] Understanding people's personalities is important because personality affects behavior as well as perceptions and attitudes.[8] Knowing about people's personalities helps you explain and predict their behavior and job performance.[9] Therefore, many organizations give personality tests to ensure a proper match between the worker and the job. For example, an outgoing personality is generally a trait of successful sales reps, and strong analytical traits are common in people who work in technical/computer jobs.

There are many personality classification methods. Two widely recognized methods are classification on the basis of single traits and classification on the basis of the big five personality dimensions.

Single Traits of Personality

Some of the single traits that make up one's personality include locus of control, optimism, risk propensity, Machiavellianism, self-esteem, and self-efficacy. Because self-esteem and self-efficacy are based on perception, they will be discussed later, in the section on perception.

LOCUS OF CONTROL

Locus of control is a trait that lies on a continuum between believing that control over one's destiny is external and believing that it is internal. *Externalizers* are people who believe that they have no control over their fate and that their behavior has little to do with their performance. *Internalizers* believe that they control their fate and that their behavior has a direct effect on their performance.[10] Internalizers have been shown to have higher levels of performance.[11]

OPTIMISM

Optimism also lies on a continuum whose opposite end is pessimism. Optimistic people believe that things will go well, and they tend to be generally happy. Pessimistic people believe that things will not go well, and they tend to be unhappy much of the time. Optimistic employees usually are more creative and have higher levels of performance.[12]

RISK PROPENSITY

Risk propensity lies on a continuum from risk taking to risk avoiding. Entrepreneurs are risk takers.[13] Successful organizations look for managers who will take risks based on research. Organizations with risk-avoiding managers often go out of business because they do not keep up with changes in their industry.

MACHIAVELLIANISM

Machiavellianism is a trait based on the belief that the ends can justify the means and power should be used to reach desired ends. *High Machs* are generally considered effective in situations in which bargaining and winning is important, such as jobs involving negotiation (purchasing, labor relations) or as commissioned sales reps. However, high Machs tend to be more concerned about meeting their own needs than helping the organization. Thus, they tend to create win-lose situations and may use unethical behavior to win.

Like most successful entrepreneurs, Larry Ellison, founder and CEO of **Oracle**, has an extremely strong internal locus of control. He is not averse to taking risk, even if his key advisers suggest that a move may be unwise. He tends to have a high level of optimism that his chosen course of action is the right one. He is also a high Mach, believing that the ends justify the means. He has been quoted as saying, "It's not enough that we win; all others must lose."[14]

Describe each of the big five personality dimensions.

The Big Five Personality Dimensions

The use of the big five personality dimensions, or traits, is the most widely accepted way to study personality. The big five are extraversion, agreeableness, emotionalism, conscientiousness, and openness to experience.[15]

EXTRAVERSION

Extraversion is measured along a continuum between extrovert and introvert. Are you outgoing? Do you like to meet new people? Extroverts do well in sales and often in management.

AGREEABLENESS

Agreeableness lies on a continuum between cooperative and competitive. Do you like to cooperate or compete with your fellow workers? Organizations with work teams whose members cooperate with each other and compete with external organizations generally have higher levels of performance than companies whose employees compete internally.

EMOTIONALISM

Emotionalism lies on a continuum between stability and instability. Someone who is emotionally stable is calm, secure, and positive, whereas an unstable person is nervous, insecure, and negative. Do you generally behave with a positive or a negative attitude? Workers with positive attitudes generally perform better.[16]

CONSCIENTIOUSNESS

Conscientiousness lies on a continuum between responsible/dependable and irresponsible/undependable. Conscientiousness also reflects whether one is a planner and organized or not. Are you responsible and dependable? Responsible employees outperform nonresponsible ones.[17]

OPENNESS TO EXPERIENCE

Openness to experience lies on a continuum between being willing to try new things and not being willing to do so. Do you like to try new experiences or do you prefer to stay with the routine? With today's fast rate of change, employees who are open to learning new things are more valuable to an organization.

I O M

Robert Johnson clearly has an internal locus of control, is optimistic, and is a risk taker. Without these personality traits, he would never have overcome prejudice and discrimination to climb the corporate ladder to the level of vice president, nor would he have started BET. However, he is not a high Mach, as he strives to create win-win situations. In terms of the big five, he is an extrovert, usually agreeable, emotionally stable, conscientious, and open to new experiences.

To review the personality dimensions and to better understand your own personality, complete the Self-Assessment on personality traits.

WorkApplication1

Identify a present or past boss's personality; refer to the personality traits in the Self-Assessment.

Personality Traits

For each trait listed below, place a check mark on the continuum to indicate how you perceive your own personality. Then, have someone who knows you well complete the assessment to see if you both perceive your personality in the same way.

Obviously, there is no "right" combination of personality traits—we are who we are. However, from a business perspective, it is generally better to recruit and retain people with traits closer to those listed at the left end of each continuum, because people with these traits are generally more productive employees.

Single Traits of Personality

Locus of Control
I'm an internalizer. ____ ____ ____ ____ ____ ____ I'm an externalizer.

Optimism
I'm an optimist. ____ ____ ____ ____ ____ ____ I'm a pessimist.

Risk Propensity
I'm a risk taker. ____ ____ ____ ____ ____ ____ I'm a risk avoider.

Machiavellianism
I'm not a power user. ____ ____ ____ ____ ____ ____ I'm a power user.

The Big Five Personality Dimensions

Extraversion
I'm an extrovert. ____ ____ ____ ____ ____ ____ I'm an introvert.

Agreeableness
I'm cooperative. ____ ____ ____ ____ ____ ____ I'm competitive.

Emotionalism
I'm calm and at ease. ____ ____ ____ ____ ____ ____ I'm worried and nervous.

Conscientiousness
I'm dependable. ____ ____ ____ ____ ____ ____ I'm not dependable.

Openness to Experience
I try new things. ____ ____ ____ ____ ____ ____ I avoid doing new things.

PERCEPTION

Oracle's Larry Ellison has many admirers. Who wouldn't admire a self-made billionaire who has built one of the most successful software companies ever? Some of his former executives, however, see a different side to Ellison. They believe he is a terrible manager.

Why do some employees view a decision made by a manager as fair while others do not?[18] Why is one employee willing to put in extra time to help a leader's plans succeed, while another employee can't wait to leave work at 5 P.M., and some want to leave their jobs completely and become entrepreneurs?[19] The answer often lies in perception.

Understanding perception is important because needs and perceptions are the starting points of behavior.[20] Employees will work harder for a manager they perceive to be a good manager than for one they don't like. If **Kodak** film is perceived to be a good product, people may buy it; if not, they won't. Perception refers to a person's interpretation of reality. In reality, is Larry

Ellison a good manager or a bad manager? It is important to realize that perceptions, right or wrong, affect behavior and performance. In this section, we discuss the perception process and perception bias.

—————————————————————— Learning Outcome 2 ——————————————————————
Explain the perception process, and identify the two factors that influence it.

The Perception Process

Perception *is the process of selecting, organizing, and interpreting environmental information.* No two people ever perceive—and thus ever experience—anything exactly the same way. One factor that determines how you select, organize, and interpret information is your own internal environment, including your personality, self-esteem, attitudes, intelligence, needs, values, and so on. *Self-esteem*, or self-concept, is your perception of yourself. Self-esteem is a personality trait; it lies on a continuum between positive and negative or between high and low.

A second factor that influences the perception process is the information available from the external environment. The more accurate the information that is received, the more closely the perception may be to reality.

WorkApplication2

Give three examples of how you (or a manager you know) have used the attribution process at work.

_____

_____

_____

_____

THE ATTRIBUTION PROCESS

One factor that affects people's attitudes and expectations is their *attributions*. **Attribution** *is the process of determining the reason for someone's behavior and whether that behavior is situational or intentional.* Situational behavior is either accidental or out of the control of the individual. A manager's response to someone else's behavior will be determined in part by whether the manager attributes the behavior to situational factors or intentional factors.[21] The attribution process is illustrated in Exhibit 9-1.

For example, suppose that Eduardo, a manager, observes an employee, Pat, coming back to work late after lunch. If Eduardo has observed that Pat is often late returning from lunch and that she is the only person in his

Exhibit 9-1 *The Attribution Process*

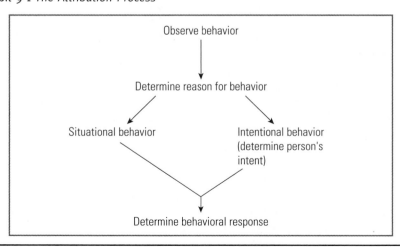

department who is late, he might conclude that Pat's lateness is intentional and that she doesn't care about being on time. In that case, Eduardo would probably decide to discipline Pat. However, if Pat is late only once, Eduardo might determine that her lateness was situational—the result of car problems, traffic, or the like—and take no action.

Bias in Perception

Different people may perceive the same behavior differently because of perception biases, including selectivity, frame of reference, stereotypes, and expectations.

SELECTIVITY
Selectivity refers to people's tendency to screen information in favor of the desired outcome. People will sometimes make great efforts to find information that supports their point of view, and ignore information that does not. In other words, people only see and hear what they want to.

FRAME OF REFERENCE
Frame of reference refers to seeing things from your own point of view. Employees often view management decisions differently than managers do. Managers and employees commonly use the same data during contract negotiations; however, managers perceive that employees want more pay and are not willing to increase productivity, whereas employees perceive managers as greedy and not willing to share the wealth that employees create. Remember that it is not your perception but others' perceptions that will influence their behavior and performance. Try to see things from others' perspective and create a win-win situation so that all parties get what they want, based on their perceptions.

STEREOTYPES
Stereotyping is the process of making generalizations about the behavior of a group and then applying the generalities to one individual. People form stereotypes about race/nationality, religion, sex, age, and so forth. Stereotyping a person can lead to perception errors, because not all individuals from a particular group possess the same traits or exhibit the same behaviors.[22] Try not to negatively stereotype employees; get to know them as individuals.

EXPECTATIONS
Read the phrase in the triangle below:

Did you read the word *the* twice? Or, like most people, did you read what you expected, only one *the*? Many people, especially those who know each other well, often do not really listen to each other. They simply hear what they expect to hear.

WorkApplication3

WorkApplication3

Give an example of a situation that you and someone else experienced together but perceived differently. Which of the biases in perception might explain the difference in perception?

_____

_____

_____

_____

Another type of expectation is the "like me" assumption—that others perceive things as you do because they are similar to you. Remember to value diversity. Don't expect others to behave as you do, and don't judge others' behavior as wrong just because it is different from yours.

Do you know any managers who think they are good managers, but whose employees think they are poor managers—or worse? **Marshall Goldsmith** is a global consultant who helps top managers achieve positive change in their behavior. One of the consulting services that Goldsmith provides is executive coaching, but he will only work with people who really want to change. He gets employees' true perceptions and confronts the manager to make him or her understand what others really think. Then Goldsmith works with the manager so that he or she learns how to apologize to employees and ask for their help in changing specific behavior. The manager is not allowed to defend past behavior; the focus is on improving future behavior.[23]

If Goldsmith worked with you, how closely do you think your self-perceptions would match those of your coworkers and family? Would you be interested in being coached so that you could change your behavior?

──────────────── Learning Outcome 3 ────────────────

Describe the interrelationship among personality, perception, and attitude, and explain the contribution of each to a manager's behavior.

ATTITUDES

Attitudes *are positive or negative evaluations of people, things, and situations.* Attitude is a major factor in determining performance.[24] Employers recruit employees with positive attitudes because they are more likely to be loyal workers who can be relied on to accomplish their tasks. J. W. Marriott, Jr., president of **Marriott Corporation**, stated, "We have found that our success depends more upon employee attitude than any other single factor."[25] You can choose to change your overall attitude to be more positive.[25] Diversity training has changed attitudes by helping to eliminate negative stereotypes.[26] In this section, we discuss how attitudes are formed and affect behavior and how managers' attitudes affect employees' performance and job satisfaction.

WorkApplication4

Give an example of how your attitude affected your behavior at work.

_____

_____

_____

_____

Attitude Formation

Attitudes are based on perceptions. Family, friends, teachers, coworkers, the mass media, and so on affect your attitude formation. Before you signed up for this course, you may have read the course description, talked to students who completed it to find out more about the course, and thought about your interest in the course. Based on what you read and heard and your interest in the subject, you may have started this course with a particular attitude. People generally find what they are looking for, so if you had a positive attitude coming into the course, you probably like it—and vice versa. However, attitudes can be changed. Has your attitude toward this course become more positive or negative? What were the primary factors that formed your present attitude toward this course?

Attitudes and Behavior

Attitudes often affect behavior. People with opposite attitudes toward a person, job, course, event, or situation often behave differently. People's attitudes toward you may affect your behavior.[27] Do you behave differently with people who like you than with those who don't?

How Managers' Attitudes Affect Performance

The **Pygmalion effect** *is the theory that managers' attitudes toward and expectations and treatment of employees largely determine their performance.* Various studies have supported this theory. The basic premise of the theory is that people fulfill expectations about themselves.[28] Thus, if managers expect employees to be productive and successful, and treat them accordingly, employees react by being productive. Conversely, if managers expect employees to be unproductive and unsuccessful, and treat them accordingly, the employees generally fulfill the expectation by not working to their potential.

Unfortunately, some managers negatively stereotype their employees as having low ability or willingness to work. This negative attitude leads to low expectations and not treating employees with respect. Their employees see and do as their managers expect.[29] These managers' expectations lead to the *self-fulfilling prophecy* of low-performing employees. As a manager, if you create win-win situations by expecting high performance and treating employees as capable, you will get the best performance from them.

------------------------------ Learning Outcome 4 ------------------------------
Explain what job satisfaction is and why it is important.

Attitudes and Job Satisfaction

Job satisfaction is a person's attitude toward his or her job, and it is generally measured along a continuum from satisfied/positive/high to dissatisfied/negative/low. Job satisfaction can be measured through an organizational development survey.

JOB SATISFACTION AND PERFORMANCE

Job satisfaction is important because it affects employee absenteeism and turnover. Employees with the personality traits of optimism and positive self-esteem tend to have greater job satisfaction. Although there has long been a debate over the expression that a happy worker is a productive worker, there is support for the idea of a positive relationship between job satisfaction and **citizenship behavior**—employee efforts that go above and beyond the call of duty.[30] Also, job satisfaction can affect satisfaction off the job, as people tend to take their jobs home with them, which affects their behavior.[31]

DETERMINANTS OF JOB SATISFACTION

Six major determinants of job satisfaction are presented in the Self-Assessment on job satisfaction. Complete it to find out your own level of job satisfaction. You can have an overall high level of job satisfaction and not like some aspects of your job; this is common.

WorkApplication5

Think of someone who really expected you to perform well (or poorly) and treated you as if you would do well (or poorly), which strongly affected your success (or failure). Explain how the Pygmalion effect influenced your performance.

Job Satisfaction

Select a present or past job. Identify your level of satisfaction by placing a check at the appropriate position on the continuum for each determinant of job satisfaction.

Personality

| I have positive self-esteem. | ___ | ___ | ___ | ___ | ___ | ___ | I have negative self-esteem. |

Work itself

| I enjoy doing the tasks I perform. | ___ | ___ | ___ | ___ | ___ | ___ | I *do not* enjoy doing the tasks I perform. |

Compensation

| I am fairly compensated. | ___ | ___ | ___ | ___ | ___ | ___ | I am *not* fairly compensated. |

Growth and upward mobility

| I have the opportunity to learn new things and get better jobs. | ___ | ___ | ___ | ___ | ___ | ___ | I have *no* opportunity to learn new things and get better jobs. |

Coworkers

| I like and enjoy working with my coworkers | ___ | ___ | ___ | ___ | ___ | ___ | I *do not* like and enjoy working with my coworkers |

Management

| I believe that managers are doing a good job. | ___ | ___ | ___ | ___ | ___ | ___ | I *do not* believe that managers are doing a good job. |

Overall Job Satisfaction

When determining your overall job satisfaction, you cannot simply add up a score based on the above six determinants, because they are most likely of different importance to you. Thus, think about your job and the above factors, and rate your overall satisfaction with your job.

| I am satisfied with my job (high level of satisfaction). | _6_ | _5_ | _4_ | _3_ | _2_ | _1_ | I am dissatisfied with my job (low level of satisfaction). |

Remember that job satisfaction is based on personality and perception; thus, it can be changed. If you work at being more positive by focusing on the good parts of your job and spend less time thinking about problems, and especially complaining to others about your job, you may increase your job satisfaction. Improving your human relationship skills can help you to get along better with coworkers and managers and increase your job satisfaction.[32] It can also increase your chances for growth and your opportunities for advancement and higher compensation.

IOM

Research has shown that African Americans face prejudice and discrimination, often based on stereotyped negative perceptions of their competence.[33] Robert Johnson overcame prejudice and discrimination because he realized that it was part of the landscape. He knew he was going to face it, but he didn't let it stop him from achieving his goals. He looked for commonalities of interest. Johnson proved that he was competent, and he overcame negative perceptions and attitudes to break the glass ceiling. Johnson believes in himself and knows there are very few things that can stop him from achieving his goals.

Join the Discussion Ethics & Social Responsibility

Smoking

1. Should employees be allowed to smoke wherever and whenever they want to at work?
2. How did your perceptions of and attitude toward smoking affect your answer to the previous question?
3. Might limiting employees' smoking change their behavior on the job? How so?
4. What kinds of personality traits might make employees resist management's efforts to restrict their smoking during working hours?
5. Is it ethical and socially responsible to restrict employees' smoking?

As you know, in many companies, the number of places where employees can smoke is limited. Smoking is restricted to certain areas within buildings or is only allowed outside, and in some cases there are even requirements that smokers stay a certain distance away from the building.

POWER

To be effective in an organization, you must understand how power is gained and used.[34] In this section, we discuss the importance of power in organizations, the types of power, and how to increase your power.

Learning Outcome 5

Define *power*, and explain the difference between position and personal power.

Organizational Power

Some people view power as the ability to make other people do what they want them to do, or the ability to do something to people or for people. These definitions may be true, but they tend to give power a manipulative, negative connotation. For our purposes, **power** *is the ability to influence others' behavior.* Larry Ellison and Robert Johnson are considered powerful people because of their ability to influence others' behavior.

Within an organization, power should be viewed in a positive sense. Without power, managers could not achieve organizational objectives.[35] Leadership and power go hand in hand. Employees are not influenced without a reason, and the reason is often the power a manager has over them.[36] You do not actually have to use power to influence others. Often it is their perception of your power, rather than actual power, that influences others.[37]

Power starts at the top of the organization, and today top managers are giving more power to employees (*empowerment*).[38] Many organizations, including **AT&T, Corning, GE**, and **Motorola**, have a team as CEO, rather than a single autocratic leader.

There are two sources of power: one's position and one's person. *Position power* is derived from top management and is delegated down the chain of command.[39] *Personal power* is derived from followers, based on an individual's

Exhibit 9-2 *Types of Power*

Position Power						Personal Power
Coercive	Connection	Reward	Legitimate	Referent	Information	Expert

behavior. Charismatic leaders have personal power. Therefore, personal power can be gained or lost. It is best to have both position power and personal power.

Recall that the opening case for Chapter 7 was about **Hewlett Packard's** former CEO Carly Fiorina. When Fiorina wanted to acquire **Compaq**, she met resistance from some of the HP board members and major shareholders. She was CEO, but she was not the chair of the board of directors. There was a proxy battle that required the stockholders to vote for or against the acquisition—which was risky for Fiorina, because if she lost she would lose not only Compaq but also some of her power. Through the use of her position power as CEO and her personal power of persuasion, Fiorina won the proxy battle to acquire Compaq. Shortly after that, she gained more control at HP by becoming the chair of the board.[40]

Types of Power and How to Increase Your Power

The seven types of power are presented in Exhibit 9-2. You can increase your power without taking power away from others. Generally, power is given to those who get results and have good human relations skills.

COERCIVE POWER

The use of *coercive power* involves threats and/or punishment to influence compliance. Out of fear of reprimands, probation, suspension, or dismissal, employees often do as their boss requests. Other examples of the use of coercive power include verbal abuse, humiliation, and ostracism. Group members may use coercive power to enforce norms. Coercive power is appropriate to use in maintaining discipline when enforcing rules. Larry Ellison, CEO of **Oracle**, admits that he often uses coercive power to get employees to do what he wants.

Generally, to have coercive power, you need to have a management job that enables you to gain and maintain the ability to hire, discipline, and fire your employees. However, some people can pressure others to do what they want without position authority.

CONNECTION POWER

Connection power is based on the user's relationship with influential people. You rely on the use of contacts or friends who can influence the person you are dealing with. The right connections can give power, or at least the perception of power. If people know you are friendly with people in power, they are more apt to do as you request. Larry Ellison's business and political contacts have given him strong connection power within the information technology industry.

Networking means developing connections. To increase your connection power, expand your network of contacts with important managers who have power. When you want something, identify the people who can help you attain it, make alliances, and win them over to your side. Connections are developed through political networking, the topic of the next section.

————————————————— **Learning** Outcome 6 —————————————————
Identify the differences among reward, legitimate, and referent power.

REWARD POWER

Reward power is based on the user's ability to influence others by providing something of value to them. In a management position, reward power involves the use of positive reinforcement or incentives, such as praise, recognition, pay raises, and promotions, to influence others' behavior. With peers, you can exchange favors or give them something of value. Let people know what's in it for them by creating a win-win situation. Larry Ellison has always made a point of rewarding **Oracle** employees for performance. For example, salespeople have received large bonuses and commissions at different points in the company's history.

To increase your reward power, you must be in a position in which you have some control over evaluating employees' performance and determining their raises and promotions. Find out what others value and try to reward them in that way.[41] Using praise can help increase your power. Employees who feel they are appreciated rather than being used will give you more power.

LEGITIMATE POWER

Legitimate power is based on the user's position power in the organization. Employees tend to feel that they ought to do what the boss says. Day-to-day manager–employee interactions are based on legitimate power.

To increase your legitimate power, you need to attain a management position.

REFERENT POWER

Referent power is based on the user's personal power relationships with others. Someone using referent power would ask another person to do something—that is, he or she would express it as a request rather than as an order. Referent

---

Join the Discussion Ethics & Social Responsibility

Following Orders

1. Is it ethical and socially responsible to teach people in the military or any other organization to follow orders without questioning authority?
2. What would you do if your boss ordered you to do something you thought might be unethical? (Some options are to just do it, to not do it and say nothing, to look more closely at what you are being asked to do, to go to your boss's boss to make sure it's okay to do it, to tell the boss you will not do it, to ask the boss to do it himself or herself, or to blow the whistle to an outside source like the government or media.)
3. Is following orders a good justification for conducting unethical practices?

Officers in the armed forces tend to use legitimate power with troops. Military recruits are conditioned to follow orders, usually without questioning authority. However, as you know, some military troops throughout the world have intentionally tortured and killed innocent people, including women and children.

power is used by people who have little or no position power; it is also used in teams where leadership is shared.

To increase your referent power, you should develop your human relations skills and make efforts to gain others' confidence.[42]

WorkApplication6

Identify the type(s) of power usually used by your current boss or a previous boss. Was there any type(s) of power that this person used only rarely?

_____

_____

_____

_____

_____

INFORMATION POWER

Information power is based on others' need for data. Managers rely on information, which is usually, but not always, related to the job. Some secretaries have more information and are more helpful in answering questions than the managers they work for. An important part of the manager's job is to convey information. Employees often come to managers for information on what to do and how to do it.

To increase your information power, know what is going on in the organization. Provide service and information to other departments. Serve on committees because doing so gives you a chance to increase both information power and connection power.

EXPERT POWER

Expert power is based on the user's skill and knowledge. Being an expert makes other people depend on you. Employees with expert power are often promoted to management positions. The fewer people who possess certain expertise, the more power the individual who does not have it will gain.[43] It's a supply-and-demand dynamic. Larry Ellison is viewed as a visionary, not just within **Oracle** but throughout the technology industry. This expert power allows him greater leeway in his actions—and mistakes—than other leaders might enjoy.

ApplyingTheConcept 1

Using Power

Identify the appropriate type of power to use in each situation.

a. coercive

b. connection

c. reward or legitimate

d. referent

e. information or expert

_____1. Bridget, one of your best workers, usually needs little direction from you. However, recently her performance level has dropped. You are quite sure Bridget has a personal problem affecting her work.

_____2. You want a new personal computer to help you do a better job. Computer purchases must be approved by a committee, and its decisions are very political in nature.

_____3. One of your best workers, Jean, wants a promotion. Jean has talked to you about getting ahead and has asked you to help prepare her for when the opportunity comes.

_____4. John, one of your worst employees, has ignored one of your directives again.

_____5. Whitney, who needs some direction and encouragement from you to maintain production, is not working to standard today. As she does occasionally, she claims that she does not feel well but cannot afford to take time off. You have to get an important customer order shipped today.

To increase your expert power, take all the training and educational programs your organization provides. Keep up with the latest technology. Volunteer to be the first to learn something new. Be willing to take on the more complex, hard-to-evaluate tasks.

As founder, chairman, and CEO of BET, Robert Johnson clearly has position power. He is well respected and thus also has personal power as well. He has position power as a member of the boards of directors of U.S. Airways, Hilton Hotels, General Mills, the United Negro College Fund, the National Cable Television Association, and the American Film Institute and the boards of governors of the Rock and Roll Hall of Fame and the Brookings Institution. These board memberships reflect Johnson's expert power and his connection power. Because of his expert power, Johnson has won several awards, including being named one of the twenty most influential people in the cable industry.

Johnson primarily uses referent power when he communicates his vision of BET as the world's preeminent African American entertainment media company. He uses his power to get the resources necessary to achieve BET's vision. Johnson's employees are motivated and empowered to pursue Johnson's vision, not coerced, and those who advance BET are well rewarded.

Why do some people seek power, whereas others will not take it even if it's offered to them? McClelland's acquired needs theory of motivation (Chapter 12) states that people have different levels of the need for power. Do you want to influence others? Do you plan to follow the suggestions in the text to increase your power?

———————————— Learning Outcome 7 ————————————
Discuss how power and politics are related.

ORGANIZATIONAL POLITICS

In this section, we discuss the nature of organizational politics, political behavior in organizations, and guidelines for developing political skills. Begin by determining your own political behavior by completing the Self-Assessment.

———————————— Learning Outcome 8 ————————————
Describe how money and politics have a similar use.

The Nature of Organizational Politics

Political skills come into play when using power.[44] **Politics** *is the process of gaining and using power.* Politics is a reality of organizational life.[45] Like power, politics is often viewed negatively, because people often abuse political power. A positive way to view politics is to realize that it is simply a medium of exchange.[46] Like money, politics in and of itself is neither good nor bad. It is simply a means of getting what we want.[47] In most economies, money is the medium of exchange; in an organization, politics is the medium of exchange.

Managers cannot meet their objectives without the help of others, including people and departments over which they have no authority, so they need to use political skills.[48] For example, Carmen, a production department manager, needs materials and supplies to make the product but must rely on the purchasing department to acquire them. If Carmen does not have a good working relationship with purchasing, materials and supplies may not be there when her department needs them.

WorkApplication7
Which of the suggestions for increasing your power are the most relevant to you? Explain.

_____
_____
_____
_____

Self-Assessment

Use of Political Behavior

Beside each statement, write the number of the choice that best describes how often you use the particular behavior on the job (or how often you imagine you will use it once you are employed).

1 = rarely   2 = seldom   3 = occasionally   4 = frequently   5 = usually

_____ 1. I get along with everyone, even those considered to be difficult to get along with.

_____ 2. I avoid giving my personal opinions on controversial issues, especially when I know others don't agree with them.

_____ 3. I try to make people feel important by complimenting them.

_____ 4. I compromise when working with others and avoid telling people they are wrong.

_____ 5. I try to get to know the key managers and find out what is going on in all the organizational departments.

_____ 6. I dress the same way as the people in power and take on the same interests (watch or play sports, join the same clubs, etc.).

_____ 7. I purposely seek contacts with higher-level managers so that they will know my name and face.

_____ 8. I seek recognition and visibility for my accomplishments.

_____ 9. I get others to help me get what I want.

_____10. I do favors for others and ask them for favors in return.

To determine your level political behavior, add the ten numbers you selected as your answers. The total will range from 10 to 50. The higher your score, the more political behavior you use. Place your score on the continuum below.

Nonpolitical   10———20———30———40———50   Political

The amount and importance of politics vary from organization to organization.[49] However, larger organizations tend to be more political, and the higher the level of management, the more important politics becomes.[50]

—————————————————— Learning Outcome 9 ——————————————————
Explain what networking, reciprocity, and coalitions have in common.

Political Behavior

Networking, using reciprocity, and coalition building are important political behaviors.

NETWORKING

As you'll recall from the appendix to Chapter 8, **networking** *is the process of developing relationships for the purpose of socializing and politicking.* Networking contributes to managerial success because it helps get the job done.[51] Successful managers spend more time networking than do average managers.

USING RECIPROCITY

Reciprocity *involves the creation of obligations and the development of alliances that are used to accomplish objectives.* When people do something for you, you incur an obligation, and they may expect to be repaid.[52] When you do something for someone else, you create a debt that you may be able to collect at a later date when you need a favor.[53] You should work on developing a network of alliances that you can call on for help in meeting your objectives.[54]

COALITION BUILDING

A **coalition** *is a network of alliances that help a manager achieve an objective.* Reciprocity is used to achieve ongoing objectives, whereas coalitions are developed for achieving a specific objective. For example, Pedro has an idea for a new service to be offered by his company. By himself, Pedro has no authority to offer a new service. To begin building a coalition, Pedro might first go to his boss or bosses. Pedro would present the idea to his boss and get approval to gain wider support. Pedro would then try to get peers and people at other levels as allies. It is important to align yourself with powerful people who can help.[55]

The former CEO of the **New York Stock Exchange (NYSE)**, Dick Grasso, is known as a powerful man who uses politics to get what he wants. Grasso used coercive power to stop brokerage firms from taking trading away from the floor of the NYSE and instead conducting it electronically on the Internet.[56] Here is another example of how Grasso used power and politics: Michael LaBranche agreed to merge his company with a smaller rival to create the largest specialist firm working on the NYSE. The merger required Grasso's approval. Grasso "strongly" recommended that his longtime friend Robert Murphy, CEO of the smaller company, be named chief executive of the new **LaBranche & Company** main operating unit after the merger.[57] In order to continue serving on the NYSE board, where Grasso wanted him, Murphy had to continue to hold a position at the top of a specialist firm.[58]

WorkApplication8
Give an example of how you used networking, reciprocity, or a coalition to achieve an organizational objective.

Guidelines for Developing Political Skills

If you want to climb the corporate ladder, you should develop your political skills.[59] Review the ten statements in the Self-Assessment on political behavior and the three political behaviors just discussed, and consciously increase your use of any or all of these behaviors. Successfully implementing these behaviors results in increased political skills. Learn what it takes in the organization where you work; the guidelines in Exhibit 9-3 can help you avoid backstabbers.[60]

LEARN THE ORGANIZATIONAL CULTURE

Learn how the organization operates, both formally and informally. Learn to read between the lines. Use political behavior to promote yourself, but be sure to use methods that are considered appropriate and ethical.[61]

LEARN THE POWER PLAYERS

It is natural, especially for young people, to take a purely rational approach to a job, without considering politics. But many business decisions are nonrational, based primarily on power and politics.[62] Furthermore, important decisions are made by "power players." Find out who those people are in your organization. And always remember that your boss is a key player for you, regardless of your personal feelings toward him or her.[63]

Exhibit 9-3 *Political Behaviors and Guidelines for Developing Political Skills*

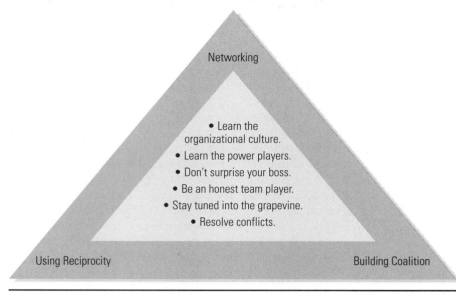

DON'T SURPRISE YOUR BOSS

If you want to get ahead, you should have a good working relationship with your boss. Get to know what your boss expects from you and do it.[64] It's common to put off telling the boss bad news, but if you are having a work problem, let your boss know early. If you are behind schedule to meet an important deadline and your boss finds out about it from others, you'll be embarrassed—especially if your boss finds out from his or her boss. When building a coalition, include your boss.

BE AN HONEST TEAM PLAYER

One unfortunate fact of life in many organizations is that some workers and managers are "backstabbers"—people who like to make others look bad by spreading untrue gossip about them. Some backstabbing gossips may get short-term benefits from their behavior, but in the long run they are generally unsuccessful because others gossip about them in return. In any organization, you must earn others' respect, confidence, and trust. Once caught in a lie, you'll find it difficult to regain people's trust. There are very few, if any, jobs in which organizational objectives can be achieved without the support of a group or team.[65] So if you are not a team player, work at being one.

STAY TUNED IN TO THE GRAPEVINE

Find out what is going on through the grapevine. The grapevine can help you to learn the organizational culture and identify key players to include in your coalitions.[66] Your grapevine should include a network of people within and outside your organization.

RESOLVE CONFLICTS

When climbing the corporate ladder, you may have to be careful not to get pushed off.[67] Following the preceding guidelines can help you avoid a political fight. However, if you are suddenly left out of the information loop, or if

WorkApplication9

Which one or two suggestions for developing political skills are the most relevant to you?

_____

_____

_____

_____

_____

Applying The Concept 2

Political Behavior

Identify the political behavior in each situation as

a. effective

b. ineffective

_____ 6. Jill is taking golf lessons so that she can join the Saturday golf group that includes some higher-level managers.

_____ 7. Paul tells his boss's boss about mistakes his boss makes.

_____ 8. Sally avoids socializing so that she can be more productive on the job.

_____ 9. John sent copies of a very positive performance report that his supervisor wrote about him to three higher-level managers to whom he does not report. They did not request copies.

_____10. Carlos has to drop off daily reports at a certain office by noon. He brings them in around 10:00 on Tuesdays and Thursdays so that he can run into some higher-level managers who meet at that time near the office. On the other days, Carlos drops the reports off around noon on his way to lunch.

your coworkers or boss start treating you differently, find out why. Confront individuals or groups suspected of instigating conflict.[68] If you did something to offend an adversary, an apology may clear the air. In any case, use the ideas in the next section to resolve the conflict.

As founder, chairman, and CEO of BET, Robert Johnson has lots of experience with organizational politics. Johnson started and expanded BET through networking. He has done favors for others, who have done favors for him (reciprocity). He focuses on having honest team players. Johnson communicates the BET vision and effectively builds consensus among broad-based coalitions of people who will achieve the vision. Johnson is able to resolve conflict effectively through consensus building. Johnson realizes that when they observe unethical politics, employees don't feel like they are part of the vision, and they won't perform as effectively. By giving employees trust and support, Johnson gets them to do their best.

I O M

MANAGING CONFLICT

A **conflict** *exists whenever people are in disagreement and opposition*. Managers need strong conflict resolution and negotiation skills if they want to be successful.[69] How well you handle conflict also affects your job satisfaction.[70]

In this section, we discuss the psychological contract, functional and dysfunctional conflict, and five conflict management styles.

The Psychological Contract

All human relations rely on the psychological contract.[71] The *psychological contract* is composed of the implicit expectations of each party.[72] At work, you have a set of expectations about what you will contribute to the organization (effort, time, and skills) and what it will provide to you (compensation and job satisfaction).[73] Often we are not aware of our expectations until they have not been met.[74]

Conflict arises when the psychological contract is broken, which happens for two primary reasons: (1) We fail to make explicit our own expectations and fail to inquire into the expectations of others. (2) We assume that others have the same expectations that we hold.[75] As long as people meet our expectations, everything is fine; when they don't meet our expectations, we are in conflict. Thus, it is important to share information and communicate expectations assertively.[76] After all, how can you expect others to meet your expectations when they don't know what they are?

Functional and Dysfunctional Conflict

People often think of conflict as "fighting" and view it as disruptive. Conflict that prevents the achievement of organizational objectives is negative, or *dysfunctional conflict*.[77] However, conflict can be positive.[78] **Functional conflict** exists when *disagreement and opposition support the achievement of organizational objectives.*

Too little or too much conflict is usually dysfunctional.[79] If people are not willing to disagree and then work toward the best solution to their conflict, or if they fight too much without resolution, objectives may not be met.[80] Challenging the status quo and presenting innovative change cause conflict, but generally lead to improved performance.[81]

────────── Learning Outcome 10──────────
List and define five conflict management styles.

Conflict Management Styles

When you are faced with conflict, you have five conflict management styles to choose from. The five styles are based on two dimensions of concern: concern for others' needs and concern for your own needs. Various levels of concern result in three types of behavior: passive, aggressive, and assertive. Each conflict management style results in a different win-loss pattern. The five styles are presented in Exhibit 9-4.

Exhibit 9-4 *Conflict Management Styles*

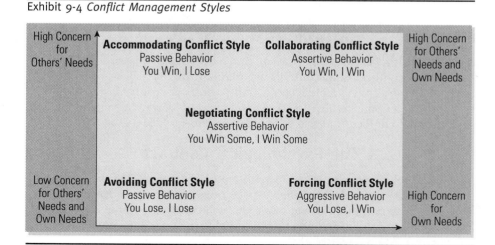

AVOIDING CONFLICT STYLE

The user of an *avoiding conflict style* attempts to passively ignore the conflict rather than resolve it.[82] When you avoid a conflict, you are being unassertive and uncooperative. People avoid conflict by refusing to take a stance, by mentally withdrawing, or by physically leaving. A lose-lose situation results because the conflict is not resolved.

The advantage of the avoiding style is that it may maintain relationships that would be hurt through conflict resolution. The disadvantage of this style is the fact that conflicts do not get resolved.[83] An overuse of this style leads to conflict within the individual who uses it; also, people tend to take advantage of an avoider. Some managers allow employees to perform poorly without confronting them. Avoiding problems usually does not make them go away; the problems often get worse. The longer you wait to confront others, the more difficult the confrontation usually is.[84]

The avoiding style is appropriate to use when (1) the conflict is trivial, (2) your stake in the issue is not high, (3) confrontation will damage an important relationship, (4) you don't have time to resolve the conflict, or (5) emotions are high. When you don't have time to resolve the conflict or when people are emotional, you should deal with the situation later. It is inappropriate to repeatedly avoid confrontation until you get so upset that you end up yelling at other people. This passive-aggressive behavior tends to make the situation worse by hurting human relations. People do not realize they are doing something that bothers you (that you are in conflict) and, when approached properly, may be willing to change.

ACCOMMODATING CONFLICT STYLE

The user of an *accommodating conflict style* attempts to resolve conflict by passively giving in to the opposing side. When you use the accommodating style, you are being unassertive but cooperative. You attempt to satisfy the needs of others but neglect your own needs by letting others get their own way. A win-lose situation is created.

A difference between the avoiding style and the accommodating style is that the latter leads you to do something you don't want to do. Suppose you are talking to someone who makes a statement you disagree with. If you are using the avoiding style, you simply say nothing and thereby avoid doing something you don't want to do (expressing an opinion that might anger the other person). However, if you and another person are working on a project together and you go along with that person's way of doing a particular task, even though you disagree with it, you are using the accommodating style. And in this case, you end up doing something you don't want to do.

The advantage of the accommodating style is that you maintain relationships by doing things other people's way. The disadvantage is that giving in may be counterproductive. The person giving in may have a better solution. An overuse of this style tends to lead to being taken advantage of.

The accommodating style is appropriate when (1) you enjoy being a follower, (2) maintaining the relationship outweighs all other considerations, (3) the changes agreed to are not important to you but are to the other person, (4) the time to resolve the conflict is limited, or (5) the person you are in conflict with uses the forcing style.

FORCING CONFLICT STYLE

The user of a *forcing conflict style* attempts to resolve conflict by using aggressive behavior to get his or her own way. When you use the forcing style, you are uncooperative and aggressive; you do whatever it takes to satisfy your own needs at the expense of others.[85] Forcers use authority, threaten, intimidate, and call for majority rule when they know they will win. Forcers commonly enjoy dealing with avoiders and accommodators. If you try to get others to change without being willing to change yourself, regardless of the means, then you use the forcing style and create a win-lose situation.

Oracle CEO Larry Ellison is well known for using the forcing conflict style in his relationships with managers, competitors, and even with customers. This is one of the reasons that many of his former executives talk so bitterly about him. Several have even started firms that compete directly with Oracle.

The advantage of the forcing style is that better organizational decisions will be made when the forcer is correct. The disadvantage is that overuse of this style leads to hostility and resentment toward its user. Forcers tend to have poor human relations skills and to care very little about people.

The forcing style is appropriate to use when (1) unpopular action must be taken on important issues, (2) commitment by others to a proposed action is not crucial to its implementation (either people will not resist doing what you want them to do or their resistance will not affect the results), (3) maintaining relationships is not critical, or (4) a resolution of the conflict is urgently needed.

NEGOTIATING CONFLICT STYLE

The user of the *negotiating conflict style*, also called the *compromising style*, attempts to resolve conflict through assertive give-and-take.[86] When you use the negotiating style, you are moderate in assertiveness and cooperation. A situation in which each side achieves a partial victory is created through compromise.

The advantages of the negotiating conflict style are that the conflict is resolved relatively quickly and working relationships are maintained. The disadvantage is that compromise often leads to counterproductive results, such as suboptimum decisions. An overuse of this style leads to game playing in which people ask for twice as much as they need in order to get what they want. This style is commonly used during collective bargaining.

The negotiating conflict style is appropriate to use when (1) the issues are complex and critical and there is no simple and clear solution, (2) parties have about equal power and are interested in different solutions, (3) a solution will be only temporary, or (4) time is short.

COLLABORATING CONFLICT STYLE

The user of a *collaborating conflict style*, also called the *problem-solving style*, assertively attempts to resolve conflict by working together with the other person to find an acceptable solution. When you use the collaborating approach, you are being assertive and cooperative. Whereas avoiders and accommodators are concerned about others' needs and forcers are concerned about their own needs, the collaborators are concerned about finding the best solution to the problem that is satisfactory to all. Unlike the forcer, the collaborator is willing to change if a better solution is presented. While negotiating is often based on secret information, collaboration is based on open and honest communication. This is the only style that creates a true win-win situation.

A difference between the negotiating and collaborating styles is in the solution each leads to. Again, suppose you and another person are working on a project and she wants to do a task in a way that you disagree with. With the negotiating style, you might do this task her way and the next task your way; you each win some and lose some. With the collaborating style, you work to develop an approach to the task that you can both agree on. The key to collaboration is agreeing that the solution picked is the best possible one. Thus, a win-win situation is achieved.

The advantage of the collaborating style is that it tends to lead to the best solution to the conflict using assertive behavior. The collaborative style offers the most benefit to the individual, group, and organization. The disadvantage is that it takes more skill, effort, and time to resolve conflict using this style than it does using the other styles. There are situations when collaboration is difficult or when a forcer prevents its use.

The collaborating style is appropriate when (1) you are dealing with an important issue that requires an optimal solution, and compromise would result in suboptimizing, (2) people are willing to place the group goal before self-interest, (3) maintaining relationships is important, (4) time is available, or (5) the conflict is between peers.

WorkApplication10

Think of one of your present or past bosses and give several examples of the conflict management style that person used most often.

_____

_____

_____

_____

Applying The Concept 3

Selecting Conflict Management Styles

Identify the most appropriate conflict management style to use in each situation.

a. avoiding style
b. accommodating style
c. forcing style
d. negotiating style
e. collaborating style

_____ 11. You have joined a committee in order to make contacts. You have little interest in what the committee actually does. While serving on the committee, you make a recommendation that is opposed by another member. You realize that you have the better idea, but the other party is using a forcing style.

_____ 12. You are on a task force that has to select a new computer. The four alternatives will all do the job, but team members disagree about the brand, price, and service.

_____ 13. You are a sales manager. Beth, one of your competent salespeople, is trying to close a big sale. The two of you are discussing the sales call she will make. You disagree on the strategy to use to close the sale.

_____ 14. You're on your way to an important meeting and running a little late. As you leave your office, at the other end of the work area you see Chris, one of your employees, goofing off instead of working.

_____ 15. You're over budget for labor this month. At the moment, the work load is light, so you ask Kent, a part-time employee, to leave work early. Kent tells you he doesn't want to go because he needs the money.

WorkApplication11
Which one of the five conflict management styles do you tend to use most often? Explain.

There is no one best style for resolving all conflicts. A person's preferred style tends to meet his or her needs. Some people enjoy forcing; others prefer to avoid conflict. Managerial success lies in one's ability to use the appropriate style to meet the situation.

Of the five styles, avoiding, accommodating, and forcing are generally the easiest to learn. If you have problems using the avoiding and accommodating styles when appropriate, you need to work at giving in to others by saying or doing nothing or by going along with others' way of doing things. For most people, the two most difficult styles to develop are the negotiating and collaborating styles. Thus, these two skills are discussed in more detail in the next section. Skill Builders 1 and 2 also focus on negotiation and collaboration skills.

IOM

As founder of BET, Robert Johnson had to negotiate to get the resources to start, expand, and continue to operate BET. He uses the collaborating conflict style to get his employees to buy into his vision of BET and to get them to work hard to achieve the vision. Johnson also negotiated a joint venture partnership, and thus collaborates with Microsoft, Liberty Digital Media, News Corporation, and USA Networks to operate BET Interactive (BET.com).

NEGOTIATION, COLLABORATION, AND MEDIATION

In this section, we discuss how to negotiate and how to use collaboration to initiate, respond to, and mediate a conflict resolution.

Negotiating

Negotiating is a process in which two or more parties in conflict attempt to come to an agreement. You have to negotiate in both your personal and your professional life.[87] There are times when negotiations are appropriate, such as in management–union collective bargaining, when buying and selling goods and services, and when discussing a job compensation offer. If there is a set "take it or leave it" deal, there is no negotiation. Also, not all negotiations end with an agreement. Power and politics are tools of negotiation.[88]

Negotiation is often a *zero-sum game* in which one party's gain is the other party's loss. For example, every dollar less that you pay for a car is your gain and the seller's loss. Negotiating is about getting what you want.[89] To get what you want, you have to sell your ideas and convince the other party to give in. Ideally, however, negotiation should be viewed by all parties as "I win some and you win some," rather than a win-lose situation; all parties should believe they got a good deal. If union employees believe that they lost and management won, they may become dissatisfied with their jobs, which could result in lower performance in the long run. If customers believe that they got a bad deal, they will not do business with the company again.

The Negotiation Process

The negotiation process has three and possibly four steps: plan, negotiate, possibly postpone, and finally, come to an agreement or no agreement.[90] These steps are summarized in Exhibit 9-5 and discussed in this section. In the course of actual negotiations, you may have to make slight adjustments to the steps in the process.

Exhibit 9-5 *The Negotiation Process*

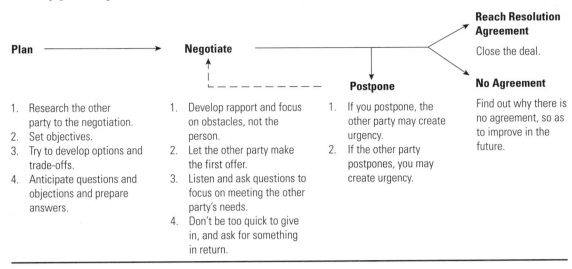

Plan ⟶ **Negotiate** ⟶

Reach Resolution Agreement

Close the deal.

Postpone

No Agreement

Find out why there is no agreement, so as to improve in the future.

1. Research the other party to the negotiation.	1. Develop rapport and focus on obstacles, not the person.
2. Set objectives.	2. Let the other party make the first offer.
3. Try to develop options and trade-offs.	3. Listen and ask questions to focus on meeting the other party's needs.
4. Anticipate questions and objections and prepare answers.	4. Don't be too quick to give in, and ask for something in return.

Postpone:
1. If you postpone, the other party may create urgency.
2. If the other party postpones, you may create urgency.

PLAN

Success or failure in negotiating is often based on preparation.[91] Be clear about what it is you are negotiating. Is it price, options, delivery time, sales quantity, or something else entirely? Planning has four steps:

Step 1. Research the other parties to the negotiation. Know the key power players. Try to find out what the other parties want and what they will and will not be willing to give up before you negotiate.[92] Find out, through your networking grapevine, their personality traits and negotiation style. The more you know about those with whom you will be negotiating, the better your chances are of reaching an agreement. If you have worked with some of the people before, think about what worked and did not work in the past.

Step 2. Set objectives. In some negotiations, your objective will be to change someone's behavior; at other times, you may be negotiating salary or benefits or a better price from a supplier. In any case, you want to set three objectives:

- A specific lower limit that you are unwilling to give up (say, a certain behavior on the part of your peer in the department, or a minimum price from your supplier). You must be willing to suspend negotiations if this lower limit is not agreed to.[93]
- A target objective that represents what you believe is fair.
- An opening objective that is more than you actually expect but that you may achieve.

Remember that the other person or party is probably also setting these kinds of objectives. The key to successful negotiation is for each person or party to achieve something between their minimum objective and their target objective.[94]

Step 3. Try to develop options and trade-offs. In some negotiating situations, you may find that you are in a position of power to achieve your target objective.[95] For example, when negotiating prices with a supplier or applying for jobs, you may be able to quote other prices or salary offers and get the other person to beat them. If you have to give up something or cannot get exactly what you want, be prepared to ask for something in return.[96] When Eastern Airlines was having financial difficulty, the company asked employees to take a pay cut. Rather than simply accept a cut, the employees asked for company stock in a trade-off. Based on your research, you should be able to anticipate the kinds of trade-offs you might expect from the other person.

Step 4. Anticipate questions and objections and prepare answers. Very likely the other party to negotiations wants an answer to the unasked question "What's in it for me?"[97] Focus on how the negotiations will benefit the other person; speak in terms of "you" and "we" rather than "I."

There is a good chance that the other person will raise objections.[98] Unfortunately, not everyone will be open about his or her real objections. Thus, you need to listen and ask questions to find out what is preventing an agreement. It will also help to project an attitude of enthusiasm and confidence. If the other person does not trust you, you will not reach an agreement.

NEGOTIATE

After you have planned, you are ready to negotiate the deal. Face-to-face negotiations are generally preferred because you can see the other person's nonverbal behavior (discussed in Chapter 11) and better understand objections. However, negotiations by telephone and written negotiations work, too. It will help to keep the following in mind as you begin negotiating.

Step 1. Develop rapport and focus on obstacles, not on the person. Use the other person's name as you greet him or her. If appropriate, open with small talk.[99] How long you wait before getting down to negotiations will depend on the particular situation and the other person's style.

Never attack the other person's personality or use negative statements such as "You always bad-mouth me to the boss" or "You're being unfair to ask for such a price cut." Statements like these will make the other person defensive, which will make it harder to reach an agreement.[100] During negotiations, people look for four things: inclusion, control, safety, and respect. If people perceive that you are pushing them into something, threatening them, or belittling them, they will not trust you and will be unlikely to come to an agreement with you.

Step 2. Let the other party make the first offer. Of course, the other party may pressure *you* to make the first offer; for example, the person may say, "Give us your best price, and we'll decide whether to take it." If so, you can counter with a question such as "What do you expect to pay?"[101]

Step 3. Listen and ask questions to focus on meeting the other party's needs. Create an opportunity for the other person to disclose reservations and objections. When you ask questions and listen, you gather information that will help you overcome the other party's objections. Determining whether the objection is a "want" criterion or a "must" criterion will help you decide how to proceed.

Step 4. Don't be too quick to give in, and remember to ask for something in return. Those who ask for more often get more. But many people—especially many women—are reluctant to ask for what they deserve.[102] You want to satisfy the other party without giving up too much yourself; remember not to go below your minimum objective, and be prepared to walk away if that minimum can't be met. When you are not getting what you want, having other options can help give you bargaining power.[103]

Though you don't want to be quick to give in, you might want to be the first to make a concession, particularly when you are negotiating complex deals. A concession makes the other party feel obligated, which gives you negotiating power. However, before making a concession, it's essential to know what all of the other party's demands are.[104] And avoid unilateral concessions.

POSTPONE

When there doesn't seem to be any progress, it may be wise to postpone negotiations.[105]

If the other party is postponing, you can try to create urgency. Suppose the other party says, "I'll get back to you." You may try to create urgency by saying, for example, "This is on sale and it ends today."[106] However, honesty is the best policy. Or, if you have other options, you can use them to create urgency, such as by saying, "I have another job offer pending. When will you let me know if you want to offer me the job?" Honesty and integrity are the most important assets a negotiator can possess.

If you are unable to create urgency and the other party says, "I'll think about it," say, "That's a good idea." Then at least review the major features the other party liked about your proposed agreement.

One thing to remember is that when the other party becomes resistant to making the agreement, a hard sell will not work. Take the pressure off by asking the other person something like "Where do you want to go from here?" or by suggesting "Why don't we think about it and discuss it some more later?"

You also need to learn to read between the lines. Some people will not come right out and tell you that there is no agreement. For example, a Japanese businessperson might say something like "It will be difficult to do business." Americans tend to perceive this to mean that they should keep trying to negotiate, but the Japanese businessperson means stop trying, but will not say so directly because doing so is impolite.

If you want to postpone, the other party may try to create urgency. If you feel you cannot agree, tell the other party you want to think about it. If the other party is creating urgency, be sure the urgency is real; don't be pressured into agreeing to something you may regret later.[107] If you do want to postpone, give the other party a specific time that you will get back to them.

AGREEMENT

Once you have resolved your conflict or come to an agreement, put things in writing, if appropriate. It is common to follow up an agreement with a letter of thanks that restates the agreement.

There will be times when you simply will be unable to resolve a conflict or come to an agreement. Rejection, refusal, and failure happen to us all; in negotiating conflict, you need to be thick-skinned.[108] The difference between the "also-rans" and the "superstars" lies in how they respond to the failure. Successful people keep trying and learn from their mistakes and continue to work hard. If you cannot resolve a conflict, analyze the situation and try to determine where you went wrong so you can improve in the future.

—————————————— Learning Outcome 11 ——————————————
List the steps in initiating and using the collaborative conflict
resolution model.

Initiating Conflict Resolution through Collaboration

An initiator is a person who confronts another person in order to resolve conflict. When trying to initiate conflict resolution, you may want to use the **collaborative conflict resolution model**. The steps of the model are (1) stating the problem in terms of behaviors, consequences, and feelings (in a BCF statement), (2) getting the other person to acknowledge the problem or conflict, (3) asking for and/or presenting alternative resolutions to the conflict, and (4) coming to an agreement. These steps are illustrated in Exhibit 9-6, which also indicates appropriate responses to the steps of the model.

Consider an example: Suppose that you don't smoke and are in fact allergic to cigarette smoke. Some of your coworkers do smoke, and although they are allowed to do so in the employees' lounge, most of them avoid smoking when you are in the lounge. One coworker, however, persists in smoking in your presence. This is a problem—you can't always avoid going into the lounge during breaks or lunch. You decide to initiate a collaborative solution to this problem. You begin by asking the smoker to help you solve your problem. This approach reduces defensiveness and establishes an atmosphere that will help maintain a good relationship.

Step 1. As noted above, the first step in the collaborative conflict resolution model is to express the problem in a **BCF statement**, *that is, a statement that describes a conflict in terms of behaviors (B), consequences (C), and feelings (F), in a way that maintains ownership of the problem.* You say to your coworker, "When you smoke around me (B), I have trouble breathing and become nauseous (C), and I feel ill and stressed (F)." Note that you can vary the sequence if a situation warrants it; for example, "I fear (F) that some viewers will respond negatively to this

---

Exhibit 9-6 *The Collaborative Conflict Resolution Model*

INITIATOR		**RESPONDER**		**MEDIATOR**	
Step 1.	State problem in terms of behavior, consequences, and feelings (a BCF statement).	*Step 1.*	Respond as appropriate to initiator's statement of the problem, using your own BCF statements.	*Step 1.*	Brings conflicting parties together and helps them resolve conflict by coaching them as they follow the steps in the model.
Step 2.	Allow other person to respond to your BCF statement and acknowledge the problem or conflict.	*Step 2.*	Acknowledge the problem or conflict.	*Step 2.*	Remains neutral, focuses on how conflict is affecting work.
Step 3.	Ask for and/or present alternative resolutions to the conflict.	*Step 3.*	Discuss alternative resolutions to the conflict.	*Step 3.*	Addresses behavior, not personalities.
Step 4.	Come to an agreement: Determine specific actions to be taken by each person.	*Step 4.*	Come to an agreement: Determine specific actions to be taken by each person.	*Step 4.*	Encourages parties to clarify their statements and responses.
				Step 5.	Follows up to make sure parties carry out the actions they agree to in Step 4.

advertisement (B) and we will lose money by running it (C)." Now, what exactly does "maintaining ownership of the problem" mean? Think about it: Is it you or the smoker who has the problem? Since the smoker is allowed to smoke in the lounge, the problem is yours. Maintaining ownership of the problem means expressing it without assigning blame or making assumptions about who is right or wrong. Fixing blame only makes people defensive, which is counterproductive in conflict resolution. Your BCF statement should be descriptive, not evaluative, and it should deal with a single issue.

Before confronting the other person, practice your BCF statement. Also, think of some possible solutions you might suggest. But be sure your ideas take into consideration the other person's point of view, not just your own. Try to put yourself in his or her position: If you were the other person, would you like the solutions you have thought of?

Step 2. You cannot resolve a conflict if the other person does not even acknowledge that it exists. After stating the problem, let the other person respond. Your coworker might say, "Oh, I didn't realize you reacted so strongly to cigarette smoke" or "Well, that explains why everybody puts out their cigarettes when you're around." On the other hand, the coworker could say, "What's the big deal? You can just stay away from the lounge if smoke bothers you." If the other person doesn't understand or acknowledge the problem, you'll need to be persistent. Repeat your statement in different terms, if necessary.

Step 3. Once the other person acknowledges the problem, ask him or her how the conflict might be resolved. Perhaps the person will suggest something that you can agree to; if so, you're well on your way to a resolution of the conflict. If not, be prepared with your own suggestions. However, remember that you are collaborating, not simply trying to change the other person. If he or she acknowledges the problem but seems unwilling to resolve it, appeal to common goals. Try to make the other person realize how he or she might also benefit from a solution to this conflict.

Step 4. The final step in the collaborative conflict resolution model is to come to an agreement. Determine what specific actions you will each take to resolve the conflict. Perhaps your coworker will agree not to smoke in your presence, now that he knows how it affects you. Perhaps you'll suggest changing your lunch hour, so you don't run into each other in the lounge. Clearly state whatever actions you each agree to.

Research suggests that collaborative conflict resolution skills can be developed.[109] Skill Builder 2 will give you a chance to practice them.

Responding to Collaborative Conflict Resolution

In the role of responder, you have a responsibility to contribute to successful conflict resolution when someone confronts you with a problem. You should keep in mind the steps in the collaborative conflict resolution model: (1) Respond to the initiator's BCF statement with descriptive, nonevaluative statements of your own. (2) Be willing to acknowledge the problem. (3) Make an effort to offer realistic suggestions to resolve the conflict. (4) Come to an agreement, and then hold up your end of the bargain. Carry out whatever specific actions you and the initiator have agreed to.

WorkApplication12

Describe a conflict in which you used (or should have used) a BCF statement.

_____

_____

_____

_____

_____

Mediation as Conflict Resolution

Frequently, parties in conflict cannot resolve their dispute alone. In these cases, a mediator may be used.[110] A **mediator** *is a neutral third party who helps resolve a conflict.* As a manager, you may be called upon to serve as a mediator between two employees. In this case, remember that you should be a mediator, not a judge. Get the employees to resolve the conflict themselves, if possible. Remain impartial, unless one party is violating company policies.

When bringing conflicting employees together, focus on how the conflict is affecting their work. Discuss the issues by addressing specific behavior, not personalities. If a person says, "We cannot work together because of a personality conflict," ask him or her to identify the specific behavior that is the root of the conflict. The discussion should make the parties aware of their behavior and of how its consequences are causing the conflict. What expectations are not being met? (What is the psychological contract?)

If the conflict cannot be resolved by mediation, an arbitrator may be used as a follow-up. *An* **arbitrator** *is a neutral third party who makes a binding decision to resolve a conflict.* The arbitrator is like a judge whose decision must be followed. However, the use of arbitration should be kept to a minimum, because it is not collaborative.

Dealing with different personality types, varying perceptions and attitudes, power, politics, and conflict can be very stressful. In the next section you will study the causes and consequences of stress and how to manage it.

STRESS

People often have internal reactions to external environmental stimuli. **Stress** *is the body's reaction to environmental demands.* This reaction can be emotional and/or physical. Some organizations offer stress management programs to enable employees to handle stress better.

Functional and Dysfunctional Stress

Stress is *functional* when it helps improve performance by challenging and motivating people to meet objectives. People perform best under some pressure. When deadlines are approaching, adrenaline flows and people rise to the occasion.

However, for the individual, too much stress can result in irritability, headaches, tension, poor digestion, heartburn, ulcers, diseases (weakened immune system, elevated blood sugar levels, high blood pressure, high cholesterol levels, and heart problems), and even premature death.[111]

Stressors *are factors that cause people to feel overwhelmed by anxiety, tension, and/or pressure.* Stress that is constant, chronic, and severe can lead to burnout over a period of time.[112] *Burnout* is a constant lack of interest and motivation to perform one's job; burnout results from stress. Stress that is severe enough to lead to burnout is *dysfunctional stress.* From the organizational point of view, dysfunctional stress results in employee job dissatisfaction, absenteeism, turnover, and lower levels of productivity.[113] One survey revealed that 71 percent of employees are stressed.[114]

Stress, like perception, is an individual matter. In the same situation, one person may be very comfortable and stress-free, while another feels stressed to the point of burnout.[115]

Causes of Job Stress

There are five common contributors to job stress: personality type, organizational culture, management behavior, type of work, and human relations.

PERSONALITY TYPE
The *Type A personality* is characterized as fast-moving, hard-driving, time-conscious, competitive, impatient, and preoccupied with work. The Type B personality is the opposite of Type A. In general, people with Type A personalities experience more stress than people with Type B personalities. If you have a

Self-Assessment

Personality Type and Stress

Identify how frequently each item applies to you at work or school. Place a number from 1 to 5 on the line before each statement.

5 = usually   4 = often   3 = occasionally   2 = seldom   1 = rarely

_____ 1. I enjoy competition, and I work/play to win.

_____ 2. I skip meals or eat fast when there is a lot of work to do.

_____ 3. I'm in a hurry.

_____ 4. I do more than one thing at a time.

_____ 5. I'm aggravated and upset.

_____ 6. I get irritated or anxious when I have to wait.

_____ 7. I measure progress in terms of time and performance.

_____ 8. I push myself to work to the point of getting tired.

_____ 9. I work on days off.

_____10. I set short deadlines for myself.

_____11. I'm not satisfied with my accomplishments for very long.

_____12. I try to outperform others.

_____13. I get upset when my schedule has to be changed.

_____14. I consistently try to get more done in less time.

_____15. I take on more work when I already have plenty to do.

_____16. I enjoy work/school more than other activities.

_____17. I talk and walk fast.

_____18. I set high standards for myself and work hard to meet them.

_____19. I'm considered a hard worker by others.

_____20. I work at a fast pace.

_____Total. Add up the numbers you assigned to all 20 items. Your score will range from 20 to 100. Indicate where your score falls on the continuum below.

Type A   Type B

100_____90_____80_____70_____60_____50_____40_____30_____20

The higher your score, the more characteristic you are of the Type A personality. The lower your score, the more characteristic you are of the Type B personality.

Type A personality, you could end up with some of the problems associated with stress. Complete the Self-Assessment to determine your personality type as it relates to stress.

ORGANIZATIONAL CULTURE

The amount of cooperation and motivation one experiences and the level of organizational morale affect stress levels. The more positive the organizational culture, the less stress there is. Organizations that push employees to high levels of performance but do little to ensure a positive work climate create a stressful situation.[116]

MANAGEMENT BEHAVIOR

The better managers are at supervising employees, the less stress there is. Calm, participative management styles are less stressful. Workers with bad bosses are more likely to report stress-related sleep loss, headaches, and upset stomachs.

TYPE OF WORK

Some types of work are more stressful than others. People who have jobs they enjoy derive satisfaction and handle stress better than those who do not. In some cases, changing to a job with enjoyable work is a wise move that can lower stress levels.

HUMAN RELATIONS

Conflicts among people who do not get along can be very stressful. People who don't really like the work they must perform but who like the people they work with can feel less stress and experience higher job satisfaction.

Stress Management

When you continually feel pressured and fear that you will miss deadlines or fail, you are experiencing stress. People watch TV or movies, drink, take drugs, eat, or sleep more than usual to escape stress.

Stress management is the process of eliminating or reducing stress. There are *five stress management techniques* you can use to decrease job stress.

TIME MANAGEMENT

Generally, people with good time management skills experience less job stress. Refer to the appendix to Chapter 5 for details on time management. Remember that procrastinating gives you more time to think about what you have to do and to get stressed before you start. If you are a perfectionist, you may do a high-quality job, but perfectionism stresses you as you perform the work.

RELAXATION

Relaxation is an excellent stress management technique. Get enough rest and sleep; have some fun and laugh.[117] If you have a Type A personality, slow down and enjoy yourself. Cultivate interests that do not relate to your job. People whose careers and personal lives are out of balance are more likely to suffer burnout.[118]

When you feel stress, you can perform relaxation exercises. One of the most popular and simplest of such exercises is deep breathing, which relaxes the entire body.[119] If you feel tension in one muscle, you may do a specific relaxation exercise. You may relax your entire body going from head to toe, or vice versa. Exhibit 9-7 lists relaxation exercises that you can do almost anywhere.

Deep breathing can be done during and/or between other relaxation exercises. Simply take a slow deep breath, preferably through your nose, hold it for a few seconds (count to five), then let it out slowly, preferably through lightly closed lips. To breathe deeply, you must inhale by expanding the stomach, not the chest. Think of your stomach as a balloon; slowly fill and then empty it.

Stress depletes your energy. Even feeling pressured and worrying about a stressor without physically doing anything depletes your energy. Mental stress can be more exhausting than physical stress. Remember that breathing and relaxation (especially sleep) are major sources of the energy you need to resist stress. Contrary to the belief of many, proper exercise increases your energy level rather than depleting it.

Exhibit 9-7 *Relaxation Exercises*

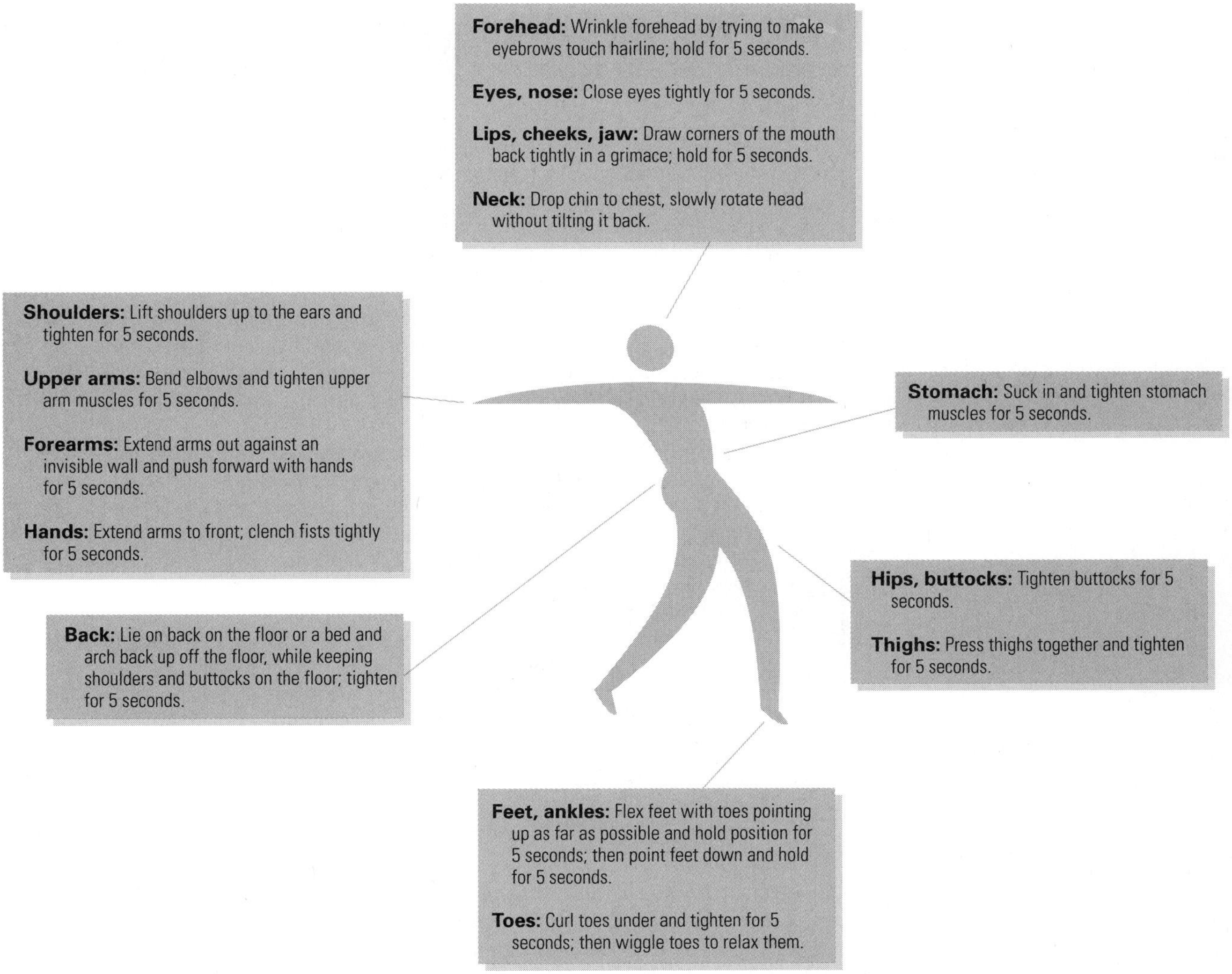

Forehead: Wrinkle forehead by trying to make eyebrows touch hairline; hold for 5 seconds.

Eyes, nose: Close eyes tightly for 5 seconds.

Lips, cheeks, jaw: Draw corners of the mouth back tightly in a grimace; hold for 5 seconds.

Neck: Drop chin to chest, slowly rotate head without tilting it back.

Shoulders: Lift shoulders up to the ears and tighten for 5 seconds.

Upper arms: Bend elbows and tighten upper arm muscles for 5 seconds.

Forearms: Extend arms out against an invisible wall and push forward with hands for 5 seconds.

Hands: Extend arms to front; clench fists tightly for 5 seconds.

Back: Lie on back on the floor or a bed and arch back up off the floor, while keeping shoulders and buttocks on the floor; tighten for 5 seconds.

Stomach: Suck in and tighten stomach muscles for 5 seconds.

Hips, buttocks: Tighten buttocks for 5 seconds.

Thighs: Press thighs together and tighten for 5 seconds.

Feet, ankles: Flex feet with toes pointing up as far as possible and hold position for 5 seconds; then point feet down and hold for 5 seconds.

Toes: Curl toes under and tighten for 5 seconds; then wiggle toes to relax them.

WorkApplication13

If you are currently experiencing stress at school or work, identify which of the stress management techniques you believe you can put into practice.

NUTRITION

Good health is essential to everyone's performance, and nutrition is a major factor in health. Underlying stress can lead to overeating and compulsive dieting, and being overweight is stressful. When you eat, take your time and relax, because rushing is stressful and can cause an upset stomach. Also, when people eat more slowly, they tend to eat less. So don't eat at your work area or desk. Taking a break generates energy and makes you more productive.

Breakfast is considered the most important meal of the day. Getting up and going to work without eating until lunch is stressful. A good breakfast increases your ability to resist stress.

Watch your intake of junk foods, which contain fat (fried meat and vegetables, including french fries and chips), sugar (pastry, candy, fruit drinks, and soda), caffeine (coffee, tea, soda), and salt. Eat more fruits and vegetables, and drink juices. Realize that poor nutrition and the use of overeating, smoking, alcohol, and drugs to reduce stress often create other stressful problems over a period of time.

Join the Discussion Ethics & Social Responsibility

Obesity

1. Is there prejudice and discrimination against obese people at work?
2. Is it ethical and socially responsible for the government to try to get people to lose weight, through ads and other methods?
3. What is the reason for the increase in obesity in the United States? Are restaurant owners and other food marketers responsible for the obesity problem, or are consumers at fault?

Being overweight places stress on the body, and poor nutrition contributes to obesity. Obesity is a major contributor to the rising cost of health care. Obesity-related medical costs hit $75 billion in 2003, and half of the cost is being paid by taxpayers. Obesity may reverse the gains in lifespan brought about by better medical care.

The federal government has reported that obesity might overtake tobacco as the leading cause of death in the United States. Health officials are trying to persuade Americans to lose weight. The government has released public service ads to convince people to get in shape and eat right. Part of the outcome will depend on whether people take personal responsibility for their own health and weight. Some people don't want to take responsibility for their obesity, but instead are trying to sue sellers of food, such as **McDonald's**.[120]

Physical exercise is an excellent way to improve health while releasing stress. Aerobic exercise, in which you increase the heart rate and maintain it for 20 to 30 minutes, is generally considered the most beneficial type of exercise. Fast walking or jogging, biking, swimming, and aerobic dance or exercise fall into this category.

EXERCISE

Before starting an exercise program, check with a doctor to make sure you are able to do so safely. Always remember that the objective is to relax and reduce stress. The "no pain, no gain" mentality applies to competitive athletes, not to stress management.

Stress Management Techniques

Identify each statement by the technique being used.

a. time management   d. exercise
b. relaxation   e. positive thinking
c. nutrition   f. support network

_____16. "I've been repeating statements to myself to be more optimistic."

_____17. "I've set up a schedule for myself."

_____18. "I've been getting up earlier and eating breakfast."

_____19. "I've been talking to my partner about my problems."

_____20. "I've been praying."

POSITIVE THINKING

People with an optimistic personality and attitude generally have less stress than pessimists. Once you start having doubts about your ability to do what you have to do, you become stressed. Make statements to yourself in the affirmative, such as "This is easy" and "I will do it." Repeat positive statements while doing deep breathing.

SUPPORT NETWORK

Talking to others in a support network can help reduce stress. Develop a network of family and friends you can go to for help with your problems. But don't continually lean on others to help you; remember that you and those in your network can reduce each other's stress.

WorkApplication14

At which of the stress management techniques are you best and worst? What can you do to improve your stress management skills?

_____

_____

_____

_____

_____

—————— Learning Outcome 12 ——————
Explain the stress tug-of-war analogy.

The Stress Tug-of-War

Think of stress as a tug-of-war with you in the center, as illustrated in Exhibit 9-8. On the left are causes of stress trying to pull you toward burnout. On the right are stress management techniques you use to keep you in the center. If the stress becomes too powerful it will pull you off center, and you suffer burnout. The stress tug-of-war is an ongoing game. On easy days, you move to the right, and on overly tough days, you move to the left. Your main objective is to stay in the center and avoid burnout.

Stress management does not require the use of all the techniques discussed in the text. Use the ones that work best for you. If you try stress management but still experience permanent burnout, you should seriously consider getting out of the situation. Ask yourself two questions: Is my long-term health

Exhibit 9-8 *The Stress Tug-of-War*

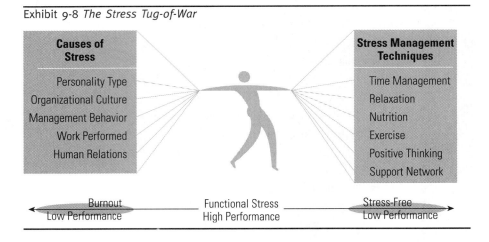

Causes of Stress	Stress Management Techniques
Personality Type	Time Management
Organizational Culture	Relaxation
Management Behavior	Nutrition
Work Performed	Exercise
Human Relations	Positive Thinking
	Support Network

Burnout   Functional Stress   Stress-Free
Low Performance   High Performance   Low Performance

important? Is this situation worth hurting my health for? If you answer yes and no, a change of situations is advisable.

Take advantage of the companion Web site for *Management Fundamentals*, where you will find a broad array of resources to help you maximize what you learn in class:

- Try a quiz
- View chapter videos
- Download slides
- Boost your vocabulary
- Work through an Internet exercise
- Find related links

Take a look for yourself at *http://lussier.swlearning.com.*

Chapter Summary

1. Describe each of the big five personality dimensions.
Extraversion lies on a continuum between extrovert and introvert; agreeableness between cooperation and competition; emotionalism between stability and instability; conscientiousness between dependable and not dependable; and openness to experience between willing to try new things and not being willing to do so.

2. Explain the perception process, and identify the two factors that influence it.
Perception is the process of selecting, organizing, and interpreting environmental information. How you select, organize, and interpret information is based on both internal individual factors, including your personality and

attitudes, and the information available from the external environment.

3. Describe the interrelationship among personality, perception, and attitude, and explain the contribution of each to a manager's behavior.
Personality affects perception and attitudes. Perception also affects attitudes, and attitudes affect perception. Thus, all three are interrelated and are important because combined they directly affect behavior and performance.

4. Explain what job satisfaction is and why it is important.
Job satisfaction is a person's attitude toward his or her job. Job satisfaction is important because it is directly related to absenteeism, turnover, and performance.

5. Define power and explain the difference between position and personal power.

Power is the ability to influence others' behavior. Position power is derived from top management and delegated down the chain of command, whereas personal power is derived from followers based on an individual's behavior.

6. Identify the differences among reward, legitimate, and referent power.

The different types of power are based on how the person with power influences others. Reward power is based on the user's ability to influence others with something of value to them. Legitimate power is based on the user's position power given by the organization. Referent power is based on the user's personality and/or his or her personal relationships with others.

7. Discuss how power and politics are related.

Power is the ability to influence the behavior of others. Politics is the process of gaining and using power. Therefore, political skills are a part of power.

8. Describe how money and politics have a similar use.

Money and politics have a similar use because they are mediums of exchange. In our economy, money is the medium of exchange. In an organization, politics is the medium of exchange.

9. Explain what networking, reciprocity, and coalitions have in common.

Networking, reciprocity, and coalitions are all political behaviors. Networking is the process of developing relationships for the purpose of socializing and politicking. Reciprocity involves the creation of obligations and the development of alliances that are used to accomplish objectives. Coalitions are networks of alliances that will help achieve an objective.

10. List and define five conflict management styles.

(1) The user of the *avoiding conflict style* attempts to passively ignore conflict rather than resolve it. (2) The user of the *accommodating conflict style* attempts to resolve conflict by passively giving in to the other party. (3) The user of the *forcing conflict style* attempts to resolve conflict by using aggressive behavior to get his or her own way. (4) The user of the *negotiating conflict style* attempts to resolve conflict through assertive give-and-take concessions. (5) The user of the *collaborating conflict style* assertively attempts to resolve conflict with the best solution agreeable to all parties.

11. List the steps in initiating and using the collaborative conflict resolution model.

The steps in the collaborative conflict resolution model are (1) stating the problem in a BCF statement, (2) getting the other party to acknowledge the conflict, (3) presenting alternative resolutions to the conflict, and (4) coming to an agreement.

12. Explain the stress tug-of-war analogy.

In the stress tug-of-war, you are in the center where stress is functional and performance is high. On your left are the causes of stress trying to pull you off center. On your right are the stress management techniques you use to keep you in the center. If the causes of stress pull you off center, you burn out and performance decreases. If there is an absence of stress, performance is also decreased.

13. Complete each of the following statements using one of this chapter's key terms.

_____ is the study of actions that affect performance in the workplace.

_____ is a combination of behavioral, mental, and emotional traits that define an individual.

_____ is the process of selecting, organizing, and interpreting environmental information.

_____ is the process of determining the reason for someone's behavior and whether that behavior is situational or intentional.

_____ are positive or negative evaluations of people, things, and situations.

The _____ is the theory that managers' attitudes toward and expectations and treatment of employees largely determine their performance.

_____ is the ability to influence others' behavior.

_____ is the process of gaining and using power.

_____ is the process of developing relationships for the purpose of socializing and politicking.

_____ is the creation of obligations and the development of alliances and that are used to accomplish objectives.

A _____ is a network of alliances that help a manager achieve an objective.

A _____ is a situation in which people are in disagreement and opposition.

_____ exists when disagreement and opposition support the achievement of organizational objectives.

The _____ calls for (1) stating the problem in a BCF statement; (2) getting the other party to acknowledge the conflict; (3) presenting alternative resolutions to the conflict; and (4) coming to an agreement.

A _____ describes a conflict in terms of behavior, consequences, and feelings.

A _____ is a neutral third party who helps resolve a conflict.

An _____ is a neutral third party who makes a binding decision to resolve a conflict.

_____ is the body's reaction to environmental demands.

_____ are factors that cause people to feel overwhelmed by anxiety, tension, and/or pressure.

Key **Terms**

arbitrator, 334
attitudes, 312
attribution, 310
BCF statement, 332
citizenship behavior, 313
coalition, 321
collaborative conflict resolution
   model, 332

conflict, 323
functional conflict, 324
mediator, 334
networking, 320
organizational behavior, 306
perception, 310
personality, 306

politics, 319
power, 315
Pygmalion effect, 313
reciprocity, 321
stress, 334
stressors, 334

Review and **Discussion** Questions

1. What are the big five personality dimensions?
2. What are four biases in perception?
3. What are the determinants of job satisfaction? Are they of equal importance to everyone?
4. What are the seven types of power?
5. Can management order that power and politics in an organization be abolished? If yes, should they?
6. Why should you learn the organizational culture and identify power players where you work?
7. How do you know when you are in conflict?

8. What is the difference between functional and dysfunctional conflict, and how does each affect performance?
9. What does it mean to "maintain ownership of a problem"?
10. What is the difference between a mediator and an arbitrator?
11. What are the characteristics of a Type A personality?
12. What are six stress management techniques?

Objective **Case**

POLITICAL BEHAVIOR OF COLLEGE FACULTY MEMBERS

Carlton Petersburg is a tenured professor of leadership at a small college in the Midwest. The Department of Leadership (DL) has nine faculty members; it is one of ten departments in the School of Arts and Sciences (SAS). The Chair of the Department of Leadership, Tina Joel, is in her first year as chair; six faculty members, including Petersburg, have been in the department longer than Joel.

When Joel asked the dean of the SAS about the college's policy on task descriptions for graduate assistants, the dean stated that there was no formal collegewide policy, but he would speak to the vice president (VP) for academic affairs. The VP and the dean discussed the matter and decided to let individual departments develop their own policies about graduate assistants and their responsibilities. Since Joel believed faculty members should have guidelines to follow,

she put use of graduate assistants on the agenda for the next department meeting.

During the meeting, Joel asked for members' views on what graduate assistants should and should not be allowed to do. Joel was hoping the department would come to a consensus on a policy. Petersburg was the only faculty member who was using graduate assistants to grade exams. One of the other faculty members spoke out against this use of graduate assistants, and other faculty members agreed, stating that it was the professor's job to grade exams. Petersburg stated that since his exams were objective, with clear correct answers, it was not necessary for him to correct them personally. He pointed out that faculty members in other departments, and across the country, were using graduate assistants to teach entire courses and to correct subjective papers and exams; therefore, he did not think it would be fair to forbid him to use graduate assistants to grade objective exams. He also stated that the department did not need a policy, and he requested that the department not set one. However, Joel, as the department chair, insisted that they set a policy. Petersburg was the only person who expressed an opposing view during the meeting, but after the meeting, another faculty member, Fred Robinson, who had said nothing during the meeting, told Petersburg that he agreed that forbidding him to use graduate assistants for grading exams would not be fair.

There was no department consensus, as Joel had hoped there would be, so Joel said she would draft a department policy, which would be discussed at a future meeting. The next day, Petersburg sent a memo to department members asking if it was ethical and legal to deny him the use of the same resources as others across the campus. He also stated that if the department set a policy against using graduate assistants to correct objective exams, he would appeal the policy decision to the dean, VP, and president.

 To learn more about graduate assistants and the duties they perform, log on to InfoTrac® College Edition at *http://infotrac.thomsonlearning.com* and use the advanced search function.

Support your answers to the following questions with specific information from the case text, or information you get from the Web or other source.

_____ 1. Which big five personality traits does Joel appear to have?

    a. extraversion
    b. agreeableness
    c. emotionalism
    d. conscientiousness
    e. openness to experience

_____ 2. Which perception bias is the major reason for the disagreement?

    a. selectivity   c. stereotypes
    b. frame of reference   d. expectations

_____ 3. Are attitudes an issue in this case?

    a. yes
    b. no

_____ 4. Which determinant of job satisfaction can be affected by the outcome of this policy issue?

    a. personalities of those involved
    b. work itself
    c. compensation
    d. growth and mobility
    e. coworkers
    f. management

_____ 5. Which type of power does Joel appear to use during the meeting?

    a. coercive   d. legitimate
    b. connection   e. referent
    c. reward   f. information

_____ 6. Which type of power does Petersburg appear to use?

    a. coercive   d. legitimate
    b. connection   e. referent
    c. reward   f. information

_____ 7. Which political behavior is stopping Petersburg from getting what he wants?

    a. networking
    b. reciprocity
    c. coalition

_____ 8. Which political behavior could be of most help to Petersburg if he wants to continue to use graduate assistants for grading exams?

    a. networking
    b. reciprocity
    c. coalition

_____ 9. Is the psychological contract relevant to this case?

    a. yes
    b. no

_____ 10. In sending his memo to the department, Petersburg used which conflict management style?

    a. avoiding   d. negotiating
    b. accommodating   e. collaborating
    c. forcing

11. Was sending the memo a wise political move? What might Petersburg have gained or lost by sending it?

12. What would you do if you were Joel? (a) Would you talk to the dean and let him know that Petersburg said he would appeal the policy decision? If so, which kind of political behavior would this approach represent? (b) Would you draft a policy directly stating that graduate assistants cannot be used to grade objective exams? (c) Would your answer to (b) be influenced by your answer to (a)?

13. If you were Petersburg, once you saw that you had no support during the meeting, would you have continued to defend your position or agreed to stop using graduate assistants to grade exams? Would your answer be different if you were not a tenured faculty member?

14. If you were Petersburg and Joel drafted a policy that department members agreed with, would you appeal the decision to the dean? Would your answer be different if you were not a tenured faculty member?

15. If you were the dean of SAS, knowing that the VP did not want to set a collegewide policy, and Petersburg appealed to you, what would you do? Would you develop a schoolwide policy for SAS?

16. (a) Should Fred Robinson have spoken up in defense of Petersburg during the meeting? If you were Robinson, would you have taken Petersburg's side against the other seven members? (b) Would your answer depend on whether you were friends with Petersburg and on whether you were a tenured professor?

Cumulative Case Questions

17. What are the ethical issues in this case, and how do perception and attitudes influence ethics? (Chapter 2)

18. At what level (collegewide, by schools, or by departments within each school) should a graduate assistant policy be set? (Chapter 5)

19. What type of change is Joel making? (Chapter 7)

20. Which of the five major reasons for resistance to change is Petersburg exhibiting? (Chapter 7)

Video Case

CANNONDALE CORPORATION

About Cannondale

This video looks at how teams at Cannondale Corporation work to fuel product design innovations and develop new, marketable products. It also provides an especially vivid picture of the roles members of high-performing teams adopt and of how they relate to each other to minimize conflict and stress.

View the Video (10–15 minutes)

View the accompanying video on Cannondale in class or at *http://lussier.swlearning.com.*

Read the Case

High-performance bicycles are finely tuned machines that are engineered for peak performance. The search for the perfect bicycle is a never-ending effort to balance a material's strength against its weight. Cannondale Corporation, based in Bethel, Connecticut, constantly makes that effort through dedicated teamwork that effectively manages workplace politics, conflicts, and stress.

Cannondale has come a long way from its beginnings in 1971, when it was housed in a loft above a pickle factory. From early efforts in manufacturing bicycle trailers and cycling apparel, the company expanded to high-performance bicycle design and production in the 1980s. Widely known for its innovative introduction of aluminum bicycle frames when its rivals were using steel, Cannondale remains the leading manufacturer of aluminum bicycles, selling more than 80 models in over 70 countries.

Maintaining position in the competitive bicycling market isn't easy. Cannondale must continually create new and revised designs, like the Jekyll 1000, that boost performance yet remain competitive in price. The goal at Cannondale is to produce a stream of innovative, quality products, using multiskilled teams and flexible manufacturing processes, to deliver those products to the market quickly, and then to back them with excellent customer service through the best specialty retailers.

Answer The Questions

1. How would you assess R&D manager John Horn's personality using the big five personality dimensions?

2. In what ways does Cannondale's use of open communication and teamwork appear to minimize workplace conflict?

3. Do the Cannondale employees seem satisfied? How do you think they would rate their level of satisfaction using the six major determinants of job satisfaction described in the Self-Assessment on page 314?

Sources: Interview with John Horn, research and development product manager at Cannondale Corporation, April 9, 2002; Cannondale Web site at *http://www.cannondale.com,* accessed May 14, 2004; Hoover's Online at *http://hoovers.com,* accessed May 14, 2004. Note: Since this video was filmed, Cannondale filed for Chapter 11 protection (in January 2003), but emerged after only 100 days as the Cannondale Bicycle Corporation, with plans to sell off its ailing motorsports business.

Skill Builder **1**
CAR DEALER NEGOTIATION[121]

Preparing for Skill Builder 1

Before beginning this Skill Builder, you should read and be sure you understand the text discussion of the negotiation process.

Objective

To develop your understanding of power and to build negotiation skills.

Experience

You will be the buyer or seller of a used car.

Procedure 1 (1–2 minutes)

Pair off and sit facing your partner so that you cannot read each other's confidential sheet. Pairs should be as far apart as possible so they cannot overhear other pairs' conversations. If there is an odd number of students in the class, one student will be an observer or work with the instructor. Decide who will be the buyer and who will be the seller of the used car.

Procedure 2 (1–2 minutes)

The instructor will give a confidential sheet to each buyer and seller. (These do not appear in this book.)

Procedure 3 (5–6 minutes)

Buyers and sellers read their confidential sheets and jot down some plans (what your basic approach will be, what you will say) for the negotiation.

_____

_____

_____

Procedure 4 (3–7 minutes)

Negotiate the sale of the car. You do not have to buy or sell the car. After you make the sale or agree not to sell, read your partner's confidential sheet and discuss the experience.

Integration (5–7 minutes)

Answer the following questions:

____ 1. What type of plan was appropriate for this situation?

    a. general single-use project plan
    b. detailed standing-policy plan

____ 2. Which type of power was most relevant in helping you to negotiate the car deal?

    a. coercive   e. referent
    b. connection   f. information
    c. reward   g. expert
    d. legitimate

____ 3. Did you experience any stress as a result of this exercise (faster heart rate, perspiration, anxiety, tension, or pressure)?

    a. yes
    b. no

____ 4. Did you set a lower limit, target, and opening price?

    a. yes
    b. no

____ 5. Did you imply that you had other options and/or develop trade-offs?

    a. yes
    b. no

____ 6. Did you anticipate questions and objections and prepare answers?

    a. yes
    b. no

____ 7. Did you develop rapport and focus on obstacles, not the person?

    a. yes
    b. no

____ 8. Did you let the other party make the first offer?

    a. yes
    b. no

____ 9. Did you listen and ask questions to focus on meeting the other party's needs?

    a. yes
    b. no

____10. Were you quick to settle for less than your target price and/or ask for something in return for giving concessions?

    a. yes
    b. no

____11. Did you reach a sales agreement?

    a. yes
    b. no

____12. If you did reach a sales agreement, which price did you receive?

    a. minimum
    b. target
    c. opening or more than expected

Conclusion

Your instructor may lead a class discussion or give the answers to the integration questions and make concluding remarks.

Apply It

What did I learn from this experience? How will I use this knowledge in the future?

_____

_____

Behavior **Modeling** 1

INITIATING CONFLICT RESOLUTION

This first scenario for this chapter shows Alex initiating resolution of a conflict over an advertising account with coworker Catherine. Alex follows the steps in Exhibit 9-6.

Objective

To better understand the collaborative conflict resolution model.

View the Video (4 1/2 minutes)

View the accompanying video in class or at _http://lussier.swlearning.com_. This video serves as a behavior model that can be used prior to conducting Skill Builder 2.

Skill Builder **2**
INITIATING CONFLICT RESOLUTION

During class you will be given the opportunity to role-play a conflict you are facing, or have faced, in order to develop your conflict resolution skills. Students and workers have reported that this exercise helped prepare them for successful initiation of conflict resolution with roommates or coworkers. Fill in the following information:

Other party/parties (you may use fictitious names): _____

_____

_____

Describe the conflict situation: _____

_____

_____

List pertinent information about the other party (i.e., relationship to you, knowledge of the situation, age, and background): _____

_____

_____

Identify the other party's possible reaction to your confrontation. (How receptive will he or she be to collaborating? What might he or she say or do during the discussion to resist change?) _____

_____

_____

How will you overcome the resistance to change? _____

_____

Following the steps in the collaborative conflict resolution model, write out your BCF statement.

_____

_____

Apply It

What did I learn from this experience? How will I use this knowledge in the future?

_____

_____

Behavior Modeling **2**

MEDIATING CONFLICT RESOLUTION

The second scenario for this chapter shows Peter bringing Alex and Catherine together to resolve their advertising account conflict. They follow the steps in Exhibit 9-6.

Objective

To better understand the collaborative conflict resolution model.

View the Video (6 1/2 minutes)

View the accompanying video in class or at *http://lussier.swlearning.com*. There is no Skill Builder to follow up this behavior modeling video.

Skill **Builder** 3

IMPROVING PERSONALITY TRAITS

We can all improve certain aspects of our personalities. Review your responses (and those of the other responder) to the Self-Assessment on personality traits (page 000). Of the traits listed, choose one you'd like to work on improving, as a way of increasing your job performance and satisfaction. For example, suppose you decided that you needed to develop a more optimistic and positive attitude and that to do so you would work on thinking and talking more positively. You might write the following specific steps for accomplishing your plan:

- I will write a list of everything that I like about my current job, and for a month I will reread the list every Monday morning before I leave for work.
- I will be aware of what I say and will focus on the positive rather than the negative; I will tell myself, for example, "I'm getting a lot done today" rather than "I'll never meet this deadline," or "I plan to do well on this 6-month evaluation" rather than "My supervisor is going to be watching every move I make that day."
- If I do find myself saying something negative to myself or to someone else, I will immediately stop and rephrase the statement.
- I will let friends and coworkers know that I am working on being more positive, and ask for their help. I will ask them not only to point out when I'm being negative but also to reinforce me when they observe a more positive attitude from me.

Identify the trait from the Self-Assessment that you would like to work on, and list the specific steps you will take to improve it.

_____

_____

_____

Zig Ziglar recommends that if you want to be more positive about your situation (at work, in school, in your family, in a romantic relationship, etc.), you need to focus on the good side, not dwell on the negative. To do so, write out a list of everything you like about the situation. Then write down some positive affirmations, such as "I have a positive attitude"; "I enjoy my job"; "I like Fred." Every morning and evening, while looking in the mirror, read your list. Or, you may record your list and play it. Do this for a month and you and others will see a changed, more positive personality.

Here are some specific steps you might list for yourself if you wanted to develop a more extraverted personality:

- I will say hi to people before they say hi to me.
- I will attend a party at which I don't know many people and I will approach people first to talk to them.
- I will go to class early (or stay after class) once a week and approach someone I don't know, or don't know well, and talk to that person for a few minutes before (or after) class.

You can also follow Zig Ziglar's recommendation and write a positive affirmation for yourself, such as "I enjoy meeting new people."

Learning Outcomes

After studying this chapter, you should be able to:

1. Describe the major differences between groups and teams. PAGE 350

2. Explain the group performance model. PAGE 351

3. List and explain the three dimensions of group types. PAGE 354

4. Define the three major roles played in groups. PAGE 358

5. State the differences between rules and norms. PAGE 359

6. Describe cohesiveness, and explain why it is important to teams. PAGE 360

10: Team Leadership

7. List the four major stages of group development, and describe the appropriate leadership style usually associated with each. PAGE 364

8. Explain the difference between a group manager and a team leader. PAGE 367

9. Discuss the three parts of meetings. PAGE 371

10. Define the following **key terms:**

group	group process
team	group process dimensions
group performance model	group roles
group structure dimensions	norms
group types	group cohesiveness
command groups	status
task groups	stages of group development
global virtual teams	team leaders
group composition	

Ideas on Management
at W. L. Gore & Associates

W. L. Gore & Associates was founded in 1958 in Newark, Delaware, by Bill and Vieve Gore in the basement of their home. It was their son Bob, however, who came up with the idea that prompted Bill and Vieve to start the business. While in college, Bob thought of using polytetrafluoroethylene (PTFE) as a better insulator for wire and cable. In 1965, W. L. Gore & Associates had gone international, and at the end of the decade its wire and cable were on the moon. By the 1970s, supercomputers were using its wire and cable, as do personal computers today.

In 1969, Bob Gore developed the firm's best-known product, GORE-TEX®, a waterproof and breathable fabric used in everything from outerwear to spacesuits. In 1991, GORE-TEX® became windproof as well. Over the years, W. L. Gore & Associates has created thousands of innovative products, which may be grouped into four general categories: (1) cable assemblies and components for the electronics industry; (2) fabrics that improve the comfort and protection of outerwear; (3) medical products that regenerate tissue destroyed by disease or trauma; and (4) innovative materials and technological solutions beneficial to a wide array of industries. You may use the company's Glide® dental floss, you most likely have heard music played on its Elixir® guitar strings, and you may also enjoy static-free cell phone calls courtesy of the Gore SnapSHOT® electromagnetic-interference shield.

© Royalty-Free/Getty Images

Today, with Bob Gore serving as chairman of the board of directors, W. L. Gore & Associates employs close to 6,000 people in 45 locations around the world. It has annual revenues of $1.35 billion and is repeatedly named one of the "100 Best Companies to Work for in America."

IOM
1. **How does W. L. Gore & Associates benefit from the use of groups and teams?**
2. **How does W. L. Gore's group structure facilitate teamwork?**
3. **How is group process managed at W. L. Gore?**
4. **What programs are in place at W. L. Gore to foster group development?**
5. **How does W. L. Gore ensure productive meetings?**

You'll find answers to these questions about groups and teams at W. L. Gore throughout the chapter.

To learn more about W. L. Gore & Associates, visit the company's Web site at *http://www.wlgore.com* or log on to InfoTrac® College Edition at *http://infotrac.thomsonlearning.com*, where you can research and read interesting articles. To access recent articles on staff evaluations, multitasking, compensation, and innovation at W. L. Gore, for instance, use the advanced search option to key in record numbers A117862594 and A109448066.

Source: Information for the opening case was taken from the second edition of this book and the W. L. Gore & Associates Web site at *http://www.gore.com*, accessed May 17, 2004.

THE LESSONS OF THE GEESE

You've no doubt seen geese heading south for the winter flying in a V formation, and so you might be interested in knowing what scientists have discovered about why they fly that way.

1. As each bird flaps its wings, it creates uplift for the bird following. By flying in a V formation, the flock's flying range is 71 percent greater than if each bird flew on its own.
   Lesson: People who share a common direction and sense of community can get where they are going quicker and easier because they are easing the trip for one another.
2. Whenever a goose falls out of formation, it suddenly is affected by the drag and resistance of trying to go it alone and quickly gets back into formation to take advantage of the lifting power of the bird immediately in front.
   Lesson: Traveling in the same direction as others with whom we share a common goal provides strength, power, and safety in numbers.
3. When the lead goose gets tired, it falls back into the formation and another goose flies point.
   Lesson: It pays to take turns doing the hard jobs.
4. The geese toward the back honk to encourage those up front to keep up their speed.
   Lesson: We all need to be encouraged with active support and praise.
5. When a goose gets sick or is wounded and falls out, two geese fall out of formation and follow the first one down. They stay with the downed goose until the crisis resolves, and then they launch out on their own to catch up with their group or join another formation.
   Lesson: We must stand by each other in times of need.

GROUPS AND TEAMS AND PERFORMANCE

Groups are the backbone of organizations because of the systems effect: Each group/department is affected by at least one other group and each department affects the performance of the total organization. Managers report spending most of their time in some form of group activity.[1] Management performance depends on team performance, and leadership behavior affects team performance.[2] The better you understand groups and their performance, the more effective you will be, both as a group member and as a leader.[3] You should make efforts to acquire some team experience.[4] If you have team experience, put it on your résumé.[5]

In this section we discuss the differences between groups and teams, some factors that affect group performance, and the effects of organizational context on performance.

Learning Outcome 1
Describe the major differences between groups and teams.

Groups and Teams

Although the terms *group* and *team* are used interchangeably, a distinction can be made between them. *A **group** has two or more members with a clear leader who perform independent jobs with individual accountability, evaluation, and*

Are You a Team Player?

Rate each of the following statements by placing a number from 1 to 5 on the line. Use the scale below.

Describes me   5   4   3   2   1   Does *not* describe me

____ 1. I focus on what I accomplish during team projects.

____ 2. I don't like to compromise.

____ 3. I depend on myself to get ahead.

____ 4. I prefer to work alone, rather than in a group, when I have a choice.

____ 5. I like to do things my way.

____ 6. I do things myself to make sure the job gets done right.

____ 7. I know that teams do better when each member has a particular contribution to make.

____ 8. I'm more productive when I work alone.

____ 9. I try to get things done my way when I work with others.

____ 10. It bothers me if I can't get the group to do things my way.

Add the numbers you assigned to the statements, and place the total on the continuum below.

Individual 50——45——40——35——30——25——20——15——10   Team Player

rewards. A **team** *has a small number of members with shared leadership who perform interdependent jobs with both individual and group accountability, evaluation, and rewards.*

Distinctions between groups and teams and their levels of autonomy are presented in Exhibit 10-1. As shown at the bottom of the exhibit, groups and teams are on a continuum; it's not always easy to make a clear distinction. The terms *management-directed, semiautonomous,* and *self-managed (or self-directed)* are commonly used to differentiate along the continuum.[6] Management-directed is clearly a group, self-directed is clearly a team, and semiautonomous is between the two. The U.S. Congress, workers on a traditional assembly line, and traditional sales forces are groups, not teams. All teams are groups, but not all groups are teams.

The trend in business today is toward the use of teams.[7] Companies such as **AES, Cooper Industries, Goodyear Tire and Rubber, Hewlett-Packard, Nucor Steel**, and **Pitney Bowes**, just to name a few, have made tremendous performance improvements because of teams.

WorkApplication1

Consider your present job or a past job. Did you work in a group or a team? Explain, using each of the six characteristics in Exhibit 10-1. *Note*: You may want to select one job and use it to answer the work applications throughout this chapter.

—————— **Learning** Outcome 2 ——————
Explain the group performance model.

The Group Performance Model

The performance of groups is based on four major factors. *According to the* **group performance model,** *group performance is a function of organizational context, group structure, group process, and group development stage.*

Exhibit 10-1 *Groups versus Teams*

Characteristics	Group	Team
Size	Two or more; can be large	Small number, often 5 to 12
Leadership	One clear leader making decisions	Shared leadership
Jobs	Members perform one clear job; individual members do one independent part of a process and pass it on to next person to do the next part.	Members share job responsibility by performing many interdependent tasks with complementary skills; the team completes an entire process.
Accountability and Evaluation	Leader evaluates individual members' performance	Members evaluate each other's individual performance and group performance
Rewards	Members are rewarded based on individual performance only	Members are rewarded for both individual and group performance
Objectives	Organizational	Organizational and those set by the team

Level of Autonomy

Group		Team
Management-Directed	Semiautonomous	Self-Directed

← →

Applying The Concept 1

Group or Team

Identify each statement as characteristic of

a. a group

b. a team

_____ 1. "My boss conducts my performance appraisals, and I get good ratings."

_____ 2. "We don't have any departmental goal; we just do the best we can to accomplish the mission."

_____ 3. "My compensation is based primarily on my department's performance."

_____ 4. "I get the assembled product from Jean; then I paint it and send it to Tony for packaging."

_____ 5. "There are about 30 people in my department."

The group performance model is illustrated in Exhibit 10-2. A number of overall organizational and environmental factors affect how groups function and their level of performance.[8] These organizational context factors have been discussed in prior chapters and are listed in the exhibit. The other three factors affecting group performance are covered in detail in the following sections.

Exhibit 10-2 *Group Performance Model*

Group Performance	(is a function of)	Organizational Context	Group Structure	Group Process	Group Development Stage
High to Low		Environment Mission Strategy Culture Structure Systems and Processes	Type Size Composition Leadership Objectives	Roles Norms Cohesiveness Status Decision making Conflict resolution	Orientation Dissatisfaction Resolution Production Termination

Join the Discussion Ethics & Social Responsibility

Team Players

1. Is it necessary to be a team player to be a successful employee at JetBlue?
2. Is it ethical and socially responsible of JetBlue to reject job candidates because they are considered not to be team players?

JetBlue Airways is not structured around teams. However, teamwork skills and attitudes are important to the success of JetBlue. In fact, JetBlue screens job candidates extensively to make sure that they are team players. In addition to checking the six or seven references the job candidate must provide, JetBlue recruiters ask the people a candidate lists as references for the names of others who can give insights into the candidate, and they call them as well.[9]

The workforce at W. L. Gore & Associates is divided into teams. Bill Gore developed a structure that eliminates assigned or assumed authority. Independent teams can be started by leaders with whom associates want to work. The teams set objectives and are responsible for achieving them. Bill Gore believed that people who know each other work better together. So he kept the plant size of all facilities to 150–200 associates. Team members select new members, and twice each year team members rank each other based on who is adding the most value to the company; this ranking does affect individual pay raises. In addition (unlike most companies, where participation is limited), W. L. Gore rewards all employees with profit-sharing and stock options. Sally Gore, leader of the company's human resources group, says that the purpose of this policy is to emphasize that we are all in this together; we are one team.

IOM

GROUP STRUCTURE

Group structure dimensions *include group type, size, composition, leadership, and objectives.* Each of these five components of group structure is described in this section.

Group Types

Group types *are formal or informal, functional or cross-functional, and command or task.*

FORMAL OR INFORMAL GROUPS

Formal groups, such as departments and smaller subparts, are created by an organization as part of its formal structure; the groups generally have their own structure for conducting business.[10] *Informal groups* are not created by the organization as part of the formal structure. They are created spontaneously when members join together voluntarily because of similar interests. Throughout this text, the focus is on formal groups and teams.

FUNCTIONAL OR CROSS-FUNCTIONAL GROUPS

The members of *functional*, or vertical, *groups* perform jobs within one limited area. A work unit or department is a functional group.[11] For example, marketing, finance, operations, and human resources departments are functional groups. The members of *cross-functional*, or horizontal, *groups* come from different areas and possibly different levels of an organization.[12] Generally, the higher the management level, the more cross-functional the responsibility.

Each manager in the organization serves as the link to other groups. Ideally, all functional groups coordinate their activities through the aid of the managers who are responsible for linking the activities together.[13] Rensis Likert calls this the *linking-pin role*. Exhibit 10-3 illustrates functional and

Exhibit 10-3 *Functional and Cross-Functional Groups*

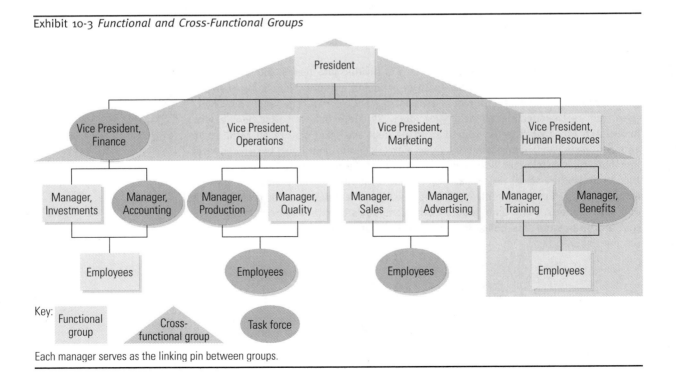

Key:
Functional group
Cross-functional group
Task force

Each manager serves as the linking pin between groups.

cross-functional groups with managers acting as linking pins. The current trend is toward using more cross-functional groups to better coordinate the functional areas of the organization.[14]

COMMAND OR TASK GROUPS

Command groups *consist of managers and the employees they supervise.* People are hired to be a part of a command group. Command groups are distinguished by department membership as functional or cross-functional.[15] In Exhibit 10-3, the president and the vice presidents are a cross-functional command group, whereas each vice president and the managers reporting to him or her form a functional command group.

Task groups *consist of employees selected to work on a specific objective.* There are two primary types of task groups: task forces and standing committees.

A *task force*, or ad hoc committee, is a temporary group formed for a specific purpose. Project teams, which use a matrix structure (Chapter 6), are a form of task group in which employees have a functional boss and work with cross-functional departments as needed. The purpose of the task force highlighted in Exhibit 10-3 is to select three top candidates to present to the board of directors as potential replacements for the current president, who will retire in six months. This task force has members from all the functional areas in the company.

A *standing committee* is a permanent task group that works on continuing organizational issues. Membership on standing committees is often rotated every year so that new ideas are brought to the group. For example, membership may be for three years, with one-third of the committee replaced every year.

There are a couple of major differences between a command group and a task group. Command group members tend to be from the same functional area, whereas task groups are often cross-functional. In addition, everyone in an organization belongs to a command group, but employees may work for an organization for many years without ever being a member of a cross-functional task group. Generally, the higher the level of management, the more time is spent in task groups and their meetings.

WorkApplication2
Identify task groups used in an organization you work for or have worked for. Specify whether each group is a task force or a standing committee.

GLOBAL VIRTUAL TEAMS

The trends toward globalization and teamwork have led to the emergence of global virtual teams. *The members of* **global virtual teams** *are physically located in different places but work together as a team.* Advances in information and telecommunications technologies are allowing new ways of structuring, processing, and distributing work and overcoming the barriers of distance and time. Thus, team members anywhere in the world in any time zone can work together on projects.[16] Work done in different time zones can be sequenced so that teams are productive over more than one work period.[17]

Hewlett Packard uses global virtual teams. For example, it might have a global virtual team of software developers in London initially code a project and transmit the code each evening to a team in the United States. The U.S. team tests the code and forwards it to Tokyo. The Tokyo team debugs the program and sends it back to London. The London team starts its next day ready to begin a new cycle of coding. However, distance and time zones can cause coordination issues because of differing work schedules, holidays, and vacations.[18]

Group Size

THERE IS NO IDEAL GROUP SIZE

There is no consensus on the ideal size for groups; some say three to nine members, others say five or six to eight, and still others say up to twenty. The number varies depending on the purpose.[19] Groups tend to be larger than teams. At **Titeflex**, teams of six to ten people manufacture fluid and gas-holding systems. EDS has project teams of eight to twelve members. **Johnsonville Foods** uses self-managed teams of around twelve.

A group that is too small limits ideas and creativity. It tends to be too cautious, and the workload is not distributed over enough members. On the other hand, a group that is too large tends to be too slow, and not everyone gets to participate.[20] With 20 or more members, there are too many members to reach consensus on many decisions, and members tend to form subgroups. In large groups, *free-riding* is also a problem. Free-riding occurs when members rely on others to carry their share of the workload.

HOW SIZE AFFECTS LEADERSHIP

Group size affects leadership and the work process. The appropriate leadership style may depend on group size. The larger the size, the more formal or autocratic the leadership needs to be to provide direction. Managers tend to be more informal and participative when they have smaller teams. Group members are more tolerant of, and at times, even appreciative of, autocratic leadership in large groups. Larger groups tend to inhibit equal participation. Generally, participation is more equal in groups of around five. This is why teams are small. The larger the group, the greater the need for formal and structured plans, policies, procedures, and rules.

LEADERSHIP IMPLICATIONS

Usually, managers have no say in the size of their command groups. However, if you have a large department, you can break this larger group into teams. As the chair of a committee, you may be able to select the group size. In doing so, keep the group size appropriate for the task and be sure to get the right group composition.

Group Composition

Group composition *is the mix of members' skills and abilities.* Regardless of type and size, group or team performance is affected by the composition.[21] Without the right mix of skills and abilities, a group will not perform at high levels.[22]

LEADERSHIP IMPLICATIONS

One of the most important group leadership functions is to attract, select, and retain the best people for the job. When selecting group or team members, be sure to include diverse individuals.[23] Diverse groups tend to outperform homogeneous groups. With teams, you want members with complementary skills, rather than people with the same skills. Cross-functional teams are likely to provide diversity and complementary skills.[24]

Group Leadership and Objectives

LEADERSHIP

To a large extent, the leader determines group structure.[25] Exhibit 10-1 pointed out that the leadership style is different in groups and teams. Group performance is affected by the team leader.[26] You will learn more about group and team leadership throughout this chapter.

OBJECTIVES

In Chapter 5, you learned the benefits of setting objectives; they apply to both individuals and groups. In groups, the objective is commonly very broad—usually to fulfill the mission. However, teams develop their own objectives.[27] One of the reasons teams tend to outperform groups is because they have their own objectives; groups do not. Objectives help to provide the structure required to identify organizational need.[28]

LEADERSHIP IMPLICATIONS

Part of a leader's responsibility is to be sure the size and composition of a group or team are appropriate for the situation. As a group or team leader, or as a member with leadership skills, be sure that the group or team has clear objectives.[29]

In summary, group structure dimensions include group type, size, composition, leadership, and objectives. Exhibit 10-4 reviews group structure dimensions.

W. L. Gore & Associates has a flat organization (Chapter 6) with a team-based structure. Gore has functional and cross-functional teams, command and task groups, and global virtual teams, but the emphasis is on cross-functional teams that can contribute to product innovation. Group size and composition vary. Teams do have leaders, and each team sets its own objectives. However, Gore is structured, in a sense, so that there are no managers and employees: *All* **employees are associates working as a team. Associates are loosely organized according to the type of work task they handle, and leaders are selected by teams based on their ability to gain consensus, offer encouragement and assistance, and interact with other teams. Bill Gore calls this arrangement a** *lattice organization.*

> **WorkApplication3**
> Identify a group or team you belong to, and describe its size, composition, leadership, and objectives.
> _____
> _____
> _____
> _____
> _____

IOM

Exhibit 10-4 *Dimensions of Group Structure*

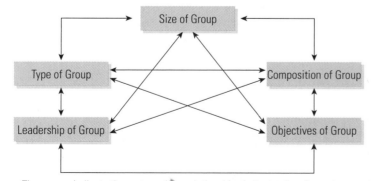

The arrows indicate the systems interrelationships between the dimensions.

GROUP PROCESS

Group process refers to the patterns of interactions that emerge as members perform their jobs. Group process is also called *group dynamics*.[30] Bill Gates advises young people to learn to work with people—to develop group dynamics skills.[31] Regardless of the type of groups you work in, your ability to understand group process and to develop these skills will affect your performance, the group's performance, and all members' job satisfaction.[32]

Group process dimensions are roles, norms, cohesiveness, status, decision making, and conflict resolution. These components are discussed in this section.

—————————————— Learning Outcome 4 ——————————————
Define the three major roles played in groups.

Group Roles

As a group works toward achieving its objectives, group members must perform certain functions. As functions are performed, people develop roles. *Job roles* are shared expectations of how group members will fulfill the requirements of their position. It is important that employees have clear roles so that they know their responsibilities.[33] Job descriptions help to clarify functional roles. People often have multiple roles within a single position.[34] For example, a professor may have the roles of teacher, researcher, writer, consultant, advisor, and committee member. Job roles vary greatly, but group roles can be classified in one of three ways.[35]

CLASSIFYING GROUP ROLES
The three primary **group roles** *are group task roles, group maintenance roles, and self-interest roles.*

Group task roles are played by members who do and say things that directly aid in the accomplishment of the group's objectives.[36] Task roles are often said to be structuring, job-centered, production-oriented, task-oriented, or directive.

Group maintenance roles are played by members who do and say things to develop and sustain the group process.[37] Terms used to describe maintenance roles include employee-centered, relationship-oriented, and supportive.

Self-interest roles are played by members who do and say things that help themselves. Usually when group members put their own needs before those of the group, the performance of the group suffers.

As a team member, watch for self-interest roles and hidden agendas. Learn to distinguish between self-interest that benefits both the individual and the organization (a win-win situation) and self-interest that benefits the individual and hurts the organization (a win-lose situation).

HOW ROLES AFFECT GROUP PERFORMANCE
To be effective, a group must have members who play task roles and maintenance roles, while minimizing self-interest roles. Groups that only have task role players may suffer performance problems because they do not deal with conflict effectively, and because the job will be boring if there is no maintenance. On the other hand, groups that have a great time but do not have members playing task roles will not get the job done. Any group whose members are mostly playing self-interest roles will not produce to its fullest potential.

WorkApplication4

Identify members of a group or team you have been on, and state the primary role each played in the group.

———————————————
———————————————
———————————————
———————————————
———————————————

Applying The Concept 2

Roles

Identify the type of role exemplified in each statement.

a. task

b. maintenance

c. self-interest

_____ 6. "Wait. We can't make the decision because we haven't heard Rodney's idea yet."

_____ 7. "I don't understand. Could you explain why we are doing this again?"

_____ 8. "We tried that before you came to work here; it did not work. My idea is much better."

_____ 9. "What does this have to do with the problem we are working on? We are getting sidetracked."

_____10. "I like Ted's idea better than mine. Let's go with his idea instead."

LEADERSHIP IMPLICATIONS

The leader of a group should be aware of the roles the group members play. If no member is playing the task or maintenance role required at a given time, the leader should play the role. The leader should also make the group aware of the need to play these roles and the need to minimize self-interest roles. Later in the chapter, you will learn about group development and how the leader should use task and maintenance roles to help the group develop.

—————— Learning Outcome 5 ——————
State the differences between rules and norms.

Group Norms

In addition to policies, procedures, and rules, all groups form their own unwritten norms about how things are done.[38] **Norms** *are expectations about behavior that are shared by members of a group.* Norms determine what should or must be done in order for the group to maintain consistent and desirable behavior.[39] Rules are formally established by management or by the group itself. Norms are not developed by management or explicitly agreed to by a group; they develop as members interact.

HOW NORMS DEVELOP

Norms develop spontaneously as the members of a group interact. Each group member has cultural values and past experience. Group members' beliefs, attitudes, and knowledge influence the type of norms that develop.[40] For example, the group decides, without ever actually talking about it, what is an acceptable level of work. If the group members develop a shared expectation that a certain level is desirable, members will produce it. Or, for example, norms develop about whether the use of certain words (such as swear words) or jokes is considered acceptable. Norms can change over time to meet the needs of the group.

Join the Discussion Ethics & Social Responsibility

Norms

1. Should employees be able to "do their own thing" without group enforcement of norms?
2. Is it ethical and socially responsible for groups to develop and enforce norms? If yes, what type of ethical standards should a group have?

Group members influence each other's behavior through the development and enforcement of norms—that is, essentially through peer pressure. In general, this process is positive, as the refusal of one person or a few people to comply with group norms can have disastrous consequences, not only for a single group but for an entire organization. On the other hand, refusing to comply with norms and instead blowing the whistle to disclose illegal or unethical business practices, as at **Enron**, can have a positive effect in lessening unethical behavior.[41]

HOW GROUPS ENFORCE NORMS

If a group member does not follow a norm, the other members try to enforce compliance.[42] Groups commonly enforce norms. For example, if Sal works at more than the accepted level of performance, other members may kid or ridicule him. If Sal continues to break the norm, members might ostracize him to enforce compliance with the norm. Members could also damage his work or take his tools or supplies to slow down his production.

LEADERSHIP IMPLICATIONS

Group norms can be positive, helping the group meet its objectives, or they can be negative, hindering the group from meeting its objectives.[43] For example, if a company's production standard is 110 units per day, a group norm of 100 is a negative norm. However, if the standard were 90, it would be a positive norm. Leaders should be aware of their group's norms. They should work toward maintaining and developing positive norms and try to eliminate negative norms.[44] Leaders should confront groups with negative norms and try to work out solutions to make them positive.

WorkApplication5

Identify at least two norms that developed in a group/team of which you were a member. Explain how you knew they were norms and how the group enforced those norms.

_____

_____

_____

_____

_____

——————————————— Learning Outcome 6 ———————————————

Describe cohesiveness, and explain why it is important to teams.

Group Cohesiveness

The extent to which members of a group abide by and enforce the group norms depends on the degree of cohesiveness. **Group cohesiveness** *is the extent to which members stick together*. The more cohesive the group, the more it sticks together as a team. The more desirable group membership is, the more willing the members are to behave according to the group's norms.[45] For example, in a highly cohesive group, all members would produce about the same amount of work. However, in a group with moderate or low cohesiveness, members could produce at different levels without the norm about production levels being enforced.

FACTORS INFLUENCING COHESIVENESS

Six factors influence group cohesiveness:

1. *Objectives*. The stronger the agreement with and commitment to the achievement of the group's objectives, the higher the cohesiveness of the group.
2. *Size*. Generally, the smaller the group, the higher the cohesiveness. Three to nine members seems to be a good group size for optimum cohesiveness.
3. *Homogeneity*. Generally, the more similar the group members are, the higher the cohesiveness (although diverse groups usually make better decisions).
4. *Participation*. Generally, the more equal the level of participation among members, the higher the group's cohesiveness.
5. *Competition*. Generally, if the group focuses on internal competition, its members will try to outdo each other, and low cohesiveness results. If the group focuses on external competition, its members tend to pull together as a team.
6. *Success*. The more successful a group is at achieving its objectives, the more cohesive it tends to become. Success tends to breed cohesiveness, which in turn breeds more success. People want to be on a winning team.

HOW COHESIVENESS AFFECTS GROUP PERFORMANCE

Many research studies have compared cohesive and noncohesive groups and concluded that cohesive groups tend to have a higher level of success at achieving their objectives with greater satisfaction.[46] Members of cohesive groups tend to miss work less often, are more trusting and cooperative, and have less tension and hostility. Cohesiveness is associated with performance in the following ways:

- Groups with the highest levels of productivity were highly cohesive and accepted management's level of productivity.
- Groups with the lowest levels of productivity were also highly cohesive, but rejected management's level of productivity; they set and enforced their own level below that of management. This can happen in organizations where employees have an "us against them" attitude.
- Groups with intermediate levels of productivity were low in cohesiveness, irrespective of their acceptance of management's level of productivity. The widest variance of individual group members' performance was among the groups with lower cohesiveness. Members of such groups tended to be more tolerant of nonconformity to group norms.

LEADERSHIP IMPLICATIONS

As a leader, you should strive to develop cohesive groups that exhibit a high level of productivity. Encouraging group members' participation helps the group develop cohesiveness and builds agreement and commitment toward the group's objectives. Some intragroup competition may be helpful, but leaders should focus primarily on intergroup competition. Recall the many advantages of managing a diverse group, and make efforts to develop a cohesive yet diversified group.

WorkApplication6
Identify the level of cohesiveness in a group or team of which you are or have been a member.

Status within the Group

Ideally, as group members interact, they develop respect for one another on numerous dimensions. The more respect, prestige, influence, and power a group member has, the higher his or her status within the group.[47] **Status** *is the perceived ranking of one member relative to other members in the group.*

THE DEVELOPMENT OF STATUS

Status is based on several factors, including members' performance, job title, wage or salary, seniority, knowledge or expertise, interpersonal skills, appearance, education, race, age, sex, and so on. Group status depends on the group's objectives, norms, and cohesiveness. Members who conform to the group's norms tend to have higher status than members who do not. A group is more willing to listen to a high-status member and to overlook such a member's breaking of the norms. High-status members also have more influence on the development of the group's norms and the decisions made by the group. Lower-status members' ideas are often ignored, and they tend to copy high-status members' behavior and to agree with their suggestions in order to be accepted.[48]

HOW STATUS AFFECTS GROUP PERFORMANCE

High-status members have a major impact on a group's performance. In a command group, the boss is usually the member with the highest status. The leader's ability to manage affects the group performance.[49] Other high-status members also affect performance. If high-status members support positive norms and high productivity, chances are the rest of the group will, too.

Another important factor influencing group performance is status congruence. *Status congruence* is the acceptance and satisfaction members receive from their group status. Members who are not satisfied with their status may not be active participants of the group. They may physically or mentally escape from the group and not perform to their full potential.[50] Or they may cause group conflict as they fight for a higher status level.[51]

LEADERSHIP IMPLICATIONS

To be effective, the leader needs to have high status within a command group. The leader should maintain good human relations with the group, particularly with the high-status informal leaders, to be sure that they endorse positive norms and objectives. In addition, the leader should be aware of conflicts that may be the result of lack of status congruence. Ideally, status should be about equal among group members.

WorkApplication7

Recall a group of which you were a member. List each member, including yourself, and identify each person's level of status within the group. Explain why each member had the level of status you identified.

Decision Making and Conflict Resolution

The decisions made by groups and teams have a direct effect on performance.[52] In groups, decision-making authority is held by the manager. However, in teams, decision-making authority is held by the members.[53] Decision making was covered in Chapter 4.

Conflict is common in groups and teams, and unresolved conflicts can have a negative effect on performance.[54] In the last chapter you developed your skills at resolving conflict.

Exhibit 10-5 *Dimensions of Group Process*

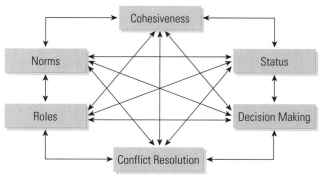

The arrows indicate the system's interrelationships between the dimensions.

W. L. Gore & Associates trains its employees in group process to help them be effective team players. Once a new associate is hired by a team, the team is responsible for the person's success. Each new associate is assigned a sponsor, or mentor, from within the team. Being a mentor to new associates is part of the team performance appraisal ranking; those who act as mentors can be rewarded with bigger raises. Mentors help new associates understand and carry out their roles within the team, learn the norms, fit in, gain status, handle conflict, and be an active part of team decision making. Gore plays down status differences with its philosophy that "we have no managers and employees; we are *all* associates working as a team."

If you understand and develop group process skills, you will be a more effective member and leader. Exhibit 10-5 summarizes the six dimensions of group process.

I O M

Applying The Concept 3

Group Process

Identify the dimension of the group process exemplified in each statement.

a. roles   d. status

b. norms   e. decision making

c. cohesiveness   f. conflict resolution

_____11. "Although we do have occasional differences of opinion, we really get along well and enjoy working together."

_____12. "When you need advice on how to do things, go see Shirley; she knows the ropes around here better than anyone."

_____13. "I'd have to say that Carlos is the peacemaker around here. Every time there is a disagreement, he tries to get the members to work out the problem."

_____14. "Kennedy, you're late for the meeting. Everyone else was on time, so we started without you."

_____15. "What does this have to do with solving the problem? We are getting sidetracked."

——————————— Learning Outcome 7 ———————————
List the four major stages of group development, and describe the
appropriate leadership style usually associated with each.

STAGES OF GROUP DEVELOPMENT AND STYLES OF LEADERSHIP

All groups have unique organizational contexts, group structure, and group processes that change over time. However, it is generally agreed that that all groups go through the same stages of development as they grow from a collection of individuals to a smoothly operating and effective group or team.[55] *The* **stages of group development** *are orientation, dissatisfaction, resolution, production, and termination.*

As groups grow and change, so should the ways in which they are led. In this section, we discuss the five stages of group development and an appropriate leadership style for each stage.

Stage 1. Orientation

The *orientation stage*, also known as the *forming stage*, is characterized by a low development level. When people first form a group, they tend to have moderate to high commitment to group goals and tasks. However, because they have not worked together, they often do not have the competence to do the job.[56]

During orientation, members have concerns about the structure, leadership, and objectives of the group.[57] Note that command groups are rarely started with all new members. This stage is more characteristic of task groups that have clear beginnings. Group process issues include anxiety over how members will fit in (status), what will be required of them (roles and norms), what the group will be like (cohesiveness), how decisions will be made, and how members will get along (conflict). These structure and process issues must be resolved if the group is to progress to the next stage of development.[58]

LEADERSHIP STYLE

During the orientation stage of group development, the appropriate leadership style is usually autocratic; that is, a manager tells group members what to do and how to do it, and closely oversees their performance. When a group first comes together, the leader needs to spend time helping the group clarify its objectives, providing clear expectations of members. The leader should also allow some time for group members to start to get to know one another.

Stage 2. Dissatisfaction

The *dissatisfaction stage*, also known as the *storming stage*, is characterized by a moderate development level. As members work together for some time, they tend to become dissatisfied with the group.[59] The psychological contract (Chapter 9) is often broken as members start asking such questions as these: Why am I a member? Is the group going to accomplish anything? Why don't other group members do what is expected? Often the task is more complex and difficult than anticipated; members become frustrated and have feelings of incompetence. However, the group does develop some competence to perform the task.

During the dissatisfaction stage, the group needs to work on resolving its structure and process issues before it can progress to the next stage of development. Groups can get stuck in this stage of development by not developing a workable psychological contract; in that case, members may never progress to being satisfied with the group and performing as a team.[60]

LEADERSHIP STYLE

During the dissatisfaction stage, the appropriate leadership style is usually consultative; that is, the manager is highly directive and oversees group members' performance, but includes their input in decision making and makes efforts to be supportive. When satisfaction drops, the leader needs to focus on playing the maintenance role to encourage members to continue to work toward objectives. The leader should help the members meet their needs as they develop the appropriate group structure and process. At the same time, the leader needs to continue to help the group develop its level of competence.

Stage 3. Resolution

The *resolution stage*, also called the *norming stage*, is characterized by high development. With time, members often resolve the differences between their initial expectations and the realities of objectives, tasks, skills, and so forth. As members develop competence, they often become more satisfied with the group. Relationships that satisfy group members' affiliation needs develop.[61] Members learn to work together as they attain a group structure and process with acceptable leadership, norms, status, cohesiveness, and decision making. During periods of conflict or change, the group needs to resolve these issues.

Commitment can vary from time to time as the group interacts. If the group does not deal effectively with group process issues, the group may regress to stage 2 or continue fluctuating in commitment and competence. If the group is successful at developing a workable group structure and process, it will move to the next stage.[62]

LEADERSHIP STYLE

During the resolution stage, the appropriate leadership style is usually participative: the manager and the group members share decision making. Once group members know what to do and how to do it, there is little need to model and encourage task behavior. The group needs the leader to play a maintenance role.

When commitment varies, it is usually because there is some problem in the group's process, such as a conflict. The leader needs to focus on maintenance behavior to get the group through the issue(s) it faces. If the leader continues to provide task directives that are not needed, the group can either become dissatisfied and regress or remain at this level.

Stage 4. Production

The *production stage*, also called the *performing stage*, is characterized by outstanding development. At this stage, commitment and competence do not fluctuate much. The group works as a team with high levels of satisfaction. The group maintains its effective group structure and process. The fact that members are very productive helps lead to positive feelings. The group structure and process may change with time, but the issues are resolved quickly and easily; members are open with each other.[63]

WorkApplication8

Recall a group from a present or past job. Identify the group's stage of development and the leadership style. Did the leader use an appropriate style? Explain what could be done to improve the group's structure and/or process.

_____

_____

_____

_____

_____

LEADERSHIP STYLE

During the production stage, the appropriate leadership style is usually empowerment—the manager gives group members the authority to do their task in their own way and to make decisions on their own. Groups that develop to this stage have members who play the appropriate task and maintenance roles; the leader does not need to play either type of role, unless there is a problem, because the group has effective shared leadership.

Stage 5. Termination

Command groups do not usually reach the _termination stage_, also called the _adjourning stage_, unless there is some drastic reorganization. However, task groups do terminate. During this stage, members experience feelings about leaving the group.

Different groups make it to different levels of development. However, to help ensure that groups develop, employees can be trained in group process skills. Teams tend to develop to higher levels than groups. As a leader or member of a group or team, be aware of the development stage and use the appropriate leadership style to help it develop to the desired productivity level.

The **BT Global Challenge** is a sailboat race around the world for amateurs, many of whom have never sailed before. The race takes around ten months to complete. Race organizers assign sailors to identical boats. The key to success is taking a group of diverse individuals through the stages of group development as quickly as possible to mold them into a high-performing team. Leaders do a lot of training and coaching as they develop the competence and commitment of each member and of the team by using the appropriate leadership style. Group structure is important as the leader gets members to set and achieve long- and short-term objectives. Group process is important as members learn their jobs (roles), develop positive norms, become cohesive, maintain status congruence, and make decisions and handle conflict through open and honest communication. At the end of the race, termination is difficult for many, who have developed close relationships that last beyond the race.

IOM **W. L. Gore & Associates faces the need for group development in three areas. First, it has ongoing teams that need to take in new members. A strong relationship between long-term members is good for teamwork and productivity, but if new hires do not feel included, they tend to quit.[64] To be successful, newcomers need to develop network relationships.[65] Gore realizes the importance of newcomer effectiveness, and this is why new hires get a mentor and why each team is responsible for newcomers' success.[66] Second, Gore is driven by its team-based approach to innovation, and thus new teams continually need to go through the stages of group development. Third, associates serve on multiple teams; thus, Gore seeks associates who are good team players.**

Changes in Group Development and Leadership Style

Two key variables in each stage of group development are competence (work on the task) and commitment. These two variables do not progress in the same manner. Competence tends to continue to increase over time, whereas commitment tends to start high, drop off, and then rise. This pattern is illustrated in Exhibit 10-6; the appropriate leadership style for each stage of development is shown at the bottom. In Skill Builder 1 at the end of this chapter, you will develop your ability to identify group development stages and to match appropriate leadership style to various real-world situations.

Exhibit 10-6 *Stages of Group Development and Leadership Styles*

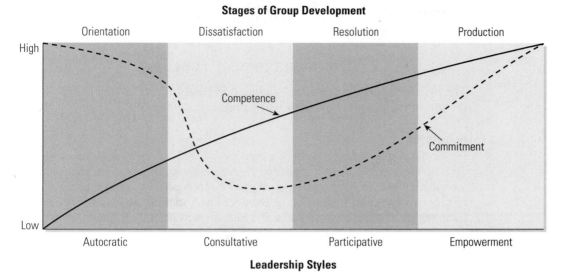

Stages of Group Development

Source: Adapted from D. Carew, E. Carew, and K. Blanchard, "Group Development and Situational Leadership," *Training & Development* (June 1986), p. 48.

Learning Outcome 8

Explain the difference between a group manager and a team leader.

DEVELOPING GROUPS INTO TEAMS

As Exhibit 10-1 pointed out, groups and teams are different. Among businesses today, the trend is toward the empowerment of teams, because teams are more productive than groups.[67] To turn a group into a team, a manager must first consider the size of the group. If the group includes 20 or more members, it can be broken into two or three teams. In this section, we discuss training, planning, organizing and staffing, leading, and controlling teams and explore the difference between a group manager and a team leader.

Training

If they are to function as a team, members need training in group process skills so that they can make decisions and handle conflict. A team-building program is also very helpful in turning groups into teams.[68]

Sabre Holdings is a world leader in travel commerce. It owns four distinct companies: **Travelocity, GetThere, Sabre Travel Network**, and **Sabre Airline Solutions**. Sabre Holdings has separate Web sites for each of its businesses.[69] It uses teams and trains employees to be team players through team building. When Sabre first established global virtual teams, members from around the globe met face to face at a resort on the coast of Mexico for three days of team-building activities. A major activity was to build a raft from everyday materials and then to take the raft out into the ocean. During their raft ride, two of the five members of one team fell in the ocean when a wave crashed into the raft, but another team member pulled them back on board, and they finished the ride together. The ride itself, as well as the entire exercise, symbolized the lesson that members of a team sink or swim together. Through this exercise, team members learned about group structure, process, and development.[70]

The Management Functions

The management functions are handled differently in groups and teams. Thus, the job of the manager changes when groups become teams.

PLANNING

Important parts of planning are setting objectives and decision making. To convert a group into a team, the manager must empower the members to set objectives, develop plans, and make decisions.[71] The manager's role changes to focusing on involving members and making sure that they know the objectives, accept them, and are committed to achieving them.

ORGANIZING AND STAFFING

The important part of organizing and staffing a team is for its members to participate in selecting, evaluating, and rewarding members.[72] Jobs on a team are interchangeable and are assigned by the members as they perform dependent parts of the entire process.

LEADING

In teams, leadership is shared. Most teams do identify a specific person as the leader, but the leader shares this responsibility.[73] The leader does not focus on telling employees what to do and assigning individuals to do it. Effective team leaders are highly skilled in group process and team building. The leader focuses on developing group structure and process. Effective leaders work to bring the team to the production stage of development; they change leadership styles with the level of group development.

CONTROLLING

As they move from being a group to being a team, members are responsible for monitoring progress, taking corrective action, and performing quality control.[74]

In summary, the roles of the group manager and team leader are different. The group manager takes responsibility for performing the four functions of management. **Team leaders** *empower members to take responsibility for performing the management functions and focus on developing effective group structure and group process and on furthering group development.* Sometimes team managers are not designated as the official leaders.

LEADERSHIP SKILLS FOR MEETINGS

As businesses begin to use more teams, meetings are taking up an increasing amount of time.[75] Therefore, the need for skills related to leading meetings is stronger than ever. Common complaints about meetings are that there are too many of them, they are too long, and they are unproductive. In this section, we discuss how to plan and conduct a meeting and how to handle problem group members.

WorkApplication9

Think about the leadership style of a present or past boss. Did that person behave as a group manager or as a team leader? What made you classify the person this way?

Planning Meetings

The quality of both leaders' and members' preparation for a meeting has a direct effect on the meeting. Unprepared leaders tend to conduct unproductive meetings. There are at least six areas where planning is needed: setting objectives, selecting participants and making assignments, preparing the agenda, setting the time and place for the meeting, determining who will lead the meeting, and preparing to use technology. A written copy of the plan should be sent to members prior to the meeting (see Exhibit 10-7).[76]

OBJECTIVES

Probably the single greatest mistake made by those who call meetings is that they often have no clear idea of the purpose for the meeting. Before calling a meeting, you should clearly define its purpose and set objectives to be accomplished during the meeting.

PARTICIPANTS AND ASSIGNMENTS

Decide who should attend the meeting. Too many people at a meeting can slow things down. Does the full group or team need to attend? Should a specialist who is not part of the team be invited to provide input? With controversial issues, the leader may find it wiser to talk with the key members before the meeting. Participants should know in advance what is expected of them at the meeting. If any preparation is expected (read material, do some research, make a report, and so forth), they should have adequate advance notice.[77]

Exhibit 10-7 *Meeting Plan*

		Example
Time	List meeting date, meeting place (unless the team always meets in the same place), and time (both beginning and ending times).	November 22, 2007, Gold Room, 9–10 A.M.
Objectives	State the objective or purpose of the meeting (Note: Objectives may be listed with agenda items, as shown in agenda item 1 below, rather than as a separate section, but wherever they are listed, they should be specific.)	
Participation and assignments	List the assignment for the entire team or, if individual members have different assignments, list each person's name and assignment. (Assignments may be listed as agenda items, as shown in agenda items 2 and 3 below.)	All members should have read the six enclosed brochures about computer systems before the meeting. Be ready to discuss your preferences.
Agenda	List each item to be covered in the meeting, in order of importance, with an approximate time limit.	1. Discussion of new computer systems; narrow down the choices to two out of six possibilities; 45 minutes 2. Venus Project report (Ted); 5 minutes 3. Presentation on proposed change in production process (Karen); 5 minutes. (Discussion will take place at our next meeting, after team members have had a chance to give the proposal some thought.)

AGENDA

The agenda tells the members what is expected and how the meeting will progress.[78] It should identify the activities that will take place in order to achieve the objective. Team members may also submit agenda items. Having a set time limit for each agenda item helps keep the group on target; needless discussion and getting off the subject are common at meetings. However, you may need to be flexible and allow more time. Agenda items that require action should have objectives listed with them.

Place agenda items in order of priority. Then, if the group does not have time to cover every item, the least important items will be carried forward to the next meeting.

DATE, PLACE, AND TIME

Get team members' input on which days of the week and times of the day are best for meetings. When members are close, it is better to have more frequent shorter meetings focusing on one or a few items. However, when members have to travel, fewer longer meetings are needed. Be sure to select an adequate place for the meeting and plan for the physical comfort of the group. Seating should allow eye contact for small discussion groups, and enough time should be allocated so that the members do not have to rush. If reservations are needed for the meeting place, make them far enough in advance to get a proper meeting room.

LEADERSHIP

The leader should determine the appropriate leadership style for the meeting. Different agenda items may need to be handled differently. For example, some items may simply call for disseminating information, but others may require a discussion, vote, or a consensus; still other items may require a report from a member. An effective way to develop group members' ability is to rotate the role of the group moderator/leader for each meeting.[79]

TECHNOLOGY

E-mail has eliminated the need for some meetings. Also, with advances in technology, telephone conferences are becoming common. Videoconferences are also gaining in popularity, especially for virtual teams.[80] These techniques save travel costs and time, and they may result in better and quicker decisions. Personal computers have been called the most useful tool for running meetings since Robert's Rules of Order. Group members can use their laptops to take notes on what took place during a meeting and distribute a hard copy or e-mail of the notes at the end of the meeting.

Conducting Meetings

THE FIRST MEETING

At its first meeting, a team is in the orientation stage. Members should be given the opportunity to spend some time getting to know one another. Introductions set the stage for subsequent interactions. A simple technique is to start with introductions, then move on to the group's purpose, objectives, and members' job roles. During or following this procedure, schedule a break that enables members to interact informally. If members find that their social needs will not be met, dissatisfaction may occur quickly.

THE THREE PARTS OF MEETINGS

Meetings should have the following three parts:

1. *Identify objectives.* Begin the meeting on time;[81] waiting for late members penalizes the members who are on time and develops a norm for coming late. Begin by reviewing progress to date, the group's objectives, and the purpose or objective for the specific meeting. Recorded minutes are usually approved at the beginning of the meeting. For most meetings, a secretary should be appointed to take minutes.
2. *Cover agenda items.* Be sure to cover agenda items in priority order. Try to keep to the approximate times, but be flexible. If the discussion is constructive and members need more time, give it to them.
3. *Summarize and review assignments.* End the meeting on time. The leader should summarize what took place during the meeting and review all of the assignments given during the meeting. The secretary and/or leader should record all assignments. If there is no accountability and follow-up on assignments, members may not complete them.

JetBlue uses a team structure, and teams have meetings, but employees make a conscious effort to avoid unproductive meetings and to be respectful of each other's time. At every meeting, there is a "time cop" who makes sure that the meeting does not last any longer than necessary. The time cop keeps the meeting on topic, allows each agenda item only its allotted time, and ends the meeting on time.

Handling Problem Members

As members work together, personality types tend to emerge. Certain personality types can cause the group to be less efficient than it could be. Some of the problem members you may have in your group are the silent type, the talker, the wanderer, the bored member, and the arguer.

SILENT TYPE

To be fully effective, all group members should participate. If members are silent, the group does not get the benefit of their input.

It is the leader's responsibility to encourage silent members to participate, without being obvious or overdoing it.[82] One technique a leader can use is the rotation method, in which all members take turns giving their input. This method is generally less threatening than being called on directly. However, the rotation method is not appropriate all the time. To build up silent members' confidence, call on them with questions they can easily answer.[83] If you are a silent type, try to participate more often. Know when to stand up for your views and be assertive; trust yourself, and take risks.

TALKER

Talkers have something to say about everything. They like to dominate the discussion. However, if they do, the other members do not get to participate. The talker can cause intragroup problems such as low cohesiveness and conflicts.

It is the leader's responsibility to slow talkers down, not to shut them up. Do not let them dominate the group.[84] The rotation method can be effective with talkers because they have to wait their turn. When not using this method, gently interrupt the talker and present your own ideas or call on other specific members to present their ideas. If you tend to be a talker, try to slow down. Give others a chance to talk and do things for themselves. Good leaders develop others' ability in these areas.

WANDERER

Wanderers distract the group from the agenda items; they tend to change the subject and often like to complain.

The leader is responsible for keeping the group on track.[85] If the wanderer wants to socialize, cut it off. Be kind, thank the member for the contribution, then throw a question out to the group to get it back on track. If you tend to be a wanderer, try to be aware of your behavior and stay on the subject at hand.

BORED MEMBER

Your group may have one or more members who are not interested in the job. The bored person may be preoccupied with other issues and not pay attention or participate in the group meeting. The bored member may also feel superior.[86]

Assign the bored member a task such as recording ideas on the board or recording the minutes. Call on bored members; bring them into the group. If you allow them to sit back, things may get worse and others may decide not to participate either. If you tend to be bored, try to find ways to help motivate yourself. Work at becoming more patient and in control of behavior that can have negative effects on other members.

WorkApplication10

Recall a meeting you have recently attended. Did you receive an agenda prior to the meeting? How well did the leader conduct the meeting? Give ideas on how the meeting could have been improved. Did the group have any problem members? How well did the leader handle them?

ARGUER

Like the talker, the arguer likes to be the center of attention. Arguers enjoy arguing for the sake of arguing, rather than helping the group.[87] They turn things into a win-lose situation, and they cannot stand losing.

The leader should resolve conflict, but not in an argumentative way.[88] Do not get into an argument with arguers; that is exactly what they want to happen. If an argument starts, bring others into the discussion. If an argument becomes personal, cut it off. Personal attacks only hurt the group.[89] Keep the discussion moving on target. If you tend to be an arguer, strive to convey your views in an assertive rather than an aggressive manner. Listen to others' views and be willing to change if they have better ideas.

WORKING WITH GROUP MEMBERS

Whenever you work in a group, do not embarrass, intimidate, or argue with any members, no matter how much they provoke you. If you do, the group will perceive them as martyrs and you as a bully. If problem members do not respond to the preceding techniques, confront them individually outside of the group. Get them to agree to work in a cooperative way.

Having a team-based organization, W. L. Gore & Associates has lots of meetings, but they are productive. Every associate is part of one or more teams, so all associates

Applying The Concept 4

Problematic Group Members

Identify the problem type described in each statement.

a. silent type   d. bored member

b. talker   e. arguer

c. wanderer

_____ 16. Charlie is always first or second to give his ideas. He is always elaborating on ideas. Because Charlie is so quick to respond, others sometimes make comments to him about it.

_____ 17. One of the usually active group members is sitting back quietly today for the first time. The other members are doing all the discussing and volunteering for assignments.

_____ 18. As the group is discussing a problem, Billy asks if they heard about the company owner and the mailroom clerk.

_____ 19. Eunice is usually reluctant to give her ideas. When asked to explain her position, she often changes her answers to agree with others in the group.

_____ 20. Dwayne enjoys challenging members' ideas. He likes getting his own way. When a group member does not agree with Dwayne, he makes sarcastic comments about the member's prior mistakes.

attend meetings. Mentors make sure that newcomers are successful, which includes being productive during team meetings. Mentors also make sure that newcomers have opportunities to sit in on important meetings with other teams to better understand the systems effect of their projects and products and to learn how Gore operates.

I O M

As we bring this chapter to a close, you should understand the growing use of teams in business settings and how to develop groups into teams. You should know that team performance is based on organizational context, group structure (type, size, composition, leadership, and objectives), group process (roles, norms, cohesiveness, status, decision making, and conflict resolution), and group development (orientation, dissatisfaction, resolution, production, and termination). You should also know how to run effective meetings.

Take advantage of the companion Web site for *Management Fundamentals*, where you will find a broad array of resources to help you maximize what you learn in class:

- Try a quiz
- View chapter videos
- Download slides
- Boost your vocabulary
- Work through an Internet exercise
- Find related links

Take a look for yourself at *http://lussier.swlearning.com.*

Chapter Summary

1. Describe the major differences between groups and teams.

The major areas of difference are size, leadership, jobs, accountability and evaluation, rewards, and objectives. A group is two or more members with a clear leader who perform independent jobs and experience individual accountability, evaluation, and rewards. A team has a small number of members with shared leadership who perform interdependent jobs and experience both individual and group accountability, evaluation, and rewards.

2. Explain the group performance model.

Group performance is a function of organizational context, group structure, group process, and group development stage.

3. List and explain the three dimensions of group types.

Groups are formal or informal, functional or cross-functional, and command or task groups. Formal groups are created as part of the organizational structure; informal groups are not. Functional group members come from one area, whereas cross-functional members come from different areas. Command groups include managers and their employees, whereas task groups include selected employees who work on a specific objective. A task force is temporary, whereas a standing committee is ongoing.

4. Define the three major roles played in groups.

Group task roles are played by members who do and say things that directly aid in the accomplishment of the group's objectives. Group maintenance roles are played by members who do and say things that develop and sustain the group process. Self-interest roles are played by members who do and say things that help themselves but hurt the group.

5. State the differences between rules and norms.

Rules are formally established by management or by the group itself. Norms are the group's shared expectations of its members' behavior. Norms are not developed by management or explicitly agreed to by the group; they develop as members interact.

6. Describe cohesiveness, and explain why it is important to teams.

Group cohesiveness is the extent to which members stick together. Group cohesiveness is important because highly cohesive groups have a higher level of productivity than groups with low levels of cohesiveness.

7. List the four major stages of group development, and describe the appropriate leadership style usually associated with each.

(1) Orientation is characterized by a low development level. The appropriate leadership style is often autocratic. (2) Dissatisfaction is characterized by moderate development level. The appropriate leadership style is often consultative. (3) Resolution is characterized by high development level. The appropriate leadership style is often participative. (4) Production is characterized by an outstanding development level. The appropriate leadership style is often empowerment.

8. Explain the difference between a group manager and a team leader.

The group manager takes responsibility for performing the four functions of management. The team leader empowers team members to take responsibility for performing the management functions and focuses on developing effective group structure, group process, and group development.

9. Discuss the three parts of meetings.

Meetings should begin with a review of the purpose and objectives for the meeting. During the meeting, agenda items should be covered in priority order. The meeting should end with a summary of what took place and assignments to be completed for future meetings.

10. Complete each of the following statements using one of this chapter's key terms.

A _____ is two or more members with a clear leader who perform independent jobs with individual accountability, evaluation, and rewards.

A _____ is a small number of members with shared leadership who perform interdependent jobs with both individual and group accountability, evaluation, and rewards.

In the _____, group performance is a function of organizational context, group structure, group process, and group development stage.

_____ are group type, size, composition, leadership, and objectives.

_____ include formal or informal, functional or cross-functional, and command or task.

_____ consist of managers and the employees they supervise.

_____ consist of employees selected to work on a specific objective.

Members of _____ are physically located in different places but work together as a team.

_____ is the mix of members' skills and abilities.

_____ is the patterns of interactions that emerge as members perform their jobs.

_____ include roles, norms, cohesiveness, status, decision making, and conflict resolution.

_____ include group task roles, group maintenance roles, and self-interest roles.

_____ are expectations about behavior that are shared by members of a group.

_____ is the extent to which members stick together.

_____ is the perceived ranking of one member relative to other members in a group.

The _____ are orientation, dissatisfaction, resolution, production, and termination.

_____ empower members to take responsibility for performing the management functions and focus on developing effective group structure, group process, and group development.

Key Terms

command groups, 355

global virtual teams, 355

group, 350

group cohesiveness, 360

group composition, 356

group performance model, 351

group process, 358

group process dimensions, 358

group roles, 358

group structure dimensions, 353

group types, 354

norms, 359

stages of group development, 364

status, 362

task groups, 355

team, 351

team leaders, 368

Review and Discussion Questions

1. Which are usually larger, groups or teams?
2. Which level of management has the most influence over organizational context?
3. Is there an ideal group size?
4. Why is diversity important to group composition?
5. Why are objectives important to groups?
6. How do groups enforce norms?
7. Which type of group tends to terminate and which does not?
8. Are the four functions of management important to both groups and teams?
9. Why is it important to keep records of meeting assignments?
10. Describe the five types of problem members in meetings. How does each cause a problem to the group?

Objective Case

THE LINCOLN ELECTRIC COMPANY

The Lincoln Electric Company is the world's largest designer and manufacturer of arc welding and cutting products. The company's products are used in metal forming and fabrication; in the construction of pipelines, buildings, bridges, and power facilities; in the transportation and defense industries; by other equipment manufacturers; and in the rental market.

In addition to its headquarters facilities in Cleveland, Ohio, the company operates one other U.S. manufacturing

location in Miami and 24 manufacturing locations in 18 foreign countries; the company has 5,992 employees worldwide. Lincoln has almost 1,000 independent welding distributors in the United States and more than 1,200 international distributors in over 160 countries. As of December 31, 2003, net sales were $1.04 billion, with net income of $54.5 million.

Lincoln has developed a global reputation for its innovative team structure and incentive program. Everyone is considered part of the team. There are no executive perks—no reserved parking spaces, no executives' washrooms or dining room—the president pays for his own meals and eats in the cafeteria—and everyone gets bonuses. Let's discuss Lincoln's team structure and its incentive program.

Unlike other companies that have more recently realized the productivity of teams, Lincoln started using a team structure 100 years ago. Lincoln has never had a formal organization chart. The objective is to ensure maximum flexibility. An open-door policy is maintained throughout the company, and employees are encouraged to take problems to people most capable of resolving the issues.

At Lincoln, leadership emerges at different times and in different ways. Teams have eliminated layers of administrative positions, but not people. A typical production supervisor oversees as many as 100 workers, which does not allow more than infrequent worker–supervisor interaction. Production workers have only two (or at most three) levels of supervision between themselves and the corporate president. The quality and enthusiasm of the Lincoln workforce makes routine supervision almost nonexistent.

Supervisors are external team members who manage the boundary between the team and the corporate organization. Each supervisor formally evaluates employees twice a year. The employee performance criteria include dependability, ideas and cooperation, and output, among eleven other items. Individual merit rating scores affect pay and normally range from 80 to 100. However, employees can receive team- and organization-based profit sharing and stock options, based on performance.

At Lincoln, management control is delegated to the team. The teams have the authority to make decisions about their work, and management provides the group with the resources and tools to continually improve their production. Teams focus on deliverables and measure results.

Teams in all functional areas work together with teams from other areas to improve performance. In some cases, project teams are created with members from a variety of department teams. Employees do not have specialized jobs; everyone pitches in and does whatever it takes to get the current job done.

Lincoln has an advisory board of employees that meets biweekly with top management, which includes the chairman, president, and other senior managers. Employees are elected by their peers to serve a term on the advisory board. Good ideas brought by the advisory board to management are implemented, with the support of management and employees.

Over the years, Lincoln has enjoyed gains in productivity far above those for manufacturing as a whole. Managers believe that workers' confidence that innovations in methods will not cost them or their colleagues their jobs has significantly contributed to Lincoln Electric's successes. Worker training and education are seen as continuous investments in productivity. Employees have the knowledge and abilities to be able to contribute effectively to corporate performance and simultaneously to increase their annual incomes.

The incentive management system at Lincoln has been in place since the early twentieth century. It is one of the oldest "pay for performance" systems in the country. Lincoln operates on the belief that two key elements—responsibility (performance) and recognition (compensation)—must be present for people to be productive.

Employees have three major responsibilities. (1) If employees do not come to work, they are not paid, and are penalized. (2) Production workers are paid on a piecework basis; they must guarantee the quality of each piece they produce or they are not paid for it. (3) The supervisor-to-worker ratio is one to 100, so employees are expected to work in teams without supervision.

Production workers are given a short period of on-the-job training before becoming part of the system of piecework pay plus bonuses. Employees are motivated through incentive management, which results in some production workers earning over $100,000 annually. At Lincoln you don't find employees wasting time hanging around doing nothing or taking long breaks.

Lincoln has coupled individual pay for performance with group-based incentive management through profit sharing and stock offering. Profit sharing, in some good years, has resulted in some employees getting a bonus larger than their annual paycheck. Employee ownership puts stock in the hands of people who are more inclined to take a long-term management view of the organization, rather than maintaining an "us against management" mentality. Employees and Lincoln family members own over 90 percent of the stock.

In addition to receiving compensation, employees are recognized through various programs. Promotion from within is used to motivate employees to aspire to the role of manager; in addition, employees vie with each other to serve on the prestigious advisory board.

Although Lincoln pays higher compensation than most companies, its tremendous productivity keeps costs low, and the company regularly lowers the prices of its products to pass along these gains to its customers. Management specialists refer to this Lincoln plan as a model for achieving high worker productivity and morale. Except for retirements, employee turnover is almost nonexistent. Lincoln's pioneering ways have had impressive results. Lincoln has not had a losing quarter for more than 58 years and has gone 44 years without layoffs. Indeed, there is some evidence that the entire corporation functions, at times, as one "super team."

To learn more about Lincoln Electric, log on to InfoTrac® College Edition at *http://infotrac. thomsonlearning.com* and use the advanced search function.

_____ 1. Based on the text definition, Lincoln teams are

    a. groups

    b. teams

_____ 2. Which element of the group process model is discussed in the case the least?

    a. organizational context   c. group process

    b. group structure   d. group development

_____ 3. Which types of groups are discussed in the case?

    a. functional

    b. cross-functional

    c. both

_____ 4. Most of the teams at Lincoln are

    a. command groups

    b. task groups

_____ 5. Which type of group is the advisory board?

    a. command group

    b. task force

    c. standing committee

_____ 6. Team leadership at Lincoln is

    a. assigned to one person

    b. shared among team members

_____ 7. Executive perks at Lincoln create large status differences between employees and managers.

    a. true

    b. false

_____ 8. Team decision making is done by the

    a. supervisor

    b. team members

_____ 9. Teams at Lincoln appear to be at the _____ stage of group development.

    a. orientation (forming)

    b. dissatisfaction (storming)

    c. resolution (norming)

    d. production (performing)

_____ 10. Team meeting skills are important at Lincoln.

    a. true

    b. false

11. Why is the team structure at Lincoln so successful?

12. What types of group norms do you think might be evident in the Lincoln teams?

13. Do you believe the teams are cohesive at Lincoln?

Cumulative Case Questions

14. Discuss the extent to which the nine organizational principles are followed at Lincoln and the type of authority used. (Chapter 6)

15. What specific types of "new" approaches to departmentalization and job design has Lincoln been using for many years? (Chapter 6)

16. Which organizational development intervention method is most relevant to Lincoln? (Chapter 7)

17. Discuss the importance of the four areas of the human resources management process at Lincoln. (Chapter 8)

Skill Builder 1

LEADERSHIP STYLES IN GROUP SITUATIONS

Objective

To determine appropriate leadership styles in group situations.

Assess Your Preferred Leadership Style

Following are twelve situations. Select the one alternative that most closely describes what you would do in each situation. Don't be concerned with trying to select the right answer; select the alternative you would really use. Circle a, b, c, or d. (Ignore the D _____ and the S _____ following each answer choice; these will be explained later.)

1.   Your group works well together; members are cohesive and have positive norms. They maintain a fairly consistent level of production that is above the organizational average, as long as you continue to play a maintenance role. You have a new assignment for them. To accomplish it, you would: D _____

a. Explain what needs to be done and tell them how to do it. Oversee them while they perform the task. S _____

b. Tell the group how pleased you are with its past performance. Explain the new assignment, but let them decide how to accomplish it. Be available if they need help. S _____

c. Tell the group what needs to be done. Encourage them to give input on how to do the job. Oversee task performance. S _____

d. Explain to the group what needs to be done. S _____

2. You have been promoted to a new supervisory position. The group you supervise appears to have little talent to do the job, but they do seem to care about the quality of the work they do. The last supervisor was fired because of the group's low productivity level. To increase productivity, you would: D ____

   a. Let the group know you are aware of its low production level, but let them decide how to improve it. S ____

   b. Spend most of your time overseeing group members as they perform their jobs. Train them as needed. S ____

   c. Explain to the group that you would like to work together to improve productivity. Work together as a team. S ____

   d. Tell the group how productivity can be improved. With their ideas, develop methods and make sure they are implemented. S ____

3. Your department continues to be one of the top performers in the organization. The members work well as a team. In the past, you generally let them take care of the work on their own. You decide to: D ____

   a. Go around encouraging group members on a regular basis. S ____

   b. Define members' roles and spend more time overseeing performance. S ____

   c. Continue things the way they are; leave them alone. S ____

   d. Hold a meeting. Recommend ways to improve and get members' ideas as well. After agreeing on changes, oversee the group to make sure it implements the new ideas and does improve. S ____

4. You have spent much of the past year training your employees. However, they do not need you to oversee production as much as you used to. Several group members no longer get along as well as they did in the past. You've played referee lately. You: D ____

   a. Have a group meeting to discuss ways to increase performance. Let the group decide what changes to make. Be supportive. S ____

   b. Continue things the way they are now. Supervise them closely and be the referee when needed. S ____

   c. Leave the group alone to work things out for themselves. S ____

   d. Continue to supervise closely as needed, but spend more time playing a maintenance role; develop a team spirit. S ____

5. Your department has been doing such a great job that it has increased in size. You are surprised at how fast the new members were integrated. The team continues to come up with ways to improve performance on its own. Because it has grown so large, the department will be moving to a larger location. You decide to: D ____

   a. Design the new layout and present it to the group to see if the members can improve on it. S ____

   b. Allow the group to design the new layout. S ____

   c. Design the new layout and put a copy on the bulletin board so employees know where to report for work after the move. S ____

   d. Hold a meeting to get employee ideas on the layout of the new location. After the meeting, think about their ideas and finalize the layout. S ____

6. You are appointed to head a task group. Because of the death of a relative, you had to miss the first meeting. At the second meeting, the group seems to have developed objectives and some ground rules. Members have volunteered for assignments that have to be accomplished. You: D ____

   a. Take over as a strong leader, and change some ground rules and assignments. S ____

   b. Review what has been done so far, and keep things as they are. However, you take charge and provide clear direction from now on. S ____

   c. Take over the leadership, but allow the group to make the decisions. Be supportive and encourage them. S ____

   d. Given the group is doing so well, leave and do not attend any more meetings. S ____

7. Your group was working at, or just below, standard. There has been a conflict within the group, and as a result, production is behind schedule. You: D ____

   a. Tell the group how to resolve the conflict. Then closely supervise to make sure people do what you say and production increases. S ____

   b. Let the group work it out. S ____

   c. Hold a meeting to work as a team to come up with a solution. Encourage the group members to work together. S ____

   d. Hold a meeting to present a way to resolve the conflict. Sell the members on its merits, ask for their input, and follow up. S ____

8. Your organization allows flextime. Two of your employees have asked if they can change work hours. You are concerned because the busy work hours need adequate coverage. The department is very cohesive with positive norms. You decide to: D ____

   a. Tell them things are going well; we'll keep things as they are now. S ____

   b. Hold a department meeting to get everyone's input, then reschedule their hours. S ____

   c. Hold a department meeting to get everyone's input; then reschedule their hours on a trial basis. Tell the group that if there is any drop in productivity, you will go back to the old schedule. S ____

d. Tell them to hold a department meeting. If the department agrees to have at least three people on the job during the busy hours, they can make changes, giving you a copy of the new schedule. S ____

9. You have arrived 10 minutes late for a department meeting. Your employees are discussing the latest assignment. This surprises you because, in the past, you had to provide clear direction and employees rarely would say anything. You: D ____

   a. Take control immediately and provide your usual direction. S ____

   b. Say nothing and just sit back. S ____

   c. Encourage the group to continue, but also provide direction. S ____

   d. Thank the group for starting without you, and encourage them to continue. Support their efforts. S ____

10. Your department is consistently very productive. However, occasionally the members fool around and someone has an accident. There has never been a serious injury. You hear a noise and go to see what it was. From a distance you can see Sue sitting on the floor, laughing, with a ball made from company material in her hand. You: D ____

    a. Say and do nothing. After all, she's OK, and the department is very productive; you don't want to make waves. S ____

    b. Call the group together and ask for suggestions on how to keep accidents from recurring. Tell them you will be checking up on them to make sure the behavior does not continue. S ____

    c. Call the group together and discuss the situation. Encourage them to be more careful in the future. S ____

    d. Tell the group that's it; from now on you will be checking up on them regularly. Bring Sue to your office and discipline her. S ____

11. You are at the first meeting of an ad hoc committee you are leading. Most of the members are second- and third-level managers from the marketing and financial areas; you are a supervisor from production. You decide to start by: D ____

    a. Working on developing relationships. Get everyone to feel as though they know each other before you talk about business. S ____

    b. Going over the group's purpose and the authority it has. Provide clear directives. S ____

    c. Asking the group to define its purpose. Because most of the members are higher-level managers, let them provide the leadership. S ____

    d. Providing both direction and encouragement. Give directives and thank people for their cooperation. S ____

12. Your department has done a great job in the past. It is getting a new computer system. You have been trained to operate the computer, and you are expected to train your employees to operate it. To train them, you: D ____

    a. Give the group instructions and work with people individually, providing direction and encouragement. S ____

    b. Get the group together to decide how they want to be instructed. Be very supportive of their efforts to learn. S ____

    c. Tell them it's a simple system. Give them a copy of the manual and have them study it on their own. S ____

    d. Give the group instructions. Then go around and supervise their work closely, giving additional instructions as needed. S ____

Scoring

To determine your preferred leadership style, follow these steps:

1. Circle the letter you selected for each situation.

	Autocratic	Consultative	Participative	Empowerment
1.	a	c	b	d
2.	b	d	c	a
3.	b	d	a	c
4.	b	d	a	c
5.	c	a	d	b
6.	a	b	c	d
7.	a	d	c	b
8.	a	c	b	d
9.	a	c	d	b
10.	d	b	c	a
11.	b	d	a	c
12.	d	a	b	c
Totals	_	_	_	_

2. Add up the number of circled items per column. The column with the most circled items represents your preferred style.

The more evenly distributed the numbers are between the four styles, the more flexible you are at leading groups. A total of 0 or 1 in any column may indicate a reluctance to use that style. Is your preferred leadership style the same as your preferred management style (Chapter 1)?

Assigning Appropriate Leadership Styles to Group Situations

Objectives

To help you understand the stages of group development and to select the appropriate leadership styles for group situations.

Preparation

You should understand the stages of group development and have completed assessment of your leadership style.

Step 1. Determine the level of development of the group in each of the twelve situations. Place the number (1, 2, 3, or 4) on the line marked D at the end of the situation.

1 = orientation stage
2 = dissatisfaction stage
3 = resolution stage
4 = production stage

Step 2. Identify the leadership style described in each answer choice. Place the letter A, C, P, or E on the line marked S following each answer choice.

A = autocratic
C = consultative
P = participative
E = empowerment

Step 3. Now circle the letter of the answer choice that represents the management style that is most appropriate for the level of development for the group in each situation.

Apply It

What did I learn from this experience? How will I use this knowledge in the future?

_____

_____

Your instructor may ask you to do part of this Skill Builder in class as a group. You may be instructed, for example, to break into teams to assign stages of development and leadership styles to each situation, or you may be asked to discuss the reasons behind your stage and style decisions.

Skill **Builder** 2
GROUP PERFORMANCE

Note: This exercise is designed for class groups that have worked together for some time. (Five or more hours of prior work are recommended.)

Objectives

To gain a better understanding of group structure, process, development and of meetings and how they affect group performance.

Answer the following questions as they apply to your class group/team.

1. Using Exhibit 10-1, would you classify your members as a group or a team? Why?

Group Structure

2. What type of group/team are you (formal/informal, functional/cross-functional, command/task)?
3. Assess the size of your group/team (too large, too small, ideal).
4. What is the group/team composition?
5. Is there a clear leader? If so, who is/are the leader[s]?
6. Does your group/team have clear objectives?
7. List some ways in which group structure could be improved to increase group performance.

_____

_____

Group Process

8. List each group member, including yourself, and the major role(s) each plays.

    1. _____   4. _____
    2. _____   5. _____
    3. _____   6. _____

9. Identify at least three group norms. Are they positive or negative? How does the group enforce them?
10. How cohesive is your group (very cohesive, moderately cohesive, minimally cohesive)?
11. List each group member, including yourself, in order of status.

    1. _____   4. _____
    2. _____   5. _____
    3. _____   6. _____

12. How are decisions made in your group/team?
13. How is conflict resolved in your group/team?
14. List some ways in which group process could be improved to increase group performance.

_____

_____

Group Development Stage

15. At what stage of development is your group/team? Explain.
16. List some ways in which your group/team can move to a higher level of development to increase group performance.

_____

_____

Meetings

17. List some ways in which your meetings could be improved to increase group performance.

_____

_____

18. Does your group have any problem members? What can be done to make them more effective?

Apply It

What did I learn from this experience? How will I use this knowledge in the future?

_____

_____

Your instructor may ask you to continue this Skill Builder in class by discussing your answers to the questions with other members of your class group. You may also be asked to jointly make specific recommendations about ways in which your team can improve its performance.

Learning Outcomes

After studying this chapter, you should be able to:

1. Describe the three ways communication flows through organizations. PAGE 384

2. List the four steps in the interpersonal communication process. PAGE 389

3. State the major advantages of oral communication and written communication. PAGE 392

4. State a general guide to channel selection. PAGE 396

5. List the five steps in the process of sending face-to-face messages. PAGE 398

6. Describe paraphrasing, and explain why it is useful. PAGE 399

11: Communicating and Information Technology

7. List and explain the three parts of the process of receiving messages. PAGE 402

8. Define reflecting responses, and state when they should be used. PAGE 406

9. Discuss what should and should not be done to calm an emotional person. PAGE 408

10. Describe the three primary types of information systems and their relationship. PAGE 409

11. List the components of an information network. PAGE 411

12. Define the following **key terms:**

communication
vertical communication
horizontal communication
grapevine
communication process
encoding
communication channel
decoding

nonverbal communication
message-sending process
feedback
paraphrasing
message-receiving process
reflecting responses
empathic listening

Ideas on Management

at Powell's Books

Michael Powell started Powell's Books back in 1970, when he was a graduate student at the University of Chicago. He borrowed $3,000 for the lease and repaid the loan in two months. His father, Walter, came to the bookstore to help for the summer. When Walter returned to Portland, Oregon, in 1971, he opened his own used bookstore.

Michael joined Walter in Portland in 1979, and together they expanded Walter's store into one with a unique new business model combining used and new, hardcover and paperback books, all on the same shelf, open 365 days a year and staffed by knowledgeable and dedicated book lovers. Powell's further expanded to six stores and went online serving customers worldwide in 1994. Within two years, Powell's entire inventory was listed on the Web (*http://www.powells.com*). Today, Powell's is one of the largest and most successful independent bookstores in America.

However, Powell's was experiencing increased competition from Barnes & Noble and Amazon.com, so Michael decided to decrease staff pay raises from 6 percent down to 3 percent. He informed employees in a memo. Not long after, he sent another memo stating that he was restructuring job responsibilities. Jobs were going to be simplified and specialized to single tasks, such as buying, selling, shipping, or returning books. Needless to say, employees were not happy with the changes. Managers and employees never talked about the changes, but employees did complain to each other. Employees organized and joined the International Longshore and Warehouse Union (ILWU). After 10 months of negotiating, a three-year contract was signed that set a minimum hiring wage and guaranteed pay increases of 6 percent a year.

© Royalty-Free/CORBIS

I O M

1. **What was the organizational communication flow of information about pay limits and restructuring at Powell's, and what was the flow of communication about employees' reactions?**
2. **Which message channel did Powell use to inform employees of the pay limits and restructuring?**
3. **Which parts of the message-sending process did Michael Powell ignore, thus creating communication problems at Powell's?**
4. **How would you rate the listening skills of managers at Powell's Books with regard to employees' reactions to pay limits and restructuring?**
5. **How would you rate Powell's managers' ability to deal with employee emotions? How could communications have been better so that the situation would not have escalated to unionization?**

To learn more about Powell's Books, visit the company's Web site at *http://www.powells.com* or log on to InfoTrac® College Edition at *http://infotrac. thomsonlearning.com*, where you can research and read articles on Powell's Books. For in-depth articles on Powell's Books and its growing business, select the advanced search option and key in record number A67591253, A94672202, or A89159843 to get started.

Source: Opening case information and answers within the chapter were taken from the second edition of this book and from Powell's Books Web site, *http://www.powells.com*, accessed May 21, 2004.

ORGANIZATIONAL COMMUNICATION AND INFORMATION TECHNOLOGY

Communication is one of the three major skills needed by managers (Chapter 1). All of the management roles (interpersonal, informational, and decisional) and management functions (planning, organizing, leading, and controlling) require effective communication skills. The organizational mission, strategy, goals, and culture must be communicated effectively.

Poor communication costs organizations money, because it leads to lack of cooperation and coordination, lower productivity, tension, gossip and rumors, and increased turnover and absenteeism.[1] Conversely, effective communication increases productivity.[2] Organizations seek employees who can communicate well.[3] Success in your personal and professional life is based on your communication skills.[4]

Communication *is the process of transmitting information and meaning.* There are two major types, or levels, of communication: organizational and interpersonal. That is, communication takes place among organizations and among their units or departments, often through the use of information technology, and communication takes place among individuals.

In this section, we discuss organizational communication and the use of information technology. In subsequent sections, we focus on interpersonal communication, and in the last section, we discuss the use of information systems at both levels.

Learning **Outcome 1**
Describe the three ways communication flows
through organizations.

Organizational communication flows formally in vertical and horizontal directions and informally through the grapevine. Exhibit 11-1 illustrates these aspects of organizational communication.

Vertical Communication

Vertical communication *is the flow of information both downward and upward through the organizational chain of command.* It is also called *formal communication* because information that flows this way is recognized as the officially sanctioned information.

DOWNWARD VERTICAL COMMUNICATION

When top-level management makes decisions or creates policies and procedures, these are often communicated down the chain of command to employees. Downward communication occurs when higher-level managers tell those below them what to do and how to do it.[5] The delegation process occurs via downward communication.

There should be official communication policies and procedures to ensure accurate and effective transmission of information.[6] Many firms have computer information systems and an executive who oversees all aspects of information technology. Generally, this executive has the title of chief information officer (CIO).

Exhibit 11-1 *Organizational Communication*

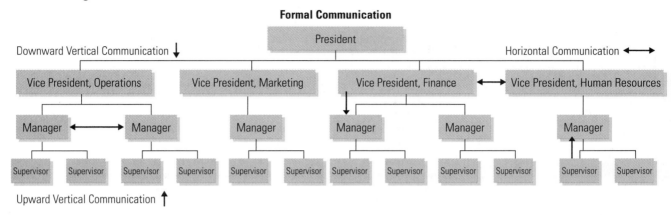

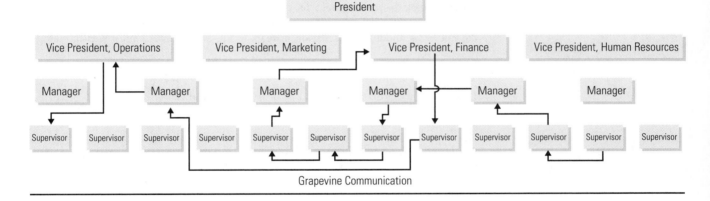

UPWARD VERTICAL COMMUNICATION

When employees send a message to their bosses, they are using upward communication. Managers learn about what is going on in the organization, and often about the actions of customers, through employees.[7]

To help facilitate upward communication, many organizations have adopted an open-door policy that allows employees to feel at ease in going to managers. **Connecticut Mutual Life Insurance** offers free breakfasts and lunches to employees who sit with managers in a no-holds-barred question-and-answer session. **Ford, Sears**, and other organizations do periodic surveys to assess employees' attitudes and opinions. Although many company managers are making an effort to know their employees, a survey revealed that only 15 percent of employees believe that senior management was well informed about what employees think and do.[8]

Horizontal Communication

Horizontal communication *is the flow of information between colleagues and peers.* It is formal communication, but it does not follow the chain of command; instead, it is multidirectional. Horizontal communication is needed to

WorkApplication1

Give an example of vertical (upward and downward), horizontal, and grapevine communication at a company where you work or have worked.

coordinate within a department, among team members, and among different departments. When the manager of the marketing department communicates with the manager of the production department, or other departments, horizontal communication takes place. Most employees spend more time communicating with peers than with managers.

Grapevine Communication

The **grapevine** *is the informal flow of information in any direction throughout an organization.* It is informal communication because it is not official or sanctioned by management. Grapevine information can begin with anyone in the organization and can flow in any direction. Employees complain, talk about sports and news events, and whisper secrets about coworkers through the grapevine. Many employees hear of layoffs through the grapevine long before the pink slips are officially sent out.

IOM

At Powell's Books, Michael Powell used downward vertical communication when he sent a memo to employees announcing that he was limiting pay raises and restructuring. The employees' reaction was to talk among themselves through the grapevine without going to management to complain. Employees also discussed unionization through the grapevine long before the formal contact with the ILWU, but management did not know about this discussion or react to the union threat until it was too late.

Information Technology

Data are unorganized facts and figures, whereas *information* is data converted into a form that helps people do their jobs. Useful information has three qualities:

- Timely—current and available when you need it
- Relevant—suited to the situation, accurate, complete but concise
- Understandable—in a form that is easy to comprehend

ApplyingTheConcept 1

Communication Flow

Identify the form of communication flow occurring for each statement.

a. vertical downward   c. horizontal
b. vertical upward   d. grapevine

_____1. "Hey, Carl, have you heard that Paul and Helen were caught . . . ?"

_____2. "Juanita, will you come here and hold this so I can get it straight?"

_____3. "Tom, here is the letter you asked me to type. Check it and I'll make changes."

_____4. "Robin, I have two new customers who want to set up charge accounts. Please rush the credit check so we can increase business."

_____5. "Ted, please take this letter to the mail room for me right now."

Information technology (IT) refers to the technology used to store, process, and distribute useful information. IT has enabled productivity gains that have reduced the cost of information and has created new opportunites.[9] IT is critical to the learning organization, which needs to be innovative in order to remain competitive.[10]

For many years, **Sears** was the leading retailer in the United States. **Kmart** took the lead for a short time, but poor management and inadequate IT led Kmart to initiate a retrenchment strategy. Today, with a total commitment to using the latest information technology, **Wal-Mart** is clearly the leading retailer. Wal-Mart took the lead in sales based on its ability to keep its costs and its prices low by effectively using IT in its warehousing, distribution, and inventory systems.

THE INTERNET

The Internet is a global collection of computer networks linked together to exchange data and information, and the *World Wide Web (WWW)* is a segment of the Internet in which information is presented in the form of Web pages that can include graphic elements as well as text. Three key information technologies used to access the Internet are computers, telephones, and handheld devices.

Over 605 million people worldwide use the Internet.[11] Many people spend more time on the Internet than they do watching TV, and online retail spending is expected to continue to increase at more than 25 percent a year.[12] Thus, online advertising will continue to increase.

Recall that Chapter 1 discussed the use of the Internet for e-business and e-commerce, as illustrated in Exhibit 1-8. Like customer-to-customer transactions, peer-to-peer (P2P) transactions allow employees to share files over the Internet, bypassing central databases, servers, control points, and Web pages. With the growing use of global virtual teams, P2P is increasing in importance.[13] The Internet has changed the way business is done.

BUSINESS PORTALS

AOL, MSN and **Yahoo**! are general-purpose portals, or windows to the Internet. A *business portal* is a specific company's gateway to Internet-based information. Computer experts develop portals to help employees get the useful information they need from within and outside the company to do their jobs and make effective decisions. Business portals allow specific categories of employees (sales reps, engineers, secretaries, or accountants) to access useful company information (inventories, production, or financials) and information from the Internet (industry news, competitor sales, and other information). The business portal saves employees hours of time looking for and at data that is not useful; it also converts data into useful information (timely, relevant, and understandable).

DATABASES

Employees can access data and information from the company database through the company intranet or the company Web site. They can access databases on the World Wide Web either directly or through business portals. Some Web sites offer free information; others charge fees to access information.

Similarly, this book came with a password that gives you access to business information and business journal articles through the InfoTrac Web site. Your college may also subscribe to other databases that you may access. Credit card companies maintain databases about customers that are accessed when a customer's credit card is scanned; the database instantly determines if the card has been reported stolen. And the database that is maintained by the issuer of your debit card tells a vendor whether you have sufficient funds to cover the transaction.

When Tim Doreck started **Monterey Express** as a sole proprietor, chartering his diving boat so that scuba divers could explore Monterey Bay National Marine Sanctuary in California, he used his answering machine to take messages. He would return calls when he was not out on a trip. He realized that he was losing some business because by the time he returned calls, the people had already found another boat. Doreck also had to spend a lot of time on the phone and e-mailing, describing his charter service, answering questions, and giving directions.

Doreck did not want the expense of paying someone to answer the phone and take reservations. The solution was to set up a Web-based reservation system, powered by Time-Trade, which enabled customers to get information and book their charters online. Doreck says his phone bills have been cut dramatically, that he spends 70 percent less time sending e-mails, and that business is up by 30 percent.[14]

WIRELESS COMMUNICATION

The trend toward wireless communication will continue, as people are becoming increasingly mobile. Handheld devices allow people to get information when and where they need it. A sales rep in a customer's office can use a cell phone or other handheld device to check inventory, set delivery dates, and close a sale. Employees can use wireless communication to e-mail, share files, and tap into the company computer anytime from anywhere.

Join the Discussion   Ethics & Social Responsibility

Revenues

1. Should **Google** use the same business practices as Yahoo! and MSN?
2. Is Google hurting its shareholders by bypassing revenues that they should benefit from?
3. Is it ethical and socially responsible for **Yahoo**! and **MSN** to present search results based on companies' fees?

Google is the leading search engine; it went public by selling stock in 2004. Unlike its two leading competitors Yahoo! and Microsoft's MSN, Google presents search results that are automatically ranked by the frequency of user access. With Yahoo! and MSN, many of the links you see as the result of a search are there because companies paid to place them there. Google makes its money selling ads, which it clearly distinguishes from search results; some Yahoo! and MSN ads can be mistaken for search results.[15]

List the four steps in the interpersonal communication process.

THE INTERPERSONAL COMMUNICATION PROCESS AND COMMUNICATION BARRIERS

The communication process takes place between a sender who encodes a message and transmits it through a channel to a receiver who decodes it and may give feedback. Exhibit 11-2 illustrates the communication process.

Stage 1. The Sender Encodes the Message and Selects the Transmission Channel

ENCODING THE MESSAGE

The *sender* of the message is the person who initiates the communication. The *message* is the information and meaning communicated.[16] Communicators should have a clear objective for their messages.[17] **Encoding** *is the sender's process of putting the message into a form that the receiver will understand.*

SELECTING THE TRANSMISSION CHANNEL

The message is transmitted through a **communication channel**; *the three primary channels are oral, nonverbal, and written.* The sender should determine the most appropriate channel to meet the needs of the situation.[18]

Stage 2. The Sender Transmits the Message

After the sender encodes the message and selects the channel, he or she transmits the message through the channel to the receiver(s).

Exhibit 11-2 *The Communication Process*

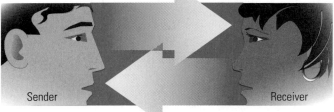

2. Message is transmitted through a channel.

1. Sender encodes the message and selects the transmission channel.

Sender

3. Receiver decodes the message and decides if feedback is needed.

Receiver

4. Feedback, response, or new message may be transmitted through a channel.

The sender and receiver continually change roles as they communicate.

WorkApplication2

Give an example of a message that might be transmitted in a work setting. Be sure to illustrate the four steps in the communication process, state the channel, and note if feedback was given.

_____

_____

_____

_____

Stage 3. The Receiver Decodes the Message and Decides If Feedback Is Needed

The person receiving the message decodes it. **Decoding** *is the receiver's process of translating a message into a meaningful form.* The receiver interprets the meaning of the message and decides if feedback, a response or a new message, is needed. With oral communication, feedback is commonly given immediately. However, with written communication, feedback may be delayed.

Stage 4. Feedback: A Response or a New Message May Be Transmitted

After the receiver decodes the message, he or she may give feedback to the sender. You should realize that the role of sender and receiver can change during a communication exchange. Remain open to messages being sent back from the receiver.

Communication Barriers

Exhibit 11-3 depicts a number of common barriers to communication.

PERCEPTION

As messages are transmitted, receivers perceive them and translate them so that they make sense.[19] *Semantics* and *jargon* can be communication barriers, because the same word often means different things to different people. For example, the phrase "wicked good" can be confusing to people not familiar with it who do not realize that it means "extremely good."

To overcome perception problems, you need to consider how the other person will most likely perceive the message and try to encode and transmit it appropriately. Thus, the choice of words is important. Be careful not to use jargon with people who are not familiar with the terminology, especially people from countries with different cultures.

INFORMATION OVERLOAD

There is a limit to the amount of information people can understand at any given time. Information overload is a common problem for new employees during the first few days, because they are often presented with too much information to comprehend in a short period of time.[20] With the widespread use of computers and with so many e-mails and information available, new managers often don't know what to do with it all.[21]

Exhibit 11-3 *Major Communication Barriers*

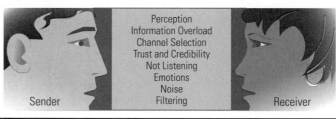

To minimize information overload, send messages in a quantity that the receiver can understand. When sending an oral message, do not talk for too long without checking to be sure the receiver understands the message as you intended. If you talk for too long, the receiver can become bored or lose the thread of the message.

CHANNEL SELECTION

Use of an inappropriate channel can result in missed communication. For example, if a manager catches an employee breaking a rule, the manager should use one-on-one, face-to-face communication. Another channel will not be as effective.

Before sending a message, give careful thought to selecting the most effective channel.

NOISE

Noise during the transmission of a message can disturb or confuse the receiver. Noise is anything that interferes with message transmission. For example, a machine or people may make noise that makes it difficult to hear, the sender may not speak loud enough for the receiver to hear well, or a radio or TV may distract the receiver, causing interpretation errors.

To overcome noise, you need to consider the physical surroundings before transmitting a message. Try to keep noise to a minimum. If possible, stop the noise or distraction or move to a quiet location.

TRUST AND CREDIBILITY

During communication, receivers take into account the trust they have in the senders, as well as the senders' credibility. When receivers do not trust senders or do not believe senders know what they are talking about, they are reluctant to accept the message.[22]

To improve others' level of trust in you, be open and honest with people. If people catch you in a lie, they may never trust you again. To gain and maintain credibility, get the facts straight before you communicate, and send clear, correct messages.[23]

POOR LISTENING

People usually hear what the sender is saying, but often they do not listen to the message or understand what is being transmitted. Poor listening is sometimes the result of not paying attention or other distractions.[24]

One method to help ensure that people listen to your message involves questioning them and having them paraphrase the message back to you. When listening, you should follow the listening tips presented later in this chapter.

EMOTIONS

Everyone has emotions, and emotions can interfere with communication and make it difficult for people to be objective and to listen.[25]

When communicating, you should remain calm and be careful not to make others emotional by your behavior. Later in this chapter you will learn how to calm an emotional employee.

WorkApplication3

Give two examples of different communication barriers you encountered at work. Explain how each barrier could have been overcome.

FILTERING

Filtering is the process of altering or distorting information to project a more favorable image. For example, when people are asked to report progress toward objectives, they may stress the positive and deemphasize, or even leave out, the negative side, or they may lie.

To help eliminate filtering, you should treat errors as a learning experience rather than as an opportunity to blame and criticize employees. You will learn about criticism later in this chapter. Using an open-door policy can create and support a two-way communication climate.

Applying The Concept 2

Communication Barriers

Identify the communication barrier indicated by each statement.

a. perception
b. information overload
c. channel selection
d. noise

e. trust and credibility
f. not listening
g. emotions
h. filtering

_____ 6. "Chill out. You shouldn't be upset."

_____ 7. "No questions" (meanwhile, thinking, "I was lost back on step one and don't know what to ask").

_____ 8. "We are right on schedule" (meanwhile, thinking, "We are actually behind, but we'll catch up").

_____ 9. "I said I'd do it in a little while. It's only been 15 minutes. Why do you expect it done by now?"

_____10. "You don't know what you are talking about. I'll do it my way."

—— **Learning** Outcome 3 ——

State the major advantages of oral communication and written communication.

MESSAGE TRANSMISSION CHANNELS

When encoding a message, the sender should give careful consideration to selecting the channel.[26] Channels (the ways in which messages are transmitted) include oral, nonverbal, and written forms. Exhibit 11-4 lists the major message transmission channels.

Oral Communication

The five most common channels for oral communication are face-to-face conversations, meetings, presentations, telephone conversations, and voice mail messages. The major advantage of oral communication is that it is usually easier and faster than written communication and encourages feedback.[27] The disadvantage is that there is usually no record of such communication.

Exhibit 11-4 *Message Transmission Channels*

Oral Communication	Nonverbal Communication	Written Communication
Face-to-face conversations	Setting	Memos
Meetings	Body language	Letters
Presentations	Facial expressions	Reports
Telephone conversations	Vocal quality	E-mail
Voice mail messages	Gestures	Faxes
	Posture	Bulletin boards
	Posters (pictures)	Posters (words)
		Newsletters

FACE-TO-FACE CONVERSATIONS

Managers should communicate one-on-one, face-to-face with employees.[28] Face-to-face communication is the appropriate channel for delegating tasks, coaching, disciplining, sharing information, answering questions, checking progress toward objectives, and developing and maintaining good interpersonal relations.

MEETINGS

Meetings were discussed in Chapter 10. The most common type of meeting is the brief, informal get-together of a manager with two or more employees. Meetings are appropriate for coordinating employee activities, delegating a task to a group, and resolving employee conflicts.[29]

PRESENTATIONS

As a manager you will very likely be required to make presentations to others on the job. Public speaking skills can help you advance. The same basic presentation skills are used for one-on-one communication and for large audiences. Begin your speech with an attention-grabbing opener. It could be a quotation, a joke, or an interesting story that will ignite interest in your topic.[30] Be sure to begin your presentation with a purpose statement and an overview of the main points to be covered; discuss your main points in the detail necessary to get the message across; and summarize the purpose, main points, and any action required of the audience.

The use of presentation software such as PowerPoint is becoming more popular. However, up-and-coming U.S. military officers were using so many "bells and whistles" in their electronic presentations that the Chairman of the Joint Chiefs of Staff ordered military personnel to tone down the technology. Listeners were complaining about too much noise, eye-popping animation, and complex graphs. The Chairman said that the medium was distracting attention from the message and that presenters ought to focus less on flash and more on getting the point across clearly and concisely.[31] Another problem with electronic slides is that people tend to just sit there and read them, which is boring. The presenter needs to communicate fully with the audience, with an outline of the key points appearing on the slides.

TELEPHONE CONVERSATIONS

The amount of time employees spend on the telephone varies greatly with the job. The telephone is the appropriate channel for quick exchanges of information and for checking up on something; phone calls often save managers from having to travel. However, a telephone conversation is an inappropriate channel for discussing or dealing with personnel matters. Increasingly, people are carrying cell phones at work, but they tend to have love-hate relationships with them. Having a cell phone can help get some tasks done faster, but a cell phone can be more annoying than an alarm clock![32]

VOICE MAIL

Voice mail is most commonly used to leave messages for people who don't answer the phone and sometimes in place of written messages. Voice mail is appropriate for sending short messages containing information that need not be in written form. An answering machine is a big help when you don't want to be disturbed.[33]

Nonverbal Communication

Every time you talk to someone face-to-face, you also use nonverbal communication. **Nonverbal communication** *consists of messages sent without words.* It includes the *setting* of the communication (physical surroundings) and *body language.* The impact of any face-to-face communication is dependent on body language, which includes (1) facial expressions (eye contact and a wink or a smile, a frown, or a dirty look);[34] (2) vocal quality (not the words used, but the way they are said—calmly or urgently, fast or slowly, softly or loudly);[35] (3) gestures (such as moving the hands, pointing and signaling, and nodding the head);[36] and (4) posture (sitting up straight or slouching, leaning back or forward, crossing arms and/or legs).

To make communication effective, you should be aware of your nonverbal communication and make sure it is consistent with your oral communication. You also want to be aware of other people's nonverbal communication because it reveals their feelings and attitudes toward the communication. When talking to people, use nonverbal communication to convey openness to messages. Smile, face the person, and use appropriate eye contact;[37] lean forward a bit and gesture frequently to convey that you are listening and are interested.[38] Do not cross your arms or legs (signs of being closed to communication), and speak in a pleasant, calm tone of voice.

Written Communication

Nothing can reveal your communication weaknesses more clearly than poorly written letters, memos, reports, e-mails, and so on. Organizations want to recruit employees with good writing skills, so you should learn to write effectively. (This chapter's appendix can help you improve your writing skills.) With the increasing use of e-mail, writing skills are becoming even more important. People frequently use e-mail rather than face-to-face communication or the telephone, as they believe it's the most effective channel.[39] The major advantage of written communication is that it provides a record of what was communicated. The major disadvantages are that it usually takes longer and it hinders feedback.

You are likely to encounter the following kinds of written communication in the workplace:

1. *Memos* are commonly used to send intraorganizational messages.
2. *Letters* are commonly used to communicate with people outside of the organization. In today's business world, memos and letters are sent electronically (in the form of e-mails or faxes) as often as they are sent through the mail. Sending written communication electronically saves time and paper.
3. *Reports* are used to convey information, evaluation, analysis, and/or recommendations to management or colleagues. Reports can also be sent by fax or as an attachment to e-mail.
4. *Bulletin board notices* usually supplement other forms of communication.
5. *Posters (or signs)* are commonly used as reminders of important information, such as a mission statement or safety instructions. Posters can also be nonverbal, or graphic, communication. An example is the universal symbol that bans or forbids some activity: a picture of what you are not supposed to do, circled and with a line through it.
6. *Newsletters* are used to convey general information to all employees.

Written communication is appropriate for transmitting general information, for saying thank-you, for messages requiring future action, for formal or official messages (especially those containing facts and figures), and for messages that affect several people in a related way.

Combining Channels

Nonverbal communication and oral communication are almost always combined. You can also combine oral and written communication (as in a presentation) or even oral, nonverbal, and written communication. Using combined

WorkApplication4
Give an example of an oral message and a written message you received at work and specify the channel of each.

_____

_____

_____

_____

Join the Discussion Ethics & Social Responsibility

Advertising

1. Is it ethical and socially responsible for food companies to use terms (like *natural*) that can be misleading?
2. How should the FDA define *natural* so that the word is not used to mislead people?

Companies use oral, nonverbal, and written communication to advertise their products in order to increase sales. Selecting the best words to sell a product or service is important. However, some of the terms used in ads are misleading or deceptive, even though the words themselves are legal. For example, some food products are labeled with the word *natural* but are highly processed, such as products including a lot of white sugar. Also, ads for some processed snack foods use the word *natural*, which leads people to think the snacks are healthy, when in fact others classify them as junk food. The obesity task force of the Food and Drug Administration (FDA) is trying to crack down on misleading labels and ads and is calling for warnings and fines for violators.[40]

Applying The Concept 3

Channel Selection

For each of the five communication situations, select the most appropriate channel for transmitting the message. If you would use a combination of channels, place the letter(s) of the additional channel you would use at the end of the situation.

Oral communication	Written communication	
a. face-to-face	e. memo	h. bulletin board
b. meeting	f. letter	i. poster
c. presentation	g. report	j. newsletter
d. telephone		

_____11. You are waiting for FedEx to deliver an important letter, and you want to know if it is in the mail room yet. _____

_____12. Employees have been leaving the lights on in the stock room when no one is in it. You want them to shut the lights off. _____

_____13. José, Jamal, and Sam will be working as a team on a new project. You need to explain the project to them. _____

_____14. John has come in late for work again; you want this practice to stop. _____

_____15. You have exceeded your departmental goals and want your boss to know about it, because this success should have a positive influence on your upcoming performance appraisal. _____

channels is appropriate when the message is important and you want to ensure that employees attend to and understand it. For example, managers sometimes send a memo, then follow up with a personal visit or telephone call to see if there are any questions. Managers often formally document a face-to-face meeting, particularly in a disciplinary situation.

IOM

Michael Powell used the written communication channel when he sent a memo to employees announcing that he was limiting pay raises and restructuring. This was one-way communication, as Powell did not ask for any feedback from employees about the memo, nor did he use a combined channel.

—————————— Learning Outcome 4 ——————————
State a general guide to channel selection.

Selecting the Message Transmission Channel

It's important to select the most appropriate channel of transmission for any message.

Media richness refers to the amount of information and meaning conveyed through a channel. The more information and meaning, the "richer" the channel. Face-to-face is the richest channel because it allows sender and receiver to take full advantage of both oral and nonverbal communication. The telephone is less rich than face-to-face because most nonverbal cues are lost when you cannot see facial expressions and gestures. All forms of oral communication are richer than written communication because oral communication allows transmission of at least some nonverbal cues, which are lost with written messages.

As a general guide, use oral channels for sending difficult and unusual messages, written channels for transmitting simple and routine messages to several people, and combined channels for important messages that recipients need to attend to and understand.

SENDING MESSAGES

Have you ever heard a manager say, "This isn't what I asked for"? When this happens, it is usually the manager's fault. A common complaint of people in all kinds of jobs is that bosses don't give clear instructions.[41] As a manager, you must take 100 percent of the responsibility for ensuring that your messages are transmitted clearly.[42]

Planning the Message

The vast majority of messages you send and receive in the workplace are quite simple and straightforward: "Please copy this document." "I'll call you when I've reviewed the specifications." "I put the report you requested on your desk." Many such messages are transmitted orally and face-to-face or in a brief memo, e-mail, or fax. Such straightforward messages need minimal planning, because they are routine. However, sometimes the message you need to transmit is difficult, unusual, or especially important. For example, you may have the difficult task of communicating to someone that he or she is to be laid off. Or, perhaps you need to communicate to workers at one plant about the changes that will be occurring as a result of closing a second plant and moving its processes to this one—an unusual situation and an important communication. As noted above, for these kinds of messages, the richer the channel, the better.

Before sending a message, you should answer these what, who, how, when, and where questions:

- *What*? What is the goal of the message? What do you want the end result of the communication to be? Set an objective.[43]
- *Who*? Determine who should receive the message.
- *How*? With the receiver(s) in mind, plan how you will encode the message so that it will be understood.[44] Select the appropriate channel(s) for the audience and situation.
- *When*? When will the message be transmitted? Timing is important. For example, if you have a message for an employee that you want to deliver in person, but it is going to take 15 minutes to transmit it, don't approach the employee 5 minutes before quitting time. Wait until the next day. Make an appointment when appropriate.
- *Where*? Decide where the message will be transmitted (setting). Will you speak to an employee in your office? Will you send a memo to a colleague's workplace?

Join the Discussion Ethics & Social Responsibility

Advertising to Underage Viewers

1. Do you believe that some ads for alcohol intentionally target underage viewers?
2. Is it ethical and socially responsible for alcoholic beverage companies to target underage viewers?
3. Do you believe the government should take action against the producers of alcoholic beverages? If so, what should it do?

Advertising spending by the alcoholic beverage industry is currently nearly $1 billion a year, and a study found that underage television viewers are often targeted. One law firm filed a suit alleging that liquor and beer companies negligently target underage drinkers in their ads.[45] Groups and individuals have contacted TV stations, pressing for fewer alcohol ads during sports broadcasts. The industry claims that its ads are not meant to target underage viewers; rather, it just happens that those viewers like the ads.

—————————————— Learning Outcome 5 ——————————————
List the five steps in the process of sending face-to-face messages.

The Message-Sending Process

As noted earlier, oral channels are richer than other channels, and face-to-face, oral communication is best when the message you must transmit is a difficult or complex one. When sending a face-to-face message, follow these steps in the **message-sending process**:

Step 1. Develop rapport. Put the receiver at ease. It is usually appropriate to begin communication with small talk related to the message.[46]

Step 2. State your communication objective. It is helpful for the receiver to know the objective (end result) of the communication before you explain the details.[47]

Step 3. Transmit your message. Tell the receiver(s) whatever you want them to know.

Step 4. Check the receiver's understanding. When giving information, you should ask direct questions and/or paraphrase.[48] Simply asking "Do you have any questions?" does not check understanding. (The next subsection describes how to check understanding.)

Step 5. Get a commitment and follow up. If the message involves assigning a task, make sure that the message recipient can do the task and have it done by a certain time or date. When employees are reluctant to commit to the necessary action, managers can use persuasive power within their authority. Follow up to ensure that the necessary action has been taken.[49]

Exhibit 11-5 lists the five steps in the message-sending process.

WorkApplication5

Recall a specific task that a boss assigned to you. Identify which steps in the face-to-face message-sending process he or she did and did not use.

_____

_____

_____

_____

_____

Exhibit 11-5 *The Message-Sending Process*

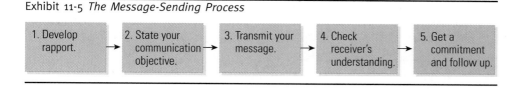

1. Develop rapport. → 2. State your communication objective. → 3. Transmit your message. → 4. Check receiver's understanding. → 5. Get a commitment and follow up.

―――――――――――――― Learning Outcome 6 ――――――――――――――
Describe paraphrasing, and explain why it is useful.

Checking Understanding: Feedback

Feedback *is information that verifies a message.* Questioning, paraphrasing, and inviting comments and suggestions are all means of obtaining feedback that check understanding. Being asked for their feedback motivates employees to achieve high levels of performance and improves retention.[50] The best way to make sure communication has taken place is to get feedback from the receiver of the message through questioning and paraphrasing.[51] **Paraphrasing** *is the process of restating a message in one's own words.*

THE COMMON APPROACH TO GETTING FEEDBACK ON MESSAGES AND WHY IT DOESN'T WORK

The most common approach to getting feedback is to send the entire message and then ask "Do you have any questions?" Feedback usually does not follow because people tend not to ask questions—for three reasons:

1. *Receivers feel ignorant.* To ask a question, especially if no one else does, is often considered an admission of not paying attention or not being bright enough to understand the message.
2. *Receivers are ignorant.* Sometimes people do not know enough about the message to judge whether it is incomplete, incorrect, or subject to interpretation. There are no questions because what was said sounds right. The receiver does not understand the message and so does not know what to ask.
3. *Receivers are reluctant to point out the sender's ignorance.* This commonly occurs when the sender is a manager and the receiver is an employee. Employees often fear that asking a question will suggest that the manager has done a poor job of preparing and sending the message or that the manager is wrong.[52] Generally, employees fear reprisal for pointing out that a message is poor or incorrect.

After managers send a message and ask if there are questions, they often make another common error. They assume that if no one asks a question, the communication is complete.[53] In fact, recipients may have misunderstood the message. When this occurs, the result is often wasted time, materials, and effort.

The most common reason that messages do not actually communicate what was intended is that senders fail to get feedback.[54] The proper use of questioning and paraphrasing can help ensure that your messages are communicated correctly.

HOW TO GET FEEDBACK ON MESSAGES

You should use the following four guidelines when seeking feedback on messages.

1. *Be open to feedback.* There are no dumb questions. When someone asks a question, you need to be responsive and patiently answer and explain things clearly. If people sense that you get upset if they ask questions, they will not ask. Also, if managers get upset with employees who bring them bad news (negative feedback), employees will tend to avoid these managers and keep bad news to themselves.[55]

   One day before the *Columbia* space shuttle disaster on February 1, 2003, **National Aeronautics and Space Administration (NASA)** engineers debated, by phone and e-mail, potential wing damage from extreme heat, similar to what investigators believe caused the tragic event. However, for some still unclear reasons, the engineers never told top NASA managers about the potential problem. Did they fear bringing bad news?[56]

2. *Be aware of nonverbal communication.* Make sure that your nonverbal communication encourages feedback. For example, if you say "I encourage questions," but you look at people as though they are stupid or you act impatient when they do ask, people will learn not to ask questions. You must also read nonverbal communication accurately. For example, if you are explaining a task to an employee and he has a puzzled look on his face, he is probably confused but may not be willing to say so. In such a case, you should stop and clarify things before going on.

3. *Ask questions.* When you send messages, you should know whether recipients understand the messages before taking action. Direct questions about the specific information you have given will indicate if the receiver has been listening and whether he or she understands enough to give an appropriate reply. If the response is not accurate, you need to repeat the message, giving more examples or elaborating further.[57]

4. *Paraphrase.* The most accurate indicator of understanding is paraphrasing. How you ask the receiver to paraphrase will affect his or her attitude. For example, saying "Tell me what I just said so that I can be sure you will not make a mistake as usual" would probably result in defensive behavior or an error by the employee. Consider these examples of proper requests for paraphrasing:

   "Now tell me what you are going to do so that we will be sure we are in agreement."

   "Would you tell me what you are going to do so that I can be sure that I explained myself clearly?"

   Notice that the second statement takes the pressure off the employee. The sender is asking for a check on his or her own ability, not that of the employee. These types of requests for paraphrasing should result in a positive attitude toward the message and the sender. They show concern for the employee and for communicating effectively.[58]

WorkApplication6

Recall a past or present boss. How effective was this person at getting feedback? Was the boss open to feedback and aware of nonverbal communication? Did the boss ask questions and ask you to paraphrase?

_____

_____

_____

_____

_____

Michael Powell's communication objective appears to have been simple and clear. However, he transmitted his message to employees by means of a memo announcing that he was limiting pay raises and restructuring. The memo did not ask for feedback from employees as to whether they understood the reasons for pay limits and restructuring. Thus, employees did not commit to the changes, nor did management follow up to see how the changes were affecting employees.

RECEIVING MESSAGES

The third step in the communication process requires the receiver to decode the message and decide if feedback is needed. With oral communication, the key to successfully understanding the message is listening.[59]

Listening Skills

Complete the Self-Assessment to determine the level and quality of your listening skills. The text provides tips for improving listening skills in the message-receiving process.

Self-Assessment

Listening Skills

For each statement, select the response that best describes how often you actually behave in the way described. Place the letter A, U, F, O, or S on the line before each statement.

A = almost always   U = usually   F = frequently
O = occasionally   S = seldom

_____ 1. I like to listen to people talk. I encourage others to talk by showing interest, smiling, nodding, and so forth.

_____ 2. I pay closer attention to people who are more similar to me than to people who are different from me.

_____ 3. I evaluate people's words and nonverbal communication ability as they talk.

_____ 4. I avoid distractions; if it's noisy, I suggest moving to a quiet spot.

_____ 5. When people interrupt me when I'm doing something, I put what I was doing out of my mind and give them my complete attention.

_____ 6. When people are talking, I allow them time to finish. I do not interrupt, anticipate what they are going to say, or jump to conclusions.

_____ 7. I tune people out who do not agree with my views.

_____ 8. While another person is talking or a professor is lecturing, my mind wanders to personal topics.

_____ 9. While another person is talking, I pay close attention to the nonverbal communication so I can fully understand what he or she is trying to communicate.

_____ 10. I tune out and pretend I understand when the topic is difficult for me to understand.

_____ 11. When another person is talking, I think about and prepare what I am going to say in reply.

_____ 12. When I think there is something missing from or contradictory in what someone says, I ask direct questions to get the person to explain the idea more fully.

_____ 13. When I don't understand something, I let the other person know I don't understand.

_____ 14. When listening to other people, I try to put myself in their position and see things from their perspective.

_____ 15. During conversations I repeat back to the other person what has been said in my own words to be sure I understand what has been said.

If people you talk to regularly answered these questions about you, would they have the same responses that you selected? To find out, have friends fill out the questions using "you" (or your name) rather than "I." Then compare answers.

To determine your score, give yourself 5 points for each A, 4 for each U, 3 for each F, 2 for each O, and 1 for each S for statements 1, 4, 5, 6, 9, 12, 13, 14, and 15. For items 2, 3, 7, 8, 10, and 11 the scores reverse: 5 points for each S, 4 for each O, 3 for each F, 2 for each U, and 1 for each A. Write the number of points on the lines next to the response letters. Now add your total number of points. Your score should be between 15 and 75. Note where your score falls on the continuum below. Generally, the higher your score, the better your listening skills.

Poor listener   Good listener

15—20—25—30—35—40—45—50—55—60—65—70—75

Listening is one of the most important business and personal skills you can develop.[60] You need to practice in order to develop active listening skills that encourage others to be more communicative.[61] You learn when you listen, and listening clues you in to the other party's needs and desires.[62] This is why listening is so important in sales, negotiation, and conflict resolution. By using the message-receiving process, you can become a better listener.

──────────────── Learning Outcome 7 ────────────────
List and explain the three parts of the process of receiving messages.

The Message-Receiving Process

The **message-receiving process** *includes listening, analyzing, and checking understanding.* To improve your listening skills, spend one week focusing your attention on listening by concentrating on what other people say and the nonverbal communication they use when they speak. Talk only when necessary. If you apply the following tips, you will improve your listening skills. The message-receiving process is illustrated in Exhibit 11-6.

LISTENING

Listening is the process of giving a speaker your undivided attention. As the speaker sends the message, you should be doing the following:

- *Paying attention.* When people begin to talk, stop what you are doing and give them your complete attention immediately. If you miss the first few words, you may miss the message.[63]
- *Avoiding distractions.* Keep your eyes on the speaker. Do not fiddle with pens, papers, or other distractions. If you are in a noisy or distracting place, suggest moving to a quiet spot or talking later.[64]
- *Staying tuned in.* While the other person is talking, try not to let your mind wander.[65] Also, do not tune out the speaker because you do not like something about the person or because you disagree with what is being said. If the topic is difficult, ask questions. Do not think about what you are going to say in reply; just listen. As you listen, mentally paraphrase the message to stay tuned in.[66]

Exhibit 11-6 *The Message-Receiving Process*

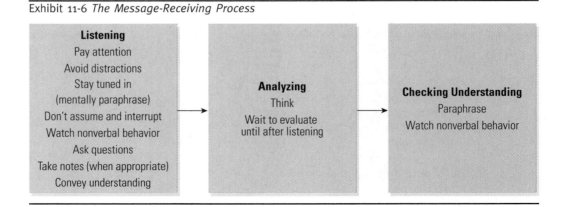

- *Not assuming and interrupting.* People make listening mistakes when they hear the first few words of a sentence, finish it in their own minds, and miss the second half. Listen to the entire message without interrupting the speaker.[67]
- *Watching nonverbal behavior.* Your goal is to understand both the feelings and the content of the message. People sometimes say one thing and mean something else. So watch as you listen to be sure that the speaker's eyes, body, and face are sending the same message as the verbal message. If something seems out of sync, get it cleared up by asking questions.
- *Asking questions.* When you feel there is something missing or contradictory in what is being said, or when you just do not understand, ask direct questions to get the person to explain the idea more fully.
- *Taking notes (when appropriate).* In work settings, part of listening is writing down important things (such as instructions) so that you can remember them later, and documenting them when necessary.[68] You should always have something to write with.
- *Conveying understanding.* The way to let the speaker know you are listening to the message is to use verbal cues, such as "uh huh," "I see," and "I understand." You should also use nonverbal communication, such as eye contact, appropriate facial expressions, nodding of the head, or leaning slightly forward in your chair to indicate you are interested and listening.

ANALYZING

Analyzing is the process of thinking about, decoding, and evaluating the message. Poor listening is caused in part by the fact that people speak at an average rate of 120 words per minute, but they are capable of listening at a rate of 600 words per minute. The ability to comprehend words more than five times faster than the speaker can talk allows the listener's mind to wander. As the speaker sends the message, you should be doing two things:

- *Thinking.* To help overcome the discrepancy between your listening speed and people's rate of speaking, use the speed of your brain positively. Listen actively by mentally paraphrasing, organizing, summarizing, reviewing, and interpreting often. These activities will help you to do an effective job of decoding the message.
- *Waiting to evaluate until after listening.* When people try to listen and evaluate what is said at the same time, they tend to miss part or all of the message. You should listen to the entire message first, then come to your conclusions. When you evaluate, base your conclusion on the facts presented rather than on stereotypes and politics.[69]

CHECKING UNDERSTANDING

Checking understanding is the process of giving feedback. After you have listened to the message (or while listening if it's a long message), check your understanding of the message by doing two things:

- *Paraphrasing.* Give feedback by paraphrasing the message back to the sender. When you can paraphrase the message correctly, you convey that you have listened and understood the other person.[70] Now you are ready

WorkApplication7

Refer to the Self-Assessment. What is your weakest listening skill? Give an example of how your listening skills have had an impact on you at work.

to offer your ideas, advice, solution, decision, or whatever the sender of the message is talking to you about.

- *Watching nonverbal behavior.* As you speak, watch the other person's nonverbal communication. If the person does not seem to understand what you are talking about, clarify the message before finishing the conversation.

Do you talk more than you listen? Ask your boss, coworkers, or friends, who will give you an honest answer. Regardless of how much you listen, if you follow the guidelines discussed in this section, you will become a better listener. Review items 1, 4, 5, 6, 9, 12, 13, 14, and 15 in the Self-Assessment, which are the statements that describe good listening skills. Effective listening requires responding to the message to ensure mutual understanding.

IOM | **Michael Powell and his managers used one-way communication and did not listen to employees or give them a chance to express their concerns about how the changes at Powell's Books would affect them and their jobs. Managers did not bother to use good listening skills with regard to decisions about pay limits and restructuring.**

RESPONDING TO MESSAGES

The fourth, and last, step in the communication process is responding to the message. However, not all messages require a response.

With oral communication, the sender often expects the receiver to respond to the message. When the receiver does respond, the roles are reversed, as the receiver now becomes the sender of a message. Roles can continue to change throughout the conversation. In this section, we discuss five response styles, how to deal with emotional people, and how to give and receive criticism.

Response Styles

As a sender transmits a message, how the receiver responds to the message directly affects the communication. The response should be appropriate for the situation. Five typical response styles are shown in Exhibit 11-7.

Suppose an employee voices the following complaint to her supervisor: "You supervise me so closely that you disrupt my ability to do my job." We will consider how a manager might respond to this complaint using each response style.

ADVISING

Advising responses provide evaluation, personal opinion, direction, or instructions.[71] Employees often come to a manager for advice on how to do something or to ask the manager to make a decision. Advising tends to close or limit discussion or direct the flow of communication away from the sender to the receiver.

Giving advice is appropriate when you are explicitly asked for it. However, automatically giving advice tends to build dependence. Managers need to develop their employees' abilities to think things through and to make decisions. When asked for advice by an employee you believe doesn't really need it, ask, "What do you think is the best way to handle this situation?"

Exhibit 11-7 *Five Typical Response Styles*

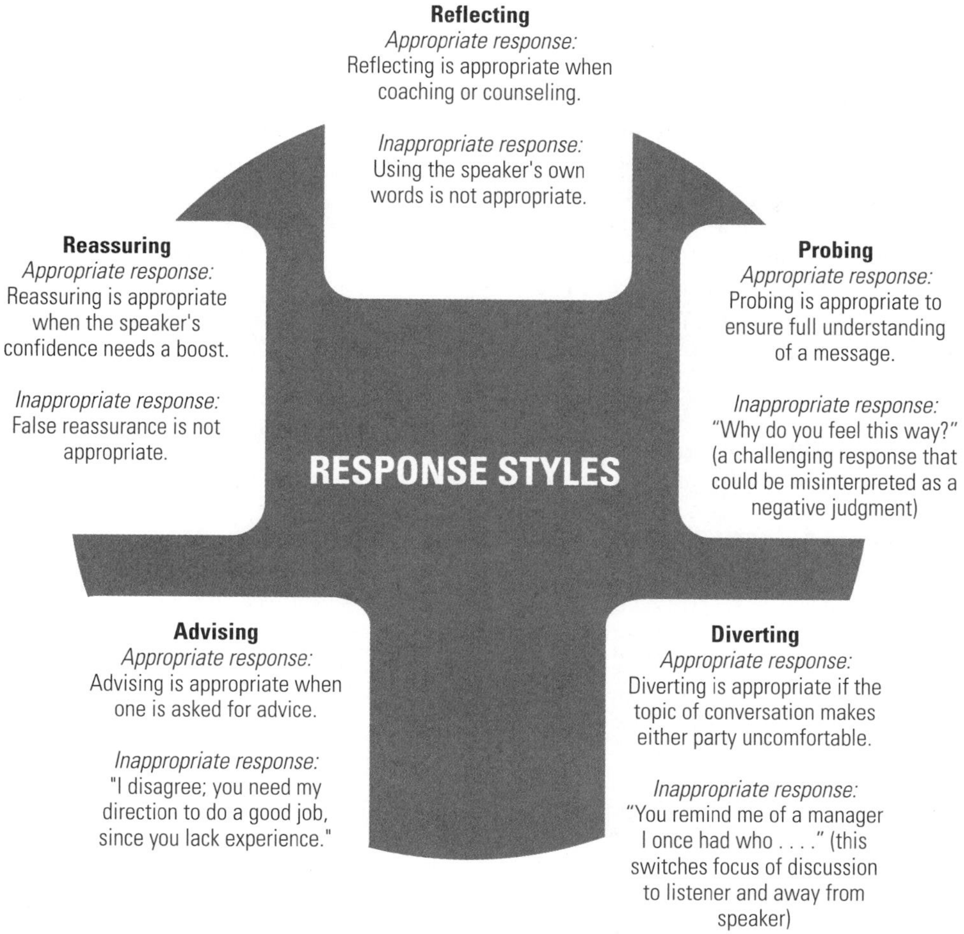

Reflecting
Appropriate response:
Reflecting is appropriate when coaching or counseling.

Inappropriate response:
Using the speaker's own words is not appropriate.

Reassuring
Appropriate response:
Reassuring is appropriate when the speaker's confidence needs a boost.

Inappropriate response:
False reassurance is not appropriate.

RESPONSE STYLES

Probing
Appropriate response:
Probing is appropriate to ensure full understanding of a message.

Inappropriate response:
"Why do you feel this way?" (a challenging response that could be misinterpreted as a negative judgment)

Advising
Appropriate response:
Advising is appropriate when one is asked for advice.

Inappropriate response:
"I disagree; you need my direction to do a good job, since you lack experience."

Diverting
Appropriate response:
Diverting is appropriate if the topic of conversation makes either party uncomfortable.

Inappropriate response:
"You remind me of a manager I once had who . . . ." (this switches focus of discussion to listener and away from speaker)

A manager's advising response to the employee's complaint might be "You need my directions to do a good job; you lack experience" or "I disagree. You need my instructions, and I need to check your work." Note that in this situation the employee did not ask for advice, but it was given anyway.

DIVERTING

Diverting responses switch the focus of the communication to a new message—in other words, they change the subject. Like advising, diverting tends to redirect, close, or limit the flow of communication. Diverting responses used during the early stages of receiving the message may cause the sender to feel that the message is not worth discussing or that the other party's message is more important.[72]

A diverting response can be appropriate when either party is uncomfortable with the topic. Diverting responses may be helpful when they share personal experiences or feelings that are similar to those of the sender, even though they change the topic.

A manager's diverting response to the employee's complaint might be: "You've reminded me of a manager I once had who . . . ."

PROBING

Probing responses ask the speaker to give more information about some aspect of the message. Probing can be useful when a listener needs to get a better understanding of the situation. When probing, "what" questions are preferable to "why" questions.

Probing is appropriate during the early stages of listening to a message to ensure that you fully understand the situation. After probing, responses in other styles are often needed.

A manager's probing response to the employee's complaint might be "What do I do to cause you to say this?" Note that "Why do you feel this way?" is *not* an appropriate probing response.

REASSURING

Reassuring responses are given to reduce the intensity of the emotions associated with the message. Essentially you're saying, "Don't worry; everything will be OK" or "You can do it." You are trying to calm the sender.

Reassuring is appropriate when the other person lacks confidence. Encouraging responses that give praise can help employees develop confidence.

A manager's reassuring response to the employee's complaint might be "Don't worry, I will not be supervising you so closely for much longer" or "Your work is improving, so I may be able to provide less direction soon."

—————————————— Learning Outcome 8 ——————————————
Define reflecting responses, and state when they should be used.

REFLECTING

Reflecting responses *paraphrase the message and communicate understanding and acceptance to the sender.* When reflecting, be sure *not* to use the sender's exact words, or the person may feel you are mimicking him or her, not understanding, or not listening closely. Reflecting in your own words leads to the most effective communication and the best human relations.

Reflecting responses should be used when coaching and counseling. Such responses help make the sender feel listened to, understood, and free to explore the topic in more depth.[73] As the communication progresses, it is often appropriate to change to other response styles.

A manager's reflecting response to the employee's complaint might be "My checking up on you annoys you?" or "You don't think I need to check up on you, is this what you mean?" Note that these responses allow the employee to express feelings and to direct the communication.

Dealing with Emotional People

As a manager, you may receive a message from an employee or customer who is in an emotional state. Emotions tend to complicate communication, but they can bring about new ideas and new ways of doing things.[74] You should understand emotions and how to deal with them.

WorkApplication8

Recall two oral messages you received and your responses to them. Identify your response style, and give examples of responses you might have given using two other response styles.

_____

_____

_____

_____

Identifying Response Styles

Identify the response style exemplified in each statement.

a. advising
b. diverting
c. probing
d. reflecting
e. reassuring

Secretary: Boss, do you have a minute to talk?

Boss: Sure, what's up?

Secretary: Can you do something about all the swearing people do in the operations department? It carries through these thin walls into my work area. It's disgusting. I'm surprised you haven't done anything.

Boss:

_____16. "I didn't know anyone was swearing. I'll look into it."

_____17. "You don't have to listen to it. Just ignore the swearing."

_____18. "Are you feeling well today?"

_____19. "So you find this swearing offensive?"

_____20. "What specific swear words are they saying that offend you?"

Understanding emotions to some extent depends on one's level of *emotional intelligence*. Emotional intelligence has five dimensions: (1) self-awareness, or understanding your own emotions; (2) self-management, the ability to manage your own emotions; (3) self-motivation, the ability to persist through failure and setbacks; (4) empathy, the ability to understand others' emotions and to see things from their perspective; and (5) social skills that allow one to handle others' emotions. Emotionally intelligent people are stable. One's level of emotional intelligence is also called one's *emotional quotient*, or EQ (to parallel the notion of intelligence quotient, or IQ). Some companies have developed EQ tests that employees can take, as emotional intelligence is considered important to individual and organizational success.[75]

When dealing with emotional people, keep the following in mind:

- Feelings are subjective; they tell us people's attitudes and needs.
- Feelings are usually disguised as factual statements. For example, when people are hot, they tend to say "It's hot in here" rather than "I feel hot." When they are bored, they tend to say "This topic is boring," rather than "I'm feeling bored by this topic."
- Most important: feelings are neither right nor wrong.

People cannot choose their feelings, or control them. However, they can control how they express feelings. For example, if Rachel, an employee, says "You *!!" (pick a word that would make you angry) to Louise, her manager, Louise will feel its impact. However, Louise has a choice about how she responds. She can express her feelings in a calm manner, or she can yell back, give Rachel a dirty look, write up a formal reprimand for Rachel's personnel file, and so on. Managers should encourage people to express their feelings in a positive way, but they can't allow employees to go around yelling at, swearing at, or intimidating others. You should avoid getting caught up in others' emotions. Staying calm when dealing with an emotional person works much better than getting emotional, too.[76]

Learning Outcome 9
Discuss what should and should not be done
to calm an emotional person.

CALMING THE EMOTIONAL EMPLOYEE

When an employee comes to you in an emotional state, *never* make condescending statements such as "You shouldn't be angry," "Don't be upset," "You're acting like a baby," or "Just sit down and be quiet." These types of statements only make the feelings stronger. You may get employees to shut up and show them who is boss, but effective communication will not take place. The problem will still exist, and your relations with the employee will suffer because of it, as will your relations with others who see or hear about what you said and did. When the employee complains to peers, some peers will feel you were too hard or easy on the person. You lose either way.

REFLECTIVE EMPATHIC RESPONDING

Empathic listening *is understanding and relating to another's feelings.* The empathic responder deals with feelings, content, and the underlying meaning being expressed in the message. Empathy is needed to develop human relationships based on trust. Don't argue with emotional people. Instead, encourage them to express their feelings in a positive way.[77] Empathically let them know that you understand how they feel. Do not agree or disagree with the feelings; simply identify them verbally. Paraphrase the feeling to the person. Use statements such as these: "You were *hurt* when you didn't get the assignment." "You *resent* Charlie for not doing his share of the work; is that what you mean?" "You are *doubtful* that the job will be done on time; is that what you're saying?"

When Carly Fiorina took over as CEO of **Hewlett-Packard**, outgoing CEO Lew Platt wanted to mentor Fiorina. However, she feared that Platt would advise slowing down her fast rate of change, so Fiorina did not seek his counsel. This did not please Platt, who talked negatively about her to HP's board. During this board meeting, Fiorina was sitting in her office, knowing that the board was talking about her behind her back. Chairman of the Board Dick Hackborn came into her office and sat down with Fiorina, and she expected the worst as they talked about Platt's concerns. But Fiorina recalls him being comforting, empathic, and supportive.[78]

After you deal with emotions, you can proceed to work on content (solving problems). It may be wise to wait until a later time if emotions are very strong. You may find that just being willing to listen to others' feelings is often the solution. Sometimes employees simply need to vent their emotions. A manager with strong listening skills may be just the solution employees need.[79]

I O M — **A major problem at Powell's Books was the fact that managers did not seek employee feedback. Rather than sending a memo, Michael Powell could have met with small groups of employees to explain the changes and why they were needed and to give employees the chance to express their emotional concerns about how the changes**

WorkApplication9

Recall a situation in which a manager had to handle an emotional employee. Did the manager follow the guidelines for calming an emotional person? Did the manager use reflective empathic responses?

**I
O
M**

would affect them and their jobs. By encouraging feedback and dealing with emotions, Powell might have avoided the build-up of negative emotions that led to unionization.

Criticism

GIVING CRITICISM

An important part of the manager's job is to improve employee performance through constructive criticism.[80] Chapter 14 will show you how to accomplish this task.

Criticism that moves upward is a different matter. Even when bosses ask, they usually don't want to hear personal criticism. If your boss asks you in a meeting for feedback on how good a manager he or she is or how he or she can improve, it may sound like the ideal opportunity to unload your complaints—but in such a situation, the first rule of thumb is to never publicly criticize your boss, even if specifically asked to do so. You are better off airing criticism in private. Don't criticize your boss behind his or her back either; bosses often find out about it.

GETTING CRITICISM

If you ask someone for critical feedback, remember that you are asking to hear things that may surprise, upset, or insult you, or hurt your feelings. If you become defensive and emotional (and it is hard not to when you feel attacked), the person will stop giving feedback.[81] The criticizer will probably tell others what happened, and others will not give you truthful feedback either. Criticism from your boss, peers, or employees is painful. People do not really enjoy being criticized, even when it is constructive.[82] Keep the phrase "no pain, no gain" in mind when it comes to criticism. If you want to improve your performance, and your chances of having a successful career, seek honest feedback. When you get criticism, whether you ask for it or not, view it as an opportunity to improve, stay calm (even when the other person is emotional), and don't get defensive. Use the feedback to improve your performance.[83]

WorkApplication10

How would you rate yourself on your ability to accept criticism without getting emotional and defensive? How could you improve your ability to accept criticism?

_____

_____

_____

_____

INFORMATION SYSTEMS

Like any system, an information system has input, transformation, and output. Information systems (IS) have data as input, and they transform the data into information to help employees do their jobs and make decisions. These systems are used to communicate with employees throughout organizations and on the interpersonal level. In this section, we discuss types of information systems and information networks.

─────────── Learning Outcome 10 ───────────

Describe the three primary types of information systems and their relationship.

Types of Information Systems

The three primary types of information systems are transaction processing systems, management information systems, and decision support systems.

TRANSACTION PROCESSING SYSTEMS (TPS)

Transaction processing systems are used to handle routine and recurring business matters.[84] Most organizations use transaction processing systems to record accounting transactions, such as accounts receivable and payable and payroll. Most large retail organizations use scanners to record sales transactions at the checkout counter. Banks process checks and deposits and record credit card transactions. Stockbrokers buy and sell stock for clients. Airlines and travel agents make flight reservations.

MANAGEMENT INFORMATION SYSTEMS (MIS)

Management information systems transform data into the information employees need to do their work. Managers' work usually consists of running their units or departments, and the information provided by management information systems is commonly used for making routine decisions.

General Motors developed the business portal **"mySocrates"** to enable GM employees to easily link GM information systems to hundreds of thousands of other GM Web sites and information services. mySocrates helps employees do their jobs more effectively, and it even allows them to update their own human resources files themselves by changing telephone numbers or addresses or the allocation of their 401(k) plans. GM hopes that mySocrates will become employees' main work and nonwork portal, replacing **Yahoo!** or other similar portals.[85]

Executive information systems (EIS) are a form of management information systems used by top-level managers. Executive information systems place greater emphasis on integrating external data and information with internal information on critical success factors, which are often industry-specific. In other words, executive information systems focus more on development and revision of strategy, whereas management information systems focus more on strategy implementation.

DECISION SUPPORT SYSTEMS (DSS)

Decision support systems use managers' insights in an interactive computer-based process to assist in making nonroutine decisions. They use decision rules, decision models, and comprehensive databases. Decision support systems are more flexible than management information systems. However, a decision support system can interact with a management information system by applying specific mathematical operations to the information available in the management information systems. These data manipulations allow managers to evaluate the possible effects of alternative decisions. For example, capital budgeting decisions (Chapter 14) can be made with the help of a decision support system. These systems can let managers know in days, rather than months, how a discounting promotion is affecting sales, for example. They can also spot a competitor's challenge before it does too much damage.

Expert systems are computer programs designed to imitate the thought processes of a human being. They build on a series of rules ("if-then" scenarios) to move from a set of data to a decision.

Boeing uses an expert system called CASE (Connector Assembly Specification Expert). CASE produces assembly procedures for each of the 5,000 electrical connectors on Boeing airplanes. It takes the computer only a few minutes to get a printout for a specific connector, which saves about 45 minutes of searching through 20,000 pages of printed material.

Applying The Concept 5

Types of Information Systems

Identify the type of information system that would be appropriate in each case.

a. transaction processing system   d. decision support system

b. management information system   e. expert systems

c. executive information system

_____ 21. A manager wants to know if an important order has been shipped yet.

_____ 22. A manager wants to determine how many checkout counters to have in a new store.

_____ 23. A small business owner wants to use an accounting software program.

_____ 24. A manager intuitively knows how to schedule customers. A top manager wants to help others do a good job of scheduling, too.

_____ 25. The CEO is working on the company's long-range plan.

— Learning Outcome 11 —

List the components of an information network.

Information Networks

Information networks apply information technology to connect all employees of an organization to each other, to suppliers, to customers, and to databases. Information networks are used to integrate information systems,[86] and at many organizations, networks are the primary means for employees to learn how to do their jobs, to find information, and to solve problems.[87] Exhibit 11-8 illustrates an information network, and its components are discussed in the following subsections.

Exhibit 11-8 *Information Network*

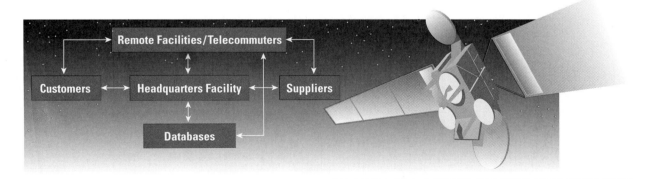

CONNECTING ALL EMPLOYEES (P2P)

Many organizations use *intranets* to connect all employees, anywhere in the world, to each other and to information through an internal Web site. An intranet uses a firewall to keep unauthorized people from getting access to the private network or to prevent employees from obtaining certain data, like confidential personnel files. Employees can share useful information using groupware. Intranets are P2P (peer to peer) networks.

CONNECTING WITH CUSTOMERS (B2C)

Information networks, in the form of *customer relationship management* (CRM) systems, are used to facilitate faster responses to customers' problems and needs. CRM software enables employees to track customers' interactions with the firm and to view information on past transactions, allowing them to provide personalized service and sales. These are known as B2C (business to customer) networks.

At **Hewlett-Packard**, when a customer calls with a technical problem, the call is routed to one of four engineering hubs around the world, depending on the time of day. This way customers have 24-hour access to technical support. The employee places data about the problem and customer into the system. All four hubs have access to information on how the problem can be solved. When other customers with the same or similar problem call, employees have relevant information to solve that problem.

CONNECTING WITH SUPPLIERS (B2B)

An information network that connects a company with suppliers can allow instant ordering of materials and supplies. With *electronic data interchange* (EDI), information from cash register scanners about current inventory levels is sent to suppliers, and orders are placed and shipped automatically to the store when stock gets low. Such a system is a B2B (business to business) network.

Ford used an information network to cut the lead time for getting new models through design and into production by one year, from 36 months down to 24. Ford also uses an information network to connect its 15,000 car dealerships around the world to manufacturing facilities to quickly supply the cars and trucks the dealers need. This network has allowed what Ford calls "manufacturing on demand." For example, it now takes less than two weeks to deliver a Mustang; in 1996 it took 50 days. Ford estimates that its information network will save it billions of dollars in inventory and fixed costs.[88]

As we bring this chapter to a close, you should understand the flow of organizational communication and the use of information techonology (IT), the interpersonal communication process, and information systems (IS).

Take advantage of the companion Web site for *Management Fundamentals*, where you will find a broad array of resources to help you maximize what you learn in class:

- Try a quiz
- View chapter videos
- Download slides
- Boost your vocabulary
- Work through an Internet exercise
- Find related links

Take a look for yourself at *http://lussier.swlearning.com.*

Chapter Summary

1. Describe the three ways communication flows through organizations.

Formal communication flows vertically downward and upward through the chain of command. Formal communication flows horizontally between colleagues and peers. Informal communication flows through the grapevine in any direction.

2. List the four steps in the interpersonal communication process.

(1) The sender encodes the message and selects the transmission channel. (2) The sender transmits the message through a channel. (3) The receiver decodes the message and decides if feedback is needed. (4) The receiver may give feedback, make a response, or send a new message through a channel.

3. State the major advantages of oral communication and written communication.

The major advantages of oral communication are that it is usually easier and faster than written communication and encourages feedback. The disadvantage is that there is usually no record of such communication.

The major advantage of written communication is that it is a record of what was communicated. The major disadvantages are that it usually takes longer and hinders feedback.

4. State a general guide to channel selection.

As a general guide, use rich oral channels for sending difficult and unusual messages, less rich written channels for transmitting simple and routine messages to several people, and combined channels for important messages that recipients need to attend to and understand.

5. List the five steps in the process of sending face-to-face messages.

The face-to-face message-sending process involves five steps: (1) Develop rapport. (2) State your communication objective. (3) Transmit your message. (4) Check the receiver's understanding. (5) Get a commitment and follow up.

6. Describe paraphrasing, and explain why it is useful.

Paraphrasing is the process of restating a message in one's own words. The receiver uses paraphrasing to check understanding of the transmitted message. If the receiver can paraphrase the message accurately, communication has taken place. If not, communication is not complete.

7. List and explain the three parts of the process of receiving messages.

The three parts of the message-receiving process are listening, analyzing, and checking understanding. Listening is the process of giving a speaker your undivided attention.

Analyzing is the process of thinking about, decoding, and evaluating the message. Checking understanding is the process of giving feedback.

8. Define reflecting responses, and state when they should be used.

Reflecting responses paraphrase the message and communicate the sender's understanding and acceptance. Reflecting responses are appropriate to use when coaching and counseling.

9. Discuss what should and should not be done to calm an emotional person.

To calm an emotional person, do not make statements that put the person down. Make reflective empathic responses that let the emotional person know that you understand how he or she feels. Paraphrase the feelings.

10. Describe the three primary types of information systems and their relationship.

Transaction process systems (TPS) are used to record routine repetitive transactions. Management information systems (MIS) transform data into information and are used by managers to perform their work and to make routine decisions. Decision support systems (DSS) are used by managers to make nonroutine decisions. TPS is related to MIS because its totals are included in MIS. DSS is related to MIS, which includes TPS totals, because it uses MIS databases.

11. List the components of an information network.

The components of an information network include connections between employees from headquarters and remote locations, suppliers and customers, and databases.

12. Complete each of the following statements using one of this chapter's key terms.

_____ is the process of transmitting information and meaning.

_____ is the flow of information both downward and upward through the organizational chain of command.

_____ is the flow of information between colleagues and peers.

The _____ is the informal flow of information in any direction throughout an organization.

The _____ is the process that takes place between a sender who encodes a message and transmits the message through a channel to a receiver who decodes it and may give feedback.

_____ is the sender's process of putting the message into a form that the receiver will understand.

A _____ is the means or medium by which a message is transmitted; the three primary channels are oral, nonverbal, and written.

_____ is the receiver's process of translating a message into a meaningful form.

_____ is messages sent without words.

The steps in the _____ are (1) developing rapport, (2) stating your communication objective, (3) transmitting your message, (4) checking the receiver's understanding, and (5) getting a commitment and following up.

_____ is information that verifies a message.

_____ is the process of restating a message in one's own words.

The _____ includes listening, analyzing, and checking understanding.

_____ paraphrase a message and communicate understanding and acceptance to the sender.

_____ is understanding and relating to another's feelings.

Key **Terms**

communication, 384
communication channels, 389
communication process, 389
decoding, 390
empathic listening, 408

encoding, 389
feedback, 399
grapevine, 386
horizontal communication, 385
message-receiving process, 402

message-sending process, 398
nonverbal communication, 394
paraphrasing, 399
reflecting responses, 406
vertical communication, 384

Review and **Discussion** Questions

1. What is the difference among vertical, horizontal, and grapevine communication?
2. What is the difference between encoding and decoding?
3. What does perception have to do with encoding and decoding?
4. What is filtering?
5. What is the difference between nonverbal setting and body language?
6. What is the difference between voice mail and e-mail?
7. What is media richness?
8. What should be included in your plan to send a message?
9. What are the four ways to get feedback on messages?
10. Why should you listen, analyze, and then check understanding?
11. Which response style do you use most often?
12. When calming an emotional employee, why shouldn't you make put-down statements to him or her?
13. What is the relationship between information and the management function?
14. What takes place during the information systems process?
15. What is the difference between a computer network and an information network?

Objective **Case**
MOBIL CREDIT CARD

In 1999, Exxon and Mobil merged and formed a new company called ExxonMobil Corporation. They merged to enhance their ability to compete effectively in a volatile world economy and in an industry that is increasingly competitive. Today ExxonMobil Corporation is a leader in almost every aspect of the energy and petrochemical business.

One aspect of business is certain: It is easier to maintain a satisfied customer than to get a new one. A gasoline credit card almost guarantees that the corporation has a repeat consumer. ExxonMobil, like most businesses, places emphasis on customer relationship management. Communication is a key to managing relations with customers, as communication can make or break a relationship. Although ExxonMobil is highly successful, like all businesses, it does make mistakes. Here is an example of a consumer relationship that broke down as a result of poor communication. In fact, this consumer no longer drives into any Mobil gasoline station.

A widow with a Mobil gasoline credit card needed to discuss an error in billing. When the Mobil credit associate she contacted asked to speak to the cardholder, her husband, who had passed away the previous month, she told the credit associate that he was not available. When the Mobil staff member said to have the cardholder call him, the widow then informed him that her husband, the cardholder, was deceased. The credit associate immediately rescinded the widow's use of the card.

At first, the widow was distraught and was "going to fight the issue." But on second thought she decided "so be it." The widow had a Visa credit card in her husband's name and could use that for all purchases, including at gasoline stations. She told the Visa representative that her husband was deceased, but the rep agreed to let her keep the card in his name. She felt good when the credit card bill came in her husband's name, for it made her feel a continuing connection with him. Not only has the Visa card become her permanent card, but she has purchased so many items using it that she has accumulated enough frequent-flier points to take some free cross-country airline trips.

What is to be learned from this particular case about communicating? How do companies and individuals get it right?

 To learn more about ExxonMobil, log on to InfoTrac® College Edition at *http://www. infotrac-college.com* and use the advanced search function.

_____ 1. This case illustrates _____ organizational communication.

    a. vertical upward   c. horizontal
    b. vertical downward   d. grapevine

_____ 2. The widow was the _____ of a message.

    a. encoder
    b. decoder

_____ 3. The major communication barrier between the Mobil credit associate and the widow was

    a. perception   e. not listening
    b. information overload   f. emotions
    c. channel selection   g. noise
    d. lack of trust and   h. filtering
       credibility

_____ 4. Communication between the widow and the Mobil credit associate was

    a. oral

    b. nonverbal
    c. written

_____ 5. The part of communication that upset the widow was

    a. oral
    b. nonverbal
    c. written

_____ 6. Which credit card representative did the best job of listening to the widow?

    a. Mobil
    b. Visa

_____ 7. What response style did the Mobil representative use with the widow?

    a. advising   d. reassuring
    b. diverting   e. reflecting
    c. probing

_____ 8. When the widow spoke to the Mobil representative she was most likely emotional.

    a. true
    b. false

_____ 9. When the Mobil representative found out about the death of the widow's husband, the best response style would have been

    a. advising   d. reassuring
    b. diverting   e. reflecting
    c. probing

_____10. Which customer representative was the most empathic?

    a. Mobil
    b. Visa

11. How could the Mobil credit associate have retained the widow as a credit card customer?

12. Do you think Mobil may have lost more than the widow as a customer? Explain.

13. Have you ever had a bad experience with a customer rep? Explain the situation and how the problem could have been avoided.

Cumulative Case Questions

14. What level of strategy is customer relations management, and what makes the planning dimension repetitive? (Chapter 5)

15. This case illustrates the need for attention to which human resource process stages? (Chapter 8)

16. Review the concepts in Chapter 9 and discuss how they relate to this case. (Chapter 9)

Skill Builder 1

GIVING INSTRUCTIONS

Objective

To develop your ability to send and receive messages (communication skills).

You will plan, give, and receive instructions for the completion of a drawing of three objects. No preparation is necessary except reading and understanding the chapter. The instructor will provide the original drawings.

Procedure (15 minutes)

In this exercise, you will work with a partner. One person will play the role of manager, and the other person will play the role of employee. You will go through the exercise twice, switching roles before the second time so that each person has a chance to give instructions in the role of manager and receive them in the role of employee.

The task is for the person in the role of manager to describe for the person in the role of employee a drawing of three objects so that the employee can duplicate the drawing, based on what the manager describes. (Your instructor will provide the drawing to those playing the role of managers; a different drawing will be used in the second run-through, when people have switched roles and partners.) The objects must be drawn to scale, and the drawing must be a recognizable reproduction of the original. The exercise has four parts.

1. *Planning.* The manager plans how to instruct the employee in the task. The manager's plans may include written instructions to be shown to the employee but may not include any drawing.
2. *Instruction.* The manager gives the instructions he or she has developed. While giving instructions, the manager is not to show the original drawing to the employee. The instructions may be given orally or in writing, or both, but the manager should not use any hand gestures. The manager must give the instructions for all three objects before the employee begins drawing them.
3. *Drawing.* The employee makes a drawing. Once the employee begins drawing, the manager should watch but may no longer communicate in any way.
4. *Evaluation.* When the employee is finished drawing or when the time is up, the manager shows the employee the original drawing. Partners should discuss how each person did and should answer the questions in the Integration section.

Integration

Answer the following questions. You may select more than one answer. The manager and employee discuss each question, and the manager, not the employee, writes the answers.

1. The goal of communication was to _____.
   a. influence
   b. inform
   c. express feelings

2. The communication was _____.
   a. vertical downward   c. horizontal
   b. vertical upward   d. grapevine

3. The manager did an _____ job of encoding the message and the employee did an _____ job of decoding the message.
   a. effective
   b. ineffective

4. The manager transmitted the message through ____ communication channel(s).
   a. oral
   b. written
   c. combined

5. The manager spent _____ time planning.
   a. too much
   b. too little
   c. the right amount of

   Questions 6 to 11 relate to the steps in the message-sending process.

6. The manager developed rapport (step 1).
   a. true
   b. false

7. The manager stated the objective of the communication (step 2).
   a. true
   b. false

8. The manager transmitted the message _____ (step 3).
   a. effectively
   b. ineffectively

9. The manager checked understanding by using _____ (step 4).
   a. direct questions   c. both
   b. paraphrasing   d. neither

10. The manager checked understanding _____.
    a. too frequently
    b. too infrequently
    c. about the right number of times

11. The manager got a commitment and followed up (step 5).
   a. true
   b. false

12. The employee did an ＿＿ job of listening, an ＿＿ job of analyzing, and an ＿＿ job of checking understanding through the message-receiving process.
   a. effective
   b. ineffective

13. The manager and/or employee got emotional.
   a. true
   b. false

14. Were the objects drawn to scale? If not, why not?

15. Did manager and employee both follow the rules? If not, why not?

16. In answering these questions, the manager was ＿＿ and the employee was ＿＿ to criticism that could help improve communication skills.
   a. open
   b. closed

17. If you could do this exercise over again, what would you do differently to improve communication?

_____

_____

Apply It

What did I learn from this experience? How will I use this knowledge in the future?

_____

_____

Behavior **Modeling**

SITUATIONAL COMMUNICATIONS

The scenario for this chapter shows two managers, Steve and Darius, meeting to discuss faulty parts. The video illustrates the four management styles explained in Skill Builder 2.

Objective

To better understand four communication styles.

View the Video (12 minutes)

View the accompanying video in class or at http://lussier.swlearning.com.

Procedure 1 (10–20 minutes)

As you watch each of the four scenes, identify the communication style used by the manager in the scene: Autocratic (A), Consultative (C), Participative (P), or Empowerment (E). Write the letter that identifies the communication style on the appropriate line below:

   Scene 1: ＿＿

   Scene 2: ＿＿

   Scene 3: ＿＿

   Scene 4: ＿＿

   Are other styles of communication appropriate in each situation? What style of communication would you have used in each situation? What styles would you *not* use in each situation? Does the manager in any scene use an inappropriate communication style?

   Your instructor may have the class discuss each scene individually.

Apply It (2–4 minutes)

What did I learn from this exercise? How will I use this knowledge in the future?

_____

_____

Skill Builder 2

ANALYZING COMMUNICATION STYLES

Preparing for Skill Builder 2

When you work with people outside your department, you have no authority to give them direct orders. You must use other means to achieve your goal. Through this Skill Builder, you will learn about communication styles and how to select the most appropriate communication style in a given situation. Begin by determining your preferred communication style by completing the Self-Assessment.

Self-Assessment: Determining Your Preferred Communication Style

To determine your preferred communication style, select the alternative that most closely describes what you would do in each of the following 12 situations. Do not be concerned with trying to pick the "correct" answer; simply circle the letter of the choice that best describes what you would actually do.

_____ 1. Wendy, a knowledgeable person from another department, comes to you, the engineering supervisor, and requests that you design a product to her specifications. You would:

　　a. Control the conversation and tell Wendy what you will do for her.

　　b. Ask Wendy to describe the product. Once you understand it, you would present your ideas. Let her know that you are concerned and want to help with your ideas.

　　c. Respond to Wendy's request by conveying understanding and support. Help clarify what she wants you to do. Offer ideas, but do it her way.

　　d. Find out what you need to know. Let Wendy know you will do it her way.

_____ 2. Your department has designed a product that is to be fabricated by Saul's department. Saul has been with the company longer than you have; he knows his department. Saul comes to you to change the product design. You decide to:

　　a. Listen to Saul explain the change and why it would be beneficial. If you believe Saul's way is better, change it; if not, explain why the original design is superior. If necessary, insist that it be done your way.

　　b. Tell Saul to fabricate it any way he wants.

　　c. Tell Saul to do it your way. You don't have time to listen and argue with him.

　　d. Be supportive; make changes together as a team.

_____ 3. Upper managers call you to a meeting and tell you they need some information to solve a problem they describe to you. You:

　　a. Respond in a manner that conveys personal support and offer alternative ways to solve the problem.

　　b. Just answer their questions.

　　c. Explain how to solve the problem.

　　d. Show your concern by explaining how to solve the problem and why it is an effective solution.

_____ 4. You have a routine work order that you typically place verbally, for work that is to be completed in three days. Sue, the receiver, is very experienced and willing to be of service to you. You decide to:

　　a. Explain your needs, but let Sue make the order decision.

　　b. Tell Sue what you want and why you need it.

　　c. Decide together what to order.

　　d. Simply give Sue the order.

_____ 5. Work orders from the staff department normally take three days to fulfill; however, you have an emergency and need the job done today. Your colleague Jim, the department supervisor, is knowledgeable and somewhat cooperative. You decide to:

　　a. Tell Jim that you need the work done by three o'clock and will return at that time to pick it up.

　　b. Explain the situation and how the organization will benefit by expediting the order. Volunteer to help in any way you can.

　　c. Explain the situation and ask Jim when the order will be ready.

　　d. Explain the situation and together come to a solution to your problem.

_____ 6. Danielle, a peer with a record of high performance, has recently had a drop in productivity. You know Danielle has a family problem. Her problem is affecting your performance. You:

　　a. Discuss the problem; help Danielle realize that the problem is affecting her work and yours. Supportively discuss ways to improve the situation.

　　b. Tell the boss about it and let him decide what to do.

　　c. Tell Danielle to get back on the job.

　　d. Discuss the problem and tell Danielle how to improve the work situation; be supportive.

_____ 7. You buy supplies from Peter regularly. He is an excellent salesperson and very knowledgeable about your situation. You are placing your weekly order. You decide to:

　　a. Explain what you want and why. Develop a supportive relationship.

　　b. Explain what you want and ask Peter to recommend products.

　　c. Give Peter the order.

　　d. Explain your situation and allow Peter to make the order.

_____ 8. Jean, a knowledgeable person from another department, has asked you to perform a routine staff function in a different way. You decide to:

　　a. Perform the task to her specifications without questioning her.

　　b. Tell her that you will do it the usual way.

　　c. Explain what you will do and why.

　　d. Show your willingness to help; offer alternative ways to do it.

____ 9. Tom, a salesperson, wants to place an order with your department but the order has a short delivery date. As usual, Tom claims it is a take-it-or-leave-it offer. He wants your decision now, or within a few minutes, because he is in the customer's office. Your action is to:

a. Convince Tom to work together to come up with a later date.

b. Give Tom a yes or no answer.

c. Explain your situation and let Tom decide if you should take the order.

d. Offer an alternative delivery date. Work on your relationship; show your support.

____10. As a time-and-motion expert, you have been called by an operator who has a complaint about the standard time it takes to perform a job. As you analyze the entire job, you realize that one element of the job should take longer, but other elements should take less time, leading to a shorter total standard time for the job. You decide to:

a. Tell the operator and foreman that the total time must be decreased and why.

b. Agree with the operator and increase the standard time.

c. Explain your findings. Deal with the operator and/or foreman's concerns, but ensure compliance with your new standard.

d. Together with the operator, develop a standard time.

____11. You approve budget allocations for projects. Marie, who is very competent in developing budgets, has come to you with a proposed budget. You:

a. Review the budget, make revisions, and explain them in a supportive way. Deal with concerns, but insist on your changes.

b. Review the proposal and suggest areas where changes may be needed. Make changes together, if needed.

c. Review the proposed budget, make revisions, and explain them.

d. Answer any questions or concerns Marie has and approve the budget as is.

____12. You are a sales manager. A customer has offered you a contract for your product but needs to have it delivered soon. The offer is open for two days. The contract would be profitable for your and the organization. The cooperation of the production department is essential to meet the deadline. Tim, the production manager, has developed a grudge against you because of your repeated requests for quick delivery. Your action is to:

a. Contact Tim and try to work together to complete the contract.

b. Accept the contract and convince Tim in a supportive way to meet the obligation.

c. Contact Tim and explain the situation. Ask him if you and he should accept the contract, but let him decide.

d. Accept the contract. Contact Tim and tell him to meet the obligation. If he resists, tell him you will go to his boss.

To determine your preferred communication style, circle the letter you selected in each situation. The column headings indicate the style you selected.

	Autocratic	Consultative	Participative	Empowerment
1.	a	b	c	d
2.	c	a	d	b
3.	c	d	a	b
4.	d	b	c	a
5.	a	b	d	c
6.	c	d	a	b
7.	c	a	b	d
8.	b	c	d	a
9.	b	d	a	c
10.	a	c	d	b
11.	c	a	b	d
12.	d	b	a	c
Total	___	___	___	___

Add up the number of circled items per column. The four totals should sum to 12. The column with the highest number represents your preferred communication style. The more evenly distributed the numbers are among the four styles, the more flexible your communications. A total of 0 or 1 in any column may indicate a reluctance to use that style. You could have problems in situations calling for the use of that style.

Selecting a Communication Style

As you saw from the Self-Assessment, communication styles can also be autocratic, consultative, participative, or empowerment.

With the **autocratic communication style**, the communication is generally controlled by the sender of the message; little, if any, response is expected from the receiver, and his or her input is not considered. The communication is structured and either directive or informative. With the **consultative communication style**, the sender of the message makes it clear that he or she desires a response and tries to elicit a response by asking questions, showing concern for the other person's point of view, and being open to the person's feelings. The **participative communication style** involves trying to elicit the other person's ideas and being helpful and supportive. A manager using the **empowerment communication style** conveys that the other person is in charge of the communication; the communication is very open.

There is no single communication style that is best for all situations. In determining the appropriate style for a given situation, managers must take into consideration four different variables: time, information, acceptance, and capability.

Time. In certain situations, there may not be enough time to engage in two-way communication. In an emergency, for example, the other three variables are not as important as the time factor; in such cases, the autocratic style is appropriate. Also, time is relative: In one situation, a few minutes may be sufficient for effective communication; in another situation, a month may be too little time.

Information. The amount of information the sender and the receiver each have helps determine which style of communication is appropriate in a given situation. For example, in a situation where an employee has little information, the manager might use an autocratic communication style; if the employee had much information, the manager would be better off using a participative style.

Acceptance. The likelihood that the receiver of a message will accept it also influences communication style. If the receiver is likely to accept a message, the autocratic style may be appropriate. However, there are situations in which acceptance is critical to success, such as when a manager is trying to implement changes. If the receiver is reluctant to accept a message or is likely to reject it, the consultative, participative, or empowerment styles may be appropriate.

Capability. An employee's capability refers to his or her ability and motivation to participate in two-way communication. If an employee has low capability, the autocratic style may be best; if an employee has outstanding capability, the empowerment communication style may be ideal. In addition, capability levels can change as situations change: The employee with whom a manager used an autocratic style might be better addressed using a participative style in a different situation.

Exhibit 11-9 *Situational Communication Model*

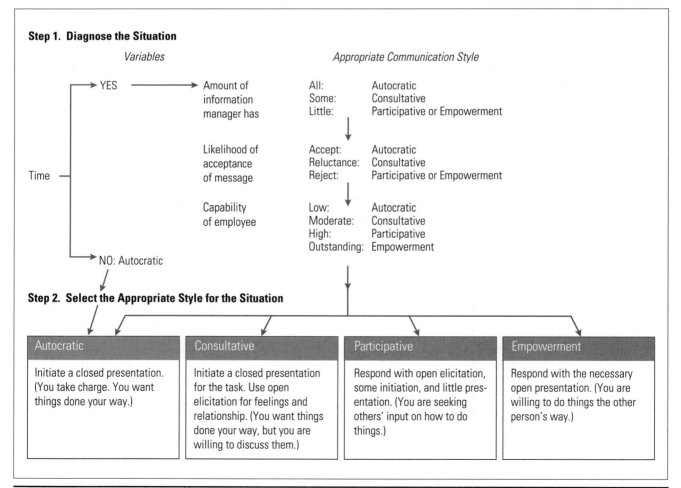

Successful managers rely on different communication styles, depending on the situation. In some situations, one of the variables discussed above may be more important than others. For example, a manager who is communicating with a highly capable employee might ordinarily use a consultative style. But if in a particular situation the manager already has the information she needs, the manager may use an autocratic style with that employee.

Reread the 12 situations in the Self-Assessment. For each one, consider the four variables discussed above. Refer to the Situational Communication Model in Exhibit 11-9. First, determine if there is sufficient time to engage in two-way communication. Second, assess the level of information you have and the other person's capability and likelihood of accepting a message. Then select the appropriate communication style for the situation, based on your analysis. Did the analysis cause you to change your earlier responses?

Apply It (2–4 minutes)

What did I learn from this experience? How will I use this knowledge in the future?

_____

_____

Written Communication

Grammar

Syntax

Rhetoric

Editing

Punctuation

Learning Outcomes

After studying this appendix, you should be able to:

1. List and define the eight parts of speech. PAGE 422

2. Explain the difference between a phrase and a clause. PAGE 423

3. Explain the 1–5–15 writing rule. PAGE 423

4. Explain three important uses of commas. PAGE 423

——————— Learning Outcome 1 ———————
List and define the eight parts of speech.

GRAMMAR

Grammar refers to the rules for using the following eight parts of speech:

1. **Nouns** are the names of people, places, or things.
2. **Pronouns** take the place of nouns.
3. **Verbs** are the action words in sentences. There are also linking and auxiliary verbs (e.g., *be*, *have*, and *do*). Verbs have number (singular or plural), which must agree with that of the accompanying noun or pronoun, tense (past, present, future), and voice (active or passive).
4. **Adjectives** modify, or give more information about, nouns.
5. **Adverbs** tell something about a verb, an adjective, or another adverb.
6. **Prepositions** (e.g., *to*, *of*, *for*, *at*, *by*, *as*, *on*, *in*, *before*, *after*) relate nouns or pronouns to other parts of a sentence.
7. **Conjunctions** (e.g., *and*, *but*, *or*, *nor*, *so*, *yet*, *because*) connect two words or parts of a sentence together.
8. An **interjection** is a word used to express feelings (e.g., *wow* for surprise or *ouch* for pain). Interjections are not commonly used in business and technical writing.

The various parts of speech are used to construct sentences, which have the following parts: The **subject** is a noun or a pronoun and is the person or thing that performs an action or is described in the sentence. The **predicate** consists of the main verb and any accompanying verbs, which express an action or describe the subject, along with complement(s) and modifier(s). Most sentences include at least one **complement**: a direct object, an indirect object, a subject complement, or an object complement. **Modifiers** include both adjectives (which modify nouns or pronouns) and adverbs (which modify verbs, adjectives, or other adverbs). **Connectives** join elements of sentences together; prepositions and conjunctions are connectives.

Learning Outcome 2

Explain the difference between a phrase and a clause.

SYNTAX

Syntax is the arrangement of words, phrases, and clauses to form sentence structure. A **sentence** needs a subject (a noun or a pronoun) and a verb, and it often also includes modifiers (adjectives and adverbs) and connectives (prepositions and conjunctions) to convey meaning. A **phrase** is a group of words that does not form a complete sentence. A **clause** is a group of words that includes a subject and a verb and often could stand alone as a sentence.

Learning Outcome 3

Explain the 1–5–15 writing rule.

RHETORIC

Rhetoric refers to the principles and rules of effective writing. **Paragraphs** should have only one main idea. Start with a topic sentence to introduce the idea, and follow with sentences that give more detail about the main idea. Generally, paragraphs in business correspondence should have a minimum of three sentences, an average of five sentences, and a maximum of eight sentences. **Sentences** should include only one idea, and that idea should relate to the paragraph's topic sentence. Sentences should average 15 words, although it is good to vary the length of your sentences. *The* **1–5–15 writing rule** *states that paragraphs should express one idea with an average of five sentences with fifteen words each.*

EDITING

Editing is a review process that improves the quality of your writing. Edit after you have finished writing, not while you are still writing; get your ideas out first. Use your computer's grammar and spell-checking functions and edit your work on screen; then use these functions again and print out your work. Finally, edit the printed draft. Does each paragraph have only one idea? Are all sentences related to that one idea? Does each paragraph have at least three sentences and a maximum of eight? Edit each sentence for punctuation. It can also be helpful to have a classmate or coworker edit your work.

Learning Outcome 4

Explain three important uses of commas.

PUNCTUATION

Punctuation is the use of special marks—commas, semicolons, colons, dashes, parentheses, and brackets—to group words, phrases, and clauses. We'll focus on the comma, which is the most important mark of internal punctuation and the one that is used incorrectly more frequently than any of the others. In this section, we discuss three major uses of commas.

1. **Commas separate items in a series**. A series contains three or more parallel words, phrases, or clauses. Do not use a comma with a series of two.

   WRONG: Smith studied the age of participants, *and* the length of their illnesses. (series of two)
   CORRECT: Smith studied the age of participants *and* the length of their illnesses.
   CORRECT: Smith studied the age of participants, the length of their illnesses, *and* their incomes. (series of three)

2. **Commas precede coordinating conjunctions that join clauses**. Conjunctions join related ideas, and using a coordinated conjunction to join related clauses can help you to avoid a series of short, choppy sentences. The primary coordinating conjunctions are *and*, *but*, *or*, *nor*, *yet*, *for*, and *so*.

   WRONG: Smith studied age *and* he also studied length of illness. (could be two sentences)
   CORRECT: Smith studied age, *and* he also studied length of illness.

   To test if you have correctly used a comma with a coordinating conjunction, replace the comma and conjunction with a period. If the result is two complete sentences, the comma is used correctly. If you do not have two complete sentences, omit the comma, because the conjunction is most likely connecting words or phrases rather than clauses.

3. **Commas set off words or phrases at the beginning, middle, or end of sentences**. A preposition and the words that follow it form a prepositional phrase. When a sentence begins with a prepositional phrase, the phrase is set off by having a comma following it. The phrase can often be moved to the middle or end of the sentence, where it does not need to be set off by a comma.

   WRONG: On the test of team skills I scored only 70%.
   CORRECT: On the test of team skills, I scored only 70%.
   CORRECT: I scored only 70% on the test of team skills.

   A comma is also used to set off a word or phrase that provides supplemental information about some part of a sentence. Supplemental information is information that is not necessary to the basic meaning of the sentence; if it were deleted from the sentence, the sentence would still be grammatically correct.

   WRONG: To improve my conflict resolution skill my weakest area I will confront others more often.
   CORRECT: To improve my conflict resolution skill, my weakest area, I will confront others more often.
   NOTE: To improve my conflict resolution skill, I will confront others more often. (a grammatically correct sentence)

   Words or phrases that provide supplemental information can also be located at the end of a sentence.

   WRONG: Smith controlled for age which makes the study more robust.
   CORRECT: Smith controlled for age, which makes the study more robust.

In summary, words or phrases that provide supplemental information can be located at the beginning, middle, or end of a sentence. Use the test of removing the word or phrase to see whether the sentence retains its grammatical form and basic meaning, in order to determine whether to insert a comma or commas. Try it by correcting the punctuation in the following exercise.

Applying The Concept 1

Punctuation

Correct the punctuation in each sentence.

1. If, I stop speaking without thinking I will improve my team skills.
2. My delegation score was 92% a good score for that area.
3. I scored 6 for planning, and 5 for conflict.
4. After reviewing the survey I will improve my team skills.
5. To improve my conflict resolution score which is too low I will confront others.
6. I will improve my team skills and I really want to let others participate more.
7. When planning with the group I will give my ideas.
8. I scored 8 on conflict resolution and I scored 7 on listening.
9. William Shakespeare the great English author wrote *Hamlet*.
10. Jose is a great guy, I like him a lot.

Appendix Summary

1. List and define the eight parts of speech.
The eight parts of speech are nouns, pronouns, verbs, adjectives, adverbs, prepositions, conjunctions, and interjections.

2. Explain the difference between a phrase and a clause.
A phrase is a group of words that does not form a complete sentence. A clause includes a subject and a verb and often can stand alone as a sentence.

3. Explain the 1-5-15 writing rule.
Paragraphs should express one idea with an average of five sentences with fifteen words each.

4. Explain three important uses of commas.
Commas separate items in a series, precede coordinating conjunctions that join clauses, and set off words or phrases at the beginning, middle, or end of sentences.

Learning Outcomes

After studying this chapter, you should be able to:

1. Illustrate the motivation process. **PAGE 428**

2. Explain the performance formula and how to use it. **PAGE 429**

3. Discuss the major similarities and differences among the four content motivation theories: hierarchy of needs theory, ERG theory, two-factor theory, and acquired needs theory. **PAGE 430**

4. Discuss the major similarities and differences among the three process motivation theories: equity theory, goal-setting theory, and expectancy theory. **PAGE 438**

5. Explain the four types of reinforcement. **PAGE 442**

6. State the major differences among content, process, and reinforcement theories. **PAGE 448**

12: Motivating for High Performance

7. Define the following **key terms:**

motivation	acquired needs theory
motivation process	process motivation theories
performance formula	equity theory
content motivation theories	goal-setting theory
hierarchy of needs theory	expectancy theory
ERG theory	reinforcement theory
two-factor theory	giving praise model

Ideas on Management
at Market America

Market America was founded in April 1992 with a business model to sell directly to consumers through UnFranchise® owners. The company markets a wide variety of high-quality products and services (including anti-aging, health, nutrition, and personal care products) through its Mall Without Walls® concept. Products are sold through approximately 100,000 independent distributors and UnFranchise® owners; both groups together are called *distributors*. Market America makes it possible for people to achieve the dream of starting their own business to achieve financial independence and freedom of time. The company offers the benefits of franchising (a proven business plan, management and marketing tools and training) without the risk and high cost (franchise fees, monthly royalties, territorial restrictions) of a traditional franchise. There

are minimal startup expenses, and most people start part-time (8 to 12 hours per week).

© Benelux Press/Index Stock Imagery

Market America is located in Greensboro, North Carolina, employing over 300 people in its sophisticated, state-of-the-art warehouse distribution systems. It also utilizes e-commerce through its Distributor Custom Web Portals and innovative Web site, *http://www.marketamerica.com*. Market America offers mass customization and the one-to-one marketing and personal service of its distributor network.

IOM

1. **What does Market America do to motivate its distributors, and how does it affect performance?**
2. **How does Market America meet its distributors' content motivation needs?**
3. **How does Market America meet its distributors' process motivation needs?**
4. **How does Market America use reinforcement theory to motivate its distributors?**
5. **Will the Market America UnFranchise® business model for motivating work in other countries?**

To learn more about Market America, visit the company's Web site at *http://www.marketamerica.com* or log on to InfoTrac® College Edition at *http://infotrac.thomsonlearning.com*, where you can research and read articles on Market America. To learn more about Market America, select the advanced search option and key in record number A76746727 or A64784709 to get started.

Sources: Opening case information and answers within the chapter were taken from the Market America Web site at *http://www.marketamerica.com*, accessed June 3, 2004.

MOTIVATION AND PERFORMANCE

In this section, we discuss what motivation is and why it is important, how motivation affects performance, and how managers affect employee motivation and performance. You will also get an overview of three major classes of theories of motivation.

—————————————— Learning Outcome 1 ——————————————
Illustrate the motivation process.

What Is Motivation, and Why Is It Important?

Motivation is an inner desire to satisfy an unsatisfied need. From a business perspective, **motivation** *is the willingness to achieve organizational objectives* or to go above and beyond the call of duty (organizational citizenship behavior).[1] People primarily do what they do to meet their needs or wants. Understanding that people are motivated by self-interest is key to understanding motivation.[2] *Through the* **motivation process,** *employees go from need to motive to behavior to consequence to satisfaction or dissatisfaction.* For example, you are thirsty (need) and have a desire (motive) to get a drink. You get a drink (behavior) that quenches your thirst (consequence and satisfaction). Satisfaction is usually short-lived. Getting that drink satisfied you, but soon you will need another drink. For this reason, the motivation process is a feedback loop:

A need or want motivates behavior.[3] However, needs and motives are complex; people don't always know what their needs are or why they do the things they do.[4] Understanding needs will help you understand behavior.[5] You will gain a better understanding of why people do the things they do.

You cannot observe motives, but you can observe behavior and infer the motive. However, it is not easy to know why people behave the way they do, because people may do the same things for different reasons. Also, people often attempt to satisfy several needs at once.[6]

Generally, people who are satisfied with their jobs are more highly motivated.[7] Managers have come to realize that a motivated and satisfied workforce can contribute powerfully to bottom-line profits.[8] Kingston Technology has been very successful at motivating its employees. As a result, the dedication and extra effort they put into their jobs has helped Kingston succeed.

More than 32 years ago, Rollin King and Herb Kelleher founded **Southwest Airlines**. Their philosophy was this: If you get your passengers to their destinations when they want to get there, on time, at the lowest possible fares, and with the fewest possible hassles, people will fly on your airline.

Kelleher, now Southwest's Chairman of the Board, said that superior performance is not achieved through ordinary employee efforts. He motivates employees by focusing on making sure that they have a good time while working. Southwest is successful because its employees are motivated to surpass what is formally required of them.[9]

The Role of Expectations in Motivation and Performance

The poor performance of employees can be caused inadvertently by managers themselves and may not result from poor skills, a lack of experience, or insufficient motivation. Recall the Pygmalion effect (Chapter 9): Managers' attitudes toward, expectations of, and treatment of employees largely determine employees' motivation and performance.[10] Managers need to have high expectations and treat employees as though they are high achievers to get the best from them. Managers need to get to know employees as individuals and motivate them in ways that will meet their unique and diverse needs.[11] In this chapter, you will learn how to motivate employees.

In addition to managers' expectations, employees' expectations also affect performance.[12] Closely related to the Pygmalion effect is the *self-fulfilling prophecy*. Henry Ford said that if you believe you can or believe you can't, you are right. If you think you will be successful, you will be. If you think you will fail, you will, because you will fulfill your own expectations. You will live up or down to your own expectations, so be positive, confident, and optimistic.[13]

--- Learning Outcome 2 ---
Explain the performance formula and how to use it.

How Motivation Affects Performance

Generally, a motivated employee will try harder than an unmotivated one to do a good job.[14] However, performance is not simply based on motivation.[15] Three interdependent factors determine the level of performance attained: ability, motivation, and resources. *The interaction of these factors can be expressed as a* **performance formula**: *performance = ability × motivation × resources*. For maximum performance, all three factors must be high. Employees who don't have competency to perform a job and those who don't contribute their best effort lower performance.[16] Strong components of the performance formula lead to outstanding performance.[17] When performance is not optimum, you must determine which performance factor needs to be improved.

As you'll recall from earlier chapters, CEO Steve Ballmer changed **Microsoft's** organizational structure. He reorganized to set up a divisional structure with seven business units that are held accountable as profit centers. All seven managers have high ability, and through the restructuring, Ballmer was also motivating those managers and giving them the resources to increase performance.[18]

Market America's primary means of affecting performance is to create self-motivation by making each distributor his or her own boss—which only succeeds with people who are interested in entrepreneurship. Market America's team approach, with more experienced distributors helping newer distributors, is key to motivating distributors to succeed. Market America has been successful at finding people who want to be their own boss, and its performance continues to improve. It has had 48 consecutive quarters of growth, and sales have reached more than $280 million. In 2004, the company achieved its goals of having more six-figure earners than any of its U.S. competitors. In terms of the performance formula, Market America's UnFranchise® approach develops the ability and motivation to sell, and the company provides the management and marketing resources to make a business grow.

I
O
M

Applying The Concept 1

The Performance Formula

Identify the factor contributing to low performance in the following five situations.

a. ability

b. motivation

c. resources

_____ 1. Latoya went on a sales call. When she reached into her briefcase she realized that she did not have her product display book. Trying to explain the products without being able to show them to the customer resulted in a lost sale.

_____ 2. Frank does not produce as much as the other department members, because he does not put much effort into the job.

_____ 3. "I practice longer and harder than my track teammates Heather and Linda. I don't understand why they beat me in the races."

_____ 4. "I could get all A's in school if I wanted to. But I'd rather relax and have a good time."

_____ 5. The production team got behind schedule because the printing press was down for repairs.

An Overview of Three Major Classes of Motivation Theories

It has been said that nothing is as practical as a good theory, and motivation theories have found numerous applications in organizations.[19] However, there is no single universally accepted theory of how to motivate people. In this chapter, we discuss three major classes of motivation theories and show how you can use them to motivate yourself and others. Exhibit 12-1 lists the major motivation theories. After studying all of these theories, you can select one theory to use, use several theories in developing your own approach, or apply the theory that best fits the specific situation.

Learning Outcome 3

Discuss the major similarities and differences among the four content motivation theories: hierarchy of needs theory, ERG theory, two-factor theory, and acquired needs theory.

CONTENT MOTIVATION THEORIES

According to content motivation theorists, if you want to have satisfied employees, you must meet their needs. When employees are asked to meet objectives, they think, but usually do not say, "What's in it for me?"[20] The key to achieving organizational objectives is to meet the needs of employees. As you create a win-win situation, you need to sell the benefits that meet employees' needs to the employees.

   Content motivation theories *focus on identifying and understanding employees' needs*. In this section, we describe and discuss the application of four content motivation theories: hierarchy of needs theory, ERG theory, two-factor theory, and acquired needs theory.

Exhibit 12-1 *Major Motivation Theories*

Class of Motivation Theories	Specific Theory (Creator)
Content motivation theories focus on identifying and understanding employees' needs.	**Hierarchy of needs theory** proposes that employees are motivated by five levels of needs: physiological, safety, social, esteem, and self-actualization. (Maslow)
	ERG theory proposes that employees are motivated by three needs: existence, relatedness, and growth. (Alderfer)
	Two-factor theory proposes that employees are motivated by motivators (higher-level needs) rather than by maintenance factors (lower-level needs). (Herzberg)
	Acquired needs theory proposes that employees are motivated by their need for achievement, power, and affiliation. (McClelland)
Process motivation theories focus on understanding how employees choose behaviors to fulfill their needs.	**Equity theory** proposes that employees will be motivated when their perceived inputs equal outputs. (Adams)
	Goal-setting theory proposes that achievable but difficult goals motivate employees. (Locke)
	Expectancy theory proposes that employees are motivated when they believe they can accomplish the task and the rewards for doing so are worth the effort. (Vroom)
Reinforcement theory proposes that the consequences of behavior will motivate employees to behave in predetermined ways. (Skinner)	**Type of reinforcement**
	Positive reinforcement is offering attractive consequences (rewards) for desirable performance to encourage the continuation of that behavior.
	Avoidance reinforcement is threatening to provide negative consequences for poor performance to encourage desirable behavior.
	Punishment is providing an undesirable consequence (punishment) for an undesirable behavior to prevent the behavior.
	Extinction is the withholding of reinforcement for a particular behavior.

Hierarchy of Needs Theory

The **hierarchy of needs theory** *proposes that employees are motivated by five levels of needs: physiological, safety, social, esteem, and self-actualization.* Abraham Maslow developed this theory in the 1940s,[21] based on four major assumptions: (1) Only unmet needs motivate. (2) People's needs are arranged in order of importance (in a hierarchy) from basic to complex. (3) People will not be motivated to satisfy a higher-level need unless the lower-level needs have been at least minimally satisfied. (4) People have five levels of needs, listed here in hierarchical order from lowest to highest:

- *Physiological needs.* These are people's basic needs for air, water, food, shelter, sex, and relief from or avoidance of pain.
- *Safety needs.* Once they satisfy their physiological needs, people are concerned with safety and security.
- *Social needs.* After establishing safety, people look for love, friendship, acceptance, and affection.
- *Esteem needs.* After they meet their social needs, people focus on acquiring status, self-respect, recognition for accomplishments, and a feeling of self-confidence and prestige.
- *Self-actualization needs.* The highest-level need is to develop one's full potential. To do so, people seek growth, achievement, and advancement.

WorkApplication1

Describe how your needs at each of Maslow's levels are addressed by an organization you work for now or were addressed by one you worked for in the past.

_____

_____

_____

_____

_____

Exhibit 12-2 *How Managers Motivate Based on Maslow's Hierarchy of Needs Theory*

Self-Actualization Needs
Organizations help employees
meet their self-actualization needs
by providing them with opportunities for
skill development, the chance to be creative,
promotions, and the ability to have complete
control over their jobs.

Esteem Needs
Organizations meet employees' esteem needs with merit pay raises,
recognition, challenging tasks, participation in decision making,
and opportunity for advancement.

Social Needs
Organizations meet employees' social needs by providing them with the opportunity
to interact with others, to be accepted, and to have friends. Many organizations schedule
employee parties, picnics, trips, and sports teams.

Safety Needs
Organizations meet employees' safety needs by providing safe working conditions, job security,
and fringe benefits (medical insurance/sick pay/pensions).

Physiological Needs
Organizations meet employees' physiological needs by providing adequate salary, work breaks, and safe working conditions.

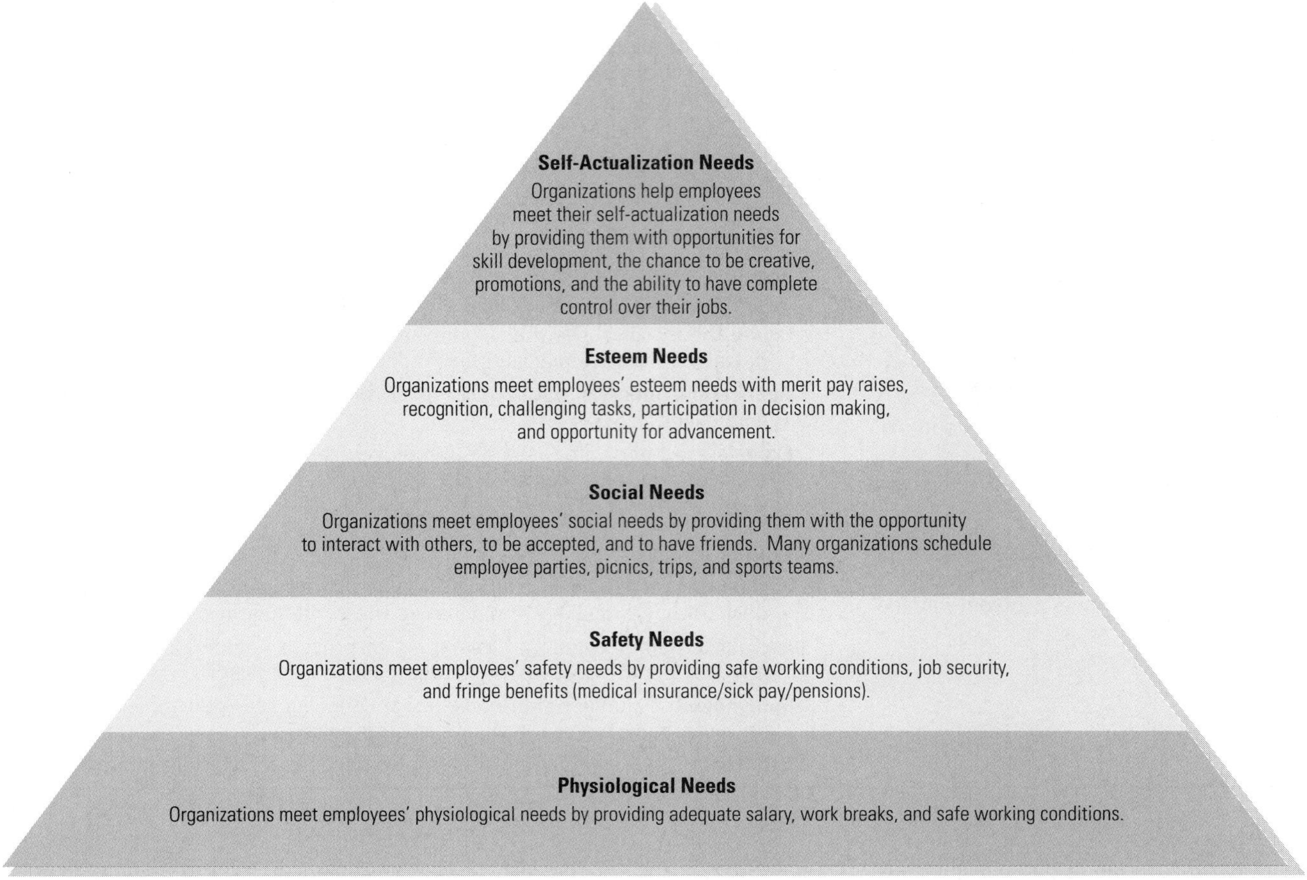

Managers should meet employees' lower-level needs so that those needs will not dominate the employees' motivational process.[22] Maslow stated that enlightened managers who truly understand that human resources are the organization's most valuable asset are rare, and this is still true today.[23] Exhibit 12-2 lists ways in which organizations attempt to meet the needs in Maslow's hierarchy.

I O M **Working for Market America allows people to meet many needs. Earning money allows them to satisfy physiological needs. Because the job involves a minimum of risk, people's safety needs are met. Customer contact and meetings satisfy some of people's social needs. The job itself offers great growth potential and thus may satisfy some distributors' esteem needs. Finally, being the boss allows people to have control over the work experience, which may help them meet self-actualization needs.**

ERG Theory

A well-known simplification of the hierarchy of needs theory, the **ERG theory,** *proposes that employees are motivated by three needs: existence, relatedness, and growth.* Clayton Alderfer reorganized Maslow's hierarchy of five types of needs into three needs: existence (physiological and safety needs), relatedness (social), and growth (esteem and self-actualization). Alderfer agreed with Maslow that unsatisfied needs motivate individuals, and he theorized that more than one need may be active at one time.[24]

To apply ERG theory, an organization must determine which employee needs have been met and which have not been met or have been frustrated and then must plan how to meet the unsatisfied needs.

Sandstrom Products Company of Port Byron, Illinois, is a manufacturer of quality product finishes, specialized coatings, and solid film lubricants. As at many companies, managers at Sandstrom did not seek employee input. Thus, most low-level employees were not motivated; only their existence needs were being met. But Sandstrom was losing money, and managers knew it had to change. Managers developed teams that were empowered to make decisions on how their jobs were done and to make changes to improve performance. The team-based approach led to higher motivation, because it helped satisfy employees' relatedness and growth needs. Sandstrom went from a loss of $100,000 to a profit of $800,000 in two years.[25]

Two-Factor Theory

In the 1950s, Frederick Herzberg classified two sets of needs that he called *factors*.[26] Herzberg combined lower-level needs into one classification he called *maintenance factors* and higher-level needs into one classification he called *motivators*. The **two-factor theory** *proposes that employees are motivated by motivators rather than by maintenance factors.* Maintenance factors are also called *extrinsic motivators*, because the motivation comes from outside the job. Motivators are called *intrinsic motivators* because the motivation comes from the work itself.[27] Exhibit 12-3 illustrates this theory. Complete the Self-Assessment to find out what motivates you.

Based on their research, Herzberg and his associates disagreed with the traditional view that satisfaction and dissatisfaction were at opposite ends of a single continuum. Instead, they proposed two continuums: one for

Exhibit 12-3 *Herzberg's Two-Factor Theory*

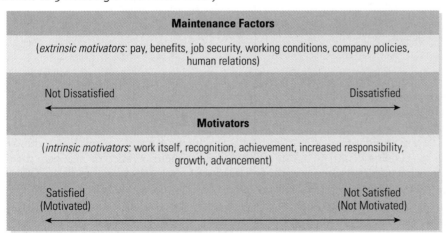

Self-Assessment

What Motivates You?

Following are 12 job factors that contribute to job satisfaction. Rate each according to how important it is to you by placing a number from 1 to 5 on the line before each factor.

Very Important	Somewhat important	Not important
5----------------4	----------------3----------------2	----------------1

_____ 1. An interesting job I enjoy doing

_____ 2. A good boss who treats people fairly

_____ 3. Getting praise and other recognition and appreciation for the work that I do

_____ 4. Satisfying interpersonal interactions on the job

_____ 5. The opportunity for advancement

_____ 6. A prestigious or high-status job

_____ 7. Job responsibility that gives me freedom to do things my way

_____ 8. Good working conditions (safe environment, nice office, cafeteria, etc.)

_____ 9. The opportunity to learn new things

_____10. Sensible company rules, regulations, procedures, and policies

_____ 11. A job I can do well and succeed at

_____12. Job security

Indicate below how you rated each factor.

Motivating Factors	_Maintenance Factors_
1. _____	2. _____
3. _____	4. _____
5. _____	6. _____
7. _____	8. _____
9. _____	10. _____
11. _____	12. _____
_____	Total points _____

Add each column vertically. Are motivators or maintenance factors more important to you?

maintenance factors (which refer to the external environment) and one for motivators. The continuum for maintenance factors runs from not dissatisfied to dissatisfied. The continuum for motivators runs from satisfied to not satisfied.

Herzberg contended that addressing maintenance factors will keep employees from being dissatisfied, but it will not make them satisfied or motivate them. For example, if employees are dissatisfied with their pay (a maintenance factor) and they get a raise, they will no longer be dissatisfied. However, before long employees will get accustomed to the new standard of living and become dissatisfied again. They will need another raise to avoid becoming dissatisfied again. This becomes a repeating cycle.

If you got a pay raise, would you be motivated and more productive? The current view of money as a motivator is that money matters more to some people than to others and that it may motivate some employees. However, money does not necessarily motivate employees to work harder. Recall (Chapter 9) that you can have overall job satisfaction without being satisfied with all determinants of job satisfaction. Herzberg says that organizations must first ensure that employees are not dissatisfied with maintenance factors. Once employees are no longer dissatisfied with their external environment, they can be motivated through their jobs.

Organizations need to ensure that employees are not dissatisfied with maintenance factors and then focus on motivating them. One successful way to motivate employees is to build challenges and opportunities for achievement into their jobs.[28] *Job enrichment* is a method for increasing motivation (Chapter 6) that is commonly used.[29] The Job Characteristics Model (also discussed in Chapter 6) has been shown to consistently predict internal work motivation, job involvement, and job satisfaction.[30]

Market America allows people to operate their own business. In terms of the two-factor theory, the focus of this organization is on motivators that allow distributors to meet their high-level needs for esteem and self-actualization. Maintenance factors are not directly addressed.

Acquired Needs Theory

The **acquired needs theory** *proposes that employees are motivated by their needs for achievement, power, and affiliation.* Henry Murray developed the general needs theory.[31] This was adapted by John Atkinson and David McClelland, who developed acquired needs theory.[32] McClelland does not have a classification for lower-level needs. His affiliation needs are the same as Maslow's social and relatedness needs, and his power and achievement needs are related to esteem, self-actualization, and growth.

Unlike the other content theories, acquired needs theory holds that needs are based on personality and are developed as people interact with the environment. All people possess the needs for achievement, power, and affiliation, but to varying degrees. One of the three needs tends to be dominant in each individual and motivates his or her behavior. Before learning more about each need, complete the Self-Assessment to determine your dominant need.

WorkApplication2

Recall a present or past job; were you dissatisfied or not dissatisfied with the maintenance factors? Were you satisfied or not satisfied with the motivators? Identify the specific maintenance factors and motivators, and explain your response.

_____

_____

_____

_____

Self-Assessment

Acquired Needs

Indicate how accurately each of the 15 statements describes you by placing a number from 1 to 5 on the line before each statement.

Like me	Somewhat like me	Not like me
5————4————3————2————1		

_____ 1. I enjoy working hard.

_____ 2. I enjoy competing and winning.

_____ 3. I enjoy having many friends.

(Continued)

Self-Assessment

Acquired Needs   (*Continued*)

_____ 4. I enjoy a difficult challenge.

_____ 5. I enjoy being in a leadership role.

_____ 6. I want other people to like me.

_____ 7. I want to know how I am progressing as I complete tasks.

_____ 8. I confront people who do things I disagree with.

_____ 9. I enjoy frequently getting together socially with people.

_____ 10. I enjoy setting and achieving realistic goals.

_____ 11. I try to influence other people so that I get my way.

_____ 12. I enjoy belonging to many groups and organizations.

_____ 13. I enjoy the satisfaction of completing a difficult task.

_____ 14. In a leaderless situation, I tend to step forward and take charge.

_____ 15. I enjoy working with others more than working alone.

To determine your dominant need, write the number you assigned to each statement in the table below. Add up the total of each column, which should be between 5 and 25 points. The column with the highest score is your dominant need.

Achievement	Power	Affiliation
1. _____	2. _____	3. _____
4. _____	5. _____	6. _____
7. _____	8. _____	9. _____
10. _____	11. _____	12. _____
13. _____	14. _____	15. _____
Totals _____	_____	_____

THE NEED FOR ACHIEVEMENT (N ACH)

People with a high need for achievement tend to want to take personal responsibility for solving problems. They are goal-oriented, and they set moderate, realistic, attainable goals. They seek challenge, excellence, and individuality; take calculated, moderate risks; desire concrete feedback on their performance; and are willing to work hard.[33] People with a high n Ach think about ways to do a better job, about how to accomplish something unusual or important, and about career progression.[34] They perform well in nonroutine, challenging, and competitive situations, whereas people low in n Ach do not perform well in such situations.

McClelland's research showed that only about 10 percent of the U.S. population has a high need for achievement. Evidence has been found for a correlation between high n Ach and high performance. People with a high n Ach tend to enjoy sales and entrepreneurial positions. Managers tend to have a high n Ach.

To motivate employees with a high n Ach, give them nonroutine, challenging tasks with clear, attainable objectives. Give them fast and frequent feedback on their performance.[35] Continually give them increased responsibility for doing new things.

THE NEED FOR POWER (N POW)

People with a high need for power tend to want to control the situation, to influence or control others, to enjoy competition in which they can win (they do not like to lose), and to be willing to confront others.[36] People with a high n Pow think about controlling a situation and others, and they seek positions of authority and status. People with high n Pow tend to have a low need for affiliation. Managers tend to have a high n Pow. They understand that power is essential for successful management.

To motivate employees with a high n Pow, let them plan and control their jobs as much as possible.[37] Try to include them in decision making, especially when the decision affects them. People with a high n Pow tend to perform best alone rather than as team members. Try to assign them to a whole task rather than just a part of it.

THE NEED FOR AFFILIATION (N AFF)

People with a high n Aff tend to seek close relationships with others, to want to be liked by others, to enjoy social activities, and to seek to belong. They join groups and organizations. People with a high n Aff think about friends and relationships. They tend to enjoy developing, helping, and teaching others. They tend to have a low n Pow. People high in n Aff seek jobs in teaching, social work, human resources management, and other helping professions. They tend to avoid management because they like to be one of the group rather than its leader.

To motivate employees with a high n Aff, be sure to let them work as part of a team. They derive satisfaction from the people they work with more than from the task itself. Give them praise and recognition. Delegate responsibility for orienting and training new employees to them. People with a high n Aff make great mentors.

Market America helps distributors meet all three acquired needs. It provides support so that they can achieve their goal of successfully running their own business, they have the power to be in control, and they can develop an affiliation with customers and other distributors.

Exhibit 12-4 compares the four content motivation theories.

WorkApplication3

Explain how your need for achievement, power, and/or affiliation has affected your motivation on the job.

_____

_____

_____

_____

_____

Exhibit 12-4 *A Comparison of Four Content Motivation Theories*

Hierarchy of Needs (Maslow)	ERG Theory (Alderfer)	Two-Factor Theory (Herzberg)	Acquired Needs Theory (McClelland)
Self-Actualization	Growth	Motivators	Achievement and Power
Esteem	Growth	Motivators	Achievement and Power
Social	Relatedness	Maintenance factors	Affiliation
Safety	Existence	Maintenance factors	(Not addressed)
Physiological	Existence	Maintenance factors	(Not addressed)
Needs must be met in a hierarchical order.	Needs at any level can be unmet simultaneously.	Maintenance factors will not motivate employees.	Motivating needs are developed through experience.

Discuss the major similarities and differences among the three process
motivation theories: equity theory, goal-setting theory, and
expectancy theory.

PROCESS MOTIVATION THEORIES

Process motivation theories *focus on understanding how employees choose behaviors to fulfill their needs.* Process motivation theories are more complex than content motivation theories. Content motivation theories focus simply on identifying and understanding employees' needs. Process motivation theories go a step further and attempt to explain why employees have different needs, why their needs change, how and why they choose to try to satisfy needs in different ways, the mental process they go through as they understand situations, and how they evaluate their need satisfaction.[38] In this section, we discuss three process motivation theories: equity theory, goal-setting theory, and expectancy theory.

Equity Theory

Equity theory, particularly the version of J. Stacy Adams, proposes that people are motivated to seek social equity in the rewards they receive (output) for their performance (input).[39] **Equity theory** *proposes that employees are motivated when their perceived inputs equal outputs.*

According to equity theory, people compare their inputs (effort, experience, seniority, status, intelligence, and so forth) and outputs (praise, recognition, pay, benefits, promotions, increased status, supervisor's approval, etc.) to those of relevant others.[40] A relevant other could be a coworker or group of employees from the same or different organizations. Notice that the definition says that employees compare their *perceived* (not actual) inputs to outputs.[41] Equity may actually exist. However, if employees believe that there is inequity, they will change their behavior to create equity. Employees must perceive that they are being treated fairly, relative to others.[42]

Unfortunately, employees tend to inflate their own efforts or performance when comparing themselves to others. They also tend to overestimate what others earn. Employees may be very satisfied and motivated until they find out that a relevant other is earning more for the same job or earning the same for doing less work. When employees perceive inequity, they are motivated to reduce it by decreasing input or increasing output.[43] A comparison with relevant others leads to one of three conclusions: The employee is either underrewarded, overrewarded, or equitably rewarded.[44]

1. *Underrewarded.* When employees perceive that they are underrewarded, they may try to reduce the inequity by increasing outputs (requesting a raise), decreasing inputs (doing less work, being absent, taking long breaks, etc.), rationalizing (finding a logical explanation for inequity), changing others' inputs or outputs (getting them to do more or receive less), leaving the situation (getting transferred or taking a better job), or changing the object of comparison.
2. *Overrewarded.* Being overrewarded does not disturb most employees. However, research suggests that employees may reduce perceived inequity

by increasing input (working harder or longer), decreasing output (taking a pay cut), rationalizing (I'm worth it), or trying to increase others' output.

3. *Equitably Rewarded.* When inputs and outputs are perceived as being equal, employees are motivated.

Using equity theory in practice can be difficult, because you don't know the employees' reference groups and their views of inputs and outcomes. However, the theory does offer some useful general recommendations:

1. Managers should be aware that equity is based on perception, which may not be correct. Possibly, managers can create equity or inequity.
2. Rewards should be equitable. When employees perceive that they are not treated fairly, morale suffers and performance problems occur. Employees producing at the same level should be given equal rewards.
3. High performance should be rewarded,[45] but employees must understand the inputs needed to attain certain outputs. When using incentive pay, managers should clearly specify the exact requirements to achieve the incentive. A manager should be able to state objectively why one person got a higher merit raise than another.

Headquartered in Bothell, Washington, **Romac Industries, Inc.** manufactures pipe fittings and tools for the waterworks industry. All Romac products are made in the United States, and the company has manufacturing and warehouse facilities on the east and west coasts.

Romac has an unusual "open-book" system, whereby all employees can see how much every employee is paid. Romac managers believe everyone finds out how much others make through the grapevine anyway, so they just tell everyone—they address equity head-on. Salary equity is open to public debate at the company. When employees want more pay, their names, pictures, current salaries, and requested increases are given to all employees, who discuss the facts and then vote by secret ballot on what, if any, raise should be given.[46]

Market America's UnFranchise® business model treats all distributors with equity. Owners have unlimited potential, as the more time and effort (inputs) they put into their business, the more potential rewards (outputs) they can reap. However, not everyone is cut out for sales, and some people who start as independent distributors drop out or stay at this level, rather than advancing to become UnFranchise® owners.

Goal-Setting Theory

Goal-setting theory is currently one of the most valid approaches to work motivation.[47] It complements the two-factor and acquired needs theories, as goals lead to higher levels of motivation and performance.[48] Goals provide challenge; thus, people set goals.[49] *The goal-setting theory proposes that achievable but difficult goals motivate employees.* Chapter 5 discussed setting objectives. Our behavior has a purpose, which is usually to fulfill a need. Goals give us a sense of purpose—why we are working to accomplish a given task.

Jack Welch, a world-renowned management consultant and former CEO of **General Electric**, has said that much of GE's success comes from setting "stretch goals," which is a lesson he learned from his mother. Also, the emphasis on boundarylessness at GE motivated ordinary employees to set goals beyond their own work areas that led them to achieve extraordinary things.[50]

WorkApplication4

Give an example of how equity theory has affected your motivation or someone else's you work with or have worked with. Be sure to specify if you were underrewarded, overrewarded, or equitably rewarded.

_____

_____

_____

_____

WorkApplication5

Give an example of how goal(s) affected your motivation and performance or that of someone you work with or have worked with.

_____

_____

_____

_____

Lou Holtz, former football coach of the **University of Notre Dame**, stated that the three keys to success are a winning attitude, positive self-esteem, and setting a higher goal.[51] Every year each player had personal goals, and the team set goals, which Coach Holtz wrote in his notebook. Holtz said, "Of all my experiences in managing people, the power of goal setting is the most incredible." All good performance starts with clear goals. When setting objectives, be sure that they are challenging, achievable, specific, measurable, have a target date for accomplishment, and are jointly set when possible (see Chapter 5 for details).[52] However, remember that setting goals is not enough. You need to formulate action plans to achieve the goals and measure progress.

IOM

Market America relies heavily on goal-setting theory. Two of its goals are to establish itself as a leader in the direct sales industry and to become a Fortune 500 company. Goal-setting is the second of five basic steps for success at Market America. (Attitude and Knowledge, Retailing, Prospecting and Recruiting, and Follow Up and Duplication are the other four.) Distributors are taught to set business and personal long-term goals for the next year and to break them down by month, week, and day. Distributors read over their goals twice a day for motivation.

Join the Discussion   Ethics & Social Responsibility

Academic Standards

1. How many hours outside of class, on average, do you and other students you know spend preparing for class each week?
2. Are college professors today assigning students 2 hours of preparation for every hour in class? If not, why do you think they have dropped this standard?
3. Are students who are essentially doing part-time work (that is, attending classes but doing little or no academic work outside of class) during college being prepared for a career after graduation (with 40–50 hour work weeks)?
4. Is it ethical and socially responsible for professors to drop standards and for colleges to award degrees for doing less work than students did 5, 10, or 20 years ago?

Successful managers set and maintain high expectations for all their employees.[53] For many students, college is preparation for life in the working world, and the standards they must meet in their college work parallel those they will be expected to meet once they enter the workforce. Have college academic standards dropped, stayed the same, or risen over the years?

The academic credit-hour system was set up many years ago to ensure that there would be some standardization across colleges throughout the country and that academics and employers had the same understanding of the workload that a college student had carried to earn a degree. The credit-hour system was based on the assumption that a student would spend 2 hours of preparation for each hour of in-class time. So, a student taking five classes should spend 15 hours per week in classes and about 30 hours preparing for classes, or a total of about 45 hours a week—which is a full-time schedule.

Expectancy Theory

Expectancy theory is based on Victor Vroom's formula: motivation = expectancy × valence.[54] *The **expectancy theory** proposes that employees are motivated when they believe they can accomplish a task and the rewards for doing so are worth the effort.* The theory is based on the following assumptions: (1) Both internal factors (needs) and external factors (environment) affect behavior; (2) behavior is the individual's decision; (3) people have different needs, desires, and goals; and (4) people make behavior decisions based on their perception of the outcome.

Two important variables in Vroom's formula determine motivation.[55]

1. *Expectancy* refers to the person's perception of his or her ability (probability) to accomplish an objective. Generally, the higher one's expectancy, the better the chance for motivation.[56] When employees do not believe that they can accomplish objectives, they will not be motivated to try. Also important is the perception of the relationship between performance and the outcome or reward, which is referred to as *instrumentality*. Generally, the higher one's expectation for a positive outcome or reward, the better the chance for motivation. If employees are certain to get a reward, they probably will be motivated.[57]
2. *Valence* refers to the value a person places on the outcome or reward. Generally, the higher the value (importance) of the outcome or reward, the better the chance of motivation.[58] For example, a supervisor, Jean, wants an employee, Sam, to work harder. Jean talks to Sam and tells him that working hard will result in a promotion. If Sam wants the promotion, he will probably be motivated. However, if Sam does not want the promotion, it will not motivate him.

Following are some keys to using expectancy theory successfully:

1. Clearly define objectives and the performance needed to achieve them.[59]
2. Tie performance to rewards. High performance should be rewarded. When one employee works harder to produce more than other employees and is not rewarded, he or she may slow down.[60]
3. Be sure rewards have value to employees.[61] Managers should get to know employees as individuals.
4. Make sure employees believe that management will do what it says it will. For example, employees must believe that management will give them a merit raise if they work hard. And management must do so to earn employees' trust.[62]

Steve and Diane Warren are co-owners of **Katzinger's Delicatessen** in Columbus, Ohio. They wanted to increase the company's performance by cutting the cost of food to below 35 percent of sales, without sacrificing quality or service. When they set this goal, they told employees that they would share 50 percent of the savings with them each month. Employees, mostly young part-timers, were well trained and knew they could cut food costs if they worked together (expectancy). In addition, more pay was important to them (valence), so they were motivated to cut food costs. Workers proposed several innovations that were implemented. During the first month, food costs fell by 2 percent, and the employees received an extra $40 each. These monthly payments went as high as $95. By the end of the year, the 35-percent goal had been met, and the food quality and service had improved.[63]

I O M Market America focuses on attracting people who have the expectancy that they can succeed at running their own business, and it provides the business model to help them succeed. Valence does vary for these people, but most UnFranchise® owners are with seeking their own business so that they can achieve financial independence and the freedom to determine how to spend their time.

Learning Outcome 5
Explain the four types of reinforcement.

REINFORCEMENT THEORY

B. F. Skinner, reinforcement motivation theorist, contended that in order to motivate employees, there is no need for managers to identify and understand needs (content motivation theories) or to understand how employees choose behaviors to fulfill them (process motivation theories). Instead, managers need to understand the relationship between behaviors and their consequences and then reinforce desirable behaviors and discourage undesirable behaviors. *The reinforcement theory proposes that the consequences of their behavior will motivate employees to behave in predetermined ways.* Reinforcement theory states that behavior is learned through experiences of positive and negative consequences. Skinner proposed that the probability that a behavior will recur is affected by the delivery of reinforcement or punishment as a consequence of the behavior:[64] Employees learn what is, and is not, desired behavior as a result of the consequences for specific behaviors, which they engage in to meet their needs and self-interest.[65]

Types of Reinforcement

The four types of reinforcement are positive, avoidance (negative), punishment, and extinction. The first two tend to encourage desirable behavior. Punishment is a consequence that tends to discourage undesirable behavior; extinction eliminates a targeted behavior.

POSITIVE REINFORCEMENT
One method of encouraging desirable behavior is to offer attractive consequences (rewards).[66] For example, an employee who arrives on time for a meeting is rewarded by thanks from the supervisor. The thank-you is used to reinforce punctuality. Other positive reinforcers are pay raises, promotions, bonuses, and so forth.[67] Positive reinforcement is an excellent motivator for increasing productivity. In fact, if desirable behavior is not positively reinforced, it may decrease or even be eliminated. (The elimination of a behavior through lack of reinforcement is called *extinction*.) For example, if employees' high performance is ignored by management, the employees may stop making extra effort, thinking "Why should I do a good job if I'm not rewarded in some way?"[68]

AVOIDANCE REINFORCEMENT
Avoidance reinforcement is also called *negative reinforcement*. Like positive reinforcement, avoidance reinforcement is used to encourage continued desirable behavior; in this case, the reinforcement occurs because the behavior prevents a negative consequence (instead of leading to a positive one).

WorkApplication6
Give an example of how expectancy theory has affected your motivation or someone else's you work with or have worked with. Be sure to specify the expectancy and the valence.

For example, an employee arrives at meetings on time to avoid the negative consequence of a reprimand. Or, a secretary makes efforts to improve the correspondence that she sends out so as to avoid hearing her supervisor complain about poor quality work. With avoidance reinforcement, it's the threat of a negative consequence that controls behavior.

PUNISHMENT

Punishment involves the actual use of a negative consequence to decrease undesirable behavior. For example, an employee who arrives late for a meeting is reprimanded immediately.[69] Other means of punishment include fines, demotions, and taking away privileges. (Note that rules, which are designed to get employees to avoid certain behaviors, are not punishment in and of themselves; punishment is only given if a rule is broken.) Using punishment may reduce the targeted behavior, but it may also cause other undesirable behavior, such as lower productivity or theft or sabotage. Punishment is very ineffective for motivating employees.[70]

Exhibit 12-5 illustrates how a manager might use reinforcement or punishment to try to improve the work of a subordinate. Clearly, the three methods are likely to lead to different results.

EXTINCTION

Positive reinforcement and avoidance reinforcement are used to encourage desirable behavior. Extinction (like punishment) is applied in an attempt to reduce or eliminate a behavior. Unlike punishment, however, which is the active application of a negative consequence, extinction involves withholding reinforcement when an undesirable behavior occurs. For example, a manager or team leader might ignore an employee who arrives late for a meeting; being ignored each time he is late should eventually cause the employee's tardiness to be extinguished. (Note that good performance or positive behaviors may also be extinguished if they are ignored.)

Join the Discussion Ethics & Social Responsibility

Airlines

1. Not using an airline ticket fully breaks the airline's rules, not any law, so it's not illegal. But is it ethical and socially responsible of travelers to do so?
2. Is it ethical and socially responsible of airlines to charge more for less travel?
3. Is it ethical and socially responsible to punish people who break the ticket rules?

Airlines often charge more for one-way tickets and for flights ending at their hubs than for round-trip tickets and for flights through their hubs to other destinations. So to save money, some travelers buy round-trip tickets but only go one way, and some buy tickets through the hub but end their travel at the hub instead of taking the connection. The airlines call this behavior breach of contract, and they have punished travel agencies for selling tickets that aren't properly used, have demanded higher fares from travelers caught using tickets improperly, and have cancelled some travelers' frequent-flier miles, saying they were fraudulently obtained.[71]

Exhibit 12-5 *Types of Reinforcement*

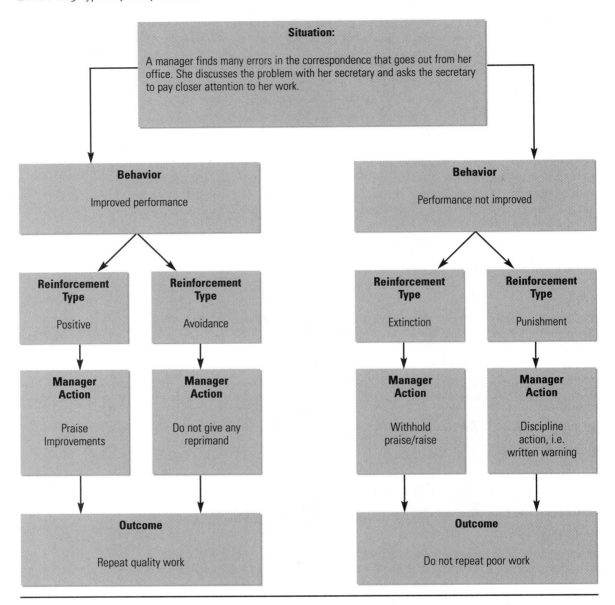

Schedules of Reinforcement

An important consideration in using positive reinforcement to control behavior is when to reinforce performance. The two major reinforcement schedules are continuous and intermittent.

CONTINUOUS REINFORCEMENT

With a continuous schedule of reinforcement, each and every desired behavior is reinforced. Examples of this approach include the use of a machine with an automatic counter that lets the employee know, at any given moment, exactly how many units have been produced; the payment of a piece rate for each unit produced; or a compliment from the manager for every positive customer report.

INTERMITTENT REINFORCEMENT

With intermittent reinforcement schedules, reinforcement is given based on the passage of time or amount of output. When the reinforcement is based on the passage of time, an *interval* schedule is being used. When reinforcement is based on output, a *ratio* schedule is being used. Ratio schedules are generally better motivators than interval schedules. When electing to use intermittent reinforcement, you have four alternatives:

1. Fixed-interval schedule (for example, giving a paycheck every week or breaks and meals at the same time every day)
2. Variable-interval schedule (giving praise only now and then)
3. Fixed-ratio schedule (giving a bonus after workers produce at a standard rate)
4. Variable-ratio schedule (operating a lottery for employees who have not been absent for a set time)

Motivating with Reinforcement

Several organizations, including **3M, Frito-Lay**, and **B. F. Goodrich**, have focused on the use of reinforcement to increase productivity. Generally, positive reinforcement is the best motivator. Continuous reinforcement is better for sustaining desired behavior; however, it is not always possible or practical. Following are some general guidelines for using reinforcement:

1. Make sure employees know what behavior is expected and reinforced.[72] Set clear objectives.[73]
2. Select appropriate rewards.[74] A reward to one person could be considered a punishment by another. Know your employees' needs.
3. Select the appropriate reinforcement schedule.
4. Do not reward mediocre or poor performance.[75]

WorkApplication7

Give a few examples of the types of reinforcement, and the schedules used, at a present or past job.

Join the Discussion Ethics & Social Responsibility

Using Reinforcement Theory

1. Does reinforcement motivate you?
2. Is reinforcement effective (does it serve to motivate) in today's global economy?
3. Is the use of reinforcement theory ethical and socially responsible or manipulative?

Reinforcement theory can be used successfully to maintain and increase performance. However, its use does have critics, who claim that it is based on the traditional hierarchical model, with managers in control of employees, a model that is no longer viable in today's global economy.[76] Some critics say that reinforcement manipulates employees, that it is the carrot-and-stick approach to motivation.

5. Look for the positive and give praise regularly, rather than focusing on the negative and criticizing.[77] Make people feel good about themselves (Pygmalion effect).[78]

6. Do things *for* your employees, instead of *to* them, and you will see productivity increases.

Giving Praise

In the 1940s, Lawrence Lindahl conducted a survey revealing that what employees want most from a job is full appreciation for work done. Similar studies have been performed over the years, with little change in results. When was the last time your boss thanked or praised you for a job well done? When was the last time your boss complained about your work? If you are a manager, when was the last time you praised or criticized your employees? What is the ratio of praise to criticism?

Being praised develops positive self-esteem in employees and leads to better performance—the Pygmalion effect. Praise is a motivator because it meets employees' needs for esteem/self-actualization, growth, and achievement. Giving praise creates a win-win situation. It is probably the most powerful, simplest, least costly, and yet most underused motivational technique.

Ken Blanchard and Spencer Johnson emphasized the importance of giving praise in their best-selling book *The One-Minute Manager*.[79] They developed a technique for feedback that involves giving one minute of praise. Exhibit 12-6 shows the steps in the **giving praise model**.

Step 1. Tell the employee exactly what was done correctly. When giving praise, look the person in the eye. Eye contact shows sincerity and concern. Be very specific and descriptive: "Mia, I just overheard you deal with that customer's complaint. You did an excellent job of keeping your cool; you were polite. That person came in angry and left happy." General statements such as "You're a good worker" are not as effective. On the other hand, don't talk for too long, or the praise loses its effectiveness.

Step 2. Tell the employee why the behavior is important. Briefly state how the organization, and/or person, benefits from the action. Also, tell the employee how you feel about the behavior. Be specific and descriptive: "Without customers, we don't have a business. One dissatisfied customer can cause hundreds of dollars in lost sales. It really made me proud to see you handle that tough situation the way you did."

Step 3. Stop for a moment of silence. Being silent is tough for many managers. The rationale for the silence is to give the employee the chance to feel the impact of the praise.

Exhibit 12-6 *Giving Praise*

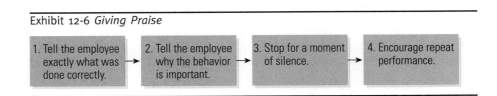

Step 4. Encourage repeat performance. This encouragement motivates the employee to continue the desired behavior. You may also make some physical gesture, if both parties feel comfortable with physical contact: "Thanks, Mia, keep up the good work" (while touching her on the shoulder or shaking hands).

As you can see, giving praise is easy and it doesn't cost a penny. Managers trained to give praise say it works wonders. It's a much better motivator than giving a raise or other monetary reward. Praise is especially effective positive reinforcement when used with a variable-interval schedule. Saying "thank you" and sending written thank-you notes are also important.[80]

Market America uses positive reinforcement with a continuous schedule, as each and every sale results in compensation. The company applies a standardized meeting

---

Applying The Concept 2

Motivation Theories

Identify the theory behind each of the following statements on how to motivate employees.

a. hierarchy of needs

b. ERG theory

c. two-factor theory

d. acquired needs theory

e. equity theory

f. goal-setting theory

g. expectancy theory

h. reinforcement theory

_____ 6. "I motivate employees by making their jobs interesting and challenging."

_____ 7. "I make sure I treat everyone fairly to motivate them."

_____ 8. "I know Kate likes people, so I give her jobs in which she works with other employees."

_____ 9. "Carl would yell in the halls because he knew it bothered me. So I decided to ignore his yelling, and he stopped."

_____ 10. "I got to know all of my employees' values. Now I can offer rewards that will motivate them when they perform a task well."

_____ 11. "Our company already offers good working conditions, salaries, and benefits, so we are working at satisfying employees' need for socialization."

_____ 12. "When my employees do a good job, I thank them using a four-step model."

_____ 13. "I used to try to improve working conditions to motivate employees. But I stopped and now focus on giving employees more responsibility so they can grow and develop new skills."

_____ 14. "I tell employees exactly what I want them to do, with a tough deadline that they can achieve."

_____ 15. "I now realize that I tend to be an autocratic manager because it helps fill my needs. I will work at giving some of my employees more autonomy in their jobs."

_____ 16. "I used to try to meet needs in a five-step sequence. After I heard about this new technique, I now focus on three needs and realize that needs can be unmet at more than one level at a time."

I
O
M **system throughout all of its areas. There are business briefings, meetings to introduce the business to interested parties, training sessions for new and existing distributors, seminars, district rallies, and a national convention. During the meetings, distributors are reinforced with praise and other recognition for accomplishments. Distributors share success stories, testimonials, voice-mail tips, tapes, and books.**

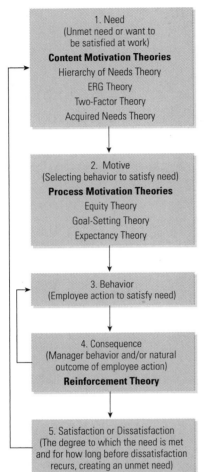

Exhibit 12-7
*The Motivation Process and
the Motivation Theories*

———————— Learning Outcome 6 ————————
State the major differences among content, process,
and reinforcement theories.

COMBINING THE MOTIVATION PROCESS AND MOTIVATION THEORIES

Motivation is important, but you may be wondering: How do these theories fit together? Is one the best? Should I try to pick the correct theory for a given situation? The groups of theories are complementary; each refers to a different stage in the motivation process or answers a different question. Content motivation theories answer this question: What needs do employees have that should be met on the job? Process motivation theories answer another question: How do employees choose behavior to fulfill their needs? Reinforcement theory answers a different question: What can managers do to get employees to behave in ways that meet the organizational objectives?

In the first section of this chapter, you learned that the motivation process moves from need to motive to behavior to consequence to satisfaction or dissatisfaction. The motivation process becomes a little more complex when we incorporate the motivation theories, in the form of answers to the preceding questions, as illustrated in Exhibit 12-7. Note that step 4 loops back to step 3 because, according to reinforcement theory, behavior is learned through consequences. Step 4 does not loop back to steps 1 or 2 because reinforcement theory is not concerned with needs, motives, or satisfaction; it focuses on getting employees to behave in certain ways through consequences provided by managers. Also, note that step 5 loops back to step 1, because meeting needs is an ongoing and never-ending process. Finally, be aware that, according to the two-factor theory, step 5, satisfaction or dissatisfaction, is not on one continuum but on two separate continuums (satisfied to not satisfied or not dissatisfied to dissatisfied), based on the level of need being met (motivator or maintenance factor).

DO MOTIVATION THEORIES APPLY GLOBALLY?

When you expand a business to other countries, diversity increases. The motivation theories you have studied were developed largely in North America. As organizations become global, managers must be aware of the cultural impact on theoretical generalizations. Geert Hofstede recognized that motivational concerns vary globally.[81] For example, a U.S. firm in Mexico gave workers a raise to motivate them to work more hours. The raise actually motivated the employees to work fewer hours, because they could make enough money to live and enjoy life (one of their primary values) in less time, so why should they work more hours? In Sweden, there is a very high tax rate on overtime pay that makes it less likely that more money will motivate employees to work more hours.

The intrinsic motivation provided by the satisfaction of higher-level needs tends to be more relevant in developed countries than in developing countries, in which most people are on a lower level of the hierarchy of needs. The term *self-actualization* cannot even be translated into some Chinese dialects. Even in developed countries, the level of needs on which people focus varies. In the United States, people tend to be motivated by higher-level needs of self-actualization and esteem; in Greece and Japan, security is more important; and in Sweden, Norway, and Denmark, people are more concerned with social needs. McClelland's need for achievement is more predominant in the United States than elsewhere. Thus, this need has limited use as a motivator outside of the United States and Canada, unless managers are willing to try to instill it in employees.

INDIVIDUALISTIC VERSUS COLLECTIVE CULTURES AND MOTIVATION

One major cultural difference that affects motivation in businesses is that between individualistic and collective societies. Individualistic societies (the United States, Canada, Great Britain, Australia) tend to value individual accomplishment. Collective societies (Japan, Mexico, Singapore, Venezuela, Pakistan) tend to value group accomplishment and loyalty. Cultural differences suggest that self-actualization, achievement, and esteem needs tend to be met through group membership in Japan and through individual accomplishments in the United States.

Expectancy theory holds up fairly well cross-culturally, because it is flexible. It allows for the possibility that there may be differences in expectations and valences across cultures. For example, social acceptance may be of higher value than individual recognition in collective societies.

Applying The Concept 3

Japanese versus American Motivation Techniques

Identify which country each statement is more closely associated with.

a. United States

b. Japan

_____ 17. The country that tends to focus on motivating groups rather than individuals

_____ 18. The country where managers would tend to get the best results with acquired needs theory

_____ 19. The country in which companies provide greater job security

_____ 20. The country where managers developed a system of giving pins/stars/etc. as symbols of high achievement.

The late W. Edwards Deming said that the United States must change from an individualistic society to a collective society if it is to survive in the global economy.[82] U.S. businesses have been moving toward the use of more teams and participative management.

IOM | **Market America's approach is working in the United States, Canada, and Australia, all of which have individualistic cultures. The company cannot be sure if its UnFranchise® approach will work in countries with more collective cultures. When Market America expands to different countries, it may need to adjust to meet diverse cultural needs.**

Take advantage of the companion Web site for *Management Fundamentals*, where you will find a broad array of resources to help you maximize what you learn in class:

- Try a quiz
- View chapter videos
- Download slides
- Boost your vocabulary
- Work through an Internet exercise
- Find related links

Take a look for yourself at *http://lussier.swlearning.com.*

Chapter Summary

1. Illustrate the motivation process.

Employees go through a five-step process to meet their needs. Note that this is a cyclical process, because needs recur.

2. Explain the performance formula and how to use it.

The performance formula proposes that performance is based on ability, motivation, and resources. If any of these three components is weak or absent, performance will be negatively affected. When a performance problem occurs, managers need to determine which component of the performance formula is weak and take appropriate action to correct the problem.

3. Discuss the major similarities and differences among the four content motivation theories: hierarchy of needs theory, ERG theory, two-factor theory, and acquired needs theory.

The similarity between the four content motivation theories is their focus on identifying and understanding employees' needs. The theories identify similar needs, but differ in the way they classify the needs. Hierarchy of needs theory classifies needs as physiological, safety, social, esteem, and self-actualization needs. ERG theory proposes existence, relatedness, and growth needs. Two-factor theory includes motivators and maintenance factors. Acquired needs theory includes achievement, power, and affiliation needs. (See

Exhibits 12-1 and 12-4 for a comparison of the four content theories of motivation.)

4. Discuss the major similarities and differences among the three process motivation theories: equity theory, goal-setting theory, and expectancy theory.

The similarity among the three process motivation theories is their focus on understanding how employees choose behaviors to fulfill their needs. However, they are very different in how they perceive employee motivation. Equity theory proposes that employees are motivated when their perceived inputs equal outputs. Goal-setting theory proposes that achievable but difficult goals motivate employees. Expectancy theory proposes that employees are motivated when they believe they can accomplish the task and the rewards for doing so are worth the effort.

5. Explain the four types of reinforcement.

Positive reinforcement is rewarding desirable behavior. Avoidance reinforcement (also called *negative reinforcement*) is the use of the threat of a negative consequence to prevent undesirable behavior; the negative consequence is not used as long as the behavior is desirable. Punishment is the actual use of a negative consequence to decrease undesirable behavior. Extinction is the withholding of reinforcement in order to reduce or eliminate (extinguish) a behavior.

6. State the major differences among content, process, and reinforcement theories.

Content motivation theories focus on identifying and understanding employees' needs. Process motivation goes a step further to understand how employees choose behavior to fulfill their needs. Reinforcement theory is not concerned about employees' needs; it focuses on getting employees to do what managers want them to do through the consequences provided for their behavior. The use of rewards is the best means of motivating employees.

7. Complete each of the following statements using one of this chapter's key terms.

_____ is the willingness to achieve organizational objectives.

The _____ is the process of moving from need to motive to behavior to consequence to satisfaction or dissatisfaction.

The _____ is performance = ability × motivation × resources.

_____ focus on identifying and understanding employees' needs.

The _____ proposes that employees are motivated by five levels of needs: physiological, safety, social, esteem, and self-actualization.

_____ proposes that employees are motivated by three needs: existence, relatedness, and growth.

_____ proposes that employees are motivated by motivators rather than by maintenance factors.

_____ proposes that employees are motivated by their need for achievement, power, and affiliation.

_____ focus on understanding how employees choose behaviors to fulfill their needs.

_____ proposes that employees are motivated when their perceived inputs equal outputs.

_____ proposes that achievable but difficult goals motivate employees.

_____ proposes that employees are motivated when they believe they can accomplish a task and the rewards for doing so are worth the effort.

_____ proposes that the consequences of their behaviors motivate employees to behave in predetermined ways.

The steps in the _____ are as follows: (1) Tell the employee exactly what was done correctly; (2) tell the employee why the behavior is important; (3) stop for a moment of silence; (4) encourage repeat performance.

Key Terms

acquired needs theory, 435
content motivation theories, 430
equity theory, 438
ERG theory, 432
expectancy theory, 441

giving praise model, 446
goal-setting theory, 439
hierarchy of needs theory, 431
motivation, 428
motivation process, 428

performance formula, 429
process motivation theories, 438
reinforcement theory, 442
two-factor theory, 433

Review and Discussion Questions

1. What is motivation, and why is it important to know how to motivate employees?
2. Do you agree that managers' attitudes and expectations affect employee motivation and performance? Explain your answer.
3. Do you agree with the performance formula? Will you use it on the job?
4. Do people really have diverse needs?
5. Which of the four content motivation theories makes the most sense to you? Why?
6. Which of the three process motivation theories makes the most sense to you? Why?
7. What reinforcement methods have been used to get you to go to work and to be on time?

8. Reinforcement theory is unethical because it is used to manipulate employees. Do you agree with this statement? Explain your answer.
9. Which motivation theory makes the most sense to you? Explain why.

10. What are the major methods and techniques you plan to use on the job as a manager to increase motivation and performance?
11. Do you agree with Deming's statement that U.S. companies need to change to a group approach to compete in a global economy?

Objective **Case**
FRIEDMAN'S MICROWAVE OVENS

Following is a conversation between Bob Lussier, this book's author, and Art Friedman, about a business technique that Friedman implemented at his business, Friedman's Appliances. At the time, Friedman's, in Oakland, California, employed 15 people.

Bob: What is the reason for your success in business?
Art: My business technique.
Bob: What is it? How did you implement it?
Art: I called my 15 employees together and told them, "From now on I want you to feel as though the company is ours, not mine. We are all bosses. From now on you decide what you're worth and tell the accountant to put it in your pay envelope. You decide which days and hours you work and when to take time off. We will have an open petty cash system that will allow anyone to go into the box and borrow money when they need it."
Bob: You're kidding, right?
Art: No, it's true. I really do these things.
Bob: Did anyone ask for a raise?
Art: Yes, several people did. Charlie asked for and received a $100-a-week raise.
Bob: Did he and the others increase their productivity to earn their raises?
Art: Yes, they all did.
Bob: How could you run an appliance store with employees coming and going as they pleased?
Art: The employees made up schedules that were satisfactory to everyone. We had no problems of under- or overstaffing.
Bob: Did anyone steal from the petty cash box?
Art: No.
Bob: Would this technique work in any business?
Art: It did work, it still works, and it will always work!

In 1976, Friedman changed his business to Friedman's Microwave Ovens. For nearly 30 years, Friedman's has been providing superior service, competitive prices, unconditional satisfaction guarantees, and cooking classes to educate customers on how to get the most from their microwaves. Friedman's also offers microwave repair and installation service.

Friedman's Microwave Ovens still utilizes Art Friedman's motivational technique of making everyone a boss at eight locations (seven in California and one in Tennessee), with over 2 million satisfied customers. Freidman's does have a Web site, and although the company does not sell microwave ovens directly through the site, it does sell accessories. The Web site provides a toll-free number and an e-mail address for customers who want to contact Friedman's customer service department.

Support your answers to the following questions with specific information from the case, the text, and/or the Web or other source.

_____ 1. Art Friedman's techniques focus on motivation and performance.
   a. true
   b. false

_____ 2. On which factor in the performance formula did Friedman focus?
   a. ability
   b. motivation
   c. resources

_____ 3. On which needs level do Friedman's employees appear to be?
   a. physiological   d. esteem
   b. safety   e. self-actualization
   c. social

_____ 4. On which level of ERG needs is Friedman focusing?
   a. existence
   b. relatedness
   c. growth

_____ 5. Which need does Friedman's technique place least emphasis on?

a. achievement
b. power
c. affiliation

_____ 6. Which of these would Herzberg say Friedman is using?

a. maintenance
b. motivators

_____ 7. Vroom would agree that Friedman uses expectancy motivation theory.

a. true
b. false

_____ 8. Adams would say Friedman uses _____.

a. equitable rewards
b. underrewards
c. overrewards

_____ 9. Friedman motivates employees through goal-setting theory.

a. true
b. false

_____10. Friedman uses which types of reinforcement?

a. positive   c. punishment
b. negative   d. extinction

11. Do you know of any organization that uses any unusual techniques to motivate employees? If yes, what is the organization's name? What does it do?

12. Could Friedman's technique work in all organizations? Explain your answer.

13. If you were in a position of authority, would you use Friedman's technique? Explain your answer.

Cumulative Case Questions

14. What does this case have to do with entrepreneurship? (Chapter 3)

15. When Friedman made the decision to change how his company was run, what was the classification of the problem? (Chapter 4)

16. What is the role of delegation and authority in this case? (Chapter 6)

17. What type of change did Friedman make? (Chapter 7)

18. How would the changes affect the human resources process at Friedman's? (Chapter 8)

Video Case

THE BUFFALO ZOO

About The Buffalo Zoo

This video explores the motivational methods and programs put in place at the zoo in Buffalo, New York, by new director Donna Fernandes. The video provides an especially vivid example of how job enrichment and increased communication and personal accountability can lead to improved job performance.

View the Video (10–15 minutes)

View the video on the Buffalo Zoo in class or at _http://lussier.swlearning.com_.

Read the Case

Donna Fernandes isn't your average manager. Her area of expertise is the behavior of slugs—the real ones that are the scourge of gardeners everywhere, not the human kind that you sometimes encounter in the workplace. She holds an MBA and a doctorate in science from Princeton University.

She's led wildlife tours in Africa, hosted her own educational TV show, and is now director of the Buffalo Zoo, where her "staff" includes elephants and hyenas.

When Fernandes arrived at the Buffalo Zoo, something had to be done to bring the 125-year-old institution (the nation's third-oldest zoo) back to life. After her appointment, Fernandes quickly outlined plans to bring the zoo back up to the standards of the American Zoo and Aquarium Association, backed by a pledge of $350,000 from Governor George Pataki, and she began finding ways to empower everyone inside and outside the organization to make the zoo the very best it could be. She abolished rigid policies that actually interfered with employees' freedom to get their jobs done and instituted new standards of communication and respect at all levels. Under Fernandes' leadership, new exhibits and exciting events are plentiful, and employees are much happier in their jobs.

Answer the Questions

1. These days, the atmosphere at the Buffalo Zoo is much more upbeat. What types of intrinsic rewards are workers now receiving from their jobs at the zoo?
2. How important is empowerment in motivating employees at the Buffalo Zoo?

Sources: James Fink, "Zoo Nears $26 Million Fund-raising Goal," *Business First*, June 16, 2004, at *http://buffalo.bizjournals.com/ buffalo/stories/2004/06/14/daily24html*, accessed June 24, 2004; Christina Abt, "Donna Fernandes, Director, Buffalo Zoological Society," *EVE*.

Behavior **Modeling**

GIVING PRAISE

This chapter's scenario shows a bank branch manager, Laura, complimenting Kelly, a teller, for successfully handling an angry customer. Laura follows the steps in Exhibit 12-6.

Objective

To better understand the process of giving praise.

View the Video

View the accompanying video in class or at *http://lussier.swlearning.com*. This video can be used prior to conducting Skill Builder 1.

Skill Builder **1**

GIVING PRAISE

Think of a job situation in which you did something well, deserving of praise and recognition. For example, you may have saved the company some money, you may have turned a dissatisfied customer into a happy one, and so on. Imagine yourself in a management position, and write out the praise you would give to an employee for doing what you did.

Briefly describe the situation:

_____

_____

Step 1. Tell the employee exactly what was done correctly.

_____

_____

_____

Step 2. Tell the employee why the behavior is important.

_____

_____

_____

Step 3. Stop for a moment of silence. (Count to five silently.)

Step 4. Encourage repeat performance.

_____

_____

_____

Apply It

What did I learn from this experience? How will I use this knowledge in the future?

_____

_____

Your instructor may ask you to do this Skill Builder in class in a group. If so, the instructor will provide you with any necessary information or additional instructions.

Skill **Builder** 2
SELF-MOTIVATION

Review the two Self-Assessment exercises.

What did you learn about yourself?

_____

_____

How can you improve your self-motivation so that you can be more successful?

_____

_____

Your instructor may ask you to do this Skill Builder in class in a group. If so, the instructor will provide you with instructions.

Learning Outcomes

After studying this chapter, you should be able to:

1. State the differences among trait, behavioral, and situational leadership theorists. **PAGE 458**

2. Explain why the terms *manager* and *leader* are not interchangeable. **PAGE 459**

3. Describe leadership trait theory, and identify Ghiselli's six significant leadership traits. **PAGE 460**

4. Discuss the major similarity and difference between two-dimensional leadership styles and the Leadership Grid®. **PAGE 464**

5. Identify the management levels at which charismatic, transformational, transactional, symbolic, and servant leadership styles are most appropriate. **PAGE 466**

13: Leading with Influence

6. State the primary difference between the contingency leadership model and other situational approaches to leadership. **PAGE 469**

7. Discuss the major criticism of both the leadership continuum model and the path-goal leadership model. **PAGE 471**

8. Describe the major characteristic of the normative leadership model. **PAGE 474**

9. Define the following **key terms**:

leadership
leadership trait theorists
behavioral leadership theorists
leadership style
two-dimensional leadership
   styles
Leadership Grid®
charismatic leadership
transformational leadership
transactional leadership
   complaint

symbolic leadership
servant leadership
situational approaches
   to leadership
contingency leadership model
leadership continuum
   model
path-goal model
Situational Leadership® model
substitutes for leadership

Ideas on Management
at American Express

American Express is best known for its credit card, but it offers much more. It has four business units: (1) Personal—individual cards with online transactions, shopping, financial services (invest, bank, borrow, local financial advice, discounts on auto insurance), and travel and entertainment (travel packages and cruises, travelers' cheques, restaurant reservations, tickets for theater, music, and more); (2) Small Business—financial solutions including cards, business loans, lines of credit, and equipment financing; (3) Merchants—businesses that accept American Express cards with online transactions, business to business, and marketing functions; (4) Corporate (businesses with more than 100 employees)—financial solutions including American Express cards, international payments, travel, asset management, financial education, retirement plans, third-party distribution, and tax and business services.

© AP Photo/Gino Domenico

Ken Chenault spent 20 years working his way up the corporate ladder to become chairman and CEO of American Express. He is one of the few African American CEOs of a Fortune 500 company. During Chenault's career at American Express, he has been well liked and has become known as a tough but fair manager who demands and gets results from the people on his team. Chenault uses candor and has courage, as he is willing to go against the old cultural norm of ignoring problems. He admits there are problems, defines them, and offers solutions. Chenault says the role of the leader is to define reality and to give hope.

Chenault became CEO just nine months before the September 11, 2001, terrorist attacks. Chenault led American Express through the crisis that cost the lives of 11 American Express employees, stranded thousands of customers, and closed its headquarters across the street from the World Trade Center.

IOM

1. What leadership traits does Ken Chenault have?
2. Which behavioral leadership styles does Ken Chenault use?
3. Is Ken Chenault a charismatic, transformational, symbolic, and/or servant leader?
4. Which situational leadership styles does Ken Chenault use?
5. Is handling complaints important at American Express?

To learn more about American Express, visit the company's Web site at http://www.americanexpress.com or log on to InfoTrac® College Edition at http://infotrac.thomsonlearning.com, where you can research and read articles on Ken Chenault and American Express. Select the advanced search option and key in record number A127933983, A120192947, or A74357799 to get started.

Sources: John A. Byrne and Heather Timmons, "Tough Time for a New CEO," *Business Week* (October 29, 2001), p. 64; Nelson D. Scwartz, "American Express: What's in the Cards for Amex," *Fortune* (January 22, 2001), p. 58.

———————————— Learning Outcome 1 ————————————

State the differences among trait, behavioral, and situational
leadership theorists.

LEADERSHIP AND TRAIT THEORY

In this section, we discuss leadership and its importance in organizations, the difference between leadership and management, and leadership trait theory.

Leadership

Leadership *is the process of influencing employees to work toward the achievement of organizational objectives.* Leadership is perhaps the most talked-about, researched, and written-about management topic.[1] Ralph Stogdill's well-known *Handbook of Leadership* contains over 3,000 references on the topic, and Bass's revision of it lists well over 5,000 publications on leadership.[2] Even in the high-tech global village, a manager needs to be 95 percent leader and 5 percent technician.[3] Leaders have a substantive effect on organization's overall performance.[4] A critical role of a CEO is to find and develop leaders.[5] As Baby Boomers retire, it is projected that one in five top management positions and nearly one in four middle management positions will become vacant.[6] Everyone has leadership potential.[7] Are you ready to lead?

As you have seen throughout the book, Carly Fiorina had to prove that she had leadership skills in order to break through the glass ceiling and become CEO of **Hewlett-Packard**. Fiorina was recognized for her effective leadership in transforming HP in order to take advantage of the global Internet economy. Fiorina's leadership skills resulted in the acquisition of **Compaq**. This acquisition was an important part of her strategic plan for HP.[8]

It is generally agreed that leadership skills can be developed.[9] This observation has resulted in a proliferation of programs and courses aimed at improving such skills.[10] Major corporations are sending managers to executive education programs offered by major universities, including Harvard, the University of Pennsylvania, the University of Michigan, and Stanford. However, it was the **Center for Creative Leadership (CCL)** that got the top rating for leadership development by *Business Week* for six consecutive years.[11]

The Center for Creative Leadership is a not-for-profit organization dedicated to promoting understanding of leadership and expanding the leadership capabilities of individuals from all types of organizations. CCL has headquarters in Greensboro, North Carolina, with additional campuses in Colorado Springs, Colorado, and San Diego, California, as well as CCL-Europe and CCL-Asia facilities. It also offers its programs through agreements with licensed and certified network associates. CCL programs develop some 20,000 leaders annually, from 3,000 organizations around the world. CCL also influences thousands of leaders around the world through its publications, products, events, and networks. More than 400,000 professionals from corporations (including **DaimlerChrysler, Microsoft, Pepsi**, and **Verizon**) and not-for-profits (including Cornell

University, the U.S. Army and U.S. Navy, and the U.S. Postal Service) have participated in CCL leadership programs.[12]

Leaders versus Managers

People tend to use the terms *manager* and *leader* interchangeably. However, managers and leaders differ.[13] Leading is one of the four management functions (planning, organizing, leading, and controlling). Thus, management is broader in scope than leadership. A manager can have this position without being a true leader. There are managers—you may know of some—who are not leaders because they do not have the ability to influence others. There are also good leaders who are not managers.[14] An informal leader, an employee group member, is a case in point. You may have worked in a situation where one of your peers had more influence in the department than the manager. Managers need to change from being the boss to being the leader.[15] You can develop your leadership skills by applying the principles in this chapter.

An important objective of management education programs is to prepare people to be outstanding managers and leaders.[16] You can develop your management and leadership skills in college, in courses like this one, and through organizational programs.[17] Major organizations spend millions to train employees annually.

General Electric (GE) has long been known for developing some of the best leaders in business, as its managers have gone on to become CEOs of other major corporations. Globally, GE invests about $1 billion annually in training and education programs. The centerpiece of GE's commitment to leadership development is the John F. Welch Leadership Center in Ossining, New York, founded in 1956 as the world's first major corporate business school. The center is named for former CEO Jack Welch, in recognition of his 20 years of support for leadership development, which he called his number-one job. Thousands of GE managers are trained at the center annually. Also, GE employees from around the globe come there to work on business problems and opportunities. Sometimes, customers, suppliers, and business colleagues participate, sharing their knowledge to enhance GE's global growth and competitiveness.[18]

As a management consultant, Jack Welch continues to develop leaders. In fact, although he was not going to vote for a Democrat in the November 2004 presidential elections, it didn't stop him from telling Democrats what to look for in a leader.[19]

——————— Learning Outcome 3 ———————
Describe leadership trait theory, and identify Ghiselli's six
significant leadership traits.

Leadership Trait Theory

The formal study of leadership began in the early 1900s. Over the years, the trait, behavioral, and situational approaches contributed to the development of an understanding of leadership.[20] In this section, we discuss leadership trait theory; in the next two sections, we examine the behavioral and situational approaches.

Early studies were based on the assumption that leaders are born, not made. (Today, research supports the opposite: Leaders are made, not born.[21]) Researchers wanted to identify a set of characteristics or traits that distinguished leaders from followers or effective leaders from ineffective ones. **Leadership trait theorists** *attempt to determine a list of distinctive characteristics that account for leadership effectiveness.* Researchers analyzed physical and psychological traits, such as appearance, aggressiveness, self-reliance, persuasiveness, and dominance, in an effort to identify a set of traits that all successful leaders possessed.

INCONCLUSIVE FINDINGS

In 70 years, over 300 trait studies were conducted.[22] However, no one was able to compile a universal list of traits that all successful leaders possess. In all cases, there were exceptions. For example, several lists identified successful leaders as being tall. However, Napoleon was short. In addition, some people were successful in one leadership position but not in another. People also questioned whether traits such as assertiveness and self-confidence were developed before or after one became a leader. Indeed, if leaders were simply born and not made (in other words, if leadership skills could not be developed), there would be no need for courses in management.

THE GHISELLI STUDY

Edwin Ghiselli conducted probably the most widely publicized trait study. He studied over 300 managers from 90 different businesses in the United States and published his results in 1971.[23] He concluded that certain traits are important to effective leadership, though not all of them are necessary for success. Ghiselli identified the following six traits, in order of importance, as being significant traits for effective leadership:

1. *Supervisory ability*—getting the job done through others (basically, the ability to perform the four functions of management you are studying in this course)
2. *Need for occupational achievement*—seeking responsibility and having the motivation to work hard to succeed
3. *Intelligence*—the ability to use good judgment and clear reasoning
4. *Decisiveness*—the ability to solve problems and make decisions competently
5. *Self-assurance*—viewing oneself as capable of coping with problems and behaving in a manner that shows others that you have self-esteem
6. *Initiative*—self-starting, or being able to get the job done with a minimum of supervision from one's boss

Ken Chenault uses supervisory ability to get subordinates to perform according to his expectations. This skill was evident early in his career when he was able to inspire managers in American Express's poorly performing merchandise unit to turn the unit into a profitable one. Chenault has also demonstrated a need for occupational achievement: He is one of only a few African Americans in top management in corporate

America. His peers and former superiors also recognize him for his intelligence, decisiveness, and initiative. All of these traits no doubt played a large role in helping Chenault to reach the CEO position at American Express.

CURRENT USE OF TRAIT THEORY

Even though it is generally agreed that no universal set of leadership traits or qualities exists, people continue to study and write about leadership traits. For example, in Chapter 1, you completed a Self-Assessment that asked this question: What are the most important traits for success as a manager? The traits included integrity, industriousness, and ability to get along with people.

PERSONALITY TRAITS

Recall from Chapter 9 that your personality is made up of traits, and thus, personality is an important part of trait theory. Organizations continue to select managers who have particular personality traits, as these affect leadership style. To be an effective leader, you must first be yourself and be aware of who you are as a leader.[24] You get to know yourself better through the self-assessment exercises throughout this book; however, you can change aspects of your personality and still be yourself.

ETHICS AND SPIRITUALITY IN THE WORKPLACE

A leader's ethical behavior is strongly based on personal values, which are also part of one's personality.[25] Related to ethics and values is spirituality. People are looking for meaning in life and at work. Organizations are offering

WorkApplication1

Of Ghiselli's six traits, which does your boss possess? Are there any that she or he does not possess?

_____

_____

_____

_____

Join the Discussion Ethics & Social Responsibility

Dilbert

1. Do you agree with Scott Adams that leadership is basically manipulation?
2. Do we really need leaders?
3. Is it ethical and socially responsible to make fun of CEOs?

Through his cartoon character Dilbert, Scott Adams makes fun of managers. Adams distrusts top-level managers and has said that leadership is really about manipulating people to get them to do something they don't want to do, when there may not be anything in it for them. According to Adams, CEOs basically pull the same scam as fortunetellers, who make up a bunch of guesses and when, by chance, one is correct, hope you forget the other errors. First, CEOs blame their predecessors for anything that is bad; then, they shuffle everything around, start a new strategic program, and wait. When things go well, the CEO takes the credit—whether deserved or not—and moves on to the next job. Adams says that we may be hung up on leadership as part of our DNA. Apparently, we have always sought to put somebody above everybody else.[26]

programs to help employees find this meaning by engaging consulting firms such as Spirit at Work.[27]

Evangelist Billy Graham identified four main character traits as personal qualities of leadership: (1) *integrity*, (2) *personal security*, (3) *sense of priority*, and (4) *vision*.[28] Zig Ziglar, a world-famous motivational speaker and best-selling author who trains people to be successful, and Peter Lowe, who conducts success seminars all over the world, both say that proper emphasis on the spiritual aspects of life is extremely important to success.[29] Research has shown that people who attend church regularly make more money, have better health, are happier with their jobs and family life, and have a much lower divorce rate. "In short, they get more of the things that money can buy and all of the things that money can't buy."[30] Of course, not all successful leaders are spiritual.

BEHAVIORAL LEADERSHIP THEORIES

By the late 1940s, most leadership research focused on the behavior of leaders, rather than on analyzing their traits. In the continuing quest to find the best leadership style for all situations, researchers attempted to identify differences in the behavior of effective leaders versus that of ineffective leaders. The focus on what leaders do also provided insight into the relationship between leaders and their followers.[31] **Behavioral leadership theorists** *attempt to determine distinctive styles used by effective leaders.* Recall that Douglas McGregor, a behavioral theorist, developed Theory X and Theory Y. Complete the Self-Assessment to determine your leadership behavior according to Theory X and Theory Y.

In this section, we discuss the basic leadership styles, two-dimensional leadership styles, the Leadership Grid, and contemporary perspectives on behavioral leadership.

Self-Assessment

Theory X and Theory Y Leadership Behavior

Beside each of the following 10 statements, place the letter (U, F, O, or S) that best describes what you would do as a manager. There are no right or wrong answers.

Usually (U)   Frequently (F)

Occasionally (O)   Seldom (S)

_____ 1. I would set the objectives for my department alone, rather than include employees' input.

_____ 2. I would allow employees to develop their own plans, rather than develop them myself.

_____ 3. I would delegate several tasks I enjoy doing to employees, rather than do them myself.

_____ 4. I would allow employees to make decisions to solve problems, rather than making them myself.

(Continued)

Theory X and Theory Y Leadership Behavior   (*Continued*)

_____ 5. I would recruit and select new employees alone, rather than using employees' input.

_____ 6. I would orient and train new employees myself, rather than have employees do it.

_____ 7. I would tell employees only what they need to know, rather than give them access to anything they want to know.

_____ 8. I would spend time praising and recognizing employees' work efforts, rather than just giving criticism.

_____ 9. I would set several controls for employees to ensure that objectives are met, rather than allowing employees to set their own controls.

_____10. I would frequently observe my employees to ensure that they are working and meeting deadlines, rather than leaving them alone.

To better understand your own behavior toward employees, score your answers. For items 1, 5, 6, 7, 9, and 10, give yourself one point for each U; two points for each F; three points for each O; and four points for each S. For items 2, 3, 4, and 8, give yourself one point for each S; two points for each O; three points for each F; and four points for each U. Total all points. Your score should be between 10 and 40.

Theory X and Theory Y are on opposite ends of a continuum. Most people's behavior falls somewhere between the two extremes. Place a check on the continuum where your score falls.

Theory X   10 ———— 20 ———— 30 ———— 40   Theory Y
Behavior   Behavior
(More Autocratic)   (More Participative)

The lower your score, the stronger your Theory X behavior, and the higher your score, the stronger your Theory Y behavior. A score of 20–30 could be considered balanced between the two theories. Your score may not be an accurate measure of how you would behave in an actual managerial position. However, it should help you anticipate how you are likely to behave.

Basic Leadership Styles

Leadership style *is the combination of traits, skills, and behaviors managers use in interacting with employees.* Note that behavioral theorists focus on the leaders' behaviors.[32] However, behaviors are based on traits and skills.

In the 1930s, before behavioral theory became popular, research was conducted on the managerial leadership style. The studies identified three basic leadership styles:

1. *Autocratic*—the leader makes decisions, tells employees what to do, and closely supervises employees (similar to Theory X behavior).
2. *Democratic*—the leader encourages employee participation in decisions, works with employees to determine what to do, and does not closely supervise employees (similar to Theory Y behavior).
3. *Laissez-faire*—the leader takes a leave-employees-alone approach, allowing them to make the decisions and decide what to do, and does not follow up.[33]

———————————— Learning Outcome 4 ————————————
Discuss the major similarity and difference between
two-dimensional leadership styles and
the Leadership Grid.

Two-Dimensional Leadership Styles

Two-dimensional leadership styles *are four possible leadership styles that are based on the dimensions of job structure and employee consideration.*

STRUCTURING AND CONSIDERATION STYLES

In 1945, the Personnel Research Board of **The Ohio State University** began a study to determine effective leadership styles.[34] In the process, researchers developed an instrument known as the Leader Behavior Description Questionnaire (LBDQ). Respondents to the questionnaire perceived leaders' behavior on two distinct dimensions:

1. *Structuring.* The extent to which the leader takes charge to plan, organize, lead, and control as the employee performs the task. This dimension focuses on getting the job done.
2. *Consideration.* The extent to which the leader communicates to develop trust, friendship, support, and respect. This dimension focuses on developing relationships with employees.

JOB-CENTERED AND EMPLOYEE-CENTERED STYLES

At approximately the same time as The Ohio State University studies began, the **University of Michigan's** Survey Research Center initiated its own leadership studies.[35] This research identified the same two dimensions, or styles, of leadership behavior as the Ohio research. However, the Michigan researchers called the two styles *job-centered* (analogous to structuring) and *employee-centered* (analogous to consideration).

USING TWO-DIMENSIONAL LEADERSHIP STYLES

When interacting with employees, the manager can focus on getting the job done through directing (structuring, or job-centered behavior) and/or through developing supportive relationships (consideration, or employee-centered behavior). Combinations of the two dimensions of leadership result in four leadership styles illustrated in Exhibit 13-1. The Ohio State University and University of Michigan leadership models differ because OSU considered the two dimensions to be independent of one another while UM placed the two dimensions at opposite ends of the same continuum.

Basketball legend Earvin Johnson founded **Magic Johnson Theatres** with partner **Loews Cineplex** to establish theatres in underserved minority communities in metropolitan areas. The company has theatres in five cities (Atlanta, Houston, Los Angeles, New York, and North Randall, Ohio) with 60 screens. Magic Johnson's dream was not only to establish theatres in poorer communities but also for each theatre to serve as a business stimulus, fostering local economic growth and financial empowerment in the community. Johnson is the chairman and plays an active role on the management committee, involving himself in strategic planning, operations, and public relations.[36]

WorkApplication2

Recall a present or past boss. Which of the four leadership styles created by Ohio State's version of the two-dimensional leadership model did your boss use most often? Describe your boss's behavior.

_____

_____

_____

_____

_____

Exhibit 13-1 *The Ohio State University and University of Michigan Two-Dimensional Leadership Styles*

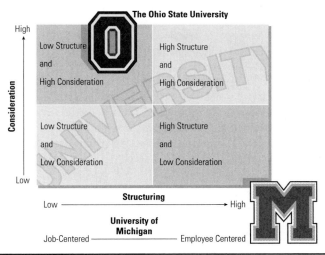

Johnson's business leadership style can be described as autocratic and structuring (job-centered). He has a team of people who advise him, including experts from Loews who taught him how to establish and run a business, but he calls the shots. Everyone knows they have to deal with Johnson.[37]

The Leadership Grid®

Robert Blake and Jane Mouton developed the Managerial Grid, which Blake and Anne Adams McCanse later transformed into the Leadership Grid.[38] The Leadership Grid is based on the same two leadership dimensions—structuring and consideration—which Blake and McCanse called "concern for production" and "concern for people." *The* **Leadership Grid®** *identifies the ideal leadership style as incorporating a high concern for both production and people.* A questionnaire is used to measure a manager's concern for people and production on a scale from 1 to 9, 1 being low concern and 9 being high concern. Five major leadership styles are highlighted on the grid:

(1, 1)   The leader with an *impoverished management style* has low concern for both production and people. The leader does the minimum required to remain employed in the position.

(9, 1)   The leader with an *authority-compliance management style* has a high concern for production and a low concern for people. The leader focuses on getting the job done; people are treated like machines.

(1, 9)   The leader with a *country club management style* has a high concern for people and a low concern for production. The leader strives to maintain a friendly atmosphere without regard for production.

(5, 5)   The leader with a *middle-of-the-road management style* has balanced, medium concern for both production and people. The leader strives to maintain minimal satisfactory performance and morale.

WorkApplication3

Recall a present or past boss. Which of the five major leadership styles did your boss use most often? Describe your boss's behavior.

_____

_____

_____

_____

_____

(9, 9)   The leader with a *team management style* has a high concern for both production and people. This leader strives for maximum performance and employee satisfaction.

According to behavioral theorists, the team leadership style is the most appropriate style to use in all situations. However, other researchers have stated that this belief is a myth.

I O M

At American Express, Ken Chenault has used the team management style most frequently since assuming his post as CEO. However, in certain situations, he has adapted his style. For example, after the World Trade Center disaster, Chenault adopted a more country club style as he expressed a higher concern for the immediate emotional and safety needs of employees while placing concerns about the company's production on the back burner.

Learning Outcome 5

Identify the management levels at which charismatic, transformational, transactional, symbolic, and servant leadership styles are most appropriate.

Contemporary Perspectives

Some current researchers focus on top-notch managers who exhibit certain behaviors that make them outstanding. These researchers focus on charismatic, transformational, transactional, symbolic, and servant leadership.

Applying The Concept 1

The Leadership Grid

Identify the leadership style described in each of the five situations.

a. impoverished   d. middle-of-the-road
b. country club   e. team
c. authority-compliance

_____ 1. The department has very high morale; its members enjoy their work. The productivity level is one of the lowest in the company. The leader is highly concerned about people but not about production.

_____ 2. The department has adequate morale and an average productivity level. The leader is somewhat concerned about both people and production.

_____ 3. The department has one of the lowest levels of morale in the company, yet is one of the top performers. The leader is highly concerned about production but not about people.

_____ 4. The department is one of the lowest producers in the company, with a low level of morale. The leader is not concerned about people or production.

_____ 5. The department is one of the top performers. The members have high morale. The leader is highly concerned about both people and production.

CHARISMATIC LEADERSHIP

Charismatic leadership *is a leadership style that inspires loyalty, enthusiasm, and high levels of performance.* The term *charismatic* has been applied to many leaders, from Pope John Paul II and Mother Teresa to Martin Luther King, Jr., Michael Jordan, and Bill Gates. Charismatic leaders have an idealized goal or vision, have a strong personal commitment to that goal, communicate the goal to others, and display self-confidence.[39] Followers in turn trust the leader's beliefs, adopt those beliefs themselves, feel affection for the leader, obey the leader, and develop an emotional involvement with the goal—all of which contribute to higher levels of performance.[40] Top-level managers of global businesses should develop the charismatic leadership style.[41]

Phil Jackson is a charismatic leader. Having won multiple championships with the **Chicago Bulls**, led by Michael Jordan, and then with the **Los Angeles Lakers**, Jackson was rated as one of the top coaches in the **National Basketball Association**. Jackson's charisma enabled him to command both the respect and the affection of his players. He was usually able to get star players to put aside their personal goals and differences to focus on the single goal of winning games and championships.

TRANSFORMATIONAL LEADERSHIP

Transformational leadership *is a leadership style that brings about continuous learning, innovation, and change.* Many charismatic leaders are also transformational leaders.[42] However, a charismatic leader is not transformational unless he or she inspires continuous innovative change.[43] Transformational leaders create significant changes as they build relationships by including followers' input in the change process.[44] They are good team leaders, allowing employees to be proactive as they match personal values to organizational values.[45] Transformational leaders believe that people do not resist change but rather resist what they don't understand.[46] Thus, these leaders are good at overcoming resistance to change. At the same time, they significantly transform organizations as they bring about changes in mission, strategy, structure, and culture. They also continue to bring about innovations in processes, products, and services. Transformational leaders are especially important to firms with growth strategies.[47] Transformational leadership has been shown to contribute to leader effectiveness, leader and follower satisfaction, follower efforts, and overall organizational performance; it is particularly effective during periods of turbulence in the external environment.[48]

Transformational leadership is important in a learning organization. CEO Jack Welch transformed **GE** from a slow bureaucracy to a learning organization that is the largest and one of the most admired and profitable firms in the world.[49]

TRANSACTIONAL LEADERSHIP

Transformational leadership has been contrasted with transactional leadership.[50] **Transactional leadership** *is a leadership style based on exchange.* The exchange involves the principle that "you do this work for me and I'll give this reward to you." The manager may engage in both structuring and consideration behaviors with employees during the exchange.[51] While transformational leaders tend to be top-level managers, transactional leadership occurs mostly among middle and first-line managers. However, top-level managers usually approve the monetary rewards used by lower-level managers in exchanges.

WorkApplication4

Recall the top manager from an organization you work for or have worked for. Would you call this CEO a charismatic or transformational leader? Why or why not?

SYMBOLIC LEADERSHIP

Symbolic leadership *is a leadership style based on establishing and maintaining a strong organizational culture.* Employees learn the culture (shared values, beliefs, and assumptions of how they should behave in the organization) through leadership.[52] After the World Trade Center disaster, Ken Chenault had to assume a symbolic leadership role to assure employees that **American Express** would continue and that their lives and roles were valued. Symbolic leadership starts with top managers and should flow down to middle and first-line managers. Symbolic leadership is also part of transformational leadership.[53]

SERVANT LEADERSHIP

Servant leadership *is a leadership style based on meeting the needs and goals of employees and the goals of the organization.* Servant leaders support employees and capitalize on the Pygmalion effect.[54] They focus on motivating employees by meeting their higher-level needs: valuing employees' input, encouraging participation, sharing power, developing self-confidence, and fostering creativity. By doing so, servant leaders motivate employees to go beyond role requirements and do what it takes to attain the goals of the organization.[55] Servant leaders can be found at all management levels, focusing on helping others, as they put the needs of others and the organization ahead of their self-interest.[56]

Land O'Lakes is a dairy cooperative, a commercial enterprise organized and jointly owned by farmers, that produces and distributes goods and is run for the benefit of its owners. Its president and CEO, Jack Gherty, is considered a servant leader. Gherty said that he became successful and Land O'Lakes is doing so well because he focuses on helping other people win; it just makes him feel good.[57]

Michael Leven is considered a servant leader because he puts integrity and the interests of the company ahead of his self-interest. Leven quit his job as president of **Days Inn** because he believed that the new owners of one of the company's largest franchises, Stanley Tollman and Monty Hundley, were unethical. They were convicted of fraud, conspiracy to commit bank fraud, and lying to banks, and Days Inn went into bankruptcy and was bought by **Cendant**.

Leven quit without any severance pay and took a job with **Holiday Inn**. Quitting cost him a lot of money, as he had no income for six months; then, when he joined Holiday Inn he took a 25 percent pay cut and a lower-level position as president of franchising. But he is not sorry for his decision to quit. He later became president and chief operating officer of Holiday Inn Worldwide.

Leven went on to start **U.S. Franchise Systems (USFS),** which has three hotel brands: **Microtel Inns & Suites, Hawthorn Suites**, and **Best Inns** and **Best Suites**. As CEO, Leven knew USFS would not meet its financial forecasts. Although he had no legal requirement to do so, and against recommendations, he went public with the announcement. USFS stock values dropped, but Leven refused to second-guess his decision. He knew it was the right thing to do.[58]

I O M

Ken Chenault is a charismatic leader, and it is his personal traits that make him charismatic. Tom Ryder, who competed with Chenault for the CEO position at American Express, said that when you work with Chenault, you feel you'll do anything for him. Chenault is also a transformational leader: Before he was CEO, he had the courage to challenge the old culture and make changes at American Express. As noted earlier,

Chenault handled the 9/11 crisis as a symbolic leader. Chenault also showed servant leadership style two weeks after the 9/11 tragedy: He gathered employees together for a "town hall meeting," personally comforted grief-stricken employees, and vowed to donate $1 million of profits to the families of American Express victims. He told them, "You represent American Express. All the people of American Express are what this company is about. In fact, you are my strength and I love you."

SITUATIONAL APPROACHES TO LEADERSHIP

Both trait and behavioral leadership theories were attempts to find the best leadership style in all situations. In the 1960s, it became apparent that no single leadership style is appropriate in all situations.

Situational approaches to leadership *attempt to determine appropriate leadership styles for particular situations.* In this section, we discuss some of the most popular situational approaches, including contingency leadership theory, the leadership continuum, path-goal theory, normative leadership theory, the Situational Leadership® model, and leadership substitutes and neutralizers.

———————————————— Learning Outcome 6 ————————————————
State the primary difference between the contingency leadership model and other situational approaches to leadership.

Contingency Leadership Model

In 1951, Fred E. Fiedler began to develop the first situational approach to leadership—the contingency theory of leader effectiveness.[59] Fiedler believed that one's leadership style reflects one's personality and remains basically constant. That is, leaders do not change styles.[60] *The* **contingency leadership model** *is used to determine if leadership style is task- or relationship-oriented and if the situation matches the style.*

LEADERSHIP STYLE

The first step is to determine whether the leadership style is task- or relationship-oriented. To do so, the manager fills in what Fiedler called the Least Preferred Coworker (LPC) scale. The LPC essentially answers this question: Are you more task-oriented or relationship-oriented in working with others? Note that unlike the model developed at Ohio State, Fiedler's model proposes two, not four, leadership styles: task-oriented leadership and relationship-oriented leadership.

SITUATIONAL FAVORABLENESS

After determining leadership style, the manager determines situational favorableness.[61] *Situational favorableness* refers to the degree to which a situation enables a leader to exert influence over followers. The three variables that determine situational favorableness, in order of importance, are as follows:

1. *Leader–follower relations.* Is the relationship between leader and followers good or poor? Do the followers trust, respect, accept, and have confidence in the leader? Is it a friendly, tension-free situation? Leaders with good leader–follower relations have more influence. The better the relations, the more favorable the situation.

2. *Task structure.* Is the task structured or unstructured? Do employees perform repetitive, routine, unambiguous, standard tasks that are easily understood? Leaders in a structured situation have more influence. The more repetitive the jobs, the more favorable the situation.

3. *Position power.* Does the leader have position power—the power to assign work, reward and punish, hire and fire, and give raises and promotions? The leader with position power has more influence. The more position power the leader has, the more favorable the situation.

WorkApplication5

Classify your present or past boss's preferred style as task- or relationship-oriented. Think of a specific situation at work and use the contingency model to determine the appropriate style to use for this situation. Did the boss use the appropriate style?

Once a manager who is using Fiedler's contingency leadership model has determined his or her leadership style and answered the three questions pertaining to situational favorableness, he or she can follow a decision tree to discover the best leadership approach to a given situation. Exhibit 13-2 shows the decision tree. If the manager's preferred leadership style is the one indicated by the decision tree, the manager proceeds. If, however, the manager's preferred leadership style is not ideal for the given situation, then the situation must be changed to match the manager's leadership style. One of the major criticisms of contingency theory is that it's often difficult to change a situation; critics say that when a manager's leadership style does not match the situation, the style should be changed.[62]

Recall from earlier chapters that CEO Steve Ballmer reorganized **Microsoft's** organizational structure. He set up a divisional structure with seven business units that are held accountable as profit centers. In doing so,

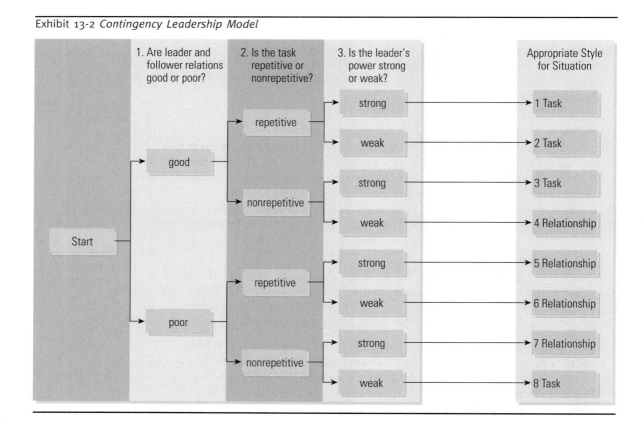

Exhibit 13-2 *Contingency Leadership Model*

Applying The Concept 2

Contingency Leadership Theory

Using Exhibit 13-2, determine the appropriate leadership style under the given conditions.

a. task-oriented   b. relationship-oriented

_____ 6. Saul, a manager, oversees the assembly of mass-produced containers. He has the power to reward and punish. Saul is viewed as a hard-nosed boss.

_____ 7. Karen is a manager from the corporate planning staff; she helps departments plan. Karen is viewed as being a dreamer who doesn't understand the company's various departments. Employees tend to be rude in their dealings with Karen.

_____ 8. Juan, a manager, oversees the processing of canceled checks for a bank. He is well liked by the employees. Juan enjoys hiring and evaluating his employees' performance.

_____ 9. Sonia, the principal of a school, assigns teachers to classes and other various duties. She hires and decides on tenure appointments. The school atmosphere is tense.

_____10. Louis, the chair of a committee charged with recommending ways to increase organizational performance, is highly regarded by the volunteer members from a variety of departments.

Ballmer changed the situational favorableness for the company's managers. First, leader–member relations changed when some employees were reassigned to other divisions headed by other managers. Task structure did not change for most employees. However, position power changed, as the seven unit heads were given more power.[63]

--------- Learning Outcome 7 ---------

Discuss the major criticism of both the leadership continuum model and the path-goal leadership model.

Leadership Continuum Model

Robert Tannenbaum and Warren Schmidt developed a model of leadership that focuses on who makes the decisions. They viewed leadership behavior on a continuum from autocratic (boss-centered) to participative (employee-centered). The continuum includes seven major styles from which a leader can choose. Exhibit 13-3 lists the seven styles.[64] *The leadership continuum model is used to determine which of seven styles of leadership, on a continuum from autocratic (boss-centered) to participative (employee-centered), is best for a given situation.*

Before selecting one of the seven leadership styles, the leader must consider the following three variables:

1. *The leader's preferred style.*
2. *The subordinates' preferred style for the leader.* Generally, the more willing and able subordinates are, the more freedom of participation should be used, and vice versa.

Exhibit 13-3 *The Leadership Continuum*

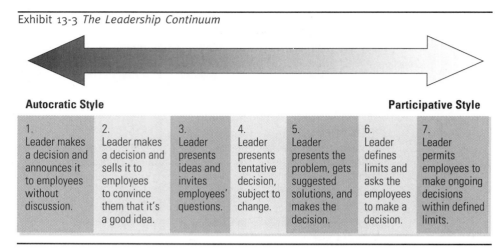

Autocratic Style						Participative Style
1. Leader makes a decision and announces it to employees without discussion.	2. Leader makes a decision and sells it to employees to convince them that it's a good idea.	3. Leader presents ideas and invites employees' questions.	4. Leader presents tentative decision, subject to change.	5. Leader presents the problem, gets suggested solutions, and makes the decision.	6. Leader defines limits and asks the employees to make a decision.	7. Leader permits employees to make ongoing decisions within defined limits.

Source: Adapted from Robert Tannenbaum and Warren Schmidt, "How to Choose a Leadership Pattern," *Harvard Business Review*, May/June, 1973.

WorkApplication6

Using the leadership continuum model, identify your boss's most commonly used leadership style. Now recall a specific situation in which this leadership style was used. Would you say this was the most appropriate leadership style in that situation? Explain.

3. *The situation.* Environmental considerations, such as the organization's size, structure, climate, goals, and technology and higher-level managers' leadership style and the time available, are also considered in selecting a leadership style.[65]

Tannenbaum and Schmidt noted that a leader should never try to trick followers into thinking that they made a decision that was actually made by the leader.[66]

Even though the continuum leadership model was very popular, one of the major criticisms of it was that the three factors to consider when selecting a leadership style are very subjective. In other words, determining which style to use in a given situation can be difficult.

The **U.S. Navy** is to some degree moving away from the old tradition of autocratic leadership to a more participative leadership style. Officers are no longer being trained simply to give orders; they are being prepared to help the Navy continually improve as a learning organization. Good ideas that come from the bottom up are being implemented immediately on many ships, and some have become standard practices throughout the Navy.[67]

Path-Goal Model

Robert House developed the path-goal leadership model. *The **path-goal model** is used to determine employee objectives and to clarify how to achieve them using one of four leadership styles.* The model focuses on how leaders influence employees' perceptions of their goals and the paths they follow toward goal attainment.[68] As summarized in Exhibit 13-4, the path-goal model uses situational factors to determine the leadership style that affects goal achievement through performance and satisfaction.[69]

SITUATIONAL FACTORS

Subordinates' situational factors are (1) authoritarianism, or the degree to which employees defer to leaders and want to be told what to do and how

Leadership Continuum

Refer to Exhibit 13-3 and indicate the leadership style exemplified in each statement.

a. 1   e. 5
b. 2   f. 6
c. 3   g. 7
d. 4

_____ 11. "Chuck, I selected you to be transferred to the new department, but you don't have to go if you don't want to."

_____ 12. "Sam, go clean off the tables right away."

_____ 13. "From now on, this is the way it will be done. Does anyone have any questions about the procedure?"

_____ 14. "These are the weeks when people can take their vacations. Let me know when you plan to take yours."

_____ 15. "I'd like your ideas on how to stop the bottleneck on the production line. Then I'll choose a solution to implement."

to do the job, (2) locus of control, or whether employees believe they control goal achievement (internal locus) or goal achievement is controlled by others (external locus), and (3) ability, or the extent of employees' ability to perform tasks to achieve goals. *Environmental* situational factors are (1) task structure, or the extent of repetitiveness in the job, (2) formal authority, or the extent of the leader's power, and (3) work group, or the extent to which coworkers contribute to job satisfaction.

LEADERSHIP STYLES

Based on the situational factors, a leader can select the most appropriate of the following leadership styles:

1. *Directive.* The leader provides high structure. Directive leadership is appropriate when subordinates want authoritarian leadership, have an external locus of control, and have low ability. Directive leadership is also appropriate when the task is complex or ambiguous, formal authority is strong, and the work group provides job satisfaction.

2. *Supportive.* The leader provides high consideration (that is, the leader makes efforts to develop the trust and respect of followers). Supportive leadership is appropriate when subordinates do not want authoritarian leadership, have an internal locus of control, and have high ability. Supportive leadership is also appropriate when the task is simple, formal authority is weak, and the work group does not provide job satisfaction.

3. *Participative.* The leader considers employee input when making decisions. Participative leadership is appropriate when subordinates want to be involved, have an internal locus of control, and have high ability. Participative leadership is also appropriate when the task is complex, authority is either strong or weak, and job satisfaction from coworkers is either high or low.

Exhibit 13-4 *A Summary of Path-Goal Factors and Styles*

Situational Factors	determine →	Leadership Styles	that affect →	Goal Achievement

Subordinate
  authoritarianism
  locus of control
  ability
Environmental
  task structure
  formal authority
  work group
		Directive
		Supportive
		Participative
		Achievement-oriented
				Performance
				Satisfaction

WorkApplication7

Identify your boss's most commonly used leadership style. Now recall a specific situation in which this style was used. From the perspective of the path-goal model, was this the most appropriate leadership style based on the situational factors? Explain.

4. *Achievement-oriented.* The leader sets difficult but achievable goals, expects subordinates to perform at their highest level, and rewards them for doing so. In essence, the leader provides both high structure and high consideration. Achievement-oriented leadership is appropriate when subordinates are open to authoritarian leadership, have an external locus of control, and have high ability. Achievement-oriented leadership is also appropriate when the environmental task is simple, authority is strong, and job satisfaction from coworkers is either high or low.

Although the path-goal model is more complex and specific than the leadership continuum model, it has been criticized for the same weakness found in that model: It is difficult to know which style to use in a given situation. Judgment calls are needed to select the appropriate style.

───────────── Learning Outcome 8 ─────────────
Describe the major characteristic of the normative leadership model.

Normative Leadership Model

Recall that Chapter 4 introduced Victor Vroom's normative participative decision-making model. The participative model is clearly a leadership model, although it focuses on making decisions. Return to Chapter 4 and review the text discussion and Exhibit 4-12. Recall your preferred leadership style in group situations, as determined in Skill Builder 1 in Chapter 10 (pages 377–380).

The normative leadership model is popular in the academic community, because it is based on research.[70] However, the model is not as popular with managers, who find it cumbersome to select from four types of decisions and an eight-question decision tree every time they have to make a decision.

Situational Leadership® Model

Paul Hersey and Ken Blanchard developed the Situational Leadership® model. *The* **Situational Leadership® model** *is used to select one of four leadership styles that match the employees' maturity level in a given situation.*[71] Hersey and Blanchard went beyond behavioral theory by developing a model that identifies which style a leader should use in a given situation. To determine leadership style, the leader determines the followers' maturity level. "Maturity level" does not mean how grown up employees act; rather, it refers to the level of employee development (competence and commitment)

WorkApplication8

Identify your boss's most commonly used normative leadership style. Now recall a specific situation in which this style was used. From the normative leadership perspective, was it the most appropriate leadership style? Explain.

or readiness to do the job (ability and willingness). If employee maturity is low, the leader uses a *telling style*, giving employees explicit directions about how to accomplish a task. If employee maturity is moderate to low, the leader uses a *selling style*, explaining decisions to gain understanding. If employee maturity is moderate to high, the leader uses the *participating style*, to facilitate decision making among subordinates. And if employee maturity is high, the leader uses a *delegating style*, giving employees responsibility for decisions and their implementation. Thus, the model identifies four leadership styles.

Hersey has used a baseball metaphor to explain how this model helps managers: "You can't give me the way to hit a home run every time at bat, but you can help me to increase my batting average."[72] Likewise, this book cannot teach you all the details of how to lead in every situation, but the models presented here can help you increase your leadership skills and managerial success.

In contrast to what Fiedler advocated with his contingency leadership model, Ken Chenault *does* change his leadership style as necessary to focus on tasks or relationships. For example, immediately after hearing that the World Trade Center had collapsed, Chenault used an autocratic style to make the decision to evacuate the American Express building across the street and to hire private planes to transport stranded American Express customers. However, his most common leadership style is participative (or facilitative, to use the terminology of the leadership continuum model).

WorkApplication9

Identify your boss's most commonly used leadership style. Would you say this is the most appropriate leadership style based on the maturity level of the employees in your team or organization? Explain.

_____

_____

_____

_____

Applying The Concept 4

Situational Leadership Styles

For each of the following situations, identify the maturity level of the employee and the leadership style the manager should use so that the job gets done.

a. Low maturity of employee: The manager should use the telling style.

b. Low to moderate maturity of employee: The manager should use the selling style.

c. Moderate to high maturity of employee: The manager should use the participating style.

d. High maturity of employee: The manager should use the delegating style.

_____16. Mary Ann has never done a report before, but you know she can do it with a minimum of help from you.

_____17. You told John to fill the customer order in a specific way. However, he deliberately ignored your directions. The customer returned the order to you with a complaint.

_____18. Tina is an enthusiastic employee. You have decided to expand her job responsibilities to include a difficult task that she has never done before.

_____19. Part of Pete's job, which he has done properly many times, is to take out the trash when the bin is full. It is full now.

_____20. Carl usually does an excellent job and gets along well with his coworkers. For the past two days, you have noticed a drop in the quality of his work, and yesterday you saw him arguing with a coworker. You want Carl to return to his usual level of performance.

Comparing Leadership Models

The behavioral and situational leadership models we've discussed are all based on two dimensions of leadership. However, as you've seen, different authors use different terms for what are basically the same dimensions. Exhibit 13-5 uses *direction* and *support* to describe these two dimensions; the columns in the exhibit are headed "High direction/Low support," "High direction/High support," and so on. The terms that appear below these headings have basically the same meanings as the column headings.

Leadership Substitutes Theory

The leadership theories and models that have been discussed so far assume that some leadership style will be effective in each situation. Steven Kerr and John Jermier argued that certain situational variables prevent leaders from affecting subordinates' attitudes and behaviors.[73] **Substitutes for leadership** *are*

Exhibit 13-5 *A Comparison of Behavioral and Situational Leadership Models*

	High direction/Low support	High direction/High support	Low direction/High support	Low direction/Low support
Behavioral Leadership Theories				
Basic leadership styles	Autocratic	Democratic		Laissez-faire
Ohio State model (Exhibit 13-1)	High structure/low consideration	High structure/high consideration	Low structure/high consideration	Low structure/low consideration
University of Michigan model (Exhibit 13-1)	Job-centered			Employee-centered
Leadership Grid®	Authority-compliance (9, 1)	Team (9, 9)	Country club (1, 9)	Impoverished (1, 1)
		Middle-of-the-road (5, 5)		

Contemporary perspectives
  Charismatic leadership
  Transformational leadership
  Transactional leadership
  Symbolic leadership
  Servant leadership				

Situational Approaches to Leadership				
Contingency leadership model (Exhibit 13-2)	Task		Relationship	
Leadership continuum model (Exhibit 13-3)	Style 1	Styles 2 and 3	Styles 4 and 5	Styles 6 and 7
Path-goal model	Directive	Achievement-oriented	Supportive	Participative
Normative leadership model	Decide	Consult	Facilitate	
Situational Leadership® model	Telling	Selling	Participating	Delegating
Leadership substitutes theory				

characteristics of the task, of subordinates, or of the organization that replace the need for a leader. These characteristics can also neutralize the effect of leadership behavior.[74] That is, the following may substitute for or neutralize leadership by providing direction and/or support:

1. *Characteristics of subordinates*—ability, knowledge, experience, training; need for independence; professional orientation; indifference toward organizational rewards
2. *Characteristics of task*—clarity, routineness, invariant methodology; provision of feedback concerning accomplishment and of intrinsic satisfaction
3. *Characteristics of the organization*—formality (explicit plans, goals, and areas of responsibility); inflexibility (rigid, unbending rules and procedures); very specific advisory and staff functions; closely knit, cohesive work groups; rewards outside of the leader's control; physical distance between superior and subordinates

Today, in their efforts to compete in the global economy, many organizations are using participative leadership styles. Top leadership gurus Jack Welch and Peter Drucker emphasize the importance of developing the leadership skills of all employees.[75] Managers at all levels who continue to use autocratic leadership styles are losing their jobs.

Jacques Nasser spent 30 years at **Ford** successfully working his way up to CEO. As CEO, Nasser set out to change Ford, in the process making autocratic decisions that upset many Ford dealers. He instituted a new performance appraisal system that required 5 percent of all managers to get at least a C performance rating each year. Anyone who received a C rating for two years in a row was dismissed, and many long-term middle and senior managers were forced out. Employees (and the UAW union) resented the new appraisal system and some brought lawsuits against Ford. Sales and product quality fell, and Nasser's autocratic methods and his leadership ability were questioned. The board of directors ended up forcing Nasser to resign.[76]

WorkApplication10

Could the characteristics of subordinates, task, or organization substitute for your present or a past boss? In other words, is your boss necessary? Explain.

_____

_____

_____

_____

WorkApplication11

Identify the one leadership theory or model you prefer. State why.

_____

_____

_____

_____

WorkApplication12

Describe the type of leader you want to be.

_____

_____

_____

_____

Join the Discussion Ethics & Social Responsibility

Leadership and Gender

1. Is it ethical and socially responsible to say that people of a particular gender make better leaders?
2. Do you think men and women lead in the same way, or not?
3. Are men or women more ethical and socially responsible as leaders?
4. Would you prefer to have a man or a woman as boss?

Are there differences in the leadership styles of men and women? Some researchers say that women tend to be more participative, relationship-oriented leaders, while men are more task-oriented. However, others say that men and women are more alike as leaders than different, and are equally effective.[77]

HANDLING COMPLAINTS

No matter how hard you try to do a good job and to satisfy all employees' and customers' needs, complaints will arise. *A* **complaint** *is an expression of dissatisfaction with a situation, often coupled with a request for change.* Many employees complain at work but do not take their complaint to a manager who can resolve it. Handling complaints requires strong leadership skills.[78] It is advisable to have an open-door policy that allows employees to feel free to come to you with a complaint. It is much better to get complaints out in the open and try to resolve them than to have employees complaining to everyone else but you. In this section, we discuss how to handle complaints; Skill Builder 2 will help you develop this skill.

Handling Employee Complaints

When employees come to you with a complaint, try not to take it personally as a reflection on you or your leadership ability. Even the best leaders have to deal with complaints. Do not become defensive or try to talk the employee out of the complaint. There are five steps you should take when an employee comes to you with a complaint.[79]

Step 1. Listen to the complaint and paraphrase it. If you cannot accurately state the complaint, you cannot resolve it. Your paraphrasing helps to clarify the complaint for everyone. When listening to the complaint, distinguish facts from opinions. At times, employees think they know the facts, when they do not. Sometimes, when managers explain the facts, complaints are dropped immediately. It is also helpful to identify the employee's feelings about the situation and his or her motives for making the complaint.

Step 2. Ask the complainer to recommend a solution. The complainer may have a good solution that you haven't thought of. However, asking about a solution does not mean that you must implement it. The recommended solution may not solve the problem, may be unfair to others, or may simply not be possible. In such cases, be sure to let the employee know why the suggestion will not be implemented.

Step 3. Schedule time to get all the facts and make a decision. Generally, the faster a complaint is resolved, the fewer the negative side effects. However, you may find it necessary to check records or talk to others about the complaint. It can also be helpful to talk to your own boss or to colleagues, who may have handled a similar complaint. Tell the employee that you will take a specific amount of time to consider the complaint; simply saying, "I'll get back to you" frustrates the employee and may make him or her think you have no intention of addressing the complaint.

Step 4. Develop a plan for addressing the complaint. You may decide to accept the employee's recommendation for a solution, or you may be able to work with the employee in coming up with a different solution. If you decide to take no action to resolve the complaint, you should clearly explain to the employee why you are choosing not to act. Remind the employee of any mechanisms that are available for appealing your decision.

Step 5. Implement the plan and follow up. It is important to make sure that the plan for resolving the complaint is implemented; following up ensures

Exhibit 13-6 *Steps in Addressing Employee Complaints*

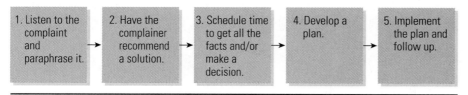

1. Listen to the complaint and paraphrase it. → 2. Have the complainer recommend a solution. → 3. Schedule time to get all the facts and/or make a decision. → 4. Develop a plan. → 5. Implement the plan and follow up.

WorkApplication13
Identify a complaint you brought to a manager. State the complaint and identify which steps in the complaint-handling model the manager did or did not follow. If you have never complained, interview someone who has.

that it is. Following up may involve meeting with the employee at some point after the solution is implemented. It is advisable to document the entire process in writing.

These steps are summarized in Exhibit 13-6.

Handling Customer Complaints

Handling a customer complaint is somewhat different from handling an employee complaint, but it is critical, because customer satisfaction is the major goal of many organizations. Unfortunately, most customers are dissatisfied with the way firms handle their complaints.[80] The steps for handling customer complaints are as follows:

Step 1. Admit the mistake and apologize. Around 60 percent of complaining customers simply want an apology, but only 5 percent receive one.[81] As when handling employees' complaints, you should listen to the customer's complaint and paraphrase it. Then admit that a mistake was made and apologize: "We're sorry the technician got dirt on your car's carpet."

Step 2. Agree on a solution. You can tell the customer what you intend to do about the problem: "I'll have a technician clean it right now." But a better approach is to ask the customer to recommend a solution to the problem: "How would you like us to handle the situation?" Customers consistently recommend solutions that cost far less than what managers might offer initially.

Step 3. Implement the solution quickly. Quick implementation has a direct effect on customer satisfaction. If the customer has to wait a week and then bring the car back to have the carpeting cleaned, he or she will be annoyed and may not do business with you again.[82]

Step 4. Prevent future complaints. Take quick corrective actions so that the mistake will not happen again.[83] For example, talk to the technician about the dirty carpet. (You'll read about coaching and disciplining employees in the next chapter.)

These steps are summarized in Exhibit 13-7.

Exhibit 13-7 *Steps in Addressing Customer Complaints*

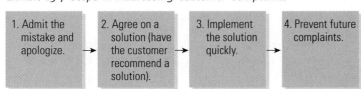

1. Admit the mistake and apologize. → 2. Agree on a solution (have the customer recommend a solution). → 3. Implement the solution quickly. → 4. Prevent future complaints.

Take advantage of the companion Web site for *Management Fundamentals*, where you will find a broad array of resources to help you maximize what you learn in class:

- Try a quiz
- View chapter videos
- Download slides
- Boost your vocabulary
- Work through an Internet exercise
- Find related links

Take a look for yourself at *http://lussier.swlearning.com.*

Chapter Summary

1. State the differences among trait, behavioral, and situational leadership theorists.

Trait theorists try to find a list of distinctive characteristics that account for leadership effectiveness. Behavioral theorists try to determine distinctive styles used by effective leaders and the one leadership style that is best in all situations. Situational theorists try to find the appropriate style for various situations and believe that the best leadership style varies from situation to situation.

2. Explain why the terms *manager* and *leader* are not interchangeable.

Management is broader in scope than leadership. Leadership is the process of influencing employees to work toward the achievement of organizational objectives. A person who is a poor leader can be a manager, and a person who is not a manager can be a good leader.

3. Describe leadership trait theory, and identify Ghiselli's six significant leadership traits.

Leadership trait theory assumes that distinctive characteristics account for leadership effectiveness. According to Ghiselli, the six traits that are significant for effective leadership are, in order of importance: supervisory ability, need for occupational achievement, intelligence, decisiveness, self-assurance, and initiative.

4. Discuss the major similarity and difference between two-dimensional leadership styles and the Leadership Grid®.

Both theories use basically the same two dimensions of leadership, although they give them different names. The major difference is that two-dimensional leadership theory has four major leadership styles (high structure/low consideration, high structure/high consideration, low structure/high consideration, low structure/low consideration), whereas the Leadership Grid® identifies five major leadership styles (impoverished, authority-compliance, country club, middle-of-the-road, and team).

5. Identify the management levels at which charismatic, transformational, transactional, symbolic, and servant leadership styles are most appropriate.

Charismatic and transformational leadership styles are most appropriate for top-level management. Transactional leadership is useful for middle and first-line management. Symbolic leadership starts with top management and should flow down to middle and first-line management. Servant leadership can be used at any level.

6. State the primary difference between the contingency leadership model and other situational approaches to leadership.

The contingency leadership model recommends changing the situation, not the leadership style. The other situational leadership approaches recommend changing the leadership style, not the situation.

7. Discuss the major criticism of both the leadership continuum model and the path-goal leadership model.

The leadership continuum model and path-goal model are subjective, and determining which leadership style to use in a given situation is difficult or unclear.

8. Describe the major characteristic of the normative leadership model.

The major characteristic of the normative leadership theory is that it provides one clear leadership style to use in a given situation.

9. Complete each of the following statements with one of this chapter's key terms.

_____ is the process of influencing employees to work toward the achievement of organizational objectives.

_____ attempt to determine a list of distinctive characteristics that account for leadership effectiveness.

_____ attempt to determine distinctive styles used by effective leaders.

_____ is the combination of traits, skills, and behaviors managers use in interacting with employees.

_____ are four possible leadership styles that are based on the dimensions of job structure and employee consideration.

The _____ identifies the ideal leadership style as incorporating a high concern for both production and people.

_____ is a leadership style that inspires loyalty, enthusiasm, and high levels of performance.

_____ is a leadership style that brings about continuous learning, innovation, and change.

_____ is a leadership style based on exchange.

_____ is based on establishing and maintaining a strong organizational culture.

_____ is based on simultaneously meeting the needs and goals of employees while meeting the organizational goals.

_____ attempt to determine appropriate leadership styles for particular situations.

The _____ is used to determine if leadership style is task- or relationship-oriented and if the situation matches the style.

The _____ is used to determine which of seven styles of leadership, on a continuum from autocratic (boss-centered) to participative (employee-centered), is best for a given situation.

The _____ is used to determine employee objectives and to clarify how to achieve them using one of four leadership styles.

The _____ is used to select one of four leadership styles that matches the maturity level of employees in a given situation.

_____ are characteristics of the task, of subordinates, or of the organization that replace the need for a leader.

A _____ is an expression of dissatisfaction with a situation, often coupled with a request for change.

Key Terms

behavioral leadership theorists, 462
charismatic leadership, 467
complaint, 478
contingency leadership model, 469
leadership, 458
leadership continuum model, 471
Leadership Grid®, 465

leadership style, 463
leadership trait theorists, 460
path-goal model, 472
servant leadership, 468
Situational Leadership® model, 474
situational approaches to leadership, 469

substitutes for leadership, 476
symbolic leadership, 468
transactional leadership, 467
transformational leadership, 467
two-dimensional leadership styles, 464

Review and Discussion Questions

1. What is leadership, and why is it important?
2. What traits do you think are important in a leader?
3. Based on the Self-Assessment, is your behavior more Theory X or Y?
4. What are the three parts of leadership style?
5. What are the two dimensions of leadership and the four possible leadership styles?
6. What are the five major leadership styles identified on the Leadership Grid?
7. What is the difference between transformational and transactional leadership?
8. What are the two leadership styles identified by the contingency leadership model?
9. What are the two styles of leadership at either end of the leadership continuum?
10. What are the four leadership styles identified by the path-goal leadership model?

11. What are the five leadership styles identified by the normative leadership model?
12. What are the four leadership styles identified by the Situational Leadership Model?

13. What are the three substitutes for leadership?
14. Do you believe men and women lead differently?

Objective **Case**
WILSON SPORTING GOODS

Wilson Sporting Goods' Humboldt, Tennessee, facility was considered to be one of the least efficient plants within the corporation. The facility produces golf balls and consistently lost money year after year. Major problems in productivity, quality, cost, safety, morale, and housekeeping caused Humboldt's lack of profitability. Management and employees both seemed to feel "It's us against them." Plant manager Al Scott wanted to change the situation by solving these problems. He wanted Humboldt to make the best golf balls and have the most efficient production facilities in the world. With this vision in mind, Scott developed the following mission statement: "Our mission is to be recognized . . . as the premier manufacturer of golf balls." To achieve the mission, Scott developed the following five guiding philosophies, or what he wanted to become shared values: employee involvement, total quality management, continuous improvement, lowest total manufacturing cost, and just-in-time manufacturing.

Scott held meetings with groups of employees to tell them about the vision, mission, and values he wanted them to share. He asked everyone to radically change their way of doing business. Scott stressed the need to change from the old "dictator" management style to the new employee involvement style. Employees were referred to as associates and empowered to find new solutions to old problems. Managers were trained in employee involvement and developed skills to include employees in decision making. The leadership style did change at Humboldt, and in turn employee loyalty, morale, enthusiasm, and performance increased.

To solve Humboldt's problems, Scott instituted a voluntary employee participation program called Team Wilson. Humboldt developed teams of associates to participate in problem solving in the areas of productivity, quality, cost, safety, morale, and housekeeping. To ensure team success, Humboldt gave all associates on teams training similar to that given to managers at the beginning of the change process.

Within a few years, 66 percent of associates had formed voluntary teams, which dramatically changed the Humboldt facility. Each team represented a specific area of the plant. Each team created its own unique logo, T-shirt, and posters to hang in the plant. Wilson holds several cookouts, picnics, and parties each year to show its appreciation to all associates. To recognize team accomplishments, Humboldt chooses three Team Wilson teams each quarter for awards. Among the accomplishments of the new team structure at

Humboldt were an increase in market share from 2 percent to 17 percent; an increase in inventory turns from 6.5 to 8.5; two-thirds reduction in inventory; 67 percent reduction in manufacturing losses caused by scrap and rework; and an increase in productivity of 121 percent. The Humboldt plant produces over 1 billion golf balls each year, and the volume is growing. *Industry Week* magazine named it one of the "Best Plants in America."

Today, Wilson is owned by the Amer Group, PLC, based in Helsinki, Finland, with corporate headquarters in Chicago. Wilson Sporting Goods Company is one of the world's leading manufacturers of sports equipment and focuses on making advanced products that help the average player play better. Its core sport categories include football, basketball, baseball, volleyball, soccer, youth sports, uniforms/apparel, golf, footwear, and racquet sports (tennis, racquetball, squash, badminton, platform tennis). The Humboldt plant is still successfully making golf balls using teams. Wilson golf balls include the Longest Spin Technology—the world's first solid wood golf ball, Solid Ball Distance (off the tee advance), and Wound Ball Spin (shot stopping spin around the green).

To see how Wilson is performing, visit Wilson's Web site at *http://www.wilson.com*.

To learn more about Wilson Sporting Goods, log on to InfoTrac® College Edition at *http:// infotrac.thomsonlearning.com* and use the advanced search function.

_____ 1. Al Scott called for a change in basic management style from _____ to _____ .

    a. democratic; laissez-faire
    b. autocratic; laissez-faire
    c. laissez-faire; democratic
    d. autocratic; democratic

_____ 2. In terms of two-dimensional leadership (Exhibit 13-1) and situational leadership, the team leader in a Team Wilson team primarily uses the _____ leadership style.

    a. telling, or high structure/low consideration
    b. selling, or high structure/high consideration
    c. participating, or low structure/high consideration
    d. delegating, or low structure/low consideration

_____ 3. Al Scott _____ be considered a charismatic leader.

a. should
b. should not

_____ 4. Al Scott should be considered a _____ leader.

a. transformational
b. transactional

_____ 5. Al Scott _____ focus on symbolic leadership at the Humboldt plant.

a. did
b. did not

_____ 6. Consider the original situation at Humboldt before Scott made changes and determine the appropriate style using Fiedler's contingency leadership model (Exhibit 13-2).

a. 1, task   e. 5, relationship
b. 2, task   f. 6, relationship
c. 3, task   g. 7, relationship
d. 4, relationship h. 8, task

_____ 7. Based on the continuum model (Exhibit 13-3), the leadership style Scott used was _____.

a. 1   e. 5
b. 2   f. 6
c. 3   g. 7
d. 4

_____ 8. In terms of the path-goal model, the management style at Humboldt was changed to the _____ leadership style.

a. directive   c. participative
b. supportive   d. achievement-oriented

_____ 9. Scott _____ create substitutes for leadership at the Humboldt plant.

a. did
b. did not

10. What role did leadership play in the improvements at Wilson's Humboldt plant?

11. Would the methods used by Al Scott work at an organization you work for or have worked for? Explain your answer.

Cumulative Case Questions

12. Which management role was the key to Humboldt's turnaround in productivity? (Chapter 1)

13. Was the internal environment or the external environment the cause of Humboldt's problems, and which factors were changed at the plant? (Chapter 2)

14. Did the Wilson plant become a learning organization? (Chapter 2)

15. How did problem solving and decision making change at Humboldt, and how did that affect performance? (Chapter 4)

16. Which OD intervention (Chapter 7) and human resources management process (Chapter 8) were discussed in this case?

17. Related to group structure, what type of group is Team Wilson? (Chapter 10)

Skill Builder 1

THE SITUATIONAL LEADERSHIP® MODEL

Think of a situation from a present or past job that required a boss to show leadership. Describe the situation in enough detail so that others can understand it and determine the maturity level of the employees. Write the information below.

_____

_____

_____

_____

For your situation, determine the maturity level of the follower(s) and select the situational leadership style appropriate for the situation (low, telling; moderate to low, selling; moderate to high, participating; high, delegating).

Apply It

What did I learn from this experience? How will I apply this knowledge in the future?

_____

_____

Behavior **Modeling**
HANDLING COMPLAINTS

This chapter's scenario illustrates a manager, Cassandra, handling a complaint from Andrew about being passed over for a promotion. Cassandra follows the steps described in the text and in Exhibit 13-7.

Objective

To better understand the process of addressing complaints.

View the Video

View the accompanying video in class or at *http://lussier.swlearning.com.*

Skill Builder 2

HANDLING COMPLAINTS

Objective

To develop experience and skills in resolving complaints.

In this activity, you will role-play handling a complaint. To begin, think of a complaint—one you actually presented to a manager, one that was presented to you, one you heard about, or one you have made up. Write down details about the situation and the complaint, including any pertinent information that will help someone else play the role of the complainer (relationship to manager, knowledge level, years of employment, background, age, etc.).

The class will be divided into groups of three. One person in each group plays the role of the manager who must handle the complaint. This person gives his or her written complaint description to the person who is to present the complaint. The two ad-lib the situation. A third person observes the role play and evaluates how the complaint is handled, writing comments on the observer form below. After each role play, group members should discuss how effectively the complaint was handled, based on the observer's comments. After the discussion, group members switch roles and do another role play, until each group member has had a chance to play each role.

Observer Form

Observe the role-play to determine whether the person playing the role of manager followed the steps below. Try to note something positive the person does at each step of the process as well as some ways the person might improve his or her handling of complaints. Be specific and descriptive in your comments, and be prepared to suggest alternative behaviors when discussing how the person might improve.

Step 1. How well did the manager listen? Was the manager open to the complaint? Did the manager try to talk the employee out of the complaint? Was the manager defensive? Did the manager get the full story without interruptions? Did the manager paraphrase the complaint?

Positive behavior: _____

_____

Ways to improve: _____

_____

Step 2. Did the manager ask the complainer to recommend a solution? How well did the manager react to the suggested solution? If the solution could not be used, did the manager explain why?

Positive behavior: _____

_____

Ways to improve: _____

_____

Step 3. Did the manager schedule time to get all the facts and/or make a decision? Was it a reasonable length of time? Did the manager set a specific time to get back to the person?

Positive behavior: _____

_____

Ways to improve: _____

_____

Step 4. Did the manager and the employee develop a plan?

Positive behavior: _____

_____

Ways to improve: _____

_____

Apply It

What did I learn from this experience? How will I use this knowledge in the future?

_____

_____

Learning Outcomes

After studying this chapter, you should be able to:

1. List the four stages of the systems process and describe the type of control used at each stage. PAGE 488

2. Describe the appropriate feedback process within and between the functional areas/departments. PAGE 492

3. List the four steps in the control systems process. PAGE 493

4. Describe the differences among the three categories of control frequency. PAGE 497

5. Explain how the capital expenditures budget is different from the expense budget. PAGE 503

6. List the three primary financial statements and what is presented in each of them. PAGE 504

14: Control Systems: Financial and Human

7. Explain the importance of positive motivational feedback in coaching. PAGE 505

8. Explain the manager's role in counseling and the role of the employee assistance program staff. PAGE 509

9. Define the following **key terms**:

controlling	operating budgets
preliminary control	capital expenditures budget
concurrent control	financial statements
rework control	coaching
damage control	management by walking around (MBWA)
control systems process	management counseling
standards	employee assistance program (EAP)
critical success factors	discipline
control frequency	
management audit	
budget	

Ideas on Management
at The Ranch Golf Club

The Ranch Golf Club, where every player is a special guest for the day, opened in 2001 in Southwick, Massachusetts. The Ranch's competitive advantage is that it is an upscale public course (peak season green fees are about $100) with links, woods, a variety of elevations, and "unsurpassed service." To communicate professionalism, all employees wear uniforms and are extensively trained to provide high-quality service. There is player assistance on the course at all times, dispensing all types of service, including offering golf tips, fetching clubs left behind, serving food and drinks, and providing cool towels on a hot day. From the start, The Ranch's goal was to be the best golf club in New England.

Peter and Korby Clark were part owners of nearly 50 Jiffy Lubes, most of which they sold to Pennzoil in 1991. At age 37, Pete stopped working full-time at Jiffy Lube. In addition to assisting his managing partner in running six Jiffy Lubes and developing three more in the Worcester, Massachusetts, area, Pete spent more time coaching, with his family, and doing community service for the Jimmy Fund. Throughout the 1990s, the Clarks had a variety of opportunities to invest in new and ongoing businesses, but nothing interested them until The Ranch came along. Unlike other businesses, which were looking simply for investors, The Ranch offered the Clarks the opportunity to create and help manage a new golf club.

© David Davis/Index Stock Imagery

Although Pete played recreational golf, what appealed to him was not so much the golf as the challenge of creating a new course and playing an ongoing part in its management. The owners agreed to have the professional golf management team of Willowbend manage day-to-day operations at The Ranch.

IOM

1. Why would the Clarks agree to pay Willowbend to manage day-to-day operations? How does The Ranch control the organizational system? How does The Ranch control the functional systems?
2. How does The Ranch use the control systems process, and how is it performing?
3. What control methods are used to achieve objectives and standards at The Ranch?
4. What are the major operating budget revenues and expenses at The Ranch?
5. How does The Ranch use capital expenditure budgets? How does The Ranch use financial statements and budgets?
6. Does Peter Clark coach his Jiffy Lube business, The Ranch, and sports teams the same way?
7. How does The Ranch get feedback to improve performance?

To learn more about The Ranch, visit the company's Web site at *http://www.theranchgolfclub.com* or log on to InfoTrac® College Edition at *http://infotrac.thomsonlearning.com*, where you can research and read articles on The Ranch Golf Club. Select the advanced search option and key in record number A94908255 or A93531784 to get started.

Source: Information for the opening case was taken from personal interviews with Peter and Korby Clark in June 2004.

ORGANIZATIONAL AND FUNCTIONAL AREA CONTROL SYSTEMS

As defined in Chapter 1, **controlling** *is the process of establishing and implementing mechanisms to ensure that objectives are achieved.* In this section, we discuss controlling the organizational system and its functional areas.

─────────── Learning Outcome 1 ───────────

List the four stages of the systems process and describe the type of control used at each stage.

Organizational Systems Control

An important part of determining performance is measuring and controlling it.[1] With multiple types of organizations and stakeholders, there is no universally accepted performance measure or control system; the control must fit the situation.[2] So the focus here will be on the importance of integrating various controls through the systems approach.[3] In Chapter 2, you learned about the systems process, which is now expanded to include types of control at each stage. Exhibit 14-1 illustrates the systems process, with appropriate types of control. The four different types of control needed at the different stages of the systems process are explained next.

The Clarks were happy to have Willowbend manage day-to-day operations at The Ranch (working on a flat fee plus bonus compensation package) for four reasons. First and foremost, they realized that they could not create and run a successful golf club without expertise in the field. Neither of them had ever worked for a golf club, and they had only played recreational golf. Second, they were happy not to have to manage The Ranch full-time. Pete was coaching high school sports, which he wanted to continue, and Pete and Korby both wanted to spend time with their family and perform community service. Third, Pete and Korby would be involved in all the important strategic decisions and have input into day-to-day operations, but Willowbend would make the day-to-day decisions. Fourth, the employees would technically work for Willowbend, which offered a good benefits package to help attract and retain employees who could meet the high-quality service standards.

PRELIMINARY CONTROL (INPUTS)

Preliminary control *is designed to anticipate and prevent possible problems.* A major difference between successful and unsuccessful managers lies in their ability to anticipate and prevent problems, rather than solving problems after they occur.

WorkApplication1

Using Exhibit 14-1, identify the primary organizational inputs, transformation process, outputs, and customers of a firm you work or have worked for. Also, identify the level of customer satisfaction.

Exhibit 14-1 *The Systems Process with Types of Controls*

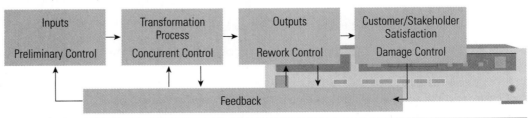

Planning and organizing are the keys to preliminary control, which is also called *feedforward control*. The organization's mission and objectives guide the use of all organizational resources. Standing plans are designed to control employee behavior in recurring situations to prevent problems,[4] and contingency plans tell employees what to do if problems occur.

A common preliminary control is preventive maintenance. Many production departments and transportation companies/departments routinely tune up their machines and engines to prevent breakdowns that would cause problems.

CONCURRENT CONTROL (TRANSFORMATION PROCESS)

Concurrent control *is action taken to ensure that standards are met as inputs are transformed into outputs.* The key to success is quality control.[5] It is more economical to reject faulty input parts than to wait and find out that the finished output does not work properly. Employees spend time checking quality during the transformation process.

REWORK CONTROL (OUTPUTS)

Rework control *is action taken to fix an output.* Rework is necessary when preliminary and concurrent controls have failed. Most organizations inspect the final output before it is sold to the customer or sent as an input to other departments within the organization. Sometimes rework is not cost-effective or possible, and outputs have to be accepted as is, discarded, or sold for salvage, which can be costly. You cannot change the past. However, past performance can be used to improve preliminary control for the next period.

DAMAGE CONTROL (CUSTOMER/STAKEHOLDER SATISFACTION)

Damage control *is action taken to minimize negative impacts on customers/ stakeholders due to faulty outputs.* When a faulty output gets to the customer, damage control is needed. Warranties, a form of damage control, require refunding the purchase price, fixing the product or reperforming the service (a form of rework), or replacing the product with a new one.

FEEDBACK

An important part of the systems process is the feedback loop, particularly from the customer and other stakeholders. The only way to continually increase customer satisfaction is to use feedback from the customer to continually improve the products. Restaurant and hotel/motel evaluation cards filled out by customers are examples of feedback.

EDS provides information technology (IT), application and business process services, and IT transformation services. Its 120,000-employee portfolio of businesses helps global clients in 60 countries maximize performance through their investment in IT.

EDS's preliminary and concurrent controls were not completely effective, leading to rework and damage control and customer feedback complaints that were not being resolved, all of which resulted in lost market share. To fix the problem, EDS developed the "Service Excellence Dashboard," an Internet-based tool that tracks critical customer service measurements such as value, timeliness, and delivery for every customer. The results are displayed on a computer desktop using a color-coded rating system. If a problem arises, a "code yellow" or "code red" alert pops up on the Dashboard, and action must

WorkApplication2

Building on Work Application 1, give examples of preliminary, concurrent, rework, and damage controls for an organization you work or have worked for.

WorkApplication3

Building on Work Applications 1 and 2 and using Exhibit 14-2, illustrate the systems process for a department you work or have worked for within an organization. Be sure to give examples of preliminary, concurrent, rework, and damage controls for your department.

Applying The Concept 1

Types of Control

Identify the type of control used or required as

a. preliminary   c. rework

b. concurrent   d. damage

_____ 1. The new shirt I bought today has a button missing.

_____ 2. I just got my monthly budget report telling me how much I spent and my balance.

_____ 3. The coach is reviewing the plays to be used during the big game on Sunday.

_____ 4. As I was scooping the ice cream, the cone split down the side.

_____ 5. The manager is using the time management system on Friday.

WorkApplication4

Building on Work Applications 1 through 3, illustrate the systems process you personally use within your department. Be sure to give examples of preliminary, concurrent, rework, and damage controls you personally use.

_____

_____

_____

_____

be taken immediately to fix the problem. Through control mechanisms, EDS improved relationships with customers and increased performance, collaboration, and communication throughout the firm, thereby regaining market share.[6]

FOCUS ON PRELIMINARY AND CONCURRENT TYPES OF CONTROL

Remember that focusing on preliminary and concurrent controls cuts down on rework and damage. Relying on rework control is not effective because it is more costly to do things twice than to do them right the first time. This approach is particularly problematic with services, such as manicures and haircuts and auto repairs, which are delivered as they are produced. The best solution is to prevent poor quality from happening in the first place. Doing so creates a win-win situation by minimizing warranty cost and maximizing customer satisfaction.

The Ranch implements various controls on the organizational system. The Ranch's major inputs that require preliminary control include the practice area, the golf course itself, the golf carts, and tee times. The transformation is the actual playing of golf, and the major concurrent control is the player assistance out on the course. If players are not satisfied, player assistance knows it early and can fix the problem quickly before the game is over. The Ranch puts the focus on preliminary and concurrent control to make sure players are satisfied, so rework and damage control (refunds or playing again at no cost) are not common. Employees are trained to get feedback from golfers to improve The Ranch experience. (We'll discuss feedback later in the section on managing by walking around.)

Functional Area/Department Control Systems

Recall from Chapters 1 and 6 that firms are commonly organized into four major functional departments: operations, marketing, human resources, and finance. Information is a fifth major functional area that may be a stand-alone department or may fall under the finance functional area.

Although in most organizations the operations department is the only functional area that actually transforms the inputs into the outputs of goods and services (which are called *products*) that are sold to customers, all functional departments use the systems process. Exhibit 14-2 illustrates how this is done. Note that damage control with the customer is primarily the function of the marketing department. The other department outputs stay within the organization and go to stakeholders, not the customer; therefore, internal damage control is necessary when outputs are faulty. You will learn more about operations in Chapter 15.

Exhibit 14-2 *Systems Processes for Functional Areas/Departments*

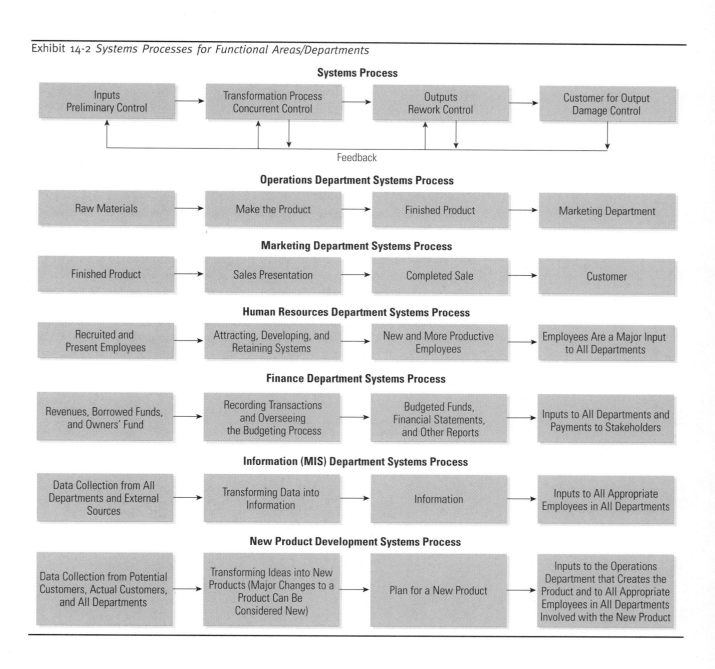

Learning Outcome 2

Describe the appropriate feedback process within and between
the functional areas/departments.

THE FEEDBACK PROCESS WITHIN AND BETWEEN FUNCTIONAL AREAS/DEPARTMENTS

Within each department, employees also use the systems process to transform inputs into outputs. Other department members, rather than other departments, may receive their outputs. For example, on a production line making the Ford Taurus, each person works on one part of the car. When the work is completed, that person's output moves down the line to become the next person's input, and so on, until the Taurus is completed. Each employee should be using preliminary, concurrent, rework, and damage control.

Feedback is needed for improvements.[7] Throughout the systems process, feedback should be circulated among all the functional areas/departments to improve organizational performance in the input, transformation, and output processes while continually increasing customer satisfaction.[8] Exhibit 14-3, illustrates an effective feedback process between the functional departments. Note that operations, marketing, finance, and human resources provide feedback to one another and to the information department. To be effective, feedback should be given to all departments, not just to the information department for dissemination to the other departments.

Several functional controls are used at The Ranch. For the operations of maintaining the golf course, Willowbend uses a sophisticated scheduling system; seeding, fertilizing, watering, mowing, and other activities are well planned and computerized. Its best marketing is word-of-mouth, but The Ranch also runs TV ads as well as print ads in newspapers and golf magazines; it maintains a cutting-edge Web site (*http://www.theranchgolfclub.com*), where players can take a virtual tour of the course. Seventy people work at The Ranch, but they are actually employees of Willowbend, which takes care of the human resources function. Willowbend also has a sophisticated information system for its four departments (golf greens and practice, Crane's Kitchen restaurant, Phil's Pub, and the functions facility and golf shop) that includes many performance measures. We'll discuss the finance function with budgeting.

Exhibit 14-3 *The Feedback Process between Functional Areas/Departments*

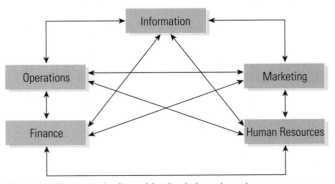

The arrows represent the flow of feedback throughout the systems process

ESTABLISHING CONTROL SYSTEMS

In this section, we discuss the four steps in the control systems process and 10 specific control methods that can be used during the process.

——————————— Learning Outcome 3 ———————————
List the four steps in the control systems process.

The Control Systems Process

The steps in the control systems process *are (1) set objectives and standards, (2) measure performance, (3) compare performance to standards, and (4) correct or reinforce.* See Exhibit 14-4 for an illustration of the control process. The same control systems process steps should be followed on an organizational level and within each functional area.

Step 1. Set objectives and standards. Part of planning should be to develop controls. Setting objectives (Chapter 4) is the starting point for both planning and controlling.[9] Setting objectives and standards is part of the input process, and the objectives and standards themselves are preliminary controls. However, additional standards are also needed to measure whether you are meeting the objectives.[10]

For standards to be complete, they must cover five major areas. **Standards** *measure performance levels in the areas of quantity, quality, time, cost, and behavior.* Incomplete standards usually lead to negative results. For example, if employees are given only high quantity standards with a fast time limit, they will tend to focus only on how many products are produced and may ignore quality. Employees respond to what is measured,[11] so the development of balanced standards is a key management function that drives business success.[12]

- *Quantity.* How many units should employees produce to earn their pay? Some examples of quantity standards include the number of words a secretary must type, the number of loans a loan officer must make, and the number of classes a professor must teach. It is relatively easy to measure performance with quantitative standards.

Exhibit 14-4 *The Control Systems Process*

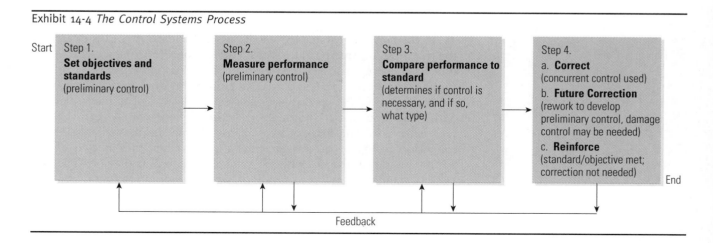

| Start | Step 1.
Set objectives and standards
(preliminary control) | Step 2.
Measure performance
(preliminary control) | Step 3.
Compare performance to standard
(determines if control is necessary, and if so, what type) | Step 4.
a. **Correct**
(concurrent control used)
b. **Future Correction**
(rework to develop preliminary control, damage control may be needed)
c. **Reinforce**
(standard/objective met; correction not needed) | End |

Feedback

- *Quality*. How well must a job be done? How many errors are acceptable? In any situation, you should set quality standards and follow through to make sure employees meet them. If you don't, employees may not produce quality work. Some examples of quality standards include the number of typing errors a secretary may make, the number or percent of delinquent loans a loan officer may make, and the acceptable number or percent of poor student evaluations a professor may get. Quality standards are often difficult to establish and measure. For example, how does an educational supervisor determine how "good" the teachers are? It's not easy, but quality must be measured and evaluated.[13]

- *Time*. When should the task be completed? Or how fast? When assigning a task, it is important to specify a time period. Deadlines are one form of time-based standard. And performance is generally measured with respect to a specific time period. Examples include how many words a secretary types per minute, how many loans a loan officer makes per month, and how many courses a professor teaches per semester or year.

- *Cost*. How much should it cost to do the job? How sophisticated a cost system should an organization have? The answers to these questions depend on the situation.[14] Some production departments use cost-accounting methods to ensure accuracy, whereas other departments have a set budget. A secretary's typing cost may be reflected in a salary limit. A loan officer's cost may include an expense account for entertaining customers, as well as the cost of an office, secretarial help, and so on, although cost could be determined on the basis of delinquent loan losses only. The professor's cost may include a salary limit and an overhead cost.

- *Behavior*. What should employees do and not do? Standing plans, especially rules, help control or limit behavior. In addition, there may be specific directives about things to do and say to customers. For example, a secretary may be expected to answer the telephone with a specific greeting. A loan officer may be expected to process a loan in a certain manner. A professor may be expected not to date current students. In many earlier chapters you learned about controlling behavior, reinforcement motivation theory being one approach. Later in this chapter we discuss coaching, counseling, and disciplining employees to control behavior.

In the previous paragraphs we discussed standards in terms of each of the five areas separately. Now we will set standards for the secretary, loan officer, and professor that combine all five areas, as effective standards should. The secretary's standard may be to type 50 words (quantity) per minute (time) with two errors or less (quality) at a maximum salary of $15.00 per hour (cost) and to answer the telephone with a specific greeting (behavior). The loan officer's standard may be to make $100,000 (quantity) in loans per quarter (time), with delinquency not to exceed $5,000 (quality and cost), while following procedures (behavior). The professor's standard may be to teach 24 semester hours (quantity) per year (time), with an acceptable department chair performance evaluation (quality), at a salary of less than $60,000 (cost), without dating current students (behavior). Each of these jobs would have additional standards as well.

Jack Welch, the former CEO of **General Electric** (the subject of previous examples from Chapters 1, 6, 7, 12, and 13), was well known for setting stretch goals and high standards, which still exist today. Welch implemented systems to align rewards and punishment with measurement. For example, GE managers were evaluated on a ranking system; the high performers got promoted, and the low performers lost their jobs at GE.[15]

Step 2. Measure performance. By measuring its performance, an organization determines to what extent it is successful and how to increase success. If you don't measure performance, how do you know if the organization's mission and objectives are being met? An important consideration in the control process is what to measure and how frequently to measure it,[16] inputs that require preliminary controls.

After setting objectives, the next step—which may take place while setting standards—is to identify the critical success factors (CSFs). **Critical success factors** *are the limited number of areas in which satisfactory results will ensure successful performance, achieving the objective/standard.* You cannot control everything, so the organization, department/team, and individual should identify the few most important things to control.[17] For example, at the organizational level in supermarkets (including **Food Mart, Kroger, Safeway**, and **Stop & Shop**), maintaining the right product mix in each local store, having the products on the shelves, having them advertised effectively to pull shoppers into the store, and having them priced correctly (since profit margins are low in this industry) are the critical success factors. At the departmental and employee level, these CSFs must be implemented and monitored.

How often should you measure performance and what methods of control should you use? It depends on the situation. Later in this section we will look at 10 specific methods you can use to control CSFs, divided into three categories based on frequency of use: constant, periodic, and occasional.

Step 3. Compare performance to standards. After determining what, when, and how frequently to measure, you must follow up by comparing the

WorkApplication5

Give an example of a standard from an organization you work or have worked for that has the five characteristics of a complete standard.

WorkApplication6

Give an example of the critical success factors for a job you have or had. Be sure to place them in priority order (most important first) and to explain why they are critical.

Join the Discussion Ethics & Social Responsibility

Academic Grades

1. Why are professors giving higher grades today than were given 5, 10, or 20 years ago?
2. Are students who are putting in less time and getting higher grades being well prepared for a career with high standards after graduation?
3. Is it ethical and socially responsible for professors to drop standards and for colleges to award higher grades today than they did 5, 10, or 20 years ago?

Recall the "Join the Discussion" about academic standards in Chapter 12. Successful managers establish and maintain high expectations for all their employees. As Lou Holtz said, we need to set a higher standard. While students are doing less work than in prior years, grades continue to go up, a trend called grade inflation. At one time, most colleges used a set grade point average (GPA) to determine honors. But today, because of grade inflation, most colleges use a system of ranking GPAs.

Exhibit 14-5 *Operations Performance Report*

Outputs and Inputs	Standard/Budget	Actual	Variance
Units produced (outputs)	10,000	9,992	−8
Production cost (inputs)			
Labor, including overtime	$70,000	$68,895	$1,105
Materials	95,500	95,763	−263
Supplies	4,750	4,700	+50
Totals	$170,250	$169,358	$ 892

WorkApplication7

Identify a situation in which corrective action was needed to meet an objective/standard. Describe the corrective action taken to meet the objective/standard.

actual results to the objective or standard in order to know if you are on schedule to achieve (or have achieved) the objective/standard.[18] This step is relatively easy if you have performed the first two steps correctly. This comparison determines the type of control, if any, needed in step 4. (The productivity section of the next chapter focuses on measuring and comparing productivity rates to standards.)

A performance or variance report, such as the one shown in Exhibit 14-5, is commonly used to measure and evaluate performance. Performance reports usually show standards, actual performance, and deviations from standards. In Exhibit 14-5, the results, although under production and over cost, are acceptable because in both cases the deviation from standard (variance divided by standard) is under 1 percent. When variances are significant, they should be explained.

Step 4. Correct or reinforce. During the transformation process, concurrent controls are used to correct performance to meet standards.[19] When performance is complete and it is too late to take corrective action to meet the standard, the appropriate corrective action is to (1) analyze why the standard was not met, (2) use the information to develop preliminary control, and (3) feed back the preliminary control so as to take the corrective action necessary to meet the objective/standard next time. When performance has affected others, also use damage control.

The CEO and top executives of **EDS** set revenue and profit objectives in their budget and measured progress with monthly reports. The CEO held monthly conference calls with 125 top executives from around the world. During the meetings, the revenue and profit figures for each unit were read aloud and compared to standard to reinforce or correct performance. Executives who missed their goals were required to explain why, and others would offer advice and suggestions for improvement in future months.[20]

When the objective/standard has been met, there is no need for corrective action. However, do not be like most managers and end the control process here. Reinforce the behavior by using techniques such as praise to reward employees for a job well done (Chapter 12). Letting employees know that they are meeting or have met objectives/standards and that you appreciate their efforts motivates them to higher levels of performance through continuous improvement.[21]

RESISTANCE TO CONTROL

When establishing control systems, especially standards, it is important to consider employee reactions to them and their possible resistance to change. Methods of managing change (Chapter 7) should be used when establishing control systems. Allowing employees to be involved in establishing the control system is very helpful at overcoming resistance to control.[22]

Each year, The Ranch (with Willowbend) sets objectives, broken down by month, for each of its four departments: golf greens and practice, Crane's Kitchen, Phil's Pub, and Functions Golf Shop. Plus Willowbend has a sophisticated computer program that has set standards. Each month, the owners and managers get a copy of the performance report for The Ranch, which compares performance this month to objectives, standards, and past months. Corrective action is taken when needed, and performance is reinforced. Willowbend has a bonus compensation package, so the better The Ranch does, the more Willowbend gets. The Ranch is quickly meeting its goal to be the best golf course in New England. In less than a year, The Ranch earned a 4-star course rating, one of only four in New England. *The New England Golf Guide* named The Ranch Golf Club "Best New Course in New England" in 2002. In the January 2003 issue of *Golf Digest*, The Ranch was rated number 3 in the country in the new upscale public golf course category.

——————————— Learning Outcome 4 ———————————
Describe the differences among the three categories of control frequency.

Control Frequency and Methods

There are 10 specific methods you can use to measure and control performance. These 10 methods fall into three categories of **control frequency**: *constant*, *periodic*, and *occasional*.

CONSTANT CONTROLS

Constant controls, which are in continuous use, include self-control, clan control, and standing plans.

- *Self-control.* If managers are not watching or somehow monitoring performance, will employees do the job? The real issue is the degree of self-control employees are given versus control imposed by managers (such as standing plans). Too much or too little imposed control can cause problems.[23]
- *Clan control.* Clan, or group, control is a form of human resources control in which the organization relies heavily on its culture and norms to ensure specific behaviors. Organizations that use teams tend to rely on clan control.[24] Self- and clan control are used in all phases of the systems process, with preliminary, concurrent, rework, and damage control.
- *Standing plans.* Policies, procedures, and rules are developed to influence employees' behavior in recurring predictable situations (Chapter 4).[25] Standards are similar to standing plans that are in constant use.[26] When standing plans and standards are developed, they are preliminary controls. When standing plans and standards are implemented, they become concurrent, rework, or damage controls.

PERIODIC CONTROLS

Periodic controls are used on a regular fixed basis, such as once per hour or day, every week, or at the end of the month, quarter, or year. Periodic controls include regular meetings and reports, budgets, and audits.

- *Regular meetings and reports.* Regular reports can be oral or written. Regularly scheduled meetings with one or more employees to discuss progress and any problems, such as the conference calls **EDS** holds with managers each month, are common in all organizations. These meetings may be scheduled daily, weekly, or monthly. Regular reports are designed as preliminary control. But the report itself is used as concurrent, rework, or damage control, depending on the situation.

- *Budgets.* Budgets are one of the most widely used control tools.[27] We discuss budgeting details in the next section of this chapter. The preparation of a new budget is a preliminary control. As the year progresses, the budget becomes a concurrent control. At year end, it is reworked for the next year. A budget may require damage control if significant changes, such as overspending, take place for some reason, such as an increase in final cost.

- *Audits.* There are two major types of audits: accounting and management. Part of the accounting function is to maintain records of the organization's transactions and assets. Most large organizations have an *internal auditing* person or department that checks periodically to make sure assets are reported accurately and to keep theft at a minimum. In addition to performing internal audits, many organizations hire a certified public accounting (CPA) firm to verify the organization's financial statements through an *external accounting audit. The* **management audit** *analyzes the organization's planning, organizing, leading, and controlling functions to look for improvements.* The analysis focuses on the past, present, and future.[28] The management audit can be conducted both internally and externally.

Audits may also serve as occasional controls when used sporadically; for example, auditors may make unannounced visits at irregular intervals. The audit is designed as a preliminary control, but it is used to ensure accurate records keeping and to control theft.

The audit control system is used to ensure that accurate records are kept of financial transactions, to protect employees, stockholders, and the public. Unfortunately, at **Enron** the internal audit did not stop Enron employees from overstating income and understating expenses. Enron's chief financial officer (CFO) Andrew Fastow pleaded guilty to cooking the books, which led to the indictment of former CEO Jeffrey Skilling.[29]

At the same time, Enron's external auditor **Arthur Andersen**, whose job it was to verify the accuracy of Enron's accounting practices, either did not know that Enron was cooking the books, when it was its job to know, or ignored it. This control system failure not only led to the demise of Enron and Arthur Andersen but also caused thousands of employees and investors to lose their jobs and retirement funds. It's a sad lesson in the need for control and ethics.

OCCASIONAL CONTROLS

Unlike periodic controls, which involve set time intervals, *occasional controls* are used on a sporadic basis when needed. They include observation, the exception principle, special reports, and project controls.

- *Observation.* Managers personally watch and talk to employees as they perform their jobs.[30] Observation is also done by video camera and electronic devices. Observation can be used for preliminary, concurrent, rework, or damage control.[31] Management by walking around (MBWA), a coaching technique that will be explained later, is a specific method of personal observation that increases performance.

- *The exception principle.* When the exception principle is used, control is left up to employees unless problems occur, in which case the employees go to the manager for help. Corrective action is then taken to get performance back on schedule.[32] The exception principle is designed as a preliminary control, but can be used for concurrent, rework, or damage control.
- *Special reports.* When problems or opportunities are identified, management often requests that a special report be compiled by one employee, a committee within the department/organization, or outside consultants who specialize in that area. Such reports vary in content and nature but are often designed to identify the cause of a problem as well as a solution—or an opportunity and a way to take advantage of it.
- *Project controls.* With nonrecurring or unique projects, the project manager needs to develop a control system to ensure the project is completed on time. Because planning and controlling are so closely linked, planning tools, such as Gantt charts and PERT networks (Chapter 15), are also project control methods.[33] Project controls are designed as preliminary controls, but can be used for concurrent, rework, or damage control.

UPS manages the flow of goods, funds, and information in more than 200 countries and territories worldwide. UPS is the world's largest package delivery company and a leading global provider of specialized transportation and logistics services. Back in 1907 when UPS started, tracking of packages was an occasional control used when packages were lost. Eventually it became *periodic*, as UPS started keeping track of where packages were at UPS facilities. But today, with information technology and the Internet, UPS, its competitor **FedEx**, and their customers have constant control knowledge of where their packages are. Every UPS driver uses a handheld computer that captures customers' signatures, as well as pickup, delivery, and timecard information, and lets the driver automatically transmit this information to the main computer via a cellular telephone network. So with a UPS account, you can go online and track your package from the time it leaves your home or office until it gets to its destination virtually anywhere in the world.[34]

Control mechanisms are critical to organizational success.[35] For a review of the systems process, with its four types of controls, and the methods of control categorized by frequency, see Exhibit 14-6. The types of control are listed separately because all four types may be used with any method and more than one method can be used at once. You need to be aware of the stage of the systems process you are in and the type of control used in that stage (Exhibit 14-1) and then select the most appropriate method(s) for the type of control.

WorkApplication8

Give an example of a constant, a periodic, and an occasional control method used by an organization you work or have worked for. Identify each by name and explain why it is classified as such.

_____

_____

_____

_____

Exhibit 14-6 *Types, Frequency, and Methods of Control*

Types of Control	Frequency and Methods of Control		
	Constant Controls	Periodic Controls	Occasional Controls
Preliminary (input)	Self	Regular Meetings and Reports	Observation
Concurrent (transformation process)			
Rework (output)	Clan	Budgets	Exception Principle
Damage (customer satisfaction)	Standing Plans	Audits	Special Reports Project

Frequency and Methods of Control

Identify the one primary method of control.

Constant	Periodic	Occasional
a. self	d. regular meetings and reports	g. observation
b. clan	e. budgets	h. the exception principle
c. standing plans	f. audits	i. special reports
		j. project

_____ 6. The boss asked an employee to meet with her to explain why the task is behind schedule.

_____ 7. Signs are posted stating that helmets must be worn throughout the factory.

_____ 8. The manager's desk is facing the employees.

_____ 9. The secretary is working alone today since the boss is out of the office.

_____10. The manager got the monthly operations performance report.

IOM

Employees at The Ranch can't be watched constantly, so managers also depend on self-control and clan control. One of the standing plans is the 10-foot rule: If you come within 10 feet of customers, you always greet them cheerfully and ask whether they need any assistance. The key to success at The Ranch is the co-managing of the Clarks and Willowbend, with clear and open communication of expectations. Pete Clark has to communicate often with his partners and managers at Willowbend, and nothing is more important to continually improving operations than sitting down face-to-face during regular weekly meetings and listening to each other. Meetings of department managers with employees continually focus on the importance of communicating the philosophy of unsurpassed professional service. As discussed, The Ranch uses budgets, and it also has audits. To offer unsurpassed service, all employees use observation. In fact, Pete Clark is so tuned in to observing that he can't really relax when he plays golf. He occasionally looks at the course to make sure everything is perfect for golfers. Player assistance uses the _exception principle_, as employees know to contact management if they can't handle any golfer's request. If any department is not meeting objectives, special reports are used to identify problems and solutions. Project control is used for golf tournaments and special events for corporate clients and other organizations, as well as the function dining facility.

In Skill Builder 1, you will be asked to develop a control system for Bolton Employment Agency, using the four steps of the control systems process.

FINANCIAL CONTROLS: THE MASTER BUDGETING PROCESS

If you want to succeed in business, you must be able to work with budgets and financial statements to make important decisions.[36] In this section, we discuss budgeting and financial statements. Important recent trends in budgeting include requiring managers to develop tighter budgets to cut costs,[37] and to use computerized spreadsheet programs such as Lotus 1-2-3 and Microsoft Excel.[38] Accounting is referred to as the language of business and is the primary measure of business success. Financial statements are needed for proper planning and control, since managers must focus on the bottom line to evaluate performance.[39]

A **budget** *is a planned quantitative allocation of resources for specific activities.* Notice that the definition of *budget* does not include money. This is because all types of resources can be allocated. For example, in Exhibit 14-5, units of output were budgeted. Human resources, machines, time, and space can also be budgeted. However, for our purposes, when we use the term *budgeting* in this chapter, we are referring to the narrower, more common use of the term to mean financial budget.

The steps in the *master budgeting process* are to develop the (1) revenue and expenditure operating budgets, (2) capital expenditures budget, and (3) financial budgeted cash flow, income statement, and balance sheet. The three steps, with their substeps, are illustrated in Exhibit 14-7. Notice the feedback loop that takes into account possible revisions in a prior budget due to other budget developments.

The budget usually covers a one-year period, broken down by month. The finance *controller* is responsible for the budgeting process that results in a *master budget* for the entire organization. Each department submits its proposed

Exhibit 14-7 *Steps in the Master Budgeting Process*

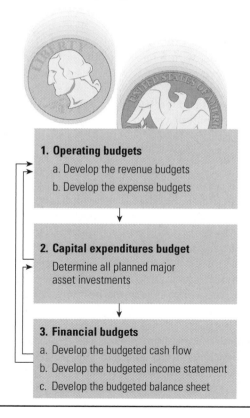

1. **Operating budgets**
   a. Develop the revenue budgets
   b. Develop the expense budgets

2. **Capital expenditures budget**
   Determine all planned major asset investments

3. **Financial budgets**
   a. Develop the budgeted cash flow
   b. Develop the budgeted income statement
   c. Develop the budgeted balance sheet

budget to the controller/committee for approval. During the budgeting process, the use of power and politics is common, and the negotiating conflict management style (Chapter 9) is typically used to resolve the conflicts that arise when allocating scarce resources.[40] The controller/committee may negotiate recommended revisions with department managers and/or use its position power to require revisions.[41]

Operating Budgets

The **operating budgets** *include the revenue and expense budgets.* You must first determine how much money you have or will have, before you can plan how you are going to spend it. Therefore, the first step in the master budgeting process is to determine the revenue, and then the expenditure budgets can be determined.

REVENUE BUDGETS

A *revenue budget* is a forecast of total income for the year. Although sales revenue is the most common form of revenue, many organizations have revenue from investments. Nonprofit organizations often get income from fees, donations, grants, and fundraisers. The revenue budget adds projected income from all sources, such as sales for each product and/or location, together. The marketing/sales department commonly provides the revenue figures for the entire firm, based on the sales forecast.

Determining revenue sounds pretty straightforward, as there are "generally accepted" accounting standards. But they are not always interpreted in the same way. For example, **Yahoo!** and **Google** (discussed in Chapter 5) have the same type of revenue but record it differently. For example, if ABC places ads on the site of XYZ through Yahoo! and the site of DEF through Google, both ads generate $5 in revenue with $3 going to the publisher of the site. But while Yahoo! counts $5 in revenue and $3 in expenses, Google records only $2 in revenue. For the first quarter of 2004, revenue plus expenses for Google totaled $390 million, but it would have been $652 million using Yahoo!'s method. Yahoo!'s total of $758 million would have been $550 million using Google's method.[42]

EXPENSE BUDGETS

An *expense budget* is a forecast of total operating spending for the year. It is common for each functional area/department manager to have an expenditure budget. Many managers fear developing budgets because they have weak math or accounting skills. In reality, budgeting requires planning skills rather than math and accounting skills. Using a computer makes the job even easier.[43] Through the systems effect, all department budgets affect the others; therefore, managers need to share information.[44] For example, the operations department needs the sales forecast to determine how much it will produce, and the human resources department needs to determine organizationwide employee needs to develop its budget.

WorkApplication9

Identify the major source(s) of revenue and expenses where you work or have worked.

_____

_____

_____

_____

_____

I O M

The Ranch's revenues come from greens and practice fees, Crane's Kitchen, Phil's Pub, and the functions facility and golf shop. Expenses include golf course and building maintenance, supplies and equipment (machines, fertilizers/chemicals, food and beverages), management and administration expenses, and employee compensation.

Join the Discussion Ethics & Social Responsibility

Expenses

1. Is it ethical and socially responsible for PricewaterhouseCoopers to charge the full rate when it gets discounts?
2. If you worked for a company and knew it did this, would you say anything to anyone about it? If yes, to whom would you speak and what would you say?

PricewaterhouseCoopers (PwC) provides independent objective accounting, auditing, tax, and business advice to clients in more than 150 countries.[45] When its employees travel to and from clients' facilities and for clients, PwC pays the cost and then charges travel expenses to the client. PwC's practice was to charge the regular rate, when in fact it was getting discounts. Clients accused PwC of overcharging them for travel. PwC said there was nothing wrong with this practice, but it agreed to a $54.5 million settlement to resolve an Arkansas lawsuit over travel rebates.[46]

Learning Outcome 5

Explain how the capital expenditures budget is different from the expense budget.

Capital Expenditures Budget

The second step in developing the master budget is to develop the capital expenditures budget. *The* **capital expenditures budget** *includes all planned major asset investments.* The major assets owned by an organization are those that last and are paid for over several years. The major assets budgeted for may include land, new buildings, whole new product lines or projects, or acquisition of an existing company. On a lower level, decisions include whether to replace existing assets such as machinery with new ones, whether to buy or lease assets, whether to make components yourself or buy them through outsourcing, and whether to rework defective outputs or sell or scrap them. In every case, the objective is to earn a satisfactory return on the invested funds.

Although controlling expenses is important, the capital expenditures budget is the most important budget because it is based on developing ways to bring in revenues through new and improved products and projects that will create customer value. Companies must continually work to develop new products and plan to take advantage of opportunities.

Prior to being a golf club, the property on which The Ranch is located was a dairy farm owned by the Hall family. The Hall family wanted to turn the farm into a golf club and solicited the help of Rowland Bates, Golf Realty Advisors, who later joined Willowbend as project coordinator. The Halls were to provide the land, and investors were to supply the capital. The Clarks did not have enough capital and approached several banks for a loan. They were told that if they wanted to build more Jiffy Lubes they could get the money, but not for a golf course when they had no experience. So Bates found a few more investors to provide the additional funding, created a one-third ownership by the Halls, one-third by the Clarks, and one-third by investors Bernard Chiu and Ronald Izen. It cost a lot of money to turn a farm into a golf course,

WorkApplication 10

Identify the major capital asset expenditures invested in by your present or a past organization.

_____

_____

_____

_____

IOM

to purchase equipment to maintain the course, and to renovate one of the old barns into Crane's Kitchen and Phil's Pub and the other into the functions facility, changing rooms, and a golf shop. It will take several years for the owners to get their investment back and start making a profit. That's what capital budgeting is all about, as it usually takes money to make money.

————————————————— Learning Outcome 6 —————————————————

List the three primary financial statements and what is presented in each of them.

Financial Budgets and Statements

The third step in the master budgeting process is to prepare financial budgets. In other words, before the year begins, the controller forecasts what each statement will be at year end. The financial budgets are prepared last because the operating and capital expenditures budget figures are needed to prepare them. If the budgeted financial statements do not meet expectations, the capital expenditures budget and/or operating budgets may need to be revised—hence the need for the feedback loop in the master budgeting process in Exhibit 14-7. Revisions are common when a net loss is projected.

Each statement commonly gives figures for the year, with each month and quarter presented. The difference between the budget, also called a pro forma statement, and actual statements is that actual statements report past results while the budget, or pro forma statement, projects future results. Budgets are a preliminary control, and actual statements are a rework control.

IOM

The Ranch prepares a financial budget (pro forma statement) for the year, and each month the budget is compared to actual financial statements as everyone tries to meet the budget. The regularly scheduled meetings devote time to financial statements. Crane's Kitchen is doing better than the original budget projected, as people who don't golf come to eat at the nicely renovated turn-of-the-century barn.

Financial statements are used by the internal managers of the firm, as well as external suppliers, creditors, and investors who make decisions about whether to conduct business with the firm by evaluating its performance.

The three primary **financial statements** are the income statement, balance sheet, and cash flow statement. (They are presented below in the order in which they appear in annual reports.)

INCOME STATEMENT

The *income statement* presents revenue and expenses and the profit or loss for the stated time period. The income statement primarily covers one year. However, monthly and quarterly income statements are also developed to measure interim performance and to be used for concurrent control when necessary. Exhibit 14-8 shows an abbreviated income statement for **IBM**.[47]

BALANCE SHEET

The *balance sheet* presents the assets and liabilities and owners' equity. Assets are owned by the organization; liabilities are debts owed to others. Owners'/stockholders' equity is the assets minus the liabilities, or the share of assets owned. The balance sheet is called by that name because the total of the assets always equals the total of the liabilities plus owners' equity for a particular point in time. Exhibit 14-8 includes a balance sheet for IBM.

Exhibit 14-8 *IBM Financial Statements (in millions)*

	Income Statement
Revenue	$ 33,018
[sales – cost = gross profit]	
Expenses	$ 22,144
[selling + administrative + R&D + taxes]	
Net Income (or Net Loss)	$ 874
[revenue – expenses]	
	Balance Sheet
Assets	$ 104,457
[current—cash/accounts receivable + inventories + property and equipment]	
Liabilities and Stockholders' Equity	
Liabilities	$ 76,593
[current—accounts payable/accrued expenses/ estimated product warranties + long-term—mortgages/notes/bonds]	
Stockholders' Equity	$ 27,864
	$ 104,457

Source: *http://www.ibm.com*, as of December, 2003.

WorkApplication11

Does the company you work for or have worked for make its financial statements available to the public? If it does, get copies and review them. Also, does the organization develop operating, capital expenditures, and financial budgets? If it does, try to get copies for review. If you are not sure, call or talk to your present or past boss to find out.

CASH FLOW STATEMENT

The *cash flow statement* presents the cash receipts and payments for the stated time period. (Checks are considered cash.) It commonly has two sections: operating and financial activities. Cash flow statements typically cover one year. However, monthly and quarterly statements are also developed to measure interim performance and to be used for concurrent control when necessary. The operating budgets and capital expenditures budget affect the cash flow statement as cash revenue is received and cash expenses and expenditures are paid.

The Ranch prepares a financial budget (pro forma statement) for the year, and each month the budget is compared to actual financial statements as everyone tries to meet the budget. The regularly scheduled meetings devote time to financial statements. Crane's Kitchen is doing better than the original budget projected, as people who don't golf come to eat at the nicely renovated turn-of-the-century barn.

HUMAN CONTROLS

In this section, we discuss how to coach, counsel, and discipline employees to maintain and increase their performance.

———————————— **Learning** Outcome 7 ————————————
Explain the importance of positive motivational feedback in coaching.

Coaching

Coaching *is the process of giving motivational feedback to maintain and improve performance.* Employees who are given more immediate, frequent, and direct feedback perform at higher levels than those who are not given such feedback.[48] Many people who hear the word *coaching* immediately think of athletes, but coaching is an important management skill that is used to get the

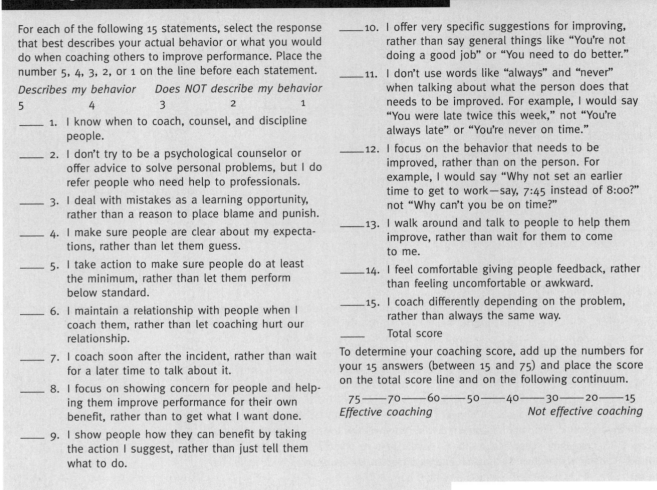

Self-Assessment

Coaching

For each of the following 15 statements, select the response that best describes your actual behavior or what you would do when coaching others to improve performance. Place the number 5, 4, 3, 2, or 1 on the line before each statement.

Describes my behavior   *Does NOT describe my behavior*
5   4   3   2   1

_____ 1. I know when to coach, counsel, and discipline people.

_____ 2. I don't try to be a psychological counselor or offer advice to solve personal problems, but I do refer people who need help to professionals.

_____ 3. I deal with mistakes as a learning opportunity, rather than a reason to place blame and punish.

_____ 4. I make sure people are clear about my expectations, rather than let them guess.

_____ 5. I take action to make sure people do at least the minimum, rather than let them perform below standard.

_____ 6. I maintain a relationship with people when I coach them, rather than let coaching hurt our relationship.

_____ 7. I coach soon after the incident, rather than wait for a later time to talk about it.

_____ 8. I focus on showing concern for people and helping them improve performance for their own benefit, rather than to get what I want done.

_____ 9. I show people how they can benefit by taking the action I suggest, rather than just tell them what to do.

_____ 10. I offer very specific suggestions for improving, rather than say general things like "You're not doing a good job" or "You need to do better."

_____ 11. I don't use words like "always" and "never" when talking about what the person does that needs to be improved. For example, I would say "You were late twice this week," not "You're always late" or "You're never on time."

_____ 12. I focus on the behavior that needs to be improved, rather than on the person. For example, I would say "Why not set an earlier time to get to work—say, 7:45 instead of 8:00?" not "Why can't you be on time?"

_____ 13. I walk around and talk to people to help them improve, rather than wait for them to come to me.

_____ 14. I feel comfortable giving people feedback, rather than feeling uncomfortable or awkward.

_____ 15. I coach differently depending on the problem, rather than always the same way.

_____ Total score

To determine your coaching score, add up the numbers for your 15 answers (between 15 and 75) and place the score on the total score line and on the following continuum.

75——70——60——50——40——30——20——15
Effective coaching   *Not effective coaching*

best results from each employee.[49] Training is an important part of coaching, as coaching is continuous development.[50]

Before reading about coaching, complete the Self-Assessment on Coaching to determine how well you do or can coach people to improve performance.

THE IMPORTANCE OF POSITIVE FEEDBACK

As implied in the definition of coaching, feedback is the central part of coaching, and it should be motivational.[51] In other words, you should give more positive than negative feedback.[52] Have you ever noticed that when athletes make good plays, the coach and team members cheer them on? The same technique motivates people in the workplace; try it!

Unfortunately, many managers spend more time giving negative criticism than praise.[53] Negative managers take the attitude "Why should I thank employees for doing their job?" The answer is simple: It motivates employees to maintain and improve performance. Managers who only criticize employees tend to *demotivate* them.[54]

Did your best boss or coach give you more positive feedback than your worst boss or coach? Did the feedback affect your motivation on the job, and why do you think of them as the best and worst boss or coach? Remember the Pygmalion effect; the "giving praise" model (Chapter 12) is a coaching technique that you should use daily.

DETERMINING CORRECTIVE COACHING ACTION

Ability and motivation have a direct effect on performance.[55] When an employee is not performing up to potential, even when acceptable standards are being met, the first step is to determine why, using the performance formula: Performance = Ability × Motivation × Resources (Chapter 12). When ability is holding back performance, training is needed. When motivation is lacking, motivational techniques, such as giving praise, may help. Talk to the employee to try to determine why motivation is lacking, and develop a plan together.[56] If motivation does not work, you may have to use discipline, which will be discussed later. When resources are lacking, work to obtain them.

Pete Clark is unique, as he spent several years managing his own Jiffy Lube franchises and coaching sports teams before managing The Ranch. He is currently the head baseball coach and assistant football coach for Agawam High School, and he was an assistant football coach at Western Maryland College and Trinity College. Plus he now combines business and sports at The Ranch. Pete says there are more similarities than differences among running a Jiffy Lube business, directing The Ranch Golf Club, and coaching sports. The focus is the same: high-quality service. You have to treat the customer or player right. Pete uses the same "3 I's" coaching philosophy at all three. You need *intensity* to be prepared to do the job right, *integrity* to do the right thing when no one is watching, and *intimacy* to be a team player. If one person does not do the job right, everyone is negatively affected. In business and sports, you need to strive to be the best. You need to set and meet challenging goals. Pete strongly believes in being positive and developing a supportive working relationship, which includes sitting down to talk and really listening to the other person.

THE COACHING MODEL

Coaching should be viewed as a way to provide ongoing feedback to employees about their job performance.[57] However, ask managers what they tend to put off doing and they'll likely say advising weak employees that they must improve their performance. Many managers are hesitant to confront employees, even to the point of jarred nerves and sleepless nights. Procrastinators hope that the employees will turn around on their own, only to find—often too late—that the situation gets worse.[58] Part of the problem is that managers don't know how to coach or are not good at coaching.[59] Thus, Exhibit 14-9 presents a four-step coaching model. And Behavior Modeling Video 1 shows a manager using the coaching model. The four steps in the coaching model are described below.

Step 1. Describe current performance. Using specific examples, describe the current behavior that needs to be changed. Tell the employees exactly what they are not doing as well as they can. Notice the positive; don't tell them only what they are doing wrong.

Exhibit 14-9 *Coaching Model*

| 1. Describe current performance. | → | 2. Describe desired performance. | → | 3. Get a commitment to the change. | → | 4. Follow up. |

For example, don't say, "You are picking up the box wrong." Say, "Billie, there is a more effective way of picking the box up off the floor than bending at the waist."

Step 2. Describe desired performance. Tell the employees exactly what the desired performance is in detail.[60] Show how they will benefit from following your advice.[61] If performance is *ability* related, demonstrate the appropriate way. If the employees know the proper way, the problem is *motivational*, and demonstration is not needed. Just describe the desired performance and ask the employees to state why the performance is important.

For example: *Ability*—"If you squat down and pick up the box using your legs instead of your back, it is easier and there is less chance of injuring yourself. Let me demonstrate for you." *Motivation*—"Why should you squat and use your legs rather than your back to pick up boxes?"

Step 3. Get a commitment to the change. When dealing with an *ability* issue, it is not necessary to get employees to verbally commit to the change if they seem willing to make it. However, if employees defend their way and you're sure it's not as effective, explain why your proposed way is better. If you cannot get the employees to understand and agree, get a verbal commitment. This step is also important for *motivation* issues, because if the employees are not willing to commit to the change, they will most likely not make the change.

For example: *Ability*—the employee will most likely be willing to pick up boxes correctly, so skip this step. *Motivation*—"Will you squat rather than use your back from now on?"

Step 4. Follow up. Remember that some employees (those with low and moderate capability for self-control) do what managers *inspect* (imposed control), not what they *expect*. You should follow up to ensure that employees are behaving as desired.[62]

When dealing with an *ability* issue, if the person was receptive and you skipped step 3, say nothing. However, watch to be sure that the activity is done correctly in the future. Coach again, if necessary. For a *motivation* problem, make a statement that you will follow up and that there are possible consequences for repeat performance.

For example: *Ability*—say nothing, but observe. *Motivation*—"Billie, picking up boxes with your back is dangerous; if I catch you doing it again, I will take disciplinary action."

WorkApplication12
How would you rate your present or past boss's coaching ability? Explain your answer using critical incidents.

Management by Walking Around

Management by walking around (MBWA) *has three major activities: listening, teaching, and facilitating.* Don't just have an open door policy; walk around and talk to employees.[63]

LISTENING

To find out what is going on, managers must do a lot more listening than talking and be open to feedback. Learn to talk last, not first. Open with a simple question like "How is it going?" Then use the communication skills from Chapter 11.

TEACHING

Teaching does not mean telling employees what to do; this is training (Chapter 8). It means helping them to do a better job by solving their own problems. Use coaching statements such as "What do you think should be done?"[64]

FACILITATING

Facilitating means taking action to help employees get their jobs done. The focus is primarily on improving the system to increase performance. By listening, find out what's getting in the way or slowing employees down.[65] The manager's job is to run interference—to remove the stumbling blocks preventing employees from improving the system.[66]

Employees who tell a manager what's going on should be told what will be done about a given problem, if anything, and when. Managers who listen but don't facilitate through corrective action will find that employees will stop talking. As a result, the manager will lose the most valuable source of input for improving the system.

Sam Walton, deceased founder and CEO of **Wal-Mart** (the subject of previous examples in Chapters 1 and 8), was a great believer in managing by walking around. While CEO, Walton would visit every one of his stores every year. He would unexpectedly go into a Wal-Mart and walk up to customers and employees and talk to them about improving Wal-Mart, writing notes on a little pad he carried around with him. Today, Wal-Mart has too many stores (3,200 facilities in the United States and more than 1,100 globally) for the CEO to visit every store annually. But, true to the philosophy of founder Sam Walton, top executives are required to visit stores every year.[67]

Feedback is critical to success at The Ranch, as it tells the Clarks and the Willowbend managers whether the players are getting quality service and how to improve. The Clarks, Willowbend managers, and employees are accepting of player criticism because they realize that the only way to improve is to listen and make changes. In fact, Pete and Korby Clark spend much of their time at The Ranch managing by walking around, as they listen to employees, teach them how to improve through coaching, and help them satisfy golfers' requests. They also talk to players about their experience, listening for suggestions for improvements and facilitating good ideas. The Clarks and the Willowbend managers set clear objectives and have regular meetings with employees to get and give feedback on how The Ranch is progressing toward meeting its objectives.

I O M

— **Learning** Outcome **8** —

Explain the manager's role in counseling and the role of the employee assistance program staff.

Counseling

When coaching, you are fine-tuning performance; with counseling and disciplining, you are dealing with a problem employee who is not performing to standards or is violating standing plans.[68] Organizations realize the need to help employees with people problems.[69]

TYPES OF PROBLEM EMPLOYEES

There are four types of problem employees:

1. Employees who do not have the *ability* to meet the job performance standards. This is an unfortunate situation, but after training reveals that such employees cannot do a good job, they should be dismissed.[70] Many employees are hired on a trial basis; this is the time to say, "Sorry, but you have to go."
2. Employees who do not have the *motivation* to meet job performance standards. These employees often need discipline.
3. Employees who intentionally *violate standing plans*. As a manager, it is your job to enforce the rules through disciplinary action.[71]
4. Employees with *problems*. These employees may have the ability but have a problem that affects job performance. The problem may not be related to the job. It is common for personal problems, such as child care and relationship/marital problems, to affect job performance.[72] Employees with problems should be counseled before they are disciplined.

Exhibit 14-10 lists some problem employees you may encounter. It is not always easy to distinguish between the types of problem employees. Therefore, it is often advisable to start with coaching/counseling and change to discipline if the problem persists.

MANAGEMENT COUNSELING

The first thing a manager should do with a person experiencing a personal problem is to attempt to help the employee solve the problem.[73] This is usually done through counseling, which is a form of coaching.

When most people hear the term *counseling*, they think of psychological counseling or psychotherapy. That type of sophisticated help should not be attempted by a noncounseling professional such as a manager.[74] Instead, **management counseling** *is the process of giving employees feedback so they realize that a problem is affecting their job performance, and referring employees with problems to the employee assistance program.*

Most managers do not like to hear the details of personal problems. Doing so is not a requirement. Instead, the manager's role is to help employees realize that they have problems and that those problems affect their work. The manager's job is getting the employee back on track.[75]

WorkApplication13

Identify a problem employee you observed on the job. Describe how the person affected the department's performance.

Exhibit 14-10 *Problem Employees*

The late employee
The absent employee
The dishonest employee
The violent or destructive employee
The alcoholic or drug user
The nonconformist
The employee with a family problem
The insubordinate employee
The employee who steals
The sexual or racial harasser
The safety violator
The sick employee
The employee who's often socializing or doing personal work

The manager should not give advice on how to solve personal problems such as a relationship difficulty. When professional help is needed, the manager should refer the employee to the human resources department for professional help through the employee assistance program.[76] *The **employee assistance program** (EAP) has a staff of people who help employees get professional assistance in solving their problems.* There has been an increase in the number of companies that offer EAPs, because they improve retention and productivity. EAPs are also offering a wider range of services to meet the needs of a diverse workforce. Most large businesses have an EAP to help solve employees' personal problems.

To make the referral, a manager could say something like "Are you aware of our employee assistance program? Would you like me to set up an appointment with Jean in the human resources department to help you get professional assistance?" However, if job performance does not return to standard, discipline is appropriate because it often makes the employee realize the seriousness of his or her problem and the importance of maintaining job performance.[77] Some time off from work, with or without pay, depending on the situation, often helps the employee deal with the problem.

A manager's first obligation is to the organization's performance rather than to individual employees.[78] Not taking action with problem employees because you feel uncomfortable confronting them, because you feel sorry for them, or because you like them does not help you or the employee. Not only do problem employees negatively affect their own productivity; they also cause more work for managers and other employees. Problem employees lower employee morale, as others resent them for not pulling their own weight. Thus, it is critical to take quick action with problem employees.[79]

Disciplining

Coaching, which includes counseling, should generally be the first step in dealing with a problem employee. However, if an employee is unwilling or unable to change or a rule has been broken, discipline is necessary.[80]

Discipline *is corrective action to get employees to meet standards and standing plans.* The major objective of discipline is to change behavior.[81] Secondary objectives may be to (1) let employees know that action will be taken when standing plans or performance requirements are not met and (2) maintain authority when challenged. Exhibit 14-11 lists eight guidelines for effective discipline.

Exhibit 14-11 *Guidelines for Effective Discipline*

A. Clearly communicate the standards and standing plans to all employees.
B. Be sure that the punishment fits the crime.
C. Follow the standing plans yourself.
D. Take consistent, impartial action when the rules are broken.
E. Discipline immediately, but stay calm and get all the necessary facts before you discipline.
F. Discipline in private.
G. Document discipline.
H. When the discipline is over, resume normal relations with the employee.

Guidelines for Effective Discipline

Identify which guideline is being followed—or not being followed—in the following statements. Use the guidelines in Exhibit 14-11 as the answers. Place the letter of the guideline (A–H) on the line before its statement.

_____ 11. "The boss must have been upset to yell that loudly."

_____ 12. "It's not fair. The manager comes back from break late all the time; why can't I?"

_____ 13. "When I leave the place a mess, the manager reprimands me. When Chris does it, nothing is ever said."

_____ 14. "The boss gave me a verbal warning for smoking in a restricted area and placed a note in my file."

_____ 15. "I want you to come into my office so that we can discuss this matter."

The human resources department handles many of the disciplinary details and provides written disciplinary procedures. These procedures usually outline grounds for specific sanctions and dismissal, based on the violation. Common offenses include theft, sexual or racial harassment, verbal or substance abuse, and safety violations.

PROGRESSIVE DISCIPLINE

Many organizations have a series of progressively more severe disciplinary actions. The progressive disciplinary steps are (1) oral warning, (2) written

Join the Discussion Ethics & Social Responsibility

Disciplining Ethical Behavior

1. Have you ever been in or known of a situation in which people were rewarded for being unethical and disciplined for being ethical? If so, describe the situation.
2. Is it ethical and socially responsible for firms to establish controls that reward unethical behavior and discipline ethical behavior to make more money?

Unfortunately, some employees are rewarded for being unethical, while others are disciplined for being ethical. For example, some auto repair shops pay a commission for work done, so mechanics are paid more if they get customers to buy new mufflers they don't need. Mechanics who have a below-average number of repairs may be considered underachievers and may be pressured, through discipline, to perform unneeded repair work. Similarly, those in the medical field may push unnecessary tests or even treatments.

warning, (3) suspension, and (4) dismissal. All four steps are commonly followed for minor violations, such as being late for work or excessive absenteeism, which cost $789 per employee in 2002, up 30 percent from 2000.[82] However, for more important violations, such as stealing, steps may be skipped. Be sure to document each step.

THE DISCIPLINE MODEL

The steps in the discipline model should be followed each time an employee must be disciplined. The five steps are presented here and summarized in Exhibit 14-12. Discipline is not solely the responsibility of managers; group members also discipline team members.[83]

Step 1. Refer to past feedback. Begin the interview by refreshing the employee's memory. If the employee has been coached/counseled about the behavior or if he or she has clearly broken a known rule, state that.

For example: *Prior coaching*—"Billie, remember my telling you about the proper way to lift boxes with your legs?" *Rule violation*—"Billie, you know the safety rule about lifting boxes with your legs."

Step 2. Ask why the undesired behavior was used. Giving the employee a chance to explain the behavior is part of getting all the necessary facts before you discipline. If you used prior coaching and the employee committed to changing the behavior, ask why the behavior did not change. If the behavior had changed, discipline would not be needed. Again, be sure to describe specific critical incidents to support your contention that behavior has not changed at all or has not changed enough to be at standard.

For example: *Prior coaching*—"Two days ago you told me that you would use your legs, rather than your back, to lift boxes. Why are you still using your back?" *Rule violation*—"Why are you breaking the safety rule and using your back, rather than your legs, to lift the box?"

Step 3. Give the discipline. If there is no good reason for the undesirable behavior, give the discipline. The discipline will vary with the stage in the disciplinary progression.

For example: *Prior coaching*—"Because you have not changed your behavior, I'm giving you an oral warning." *Rule violation*—"Because you have violated a safety rule, I'm giving you an oral warning."

Step 4. Get a commitment to change and develop a plan. Try to get a commitment to change. If the employee will not commit, make note of the fact in the critical incidents file or use the procedures for a written warning. If a plan for change has been developed in the past, try to get the employee to commit to it again. Or develop a new plan, if necessary.

Exhibit 14-12 *The Discipline Model*

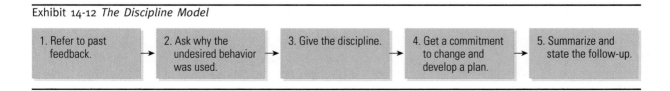

A statement such as "Your previous attempt has not worked; there must be a better way" is often helpful. With a personal problem, offer professional help again.

For example: *Prior coaching or rule violation*—"Will you lift with your legs from now on?" "Is there a way to get you to remember to use your legs instead of your back when you lift?"

Step 5. Summarize and state the follow-up. Summarize the discipline and state the follow-up disciplinary action to be taken. Part of follow-up is to document the discipline. At the written warning and suspension stages, get the employee's signature. If necessary, take the next step in the discipline model: dismissal.

For example: *Prior coaching or rule violation*—"So you agree to use your legs instead of your back when you lift. If I catch you again, you will be given a written warning, which is followed by a suspension and dismissal if necessary."

Take advantage of the companion Web site for *Management Fundamentals*, where you will find a broad array of resources to help you maximize what you learn in class:

- Try a quiz
- View chapter videos
- Download slides
- Boost your vocabulary
- Work through an Internet exercise
- Find related links

Take a look for yourself at *http://lussier.swlearning.com.*

WorkApplication14

Review the discipline guidelines. Identify any guidelines your present or past boss did not follow.

_____

_____

_____

_____

Chapter Summary

1. List the four stages of the systems process and describe the type of control used at each stage.

The first stage of the systems process is inputs. Preliminary control is designed to anticipate and prevent possible input problems. The second stage is the transformation process. Concurrent control is action taken to ensure that standards are met as inputs are transformed into outputs. The third stage is outputs. Rework control is action taken to fix an output. The fourth stage is customer/stakeholder satisfaction. Damage control is action taken to minimize negative impacts on customers/stakeholders due to faulty outputs. During the four stages, feedback is used to improve upon the process to continually increase customer satisfaction.

2. Describe the appropriate feedback process within and between the functional areas/departments.

Throughout the systems process, feedback is circulated among all the functional areas to improve organizational performance in the input, transformation, and output processes and to continually increase customer satisfaction.

3. List the four steps in the control systems process.

The steps in the control systems process are (1) set objectives and standards, (2) measure performance, (3) compare performance to standards, and (4) correct or reinforce, with a feedback loop for continuous improvement.

4. Describe the differences among the three categories of control frequency.

Constant controls are in continuous use. Periodic controls are used on a regular, fixed basis such as once a day or week. Occasional controls are used on a sporadic basis when needed.

5. Explain how the capital expenditures budget is different from the expense budget.

The capital expenditures budget includes all planned major asset investments. It shows funds allocated for investments in major assets that will last and be paid for over several years. The expense budget shows funds allocated to pay for operating costs during the budgeting year. With expense budgets, the focus is on cost control. With capital expenditures budgets, the focus is on the more important role of developing ways to bring in revenues through new and improved products and projects that will create customer value.

6. List the three primary financial statements and what is presented in each of them.

The income statement presents revenue and expenses and the profit or loss for the stated time period. The balance sheet presents assets, liabilities, and owners' equity. The cash flow statement presents the cash receipts and payments for the stated time period.

7. Explain the importance of positive motivational feedback in coaching.

The objective of coaching is to improve performance. Positive feedback, such as praise, is used to motivate employees to maintain and improve their performance.

8. Explain the manager's role in counseling and the role of the employee assistance program staff.

The manager's role in counseling is to give employees feedback so they realize that a problem is affecting their job performance, and to refer employees with problems to the employee assistance program. The role of the employee assistance program staff is to assist employees who need professional help to solve their problems.

9. Complete each of the following statements using one of this chapter's key terms.

_____ is the process of establishing and implementing mechanisms to ensure that objectives are achieved.

_____ is designed to anticipate and prevent possible problems.

_____ is action taken to ensure standards are met as inputs are transformed into outputs.

_____ is action taken to fix an output.

_____ is action taken to minimize negative impacts on customers/stakeholders due to faulty outputs.

The _____ steps are (1) set objectives and standards, (2) measure performance, (3) compare performance to standards, and (4) correct or reinforce.

_____ measure performance levels in the areas of quantity, quality, time, cost, and behavior.

_____ are the limited number of areas in which satisfactory results will ensure successful performance, achieving the objective/standard.

Categories of _____ include constant, periodic, and occasional.

The _____ analyzes the organization's planning, organizing, leading, and controlling functions to look for improvements.

A _____ is a planned quantitative allocation of resources for specific activities.

The _____ include the revenue and expense budgets.

The _____ includes all planned major asset investments.

The three primary _____ are the income statement, balance sheet, and cash flow statement.

_____ is the process of giving motivational feedback to maintain and improve performance.

_____ has three major activities: listening, teaching, and facilitating.

_____ is the process of giving employees feedback so they realize that a problem is affecting their job performance, and referring employees with problems to the employee assistance program.

The _____ is staffed by people who help employees get professional assistance in solving their problems.

_____ is corrective action to get employees to meet standards and standing plans.

Key Terms

budget, 501
capital expenditures budget, 503
coaching, 505
concurrent control, 489
control frequency, 497
controlling, 488
control systems process, 493

critical success factors, 495
damage control, 489
discipline, 511
employee assistance program (EAP), 511
financial statements, 504
management audit, 498

management by walking around (MBWA), 508
management counseling, 510
operating budgets, 502
preliminary control, 488
rework control, 489
standards, 493

Review and Discussion Questions

1. Why is damage control important?
2. Why should you focus on preliminary and concurrent types of control rather than rework and damage control?
3. Who are the primary customers/stakeholders for the outputs of the operations, marketing, human resources, finance, and information functional areas/departments?
4. What are the five areas of performance that standards measure?
5. Why is measuring performance important to an organization?
6. What is shown in a performance report?
7. What is the role of reinforcement in the control systems process?
8. What are the three constant control methods, the three periodic control methods, and the four occasional control methods?
9. What are the three steps in the master budgeting process?
10. Why is the capital expenditures budget the most important budget?
11. What is the difference between financial statements and financial budgets?
12. What is the objective of coaching?
13. How do managers commonly demotivate employees?
14. What is the performance formula, and how is it used with coaching?
15. What are the three activities of management by walking around, and what is the role of facilitating?
16. What are the differences among coaching, counseling, and disciplining?
17. Which of the eight discipline guidelines is most relevant to you personally? Explain.

Objective Case

RODRIGUEZ CLOTHES MANUFACTURING

Carmen Rodriguez started his small business about 15 years ago in the Garment District in New York City. Rodriguez Clothes Manufacturing employs around 50 people. The five teams at Rodriguez work in one big room in which all clothes are made. One of the teams makes quality shirts for men's clothing stores.

Carmen works in a separate office and spends most of his time on marketing, finance, and human resources management. He does not spend much time with the manufacturing employees. Team leaders are responsible for keeping team production records and hours worked, training team members, and helping them when there is a problem. Team leaders do not get involved with discipline.

Unlike some of his competitors, Carmen does not want to run a sweatshop, so he pays employees a salary rather than a low piece rate for actual work performed. However, if employees don't produce an average of 48 shirts, they lose their jobs. Carmen's employees have

a higher rate of job satisfaction than competitors' employees do, and Rodriguez has a quality reputation.

With all the competition, Carmen is not making much money. He wants to get employees to produce more shirts. Carmen thought about buying new machines as a capital expenditure, but he really did not have the money or the desire, because his current machines were working fine. Carmen also considered changing to piece-rate pay. However, he figured that paying employees more to produce more would have an offsetting effect and would not benefit him much. He also feared that if he went to piece-rate pay he might have quality problems, which he did not want to risk. Carmen prides himself on being ethical and socially responsible to all stakeholders.

Carmen came up with the idea of setting a new quota in addition to the 48-shirt standard. Employees could leave work early once they had met the new 53-shirt quota. Carmen figured that he was not pushing his employees too hard and that they could get out of work around a half-hour earlier each day.

Carmen met with the employees in the shirt team and told them, "I want to try a new idea, which I think is fair to everyone, for the next two weeks. If you produce 53 shirts, you can go home for the day and get your full pay. I figure you can get out around 4:30 instead of 5 o'clock without having to rush your work. The same level of quality is required, and quality will be checked as usual. If you want, you can continue to produce 48 shirts and work the full eight hours." They discussed the new system, and they all liked the idea of working less hours for the same pay. If it did not work, they would go back to the old system.

On the Monday following the first week, Carmen got his weekly production reports, which state the number of units made by each worker and the hours each employee worked, arranged by team. Carmen got around to reading them after closing time, as usual. He went right to the shirt team report to see how the new system was working. Carmen was happy to see that everyone was producing 53 shirts and getting out around 4:30. However, on Friday, Maria made 53 shirts and left at 2:30. Carmen did not understand how this was possible. He decided to talk to Maria to see what was going on.

On Tuesday morning, Carmen visited Maria at work and asked her how it was possible to get out at 2:30. Maria said, "All I did was adjust my machine and place this new gadget on it to speed it up. Plus I developed a new procedural sequence in which I make shirts. Watch how much faster I can sew now; especially placing buttons on is so much faster." Carmen watched her in amazement as she made a shirt. He did not know what to say. He told her to keep up the good work and went back to his office.

As Carmen walked back to his office, he wondered to himself: "Should I continue to let her leave that early? Do the other workers think it's fair for Maria to get out so much earlier than they do? This is only a two-week trial, subject to changes that are fair to everyone. What is the fair thing to do?"

Be sure that you are prepared to explain your answers to the following questions.

_____ 1. Carmen's allowing employees to go home early when they finished their work was a _____ control.

    a. preliminary   c. rework
    b. concurrent   d. damage

_____ 2. The primary customer for the operations products is _____.

    a. customers
    b. marketing
    c. finance

_____ 3. Carmen's new standard was not clear in the area of _____.

    a. quantity   d. cost
    b. quality   e. behavior
    c. time

_____ 4. Which was the primary control method Carmen used in letting employees leave when they had met the quota/standard?

Constant	Periodic	Occasional
a. self	d. regular	g. observation
b. clan	reports	h. exception
c. standing	e. budgets	principle
plans	f. audits	i. special reports
		j. project

_____ 5. In this case, Carmen was focusing on _____.

    a. operating budgets
    b. capital expenditures
    c. financial budgets
    d. productivity

_____ 6. Carmen's new leave-early control system had a meaningful direct effect on _____.

    a. the income statement   c. the cash flow
    b. the balance sheet   d. none of these

_____ 7. A change in which part of the performance formula was the primary reason for Maria's increase in productivity?

    a. ability
    b. motivation
    c. resources

_____ 8. A customer's returning a shirt because the sleeves are not the same length is an example of a _____ system control.

    a. preliminary   c. rework
    b. concurrent   d. damage

_____ 9. With his new leave-early method, Carmen followed all four steps in the control systems process. (State the steps he did and/or did not follow.)

    a. true
    b. false

_____10. Carmen uses management by walking around (MBWA).

    a. true
    b. false

11. Is there any potential problem with Maria's adjusting her machine?

12. Should Carmen keep the control system the way it is now and continue to let Maria leave two hours earlier than the other employees? If not, what should he do?

13. Does the increased production/productivity pose any potential threat to employees? Explain.

Cumulative Case Questions

14. Which internal environmental factor is the major issue in this case? (Chapter 2)

15. How does the global village affect Rodriguez Clothes? (Chapter 3)

16. (a) Was the change at Rodriguez a strategic or operational one? (b) What was the role of objectives in this case? (c) Which functional area was affected? (Chapter 5)

17. Which job design did Maria use to increase productivity? (Chapter 6)

18. What type of change was made by Maria to increase productivity? (Chapter 7)

19. What (a) content, (b) process, and (c) reinforcement motivation theories were used by Carmen when he changed the standard to allow employees to go home early? (Chapter 12)

Skill Builder 1

BOLTON CONTROL SYSTEM

Objective

To improve your skill at developing a control system for an organization/department.

Situation

Marie Bolton owns and operates the Bolton Clerical Employment Agency. As the name indicates, her agency focuses on providing clerical employees to its business clients. It has a file of clerical employees looking for jobs or better jobs. When employers place job orders with the agency, the agency recruiter tries to find a person who fits the job specifications. The agency sends possible candidates to the employer. The employment agency charges the employer a fee only when one of its referred candidates is hired by the company. The fee is based on the employee's first-year salary. The average fee paid by employers is $1,000.

Each agency recruiter gets 35 percent of the fee charged as a salary. Pay is 100 percent commission. Refunds are made if the person placed does not stay on the job for three months.

Marie has two employees called recruiters. With only two employees, Marie is also a full-time recruiter. She does the management functions in addition to recruiting.

Marie has no formal control methods because her two recruiters are very competent professionals who are paid

only by commission; she places minimal restrictions on them. Marie is somewhat satisfied with the way her business is operating. However, through a professional association she found out that her business is not doing as well as the average employment agency. Being competitive by nature, Marie does not want to be below average.

Marie has asked you to set up a control system to help her improve her agency's performance. She has provided you with the following performance report, comparing her agency figures to those of the average agency. The professional association forecasts that revenues for next year will not increase for the industry.

Performance Information Report for Last Year

	Bolton	Average
Placement Revenue (refunds deducted, not taxes)	$230,000	$250,000
Recruiter commissions paid	$80,500	$87,500
Refunds	$8,000	$10,000
Number of placements	230	250
Number of company interviews	*	1,000
Number of full-time recruiters (including owners who recruit)	3	3

*Bolton does not keep records of the number of candidates it sends to companies for interviews.

Procedure

Identify the systems process for Bolton by identifying its primary inputs, transformation process, outputs, and customers/stakeholders:

Inputs	Transformation Process	Outputs	Customers/ Stakeholders

Identify major types of control for each stage of the systems process:

Preliminary	Concurrent	Rework	Damage

To set up a control system for Bolton, follow the steps in the control systems process.

Step 1. Setting Objectives and Standards

Marie's objective is to earn $250,000 in revenue for the next year, which is the industry average. Establish standards for the year that will enable Marie to reach her objective.

Quantity of interviews per recruiter: _____

Quantity of placements per recruiter: _____

Calculate the number of additional interviews needed to meet the standard per recruiter: _____

Calculate the percent increase: _____ %

Quality. State the dollar value of acceptable refunds per recruiter: $ _____

State the corresponding number of refunds: _____

Time. State the time period in which the quantity and quality standards should be met: _____

Cost. State the cost based on commissions per recruiter: $_____

Behavior. Identify any behaviors employees should change to help them meet the standards.

_____

_____

Step 2. Measuring Performance

What are the critical success factors for employment agencies? Have you identified the critical success factors within your standards? If not, rework them.

How often should Marie measure performance and what methods of control should she use?

Time frequency for measuring performance: _____

Quantity of interviews per recruiter for time period: _____

Quantity of placements per recruiter for time period: _____

Specific control methods to use:

_____

_____

Step 3. Comparing Performance to Standards

How should Marie compare her agency's performance to her new standards?

_____

_____

Step 4. Correcting or Reinforcing

What type of corrective action should Marie take if standards are not being met or what type of reinforcement if they are?

_____

_____

Assume that Bolton does exactly meet the standard.

1. Calculate the rate of productivity for Bolton's past performance (average agency): _____
    Calculate the rate of productivity for the new performance standard: _____
    Is there a change in productivity? _____ yes _____ no
    If yes, by what percent did it increase or decrease? _____
    Base the inputs on recruiter commissions only.

2. Calculate the past commission per employee (average agency): _____
    Calculate the new commission per employee: _____
    What percent pay increase do recruiters get? _____

3. Do profits increase when the new standards are met? _____

    How do you think the employees will react to your proposed control system? Do you think they will resist the control? Why or why not?

_____

_____

Apply It

What did I learn from this exercise? How will I use this knowledge in the future?

_____

_____

Your instructor may ask you to do this Skill Builder in class in a group. If so, the instructor will provide you with any necessary information or additional instructions.

Behavior **Modeling** 1
COACHING

This chapter's first scenario shows Sarah coaching Dan. Dan is an Internet Web page designer who is not meeting deadlines. Sarah follows the steps in Exhibit 14-9.

Objective

To better understand the coaching process.

View the Video

View the accompanying video in class or at *http://lussier.swlearning.com*. This video can be used prior to conducting Skill Builder 2.

Skill Builder 2

COACHING

Objective

To develop your skill at improving performance through coaching.

Procedure 1 (2–4 minutes)

Break into groups of three. Make some groups of two, if necessary. Each member selects one of the following three situations in which to be the manager, and a different one in which to be the employee. In each situation, the employee knows the standing plans; he or she is not motivated to follow them. You will take turns coaching and being coached.

Three Problem Employee Situations

1. Employee 1 is a clerical worker. The person uses files, as do the other 10 employees in the department. The employees all know that they are supposed to return the files when they are finished so that others can find them when they need them. Employees should have only one file out at a time. The supervisor notices that Employee 1 has five files on the desk, and another employee is looking for one of them. The supervisor thinks that Employee 1 will complain about the heavy workload as an excuse for having more than one file out at a time.
2. Employee 2 is a server in an ice cream shop. The employee knows that the tables should be cleaned up quickly after customers leave so that new customers do not have to sit at dirty tables. It's a busy night. The supervisor finds dirty dishes on two of this employee's occupied tables. Employee 2 is socializing with some friends at one of the tables. Employees are supposed to be friendly; Employee 2 will probably use this as an excuse for the dirty tables.
3. Employee 3 is an auto technician. All employees at the garage where this person works know that they are supposed to put a paper mat on the floor of each car so that the carpets don't get dirty. When the service supervisor got into a car Employee 3 repaired, the car did not have a mat and there was grease on the carpet. Employee 3 does excellent work and will probably make reference to this fact when coached.

Procedure 2 (3–7 minutes)

Prepare for coaching to improve performance. Below, each group member writes an outline of what he or she will say when coaching Employee 1, 2, or 3, following the steps below:

1. Describe current performance.

   _____

   _____

2. Describe the desired behavior. (Don't forget to have the employee state why it is important.)

   _____

   _____

3. Get a commitment to the change.

   _____

   _____

4. Follow up.

_____

_____

Procedure 3 (5–8 minutes)

Role Playing. The manager of Employee 1, the clerical worker, coaches him or her as planned. (Use the actual name of the group member playing Employee 1.) Talk—do not read your written plan. Employee 1, put yourself in the worker's position. You work hard; there is a lot of pressure to work fast. It's easier when you have more than one file. Refer to the workload while being coached. Both the manager and the employee will have to ad lib.

The person not playing a role is the observer. He or she makes notes on the observer form below. Try to make positive comments and point out areas for improvement. Give the manager alternative suggestions about what he or she could have said to improve the coaching session.

Observer Form

1. How well did the manager describe current behavior?

_____

_____

2. How well did the manager describe desired behavior? Did the employee state why the behavior is important?

_____

_____

3. How successful was the manager at getting a commitment to the change? Do you think the employee will change?

_____

_____

4. How well did the manager describe how he or she was going to follow up to ensure that the employee performed the desired behavior?

_____

_____

Feedback. The observer leads a discussion of how well the manager coached the employee. (This should be a discussion, not a lecture.) Focus on what the manager did well and how the manager could improve. The employee should also give feedback on how he or she felt and what might have been more effective in getting him or her to change. Do not go on to the next interview until you are told to do so. If you finish early, wait for the others to finish.

Procedure 4 (5–8 minutes)

Same as procedure 3, but change roles so that Employee 2, the server, is coached. Employee 2 should make a comment about the importance of talking to customers to make them feel welcome. The job is not much fun if you can't talk to your friends.

Procedure 5 (5–8 minutes)

Same as procedure 3, but change roles so that Employee 3, the auto technician, is coached. Employee 3 should comment on the excellent work he or she does.

Apply It

What did I learn from this experience? How will I use this knowledge in the future?

_____

_____

Behavior **Modeling** 2
DISCIPLINE

In this scenario, Dan continues to miss deadlines, so Sarah disciplines him following the steps in Exhibit 14-12.

Objective

To better understand the discipline model.

View the Video

View the accompanying video in class or at *http://lussier.swlearning.com.* This video can be used prior to conducting Skill Builder 3.

Skill Builder 3

DISCIPLINING

Objective

To develop your ability to discipline an employee.

Procedure 1 (2–4 minutes)

Break into groups of three. Make some groups of two, if necessary. Each member selects one of the three situations from Skill Builder 2. Decide who will discipline Employee 1, the clerical worker; Employee 2, the ice cream shop server; and Employee 3, the auto technician. Also select a different group member to play the employee being disciplined.

Procedure 2 (3–7 minutes)

Prepare for the discipline session. Write a basic outline of what you will say to Employee 1, 2, or 3; follow the steps in the discipline model below.

1. Refer to past feedback. (Assume that you have discussed the situation before, using the coaching model.)

   _____

   _____

2. Ask why the undesired behavior was used. (The employee should make up an excuse for not changing.)

   _____

   _____

3. Give the discipline. (Assume that an oral warning is appropriate.)

   _____

   _____

4. Get a commitment to change and develop a plan.

   _____

   _____

5. Summarize and state the follow-up.

   _____

   _____

Procedure 3 (5–8 minutes)

Role Playing. The manager of Employee 1, the clerical worker, disciplines him or her as planned. (Use the actual name of the person playing the employee.) Talk—do not read your written plan. Employee 1, put yourself in the worker's

position. You work hard; there is a lot of pressure to work fast. It's easier when you have more than one file. Both the manager and the employee will need to ad lib.

The person not playing a role is the observer. He or she makes notes on the observer form below. For each of the following steps, try to make a statement about the positive aspects of the discipline and a statement about how the manager could have improved. Give alternative things the manager could have said to improve the discipline session. Remember, the objective is to change behavior.

Observer Form

1. How well did the manager refer to past feedback?

   _____

   _____

2. How well did the manager ask why the undesired behavior was used?

   _____

   _____

3. How well did the manager give the discipline?

   _____

   _____

4. Did the manager get a commitment to change? Do you think the employee will change his or her behavior?

   _____

   _____

5. How well did the manager summarize and state the follow-up? How effective will the follow-up be?

   _____

   _____

Feedback. The observer leads a discussion of how well the manager disciplined the employee. The employee should also give feedback on how he or she felt and what might have been more effective in getting him or her to change. Do not go on to the next interview until you are told to do so. If you finish early, wait until the others finish or the time is up.

Procedure 4 (5–8 minutes)

Same as procedure 3, but change roles so that Employee 2, the ice cream server, is disciplined. Employee 2, put yourself in the worker's position. You enjoy talking to your friends, and you're supposed to be friendly to the customers.

Procedure 5 (5–8 minutes)

Same as procedure 3, but change roles so that Employee 3, the auto technician, is disciplined. Employee 3, put yourself in the worker's position. You are an excellent technician. Sometimes you forget to put the mat on the floor.

Apply It

What did I learn from this experience? How will I use this knowledge in the future?

_____

_____

Learning Outcomes

After completing this chapter, you should be able to:

1. Describe time-based competition and why it is important. **PAGE 526**

2. Explain the differences among operations systems with respect to tangibility of products, levels of customer involvement, operations flexibility, and management of resources and technology. **PAGE 527**

3. Discuss what is meant by "Quality is a virtue of design." **PAGE 533**

4. Explain product, process, cellular, and fixed-position facility layouts in terms of their level of customer involvement and flexibility. **PAGE 534**

5. Describe the similarities and differences among the planning sheet, Gantt chart, and PERT network. **PAGE 539**

6. Explain the relationship among inventory control, just-in-time (JIT) inventory, and materials requirement planning (MRP). **PAGE 543**

15: Operations, Quality, and Productivity

7. Explain how statistical process control (SPC) charts and the exception principle are used in quality control. **PAGE 549**

8. Describe how to measure productivity and list three ways to increase it. **PAGE 552**

9. Define the following **key terms:**

time-based competition	PERT
operations	critical path
product	inventory
customer involvement	inventory control
operations flexibility	just-in-time (JIT) inventory
technology	materials requirement planning (MRP)
facility layout	supply chain management
capacity	quality control
routing	International Standards Organization (ISO)
priority scheduling	statistical process control (SPC)
planning sheet	productivity
Gantt chart	balanced scorecard (BSC)

Ideas on Management

at Frito-Lay

Pepsi-Cola was created in the late 1890s by Caleb Bradham. In the 1930s, Elmer Doolin founded The Frito Company and Herman Lay founded H. W. Lay Company, each borrowing around $100 to start his business. In 1961, the Frito and Lay companies merged to form Frito-Lay, Inc. In 1965, that company merged with Pepsi-Cola to form PepsiCo, with the two former companies run as separate operating divisions. At the time, Pepsi also owned Pizza Hut, Kentucky Fried Chicken, and Taco Bell, but PepsiCo made the strategic decision to sell the restaurants in order to focus on packaged goods. In 1998, PepsiCo acquired Tropicana Products. The Quaker Oats Company, with its Gatorade products, merged with PepsiCo in 2001, making it the fourth-largest consumer-goods company in the world. Today, PepsiCo has five major division brands: Pepsi, Frito-Lay, Quaker, Tropicana, and Gatorade.

In this chapter, we will discuss operations at Frito-Lay, as Americans continue to eat more than 20 pounds of snacks a year. Frito-Lay is the world's leading snack food company, with sales in nearly every corner of the globe. Frito-Lay thinks globally and acts locally. To ensure that its products are developed to satisfy the taste preferences of people in various countries around the world, Frito-Lay has acquired foreign operations and brands through direct investment. Even in the United States, some products are not available in all areas, as products that don't sell well are removed or replaced. Frito-Lay acquired Smartfood and Cracker Jack brands, and it also sells Quaker snack and breakfast products. The reasons why Frito-Lay is so successful include aggressive marketing, an extensive distribution system, operating discipline to control consistent quality, and new product innovation.

© AP/Wide World Photos

I O M

1. **How would Frito-Lay's operations systems be classified?**
2. **How would Frito-Lay's operations systems be described in terms of design?**
3. **How does Frito-Lay manage its operations systems and supply chain?**
4. **How does Frito-Lay control quality?**
5. **What are Frito-Lay's three top-selling products in the United States, and are its performance and productivity improving?**

To learn more about Frito-Lay, visit the company's Web site at *http://www.fritolay.com* or log on to InfoTrac® College Edition at *http://infotrac.thomsonlearning.com*, where you can research and read articles on Frito-Lay and its operations. Select the advanced search option and key in record number A127287379, A123637408, CJ128115459, or A116363664 to get started.

Source: The PepsiCo and Frito-Lay Web sites, *http://www.pepsico.com* and *http://www.fritolay.com*, accessed June 24, 2004.

<hr>

Learning Outcome **1**

Describe time-based competition and why it is important.

TIME-BASED COMPETITION AND OPERATIONS

Time-based competition *refers to the use of strategies to increase the speed with which an organization goes from creativity to delivery.* An organization that can turn a creative idea into an innovation, sell it, and deliver it to increase customer value has a first-mover competitive advantage.[1] The time required to complete this process is called *throughput time*.[2]

With globalization, the speed of competition has increased.[3] Speed, efficiency, and cost control are the common goals of savvy companies,[4] such as **Toyota**. Through time-based competition, **3M** reduced its new product development time from two years to two months, **Motorola** cut its production lead time for cellular phones from several weeks to four hours, and **Johnson & Johnson** became the top seller of contact lenses (largely due to its rapid and reliable delivery of disposable contacts). **Levi Strauss** reduced its reorder cycle time from nine weeks to four days, resulting in lower costs, fewer stockouts, and greater flexibility. Because the mission of all organizations revolves around providing products, the operations department is the primary focus of efforts to improve speed.[5] And remember that people, rather than machinery, are the force behind operations.[6] So keep moving; speed is vital to your career success.[7]

Charles Darwin said that it is not the strongest or most intelligent that survive, but those most responsive to change. **Eastman Kodak** is an example of a company that has not kept up with changes in its industry. Although attention to time is critical to survival,[8] Kodak was slow to come out with instant photography. Once it did, **Polaroid** sued it for patent infringement. Then it missed the industry transition to 35-millimeter cameras, losing market share to the Japanese. More recently, it was slow to recognize the popularity of digital cameras. Unable to keep up to speed in digital photography and experiencing a drop in film sales, Kodak planned to reduce its workforce by up to 15,000.[9]

Operations *is the function concerned with transforming resource inputs into product outputs. A* **product** *is a good, a service, or a combination of the two.* Exhibit 15-1 lists the ways systems to manage operations are classified, designed, and managed.

WorkApplication1

Is your present or past organization concerned about time-based competition? If so, what functional areas are primarily responsible for speed?

_____

_____

_____

_____

_____

Exhibit 15-1 *How Operations Systems Are Classified, Designed, and Managed*

Classifying Operations Systems	Designing Operations Systems	Managing Operations Systems
• Tangibility of products • Level of customer involvement • Operations flexibility • Resources and technology management	• Product mix and design • Facility layout • Facility location • Capacity planning	• Planning schedules and product management • Inventory control • Materials requirement planning (MRP) • Supply chain management • Quality control

——————— Learning Outcome 2 ———————
Explain the differences among operations systems with respect to tangibility of products, levels of customer involvement, operations flexibility, and management of resources and technology.

CLASSIFYING OPERATIONS SYSTEMS

Operations systems can be classified by the tangibility of products, level of customer involvement, operations flexibility, and management of resources and technology.

Tangibility of Products

The *tangibility of products* refers to whether the products are tangible, intangible, or mixed.

TANGIBLE PRODUCTS
Goods, such as **Toyota** automobiles, **Gateway** 2000 computers, and this textbook, are *tangible products*.

INTANGIBLE PRODUCTS
Services, such as haircuts, dry cleaning, and legal advice, are *intangible products*.

MIXED PRODUCTS
Mixed products are made up of both tangible products, such as **USAir** airplanes, and intangible services, such as the airline flight. Today, many organizations focus on mixed products. For example, major appliance retail stores, like Sears Brand Central, not only sell appliances but also offer extended warranties and service what they sell.

Level of Customer Involvement

It is important to view operations from the customer's perspective.[10] The level of **customer involvement** *refers to the amount of input from customers, which determines whether operations are make-to-stock, assemble-to-order, or make-to-order.*

MAKE-TO-STOCK (MTS) OPERATIONS
Make-to-stock operations produce products with a common design and price, in anticipation of demand. Therefore, there is a low level of customer involvement. Most goods that you see in retail stores are from make-to-stock operations. While most services, such as hair cuts, cannot be made to stock, some, such as scheduled transportation on airline flights, can.

ASSEMBLE-TO-ORDER (ATO) OPERATIONS
Assemble-to-order operations produce a standard product with some customized features. Some services and goods, such as those built with optional features, can be produced only after the receipt of an order. Therefore, there is a moderate level of customer involvement. Relatively expensive goods, such as automobiles, mainframe computer systems, and furniture, are commonly assembled to order. **McDonald's** hamburgers and other products

are primarily made to stock, whereas **Burger King** emphasizes "having it your way," using assemble-to-order operations to offer a standard burger with customized toppings.

Services can also be assembled to order. For example, standard training consulting packages and accounting and legal services can be customized to fit the needs of an organization.

MAKE-TO-ORDER (MTO) OPERATIONS

Make-to-order operations are carried out only after an order has been received from a specific customer. Here, there is a high level of customer involvement. Many services, such as auto repair, tailoring, development of a business's accounting system, criminal legal defense, and medical services, have to be made to order. Some goods, such as custom clothing and family portraits, are also made to order.

Operations Flexibility

Operations flexibility *refers to the amount of variety in the products an operation produces, which determines whether the products are produced continuously, repetitively, in batches, or individually.* Flexibility is based on product volume (how many units of one product are produced), and variety (how many different products the operation produces). The trend is toward more flexible manufacturing.[11]

CONTINUOUS PROCESS OPERATIONS (CPO)

Continuous process operations produce outputs that are not in discrete units, such as gas and oil, electricity, chemicals, and pulp. They tend to produce goods rather than services. With little to no variety and high volume, continuous process operations are the least flexible of the operations systems. Therefore, they are used for made-to-stock goods.

Applying The Concept 1

Level of Customer Involvement

Identify each product by its level of customer involvement.

a. make-to-stock
b. assemble-to-order
c. make-to-order

_____ 1. A haircut by Pierre.

_____ 2. A soft drink by 7-Up in a can.

_____ 3. Coffee ice cream in a sugar cone from Friendly's.

REPETITIVE PROCESS OPERATIONS (RPO)

Repetitive process operations produce outputs in an assembly-line structure, where employees and equipment are quite specialized in function and location. Each unit of output follows the same path through labor and equipment. All kinds of consumer and industrial goods, such as automobiles and tableware, are repetitive process operations outputs. Some services can also be assembly-line oriented, such as an automatic car wash or dog grooming service. Repetitive process operations have some variety and a high volume of similar units. Therefore, they are primarily used for made-to-stock or assembled-to-order goods. Most traditional automotive plants use repetitive process operations—work flows continuously along an assembly line, with workers repeatedly performing standard tasks.

BATCH PROCESS OPERATIONS (BPO)

Batch process operations produce different outputs with the same resources. When both the volume and the variety of products are moderate, flexibility is needed, especially if the organization cannot justify the investment required to dedicate labor or equipment to a single product. For example, a wood furniture maker might use the same people and machines to make dining room tables and chairs, desks, and bedroom dressers. A few services, such as cleaning services with business accounts, can also use batch process operations. With moderate variety and volume of similar units, batch process operations are primarily used for made-to-stock or assembled-to-order goods.

Batch process operations require more controls than do continuous process and repetitive process operations to monitor the coordination of inputs, the transformation process, and the inventory of finished outputs. Businesses using batch process operations have to be sure not to sell all of one product or have too much of one product in stock.

INDIVIDUAL PROCESS OPERATIONS (IPO)

Individual process operations produce outputs to customer specifications. They have high variety and low volume and so are used for made-to-order goods and services. In manufacturing, individual process operations are known as *job shops*. Used by the large majority of retailers and service organizations, individual process operations have the most flexibility.

Like batch process operations, individual process operations require controls to monitor the coordination of inputs and the transformation process. The idea is to maintain an even flow of business.

PROJECT PROCESS OPERATIONS (PPO)

Project process operations are another type of process operation that is low in volume and high in variety. They produce outputs that require a relatively long period of time to complete. Commonly completed by sending the resources to the customer's site, rather than working on the project at the seller's facilities, project process operations are used, for example, in the construction industry. Consulting services often blend individual process with project process operations: A client gives the consultant a project to complete, and the work may be divided between the two sites.

Flexibility of Operations

Identify the operations system that would be used to produce each product.

a. CPO
b. RPO
c. BPO

d. IPO
e. PPO

_____ 4. A Whirlpool refrigerator.

_____ 5. A swimming pool sold and installed by Teddy Bear Pools.

_____ 6. The asphalt for a driveway delivered by Juan's Asphalt Company.

_____ 7. Packages of Trident gum.

Resources and Technology Management

Operations is the function through which inputs are transformed into product outputs, but **technology** *is the process used to transform inputs into outputs.* Important operations decisions concerning the management of resources and technology include how labor- and capital-intensive the operations to make the product will be, how the customer will be served, and how the manufacturing or service technology will be managed.[12]

INTENSITY

In *capital-intensive operations*, machines do most of the work. Manufacturing companies that use continuous and repetitive operations processes (such as oil, automobile, and steel companies) are generally capital-intensive. These companies tend to use high levels of technology, much of which has been developed by other companies, such as **Modern Controls**.

In *labor-intensive operations*, human resources do most of the work. Organizations that use individual process operations tend to be labor intensive. Retail and service organizations are generally less capital-intensive than manufacturing firms and tend to use lower levels of technology. Education and consulting, as well as personal services such as hair cutting, auto repair, accounting, and legal services, tend to be very labor-intensive.

Manufacturing firms use a balance of capital and labor in batch and individual process operations, because it takes skilled workers to use flexible machines. Many large retailers have a balance of capital (because of the high cost of renting space at malls or buying a store in a good location) and labor (because they have a lot of employees). **Toyota** is an example of a balanced-intensity operation. Toyota's emphasis on quality and teamwork requires a skilled and well-trained labor force, but the company also makes capital investments in production machinery and technology.

WAYS OF SERVING CUSTOMERS

Customers can be served by people, machines, or both. Banks, for instance, provide service via tellers, automated teller machines, the Internet, and the telephone. Another consideration is where customers will be served. Today, some banks will send a loan officer to your home or office to take a mortgage loan application; others will do it over the phone. **Toyota**, like many businesses, relies on intermediaries—a network of dealers—to serve and sell to customers.

WAYS OF MANAGING MANUFACTURING TECHNOLOGY

Two important forms of manufacturing technology used in organizations are *automation*, using machines to perform work, and *computer-assisted manufacturing*, using computers to design or manufacture goods. Computer-assisted manufacturing includes *computer-aided design (CAD)*, *computer-aided manufacturing (CAM)*, and *computer-integrated manufacturing (CIM)*. In CAD, computers are used to design parts and complete goods and to simulate performance so that a prototype does not need to be constructed. **Ford** used it to speed up car design, **GE** has used it to change the design of circuit breakers, and **Benneton** has used it to design new styles and products. CAD is usually combined with CAM to ensure that design and production are coordinated. CAM is especially useful with individual process operations when reorders come in, because it can be used to quickly produce the desired product, prepare labels and copies of orders, and deliver the product.

Computer-integrated manufacturing links CAD and CAM. With CIM, the computer can access the company's information systems and adjust machine placements and settings automatically, enhancing both the complexity and the flexibility of scheduling. Robots perform functions ordinarily thought to be appropriate only for human beings. CIM is a powerful and complex management control system. It is relatively expensive and, therefore, is most commonly used with high-volume continuous and repetitive process operations.

Manufacturing technology can be used to create a competitive advantage.[13] **Cemex** used technology to automate its factory and office operations. In less than 10 years, Mexican Cemex went global, using a network of over 300 servers, 7,000 PCs, and 80 workstations to become the most efficient and the third-largest cement company in the world. Cemex trucks have onboard computers linked by GPS that relay pouring status and location, and the closest preloaded trucks fill orders immediately. The company offers an on-time delivery guaranty with a 5 percent rebate for orders delivered more than 20 minutes late. Cemex changed the concrete industry by replacing "old economy" supply operations with a "new economy" sophisticated transport logistics service.[14]

WAYS OF MANAGING SERVICE TECHNOLOGY

Manufacturers often create innovative products, such as computer hardware and software for the Internet, which are then commonly used by service firms to gain a competitive advantge.[15] For example, **VISA** customers' credit card transactions are recorded and billed electronically. Hotels use technology to accept and record room reservations. Health care providers use technology to manage patient records, dispatch ambulances, and monitor patients' vital signs.

WorkApplication2

Using Exhibit 15-2, identify the operations system where you work or have worked based on product tangibility, customer involvement, flexibility, and resources.

_____

_____

_____

_____

_____

Exhibit 15-2 *Classifying Operations Systems*

	Tangibility of Products	
Tangible		Intangible
Goods	Mixed Products	Services

	Level of Customer Involvement	
Low		High
Make-to-Stock	Assemble-to-Order	Make-to-Order

	Operations Flexibility		
Inflexible—high volume, low variety		Flexible—high variety, low volume	
Continuous Process Operations	Repetitive Process Operations	Batch Process Operations	Individual and Project Process Operations

	Resources and Technology Management	
Developers and users of technology— higher level of technology commonly used		Users of technology— lower level of technology commonly used
Capital-Intensive	Balanced Intensity	Labor-Intensive

Multiple Classifications

Exhibit 15-2 shows the four criteria for classifying operations systems. Notice that the focus on the left side of the exhibit is on manufacturing goods, while the focus on the right side is on providing services. However, it is not always easy to classify an organization's operations system, either because it falls at some intermediate point on the continuum in Exhibit 15-2 or because it encompasses more than one type of operation.

Frito-Lay offers tangible goods produced through make-to-stock operations. The company actually has two customer groups—consumers (who eat the products) and customers (who sell the products). Frito-Lay uses a repetitive process for its high-volume products and a batch process for its lower-volume products. A batch process is also used for different-sized portions of the same product. Frito-Lay's resources are balanced in intensity, as its manufacturing plants and trucks are expensive but it also has thousands of well-paid employees. Customer service is important, and that is why Frito-Lay makes frequent deliveries and stocks shelves for customers. New manufacturing and information technologies have increased productivity globally.[16] Frito-Lay uses the latest technology: computer-integrated manufacturing. Its sales staff was one of the first to use handheld computers to transmit sales and inventory data back to headquarters so that everyone with access could find out how many of each product had been sold, were in warehouses, and were en route to delivery.

DESIGNING OPERATIONS SYSTEMS

In a changing environment, operations systems must be continually redesigned. The interrelated areas of product mix and design, facility layout, facility location, and capacity planning must all be considered.

Product Mix and Design

Based on the organization's mission and objectives, top-level managers select the product mix. The *product mix* includes the number of product lines, the number of products offered within each line, and the mixture of goods and services within each line.

Apple expanded its product mix to include the iPod digital music player and iTunes, for downloading music. In its first year, iTunes sold more than 70 million songs.[17] Based on iPod sales, Apple reported that its first quarter 2004 revenues jumped 29 percent and its net income tripled.[18]

Apple teamed up with auto maker **BMW** to offer its iPod adapter as a car accessory. With the installation of an integrated adapter developed by both firms, BMW drivers can now control iPods through their existing audio system and multifunction steering wheel. Visit *http://ww.ipodyourbmw.com* for more information.[19]

Product design refers to new or improved product development. Successful companies integrate design and manufacturing rather than treating them as separate steps in product development.[20]

Toyota views product design as a continuous two-way flow through design, assembly, and distribution. The firm depends on customer feedback in order to develop new products that solve consumer problems and meet customers' needs. At the same time, the company attempts to achieve quality by linking engineering with manufacturing so that potential problems can be identified and resolved before production occurs. To better design cars for the U.S. market, Toyota nearly doubled the number of engineers at its Michigan center.[21]

WorkApplication3
List the product mix for an organization for which you work or have worked. Be sure to identify the number of major product lines, the number of products within one of the major lines offered, and the mixture of goods and services within that one major line.

_____

_____

_____

_____

————— Learning Outcome 3 —————

Discuss what is meant by "Quality is a virtue of design."

QUALITY IS A VIRTUE OF DESIGN

The throughput stages, Exhibit 15-3, must be well coordinated and controlled.[22] As you can see, the first stage is to design the product. "Quality is a virtue of design" means that if products are well designed, with cross-functional team input to ensure customer value, there will be fewer operations problems, the product will be easier to sell, and servicing the product will be less costly. Therefore, it is important for all functional areas to work together on the design of new products.[23]

BALANCING TIME-BASED COMPETITION AND DESIGN

While companies need to increase innovation and speed products to market,[24] they also need to have quality products to succeed.[25] Rushing through the design process can lead to operations problems that can't be easily fixed, in turn leading to sales problems and high repair costs. Thus, it can result in companies' losing money rather than making profits.

Exhibit 15-3 *Throughput Stages*

| Design | → | Operations | → | Sales | → | Service |

GM's Pontiac Fiero sports car lacked virtue of design. One design error was that the trunk contained a small spare tire. When a driver got a flat tire and put on the spare, the regular tire would not fit into the trunk and there was really no room for the tire in the small two-seat interior. In addition, some of the cars' engines caught on fire, and a multitude of small problems ran up service costs. Because of these problems, the Fiero was hard to sell and had one of the worst records for repeat buyers. Pontiac eventually discontinued the Fiero.

Learning Outcome 4

Explain product, process, cellular, and fixed-position facility layouts in terms of their level of customer involvement and flexibility.

Facility Layout

Facilities are the physical resources used in the operations process. The building, machines, furniture, and so on, are part of the facility. **Facility layout** refers to *the spatial arrangement of physical resources relative to each other.* Operations use product, process, cellular, or fixed-position layouts. The type of facility layout selected is based on the classification of the operations system and the product design. An important consideration in layout is the flow of the product throughout its transformation.[26]

PRODUCT LAYOUT

Product layout is associated with make-to-stock and assemble-to-order levels of customer involvement, relatively inflexible repetitive process or continuous process operations, and capital intensity.

Organizations with high volume and low variety have to decide what the sequence of assembly-line flow will be. **Hewlett-Packard** produces PCs using a product layout. **American, Southwest,** and other airlines provide a service using a product layout.

PROCESS LAYOUT

Process, or *functional, layout* is associated with a make-to-order level of customer involvement, flexible individual process operations, and labor intensity or a balanced intensity.

Organizations with high variability and low volume, whose products/customers have different needs and use only some processes/functions, have to decide how the layout should be arranged. Most offices are set up functionally, with assigned areas/departments such as human resources and finance. Retail stores use process layouts so that customers can go to particular departments to find what they need. Upscale restaurants make each meal to order and locate the kitchen away from the dining area. In a health care facility, a patient is sent to the functions necessary for his or her treatment, such as x-ray, a diagnostic laboratory, the pharmacy, and so on.

CELLULAR LAYOUT

Cellular layout is associated with make-to-stock and assemble-to-order levels of customer involvement, relatively flexible batch process operations, and a balanced intensity.

Organizations with products of moderate variability and volume must decide how to group technology so that all the activities involved in creation of a product are located near one another. Grouping technology into cells provides some of the efficiencies of both product and process layouts. Multiple cells make it easy for employees with different skills to work together to deliver the final product. **Edy's Ice Cream** uses cells with self-managed teams to make its various flavors in batches.

By using automated technology, *flexible manufacturing systems* group technology to take advantage of a product layout to produce both high-volume and high-variety products.[27] Without creating a batch environment, they still produce in batches. For example, **Mazda's** Japan Ujina plant can build up to eight different car models on a single assembly line. (Most U.S. assembly lines, which can be an entire facility, make only one model.) However, flexible systems must deal with the control issues of batch process operations.

FIXED-POSITION LAYOUT

Fixed-position layout is associated with make-to-order and assemble-to-order levels of customer involvement, flexible project process operations, and balanced intensity.

Organizations with low-volume products that take a relatively long time to complete must determine the sequence of steps required of workers during the construction of each unit. Contractors construct buildings and Boeing makes planes using fixed-position layout.

Exhibit 15-4 compares the four types of layouts with respect to their level of customer involvement and flexibility of operations and provides an illustration of each systems process.

Facility Location

Location is the physical geographic site of facilities. The facility location must be determined based on the classification of the operations system and the

WorkApplication4
Identify the facility layout used where you work or have worked. Draw the physical arrangement of the facilities.

_____

_____

_____

_____

Applying The Concept 3

Facilities Layout

Identify the facility layout that would be used to produce each product.

a. product
b. process
c. cellular
d. fixed-position

_____ 8. A container of blueberry ice cream at Bonnie's Gourmet Ice Cream Shop.

_____ 9. A DVD player by RCA.

_____ 10. A bridge being built by Smith Contractors, Inc.

_____ 11. A set of fingernails by Jean's Manicures.

Exhibit 15-4 *Facility Layout*

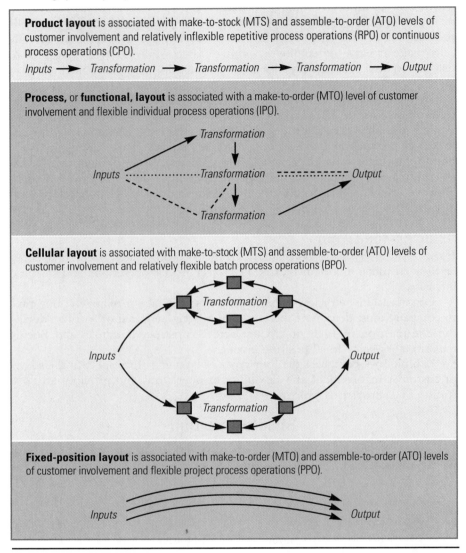

Product layout is associated with make-to-stock (MTS) and assemble-to-order (ATO) levels of customer involvement and relatively inflexible repetitive process operations (RPO) or continuous process operations (CPO).

Inputs → *Transformation* → *Transformation* → *Transformation* → *Output*

Process, or **functional, layout** is associated with a make-to-order (MTO) level of customer involvement and flexible individual process operations (IPO).

Cellular layout is associated with make-to-stock (MTS) and assemble-to-order (ATO) levels of customer involvement and relatively flexible batch process operations (BPO).

Fixed-position layout is associated with make-to-order (MTO) and assemble-to-order (ATO) levels of customer involvement and flexible project process operations (PPO).

organization's product mix, layout requirements, and capacity planning. Major factors that are considered when making the location decision include cost; proximity to inputs, customers, and/or competitors; transportation; access to human resources; and number of facilities.

COST

Cost includes the cost of buying or renting land and the facility, as well as operating expenses such as utilities, taxes, and insurance.

Tyco International Ltd. is a diversified manufacturing and service company with over 267,000 employees, operations in all 50 U.S. states and more than 100 other countries, and millions of customers throughout the world. Some of its businesses and products are world leaders in the electronics, fire and security, health care, plastics and adhesives, and engineered products and services industries.[28] Although Tyco is primarily a U.S. company, it is incorporated in Bermuda. Its board of directors recommended that its headquarters location remain there for cost reasons—to minimize American corporate taxes.[29]

PROXIMITY TO INPUTS, CUSTOMERS, AND/OR COMPETITORS

General Mills and Pillsbury are both located in Minneapolis, Minnesota, where they can get easy access to grains for processing into flour and other products. Retail stores are commonly located in malls in major suburbs. Fast-food restaurants are usually located on major thoroughfares, and **McDonald's** and **Burger King** are often located near each other.

TRANSPORTATION

Manufacturers need access to air, rail, truck, and water transportation to get inputs and to deliver outputs. For retailers, transportation includes getting merchandise delivered and getting employees and customers to the store. Lack of parking is one of the problems that has caused the failure of many downtown businesses.

ACCESS TO HUMAN RESOURCES

Certain types of skilled labor can be found more easily in certain locations. For example, high-tech firms tend to locate on the technology highway—Route 128 in the Boston area and Silicon Valley in California. Another consideration is that the cost of labor can be much lower in other countries.

NUMBER OF FACILITIES

Global companies have headquarters in one country and facilities in others. Companies need to determine the right number of facilities for ease of distribution.

Join the Discussion Ethics & Social Responsibility

Factory Conditions

1. Should Gap let local authorities monitor its factory conditions?
2. Is it ethical and socially responsible for Gap to revoke contracts, causing poor workers to lose their jobs?
3. Is it ethical and socially responsible to Gap's stockholders to pay higher labor costs than necessary, thus possibly reducing profits and their dividends?

Gap, the subject of the opening case in Chapter 1, has 3,000 factories in about 50 countries, making clothes for its Gap, Old Navy, and Banana Republic clothing-store chains. Gap is the largest specialty-apparel retailer, with over $15 billion in sales. Many companies, including Gap, have been criticized for not monitoring factory conditions. To address the criticism, the firm set standards for its manufacturers. In 2003, Gap revoked its contracts with 136 factories for persistent or severe violations of standards.[30]

Join the Discussion Ethics & Social Responsibility

Oil Reserves

1. Do you think Shell made an honest mistake, or did it intentionally overstate its reserves?
2. What implications does this overstatement have for Shell's capacity planning?

When the **Royal Dutch/Shell Group** disclosed that it had overstated its proven oil and natural gas reserves by 20 percent, or the equivalent of 3.9 million barrels of oil, investors were very worried about the future value of the stock. After all, Shell's reserves are the basis for its capacity planning.[31]

Capacity Planning

Another part of the facility decision is capacity planning. **Capacity** *is the amount of products an organization can produce.* Should a facility be built to produce 2,000 or 5,000 units per day? How many checkout/teller stations should a supermarket/bank have? Should a restaurant have 50 or 100 tables? How many rooms should a hotel build? How many beds should an intensive care unit of a hospital have? Computerized mathematical models can be used to make these decisions.

In most cases, capacity planning is done under conditions of uncertainty and high risk (Chapter 4), because it usually requires a large capital investment and is based on a long-term sales forecast. After capacity is set, some scheduling techniques can be used to help optimize it. This topic is discussed in the next section.

Frito-Lay has expanded its convenience food product mix in recent years. It now has a wider variety of salty snacks, as well as Grandma's cookies, Oberto meat snacks, nuts, and trail mix. With Quaker, it has expanded its product mix to include cereal, snack, and granola bars and toaster pastry. Frito-Lay is also focusing on "better-for-you" snacks, with less fat, sugar, sodium, and calories. It has removed trans fats from some of its products, offering Baked Lays, WOW! fat-free products, and Natural snacks without preservatives and artificial flavor or color. It also offers ethnic products, using guacamole flavoring. Product packaging and design are important to make the product stay fresh longer and look good to potential buyers. Frito-Lay uses product and cellular layouts to make the snacks, and it has 22 facility locations in the United States, with flexible capacity to meet fluctuating demand and optimize production and distribution.

MANAGING OPERATIONS SYSTEMS AND THE SUPPLY CHAIN

After operations systems have been designed, they must be managed. The principles of organization—authority, delegation, and especially organizational and job design (Chapter 6)—must be used,[32] as well as the leadership theories in Chapter 13. In this section, we look at planning schedules and project management, inventory control, materials requirement planning, and supply chain management.

—————————— Learning Outcome 5 ——————————
Describe the similarities and differences among the planning sheet, Gantt chart, and PERT network.

Planning Schedules and Project Management

Today, computer software packages are used for all types of scheduling, from simple calendars and to-do lists to complex PERT networks. **Westhoff Tool and Die** uses a computer program to track 80 projects. The software schedules each machine in the plant on a chart, which is then given to the six managers, who supervise 60 machine operators. This section will discuss three scheduling techniques—the planning sheet, the Gantt chart, and the PERT network—which are often designed for specific projects.

Scheduling is the process of listing activities that must be performed to accomplish an objective; the activities are listed in sequence, along with the time needed to complete each one. Scheduling answers the planning questions: Which employees will make which products? What specific products will be produced? When will they be produced? Where will they be produced? How will they be produced? How many of each will be produced?

An important part of scheduling is routing. **Routing** *is the path and sequence of the transformation of a product into an output.* Routing for each of the four facility layouts is illustrated with arrows in Exhibit 15-4. Notice that with process and cellular layouts, routing is complex.

Priority scheduling *is the continuing evaluation and reordering of the sequence in which products will be produced.* The method of priority scheduling depends on the layout used. Three simple methods are used to schedule operations:

- *First come–first served.* Jobs are scheduled in the order in which they are received. This method is common in service organizations.
- *Earliest due date.* The job with the earliest promised delivery date is scheduled first.
- *Shortest operating time.* Jobs that take the least amount of time are scheduled first.

Many organizations use a combination of the three methods.

THE PLANNING SHEET

Planning sheets *state an objective and list the sequence of activities required to meet the objective, when each activity will begin and end, and who will complete each activity.* The planning sheet in Exhibit 15-5 shows the transformation process for a monthly marketing letter, which is mailed to 300 potential customers.

GANTT CHART

Gantt charts *use bars to graphically illustrate a schedule and progress toward the objective over a period of time.* The different activities to be performed are usually listed vertically, with time shown horizontally. The resources to be allocated, such as people or machines, are also commonly shown on the vertical axis. Gantt charts, like planning sheets, are appropriate when independent sequential steps are needed to accomplish the objective. The Gantt chart has an advantage over the planning sheet in that it places progress toward the

WorkApplication5
Identify which priority scheduling method(s) the organization for which you work or have worked uses.

WorkApplication6
Give an example of a project in an organization for which you work or have worked that is suitable for scheduling using the planning sheet.

Exhibit 15-5 *Planning Sheet*

OBJECTIVE: To mail a personalized form letter to all target clients by the 15th of each month.

Responsible: Latoya/Joel   **Starting date**: 1st of each month
Due date: 15th of each month   **Priority**: High
Control checkpoints: 7th and 12th of each month

| | When | | |
Activities	Start		End	Who
1. Type letter on word processor.	1st		2nd	Latoya
2. Deliver letter to printer.	3rd	or	4th	Joel
3. Print letters on company stationery.	5th		6th	printer
4. Pick up letters at printer.	6th	or	7th	Joel
5. Use mail merge to type names and addresses on letters and envelopes.	7th		9th	Joel
6. Sign each letter.	9th	or	10th	Latoya
7. Fold each letter and put in an envelope.	10th		11th	Joel
8. Bundle letters to meet bulk mailing specifications.	12th		13th	Joel
9. Deliver to U.S. Postal Bulk Mail Center.	13th			Joel
10. Mail letters.	14th	or	15th	U.S. Mail

WorkApplication7

Give an example of a project in an organization for which you work or have worked that would be appropriate to schedule using a Gantt chart.

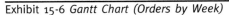

objective on the chart as a control technique. In other words, a Gantt chart is both a planning and a control tool. Another important advantage of the Gantt chart over the planning sheet and PERT is that it can show multiple projects on one chart. This helps in prioritizing and scheduling project activities that use the same resources.[33]

Exhibit 15-6 illustrates a Gantt chart for multiple orders in an operations department. Each bar extends from the start time to the end time, with the shaded portion indicating the part completed to date. Using the chart, you can see at a glance how orders are progressing. If you become aware that a project is behind schedule, you can take corrective action to get it back on schedule. If today is day 1 of week 3 in May, the end of the shaded portion of the bar will

Exhibit 15-6 *Gantt Chart (Orders by Week)*

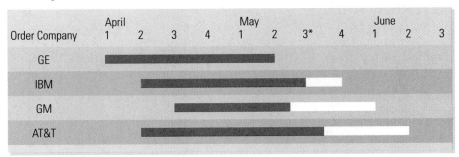

* Indicates today's date—the first day of the third week of May.
Ends of bars indicate scheduled starting and ending dates of project. The shaded part of the bar indicates the part of the project completed to date, while the blank space to the end of the bar indicates work still to be completed. The GE project is done. The IBM project is right on schedule and should be completed this week. The GM project is behind schedule and should be completed during the fourth week in May. The AT&T project is ahead of schedule and should be completed during the first week of June.

be directly under the second 3 if the project is exactly on schedule. What is the status of each of the four projects on the chart in Exhibit 15-6? The answer is at the bottom of the exhibit.

PERFORMANCE EVALUATION AND REVIEW TECHNIQUE (PERT)

Multiple activities are considered to be independent when they can be performed simultaneously; they are considered to be dependent when one must be completed before the next activity can begin. Planning sheets and Gantt charts are useful tools when the activities follow each other in a dependent series. However, when some activities are dependent and some are independent, PERT (critical path) is more appropriate. **PERT** *is a network scheduling technique that illustrates the dependence of activities.* Exhibit 15-7 shows a PERT network.

The key components of PERT are activities, events, times, and the critical path. With complex projects, it is common to have multiple activities represented as one event.[34] For example, in automobile production, building the engine would be an event that requires multiple activities to complete. Time can be measured in a variety of ways (seconds, minutes, hours, days, weeks, months, years, etc.) to determine the critical path. *The* **critical path** *is the most time-consuming series of activities in a PERT network.* The critical path is important to know because it determines the length of time it will take to complete a project. It is shown by the double lines in Exhibit 15-7. Any delay in the steps in the critical path will delay the entire project. The cost of each activity is sometimes shown with the time.

The following steps explain how the PERT network in Exhibit 15-7 was completed.

Step 1. List all the activities/events that must be completed to reach the specific objective. Assign a letter to each one. Exhibit 15-7 shows 10 activities, labeled A through J.

Exhibit 15-7 *PERT Network*

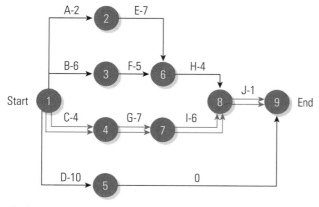

Circles = events
Arrows and letters = activities
Numbers = time in days
Double arrows = the critical path

Step 2. Determine the time it will take to complete each activity/event. In Exhibit 15-7, time is measured in number of days as follows: A, 2 days; B, 6 days; C, 4 days; D, 10 days; E, 7 days; F, 5 days; G, 7 days; H, 4 days; I, 6 days; and J, 1 days.

Step 3. Arrange the tasks on the diagram in the sequence in which they must be completed. In Exhibit 15-7, A must be completed before E can begin; E must be completed before H can begin; and H must be completed before J can begin. For example, before you can place a box of cereal on a shelf for sale (J), it must be ordered (A), received (E), and priced (H). Notice that activity D is independent. An arrow, as well as a letter, represents each activity. The numbered circles signify the completion of an event leading to the desired outcome. All activities originate and terminate at a circle. In Exhibit 15-7, 1 represents the start of the project, and 9 its end or completion.

Step 4. Determine the critical path. To do this, you must total the time required for each path from start (1) to end (9). Path 1–2–6–8–9 takes 2 + 7 + 4 + 1 days, for a total of 14 days. Path 1–3–6–8–9 takes 6 + 5 + 4 + 1 days, for a total of 16 days. Path 1–4–7–8–9 takes 4 + 7 + 6 + 1 days, for a total of 18 days. Path 1–5–9 takes 10 + 0 days, for a total of 10 days.

The critical path, indicated by the double arrow, is 1–4–7–8–9. The program or project should take 18 days to complete. If the job was supposed to be done in two weeks, you would know before you even started that it could not be done on time. You would have to change the completion date or maybe abandon the project.

To summarize, planning sheets and Gantt charts are commonly used to develop procedures for routine standing plans, whereas PERT is commonly used for single-use program plans for a complex project with dependent activities.[35] However, all three types of schedules can be used for either standing or single-use plans.

WorkApplication8

Give an example of a project in an organization for which you work or have worked that would be appropriate to schedule using a PERT network.

<hr>

ApplyingTheConcept 4

Scheduling Tools

Select the most appropriate scheduling tool for each situation.

a. planning sheet

b. Gantt chart

c. PERT network

_____12. A production department wants to schedule the making of eight products on six different types of machines.

_____13. Ted will develop a plan for building a new house.

_____14. Karen will develop procedures for a new method of providing a service.

_____15. A plan will be created for building a new submarine.

_____16. The training department wants to schedule the use of its rooms and courses.

— Learning Outcome 6 —
Explain the relationship among inventory control, just-in-time (JIT)
inventory, and materials requirement planning (MRP).

Inventory Control

Inventory *is the stock of materials held for future use.* Thus, inventory is an idle resource. Inventory control, also called *materials control*, is an important responsibility of the operations manager, because in many organizations purchasing, moving, storing, insuring, and controlling materials is the single major cost.[36] Clearly, decisions that determine the control of materials through operations have a significant effect on whether a firm meets its objective.[37]

Inventory control *is the process of managing raw materials, work-in-process, finished goods, and in-transit goods.*

- *Raw materials.* Raw materials are input materials that have been received but have not yet been transformed in any way by the operations department, such as eggs at a restaurant or steel at an auto maker. Important preliminary controls include purchasing raw materials and scheduling their delivery to your facility so that they will be there when needed.
- *Work-in-process.* Work-in-process is material that has had some transformation but is not yet an output, such as an egg that is being cooked or a car on the assembly line. Concurrent controls are used to ensure that products meet standards before they become finished goods.
- *Finished goods.* Finished goods are transformed outputs that have not yet been delivered to customers, such as cooked eggs sitting on a plate waiting to be served to a customer or a car sitting at the factory waiting to be shipped to a dealer. Rework control may be needed, such as reheating of the eggs if they get cold while waiting for the server or fixing of the car if it cannot be driven off the assembly line.
- *In-transit (pipeline) goods.* In-transit goods are finished goods being delivered to the customer, such as eggs being carried to the table by a server or cars being delivered by truck to the dealer. Damage control may be needed. For example, if the server drops the eggs on the way to the table, the order must be redone; or if the car is damaged in delivery, it will need to be returned or fixed by the dealer at the manufacturer's expense. Deliverers of products commonly have insurance to cover the cost of damaged and lost goods.

Exhibit 15-8 illustrates how inventory control fits into the systems process.

Exhibit 15-8 *Inventory Control within the Systems Process*

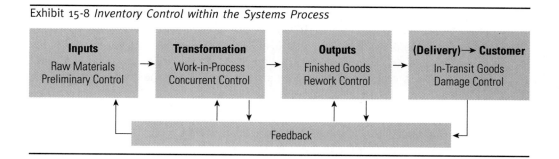

It is important to balance responsiveness (how fast the product gets to the customer) and efficiency (cost control). For example, having more facilities increases responsiveness, but it also decreases efficiency, as does having lots of inventory on hand. Using a fast delivery service like **FedEx** again increases responsiveness but decreases efficiency. Information is key to balancing responsiveness and efficiency, as the firm that understands customer demand can respond quickly and efficiently.[38]

Caterpillar (Cat) is a manufacturer of heavy earth-moving equipment. With capital-intensive equipment, avoiding downtime is important to customers. Thus, Cat's competitive advantage is its superior parts-supply capability, which gets needed parts to stranded machines quickly. Working with FedEx, Cat possesses what may be the fastest and most comprehensive parts-supply capability in the world. Its global IT system makes this precision and speed possible, as factories, dealers, and distribution centers are all networked through Cat's intranet. Cat is working toward zero downtime by placing into key working parts microchips that signal a breakdown before it occurs, so that the parts can be replaced before the equipment actually breaks down.[39]

RETAILING AND SERVICES INVENTORY
Retail inventory control, including *purchasing*, is concerned almost exclusively with finished goods for resale as is. However, many retailers, such as the Home **Shopping Network**, catalog seller **L.L. Bean**, and major furniture and appliance stores, do have in-transit inventory.

Most service organizations deal only with the finished-goods inventory they create by providing the service. However, some services have in-transit inventory—for example, accounting statements and legal documents are commonly delivered to clients.

A major reason why **Wal-Mart** overtook **Kmart** to become the nation's largest retailer lies in its use of inventory control. In March 2004, Kmart reported its first quarterly profit, which it attributed to improvements in inventory management and pricing. Kmart is also working to provide a more shopper-friendly layout in its stores. But it still has a long way to go to catch up to Wal-Mart, as Wal-Mart and **Target** both had increases in same-store sales, while Kmart, although now profitable, had a decline in same-store sales.[40]

JUST-IN-TIME (JIT) INVENTORY
The objective of inventory control is to have the correct amount of all four types of inventory available when and where they are needed, while minimizing waste and the total cost of managing and storing inventory.[41] To accomplish this objective, many organizations now use JIT.[42] **Just-in-time (JIT) inventory** *is a method in which necessary parts and raw materials are delivered shortly before they are needed.*

Toyota was a pioneer in JIT inventory management. Very few parts are stored at the plant, waiting to be installed as cars move through the assembly line. Instead, the factories rely on suppliers to get the needed raw materials and parts to the factory floor when they are required during the production process.

Materials Requirement Planning (MRP)

Materials requirement planning (MRP) *is a system that integrates operations and inventory control with complex ordering and scheduling.* MRP involves developing a process for ordering raw materials and components at the right time

---

WorkApplication9

Identify the type of inventory and how it is controlled where you work or have worked.

and in the right quantity so that they arrive shortly before their scheduled transformation into outputs, and appropriate work-in-process is ready as needed. JIT is part of inventory control, which is part of MRP.

MRP is commonly used by firms that have different delivery systems and lead times. **Boise-Cascade, Lockheed, Texas Instruments,** and **Westinghouse** all use MRP because they need hundreds of parts in vastly different quantities, with arrival times that vary from hours to months. Coordinating and controlling such a complex system is virtually impossible for any manager. However, MRP software can manage such a system fairly easily.[43]

Dell's competitive advantage, making it so successful, comes from its speedy delivery of low-cost products. Recall from Chapter 1 that Dell does not stock monitors, instead using just-in-time inventory, and leaving it to shippers to match monitors to computers ordered by Dell customers. Good relationships with key suppliers permit Dell to get parts in minutes rather than days. Dell's just-in-time system allows it to custom-build and ship 85 percent of orders within eight hours. Its OptiPlex factory, in Austin, Texas, uses materials requirements planning—a system it calls Metric 12—to integrate just-in-time inventory delivery with a complicated computer system. The operations goal is to cut cost and save time by decreasing the number of worker "touches" per machine. Unlike competitors, which use an assembly-line product layout, Dell uses a cellular layout, with small teams building a complete machine by using components that arrive in racks at their workstations.[44]

ENTERPRISE RESOURCE PLANNING (ERP)

ERP takes MRP a step further, as it collects, processes, and provides information about a firm's entire enterprise. Ordering, product design, production, purchasing, inventory, distribution, human resources, receipt of payments, and forecasting of future demand are incorporated into one network system.[45] For example, anyone with access can check the current inventory, a sales rep can enter an order and see what the actual delivery date will be, and an engineer can see how a decision about product design will affect production schedules and resource needs. SAP R/3 software, as well as other software by companies such as Oracle, makes ERP possible.

Harman Music Group (HMG), of Salt Lake City, Utah, designs, manufactures, and markets signal-processing equipment for professional musicians, recording studios, and live sound applications, under the most respected brand names in the music industry (DigiTech, DOD, and dbx).[46] HMG wanted to improve its operations, so it hired **Hewlett-Packard** to develop a new enterprise resource planning system. A five-person HP team began by developing a blueprint of how HMG operated—interviewing employees, mapping out exactly how information traveled through the organization, and analyzing which managers needed which kinds of information. Then, the team developed the ERP software. HMG's new ERP system updates the sales forecast whenever an order is received, automatically updates production plans, and provides HMG managers with a real-time estimate of the profitability of each product.[47]

ECONOMIC ORDER QUANTITY (EOQ)

The EOQ is the optimal quantity of a product to order, determined on the basis of a mathematical model. The more often you order, the higher the ordering cost—but if you order less often, your holding cost goes up. By using the EOQ, you can minimize ordering and holding costs without running out of stock.

Calculating EOQs is a part of MRP. However, many small businesses that want to calculate EOQs don't need MRP.[48] Such businesses can determine EOQ using a calculator, as follows:

$$EOQ = \sqrt{\frac{2RS}{H}} = \sqrt{\frac{2(5,000)(25)}{2}} = \sqrt{5,000(25)} = \sqrt{125,000} = 353.55$$

where
- EOQ = optimal quantity to reorder
- R = total required over planning horizon (usually one year); here, 5,000
- S = cost of preparing one order (or setup); here, $25
- H = cost of holding one unit for the planning horizon; here, $2

Supply Chain Management

Supply chain management *is the process of coordinating all the activities involved in producing a product and delivering it to the customer.* To provide high-quality products at the lowest cost, supply chain management starts with forecasting demand for a product and then moves on to planning and managing supply and demand, acquiring materials, scheduling and producing the product, warehousing, controlling inventory, distributing the product, and delivering it. The final stage involves customer service. Supply chain management focuses heavily on purchasing and inventory control. Raw materials, including component parts, are expensive for many manufacturers. Thus, keeping inventory costs down while ensuring that good-quality materials are available when needed is important in the supply chain.[49] Just-in-time inventory is used to control costs and to avoid stocking inventories that may not be sold.[50]

The supply chain includes every organization your firm buys supplies from, as well as those that help you sell and deliver your products to final customers.[51] Like any chain, your supply chain is only as good as its weakest link, so your firm needs to establish strong relationships throughout the chain. Good relationships are based on information, which is potentially the biggest driver of performance in the supply chain, as it directly affects the other three drivers—operations facilities, inventory, and transportation—enabling the entire chain to be more responsive and efficient.[52] Global leaders are those companies that add the most value as they handle transactions through the supply chain.[53]

Dell is a global leader because it is so successful at supply chain management. It does not make monitors or keep them in inventory, and it buys most of its computer components on a just-in-time basis. Dell specializes in customizing computers, putting suppliers' components together to customer specifications. By selling directly to the customer, it has eliminated entire steps in the supply chain, thus keeping inventory to a bare minimum.[54]

Eastman Kodak is an example of a company that is having a supply chain management problem, as it is losing its supply chain member *Walgreen Co.* to Japanese rival **Fuji Photo Film Co. Walgreen** is America's largest drug chain. With 4,290 outlets, it sells more than two billion photo prints a year, a volume second only to **Wal-Mart's.** Kodak used to be Walgreen's exclusive provider of photo-developing services. But Walgreen has now installed Fuji's one-hour developing equipment in 1,500 stores and more than 4,000 computer kiosks, allowing customers to get prints in minutes from their filmless digital cameras.[55]

When you think of **UPS** and **FedEx**, you probably think of shipping packages. But both offer much more, including supply chain management help to businesses of all sizes. On their Web sites, they offer a link to "Supply Chain Solutions," where you can find details about how these firms can help your company improve its supply chain. With the growth in online sales, deliveries are on the increase, and managing the delivery portion of the supply chain is becoming an increasingly important part of doing business.

Frito-Lay plans and schedules the production and delivery of its products. Its raw materials include tons of potatoes, corn, cheese, and many other ingredients, which it buys on a just-in-time basis from suppliers to make the products (work-in-process and finished goods inventory) that are shipped to customers. It offers just-in-time inventory to most of its customers, as it restocks shelves frequently so that many customers carry no inventory at all—it's all on the shelves. Within its supply chain management program, Frito-Lay uses enterprise resource planning to integrate all its B2B and EDI activities with those of suppliers and customers. When products are delivered and sold, data are sent in real time so that supply, production, and inventory information can be adjusted quickly for effective inventory control.

Quality Control

Quality control is one of the most important functions of managing an operations system. Because quality is such an important issue, it has been covered throughout the text; however, in this section we discuss it in more detail as we look at customer quality control, TQM, the International Standards Organization, Six Sigma, statistical quality control, and contributions made by quality gurus.

Quality control *is the process of ensuring that all types of inventory meet standards.* As you can tell by the definition, quality control and inventory control overlap. The top row in Exhibit 15-8 shows the systems process steps, the second row shows the four inventory stages, and the third row shows the four types of quality control. Quality control is just as important for goods as it is for services; it applies to the scrambled eggs in a restaurant as well as the car produced by an auto maker.

Quality assurance requires that you "build in" quality; you cannot "inspect it in." Recall from Chapter 14 that the quality focus should be on preliminary and concurrent control, not rework and damage control, and that quality is a virtue of design.

CUSTOMER QUALITY CONTROL

Throughout this entire book we have been focusing on creating customer value. Exhibit 15-9 lists five rules that will help ensure quality customer service. If you follow these rules, you will increase your chances of developing effective human relations skills and ensuring a high-quality product for your customer. And remember that everyone you deal with is a customer.

TQM

The four major TQM principles are (1) focus on delivering customer value, (2) continually improve systems and processes, (3) focus on managing processes rather than people, and (4) use teams to continually improve.

Exhibit 15-9 *Five Rules of Customer Human Relations*

> 1. Put people before things.
> 2. Always be nice—no matter how busy you are.
> 3. Take your time with people.
> 4. Be polite; say "please," "thank you," and "you're welcome."
> 5. Don't discriminate with your service (treat everyone well).

A few of the differences between TQM (discussed in Chapter 2) and quality control follow:

- TQM is much broader in scope than quality control because part of its core value is to make it the job of everyone in the organization to improve quality.[56] Under quality control, the operations department is solely responsible for product quality.
- With TQM, quality is determined by customers, who compare actual use with requirements to determine value, or purchasing benefits.[57] With quality control, quality is determined by the standards set for acceptability.
- The focus in TQM is not on acceptance or rejection of the product,[58] but on continuous improvement.[59] With quality control, if products don't meet quality requirements, corrective action is taken to make them acceptable or they are rejected.

THE INTERNATIONAL STANDARDS ORGANIZATION

The **International Standards Organization (ISO)** *certifies firms that meet set quality standards.* Both manufacturing and services sectors are applying for ISO certification to improve their management systems and operational control.[60] JIT and TQM are part of ISO 9000 certification, as organizations must document policies that address quality management, continuous improvement, and customer satisfaction. Most multinational corporations have ISO 9000 certification, and they require the suppliers they do business with to be certified, to ensure the quality of materials used. The implementation of ISO 9000 has greatly improved the efficiency of the Department of Agriculture's Meat Grading and Certification Branch.

SIX SIGMA

The cost of poor quality is typically 20 to 30 percent of revenues. Six Sigma is a revolutionary quality initiative that is fast becoming a world standard.[61] It is based on the reality that higher levels of quality at lower cost are urgently required to compete in the challenging global economy. Six Sigma can reduce costs, rejects, lead times, and capital spending while raising employee skill levels and strengthening overall financial results.[62]

Six Sigma's goal is only 3.4 defects or mistakes per million operations. *Sigma* is a letter from the Greek alphabet, used to represent a statistical measure of deviations from a standard. Most companies operate at the Three-Sigma level of 66,000 defects per million.[63] Six Sigma is grounded in math, statistics,

Join the Discussion Ethics & Social Responsibility

Social Accountability International

1. Should global multinationals eliminate sweatshops by having SA8000-certified facilities?
2. Should global multinationals require all their suppliers to get SA8000 certification?
3. How might working toward SA8000 certification affect cost, revenues, and profits?

Social Accountability International, or **SAI** (*http://www.sa-intl.org*), is a U.S.-based nonprofit organization dedicated to the development, implementation, and oversight of voluntary verifiable social accountability standards. SAI works to improve workplaces and combat sweatshops through the expansion and further development of the current international workplace standards. SAI gets key stakeholders to develop consensus-based voluntary standards and promotes understanding and implementation of standards worldwide. Like ISO 9000 certification, SA8000 certification verifies compliance of qualified organizations with international workplace standards. Most multinationals have social responsibility sections in their annual reports, but not too many have facilities that are SA8000 certified. As of May 2004, 400 facilities in 40 countries, representing 40 industries, were certified.[64]

data analysis, finance, and computer skills. There is a heavy emphasis on measurement and achieving measurable bottom-line results.[65]

Motorola first advanced Six Sigma about 1986.[66] Since then Motorola has saved $15 billion over 11 years, and GE has produced more than $2 billion in benefits.[67]

Ford Motor Company is the first and only auto maker to use Six Sigma in all of its operations. "Consumer Driven 6-Sigma," used by Ford to achieve breakthrough improvements in quality and customer satisfaction, is a data-driven methodology that employs statistical tools to reduce variability and defects in processes. Consumer Driven 6-Sigma focuses on customers by selecting projects that target their most important satisfaction issues. Critical to Ford's strategy of achieving best-in-class customer satisfaction, 6-Sigma is leading a culture change at Ford. Ford has saved more than $675 million globally by using 6-Sigma.[68]

––––––––––––––––– Learning Outcome 7 –––––––––––––––––
Explain how statistical process control (SPC) charts and the exception principle are used in quality control.

STATISTICAL QUALITY CONTROL

Statistical quality control is a management science technique that uses a variety of statistical tests based on probability to improve the quality of decision making. Statistics are employed to improve the probability of identifying and eliminating quality problems. The most common test is statistical process control, a standard TQM technique that is part of Six Sigma.

Statistical process control (SPC) *aids in determining whether quality is within an acceptable standard range.* It is called a process control because it is concurrent; quality is measured and corrected during the transformation process.[69] SPC is used to monitor operations and to minimize variances in the quality of products. **McDonald's**, for example, goes to great lengths to ensure that the quality of its Big Mac is the same all over the country. Implementing SPC requires four steps.

Step 1. Set the desired quality standard and a range. The range includes the highest (upper control limit, or UCL) and the lowest (lower control limit, or LCL) level of acceptable quality, with the desired standard in the middle. This desired standard is called the *mean*, which is an average. The narrower the range, the higher the quality consistency between products.

Step 2. Determine the sampling technique and the frequency of measuring performance. The *sampling technique* determines how many products will be inspected; the range is from 0 to 100 percent. Statistical models can help determine the percentage. As a general rule, the more critical it is to stay within quality range, the more frequent the measures and the larger the sample inspected.

Step 3. Measure performance and plot it on an SPC chart. The variance of each sample mean from the desired mean can then be statistically analyzed.

Step 4. Use the exception principle. Do nothing if performance is within the acceptable range, but take corrective action if it is out of the control limits.

An example of an SPC chart for 16-ounce bags of Lay's Potato Chips is shown in Exhibit 15-10. As long as the bags of chips weigh between 15.80 and 16.20 ounces, the machine continues to produce them. However, if the measured weight goes out of this range, as it did at 10:00, the machine stops and is adjusted so as to produce the desired mean weight of 16 ounces, as shown at 10:30.

Service organizations can also benefit from statistical process control. An SPC system was created to help a credit company achieve timeliness goals for its car loans and to monitor the creation of accounts for customer groups. By helping the loan-processing department dispatch labor assignments and speed

WorkApplication10

Explain quality control in an organization where you work or have worked.

_____

_____

_____

_____

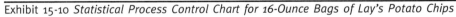

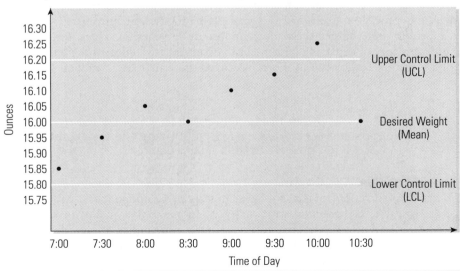

Exhibit 15-10 *Statistical Process Control Chart for 16-Ounce Bags of Lay's Potato Chips*

up other operating procedures, SPC increased labor productivity, improved response times, and minimized the duration of poor service.

Frito-Lay is very concerned about the quality of its products. It uses TQM to make sure that all of its ingredients (potatoes, corn, cheese, etc.) are of consistent quality and uniformly combined in its manufacturing plants so that each product always tastes the same. Packing supplies are also important so that products remain fresh until the expiration date on the package. Frito-Lay is ISO 9000 certified and requires its manufacturing suppliers to be certified too. As illustrated in Exhibit 15-10, Frito-Lay uses SPC to ensure quality.

I
O
M

CONTRIBUTIONS BY QUALITY GURUS

The beginning of the quality revolution dates back to May 16, 1924, when Walter Shewhart wrote a memo to his boss at Bell Labs stating that he wanted to use statistics to improve the quality of Bell telephones. Shewhart started the focus on concurrent control by delegating the role of inspector to employees.

W. Edwards Deming.   In the 1950s, W. Edwards Deming went to Japan to teach quality and is credited with being instrumental in turning Japanese industry into an economic world power. In fact, the highest Japanese award for quality is the Deming Prize. Deming said that improving quality would automatically improve productivity and called for a focus on customer value and continuous improvement. He directed managers' attention to the fact that most quality problems—up to 90 percent—are not the fault of employees; rather, the system is to blame. Deming developed the world-famous 14 points to improve quality.

Joseph M. Juran.   Joseph M. Juran stated that 20 percent of the reasons for out-of-control performance cause 80 percent of the quality problems. He called this the *Pareto principle*, more commonly known as the *80–20 rule*. When performance is out of control, manufacturers should first look at the usual "vital few" reasons (20 percent), and most of the time (80 percent) they will have a standing-plan solution. Have you ever noticed how manufacturers commonly have a place in the product manual that says, "If you have a problem, try 1, 2, 3, 4"?

Armand V. Feigenbaum.   Armand V. Feigenbaum made his mark in the 1950s by publishing material on "total quality control," now more commonly called TQM. Feigenbaum worked to fight the myth that maintaining quality is expensive and focused on improving quality as an important way to lower costs. In fact, he said that investing in quality improvement pays better dividends than any other investment a company can make, hence the emphasis on quality in capital budgeting.

Philip B. Crosby.   Philip B. Crosby popularized the concepts "quality is free," "do it right the first time," and "zero defects" in the late 1970s. Crosby believed that it was possible, and necessary, to measure the costs of poor quality in order to combat the notion that quality was expensive. He stressed that quality is not only free, but easy to achieve.

Genichi Taguchi.   Genichi Taguchi advocated designing quality into each product. Hence, he emphasized quality as a virtue of design.

Steven Kerr.   Although not a TQM guru, Steven Kerr contributed indirectly to TQM by popularizing the idea that "you get what you reward." In other words, if you want people to do a quality job, you have to develop a system that really rewards employees for doing a quality job.

WorkApplication11

Are any of the gurus' quality contributions used where you work or have worked? Explain how.

_____

_____

_____

_____

_____

PRODUCTIVITY AND THE BALANCED SCORECARD

Employees would like to get paid more. However, if they are paid more without producing more, a company must cut costs and/or raise product prices to offset the additional wage cost in order to maintain profits.[70] This causes inflation. The only real way to increase our standard of living is to increase productivity.[71] As a manager, you need to understand how to measure and increase productivity.[72] The long-term productivity trend appears to show that efficiency is improving.[73] Recall that managers have a major impact on employee productivity through the Pygmalion effect, and that effective human resource management increases productivity.[74]

Measuring Productivity

The U.S. government measures productivity on a macro level for various industries. Measuring productivity can be complex, but it doesn't have to be.[75] This section outlines a simple, yet realistic, approach for you to use on the job. This approach focuses on measuring productivity on a micro level.

Productivity *is a performance measure relating outputs to inputs.* In other words, productivity is measured by dividing the outputs by the inputs.[76] For example, suppose a trucking company wants to measure productivity of a delivery. The truck traveled 1,000 miles and used 100 gallons of gas. Its productivity was 10 miles to the gallon:

$$\frac{\text{Output}}{\text{Input}} = \text{Productivity}$$

$$\frac{1,000 \text{ miles}}{100 \text{ gallons}} = 10 \text{ mpg}$$

The inputs can be in a variety of forms. In the preceding example, the inputs were gallons of gas. Inputs could also be labor hours, machine hours, number of workers, the cost of labor, and so on.

Following is another fairly simple example, involving measuring the productivity of an accounts payable department.

Step 1. Select a base period of time, such as an hour, day, week, month, quarter, or year. In this example we will use a week.

Step 2. Determine how many bills were sent out during that period of time (outputs). The records show that 800 bills were sent out.

Step 3. Determine the cost of sending out the bills (inputs). Determining cost can become complicated if you include overhead, depreciation, and so forth. In this instance, calculate cost based on direct labor charges for three employees who are each paid $7 per hour. They each worked 40 hours during the week, or a total of 120 hours. The total cost is $7 per hour times 120 hours, or $840.

Step 4. Divide the number of outputs (bills) by the inputs (labor costs) to determine the productivity rate of .95 (800 ÷ $840 = .95).

Performance is usually stated as a ratio (in this case, .95:1) or as a percentage (95%). It can also be stated as a labor cost per unit. To determine the *labor cost per unit*, reverse the process and divide the input by the output. In this case, it cost $1.05 to send out each bill ($840 ÷ 800).

Today's workers are stressed, as they are pressed to increase productivity while organizations cut staff.[77] One of the key reasons jobs did not increase at a faster rate in 2000, despite the growing economy, was that fewer workers maintained or increased production levels.[78] Many firms outsourced tasks to companies that specialized in particular functions or areas, such as human resources or computer work. The outsourcing of computer work increased productivity, allowing firms to increase jobs by 90,000 in 2003.[79]

Japanese car makers, led by **Toyota**, are known to have high rates of productivity and quality. Although U.S. car makers, led by **GM**, are coming close to matching their Japanese rivals, the Japanese still make more profit per car than the Americans.[80]

CALCULATING PRODUCTIVITY PERCENTAGE CHANGES

The .95 productivity rate is set as the base standard. The next week, the accounting department again sent out 800 bills, but because of machine problems, concurrent corrective action of having employees work overtime was needed to meet the standard output, at an additional cost of $100. The productivity rate went down to .85 (800 ÷ $940). The labor cost per unit went up to $1.175 ($940 ÷ 800). To determine the percentage change, use this formula:

$$
\begin{array}{lr}
\text{Current productivity rate} & 85 \\
-\ \text{Base standard productivity rate} & -95 \\
\hline
\text{Change} & 10
\end{array}
$$

Change ÷ base productivity rate = 10 ÷ 95 = .1053

There was a 10.53 percent decrease in productivity. Note that it is not necessary to use the decimals on .95 and .85 in this calculation. Also, when the current productivity rate is less than the standard, there is a decrease in productivity, but it is not necessary to use a negative number.

PRODUCTION VERSUS PRODUCTIVITY

It is important to calculate productivity rather than just production output, because it is possible to increase production but decrease productivity. For example, if the accounts payable department sends out 850 bills (production) but uses 10 hours of overtime to do so (time-and-a-half at $10.50 per hour × 10 hours = $105), productivity has decreased from .95 to .90 (850 ÷ 945). In other words, if you measure only output production and it increases, you can be fooled into thinking you are doing a better job when in reality you are doing a worse job.

PRODUCTIVITY COMPARISONS

Productivity measures are more meaningful when they are compared to other productivity rates.[81] For example, you can compare your department's productivity to that of other organizations and/or departments. This was done in Skill Builder 1 in Chapter 14. Most important, you should compare your department's productivity during one period to its productivity in other periods. This comparison will enable you to identify increases or decreases in productivity over time. A productivity rate can also be set as the standard, and you can compare your department's productivity to the standard on an ongoing basis. This is done in Applying the Concept 5.

Measuring Productivity

The standard monthly productivity rate in your department is

$$\frac{\text{Outputs of 6,000 units}}{\text{Inputs of \$9,000 cost}} = .67$$

For the first five months of the year, calculate the current productivity rate and show it as a ratio and a percentage. Also, calculate the percentage productivity change, compared to the standard, stating whether it is an increase or a decrease.

17. January: outputs of 5,900, inputs of $9,000

_____ ratio, _____ %, increase/decrease of _____ %

18. February: outputs of 6,200, inputs of $9,000

_____ ratio, _____ %, increase/decrease of _____ %

19. March: outputs of 6,000, inputs of $9,300

_____ ratio, _____ %, increase/decrease of _____ %

20. April: outputs of 6,300, inputs of $9,000

_____ ratio, _____ %, increase/decrease of _____ %

21. May: outputs of 6,300, inputs of $8,800

_____ ratio, _____ %, increase/decrease of _____ %

Increasing Productivity

Productivity has been referred to as a state of mind because everyone should be constantly thinking of ways to increase it.[82] As a manager, you should work with your employees to measure productivity and continually increase it to provide better customer value.

There are three ways to increase productivity:

1. Increase the value of the outputs but maintain the value of the inputs ($\uparrow$ O $\leftrightarrow$ I)
2. Maintain the value of the outputs but decrease the value of the inputs ($\leftrightarrow$ O $\downarrow$ I)
3. Increase the value of the outputs but decrease the value of the inputs ($\uparrow$ O $\downarrow$ I)

Productivity Measures for the Functional Areas

The basic concepts of productivity measurement can be applied to all functional areas in the organization. All productivity measures are indications of how well an organization is managed. See Exhibit 15-11 for a list of ratios in the functional areas. Although the ratios are separated by function, they are interrelated because of the systems effect.

Frito-Lay's three top-selling products in the United States are Lay's Potato Chips, Doritos, and Cheetos. The company continues to be the dominant seller of salty snack

Exhibit 15-11 *Functional Area Ratios*

Area	Ratio	Calculation	Information Provided
Finance Profitability	Gross profit margin	$\dfrac{\text{Sales} - \text{COGS}}{\text{Sales}}$	Efficiency of operations and product pricing
	Net profit margin	$\dfrac{\text{Net profit/income}}{\text{Sales}}$	Product profitability
	Return on investment	$\dfrac{\text{Net profit/income}}{\text{Total assets}}$	Return on total capital expenditures or ability of assets to generate profit
Liquidity	Current ratio	$\dfrac{\text{Current assets}}{\text{Current liabilities}}$	Ability to pay short-term debt
	Quick ratio	$\dfrac{\text{Current assets} - \text{inventory}}{\text{Current liabilities}}$	Stronger measure of bill-paying ability because inventory may be slow to sell for cash
Leverage	Debt to equity	$\dfrac{\text{Total liabilities}}{\text{Owners' equity}}$	Proportion of assets owned by an organization; the higher the ratio, the more solvent the firm and the easier it will be to get credit/funds.
Operations	Inventory turnover	$\dfrac{\text{Cost of goods sold}}{\text{Average inventory}}$	Efficiency of controlling investment in inventory; the larger the number, the better, because products are sold faster.
Marketing	Market share	$\dfrac{\text{Company sales}}{\text{Total industry sales}}$	Organization's competitive position; the larger the number, the better, because it is outselling competitors.
	Sales to presentation	$\dfrac{\text{Sales completed}}{\text{Sales presentations made}}$	How many presentations it takes to make one sale; the lower the number, the better, because less time is spent making nonproductive presentations.
Human Resources	Absenteeism	$\dfrac{\text{No. of employees absent}}{\text{Total no. of employees}}$	Ratio/percentage of employees not at work for a given time period
	Turnover	$\dfrac{\text{No. of employees leaving}}{\text{Total no. of employees}}$	Ratio/percentage of employees who must be replaced in a given period, usually one year
	Workforce composition	$\dfrac{\text{No. of a specific group}}{\text{Total no. of employees}}$	Ratio/percentage of women, Hispanics, African-Americans, and so on

foods, with no close national competitor. Frito-Lay has the number-one-selling brands of potato chips, corn chips, tortilla chips, and pretzels. Sales continue to grow as productivity increases.

The Balanced Scorecard

Is your organization achieving its mission? If you don't have a quick and accurate answer, then, besides financial measures, you need a balanced scorecard (BSC). The BSC is one of the most highly touted management tools today.[83] A survey found that approximately 50 percent of the Fortune 1000 companies in North America and 40 percent of those in Europe use a version of the

Financial Ratios

Using the figures below, determine the following ratios, using the calculations in Exhibit 15-11 on page 555.

Income Statement		Balance Sheet	
Sales	$10,612,752	Current assets	$ 9,843,115
Cost of goods sold	$ 3,941,933	Current liabilities	$ 1,585,324
Average inventory	$ 1,733,766		
Net profit	$ 1,852,977	Total assets	$13,128,371
		Total liabilities	$ 1,614,324
		Owners' equity	$11,514,047

_____ %   22. Net profit margin. (Profitability ratios are commonly reported as percentages.)

_____ %   23. Return on investment.

_____ : 1   24. Current ratio. (Liquidity ratios are commonly reported as a ratio compared to one.)

_____ : 1   25. Debt to equity. (Leverage ratios are commonly reported as ratios.)

_____   26. Inventory turnover. (Operations ratios are reported as number of times per year.)

How would you say this company is doing financially based on these ratios?

BSC.[84] Researchers Robert Kaplan and David Norton concluded that financial measures alone were not sufficient to measure performance; other factors in the new economy were missing from traditional financial reporting.[85] *The* **balanced scorecard (BSC)** *measures financial, customer service, and internal business performance, as well as learning and growth performance.* All four dimensions of the scorecard are equally important, and results relate to one another through the systems effect. See Exhibit 15-12 for an overview of the BSC and Exhibit 15-13 for a sample balanced scorecard.

Employees develop a control system with targets, measures, outcomes, and initiatives to guide improvement in all four dimensions of the BSC. *Targets* are objectives (or metrics) that employees set to improve in the areas critical to success. *Measures* are compared to *outcomes* to determine whether targets are being achieved. *Initiatives* are the strategies and tactics (plans) designed to achieve targets. Rather than simply measuring the past, the targets and measures create focus for the future, as the BSC is both a planning and a control method.[86]

As you can see, the BSC plays to the well-known management adage "If you want to manage it, you've got to measure it, and you get what you measure and reinforce." If you are not measuring your financial, customer service, internal business, and learning and growth performance, you and other stakeholders really don't know how well you are doing.[87] If your team is without a scorecard, it isn't playing the game; it's only practicing.[88]

Exhibit 15-12 *The Balanced Scorecard*

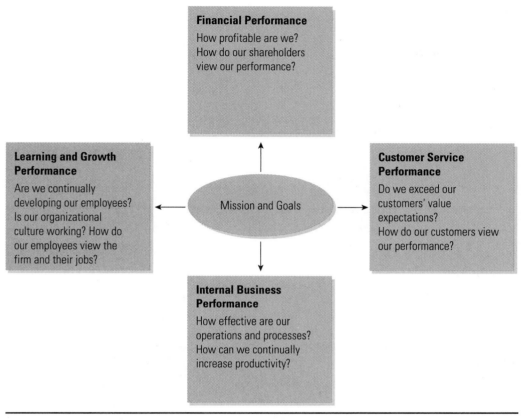

Financial Performance

How profitable are we?
How do our shareholders
view our performance?

**Learning and Growth
Performance**

Are we continually
developing our employees?
Is our organizational
culture working? How do
our employees view the
firm and their jobs?

Mission and Goals

**Customer Service
Performance**

Do we exceed our
customers' value
expectations?
How do our customers view
our performance?

**Internal Business
Performance**

How effective are our
operations and processes?
How can we continually
increase productivity?

Source: Based on Robert Kaplan and David Norton, "Using the Balanced Scorecard as a Strategic Management System," *Harvard Business Review*, January–February 1996, pp. 75–85.

Ford uses a balanced scorecard to help direct long-term and annual business planning activities. The scorecard transforms Ford's vision and strategy into a comprehensive set of performance measures. Each business plan is translated into a BSC to establish priorities, targets, and metrics. Ford has targets for quality, customer and employee satisfaction, and environmental performance. BSC metrics determine the objectives for performance reviews of business units and individuals, which influence compensation.[89]

Take advantage of the companion Web site for *Management Fundamentals*, where you will find a broad array of resources to help you maximize what you learn in class:

- Try a quiz
- View chapter videos
- Download slides
- Boost your vocabulary
- Work through an Internet exercise
- Find related links

Take a look for yourself at *http://lussier.swlearning.com.*

Exhibit 15-13 *Futura Industries' Balanced Scorecard, 2003*

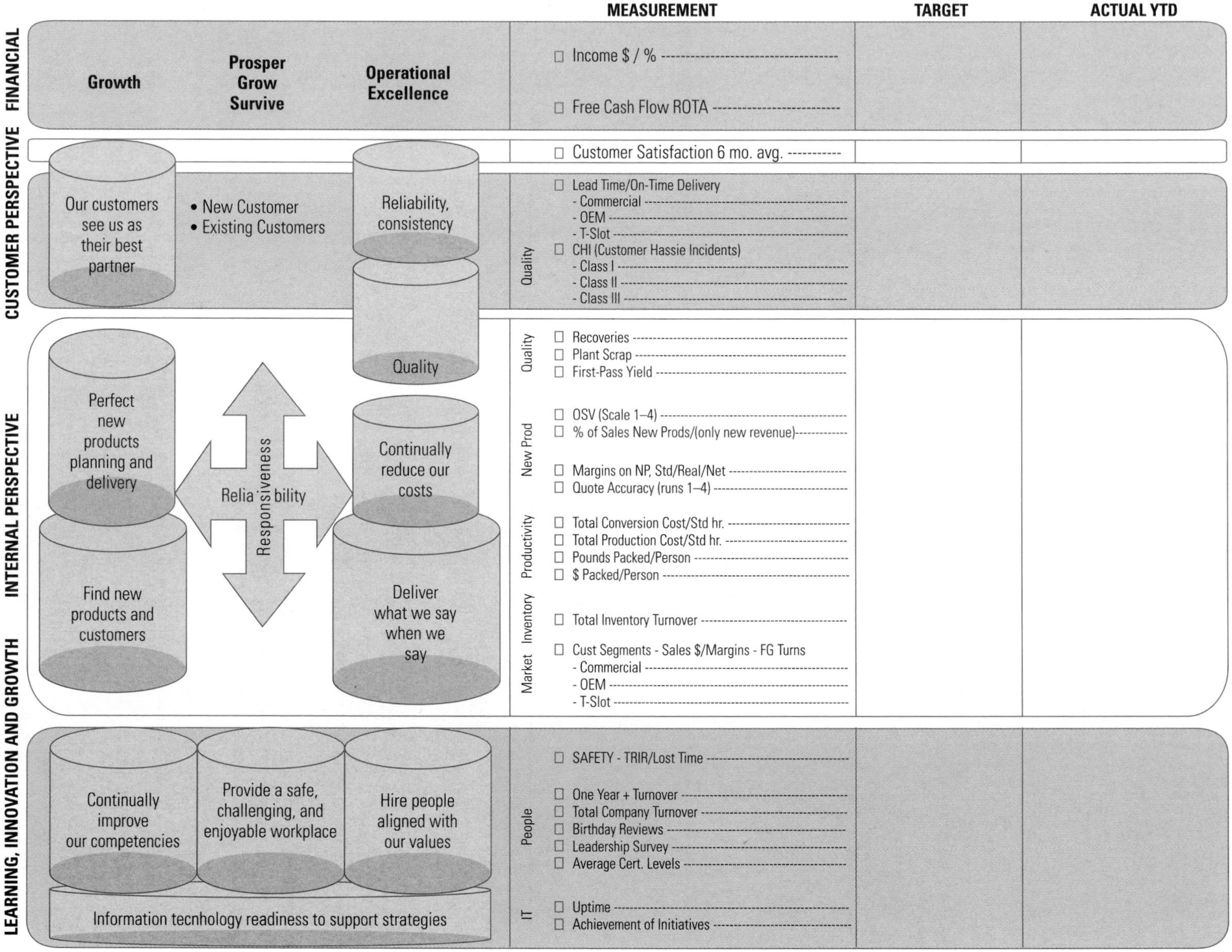

	Growth	Prosper Grow Survive	Operational Excellence		MEASUREMENT	TARGET	ACTUAL YTD

FINANCIAL

- ☐ Income $ / %
- ☐ Free Cash Flow ROTA

CUSTOMER PERSPECTIVE

Our customers see us as their best partner — • New Customer • Existing Customers — Reliability, consistency

- ☐ Customer Satisfaction 6 mo. avg.

Quality

- ☐ Lead Time/On-Time Delivery
  - Commercial
  - OEM
  - T-Slot
- ☐ CHI (Customer Hassle Incidents)
  - Class I
  - Class II
  - Class III

INTERNAL PERSPECTIVE

Perfect new products planning and delivery / Find new products and customers — Responsiveness / Reliability — Quality / Continually reduce our costs / Deliver what we say when we say

Quality
- Recoveries
- Plant Scrap
- First-Pass Yield

New Prod
- OSV (Scale 1–4)
- % of Sales New Prods/(only new revenue)
- Margins on NP, Std/Real/Net
- Quote Accuracy (runs 1–4)

Productivity
- Total Conversion Cost/Std hr.
- Total Production Cost/Std hr.
- Pounds Packed/Person
- $ Packed/Person

Inventory
- Total Inventory Turnover

Market
- Cust Segments - Sales $/Margins - FG Turns
  - Commercial
  - OEM
  - T-Slot

LEARNING, INNOVATION AND GROWTH

Continually improve our competencies / Provide a safe, challenging, and enjoyable workplace / Hire people aligned with our values / Information technology readiness to support strategies

People
- ☐ SAFETY - TRIR/Lost Time
- ☐ One Year + Turnover
- ☐ Total Company Turnover
- ☐ Birthday Reviews
- ☐ Leadership Survey
- ☐ Average Cert. Levels

IT
- ☐ Uptime
- ☐ Achievement of Initiatives

558

Putting It All Together

For this self-assessment, refer to prior self-assessments; write down a few things you have learned about yourself, focusing on strengths and areas for improvement.

Chapter 1, Management Traits, p. 7

_____

Chapter 2, How Ethical Is Your Behavior?, p. 61

_____

Chapter 3, Country of Origin of Products, p. 79

_____

Chapter 3, Entrepreneurial Qualities, p. 92

_____

Chapter 4, Decision-Making Styles, p. 112

_____

Chapter 5, Effective Planning, p. 148

_____

Chapter 5 Appendix, Time Management Techniques, p. 190

_____

Chapter 6, Personal Priorities, p. 214

_____

Chapter 7, Women at Work, p. 245

_____

Chapter 8, Career Development, p. 270

_____

Chapter 9, Personality Traits, p. 309

_____

Chapter 9, Job Satisfaction, p. 314

_____

Chapter 9, Use of Political Behavior, p. 320

_____

Chapter 9, Personality Type and Stress, p. 335

_____

Chapter 10, Are You a Team Player?, p. 351

_____

Chapter 10 Skill Builder 1, Your Preferred Leadership Style, p. 377

_____

Chapter 11, Listening Skills, p. 401

_____

Chapter 11 Skill Builder 2, Analyzing Communication Styles, p. 418

_____

Chapter 12, What Motivates You?, p. 434

_____

Chapter 12, Acquired Needs, p. 435

_____

Chapter 13, Theory X and Theory Y Leadership Behavior, p. 462

_____

Chapter 14, Coaching, p. 506

_____

Based on your review, how can you use this knowledge to help you in your career development?

_____

Develop a plan to apply your self-assessments in both your personal and your professional life. What specific areas will you work on improving? How will you improve? How will you know if you have improved?

_____

Chapter Summary

1. Describe time-based competition and why it is important.
Time-based competition refers to the use of strategies to increase the speed with which an organization goes from creativity to delivery. It is important because speed gives an organization a first-mover competitive advantage.

2. Explain the differences among operations systems with respect to tangibility of products, levels of customer involvement, operations flexibility, and management of resources and technology.
A product can be a tangible good, an intangible service, or a combination of the two. The three levels of customer involvement refer to whether a standard product is made to stock, customer-specific products are made to order, or a standard product with some customized features is assembled to order. Operations flexibility refers to whether the products are produced continuously in nondiscrete units, repetitively on an assembly line for one product, in batches with the same resources used for multiple products, individually to customer specifications at the seller's facilities, or individually over a long period of time at sites including the customer's facilities. Resources may be capital intensive (if machines do most of the work), labor intensive (if human resources do most of the work), or a balance of the two.

3. Discuss what is meant by "Quality is a virtue of design."
"Quality is a virtue of design" means that if products are well designed, with cross-functional team input to ensure customer value, there will be fewer operations problems, the product will be easier to sell, and servicing the product will be less costly. Therefore, it is important for cross-functional teams to work together on the design of new products.

4. Explain product, process, cellular, and fixed-position facility layouts in terms of their level of customer involvement and flexibility.
Product layout is associated with make-to-stock and assemble-to-order levels of customer involvement and relatively inflexible repetitive or continuous process operations. Process layout is associated with a make-to-order level of customer involvement and flexible individual process operations. Cellular layout is associated with make-to-stock and assemble-to-order levels of customer involvement and relatively flexible batch process operations. Fixed-position layout is associated with make-to-order and assemble-to-order levels of customer involvement and flexible project process operations.

5. Describe the similarities and differences among the planning sheet, Gantt chart, and PERT network.
Similarities include the fact that all three are scheduling techniques and list activities that must be performed to accomplish an objective. Activities are listed in sequence, with the time needed to complete each. The primary differences concern their format and use.

Planning sheets state an objective and list the sequence of activities required to meet the objective, when each activity will begin and end, and who will complete each activity. Gantt charts use bars to graphically illustrate a schedule and progress toward the objective over a period of time. Gantt charts, like planning sheets, are appropriate when independent sequential steps are needed to accomplish the objective. The Gantt chart has an advantage over the planning sheet in that it places progress toward the objective on the chart as a control technique. PERT is a network scheduling technique that illustrates the dependence of activities. When some activities are dependent and some independent, PERT is more appropriate.

6. Explain the relationship among inventory control, just-in-time (JIT) inventory, and materials requirement planning (MRP).
Inventory control is the process of managing raw materials, work-in-process, finished goods, and in-transit goods. JIT is an inventory method in which necessary parts and raw materials are delivered shortly before they are needed. MRP is a system that integrates operations and inventory control. JIT is part of inventory control, and both are part of MRP.

7. Explain how statistical process control (SPC) charts and the exception principle are used in quality control.
The statistical process control chart is used to graph actual performance to see whether it is within an acceptable standard range. According to the exception principle, if performance is within the acceptable range, do nothing; if it is out of the control limits, take corrective action.

8. Describe how to measure productivity and list three ways to increase it.
Productivity is measured by dividing outputs by inputs. Productivity can be increased by (1) increasing the value of the outputs while maintaining the value of the inputs, (2) maintaining the value of the outputs while decreasing the value of the inputs, or (3) increasing the value of the outputs while decreasing the value of the inputs.

9. Complete each of the following statements using one of this chapter's key terms.

_____ refers to the use of strategies to increase the speed with which an organization goes from creativity to delivery.

_____ is the function concerned with transforming resource inputs into product outputs.

A _____ is a good, a service, or a combination of the two.

_____ refers to the amount of input from customers, which determines whether operations are make-to-stock, assemble-to-order, or make-to-order.

_____ refers to the amount of variety in the products an operation produces, which determines whether products are produced continuously, repetitively, in batches, or individually.

_____ is the process used to transform inputs into outputs.

_____ refers to the spatial arrangement of physical resources relative to each other.

_____ is the amount of products an organization can produce.

_____ is the path and sequence of the transformations of a product into an output.

_____ is the continuing evaluation and reordering of the sequence in which products will be produced.

A _____ states an objective and lists the sequence of activities required to meet the objective, when each activity will begin and end, and who will complete each activity.

A _____ uses bars to graphically illustrate a schedule and progress toward the objective over a period of time.

_____ is a network scheduling technique that illustrates the dependence of activities.

The _____ is the most time-consuming series of activities in a PERT network.

_____ is the stock of materials held for future use.

_____ is the process of managing raw materials, work-in-process, finished goods, and in-transit goods.

_____ is an inventory method in which necessary parts and raw materials are delivered shortly before they are needed.

_____ is a system that integrates operations and inventory control with complex ordering and scheduling.

_____ is the process of coordinating all the activities involved in producing a product and delivering it to the customer.

_____ is the process of ensuring that all types of inventory meet standards.

The _____ certifies firms that meet set quality standards.

_____ aids in determining whether quality is within an acceptable standard range.

_____ is a performance measure relating outputs to inputs.

A _____ measures financial, customer service, and internal business performance, as well as learning and growth performance.

Key Terms

balanced scorecard (BSC), 555
capacity, 538
critical path, 541
customer involvement, 527
facility layout, 534
Gantt chart, 539
International Standards Organization (ISO), 548
inventory, 543

inventory control, 543
just-in-time (JIT) inventory, 549
materials requirement planning (MRP), 544
operations, 526
operations flexibility, 528
PERT, 541
planning sheets, 539
priority scheduling, 539

product, 526
productivity, 552
quality control, 547
routing, 539
statistical process control (SPC), 550
supply chain management, 546
technology, 530
time-based competition, 526

Review and Discussion Questions

1. What does the operations department do?
2. Is the level of customer involvement highest with make-to-stock, assemble-to-order, or make-to-order operations? Why?
3. Which type of process operation is the most flexible? Least flexible?
4. Which type of process operation is most commonly used by retailers and service organizations?
5. Are services generally more capital- or labor-intensive than manufacturing? Why?
6. Why is it important to balance time-based competition and design?
7. Which two facility layouts are the most flexible? Which two layouts are the least flexible?
8. Why is capacity planning so important?
9. Why is scheduling important?

10. What does a Gantt chart show that a planning sheet and PERT network don't show?
11. When would you use a PERT network rather than a Gantt chart?
12. What are the four types of inventory?
13. What does materials requirement planning integrate?
14. What is the relationship between inventory and quality control?
15. What are the five rules of customer relations?
16. Why should you measure productivity rather than just production?
17. What are some of the major ratio measures in the functional areas of finance, marketing, and human resources?

Objective Case

THE RETAIL GROCERY INDUSTRY

In the grocery industry, the term "center store" refers to the fast-moving lines of beverages, snacks, health and beauty care items, and other nonperishable products that a supermarket carries. Along with groceries, the center store has traditionally been a cash engine at supermarkets. Lund Food Holdings, a 20-unit supermarket chain headquartered in Minneapolis, believes that one way to prevent stock-out problems is to ensure adequate staffing. At Lund, proper staffing means having the right people in the center store aisles where they are needed most, whether it's to build displays or to prevent stock-outs.

For consumers, one of the most frustrating aspects of shopping—particularly when they are stopping off at the grocery to buy dinner for the evening—is finding merchandise out of stock. Such frustration undermines all the service and customer-satisfaction programs that retailers put in place to enhance the shopping experience at their stores. Although it is difficult for most consumers to believe that an efficient supermarket chain would have stock-out problems, inventory maintenance is probably the most difficult challenge that a supermarket manager encounters, aside from unexpected crises such as power failures. A hole on a shelf is a significant problem.

Poor staffing decisions aren't the only source of stock-out problems. The number of new products and promotions is increasing annually. Changes in product assortments and additional product options (should the store stock a brand of shampoo and conditioner as individual units or as two-in-a-pack bundles?) also put pressure on managers to plan ahead. They must be sensitive to switches in customer shopping preferences so that they have the right mix of products on their shelves to stay in front of their competitors.

Supermarket retailers and manufacturers have formed partnerships to help solve stock-out problems. Retailers have been investing in technologies that automate manual processes, allowing them to deploy their in-store labor more efficiently. Stores are also relying on vendors, rather than on store personnel, to better manage product inventories. Some vendors deliver products directly to the shelves, rather than to the store's loading docks. A new contract recently negotiated by Lund with its union gives the corporation permission to have vendors come into its stores to stock many categories of products. Turning increasingly to "category management," grocery retailers are working with leading manufacturers such as Procter & Gamble, Unilever, and Pepsi to better understand and manage consumer demand. Category management ensures that best practices are adopted with respect to product assortment decisions, merchandising, and other in-store operations.

Another innovation that is helping stores avoid stock-outs and thus maintain customer purchasing and motivation is scan-based trading. With this arrangement, retailers lower their inventory costs by allowing manufacturers to retain ownership of their products until the items are rung up at the point of sale. Scan-based trading, facilitated by scannable uniform product code (UPC) labels, offers incentives to suppliers to ensure optimal on-shelf positions and helps retailers to save on inventory and store-level labor costs.

Retailers are also finding better ways to motivate their own employees to meet higher productivity standards. Lund Food Holdings sets productivity standards and then challenges employees with rewards for exceeding those standards. Lund may have a standard that employees need to stock 25 cases of a certain product in an hour. If Lund can get its employees to bring that standard up, it may save 15 hours of employee time a week. The goal is not to cut those hours permanently from the payroll, but to put them to better use to drive sales.

Stop & Shop, headquartered in Massachusetts, has introduced self-checkout systems to help reduce labor costs at the front end. However, Stop & Shop has not cut back on employee hours. To make center store shopping more interactive, employees known as sales associates walk around the store offering help to customers in need of service. The program is as yet too new to measure cost-effectiveness, but customer reaction has been positive.

Grocery retailers who optimize labor and combine cost efficiency with customer service will be able to deal more effectively with encroachment from Wal-Mart. In some instances, the retail grocery industry is beginning to initiate creative problem solving, rather than just reordering products when a set number remain on the shelf. When a Wal-Mart superstore with groceries comes to town, it is common for one of the supermarkets in the area to go out of business. One major advantage Wal-Mart has over supermarkets is nonunion employees who work for less, keeping costs down.

One model that is being tested in the grocery industry to help supermarkets compete with Wal-Mart is the Six Sigma quality program. Rob Garf, a retail analyst for Boston-based AMR Research, has stated that Six Sigma is intended to remove variability from store operations. The aspects of store operations that most directly prevent stock-outs are employee efficiency, product availability, and customer intimacy.

The Six Sigma model looks at the customer's experience and tracks processes backward through the store and the supply chain. All operations are mapped from the customer backward. Rather than assuming that the goal is to get product to the customer, Six Sigma puts the customer at the center of the supply chain. The model tries to identify all the things in the supply chain that are good, so that managers will know what to keep. Things that lead to bad customer experiences are identified, focused on, and fixed.

Six Sigma can show whether cutting labor hours will result in stock-outs, lost sales, or a negative shopping experience. Six Sigma does not look at labor in a vacuum. It factors into the equation task management, inventory management, and customer service. Albertsons is beginning to use Six Sigma to reengineer its major processes in every function, with the goal of moving the major supermarket chain to a new level of productivity and customer service.

 To learn more about the retail grocery industry, log on to InfoTrac® College Edition at *http:/infotrac. thomsonlearning.com* and use the advanced search function.

_____ 1. The products of supermarket operations systems are classified as _____ products.

    a. tangible
    b. intangible
    c. mixed

_____ 2. Based on their level of customer involvement, supermarket operations are classified primarily as _____ operations.

    a. make-to-stock
    b. make-to-order
    c. assemble-to-order

_____ 3. Based on their level of flexibility, supermarket operations are classified as _____ process operations.

    a. continuous   d. individual
    b. repetitive   e. project
    c. batch

_____ 4. Based on the resources they require, supermarket operations are classified as _____.

    a. capital-intensive
    b. labor-intensive
    c. balanced in intensity

_____ 5. The facility layout used by a supermarket is classified as a _____ layout.

    a. product   c. cellular
    b. process   d. fixed-position

_____ 6. The primary consideration in supermarket facility location is _____.

    a. cost
    b. nearness to inputs
    c. nearness to customers
    d. nearness to competitors
    e. nearness to transportation
    f. nearness to human resources

_____ 7. Supermarket inventory is primarily _____ inventory.

    a. raw material   c. finished goods
    b. work-in-process   d. in-transit

_____ 8. Not being manufacturers of groceries, supermarkets are not concerned with just-in-time inventory and materials requirement planning. (Discuss.)

    a. true
    b. false

_____ 9. Not being manufacturers of groceries, supermarkets are not concerned with supply chain management. (Discuss.)

    a. true
    b. false

_____10. Six Sigma cannot really be of much help to supermarkets because they are not manufacturers. (Discuss.)

    a. true
    b. false

_____11. It is difficult to measure productivity in supermarkets.

    a. true
    b. false

_____12. According to the case, which of the following profitability ratios is most relevant to supermarkets?

    a. gross profit margin
    b. net profit margin
    c. return on investment

_____13. According to the case, which of the following ratios is most relevant to supermarkets?

    a. liquidity
    b. leverage
    c. operations

_____14. Which human resources ratio is becoming more of a problem for supermarkets?

    a. absenteeism
    b. turnover
    c. workforce composition

_____15. The balanced scorecard is not really needed in supermarkets.

    a. true
    b. false

Cumulative Case Questions

16. Discuss the importance of the interrelationship of the manager's resources in Six Sigma. (Chapter 1)

17. Explain the systems process for supermarkets. (Chapter 2)

18. Discuss how the global borderless Internet environment is affecting the retail grocery industry. (Chapter 3)

19. What type of decision was implementing Six Sigma at Albertsons? (Chapter 4)

20. Which functional-level strategy is the focus of this case? (Chapter 5)

21. What type of departmentalization is used by supermarket chains? (Chapter 6)

22. How would you rate supermarkets' ability to change through innovation, and what type of changes have they been making? (Chapter 7)

23. Having employees walk around to help customers requires a change in which human resource management process? (Chapter 8)

24. Discuss why negotiation skills are so important to supermarkets. (Chapter 9)

25. Discuss the need for a team approach in supermarkets. (Chapter 10)

26. Why is communication important for supermarkets—what is communicated and how is it communicated? (Chapter 11)

27. Discuss the importance of motivation (Chapter 12) and leadership (Chapter 13) for supermarkets.

28. Discuss some of the important issues surrounding financial and human controls in supermarkets. (Chapter 14)

Skill Builder 1

DEVELOPING A PLAN TO OPEN A MUSIC SHOP

Objective

To develop your skills in planning using a Gantt chart and PERT network. You have decided to open and manage Smith (your last name) Music Shop on April 1. It is now late December. You plan to move in one month before the store opens in order to set up. During March, your assistant will help you set up while you train him or her.

Assume that you have decided to use (1) a Gantt chart and (2) a PERT network. Develop both, in whichever order you prefer, following the text guides for their development. Assume that you have identified the activities and completion times listed below (the activities may not be given in sequence) and that you will start to implement the plan on January 2.

a. Lease the fixtures necessary to display your tapes and CDs; it will take two weeks to get them.
b. Order and receive tapes and CDs. This will take one week.
c. Recruit and select an assistant (three weeks or less).
d. Install the fixtures, paint, decorate, and so on (two weeks).
e. Form a corporation (four weeks).
f. Make arrangements to buy tapes and CDs on credit (two weeks).
g. Find a store location (six weeks or less).
h. Unpack and display the tapes and CDs (one week).
i. Train the assistant (one week).

j. Select the tapes and CDs you plan to stock (one week).
k. Determine start-up costs and cash outflows per month through April 30; your rich uncle will lend you this amount (one week).

Gantt Chart

When developing the Gantt chart, use the following format, based on weeks. You may want to change the letter sequence to match the starting dates.

Gantt Chart

Activity letter	January 1 2 3 4	February 1 2 3 4	March 1 2 3 4	April 1
_____				
_____				
_____				
_____				
_____				
_____				
_____				
_____				
_____				

PERT

When developing the PERT chart, draw arrows from the start to your circles for the independent activities. Place the letter of the activity inside the circle. On the arrow to the activity, place the number of weeks needed to complete it. Then draw an arrow to the end. Also from the start, draw the first dependent activity, followed by the next dependent activity, and so on, until you get to the last one; then draw an arrow to the end. Be sure to put the number of weeks and activity/event letters on your network. After all activities have been listed, determine the critical path and draw the second arrow to indicate it. *Hint*: You should have five arrows to activities coming from the start; you can begin the process with either selecting music or finding a store location.

PERT
(with critical path)

Start   End

Conclusion

Is Gantt or PERT more appropriate for this type of plan?

Apply It

What did I learn from this experience? How can I use this knowledge in the future?

_____

_____

Skill **Builder** 2
ECONOMIC ORDER QUANTITY

Objective

To develop your skill at calculating EOQ.

Calculate the EOQ for each of the following four situations:

—— 1. $R = 2,000$, $S = \$15.00$, $H = \$5.00$

—— 2. $H = \$10.00$, $R = 7,500$, $S = \$40.00$

—— 3. $R = 500$, $H = \$15.00$, $S = \$35.00$

—— 4. $S = \$50.00$, $H = \$25.00$, $R = 19,000$

Apply It

What did I learn from this experience? How will I use this knowledge in the future?

_____

_____

Skill **Builder** 3

YOUR COURSE SELF-ASSESSMENT

Objective

To review your course Self-Assessments.

Break into groups and discuss your answers to the Self-Assessment, Putting It All Together. Focus on helping each other improve career development plans.

Apply It

What did I learn from this experience? How will I use this knowledge in the future?

_____

_____

Endnotes

Chapter 1

1. J. P. Doh, "Can Leadership Be Taught? Perspectives from Management Educators," *Academy of Management Learning and Education* (2003), Vol. 2, No. 1, pp. 54–67.

2. S. A. Zahra, "*The Practice of Management*: Reflections on Peter F. Drucker's Landmark Book," *Academy of Management Executive* (2003), Vol. 17, No. 3, pp. 16–23.

3. G. Chen and R. J. Klimoski, "The Impact of Expectations on Newcomer Performance in Teams as Mediated by Work Characteristics, Social Exchanges, and Empowerment," *Academy of Management Journal* (2003), Vol. 48, No. 5, pp. 591–607.

4. L. A. Burke and J. E. Moore, "A Perennial Dilemma in OB Education: Engaging the Traditional Student," *Academy of Management Learning and Education* (2003), Vol. 2, No. 1, pp. 37–52.

5. S. A. Zahra, "Introduction: Peter F. Drucker's *The Practice of Management*," *Academy of Management Executive* (2003), Vol. 17, No. 3, pp. 7–8.

6. M. A. Boland and J. P. Katz, "Jack Gherty, President and CEO of Land O'Lakes, on Leading a Branded Food and Farm Supply Cooperative," *Academy of Management Executive* (2003), Vol. 17, No. 3, pp. 24–30.

7. J. Child and R. G. McGrath, "Organizations Unfettered: Organizational Form in an Information-Intensive Economy," *Academy of Management Journal* (2001), Vol. 44, No. 6, pp. 1135–1146.

8. G. DeSanctis, J. T. Glass, and I. M. Ensing, "Organization Designs for R&D," *Academy of Management Executive* (2002), Vol. 16, No. 3, pp. 55–61.

9. J. Magretta, *What Management Is: How It Works and Why It's Everyone's Business* (New York: The Free Press, 2002).

10. J. S. Bunderson, "Team Member Functional Background and Involvement in Management Teams: Direct Effects and the Moderating Role of Power Centralization," *Academy of Management Journal* (2003), Vol. 48, No. 4, pp. 458–474.

11. Zahra, "Drucker's Landmark Book," 16–23.

12. B. J. Tepper and E. C. Taylor, "Relationships Among Supervisors' and Subordinates' Procedural Justice Perceptions and Organizational Citizenship Behaviors," *Academy of Management Journal* (2003), Vol. 46, No. 1, pp. 97–105.

13. *Wall Street Journal* (November 14, 1980), p. 33.

14. L. E. Greiner, A. Bhambri, and T. G. Cummings, "Searching for a Strategy to Teach Strategy," *Academy of Management Learning and Education* (2002), Vol. 2, No. 4, pp. 402–420.

15. Doh, "Can Leadership Be Taught?" 54–67.

16. R. Katz, "Skills of an Effective Administrator," *Harvard Business Review* (September/October 1974), pp. 90–102.

17. S. L. Rynes, A. M. Lawson, and R. Ilies, "Behavioral Coursework in Business Education: Growing Evidence of a Legitimacy Crisis," *Academy of Management Learning and Education* (2003), Vol. 2, No. 3, pp. 269–283.

18. M. J. Lankau and T. A. Scandura, "An Investigation of Personal Learning in Mentoring Relationships: Content, Antecedents, and Consequences," *Academy of Management Journal* (2002), Vol. 45, No. 4, pp. 779–790.

19. B. L. Kirkman, B. Rosen, C. B. Gibson, P. E. Tesluk, and S. O. McPherson, "Five Challenges to Virtual Team Success: Lessons from Sabre, Inc.," *Academy of Management Executive* (2002), Vol. 16, No. 3, pp. 67–76.

20. Burke and Moore, "A Perennial Dilemma in OB Education," 37–52.

21. B. Gates, "My Advice to Students: Get a Sound, Broad Education," *The Costo Connection* (February 1999), p. 13.

22. L. Gratton and C. Truss, "The Three-Dimensional People Strategy: Putting Human Resources Policies into Action," *Academy of Management Executive* (2003), Vol. 17, No. 3, pp. 74–86.

23. G. Detrick, "Interview with Russell Ackoff," *Academy of Management Learning and Education* (2002), Vol. 1, No. 1, pp. 56–63.

24. R. E. Boyatzis, E. C. Stubbs, and S. N. Taylor, "Learning Cognitive and Emotional Intelligence Competencies through Graduate Management Education," *Academy of Management Learning and Education* (2002), Vol. 1, No. 2, pp. 150–162.

25. J. Ussem, "A Manager for All Season," *Fortune* (April 30, 2001), pp. 66–72.

26. E. Ghiselli, *Explorations in Management Talent* (Santa Monica, CA: Goodyear Publishing, 1971).

27. Zahra, "Drucker's Landmark Book," 16–23.

28. "Student Projects," *Planning* (March 2001), Vol. 67, No. 3, p. 34.

29. F. S. Seo, "Advancing the Cause," *Planning* (January 2001), Vol. 67, No. 1, p. 42.

30. Lankau and Scandura, "Personal Learning in Mentoring Relationships," 779–790.

31. Child and McGrath, "Organizations Unfettered," 1135–1146.

32. M. G. Seo, "Overcoming Emotional Barriers, Political Obstacles, and Control Imperatives in the Action-Science Approach to Individual and Organizational Learning," *Academy of Management Learning and Education* (2003), Vol 2, No. 1, pp. 7–21.

33. R. Hogan and R. Warrenfeltz, "Education of the Modern Manager," *Academy of Management Learning and Education* (2003), Vol. 2, No. 1, pp. 74–84.

34. T. Pollock, "Mind Your Own Business," *Supervision* (February 2001), Vol. 62, No. 2, p. 16.

35. Tepper and Taylor, "Supervisors' and Subordinates' Procedural Justice Perceptions," 97–105.

36. DeSanctis, Glass, and Ensing, "Organization Designs for R&D," 55–61.

37. C. Argyris, "Double-Loop Learning, Teaching, and Research," *Academy of Management Learning and Education* (2002), Vol. 1, No. 2, pp. 206–218.

38. Boyatzis, Stubbs, and Taylor, "Learning Cognitive and Emotional Intelligence Competencies," 150–162.

39. R. Zomke, "Systems Thinking," *Training* (February 2001), Vol. 38, No. 2, p. 40.

40. Detrick, "Interview," 56–63.

41. Zahra, "Drucker's Landmark Book," 16–23.

42. L. Kurke and H. Aldrich, "Mintzberg Was Right! A Replication and Extension of *The Nature of Managerial Work*," *Management Science* (1983), Vol. 29, pp. 975–984; C. Avert and A. Al, "Managerial Work: The Influence of Hierarchical Level and Functional Specialty," *Academy of Management Journal* (1983), Vol. 26, pp. 170–177; C. Hales, "What Do Managers Do? A Critical Review of the Evidence," *Journal of Management Studies* (1986), Vol. 23, pp. 88–115.

43. H. Mintzberg, *The Nature of Managerial Work* (New York: Harper & Row, 1973).

44. Magretta, *What Management Is*.

45. Hogan and Warrenfeltz, "Education of the Modern Manager," 74–84.

46. L. Gomes, "Growth of the Internet May Take Nothing Short of a Revolution," *Wall Street Journal*, (December 22, 2003), B1.

47. J. Weaver, "Fuel the Fire," *Entrepreneur* (December 2003), p. 98.

48. M. Campanelli, "A World of Goods," *Entrepreneur* (December 2003), p. 60.

49. DeSanctis, Glass, and Ensing, "Organization Designs for R&D," 55–61.

50. "The Global Giants," *Wall Street Journal* (September 22, 2003), p. R9.

51. J. Welch and J. Byrne, "Jack: Straight from the Gut," *Journal of Small Business Strategy* (Fall/Winter 2002), Vol. 13, No. 2, pp. 97–99.

52. M. Murry and J. Sapsford, "GE Reshuffles Its Dot-Com Strategy to Focus on Internal Digitizing," *Wall Street Journal* (May 4, 2001), pp. B1, B4.

53. "The Global Giants," R9.

54. Seo, "Overcoming Emotional Barriers," 7–21.

55. Zahra, "Drucker's Landmark Book," 16–23.

56. R. Coff, "Bidding Wars over R&D-Intensive Firms: Knowledge, Opportunism, and the Market for Corporate Control," *Academy of Management Journal* (2003), Vol. 46, No. 1, pp. 74–85; Lankau and Scandura, "Personal Learning in Mentoring Relationships," 779–790.

57. Child and McGrath, "Organizations Unfettered," 1135–1146.

58. Zahra, "Drucker's Landmark Book," 16–23.

59. Boyatzis, Stubbs, and Taylor, "Learning Cognitive and Emotional Intelligence Competencies," 150–162.

60. Lankau and Scandura, "Personal Learning in Mentoring Relationships," 779–790.

61. S. Nadkarni, "Instructional Methods and Mental Models of Students: An Empirical Investigation," *Academy of Management Learning and Education* (2003), Vol. 2, No. 4, pp. 335–351.

62. Greiner, Bhambri, and Cummings, "Searching for a Strategy," 402–420; E. A. Locke, "The Epistemological Side of Teaching Management: Teaching Through Principles," *Academy of Management Learning and Education* (2002), Vol. 1, No. 2, pp. 195–205.

63. J. P. Meyer, "Four Territories of Experience: A Developmental Action Inquiry Approach to Outdoor-Adventure Experiential Learning," *Academy of Management Learning and Education* (2003), Vol. 2, No. 4, pp. 352–363.

64. Detrick, "Interview," 56–63.

65. J. Nirenberg, *Power Tools* (Upper Saddle River, NJ: Prentice-Hall, 1997), p. iv.

66. Nadkarni, "Instructional Methods and Mental Models," 335–351.

67. Magretta, *What Management Is*; Argyris, "Double-Loop Learning," 206–218.

68. Doh, "Can Leadership Be Taught?" 54–67.

69. Hogan and Warrenfeltz, "Education of the Modern Manager," 74–84.

70. Seo, "Overcoming Emotional Barriers," 7–21.

71. Boland and Katz, "Jack Gherty," 24–30.

72. Zahra, "Drucker's Landmark Book," 16–23.

73. Zahra, "Introduction," 7–8.

74. DeSanctis, Glass, and Ensing, "Organization Designs for R&D," 55–61.

75. V. U. Druskat and J. V. Wheeler, "Managing from the Boundary: The Effective Leadership of Self-Managing Work Teams," *Academy of Management Journal* (2003), Vol. 46, No. 4, pp. 435–457.

76. J. M. Ivancevich, T. N. Duening, J. A. Gilbert, and R. Konopaske, "Deterring White-Collar Crime," *Academy of Management Executive* (2003), Vol. 17, No. 2, pp. 114–127.

77. R. L. Jenkins, "Crisis in Confidence in Corporate America," *Mid-American Journal of Business* (2003), Vol. 18, No. 3, p. 5.

78. E. W. Morrison, "Newcomers' Relationships: The Role of Social Network Ties During Socialization," *Academy of Management Journal* (2002), Vol. 45, No. 6, pp. 1149–1160.

79. Druskat and Wheeler, "Managing from the Boundary," 435–457.

80. Welch and Byrne, "Jack: Straight from the Gut," 97–99.

81. "Global Giants," R9.

82. Information taken from the Dell Computer Web site at *http://www.dell.com,* accessed January 12, 2004.

83. N. Wingfield, "E-tailing Comes of Age," *Wall Street Journal,* (December 8, 2003), B1.

84. J. Pfeffer and R. I. Sutton, *The Knowing–Doing Gap* (Boston: Harvard Business School Publishing, 2000).

85. Magretta, *What Management Is.*

Appendix

1. F. W. Taylor, *Principles of Scientific Management* (New York: Harper & Brothers, 1911).

2. H. Fayol, *General and Industrial Management,* trans. by J. A. Conbrough (Geneva: International Management Institute, 1929).

3. F. Roethlisberger and W. Dickson, *Management and the Worker* (Boston: Harvard University Press, 1939).

4. A. Maslow, *Motivation and Personality,* 2nd ed. (New York: Harper & Row, 1970).

5. D. McGregor, *The Human Side of Enterprise* (New York: McGraw-Hill, 1960).

6. R. Ackoff, *Creating the Corporate Future* (New York: Wiley, 1981).

7. H. Koontz, "The Management Theory Jungle Revisited," *Academy of Management Review* (April 1980), Vol. 5, p. 175; D. Katz and R. Khan, *The Social Psychology of Organizations,* 2nd ed. (New York: Wiley, 1978).

8. E. L. Trist and K. W. Bamforth, "Some Social and Psychological Consequences of the Longwall Method of Coalgetting," *Human Relations* (1951), Vol. 4, pp. 3–38; F. E. Emery and E. L. Trist, *Socio-Technical Systems, Vol. 2*

of Management Science: Methods and Techniques (London: Pergamon, 1960).

9. T. Burns and G. Stalker, *The Management of Innovation* (London: Tavistock, 1961).

Chapter 2

1. M. J. McDermott, "Listening with a Purpose," *Chief Executive (U.S.)* (February 2001), p. 35.

2. S. A. Zahra, "The Practice of Management: Reflections on Peter F. Drucker's Landmark Book," *Academy of Management Executive* (2003), Vol. 17, No. 3, pp. 16–23.

3. J. Magretta, *What Management Is: How It Works and Why It's Everyone's Business* (New York: The Free Press, 2002).

4. "Student Projects," *Planning* (March 2001), Vol. 67, No. 3, p. 34.

5. Zahra, "Drucker's Landmark Book," 16–23.

6. R. Hogan and R. Warrenfeltz, "Education of the Modern Manager," *Academy of Management Learning and Education* (2003), Vol. 2, No. 1, pp. 74–84.

7. M. T. Bolko and V. O. Hansen, "T-Shaped Managers; Knowledge Management's Next Generation," *Harvard Business Review* (March 2001), Vol. 79, No. 3, p. 106.

8. P. F. Hewlin, "And the Award for Best Actor Goes to . . .: Facades of Conformity in Organizational Settings," *Academy of Management Review* (2003), Vol. 28, No. 4, pp. 633–642.

9. A. R. Jassawalla and H. C. Sashittal, "Cultures That Support Product-Innovation Processes," *Academy of Management Executive* (2002), Vol. 16, No. 3, pp. 42–43.

10. S. A. Zahra, "Introduction: Peter F. Drucker's *The Practice of Management*," *Academy of Management Executive* (2003), Vol. 17, No. 3, pp. 7–8.

11. A. Davis, "Merrill's O'Neal Walks Tightrope as He Revamps Firm's Mission," *Wall Street Journal* (September 2, 2003), p. A1.

12. K. D. I. Tuzaman, "Glad That's Over," *Entrepreneur* (December 2002), p. 38.

13. FedEx mission statement taken from the company's Web site at *http://www.fedex.com,* accessed January 16, 2004.

14. Zahra, "Drucker's Landmark Book," 16–23.

15. J. Florin, M. Lubatkin, and W. Schulze, "A Social Capital Model of High-Growth Ventures," *Academy of Management Journal* (2003), Vol. 46, No. 3, pp. 374–384.

16. A. J. Hillman and G. D. Keim, "Shareholder Value, Stakeholder Management, and Social Issues: What's the Bottom Line?" *Strategic Management Journal* (February 2001), Vol. 22, No. 2, pp. 125–140.

17. S. G. Scott and V. R. Lane, "A Stakeholder Approach to Organizational Identity," *Academy of Management Review* (2000), Vol. 25, No. 1, pp. 43–62.

18. B. L. Kirkman, B. Rosen, C. B. Gibson, P. E. Tesluk, and S. O. McPherson, "Five Challenges to Virtual Team Success:

Lessons from Sabre, Inc.," *Academy of Management Executive*, 2002, Vol. 16, No. 3, pp. 67–76.

19. G. Detrick, "Interview with Russell L. Ackoff," *Academy of Management Learning and Education* (2002), Vol. 1, No. 1, pp. 56–63.

20. J. B. Miner, "The Rated Importance, Scientific Validity, and Practical Usefulness of Organizational Behavior Theories: A Quantitative Review," *Academy of Management Learning and Education* (2003), Vol. 2, No. 3, pp. 250–268.

21. Kirkman et al., "Five Challenges," 67–76.

22. M. J. Lankau and T. A. Scandura, "An Investigation of Personal Learning in Mentoring Relationships: Content, Antecedents, and Consequences," *Academy of Management Journal* (2002), Vol. 45, No. 4, pp. 779–790.

23. M. G. Seo, "Overcoming Emotional Barriers, Political Obstacles, and Control Imperatives in the Action-Science Approach to Individual and Organizational Learning," *Academy of Management Learning and Education* (2003), Vol. 2, No. 1, pp. 7–21.

24. Zahra, "Introduction," 7–8.

25. McDermott, "Listening with a Purpose," 35.

26. M. C. Bolino and W. H. Turnley, "Going the Extra Mile: Cultivating and Managing Employee Behavior in Organizations," *Academy of Management Executive* (2003), Vol. 17, No. 3, pp. 60–71.

27. McDermott, "Listening with a Purpose," 35.

28. Hewlin, "And the Award for Best Actor," 633–642; J. A. Howard-Grenville and A. J. Hoffman, "The Importance of Cultural Framing to the Success of Social Initiatives in Business," *Academy of Management Executive* (2003), Vol. 17, No. 2, pp. 70–86.

29. Jassawalla and Sashittal, "Product-Innovation Processes," 42–43.

30. G. T. M. Hult, D. J. Ketchen, Jr., and E. L. Nichols, Jr., "An Examination of Cultural Competitiveness and Order Fulfillment Cycle Time within Supply Chains," *Academy of Management Journal* (2002), Vol. 45, No. 3, pp. 577–586.

31. Hult, Ketchen, and Nichols, "Cultural Competitiveness," 577–586.

32. Hewlin, "And the Award for Best Actor," 633–642.

33. S. D. Friedman and S. Lobel, "The Happy Workaholic: A Role Model for Employees," *Academy of Management Executive* (2003), Vol. 17, No. 3, pp. 87–98.

34. M. Alavi and R. B. Gallupe, "Using Information Technology in Learning: Case Studies in Business and Management Education Programs," *Academy of Management Learning and Education* (2003), Vol. 2, No. 2, pp. 139–153.

35. Jassawalla and Sashittal, "Product-Innovation Processes," 42–43.

36. E. W. Morrison, "Newcomers' Relationships: The Role of Social Network Ties During Socialization," *Academy of Management Journal* (2002), Vol. 45, No. 6, pp. 1149–1160.

37. R. A. Guth, "Midlife Correction: Inside Microsoft, Financial Managers Win New Clout," *Wall Street Journal* (July 23, 2003), p. A1.

38. M. Crossan, "Altering Theories of Learning and Action: An Interview with Chris Argyris," *Academy of Management Executive* (2003), Vol. 17, No. 2, pp. 40–46; M. Crossan, "Chris Argyris and Donald Schon's Organizational Learning: There Is No Silver Bullet," *Academy of Management Executive* (2003), Vol. 17, No. 2, pp. 38–39.

39. Hogan and Warrenfeltz, "Education the Modern Manager," 74–84; J. S. Lublin, "How to Win Support from Colleagues at Your New Job," *Wall Street Journal* (November 25, 2003), p. B1.

40. P. M. Senge, "Taking Personal Change Seriously: The Impact of Organizational Learning on Management Practice," *Academy of Management Executive* (2003), Vol. 17, No. 2, pp. 47–50.

41. Bolko and Hansen, "T-Shaped Managers," 106–107.

42. J. R. Detert, R. G. Schroeder, and J. J. Mauriel, "A Framework for Linking Culture and Improvement Initiatives in Organizations," *Academy of Management Review* (2000), Vol. 25, No. 4, pp. 850–863.

43. Senge, "Taking Personal Change Seriously," 47–50.

44. G. Hyatt, "Creating Connection with Contact Collaboration Technologies," *The Rhythm of Business* (September 24, 2003).

45. B. Farber, "Star Power," *Entrepreneur* (December 2003), p. 102.

46. Seo, "Overcoming Emotional Barriers," 7–21.

47. K. T. Gordon, "Evolution Theory," *Entrepreneur* (January 2003), p. 74.

48. "What Goes Around Comes Around," *News from . . . Curtis* [no year listed], Vol. 8, No. 1.

49. "How to Satisfy Customers," *Communication Briefings* (2003), Vol. XX, No. 1, p. 6.

50. M. J. Benner and M. L. Tushman, "Exploitation, Exploration and Process Management: The Productivity Dilemma Revisited," *Academy of Management Review* (2003), Vol. 28, No. 2, pp. 238–256.

51. M. M. Phillips, "Detroit Big Three Automakers," *Wall Street Journal* (January 6, 2004), p. A1.

52. N. Shirouzu, "As Toyota Pushes Hard in China, A Lot Is Riding on the Outcome," *Wall Street Journal* (December 8, 2003), p. A1.

53. Howard-Grenville and Hoffman, "The Importance of Cultural Framing," 70–86.

54. P. A. Gompers and A. Wetrick, "Corporate Governance and the Individual Investor," *TIAA-CREF Investment Forum* (June 2003), pp. 11–12.

55. F. R. Post, "The Social Responsibility of Management: A Critique of the Shareholder Paradigm and Defense of Stakeholder Primacy," *Mid-American Journal of Business* (2003), Vol. 18, No. 2, pp. 57–58.

56. N. W. Van Yperen and O. Janssen, "Fatigued and Dissatisfied or Fatigued but Satisfied? Goal Orientations and Responses to High Job Demands," *Academy of Management Journal* (2002), Vol. 45, No. 6, pp. 1161–1171.

57. S. V. Yoder, "Beware the Coming Corporate Backlash," *Industry Week* (April 2, 2001), Vol. 250, No. 5, p. 38; K. Chen, "Nike Gets Traction from Sweatshop Spat," *Wall Street Journal* (February 28, 2001), p. B14.

58. S. Greengard, "Surviving Internet Speed," *Workforce* (April 2001), Vol. 80, No. 4, p. 38.

59. W. F. Cascio, "Managing a Virtual Workplace," *Academy of Management Executive* (2000), Vol. 14, No. 3, pp. 81–90.

60. L. Greenhalgh, "Ford Motor Company's CEO Jac Nasser on Transformational Change, E-Business, and Environmental Responsibility," *Academy of Management Executive* (2000), Vol. 14, No. 3, pp. 46–51.

61. "Hiring Will Pick Up . . . ," *Wall Street Journal* (January 2, 2004), p. A1.

62. M. M. Arthur, "Share Price Reactions to Work-Family Initiatives: An Institutional Perspective," *Academy of Management Journal* (2003), Vol. 46, No. 4, pp. 497–505.

63. E. R. E. O'Higgins, "Government and the Creation of the Celtic Tiger: Can Management Maintain the Momentum?" *Academy of Management Executive* (2002), Vol. 16, No. 3, p. 104.

64. A. McWilliams and D. Siegel, "Corporate Social Responsibility: A Theory of the Firm Perspective," *Academy of Management Review* (2001), Vol. 26, No. 1, pp. 117–127.

65. Alavi and Gallupe, "Using Information Technology," 139–153.

66. R. Ackoff, *Creating the Corporate Future* (New York: Wiley, 1981).

67. McWilliams and Siegel, "Corporate Social Responsibility," 117–127.

68. M. D. Lord, "Constituency Building as the Foundation for Corporate Political Strategy," *Academy of Management Executive* (2003), Vol. 17, No. 1, pp. 112–123.

69. Exhibit 2-6 is based on systems theory and was designed by Dr. Abbas Nadim of the University of New Haven. The author added the word *culture* in the segment whose label now reads "Management and Culture."

70. R. L. Jenkins, "Crisis in Confidence in Corporate America," *Mid-American Journal of Business* (2003), Vol. 18, No. 3, p. 5.

71. "Good as Gold," *Entrepreneur* (August 2003), p. 60; A. P. Brief, "Editor's Comments: Taking Ethics Seriously— A Mission Now More Possible," *Academy of Management Review* (2003), Vol. 28, No. 3, pp. 363–366.

72. R. L. Hughes, R. C. Ginnett, and G. J. Curphy, *Leadership: Enhancing the Lessons of Experience*, 4/e (Burr Ridge, IL: McGraw-Hill, 2002).

73. J. Jusko, "Why Leaders Fail," *Industry Week* (March 25, 2002), pp. 15–16.

74. J. P. Doh, "Can Leadership Be Taught? Perspectives from Management Educators," *Academy of Management Learning and Education* (2003), Vol. 2, No. 1, pp. 54–67.

75. "Good as Gold," p. 60; "Trust Me?" *Entrepreneur* (February 2003), pp. 26–29; L. Gratton and C. Truss, "The Three-Dimensional People Strategy: Putting Human Resources Policies into Action," *Academy of Management Executive* (2003), Vol. 17, No. 3, pp. 74–86.

76. B. Farber, "Star Power," *Entrepreneur* (December 2003), p. 102.

77. J. Kurlantzick, "Liar, Liar: A Culture of Lying Is Infecting American Business. Can You Help Stop the Epidemic?" *Entrepreneur* (October 2003), pp. 68–71.

78. M. Diener, "Looking for a Punch in the Nose?" *Entrepreneur* (March 2003), p. 63.

79. Kurlantzick, "Liar, Liar," 68–71.

80. M. J. Gundlach, S. C. Douglas, and M. J. Martinko, "The Decision to Blow the Whistle: A Social Information Processing Framework," *Academy of Management Review* (2003), Vol. 28, No. 1, pp. 107–123.

81. Kurlantzick, "Liar, Liar," 68–71.

82. D. E. Warren, "Constructive and Destructive Deviance in Organizations," *Academy of Management Review* (2003), Vol. 28, No. 4, pp. 622–632.

83. S. S. Ariss, "Employee Involvement to Improve Safety in the Workplace: An Ethical Imperative," *Mid-American Journal of Business* (2003), Vol. 18, No. 2, pp. 9–18.

84. C. Wittmeyer, "The Practice of Management: Timeless Views and Principles," *Academy of Management Executive* (2003), Vol. 17, No. 3, pp. 13–15.

85. L. Chordas, "Code of Ethics," *Best's Review* (March 2001), Vol. 101, No. 11, p. 47.

86. Warren, "Constructive and Destructive Deviance," 622–632.

87. "Whistleblowing," *Wall Street Journal* (October 30, 2002), p. D1.

88. J. L. Lunsford and A. M. Squeo, "Boeing Dismisses Two Executives for Violating Ethical Standards," *Wall Street Journal* (November 25, 2003), p. A1.

89. T. J. Rowley and M. Moldoveanu, "When Will Stakeholder Groups Act? An Interest- and Identity-Base Model of Stakeholder Group Mobilization," *Academy of Management Review* (2003), Vol. 28, No. 2, pp. 204–219.

90. J. A. Aragon-Correa and S. Sharma, "A Contingent Resource-Base View of Proactive Corporate Environmental Strategy," *Academy of Management Review* (2003), Vol. 28, No. 1, pp. 71–88.

91. Ariss, "Safety in the Workplace," 9–18.

92. McWilliams and Siegel, "Corporate Social Responsibility," 117–127.

93. D. A. Rondinelli and T. London, "How Corporations and Environmental Groups Cooperate: Assessing Cross-Sector

Alliances and Collaborations," *Academy of Management Executive* (2003), Vol. 17, No. 1, pp. 61–76.

94. Information taken from Ben & Jerry's Web site, *http://www.benjerry.com*, accessed January 18, 2004.

Chapter 3

1. R. Harborne, "Wisdom of the CEO: The Challenge to Business Leadership in the 21st Century." Research conducted by PricewaterhouseCoopers, presented at the New England Business Administration Association International Conference, New Haven, CT, April 28, 2000. Information taken from presenter handout.

2. R. N. Lussier, R. Baeder, and J. Corman, "Measuring Global Practices: Global Strategic Planning Through Company Situational Analysis," *Business Horizons* (October 1994), Vol. 37, No. 5, pp. 56–63.

3. J. Welch and J. Byrne, "Jack: Straight from the Gut," *Journal of Small Business Strategy* (2002), Vol. 13, No. 2, pp. 97–99.

4. F. C. Broadbeck, M. Frese, and M. Javidan, "Leadership Made in Germany: Low on Compassion, High on Performance," *Academy of Management Executive* (2002), Vol. 16, No.1, pp. 16–29.

5. C. Wittmeyer, "The Practice of Management: Timeless Views and Principles," *Academy of Management Executive* (2003), Vol. 17, No. 3, pp. 13–15.

6. P. C. Earley and E. Mosakowski, "Creating Hybrid Team Cultures: An Empirical Test of Transnational Team Function," *Academy of Management Journal* (2000), Vol. 43, No. 1, pp. 26–49.

7. M. Alavi and R. B. Gallupe, "Using Information Technology in Learning: Case Studies in Business and Management Education Programs," *Academy of Management Learning and Education* (2003), Vol. 2, No. 2, pp. 139–153.

8. Answers are taken from "The Global Giants," *Wall Street Journal* (September 22, 2003), p. R9.

9. S. Cooper, "Global Village," *Entrepreneur* (April 2003), p. 30.

10. P. Burrows, "The Radical Carly Fiorina's Bold Management Experiment at HP," *Business Week* (February 19, 2001), pp. 70–80.

11. Information taken from Hewlett-Packard Web site, *http://www.hp.com*, accessed January 21, 2004.

12. D. A. Whetten and A. L. Delbecq, "Saraide's Chairman Hatim Tyabji on Creating and Sustaining a Values-Based Organizational Culture," *Academy of Management Executive* (2000), Vol. 14, No. 4, pp. 32–33.

13. Harborne, "Wisdom of the CEO."

14. E. R. E. O'Higgins, "Government and the Creation of the Celtic Tiger: Can Management Maintain the Momentum?" *Academy of Management Executive* (2002), Vol. 16, No. 3, p. 104.

15. B. Bahree and S. Warren, "OPEC Seeks High Oil Prices to Offset Weak Dollar," *Wall Street Journal* (December 4, 2003), p. A1.

16. "Japanese Officials Reiterated . . .," *Wall Street Journal* (January 7, 2003), p. A1.

17. J. P. Doh, P. Rodriguez, K. Uhlenbruck, J. Collins, and L. Eden, "Coping with Corruption in Foreign Markets," *Academy of Management Executive* (2003), Vol. 17, No. 3, pp. 114–127.

18. O'Higgins, "Celtic Tiger," 104.

19. J. Kurlantzick, "Promised Land," *Entrepreneur* (January 2004), pp. 66–69.

20. D. Davis, "U.S. Battles Europe to Narrow Global Treaty Banning Corruption," *Wall Street Journal* (June 17, 2003), p. A1.

21. "America's Leaders," *Wall Street Journal* (April 23, 2001), p. 1.

22. Lussier, Baeder, and Corman, "Measuring Global Practices," 56–63.

23. Doh et al., "Coping with Corruption," 114–127.

24. S. M. Toh and A. S. Denisi, "Host Country National Reactions to Expatriate Pay Policies: A Model and Implications," *Academy of Management Review* (2003), Vol. 28, No. 4, pp. 606–621.

25. J. Barthelemy, "The Seven Deadly Sins of Outsourcing," *Academy of Management Executive* (2003), Vol. 17, No. 2, pp. 87–98.

26. N. L. Torres, "Take It Outside," *Entrepreneur* (February 2003), p. 20.

27. J. Kurlantzick, "Made in America?" *Entrepreneur* (October 2003), p. 73.

28. "Lehman and Bear Stearns," *Wall Street Journal* (December 18, 2003), p. A1.

29. K. J. Delaney, "Indian Tech Companies Step up Rivalry with West," *Wall Street Journal* (December 16, 2003), p. B1.

30. "Global Giants," R9.

31. Information taken from the IBM Web site, *http://www.ibm.com*, accessed January 22, 2004.

32. W. M. Bulkeley, "IBM to Export Highly Paid Jobs to India, China," *Wall Street Journal* (December 15, 2003), pp. B1, B3.

33. W. M. Bulkeley, "IBM Document Gives Rare Look at Sensitive Plans on Offshoring," *Wall Street Journal* (November 19, 2004), p. A1.

34. "Oracle's Earnings Rose," *Wall Street Journal* (December 16, 2003), p. A1.

35. S. Parise and A. Casher, "Alliance Portfolios: Designing and Managing Your Network of Business-Partner Relationships," *Academy of Management Executive* (2003), Vol. 17, No. 4, pp. 25–37.

36. M. Zeng and X. P. Chen, "Achieving Cooperation in Multiparty Alliances: A Social Dilemma Approach to Partnership Management," *Academy of Management Review* (2003), Vol. 28, No. 4, pp. 587–605; K. T. Gordon, "Friends and Foes," *Entrepreneur* (March 2003), p. 69.

37. M. J. McDermott, "Listening with a Purpose," *Chief Executive (U.S.)* (February 2001), p. 35.

38. J. Corman, R. N. Lussier, and R. Baeder, "Global Strategies for the Future: Large vs. Small Business," *Journal of Business Strategies* (Fall 1991), Vol. 8, No. 2, pp. 86–93.

39. Toh and Denisi, "Reactions to Expatriate Pay," 606–621.

40. G. DeSanctis, J. T. Glass, and I. M. Ensing, "Organization Design for R&D," *Academy of Management Executive* (2002), Vol. 16, No. 3, pp. 55–61.

41. N. Hewitt-Dundas, "Resource and Capability Constraints to Innovation—An Examination of Small and Larger Firms," *SBANC Newsletter* (December 17, 2003), No. 302.

42. E. White and J. A. Trachtenberg, "One Size Doesn't Fit All," *Wall Street Journal* (October 1, 2003), p. B1.

43. C. E. Griffin, "Welcome to the Jungle," *Entrepreneur* (March 2001), p. 39.

44. S. A. Zahra, "Introduction: Peter F. Drucker's *The Practice of Management*," *Academy of Management Executive* (2003), Vol. 17, No. 3, pp. 7–8.

45. "What Makes an Entrepreneur?" *Monthly Labor Review* (2001), Vol. 124, No. 1, p. 35.

46. S. A. Zahra, "An Interview with Peter Drucker," *Academy of Management Executive* (2003), Vol. 17, No. 3, pp. 9–12.

47. D. Worrell, "The Best-Relaid Plans" *Entrepreneur* (March 2003), p. 45.

48. C. Ansberry, "Small Companies Slowly Build Momentum in the Job Market," *Wall Street Journal* (December 4, 2003), p. A1.

49. R. N. Lussier and M. C. Sonfield, "Family Business Management Activities, Styles and Characteristics: A Correlational Study," *Mid-American Journal of Business* (2004), Vol. 19, No. 1, pp. 47–53.

50. C. Elliott, "Safety First," *Entrepreneur* (February 2003), p. 19.

51. S. H. Tucker and K. L. Hill, "Women's Status in the U.S. Workforce 2000+," *Academy of Entrepreneurship Journal* (2002), Vol. 8, No. 2, pp. 17–33; D. Worrell, "Our Little Angels," *Entrepreneur* (January 2003), p. 45–46.

52. J. Amadio, "New-Car Smell," *Entrepreneur* (February 2003), p. 22.

53. "You're Not So Hot," *Business Week* (April 23, 2001), No. 3729, p. 5.

54. A. Greve and J. W. Salaff, "Social Networks and Entrepreneurship," *Entrepreneurship Theory and Practice* (2003), Vol. 28, No. 1, pp. 1–12; "Why Goliath Needs David," *The Rhythm of Business* (October 31, 2003), p. 1.

55. Ansberry, "Small Companies Slowly Build Momentum," A1.

56. "Wire Your Filing to the Agency and Avoid All the Painstaking Pencilwork," *Entrepreneur* (December 2002), p. 77.

57. M. A. Razi and J. M. Tarn, "ERP System Solutions for Small Companies: Readiness and Selection," *Journal of Small Business Strategy* (2003), Vol. 14, No. 1, pp. 71–85.

58. S. Cooper, "Creative Endeavors," *Entrepreneur* (January 2003), pp. 126–127.

59. J. D. Arthurs and L. W. Busenitz, "The Boundaries and Limitations of Agency Theory and Stewardship Theory in the Venture Capitalist/Entrepreneur Relationship," *Entreprenuship Theory and Practice* (2003), Vol. 28, No. 2, pp. 145–152.

60. M. T. Manion, "Creative Thinking or Concept Development? The Process of Recognizing Successful Opportunities for Technologically Complex New Ventures," *Academy of Entrepreneurship Journal* (2002), Vol. 8, No. 2, pp. 115–134.

61. J. Corman and R. N. Lussier, *Entrepreneurial New Ventures* (Cincinnati: Dame Publishing, 2001).

62. C. Achua and R. N. Lussier, "Small-Town Merchants Are Not Using the Recommended Strategies to Compete Against National Discount Chains: A Prescriptive vs. Descriptive Study," *Journal of Small Business Strategy* (2003), Vol. 13, No. 1, pp. 80–87.

63. M. C. Bolino, W. H. Turnley, and J. M. Bloodgood, "Citizenship Behavior and the Creation of Social Capital in Organizations," *Academy of Management Review* (2002), Vol. 27, No. 4, pp. 505–522.

64. J. Florin, M. Lubatkin, and W. Schulze, "A Social Capital Model of High-Growth Ventures," *Academy of Management Journal* (2003), Vol. 46, No. 3, pp. 374–384.

65. J. A. Aragon-Correa and S. Sharma, "A Contingent Resource-Based View of Proactive Corporate Environmental Strategy," *Academy of Management Review* (2003), Vol. 28, No. 1, pp. 71–88.

66. R. N. Lussier, M. C. Sonfield, J. Corman, and M. McKinney, "Strategies Used by Small Business Entrepreneurs," *Mid-American Journal of Business* (Spring 2001), Vol. 16, No. 1, p. 29.

67. "Best Path to Entrepreneurship," *Inc.* (January 1, 2001), p. 36.

68. J. S. Osteryoung and D. L. Denslow, *So You Need to Write a Business Plan!* (Madison, OH, South-Western, 2003).

69. Worrell, "Best-Relaid Plans," 45.

70. R. McGarvey, "Grow Up," *Entrepreneur* (April 2001), p. 32.

71. "Develop a Winning Business Plan with Tips from Oracle VentureNetwork," *123Jump* (April 27, 2001), pp. 40–43; McGarvey, "Grow Up," 32.

72. J. C. Kennedy, "Leadership in Malaysia: Traditional Values, International Outlook," *Academy of Management Executive* (2002), Vol. 16, No. 3, pp. 15–24; W. P. Wan and R. E. Hoskisson, "Home Country Environments, Corporate Diversification Strategies, and Firm Performance," *Academy of Management Journal* (2003), Vol. 46, No. 1, pp. 27–45; S. L. Rynes, A. M. Mullenix, and C. Q. Trank, "Do Behavioral Skills Increase the Employability of Business Students?" *Journal of Career Centers* (Summer 2001), pp. 40–43.

73. Greve and Salaff, "Social Networks and Entrepreneurship," 1–12.

74. C. Penttila, "Employee Interrupted," *Entrepreneur* (February 2003), pp. 66–67.

75. G. Hofstede, "The Cultural Relativity of the Quality of Life Concept," *Academy of Management Review* (1984), Vol. 9, pp. 389–398.

76. The original terms used by Hofstede were *masculinity* and *femininity*. The author has elected to use the terms *achievement orientation* and *relationship oientation* to avoid the appearance of sexism.

77. H. K. Steensma, L. Marino, and K. M. Weaver, "Attitudes Toward Cooperative Strategies: A Cross-Cultural Analysis of Entrepreneurs," *Journal of International Business Studies* (2000), Vol. 31, No. 4, p. 591.

78. "The Leadership Connection," *Entrepreneur* (March 2003), p. 50.

79. E. White, and J. A. Trachtenberg, "One Size Doesn't Fit All," *Wall Street Journal* (October 1, 2003), p. B1.

80. Information taken from McDonald's Web site at *http://www.mcdonalds.com*, accessed January 24, 2004.

81. D. Ucbanaran, A. Lockett, M. Wright, and P. Westhead, "Entrepreneurial Founder Teams: Factors Associated with Member Entry and Exit," *Entrepreneurship Theory and Practice* (2003), Vol. 28, No. 2, pp. 107–118.

Chapter 4

1. B. L. Kirkman, B. Rosen, C. B. Gibson, P. E. Tesluk, and S. O. McPherson, "Five Challenges to Virtual Team Success: Lessons from Sabre, Inc.," *Academy of Management Executive* (2002), Vol. 16, No. 3, pp. 67–76.

2. J. S. Bunderson, "Team Member Functional Background and Involvement in Management Teams: Direct Effects and the Moderating Role of Power Centralization," *Academy of Management Journal* (2003), Vol. 48, No. 4, pp. 458–474.

3. L. E. Greiner, A. Bhambri, and T. G. Cummings, "Searching for a Strategy to Teach Strategy," *Academy of Management Learning and Education* (2002), Vol. 2, No. 4, pp. 402–420.

4. S. Nadkarni, "Instructional Methods and Mental Models of Students: An Empirical Investigation," *Academy of Management Learning and Education* (2003), Vol. 2, No. 4, pp. 335–351.

5. Greiner, Bhambri, and Cummings, "Strategy to Teach Strategy," 402–420.

6. Kirkman et al., "Five Challenges to Virtual Team Success," 67–76.

7. C. J. Collins and K. D. Clark, "Strategic Human Resource Practices, Top Management Team Social Networks, and Firm Performance: The Role of Human Resource Practices in Creating Organizational Competitive Advantage," *Academy of Management Journal* (2003), Vol. 46, No. 6, pp. 740–751.

8. "Tips of the Month," *Communication Briefings* (2003), Vol. XX, No. 1, p. 1.

9. G. Detrick, "Interview with Russell L. Ackoff," *Academy of Management Learning and Education* (2002), Vol. 1, No. 1, pp. 56–63.

10. M. Crossan, "Chris Argyris and Donald Schon's Organizational Learning: There Is No Silver Bullet," *Academy of Management Executive* (2003), Vol. 17, No. 2, pp. 38–39.

11. S. A. Zahra, "*The Practice of Management*: Reflections on Peter F. Drucker's Landmark Book," *Academy of Management Executive* (2003), Vol. 17, No. 3, pp. 16–23.

12. Review of P. C. Nutt's *Why Decisions Fail: Avoiding the Blunders and Traps That Lead to Debacles*, *Academy of Management Executive* (February 2003), pp. 130–131.

13. L. A. Perlow, G. A. Okhuysen, and N. P. Repenning, "The Speed Trap: Exploring the Relationship Between Decision Making and Temporal Context," *Academy of Management Journal* (2002), Vol. 45, No. 5, pp. 931–955.

14. "Leadership Test," *Communication Briefings* (2003), Vol. XX, No. 1, p. 2.

15. Perlow, Okhuysen, and Repenning, "The Speed Trap," 931–955.

16. K. Atuahene Gima, "The Effects of Centrifugal and Centripetal Forces on Product Development Speed and Quality: How Does Problem Solving Matter?" *Academy of Management Journal* (2003), Vol. 46, No. 3, pp. 359–373.

17. M. L. Lengnick-Hall and C. A. Lengnick-Hall, " HR's Role in Building Relationship Networks," *Academy of Management Executive* (2003), Vol. 17, No. 4, pp. 53–65.

18. C. Olofson, "So Many Decisions, So Little Time," *Fast Company* (October 1999), p. 62.

19. N. J. Adler, *International Dimensions of Organizational Behavior*, 4th ed. (Cincinnati: South-Western, 2002), pp. 182–189.

20. Review of Nutt, *Why Decisions Fail*, 130–131.

21. B. C. Skaggs and T. R. Huffman, "A Customer Interaction Approach to Strategy and Production Complexity Alignment in Service Firms," *Academy of Management Journal*, 2003, Vol. 46, No. 6, pp. 775–786; Nadkarni, "Instructional Methods and Mental Models," 335–351.

22. P. K. Mills and G. R. Ungson, "Reassessing the Limits of Structural Empowerment: Organizational Constitution and Trust as Controls," *Academy of Management Review* (2003), Vol. 28, No. 1, pp. 143–153.

23. S. G. Green, M. A. Welsh, and G. E. Dehler, "Advocacy, Performance, and Threshold Influences on Decisions to Terminate New Product Development," *Academy of Management Journal* (2003), Vol. 46, No. 4, pp. 419–434.

24. M. R. Subramani and N. Venkatraman, "Safeguarding Investments in Asymmetric Interorganizational Relationships: Theory and Evidence," *Academy of Management Journal* (2003), Vol. 46, No. 1, pp. 46–62.

25. S. S. Ariss, "Employee Involvement to Improve Safety in the Workplace: An Ethical Imperative," *Mid-American Journal*

of Business (2003), Vol. 18, No. 2, pp. 9–18; S. S. K. Lam, X. P. Chen, and J. Schaubroeck, "Participative Decision Making and Employee Performance in Different Cultures: The Moderating Effects of Allocentrism/Idiocentrism and Efficacy," *Academy of Management Journal* (2003), Vol. 45, No. 5, pp. 905–914.

26. V. U. Druskat and J. V. Wheeler, "Managing from the Boundary: The Effective Leadership of Self-Managing Work Teams," *Academy of Management Journal* (2003), Vol. 46, No. 4, pp. 435–457.

27. Detrick, "Interview," 56–63.

28. Information taken from Sun Microsystems Web site at *http://www.sun.com*, accessed January 29, 2004.

29. K. Carney, "Successful Performance Measurement: A Checklist," Harvard Management Update (No. U991B), 1999.

30. J. Magretta, *What Management Is: How It Works and Why It's Everyone's Business* (New York: The Free Press, 2002); M. J. Benner and M. L. Tushman, "Exploitation, Exploration and Process Management: The Productivity Dilemma Revisited," *Academy of Management Review* (2003), Vol. 28, No. 2, pp. 238–256; M. T. Manion, "Creative Thinking or Concept Development? The Process of Recognizing Successful Opportunities for Technologically Complex New Ventures," *Academy of Entrepreneurship Journal* (2002), Vol. 8, No. 2, pp. 115–134.

31. C. Wittmeyer, "*The Practice of Management*: Timeless Views and Principles," *Academy of Management Executive* (2003), Vol. 17, No. 3, pp. 13–15.

32. J. B. Miner, "The Rated Importance, Scientific Validity, and Practical Usefulness of Organizational Behavior Theories: A Quantitative Review," *Academy of Management Learning and Education* (2003), Vol. 2, No. 3, pp. 250–268.

33. Zahra, "Drucker's Landmark Book," 16–23.

34. Manion, "Creative Thinking," 115–134.

35. S. J. Shin and J. Zhou, "Transformational Leadership, Conservation, and Creativity: Evidence from Korea," *Academy of Management Journal* (2003), Vol. 46, No. 6, pp. 703–714.

36. Lengnick-Hall and Lengnick-Hall, "HR's Role," 53–65.

37. N. Madjar, G. R. Oldham, and M. G. Pratt, "There's No Place Like Home? The Contributions of Work and Nonwork Creativity Support to Employees' Creative Performance," *Academy of Management Journal* (2002), Vol. 45, No. 4, pp. 757–767.

38. S. M. Farmer, P. Tierney, and K. Kung-McIntyre, "Employee Creativity in Taiwan: An Application of Role Identity Theory," *Academy of Management Journal* (2003), Vol. 46, No. 5, pp. 618–630.

39. M. Diener, "Out of Nowhere," *Entrepreneur* (February 2003), p. 69.

40. P. Tierney and S. M. Farmer, "Creative Self-Efficacy, Its Potential Antecedents and Relationship to Creative Performance," *Academy of Management Journal* (2002), Vol. 45, No. 6, pp. 1137–1148.

41. R. J. Sternberg, "WICS: A Model of Leadership in Organizations," *Academy of Management Learning and Education* (2003), Vol. 2, pp. 386–401.

42. C. Penttila, "An Art in Itself," *Entrepreneur* (December 2003), pp. 96–97.

43. Lengnick-Hall and Lengnick-Hall, "HR's Role," 53–65.

44. J. E. Perry-Smith and C. E. Shalley, "The Social Side of Creativity: A Static and Dynamic Social Network Perspective," *Academy of Management Review* (2003), Vol. 28, No. 1, pp. 89–106.

45. Manion, "Creative Thinking," 115–134.

46. M. Henricks, "Worth a Try," *Entrepreneur* (February 2003), pp. 65–66.

47. M. Orlitzky and J. D. Benjamin, "The Effects of Sex Composition on Small-Group Performance in a Business School Case Competition," *Academy of Management Learning and Education* (2003), Vol. 2, No. 2, pp. 128–138.

48. L. Thompson, "Improving the Creativity of Organizational Work Groups," *Academy of Management Executive* (2003), Vol. 17, No. 1, pp. 96–109.

49. W. B. Swann, Jr., J. T. Polzer, D. C. Seyle, and S. J. Ko, "Finding Value in Diversity: Verification of Personal and Social Self-Views in Diverse Groups," *Academy of Management Review* (2004), Vol. 29, No. 1, pp. 9–27.

50. Thompson, "Creativity of Organizational Work Groups," 96–109.

51. Swann et al., "Finding Value in Diversity," 9–27.

52. Thompson, "Creativity of Organizational Work Groups," 96–109.

53. Orlitzky and Benjamin, "Effects of Sex Composition," 128–138.

54. Thompson, "Creativity of Organizational Work Groups," 96–109.

55. F. S. Seo, "Advancing the Cause," *Planning* (January 2001), Vol. 67, No. 1, p. 42.

56. Tierney and Farmer, "Creative Self-Efficacy," 1137–1148.

57. Information taken from the *Art Calendar* Web site at *http://www.artcalendar.com*, accessed February 3, 2004.

58. Thompson, "Creativity of Organizational Work Groups," 96–109.

59. Bill Gates, *Business @ the Speed of Thought* (NY: Warner Books, 2000).

60. S. L. Rynes, K. G. Brown, and A. E. Colbert, "Seven Common Misconceptions about Human Resource Practices: Research Findings versus Practitioner Beliefs," *Academy of Management Executive* (2003), Vol. 16, No. 3, pp. 92–104.

61. C. Parry, "Planning Process Called into Question," *Leisure & Hospitality Business* (January 11, 2001), p. 19.

62. Review of Nutt, *Why Decisions Fail*, 130–131.

63. "Doing What's Right," *Entrepreneur* (March 2003), p. 52.

64. "Doing What's Right," 52.

65. Review of Nutt, *Why Decisions Fail*, 130–131.

66. M. J. McDermott, "Listening with a Purpose," *Chief Executive (U.S.)* (February 2001), p. 35.

67. C. M. Fiol and E. J. O'Connor, "Waking Up! Mindfulness in the Face of Bandwagons," *Academy of Management Review* (2003), Vol. 28, No. 1, pp. 54–70.

68. A. Zardkoohi, "Do Real Options Lead to Escalation of Commitment?" *Academy of Management Review* (2004), Vol. 29, No. 1, pp. 111–119.

69. V. H. Vroom and P. W. Yetton, *Leadership and Decision Making* (Pittsburgh: University of Pittsburgh Press, 1973); V. H. Vroom and A. G. Jago, *The New Leadership: Managing Participation in Organizations* (Englewood Cliffs, NJ: Prentice-Hall, 1988).

70. V. H. Vroom, "Leadership and the Decision-Making Process," *Organizational Dynamics 28* (Spring 2000), pp. 82–94.

Chapter 5

1. F. S. Seo, "Advancing the Cause," *Planning*, 2001, Vol. 67, No. 1, p. 42.

2. D. M. Brown, "Review of *Business @ the Speed of Thought*," *Mid-American Journal of Business* (2002), Vol. 17, No. 2, pp. 57–58.

3. J. Kickul and M. A. Liao-Troth, "The Meaning Behind the Message: Climate Perceptions and the Psychological Contract," *Mid-American Journal of Business* (2003), Vol. 18, No. 2, pp. 23–36; L. Thompson, "Improving the Creativity of Organizational Work Groups," *Academy of Management Executive* (2003), Vol. 17, No. 1, pp. 96–109.

4. E. Biech, "Executive Commentary," *Academy of Management Executive* (2003), Vol. 17, No. 4, p. 92.

5. R. Wolter, "A Wild Ride," *Entrepreneur* (October 2003), pp. 124–125; T. G. Pollock, J. F. Porac, and J. B. Wade, "Constructing Deal Networks: Brokers as Network 'Architects' in the U.S. IPO Market and Other Examples," *Academy of Management Review* (2004), Vol. 29, No. 1, pp. 50–72.

6. S. A. Zahra, "Introduction: Peter F. Drucker's *The Practice of Management*," *Academy of Management Executive* (2003), Vol. 17, No. 3, pp. 7–8.

7. D. K. Bermn, "Telecoms Embrace Internet Calling, But Is It Trouble?" *Wall Street Journal* (December 29, 2003), p. B1; J. A. Howard-Grenville and A. J. Hoffman, "The Importance of Cultural Framing to the Success of Social Initiatives in Business," *Academy of Management Executive* (2003), Vol. 17, No. 2, pp. 70–86.

8. S. A. Zahra, "An Interview with Peter Drucker," *Academy of Management Executive* (2003), Vol. 17, No. 3, pp. 9–12.

9. S. A. Zahra, "*The Practice of Management*: Reflections on Peter F. Drucker's Landmark Book," *Academy of Management Executive* (2003), Vol. 17, No. 3, pp. 16–23.

10. Zahra, "Introduction," pp. 7–8.

11. "Leadership Test," *Communication Briefings* (2003), Vol. XX, No. 1, p. 2.

12. H. B. Gregersen and J. H. Dyer, "Lockheed Martin Chairman and CEO Vance Coffman on Achieving Mission Success," *Academy of Management Executive* (2002), Vol. 16, No. 3, pp. 31–42.

13. J. C. Kennedy, "YTL Corporation's CEO Tan Sri Dato Francis Yeoh on Providing World-Class Products at Third-World Prices," *Academy of Management Executive* (2002), Vol. 16, No. 3, pp. 27–28.

14. Zahra, "Interview," 9–12.

15. Information taken from the YTL Corporation Berhad Web site at *http://www.ytl.com.my*, accessed February 16, 2004; Kennedy, "World-Class Products," 27–28.

16. D. A. Rondinelli and T. London, "How Corporations and Environmental Groups Cooperate: Assessing Cross-Sector Alliances and Collaborations," *Academy of Management Executive* (2003), Vol. 17, No. 1, pp. 61–76.

17. Kickul and Liao-Troth, "Meaning Behind the Message," 23–36.

18. J. Magretta, *What Management Is: How It Works and Why It's Everyone's Business* (New York: The Free Press, 2002).

19. C. M. Fiol and E. J. O'Connor, "Waking Up! Mindfulness in the Face of Bandwagons," *Academy of Management Review* (2003), Vol. 28, No. 1, pp. 54–70.

20. D. J. Ketchen, Jr., "Introduction: Raymond E. Miles and Charles C. Snow's *Organizational Strategy, Structure, and Process*," *Academy of Management Executive* (2003), Vol. 17, No. 4, pp. 95–105.

21. M. Porter, "How Competitive Forces Shape Strategy," *Harvard Business Review* (1979), Vol. 57, No. 2, pp. 137–145.

22. M. L. Lengnick-Hall and C. A. Lengnick-Hall, "HR's Role in Building Relationship Networks," *Academy of Management Executive* (2003), Vol. 17, No. 4, pp. 53–65.

23. K. T. Gordon, "Friends and Foes," *Entrepreneur* (March 2003), p. 69.

24. L. A. Perlow, G. A. Okhuysen, and N. P. Repenning, "The Speed Trap: Exploring the Relationship Between Decision Making and Temporal Context," *Academy of Management Journal* (2002), Vol. 45, No. 5, pp. 931–955.

25. Zahra, "Drucker's Landmark Book," 16–23.

26. R. C. Ford, "Pierre Bellon, Founder and President-Director General of Sodexho Alliance, on Working Hard and Having Fun," *Academy of Management Executive* (2003), Vol. 17, No. 1, pp. 38–45.

27. J. Florin, M. Lubatkin, and W. Schulze, "A Social Capital Model of High-Growth Ventures," *Academy of Management Journal* (2003), Vol. 46, No. 3, pp. 374–384.

28. C. J. Collins and K. D. Clark, "Strategic Human Resource Practices, Top Management Team Social Networks, and Firm

Performance: The Role of Human Resource Practices in Creating Organizational Competitive Advantage," *Academy of Management Journal* (2003), Vol. 46, No. 6, pp. 740–751.

29. M. A. Boland and J. P. Katz, "Jack Gherty, President and CEO of Land O'Lakes, on Leading a Branded Food and Farm Supply Cooperative," *Academy of Management Executive* (2003), Vol. 17, No. 3, pp. 24–30.

30. M. Diener, "Don't Cry Over . . . ," *Entrepreneur* (December 2003), p. 99.

31. S. M. Lee, "Samsung CEO Ki Tae Lee on Expanding the Global Market," *Academy of Management Executive* (2003), Vol. 17, No. 2, pp. 27–29.

32. P. J. Brews and C. L. Tucci, "Internetworking: Building Internet-Generation Companies," *Academy of Management Executive* (2003), Vol. 17, No. 4, pp. 8–20.

33. M. J. Lankau and T. A. Scandura, "An Investigation of Personal Learning in Mentoring Relationships: Content, Antecedents, and Consequences," *Academy of Management Journal* (2002), Vol. 45, No. 4, pp. 779–790.

34. Zahra, "Introduction," 7–8.

35. L. Gratton and C. Truss, "The Three-Dimensional People Strategy: Putting Human Resources Policies into Action," *Academy of Management Executive* (2003), Vol. 17, No. 3, pp. 74–86.

36. B. Farber, *Entrepreneur* (April 2003), p. 83.

37. M. E. Douglas, Indiana State University.

38. S. Hanschild, T. Licht, and W. Stein, "Creating a Knowledge Culture," *The McKinsey Quarterly* (Winter 2001), p. 74.

39. E. A. Locke, "The Epistemological Side of Teaching Management: Teaching Through Principles," *Academy of Management Learning and Education* (2002), Vol. 1, No. 2, pp. 195–205.

40. M. J. McDermott, "Listening with a Purpose," *Chief Executive (U.S.)* (February 2001), p. 35.

41. J. Kurlantzick, "There's Something To Be Said for Doing Things Your Way," *Entrepreneur* (November 2003), p. 89; H. Schultz, "It's a Grande-Latte World," *Wall Street Journal* (December 15, 2003), p. B1.

42. D. Knight, C. C. Durham, and E. A. Locke, "The Relationship of Team Goals, Incentives, and Efficacy to Strategic Risk, Tactical Implementation, and Performance," *Academy of Management Journal* (2001), Vol. 44, No. 2, pp. 326–338; J. Welch and J. Byrne, "Jack: Straight from the Gut," *Journal of Small Business Strategy* (2002), Vol. 13, No. 2, pp. 97–99.

43. "Doing What's Right," *Entrepreneur* (March 2003), p. 52.

44. N. W. Van Yperen and O. Janssen, "Fatigued and Dissatisfied or Fatigued but Satisfied? Goal Orientations and Responses to High Job Demands," *Academy of Management Journal* (2002), Vol. 45, No. 6, pp. 1161–1171.

45. P. K. Mills and G. R. Ungson, "Reassessing the Limits of Structural Empowerment: Organizational Constitution and Trust as Controls," *Academy of Management Review* (2003), Vol. 28, No. 1, pp. 143–153.

46. Zahra, "Drucker's Landmark Book," 16–23.

47. McDermott, "Listening with a Purpose," 35.

48. E. C. Hollensbe and J. P. Guthrie, "Group Pay-Performance Plans: The Role of Spontaneous Goal Setting," *Academy of Management Review* (2001), Vol. 25, No. 4, pp. 864–872.

49. Ketchen, "Introduction," 95–105.

50. D. Worrell, "The Best-Relaid Plans" *Entrepreneur* (March 2003), p. 45.

51. Information taken from the McDonald's Web site at *http://www.mcdonalds.com*, accessed February 20, 2004; S. Leung, "McDonald's Makeover," *Wall Street Journal* (January 28, 2004), p. B1; S. Leung, "McDonald's to Shed Only 2 Brands," *Wall Street Journal* (December 16, 2003), p. B1; Zahra, "Drucker's Landmark Book," 16–23.

52. "Apple Plans," *Wall Street Journal* (May 16, 2001), p. A1.

53. G. DeSanctis, J. T. Glass, and I. M. Ensing, "Organization Design for R&D," *Academy of Management Executive* (2002), Vol. 16, No. 3, pp. 55–61.

54. W. P. Wan and R. E. Hoskisson, "Home Country Environments, Corporate Diversification Strategies, and Firm Performance," *Academy of Management Journal* (2003), Vol. 46, No. 1, pp. 27–45.

55. M. Zeng and X. P. Chen, "Achieving Cooperation in Multiparty Alliances: A Social Dilemma Approach to Partnership Management," *Academy of Management Review* (2003), Vol. 28, No. 4, pp. 587–605.

56. L. C. Abrams, R. Cross, E. Lesser, and D. Z. Levin, "Nurturing Interpersonal Trust in Knowledge-Sharing Networks," *Academy of Management Executive* (2003), Vol. 17, No. 4, pp. 64–71.

57. M. Peers, "Tuning Up Time Warner," *Wall Street Journal* (December 11, 2003), p. B1.

58. J. Sapsford, L. P. Cohen, and M. Langley, "J. P. Morgan Chase to Buy Bank One," *Wall Street Journal* (January 15, 2004), p. A1.

59. "The Dollar Limped to the Finish Line," *Wall Street Journal* (January 2, 2004), p. A1.

60. N. Shirouzu, "As Toyota Pushes Hard in China, a Lot is Riding on the Outcome," *Wall Street Journal* (December 8, 2003), p. A1.

61. Magretta, *What Management Is.*

62. M. Sonfield and R. N. Lussier, "The Entrepreneurial Strategy Matrix: A Model for New and Ongoing Ventures," *Business Horizons* (May/June 1997), Vol. 40, pp. 73–77.

63. R. N. Lussier, M. C. Sonfield, J. Corman, and M. McKinney, "Strategies Used by Small Business Entrepreneurs," *Mid-American Journal of Business* (2001), Vol. 16, No. 1, p. 29.

64. O. C. Richard, "Racial Diversity, Business Strategy, and Firm Performance: A Resource-Based View," *Academy of Management Journal* (2001), Vol. 43, No. 2, pp. 164–177.

65. D. J. Ketchen, Jr., "An Interview with Raymond E. Miles and Charles C. Snow," *Academy of Management Executive* (2003), Vol. 17, No. 4, pp. 97–103.

66. M. Mangalindan, "Yahoo! Gets Set to Give Google Run for Money," *Wall Street Journal* (January 6, 2004), p. B1.

67. S. E. Brunk, "From Theory to Practice: Applying Miles and Snow's Ideas to Understand and Improve Firm Performance," *Academy of Management Executive* (2003), Vol. 1, No. 4, pp. 105–108.

68. M. Porter, *Competitive Strategy: Techniques for Analyzing Industries and Competitors* (New York: The Free Press, 1980), p. 15.

69. "Searching for New Value," *Entrepreneur* (June 2003), p. 70.

70. "Good Advice," *Entrepreneur* (June 2003), p. 70.

71. K. T. Gordon, "Evolution Theory," *Entrepreneur* (January 2003), p. 74.

72. R. Harborne, "Wisdom of the CEO: The Challenge to Business Leadership in the 21st Century." Research conducted by PricewaterhouseCoopers, presented at the New England Business Administration Association International Conference, New Haven, CT, April 28, 2000. Information taken from presenter handout.

73. M. Gros, "Going Somewhere?" *Entrepreneur* (September 2003), p. 50.

74. T. J. Douglas and W. Q. Judge, "Total Quality Management Implementation and Competitive Advantage: The Role of Structural Control and Exploration," *Academy of Management Journal* (2001), Vol. 44, No. 1, pp. 158–169.

75. Zahra, "Interview with Peter Drucker," 9–12.

76. Ketchen, "Introduction," 95–105.

77. J. S. Bunderson and K. M. Sutcliffe, "Comparing Alternative Conceptualizations of Functional Diversity in Management Teams: Process and Performance Effects," *Academy of Management Journal* (2002), Vol. 45, No. 5, pp. 875–893.

78. C. Rhoads, "Success Stories," *Wall Street Journal* (September 22, 2003), pp. R1–R3.

79. Information taken from the DuPont Web site at *http://www.dupont.com*, accessed February 24, 2004; "DuPont," *Wall Street Journal* (December 2, 2003), p. A1.

80. D. Worrell, "Our Little Angels," *Entrepreneur* (January 2003), pp. 45–46.

81. M. Crossan, "Altering Theories of Learning and Action: An Interview with Chris Argyris," *Academy of Management Executive* (2003), Vol. 17, No. 2, pp. 40–46.

82. A. A. Grandey, "When 'The Show Must Go On': Surface Acting and Deep Acting as Determinants of Emotional Exhaustion and Peer-Rated Service Delivery," *Academy of Management Journal* (2003), Vol. 46, No. 1, pp. 86–96.

83. K. A. Eddleston, D. L. Kidder, and B. E. Litzky, "Who's the Boss? Contending with Competing Expectations from Customers and Management," *Academy of Management Executive* (2002), Vol. 16, No. 4, pp. 85–95.

84. A. Zardkoohi, "Do Real Options Lead to Escalation of Commitment?" *Academy of Management Review* (2004), Vol. 29, No. 1, pp. 111–119.

85. Ketchen, "Interview," 97–103.

Appendix

1. Q. R. Jett and J. M. George, "Work Interrupted: A Closer Look at the Role of Interruptions in Organizational Life," *Academy of Management Review* (2003), Vol. 28, No. 3, pp. 494–507.

2. D. A. Harrison, K. H. Price, J. H. Gavin, and A. T. Florey, "Time, Teams, and Task Performance: Changing Effects of Surface- and Deep-Level Diversity on Group Functioning," *Academy of Management Journal* (2002), Vol. 45, No. 5, pp. 1029–1045.

3. M. Diener, "Looking for a Punch in the Nose?" *Entrepreneur* (March 2003), p. 63.

4. "Buddy, Can You Spare Some Time?" *Wall Street Journal* (January 26, 2004), p. B1.

5. Jett and George, "Work Interrupted," 494–507.

6. Magretta, *What Management Is: How It Works and Why It's Everyone's Business* (New York: The Free Press, 2002.

7. E. K. Yakura, "Charting Time: Timelines as Temporal Boundary Objects," *Academy of Management Journal* (2002), Vol. 45, No. 5, pp. 956–970.

8. Harrison et al., "Time, Teams, and Task Performance," 1029–1045.

9. Yakura, "Charting Time," 956–970.

10. J. Magretta, *What Management Is*.

11. Yakura, "Charting Time," 956–970.

12. M. J. Waller, M. E. Zellmer-Bruhn, and R. C. Giambatista, "Watching the Clock: Group Pacing Behavior Under Dynamic Deadlines," *Academy of Management Journal* (2002), Vol. 45, No. 5, pp. 1046–1055.

13. Waller, Zellmer-Bruhn, and Giambatista, "Watching the Clock," 1046–1055.

14. C. Penttila, "Employee Interrupted," *Entrepreneur* (February 2003), pp. 66–67.

Chapter 6

1. J. Magretta, *What Management Is: How It Works and Why It's Everyone's Business* (New York: The Free Press, 2002).

2. S. A. Zahra, *The Practice of Management*: Reflections on Peter F. Drucker's Landmark Book," *Academy of Management Executive* (2003), Vol. 17, No. 3, pp. 16–23.

3. G. DeSanctis, J. T. Glass, and I. M. Ensing, "Organization Designs for R&D," *Academy of Management Executive* (2002), Vol. 16, No. 3, pp. 55–61.

4. J. Child and R. G. McGrath, "Organizations Unfettered: Organizational Form in an Information-Intensive Economy,"

Academy of Management Journal (2001), Vol. 44, No. 6, pp. 1135–1146.

5. W. F. Cascio, "Strategies for Responsible Restructuring," *Academy of Management Executive* (2002), Vol. 16, No. 3, pp. 80–81.

6. "H-P Plans to Reorganize," *Wall Street Journal* (December 9, 2003), p. A1.

7. "GE Announces a Reorganization," *Wall Street Journal* (December 5, 2003), p. A6.

8. S. L. Rynes, A. M. Mullenix, and C. Q. Trank, "Do Behavioral Skills Increase the Employability of Business Students?," *Journal of Career Centers* (Summer 2001), pp. 40–43.

9. "Managers Oversee," *Wall Street Journal* (January 9, 2001), p. A1.

10. L. Thompson, "Improving the Creativity of Organizational Work Groups," *Academy of Management Executive* (2003), Vol. 17, No. 1, pp. 96–109; Cascio, "Responsible Restructuring," 80–81.

11. N. L. Torres, "Top-Heavy," *Entrepreneur* (January 2004), pp. 30–31; C. Bendersky, "Organizational Dispute Resolution Systems: A Complementarities Model," *Academy of Management Review* (2003), Vol. 29, No. 4, pp. 643–656.

12. P. Lawrence and J. Lorsch, *Organization and Environment* (Burr Ridge, IL: Irwin, 1967).

13. Zahra, "Drucker's Landmark Book," 16–23.

14. DeSanctis, Glass, and Ensing, "R&D," 55–61.

15. Thompson, "Organizational Work Groups," 96–109.

16. B. C. Skaggs and T. R. Huffman, "A Customer Interaction Approach to Strategy and Production Complexity Alignment in Service Firms," *Academy of Management Journal* (2003), Vol. 46, No. 6, pp. 775–786.

17. M. M. Montoya-Weiss, A. P. Massey, and M. Song, "Getting It Together: Temporal Coordination and Conflict Management in Global Virtual Teams," *Academy of Management Journal* (2001), Vol. 44, No. 6, pp. 1251–1262.

18. Zahra, "Drucker's Landmark Book," 16–23.

19. L. Bossidy, "The Job No CEO Should Delegate," *Harvard Business Review* (2001), Vol. 79, No. 3, p. 47.

20. P. K. Mills and G. R. Ungson, "Reassessing the Limits of Structural Empowerment: Organizational Constitution and Trust as Controls," *Academy of Management Review* (2003), Vol. 28, No. 1, pp. 143–153.

21. S. K. Majumdar and A. A. Marcus, "Rules Versus Discretion: The Productivity Consequences of Flexible Regulation," *Academy of Management Journal* (2001), Vol. 44, No. 1, pp. 170–179.

22. K. A. Eddleston, D. L. Kidder, and B. E. Litzky, "Who's the Boss? Contending with Competing Expectations from Customers and Management," *Academy of Management Executive* (2002), Vol. 16, No. 4, pp. 85–95.

23. D. J. Ketchen, Jr., "An Interview with Raymond E. Miles and Charles C. Snow," *Academy of Management Executive* (2003), Vol. 17, No. 4, pp. 97–103.

24. N. W. Van Yperen and M. Hagedoorn, "Do High Job Demands Increase Intrinsic Motivation or Fatigue or Both? The Role of Job Control and Job Social Support," *Academy of Mangement Journal* (2003), Vol. 46, No. 3, pp. 339–348.

25. N. W. Biggart and R. Delbridge, "Systems of Exchange," *Academy of Management Review* (2004), Vol. 29, No. 1, pp. 28–49.

26. J. S. Bunderson, "Team Member Functional Background and Involvement in Management Teams: Direct Effects and the Moderating Role of Power Centralization," *Academy of Management Journal* (2003), Vol. 48, No. 4, pp. 458–474.

27. R. C. Ford, "Pierre Bellon, Founder and President-Director General of Sodexho Alliance, on Working Hard and Having Fun," *Academy of Management Executive* (2003), Vol. 17, No. 1, pp. 38–45.

28. Bendersky, "Dispute Resolution Systems," 643–656.

29. R. A. Guth, "Midlife Correction: Inside Microsoft, Financial Managers Win New Clout," *Wall Street Journal* (July 23, 2003), p. A1.

30. DeSanctis, Glass, and Ensing, "Organization Designs for R&D," 55–61.

31. H. B. Gregersen and J. H. Dyer, "Lockheed Martin Chairman and CEO Vance Coffman on Achieving Mission Success," *Academy of Management Executive* (2002), Vol. 16, No. 3, pp. 31–42.

32. Mills and Ungson, "Limits of Structural Empowerment," 143–153.

33. M. A. Schilling and H. K. Steensma, "The Use of Modular Organizational Forms: An Industry-Level Analysis," *Academy of Management Journal* (2001), Vol. 44, No. 6, pp. 1149–1168.

34. Zahra, "Drucker's Landmark Book," 16–23.

35. J. S. Bunderson and K. M. Sutcliffe, "Comparing Alternative Conceptualizations of Functional Diversity in Management Teams: Process and Performance Effects," *Academy of Management Journal* (2002), Vol 45, No. 5, pp. 875–893.

36. Bunderson, "Team Member Functional Background," 458–474.

37. J. Kurlantzick, "There's Something to Be Said for Doing Things Your Way," *Entrepreneur* (November 2003), p. 89; Information taken from the Subway Web site at *http://www.subway.com*, accessed March 9, 2004; Information taken from the TGI Friday's Web site at *http://www.tgifridays.com*, accessed March 9, 2004.

38. Thompson, "Creativity of Organizational Work Groups," 96–109.

39. Thompson, "Creativity of Organizational Work Groups," 96–109.

40. W. P. Wan and R. E. Hoskisson, "Home Country Environments, Corporate Diversification Strategies, and Firm

Performance," *Academy of Management Journal* (2003), Vol. 46, No. 1, pp. 27–45.

41. J. C. Kennedy, "YTL Corporation's CEO Tan Sri Dato Francis Yeoh on Providing World-Class Products at Third-World Prices," *Academy of Management Executive* (2002), Vol. 16, No. 3, pp. 27–28.

42. G. Chen and R. J. Klimoski, "The Impact of Expectations on Newcomer Performance in Teams, as Mediated by Work Characteristics, Social Exchanges, and Empowerment," *Academy of Management Journal* (2003), Vol. 48, No. 5, pp. 591–607.

43. E. W. Morrison, "Newcomers' Relationships: The Role of Social Network Ties During Socialization," *Academy of Management Journal* (2002), Vol. 45, No. 6, pp. 1149–1160.

44. T. G. Pollock, J. F. Porac, and J. B. Wade, "Constructing Deal Networks: Brokers as Network 'Architects' in the U.S. IPO Market and Other Examples," *Academy of Management Review* (2004), Vol. 29, No. 1, pp. 50–72.

45. F. J. Flynn, "How Much Should I Give and How Often? The Effects of Generosity and Frequency of Favor Exchange on Social Status and Productivity," *Academy of Management Journal* (2003), Vol. 46, No. 5, pp. 539–553.

46. J. Welch and J. Byrne, "Jack: Straight from the Gut," *Journal of Small Business Strategy* (2002), Vol. 13, No. 2, pp. 97–99.

47. M. R. Subramani and N. Venkatraman, "Safeguarding Investments in Asymmetric Interorganizational Relationships: Theory and Evidence," *Academy of Management Journal* (2003), Vol. 46, No. 1, pp. 46–62.

48. Pollock, Porac, and Wade, "Constructing Deal Networks," 50–72.

49. M. G. Seo, "Overcoming Emotional Barriers, Political Obstacles, and Control Imperatives in the Action-Science Approach to Individual and Organizational Learning," *Academy of Management Learning and Education* (2003), Vol. 2, No. 1, pp. 7–21.

50. P. M. Senge, "Taking Personal Change Seriously: The Impact of Organizational Learning on Management Practice," *Academy of Management Executive* (2003), Vol. 17, No. 2, pp. 47–50.

51. A. E. Schreifer, "Beyond Cyberspace: The Workplace of the Future," *Strategy & Leadership* (2001), Vol. 29, No. 1, p. 3.

52. Child and McGrath, "Organizations Unfettered," 1135–1146.

53. M. L. Lengnick-Hall and C. A. Lengnick-Hall, " HR's Role in Building Relationship Networks," *Academy of Management Executive* (2003), Vol. 17, No. 4, pp. 53–65.

54. Zahra, "Drucker's Landmark Book," 16–23.

55. C. R. Leana and B. Barry, "Stability and Change as Simultaneous Experiences in Organizational Life," *Academy of Management Review* (2001), Vol. 25, No. 4, pp. 753–759.

56. Van Yperen and Hagedoorn, "High Job Demands," 339–348.

57. M. C. Bolino, W. H. Turnley, and J. M. Bloodgood, "Citizenship Behavior and the Creation of Social Capital in Organizations," *Academy of Management Review* (2002), Vol. 27, No. 4, pp. 505–522.

58. Chen and Klimoski, "Impact of Expectations," 591–607.

59. Flynn, "How Much Should I Give," 539–553.

60. J. E. Perry-Smith and C. E. Shalley, "The Social Side of Creativity: A Static and Dynamic Social Network Perspective," *Academy of Management Review* (2003), Vol. 28, No. 1, pp. 89–106; R. Hackman and G. Oldham, *Work Redesign* (Reading, MA: Addison-Wesley, 1980).

61. J. B. Miner, "The Rated Importance, Scientific Validity, and Practical Usefulness of Organizational Behavior Theories: A Quantitative Review," *Academy of Management Learning and Education* (2003), Vol. 2, No. 3, pp. 250–268.

62. J. Kickul and M. A. Liao-Troth, "The Meaning Behind the Message: Climate Perceptions and the Psychological Contract," *Mid-American Journal of Business* (2003), Vol. 18, No. 2, pp. 23–36.

63. "Ideas to Use When Delegating," *Communication Briefings* (2003), Vol. XX, No. 1, p. 8.

64. Zahra, "Drucker's Landmark Book," 16–23.

65. S. Shellenbarger, "Taking an 'Inner Vacation': How to Relax When You're Chained to Your Desk," *Wall Street Journal* (October 9, 2003), p. D1.

66. This section and Skill Builder 1 are adapted from Harbridge House training materials (Boston).

67. Shellenbarger, "Taking an 'Inner Vacation,'" D1.

68. R. Wolter, "Take a Breather," *Entrepreneur* (December 2003), pp. 134–135.

69. K. D. I. Tuzaman, "Glad That's Over," *Entrepreneur* (December 2002), p. 38.

70. Wolter, "Take a Breather," 134–135.

71. T. Pollock, "Mind Your Own Business," *Supervision* (2001), Vol. 62, No. 2, p. 16.

72. C. Wittmeyer, "*The Practice of Management*: Timeless Views and Principles," *Academy of Management Executive* (2003), Vol. 17, No. 3, pp. 13–15.

73. Guth, "Midlife Correction," A1.

74. "Ideas to Use When Delegating," 8.

75. M. J. Waller, M. E. Zellmer-Bruhn, and R. C. Giambatista, "Watching the Clock: Group Pacing Behavior Under Dynamic Deadlines," *Academy of Management Journal* (2002), Vol. 45, No. 5, pp. 1046–1055.

76. Pollock, "Mind Your Own Business," 16.

77. "Ideas to Use When Delegating," 8.

78. "Ideas to Use When Delegating," 8.

Chapter 7

1. M. G. Seo, "Overcoming Emotional Barriers, Political Obstacles, and Control Imperatives in the Action-Science Approach to Individual and Organizational Learning," *Academy of Management Learning and Education* (2003), Vol 2, No. 1, pp. 7–21; R. Hogan and R. Warrenfeltz, "Education of the Modern Manager," *Academy of Management Learning and Education* (2003), Vol. 2, No. 1, pp. 74–84.

2. J. Loewenstein and L. Thompson, "Analogical Learning in Negotiation Teams: Comparing Cases Promotes Learning and Transfer," *Academy of Management Learning and Education* (2003), Vol. 2, No. 2, pp. 119–127; S. L. Rynes, A. M. Mullenix, and C. Q. Trank, "Do Behavioral Skills Increase the Employability of Business Students?" *Journal of Career Centers* (Summer 2001), pp. 40–43.

3. G. S. Van Der Vegt, E. Van De Vliert, and A. Oosterhof, "Informational Dissimilarity and Organizational Citizenship Behavior: The Role of Intrateam Interdependence and Team Identification," *Academy of Management Journal* (2003), Vol. 46, No. 6, pp. 715–727.

4. M. Peers and N. Wingfield, "Blockbuster Set to Offer Movies by Mail," *Wall Street Journal* (February 11, 2004), pp. D1, D4.

5. T. G. Pollock, J. F. Porac, and J. B. Wade, "Constructing Deal Networks: Brokers as Network 'Architects' in the U.S. IPO Market and Other Examples," *Academy of Management Review* (2004), Vol. 29, No. 1, pp. 50–72.

6. G. DeSanctis, J. T. Glass, and I. M. Ensing, "Organization Design for R&D," *Academy of Management Executive* (2002), Vol. 16, No. 3, pp. 55–61.

7. A. Chang, P. Bordia, and J. Duck, "Punctuated Equilibrium and Linear Progression: Toward a New Understanding of Group Development," *Academy of Management Journal* (2003), Vol. 46, No. 1, pp. 106–117.

8. Hogan and Warrenfeltz, "Education of the Modern Manager," 74–84.

9. S. A. Zahra, "Introduction: Peter F. Drucker's *The Practice of Management*," *Academy of Management Executive* (2003), Vol. 17, No. 3, pp. 7–8.

10. B. L. Kirkman, B. Rosen, C. B. Gibson, P. E. Tesluk, and S. O. McPherson, "Five Challenges To Virtual Team Success: Lessons from Sabre, Inc.," *Academy of Management Executive* (2002), Vol. 16, No. 3, pp. 67–76.

11. P. M. Senge, "Taking Personal Change Seriously: The Impact of Organizational Learning on Management Practice," *Academy of Management Executive* (2003), Vol. 17, No. 2, pp. 47–50.

12. M. J. Lankau and T. A. Scandura, "An Investigation of Personal Learning in Mentoring Relationships: Content, Antecedents, and Consequences," *Academy of Management Journal* (2002), Vol. 45, No. 4, pp. 779–790.

13. M. J. McDermott, "Listening with a Purpose," *Chief Executive (U.S.)* (February 2001), p. 35.

14. M. J. Benner and M. L. Tushman, "Exploitation, Exploration and Process Management: The Productivity Dilemma Revisited," *Academy of Management Review* (2003), Vol. 28, No. 2, pp. 238–256.

15. Seo, "Overcoming Emotional Barriers," 7–21.

16. C. J. Collins and K. D. Clark, "Strategic Human Resource Practices, Top Management Team Social Networks, and Firm Performance: The Role of Human Resource Practices in Creating Organizational Competitive Advantage," *Academy of Management Journal* (2003), Vol. 46, No. 6, pp. 740–751; Seo, "Overcoming Emotional Barriers," 7–21.

17. Seo, "Overcoming Emotional Barriers," 7–21.

18. Collins and Clark, "Strategic Human Resource Practices," 740–751.

19. Information taken from the NCR Web site at *http://www.ncr.com*, accessed March 16, 2004.

20. C. W. L. Hill and F. T. Rothaermel, "The Performance of Incumbent Firms in the Face of Radical Technological Innovation," *Academy of Management Review* (2003), Vol. 28, No. 2, pp. 257–274.

21. R. L. Rundle, "Web School Lets Young Athletes Study and Play," *Wall Street Journal* (March 9, 2004), pp. B1, B8.

22. S. A. Zahra, "*The Practice of Management*: Reflections on Peter F. Drucker's Landmark Book," *Academy of Management Executive* (2003), Vol. 17, No. 3, pp. 16–23.

23. S. M. Lee, "Samsung CEO Ki Tae Lee on Expanding the Global Market," *Academy of Management Executive* (2003), Vol. 17, No. 2, pp. 27–29.

24. L. Varricchionne, "Session Examines Transformational Leadership Skills," *Nation's Cities Weekly* (March 19, 2001), Vol. 24, No. 11, p. 13.

25. J. C. Quick and J. H. Gavin, "The Next Frontier: Edgar Schein on Organization Therapy," *Academy of Management Executive* (2000), Vol. 14, No. 1, pp. 31–38.

26. N. L. Torres, "Playing Well with Others," *Entrepreneur* (February 2003), p. 30.

27. "More Top Tips," *Communication Briefings* (2003), Vol. XX, No. 1, p. 8.

28. Torres, "Playing Well with Others," 30.

29. Quick and Gavin, "The Next Frontier," 31–38.

30. T. J. Rowley and M. Moldoveanu, "When Will Stakeholder Groups Act? An Interest- And Identity-Base Model of Stakeholder Group Mobilization," *Academy of Management Review* (2003), Vol. 28, No. 2, pp. 204–219.

31. B. Farber, "Star Power," *Entrepreneur* (December 2003), p. 102.

32. K. Hultman, *The Path of Least Resistance* (Austin, TX: Learning Concepts, 1979).

33. N. Madjar, G. R. Oldham, and M. G. Pratt, "There's No Place Like Home? The Contributions of Work and Nonwork Creativity Support to Employees' Creative Performance,"

Academy of Management Journal (2002), Vol. 45, No. 4, pp. 757–767.

34. A. R. Jassawalla and H. C. Sashittal, "Cultures That Support Product-Innovation Processes," *Academy of Management Executive* (2002), Vol. 16, No. 3, pp. 42–43.

35. Information taken from the Intel Web site at *http://ww.intel.com*, accessed March 17, 2004.

36. D. J. Ketchen, Jr., "An Interview with Raymond E. Miles and Charles C. Snow," *Academy of Management Executive* (2003), Vol. 17, No. 4, pp. 97–103; S. G. Green, M. A. Welsh, and G. E. Dehler, "Advocacy, Performance, and Threshold Influences on Decisions to Terminate New Product Development," *Academy of Management Journal* (2003), Vol. 46, No. 4, pp. 419–434; L. C. Abrams, R. Cross, E. Lesser, and D. Z. Levin, "Nurturing Interpersonal Trust in Knowledge-Sharing Networks," *Academy of Management Executive* (2003), Vol. 17, No. 4, pp. 64–71.

37. S. A. Zahra, "An Interview with Peter Drucker," *Academy of Management Executive* (2003), Vol. 17, No. 3, pp. 9–12.

38. M. Henricks, "Worth a Try," *Entrepreneur* (February 2003), pp. 65–66.

39. D. K. Berman, "Telecoms Embrace Internet Calling, But Is It Trouble?" *Wall Street Journal* (December 29, 2003), p. B1.

40. Hogan and Warrenfeltz, "Education of the Modern Manager," 74–84.

41. Jassawalla and Sashittal, "Cultures That Support Product-Innovation Processes," 42–43; "Walk the Talk," *Communication Briefings* (2003), Vol. XX, No. 1, p. 4; McDermott, "Listening with a Purpose," 35; J. Weaver, "Fuel the Fire," *Entrepreneur* (December 2003), p. 98; W. B. Swann, Jr., J. T Polzer, D. C. Seyle, and S. J. Ko, "Finding Value in Diversity: Verification of Personal and Social Self-Views in Diverse Groups," *Academy of Management Review* (2004), Vol. 29, No. 1, pp. 9–27.

42. Information taken from the SAP Web site at *http://www.sap.com*, accessed March 17, 2004.

43. Information taken from the Fluor Web site at *http://www.fluor.com*, accessed March 17, 2004.

44. K. J. Delaney and D. Bank, "Large Software Customers Refuse to Get with the Program," *Wall Street Journal* (January 2, 2004), p. A1, A6.

45. A. E. Randel and K. S. Jaussi, "Functional Background Identity, Diversity, and Individual Performance in Cross-Functional Teams," *Academy of Management Journal* (2003), Vol. 46, No. 6, pp. 763–774; Swann et al., "Finding Value in Diversity," 9–27.

46. S. H. Tucker, and K. L. Hill, "Women's Status in the US Workforce 2000+," *Academy of Entrepreneurship Journal* (2002), Vol. 8, No. 2, pp. 17–33.

47. C. Bendersky, "Organizational Dispute Resolution Systems: A Complementarities Model," *Academy of Management Review* (2003), Vol. 29, No. 4, pp. 643–656.

48. "Nonwhite Public Ratio," *Wall Street Journal* (June 24, 2003), p. A1.

49. "The Number of Immigrants," *Wall Street Journal* (March 10, 2003), p. A1; B. Farber, "Back to Basics," *Entrepreneur* (January 2004), pp. 78–79.

50. "Census 2000," *Wall Street Journal* (March 8, 2001), p. A24.

51. O. C. Richard, "Racial Diversity, Business Strategy, and Firm Performance: A Resource-Based View," *Academy of Management Journal* (2001), Vol. 43, No. 2, pp. 164–177.

52. S. Brickson, "The Impact of Identity Orientation on Individual and Organizational Outcomes in Demographically Diverse Setting," *Academy of Management Review* (2001), Vol. 25, No. 1, pp. 82–101.

53. J. A. Howard-Grenville and A. J. Hoffman, "The Importance of Cultural Framing to the Success of Social Initiatives in Business," *Academy of Management Executive* (2003), Vol. 17, No. 2, pp. 70–86.

54. D. Ucbanaran, A. Lockett, M. Wright, and P. Westhead, "Entrepreneurial Founder Teams: Factors Associated with Member Entry and Exit," *Entrepreneurship Theory and Practice* (2003), Vol. 28, No. 2, pp. 107–118.

55. Swann et al., "Finding Value in Diversity," 9–27.

56. Tucker and Hill, "Women's Status," 17–33.

57. S. Shellenbarger, "Number of Women Managers Rises," *Wall Street Journal* (September 30, 2003), p. D2.

58. Tucker and Hill, "Women's Status," 17–33.

59. C. Hymowitz, "In Turbulent Climate, Pioneering Women Face Special Scrutiny," *Wall Street Journal* (March 31, 2001).

60. Shellenbarger, "Women Managers," D2; Tucker and Hill, "Women's Status," 17–33.

61. S. C. de Janasz, S. E. Sullivan, and V. Whiting, "Mentor Networks and Career Success: Lessons for Turbulent Times," *Academy of Management Executive* (2003), Vol. 17, No. 4, pp. 78–85.

62. J. S. Lublin, "How to Win Support from Colleagues at Your New Job," *Wall Street Journal* (November 25, 2003), p. B1.

63. C. Hymowitz, "Women Put Noses to the Grindstone, and Miss Opportunities," *Wall Street Journal* (February 19, 2004), p. B1.

64. E. Biech, "Executive Commentary," *Academy of Management Executive* (2003), Vol. 17, No. 4, p. 92.

65. M. Crossan, "Altering Theories of Learning and Action: An Interview with Chris Argyris," *Academy of Management Executive* (2003), Vol. 17, No. 2, pp. 40–46.

66. M. Crossan, "Chris Argyris and Donald Schon's *Organizational Learning*: There Is No Silver Bullet," *Academy of Management Executive* (2003), Vol. 17, No. 2, pp. 38–39.

67. R. Coff, "Bidding Wars over R&D-Intensive Firms: Knowledge, Opportunism, and the Market for Corporate Control," *Academy of Management Journal* (2003), Vol. 46, No. 1, pp. 74–85.

68. Hogan and Warrenfeltz, "Education of the Modern Manager," 74–84.

69. Information taken from the Fortune Web site at *http://www.fortune.com*, accessed March 17, 2004.

70. P. J. Brews and C. L. Tucci, "Internetworking: Building Internet-Generation Companies," *Academy of Management Executive* (2003), Vol. 17, No. 4, pp. 8–20.

71. B. Beersma, J. R. Hooenbeck, H. Moon, D. E. Conlon, and D. R. Ilgen, "Cooperation, Competition, and Team Performance: Toward a Contingency Approach," *Academy of Management Journal* (2003), Vol. 46, No. 5, pp. 572–590.

72. J. S. Bunderson and K. M. Sutcliffe, "Comparing Alternative Conceptualizations of Functional Diversity in Management Teams: Process and Performance Effects," *Academy of Management Journal* (2002), Vol. 45, No. 5, pp. 875–893.

73. Bunderson and Sutcliffe, "Conceptualizations of Functional Diversity," 875–893.

74. R. Daft and D. Marcic, *Understanding Management*, 4e (Mason, OH: South-Western, 2004).

Chapter 8

1. I. O. Williamson and D. M. Cable, "Organizational Hiring Patterns, Interfirm Network Ties, and Interorganizational Imitation," *Academy of Management Journal* (2003), Vol. 46, No. 3, pp. 349–358.

2. M. P. Brown, M. C. Thurman, and M. J. Simmering, "Compensation Policy and Organizational Performance: The Efficiency, Operational, and Financial Implications of Pay Levels and Pay Structure," *Academy of Management Journal* (2003), Vol. 46, No. 6, pp. 752–762.

3. S. L. Rynes, K. G. Brown, and A. E. Colbert, "Seven Common Misconceptions about Human Resource Practices: Research Findings versus Practitioner Beliefs," *Academy of Management Executive* (2003), Vol. 16, No. 3, pp. 92–104.

4. M. L. Lengnick-Hall and C. A. Lengnick-Hall, "HR's Role in Building Relationship Networks," *Academy of Management Executive* (2003), Vol. 17, No. 4, pp. 53–65; B. S. Klass, "Professional Employer Organizations and Their Role in Small and Medium Enterprises: The Impact of HR Outsourcing," *Entrepreneurship Theory and Practice* (2003), Vol. 28, No. 1, pp. 43–51.

5. Rynes, Brown, and Colbert, "Seven Common Misconceptions," 92–104.

6. B. L. Kirkman, B. Rosen, C. B. Gibson, P. E. Tesluk, and S. O. McPherson, "Five Challenges to Virtual Team Success: Lessons from Sabre, Inc.," *Academy of Management Executive* (2002), Vol. 16, No. 3, pp. 67–76.

7. Information taken from the KnowledgePoint Web site at *http://www.knowledgepoint.com*, accessed March 23, 2004.

8. "They Ask What?" *Wall Street Journal* (March 27, 2001).

9. L. Gratton and C. Truss, "The Three-Dimensional People Strategy: Putting Human Resources Policies into Action," *Academy of Management Executive* (2003), Vol. 17, No. 3, pp. 74–86.

10. J. Barthelemy, "The Seven Deadly Sins of Outsourcing," *Academy of Management Executive* (2003), Vol. 17, No. 2, pp. 87–98.

11. Information taken from the Young Electric Sign Web site at *http://www.yesco.com*, accessed March 19, 2004; R. Daft and D. Marcic, *Understanding Management*, 4e (Mason, OH: South-Western, 2004).

12. Information taken from the Ceridian Web site at *http://www.ceridian.com*, accessed on March 19, 2004.

13. J. Magretta, *What Management Is: How It Works and Why It's Everyone's Business* (New York: The Free Press, 2002).

14. C. J. Collins and K. D. Clark, "Strategic Human Resources Practices, Top Management Team Social Networks, and Firm Performance: The Role of Human Resource Practices in Creating Organizational Competitive Advantage," *Academy of Management Journal* (2003), Vol. 46, No. 6, pp. 740–751.

15. Gratton and Truss, "Three-Dimensional People Strategy," 74–86.

16. S. A. Zahra, "Introduction: Peter F. Drucker's *The Practice of Management*," *Academy of Management Executive* (2003), Vol. 17, No. 3, pp. 7–8.

17. Williamson and Cable, "Organizational Hiring Patterns," 349–358.

18. Information taken from the Job Descriptions Web site at *http://www.jobdescription.com*, accessed March 23, 2004.

19. D. Newton, "Of One Mind," *Entrepreneur* (August 2003), p. 23.

20. J. Sandberg, "Short Hours, Big Pay and Other Little Lies from Your Future Boss," *Wall Street Journal* (October 22, 2003), p. B1.

21. R. Hogan and R. Warrenfeltz, "Education of the Modern Manager," *Academy of Management Learning and Education* (2003), Vol. 2, No. 1, pp. 74–84.

22. S. D. Friedman and S. Lobel, "The Happy Workaholic: A Role Model for Employees," *Academy of Management Executive* (2003), Vol. 17, No. 3, pp. 87–98.

23. "Good as Gold," *Entrepreneur* (August 2003), p. 60.

24. "The Checkoff," *Wall Street Journal* (December 12, 2000), p. C1.

25. M. C. Bolino and W. H. Turnley, "Going the Extra Mile: Cultivating and Managing Employee Citizenship Behavior," *Academy of Management Executive* (2003), Vol. 17, No. 3, pp. 60–71.

26. S. L. Rynes, A. M. Mullenix, and C. Q. Trank, "Do Behavioral Skills Increase the Employability of Business Students?" *Journal of Career Centers* (Summer 2001), pp. 40–43.

27. Bolino and Turnley, "Going the Extra Mile," 60–71.

28. Williamson and Cable, "Organizational Hiring Patterns," 349–358.

29. Williamson and Cable, "Organizational Hiring Patterns," 349–358.

30. "A Question for Candidates," *Communication Briefings* (2003), Vol. XX, No. 1, p. 7.

31. Bolino and Turnley, "Going the Extra Mile," 60–71.

32. Adapted from R. Lussier, "Selecting Qualified Candidates through Effective Job Interviewing," *Clinical Laboratory Management Review* (1995), Vol. 9, No. 4, pp. 267–275.

33. A. Jehan, "Will Work for Pizza," *Entrepreneur* (January 2003), p. 38.

34. J. Schaubroeck and S. S. K. Lam, "How Similarity to Peers and Supervisor Influences Organizational Advancement in Different Cultures," *Academy of Management Journal* (2002), Vol. 45, No. 6, pp. 1120–1136.

35. J. Loewenstein and L. Thompson, "Analogical Learning in Negotiation Teams: Comparing Cases Promotes Learning and Transfer," *Academy of Management Learning and Education* (2003), Vol. 2, No. 2, pp. 119–127.

36. S. A. Zahra, "The Practice of Management: Reflections on Peter F. Drucker's Landmark Book," *Academy of Management Executive* (2003), Vol. 17, No. 3, pp. 16–23.

37. A. Argyris, "Double-Loop Learning, Teaching, and Research," *Academy of Management Learning and Education* (2002), Vol. 1, No. 2, pp. 206–218.

38. G. Detrick, "Interview with Russell L. Ackoff," *Academy of Management Learning and Education* (2002), Vol. 1, No. 1, pp. 56–63.

39. J. Pfeffer and R. I. Sutton, *The Knowing–Doing Gap* (Harvard Business School Publishing, 2000).

40. "Intel Cost-Cutting Spares a College Tour," *Wall Street Journal* (June 14, 2001), p. A1.

41. Bolino and Turnley, "Going the Extra Mile," 60–71.

42. Gratton and Truss, "Three-Dimensional People Strategy," 74–86.

43. Bolino and Turnley, "Going the Extra Mile," 60–71.

44. Gratton and Truss, Three-Dimensional People Strategy," 74–86.

45. "Performance Appraisal Discussion," *WFCR Public Radio* (January 3, 2001).

46. C. Hymowitz, "How to Tell Employees All the Things They Don't Want to Hear," *Management* (August 22, 2001), p. B1.

47. Bolino and Turnley, "Going the Extra Mile," 60–71.

48. Schaubroeck and Lam, "Similarity to Peers and Supervisor," 1120–1136.

49. Information taken from the Performance Reviews Web site at *http://www.performancereviews.com*, accessed March 25, 2004.

50. G. Toegel and J. A. Conger, "360-Degree Assessment: Time for Reinvention," *Academy of Management Learning and Education* (2003), Vol. 2, No. 3, pp. 297–311.

51. E. Biech, "Executive Commentary," *Academy of Management Executive* (2003), Vol. 17, No. 4, p. 92.

52. P. Brandes, R. Dharwadkar, and G. V. Lemesis, "Effective Employee Stock Option Design: Reconciling Stakeholder, Strategic, and Motivational Factors," *Academy of Management Executive* (2003), Vol. 17, No. 1, pp. 77–93.

53. T. R. Mitchell, B. C. Holtom, and T. W. Lee, "How to Keep Your Best Employees: Developing an Effective Retention Policy," *Academy of Management Executive* (2001), Vol. 15, No. 4, pp. 96–108.

54. Friedman and Lobel, "The Happy Workaholic," 87–98.

55. Hogan and Warrenfeltz, "Education of the Modern Manager," 74–84.

56. Mitchell, Holtom, and Lee, "Keep Your Best Employees," 96–108.

57. Brandes, Dharwadkar, and Lemesis, "Effective Employee Stock Option Design," 77–93.

58. Brown, Sturman, and Simmering, "Compensation Policy and Organizational Performance," 752–762.

59. R. Griffin, *Fundamentals of Management*, 3e (Boston: Houghton Mifflin, 2003), p. 240.

60. A. Zimmerman, "Costco's Dilemma: Be Kind to Its Workers, or Wall Street?" *Wall Street Journal* (March 26, 2004), pp. B1–B3.

61. Information taken from the Putnam Web site at *http://www.putnam.com*, accessed March 30, 2004; "Putnam Is Dropping Its . . . ," *Wall Street Journal* (November 26, 2003), pp. A1, C1.

62. Zahra, "Drucker's Landmark Book," 16–23.

63. Bolino and Turnley, "Going the Extra Mile," 60–71.

64. J. G. Combs and M. S. Skill, "Managerialist and Human Capital Explanations for Key Executive Pay Premiums: A Contingency Perspective," *Academy of Management Journal* (2003), Vol. 46, No. 1, pp. 63–73.

65. M. G. Pratt and J. A. Rosa, "Transforming Work-Family Conflict into Commitment in Network Marketing Organizations," *Academy of Management Journal* (2003), Vol. 46, No. 4, pp. 395–418.

66. "How Loyalty Comes by Degrees," *Wall Street Journal* (May 17, 2001), p. C1.

67. R. Lieber and B. Martinez, "Companies Pass the Buck on Benefits," *Wall Street Journal* (November 26, 2002), p. D1.

68. "Employer Health Benefit Costs Rose," *Wall Street Journal* (December 9, 2002), p. A1.

69. M. M. Arthur, "Share Price Reactions to Work-Family Initiatives: An Institutional Perspective," *Academy of Management Journal* (2003), Vol. 46, pp. 497–505.

70. Bolino and Turnley, "Going the Extra Mile," 60–71.

71. M. Henricks, "Take Your Pick," *Entrepreneur* (May 2003), p. 69.

72. S. S. Ariss, "Employee Involvement to Improve Safety in the Workplace: An Ethical Imperative," *Mid-American Journal of Business* (2003), Vol. 18, No. 2, pp. 9–18.

73. M. Prince, "Violence in the Workplace on the Rise; Training, Zero Tolerance Can Prevent Aggression," *Business Insurance* (May 12, 2003), p. 1.

74. J. P. Guthrie, "High-Involvement Work Practices, Turnover, and Productivity: Evidence from New Zealand," *Academy of Management Journal* (2001), Vol. 44, No. 1, pp. 180–190.

75. "Grading Employees," *Wall Street Journal* (February 20, 2001), p. A1.

76. Information taken from the HRTools Web site at *http://www.hrtools.com*, accessed March 30, 2004.

Appendix

1. R. D. Ramsey, "15 Time Wasters for Supervisors," *Supervision* (2000), Vol. 61, No. 6, p. 10.

2. T. Pollock, "A Personal File of Stimulating Ideas, Little-Known Facts and Daily Problem Solvers," *Supervision* (2000), Vol. 61, No. 3, p. 13.

3. J. Pollock, "Stimulating Ideas," 13.

4. Collins and K. D. Clark, "Strategic Human Resource Practices, Top Management Team Social Networks, and Firm Performance," *Academy of Management Journal* (2003), Vol. 46, No. 6, pp. 740–751.

5. "Deflect Minor Interruptions," *Communication Briefings* (2003), Vol. XX, No. 1, p. 3.

6. T. Pulliam, "Plan Your Work and Work Your Plan," *South Florida Business Journal* (2000), Vol. 20, No. 34, p. 47.

7. J. S. Lublin, "How to Win Support from Colleagues at Your New Job," *Wall Street Journal* (November 25, 2003), p. B1; M. J. Lankau and T. A. Scandura, "An Investigation of Personal Learning in Mentoring Relations," *Academy of Management Journal* (2002), Vol. 45, No. 4, pp. 779–790.

8. "The 5 Major Time Wasters," *Communication Briefings* (2003), Vol. XX, No.1, p. 5.

9. A. Gumbus, "Networking: A Long-Term Strategy," *Clinical Leadership & Management Review* (2003), Vol. 17, No. 3, pp. 151–156.

10. "How to Succeed in Business by Really Trying," *Journal of Accountancy* (2000), Vol. 190, No. 1, p. 12.

11. Information taken from the Proven Resumes Web site at *http://www.provenresumes.com*, accessed April 1, 2004.

12. R. A. Baron and G. D. Markman, "Beyond Social Capital: How Social Skills Can Enhance Entrepreneurs' Success," *Academy of Management Executive* (2000), Vol. 14, No. 1, pp. 106–116; V. U. Druskat and J. V. Wheeler, "Managing from the Boundary," *Academy of Management Journal* (2003), Vol. 46, No. 4, pp. 435–457; E. W. Morrison, "Newcomers Relationships: The Role of Social Network Ties During Socialization," *Academy of Management Journal* (2002), Vol. 45, No. 6, pp. 1149–1160.

13. P. Tharenou, "Going Up? Do Traits and Informal Social Processes Predict Advancing in Management?" *Academy of Management Journal* (2001), Vol. 44, No. 5, pp. 1005–1017.

14. S. C. de Janasz, S. E. Sullivan, and V. Whiting, "Mentor Networking and Career Success," *Academy of Management Executive* (2003), Vol. 17, No. 4, pp. 78–85.

15. S. Shellenbarger, "Along with Benefits and Pay, Employees Seek Friends on the Job," *Wall Street Journal* (February 20, 2002), p. B1.

16. A. Gumbus, "Networking: A Long-Term Strategy," *Clinical Leadership & Management Review* (2003), Vol. 17, No. 3, pp. 151–156.

17. A. Fisher, "Surviving the Downturn," *Fortune* (April 2, 2001), pp. 98–106.

18. Morrison, "Newcomers Relationships," 1149–1160.

19. A. Greve and J. W. Salaff, "Social Networks and Entrepreneurship," *Entrepreneurship Theory and Practice* (2003), Vol. 28, No. 1, pp. 1–12.

20. J. Gitomer, "The Best Places for Successful Networking," *Business Record* (2002), Vol. 18, No. 17, pp. 23–24.

21. This section is adapted with permission from A. Gumbus and R. N. Lussier, "Career Development: Enhancing Your Networking Skill," *Clinical Leadership & Management Review* (2003), Vol. 17, No. 1, pp. 16–20.

22. P. S. Adler and S. W. Kwon, "Social Capital: Prospects for a New Concept," *Academy of Management Review* (2002), Vol. 27, No. 1, pp. 17–41.

23. I. O. Williamson and D. M. Cable, "Organizational Hiring Patterns, Interfirm Network Ties, and Interorganizational Imitation," *Academy of Management Journal* (2003), Vol. 46, No. 3, pp. 349–358.

24. T. Raz, "The 10 Secrets of a Master Networker," *Inc.*, *http://www.bcentral.com*, accessed September 4, 2003.

25. A. C. Kooser, "Six Degrees," *Entrepreneur* (January 2004), p. 27.

26. B. Farber, "Booster Club," *Entrepreneur* (February 2003), p. 72.

27. B. Farber, "People Who Need People," *Entrepreneur* (May 2003), pp. 76–77.

28. A. Philippidis, "Hello, Now What? The Joys of Networking," *Westchester County Business Journal* (2002), Vol. 40, No. 6, pp. 9–10.

29. H. Clancy, "What's the Story," *Entrepreneur* (February 2003), p. 45.

30. T. G. Pollock, J. F. Porac, and J. B. Wade, "Constructing Deal Networks," *Academy of Management Review* (2002), Vol. 29, No. 1, pp. 50–72.

31. J. Quinn, "Getting Past Today's Layoffs," *Newsweek* (February 5, 2001), p. 46.

Chapter 9

1. L. A. Burke and J. E. Moore, "A Perennial Dilemma in OB Education: Engaging the Traditional Student," *Academy of Management Learning and Education* (2003), Vol. 2, No. 1, pp. 37–52.

2. B. Miner, "The Rated Importance, Scientific Validity, and Practical Usefulness of Organizational Behavior Theories: A Quantitative Review," *Academy of Management Learning and Education* (2003), Vol. 2, No. 3, pp. 250–268.

3. S. L. Rynes, A. M. Mullenix, and C. Q. Trank, "Do Behavioral Skills Increase the Employability of Business Students?" *Journal of Career Centers* (Summer 2001), pp. 40–43.

4. M. J. Lankau and T. A. Scandura, "An Investigation of Personal Learning in Mentoring Relationships: Content, Antecedents, and Consequences," *Academy of Management Journal* (2002), Vol. 45, No. 4, pp. 779–790.

5. J. Schaubroeck and S. S. K. Lam, "How Similarity to Peers and Supervisors Influences Organizational Advancement in Different Cultures," *Academy of Management Journal* (2002), Vol. 45, No. 6, pp. 1120–1136.

6. "Reacting to Difficult Types," *Communication Briefings* (2003), Vol. XX, No. 1, p. 8.

7. "Getting Along with Your Boss," *Communication Briefings* (2003), Vol. XX, No. 1, p. 6.

8. N. E. Peterman and J. Kennedy, "Enterprise Education: Influencing Students' Perceptions," *Entrepreneurship Theory and Practice* (2003), Vol. 28, No. 2, pp. 129–136.

9. Miner, "Organizational Behavior Theories," 250–268.

10. P. Perrewe, K. Zellars, G. Ferris, A. Rossi, C. Kacmar, and D. Ralston, "Neutralizing Job Stressors: Political Skills as an Antidote to the Dysfunctional Consequences of Role Conflict," *Academy of Management Journal* (2004), Vol. 47, No. 1, pp. 141–152.

11. S. S. K. Lam and J. Schaubroeck, "The Role of Locus of Control in Reactions to Being Promoted and to Being Passed Over: A Quasi-Experiment," *Academy of Management Journal* (2001), Vol. 43, No. 1, pp. 66–78.

12. N. Madjar, G. R. Oldham, and M. G. Pratt, "There's No Place Like Home? The Contributions of Work and Nonwork Creativity Support to Employees" Creative Performance," *Academy of Management Journal* (2002), Vol. 45, No. 4, pp. 757–767; H. E. Allerton, "Secrets of Leaders," *Training and Development* (March 2001), Vol. 55, No. 3, p. 15.

13. Peterman and Kennedy, "Enterprise Education," 129–136.

14. D. Kirkpatrick, "Larry to Everyone: King Me!" *Fortune* (March 5, 2001), p. 53.

15. H. Liao and A. Chuang, "A Multilevel Investigation of Factors Influencing Employee Services Performance and Customer Outcomes," *Academy of Management Journal* (2004), Vol. 47, No. 1, pp. 41–58.

16. M. C. Bolino and W. H. Turnley, "Going the Extra Mile: Cultivating and Managing Employee Citizenship Behavior," *Academy of Management Executive* (2003), Vol. 17, No. 3, pp. 60–71.

17. Bolino and Turnley, "Going the Extra Mile," 60–71.

18. B. J. Tepper and E. C. Taylor, "Relationships Among Supervisors' and Subordinates' Procedural Justice Perceptions and Organizational Citizenship Behaviors," *Academy of Management Journal* (2003), Vol. 46, No. 1, pp. 97–105.

19. Peterman and Kennedy, "Enterprise Education," 129–136.

20. Miner, "Organizational Behavior Theories," 250–268.

21. M. J. Gundlach, S. C. Douglas, and M. J. Martinko, "The Decision to Blow the Whistle: A Social Information Processing Framework," *Academy of Management Review* (2003), Vol. 28, No. 1, pp. 107–123.

22. D. A. Harrison, K. H. Price, J. H. Gavin, and A. T. Florey, "Time, Teams, and Task Performance: Changing Effects of Surface- and Deep-Level Diversity on Group Functioning," *Academy of Management Journal* (2002), Vol. 45, No. 5, pp. 1029–1045.

23. L. MacFarquhar, "The Better Boss," *The New Yorker* (April 22, 2002), pp. 114–136.

24. B. Farber, "Star Power," *Entrepreneur* (December 2003), p. 102.

25. P. Camilli, Review of *Fish! A Remarkable Way to Boost Morale and Improve Results*, *Mid-American Journal of Business* (2003), Vol. 18, No. 2, p. 62.

26. Lankau and Scandura, "Personal Learning in Mentoring Relationships," 779–790.

27. N. L. Torres, "Playing Well with Others," *Entrepreneur* (February 2003), p. 30.

28. G. Chen and R. J. Klimoski, "The Impact of Expectations on Newcomer Performance in Teams as Mediated by Work Characteristics, Social Exchanges, and Empowerment," *Academy of Management Journal* (2003), Vol. 46, No. 5, pp. 591–607.

29. M. C. Bolino, W. H. Turnley, and J. M. Bloodgood, "Citizenship Behavior and the Creation of Social Capital in Organizations," *Academy of Management Review* (2002), Vol. 27, No. 4, pp. 505–522.

30. Bolino and Turnley, "Going the Extra Mile," 60–71.

31. J. E. P. Smith and C. E. Shalley, "The Social Side of Creativity," *Academy of Management Review* (2003), Vol. 28, No. 1, pp. 89–106.

32. Bolino, Turnley, and Bloodgood, "Citizenship Behavior," 505–522.

33. Harrison et al., "Time, Teams, and Task Performance," 1029–1045; P. F. Hewlin, "And the Award for Best Actor Goes to . . .: Facades of Conformity in Organizational Settings," *Academy of Management Review* (2003), Vol. 28, No. 4, pp. 633–642; S. E. Moss and J. I. Sanchez, "Are Your Employees Avoiding You?" *Academy of Management Executive* (2004), Vol. 18, No. 1, pp. 32–44.

34. C. M. Fiol, E. J. O'Connor, and H. Aguinis, "All for One and One for All? The Development and Transfer of Power across Organizational Levels," *Academy of Management Review* (2001), Vol. 26, No. 2, pp. 224–242.

35. T. G. Pollock, H. M. Fischer, and J. Wade, "The Role of Power and Politics in the Repricing of Executive Options,"

Academy of Management Journal (2002), Vol. 45, No. 1, pp. 63–73.

36. M. G. Seo, "Overcoming Emotional Barriers, Political Obstacles, and Control Imperatives in the Action-Science Approach to Individual and Organizational Learning," *Academy of Management Learning and Education* (2003), Vol. 2, No. 1, pp. 7–21.

37. Fiol, O'Connor, and Aguinis, "All for One and One for All?" 224–242.

38. S. A. Zahra, *The Practice of Management*: Reflections on Peter F. Drucker's Landmark Book," *Academy of Management Executive* (2003), Vol. 17, No. 3, pp. 16–23.

39. J. G. Combs and M. S. Skill, "Managerialist and Human Capital Explanations for Key Executive Pay Premiums: A Contingency Perspective," *Academy of Management Journal* (2003), Vol. 46, No. 1, pp. 63–73.

40. "Carly Fiorina, Up Close," *Wall Street Journal* (January 13, 2003), pp. B1, B6.

41. J. A. Thompson and J. S. Bunderson, "Violations of Principle: Ideological Currency in the Psychological Contract," *Academy of Management Review* (2003), Vol. 28, No. 4, pp. 571–586.

42. J. S. Bunderson, "Team Member Functional Background and Involvement in Management Teams: Direct Effects and the Moderating Role of Power Centralization," *Academy of Management Journal* (2003), Vol. 46, No. 4, pp. 458–474; J. S. Lublin, "How to Win Support from Colleagues at Your New Job," *Wall Street Journal* (November 5, 2003), p. B1.

43. "How to Deal with Conflict," *Communication Briefings* (2003), Vol. XX, No. 1, p. 1.

44. Seo, "Overcoming Emotional Barriers," 7–21.

45. R. B. Pickett and M. M. Kennedy, "Career Development Strategies: Understanding and Using Organizational Politics, Part One," *Clinical Leadership and Management Review* (March/April 2004), pp. 120–122.

46. N. W. Biggart and R. Delbridge, "Systems of Exchange," *Academy of Management Review* (2004), Vol. 29, No. 1, pp. 28–49.

47. Thompson and Bunderson, "Violations of Principle," 571–586.

48. Perrewe et al., "Neutralizing Job Stressors," 141–152.

49. S. G. Green, M. A. Welsh, and G. E. Dehler, "Advocacy, Performance, and Threshold Influences on Decisions to Terminate New Product Development," *Academy of Management Journal* (2003), Vol. 46, No. 4, pp. 419–434.

50. S. Clinebell and D. J. Rowley, "Former CEO of the Security Traders Association Lee Korins on Managing Through Chaos," *Academy of Management Executive* (2003), Vol. 17, No. 2, pp. 30–36.

51. Lublin, "How to Win Support from Colleagues," p. B1.

52. F. J. Flynn, "How Much Should I Give and How Often? The Effects of Generosity and Frequency of Favor Exchange on Social Status and Productivity," *Academy of Management Journal* (2003), Vol. 46, No. 5, pp. 539–553.

53. T. M. Glomb and H. Liao, "Interpersonal Aggression in Work Groups: Social Influence, Reciprocal, and Individual Effects," *Academy of Management Journal* (2003), Vol. 46, No. 4, pp. 486–496.

54. A. Stewart, "Help One Another, Use One Another: Toward an Anthropology of Family Business," *Entrepreneurship Theory and Practice* (Summer 2003), pp. 383–396.

55. Bunderson, "Team Member Functional Background," 458–474.

56. G. Ip, K. Kelly, S. Craig, and I. J. Dugan, "How Grasso's Rule Kept NYSE on Top but Hid Deep Trouble," *Wall Street Journal* (December 30, 2003), pp. A1, A6.

57. K. Kelly, "Grasso, Spitzer Keep Door Open for a Deal Despite Tough Talk," *Wall Street Journal* (April 27, 2004), p. B1.

58. Ip et al., "Grasso's Rule," A1, A6.

59. Pickett and Kennedy, "Career Development Strategies," 120–122.

60. J. Sandberg, "Sabotage 101: The Sinister Art of Backstabbing," *Wall Street Journal* (February 11, 2004), p. B1.

61. Lublin, "How to Win Support from Colleagues," B1.

62. Pickett and Kennedy, "Career Development Strategies," 120–122.

63. K. Maher, "The Jungle: Focus on Recruitment, Pay and Getting Ahead," *Wall Street Journal* (October 21, 2003), p. D6.

64. Maher, "The Jungle," D6.

65. Maher, "The Jungle," D6.

66. Lublin, "How to Win Support from Colleagues," B1.

67. Sandberg, "Sabotage 101," B1.

68. "How to Deal with Conflict," 1.

69. C. Bendersky, "Organizational Dispute Resolution Systems: A Complementarities Model," *Academy of Management Review* (2003), Vol. 29, No. 4, pp. 643–656.

70. J. S. Bunderson and K. M. Sutcliffe, "Comparing Alternative Conceptualizations of Functional Diversity in Management Teams: Process and Performance Effects," *Academy of Management Journal* (2002), Vol. 45, No. 5, pp. 875–893.

71. J. Kickul and M. A. Liao-Troth, "The Meaning Behind the Message: Climate Perceptions and the Psychological Contract," *Mid-American Journal of Business* (2003), Vol. 18, No. 2, pp. 23–26.

72. D. M. Rousseau, "Psychological Contracts in the Workplace: Understanding the Ties that Motivate," *Academy of Management Review* (2004), Vol. 18, No. 1, pp. 120–127.

73. M. G. Pratt and J. A. Rosa, "Transforming Work-Family Conflict into Commitment in Network Marketing

Organizations," *Academy of Management Journal* (2003), Vol. 46, No. 4, pp. 395–418.

74. K. A. Eddleston, D. L. Kidder, and B. E. Litzky, "Who's the Boss? Contending with Competing Expectations from Customers and Management," *Academy of Management Executive* (2002), Vol. 16, No. 4, pp. 85–95.

75. Thompson and Bunderson, "Violations of Principle," 571–586.

76. Rousseau, "Psychological Contracts in the Workplace," 120–127.

77. S. B. Bacharach, P. A. Bamberger, and W. J. Sonnenstuhl, "Driven to Drink: Managerial Control, Work-Related Risk Factors, and Employee Problem Drinking," *Academy of Management Journal* (2002), Vol. 45, No. 4, pp. 637–658.

78. N. L. Torres, "Animal Instincts," *Entrepreneur* (February 2003), pp. 26–27.

79. M. M. Montoya-Weiss, A. P. Massey, and M. Song, "Getting It Together: Temporal Coordination and Conflict Management in Global Virtual Teams," *Academy of Management Journal* (2001), Vol. 44, No. 6, pp. 1251–1262.

80. Bendersky, "Organizational Dispute Resolution Systems," 643–656.

81. Bunderson and Sutcliffe, "Conceptualization of Functional Diversity," 875–893.

82. Moss and Sanchez, "Are Your Employees Avoiding You?" 32–44.

83. Torres, "Animal Instincts," 26–27.

84. Moss and Sanchez, "Are Your Employees Avoiding You?" 32–44.

85. Torres, "Animal Instincts," 26–27.

86. "How to Deal with Conflict," 1.

87. M. Diener, "Nothing Personal," *Entrepreneur* (October 2003), p. 85.

88. M. R. Subramani and N. Venkatraman, "Safeguarding Investments in Asymmetric Interorganizational Relationships: Theory and Evidence," *Academy of Management Journal* (2003), Vol. 46, No. 1, pp. 46–62.

89. Diener, "Nothing Personal," 85.

90. R. Lussier, "The Negotiation Process," *Clinical Leadership & Management Review* (2000), Vol. 14, No. 2, pp. 55–59.

91. M. Diener, "What's Your Hurry?" *Entrepreneur* (April 2004), p. 81.

92. B. Farber, "Fishing for Trouble," *Entrepreneur* (December 2002), p. 112.

93. B. Farber, "Back to Basics," *Entrepreneur* (January 2004), pp. 78–79.

94. Diener, "Nothing Personal," 85.

95. Subramani and Venkatraman, "Safeguarding Investments," 42–62.

96. Farber, "Fishing for Trouble," 112.

97. Diener, "What's Your Hurry?" 81.

98. B. Farber, "Target Practice," *Entrepreneur* (August 2003), p. 72.

99. B. Farber, "People Who Need People," *Entrepreneur* (May 2003), pp. 76–77.

100. Diener, "Nothing Personal," 85.

101. M. Diener, "Looking for a Punch in the Nose?" *Entrepreneur* (March 2003), p. 63.

102. C. Hymowitz, "Women Put Noses to the Grindstone and Miss Opportunities," *Wall Street Journal* (February 19, 2004), p. B1.

103. V. Patterson, "How to Negotiate Pay in a Tough Economy," *Wall Street Journal* (March 29, 2004), p. R7.

104. M. Diener, "A Tug of War," *Entrepreneur* (September 2003), p. 81.

105. Diener, "Nothing Personal," 85.

106. B. Farber, "Star Power," *Entrepreneur* (December 2003), p. 102.

107. Diener, "What's Your Hurry?" 81.

108. Diener, "Nothing Personal," 85.

109. J. Loewenstein and L. Thompson, "Analogical Learning in Negotiation Teams: Comparing Cases Promotes Learning and Transfer," *Academy of Management Learning and Education* (2003), Vol. 2, No. 2, pp. 119–127.

110. M. Diener, "Making Peace," *Entrepreneur* (January 2004), p. 75.

111. J. Dietz, S. Robinson, R. Folger, R. Baron, and M. Schulz, "The Impact of Community Violence and an Organization's Procedural Justice Climate on Workplace Aggression," *Academy of Management Journal* (2003), Vol. 46, No. 3, pp. 317–326.

112. A. A. Grandey, "When 'The Show Must Go On': Surface Acting and Deep Acting as Determinants of Emotional Exhaustion and Peer-Rated Service Delivery," *Academy of Management Journal* (2003), Vol. 46, No. 1, pp. 86–96.

113. Dietz et al., "Workplace Aggression," 317–326.

114. Margin note, *Entrepreneur* (February 2003), p. 22.

115. Perrewe, "Neutralizing Job Stressors," 141–152.

116. Bacharach, Bamberger, and Sonnenstuhl, "Driven to Drink," 637–658.

117. S. Shellenbarger, "The Power Nap's 15 Minutes Is Over," *Wall Street Journal* (October 23, 2003), p. D1.

118. S. Shellenbarger, "Polish Your Resume: E-Mail in Bed," *Wall Street Journal* (December 18, 2003), p. D1.

119. S. Shellenbarger, "Taking an 'Inner Vacation': How to Relax When You're Chained to Your Desk," *Wall Street Journal* (October 9, 2003), p. D1.

120. "Health-Care Spending Rose," *Wall Street Journal* (January 9, 2004), p. B1; "Obesity-Tied Medical Costs,"

Wall Street Journal (January 22, 2004), p. B1; "Obesity Worries," *Wall Street Journal* (March 9, 2004), p. D1; "Government Ads Urge Americans to Shed Pounds," *Wall Street Journal* (March 10, 2004), p. B1; "The House Voted," *Wall Street Journal* (March 11, 2004), p. A1.

121. The Car Dealer Negotiations confidential information is from A. G. Woodside, Tulane University. The Car Dealer Game is part of a paper, "Bargaining Behavior in Personal Selling and Buying Exchanges," presented by Dr. Woodside at the Eighth Annual Conference of the Association for Business Simulation and Experiential Learning (ABSEL), Orlando, Florida, 1980. It is used with Dr. Woodside's permission.

Chapter 10

1. L. R. Offerman and R. K. Spiros, "The Science and Practice of Team Development: Improving the Link," *Academy of Management Journal* (2001), Vol. 44, No. 2, pp. 376–392.

2. G. S. Van Der Vegt, E. Van De Vliert, and A. Oosterhof, "Informational Dissimilarity and Organizational Citizenship Behavior: The Role of Intrateam Interdependence and Team Identification, *Academy of Management Journal* (2003), Vol. 46, No. 6, pp. 715–727.

3. G. Chen, L. M. Donahue, and R. Klimoski, "Training Undergraduates to Work in Organizational Teams," *Academy of Management Learning and Education* (2003), Vol. 3, No. 1, pp. 27–40.

4. D. Harrison, K. Price, J. Gavin, and A. Florey, "Time, Teams, and Task Performance: Changing Effects of Surface- and Deep-Level Diversity on Group Functioning," *Academy of Management Journal* (2002), Vol. 45, No. 5, pp. 1029–1045.

5. L. Thompson, "Improving the Creativity of Organizational Work Groups," *Academy of Management Executive* (2003), Vol. 17, No. 1, pp. 96–109.

6. M. Waller, M. Z. Bruhn, and R. Giambastista, "Watching the Clock: Group Pacing Behavior Under Dynamic Deadlines," *Academy of Management Journal* (2002), Vol. 45, No. 5, pp. 1046–1055.

7. G. Chen and R. J. Klimoski, "The Impact of Expectations on Newcomer Performance in Teams as Mediated by Work Characteristics, Social Exchanges, and Empowerment," *Academy of Management Journal* (2003), Vol. 46, No. 5, pp. 591–607.

8. B. Beersma, J. R. Hooenbeck, H. Moon, D. E. Conlon, and D. R. Ilgen, "Cooperation, Competition, and Team Performance: Toward a Contingency Approach," *Academy of Management Journal* (2003), Vol. 46, No. 5, pp. 572–590.

9. Information taken from the JetBlue Web site at *http://www.jetblue.com*, accessed May 17, 2004.

10. Van Der Vegt et al., "Informational Dissimilarity," 715–727.

11. J. H. Grenville and A. Hoffman, "The Importance of Cultural Framing to the Success of Social Initiatives in Business," *Academy of Management Executive* (2003), Vol. 17, No. 2, pp. 70–86.

12. A. Jassawalla and H. Sashittal, "Cultures That Support Product-Innovation Processes," *Academy of Management Executive* (2002), Vol. 16, No. 3, pp. 42–54.

13. Chen et al., "Training Undergraduates," 27–40.

14. Jassawalla and Sashittal, "Product-Innovation Processes," 42–54.

15. Van der Vegt et al., "Informational Dissimilarity," 715–727.

16. M. M. Weiss, A. Massey, and M. Song, "Getting It Together: Temporal Coordination and Conflict Management in Global Virtual Teams," *Academy of Management Journal* (2001), Vol. 44, No. 6, pp. 1251–1262.

17. C. Saunders, C. Van Slyke, and D. R. Vogel, "My Time or Yours? Managing Time Visions in Global Virtual Teams," *Academy of Management Executive* (2004), Vol. 18, No. 1, pp. 19–31.

18. Saunders et al., "My Time or Yours?" 19–31.

19. E. W. Morrison, "Newcomers' Relationships: The Role of Social Network Ties During Socialization," *Academy of Management Journal* (2002), Vol. 45, No. 6, pp. 1149–1160.

20. Thompson, "Improving Creativity," 96–109.

21. M. Orlitzky and J. Benjamin, "The Effects of Sex Composition on Small-Group Performance in a Business School Case Competition," *Academy of Management Learning and Education* (2003), Vol. 2, No. 2, pp. 128–138.

22. D. Ucbasaran, A. Lockett, M. Wright, and P. Westhead, "Entrepreneurial Founder Teams: Factors Associated with Member Entry and Exit," *Entrepreneurship Theory and Practice* (2003), Winter, pp. 107–118.

23. J. S. Bunderson and K. M. Sutcliffe, "Comparing Alternative Conceptualizations of Functional Diversity in Management Teams; Process and Performance Effects," *Academy of Management Journal* (2002), Vol. 45, No. 5, pp. 875–893.

24. Beersma et al., "Cooperation, Competition, and Team Performance," 572–590.

25. R. Hogan and R. Warrenfeltz, "Educating the Modern Manager," *Academy of Management Learning and Education* (2003), Vol. 2, No. 1, pp. 74–84.

26. V. U. Druskat and J. V. Wheeler, "Managers from the Boundary: The Effective Leadership of Self-Managing Work Teams," *Academy of Management Journal* (2003), Vol. 46, No. 4, pp. 435–457.

27. E. C. Hollensbe and J. P. Guthrie, "Group Pay-Performance Plans: The Role of Spontaneous Goal Setting," *Academy of Management Review* (2001), Vol. 25, No. 4, pp. 864–872.

28. Chen and Klimoski, "Newcomer Performance in Teams," 591–607.

29. D. Knight, C. C. Durham, and E. A. Locke, "The Relationship of Team Goals, Incentives, and Efficacy to Strategic Risk, Tactical Implementation, and Performance,"

Academy of Management Journal (2001), Vol. 44, No. 2, pp. 326–338.

30. Saunders et al., "My Time or Yours?" 19–31.

31. B. Gates, "My Advice to Students: Get a Sound, Broad Education," *The Costo Connection* (February 1999), p. 13.

32. A. Chang, B. Bordia, and J. Duck, "Punctuated Equilibrium and Linear Progression: Toward a New Understanding of Group Development," *Academy of Management Journal* (2003), Vol. 46, No. 1, pp. 106–117.

33. Waller et al., "Watching the Clock," 1046–1055.

34. A. E. Randel and K. S. Jaussi, "Functional Background Identity, Diversity, and Individual Performance in Cross-Functional Teams," *Academy of Management Journal* (2003), Vol. 46, No. 6, pp. 763–774.

35. Morrison, "Newcomers' Relationships," 1149–1160.

36. Knight et al., "Team Goals, Incentives, and Efficacy," 326–338.

37. C. Gomez, B. L. Kirkman, and D. L. Shapiro, "The Impact of Collectivism and In-Group/Out-Group Membership on the Evaluation of Generosity of Team Members," *Academy of Management Journal* (2000), Vol. 43, No. 6, pp. 1097–1106.

38. S. Bacharach, P. Bamerger, and W. Sonnenstuhl, "Driven to Drink: Management Control, Work-Related Risk Factors, and Employee Problem Drinking," *Academy of Management Journal* (2002), Vol. 45, No. 4, pp. 637–658.

39. I. O. Williamson and D. M. Cable, "Organizational Hiring Patterns, Interfirm Network Ties, and Interorganizational Imitation," *Academy of Management Journal* (2003), Vol. 46, No. 3, pp. 349–358.

40. L. K. Scheer, N. Kumar, and J. B. Steenkamp, "Reaction to Perceived Inequities in U.S. and Dutch Interorganizational Relationships," *Academy of Management Journal* (2003), Vol. 46, No. 3, pp. 303–316.

41. Warren, "Constructive and Destructive Deviance," 622–632.

42. D. E. Warren, "Constructive and Destructive Deviance in Organizations," *Academy of Management Review* (2003), Vol. 28, No. 4, pp. 622–632.

43. P. F. Hewlin, "And the Award for Best Actor Goes to . . .": Facades of Conformity in Organizational Settings," *Academy of Management Review* (2003), Vol. 28, No. 4, pp. 633–642.

44. Williamson and Cable, "Organizational Hiring Patterns," 349–358.

45. W. Swann, J. Polzer, D. D. Seyle, and S. Ko, "Finding Value in Diversity: Verification of Personal and Social Self-Views in Diverse Groups," *Academy of Management Review* (2004), Vol. 29, No. 1, pp. 9–27.

46. Swann et al., "Finding Value in Diversity," 9–27.

47. Hogan and Warrenfeltz, " Educating the Modern Manager," 74–84.

48. F. J. Flynn, "How Much Should I Give and How Often? The Effects of Generosity and Frequency of Favor Exchange on Social Status and Productivity," *Academy of Management Journal* (2003), Vol. 46, No. 5, pp. 539–553.

49. Druskat and Wheeler, "Managers from the Boundary," 435–457.

50. C. Penttila, "Out with the In," *Entrepreneur* (October 2003), pp. 78–79.

51. Flynn, "How Much Should I Give," 539–553.

52. J. S. Bunderson, "Team Member Functional Background and Involvement in Management Teams: Direct Effects and the Moderating Role of Power Centralization," *Academy of Management Journal* (2003), Vol. 46, No. 4, pp. 458–474.

53. Knight et al., "Team Goals, Incentives, and Efficacy," 326–338.

54. Bunderson and Sutcliffe, "Alternative Conceptualizations of Functional Diversity," 875–893; Chen et al., "Training Undergraduates," 27–40.

55. Chang et al., "Punctuated Equilibrium," 106–117.

56. Morrison, "Newcomers' Relationships," 1149–1160.

57. G. L. Stewart, "Team Structure and Performance: Assessing the Mediating Role of Intrateam Process and the Moderating Role of Task Type," *Academy of Management Journal* (2000), Vol. 43, No. 2, pp. 135–148.

58. Chen and Klimoski, "Newcomer Performance in Teams," 591–607.

59. P. C. Earley and E. Mosakowski, "Creating Hybrid Team Cultures: An Empirical Test of Transnational Team Function," *Academy of Management Journal* (2000), Vol. 43, No. 1, pp. 26–49.

60. Chang et al., "Punctuated Equilibrium," 106–117.

61. Harrison et al., "Time, Teams, and Task Performance," 1029–1045.

62. Chang et al., "Punctuated Equilibrium," 106–117.

63. Chang et al., "Punctuated Equilibrium," 106–117.

64. Penttila, "Out with the In," 78–79.

65. Morrison, "Newcomers' Relationships," 1149–1160.

66. Chen and Klimoski, "Newcomer Performance in Teams," 591–607.

67. Harrison et al., "Time, Teams, and Task Performance," 1029–1045.

68. Knight et al., "Team Goals, Incentives, and Efficacy," 326–338.

69. Information taken from the Sabre Holdings Web site at *http://www.sabre-holdings.com*, accessed May 20, 2004.

70. B. Kirkman, B. Rosen, C. Gibson, P. Tesluk, and S. McPherson, "Five Challenges to Virtual Team Success: Lessons from Sabre," *Academy of Management Executive* (2002), Vol. 16, No. 3, pp. 67–76.

71. Bunderson, "Team Member Functional Background," 458–474.

72. T. R. Zenger and C. R. Marshall, "Determinants of Incentive Intensity in Group-Based Rewards," *Academy of Management Journal* (2000), Vol. 43, No. 2, pp. 149–163.

73. Druskat and Wheeler, "Managers from the Boundary," 435–457.

74. Bacharach et al., "Driven to Drink," 637–658.

75. P. G. Clampitt, R. J. DeKoch, and T. Cashman, "A Strategy for Communicating about Uncertainty," *Academy of Management Executive* (2000), Vol. 14, No. 1, pp. 41–60.

76. "How to Run a Good Meeting," *Communication Briefings* (2003), Vol. XX, No. 1, p. 3.

77. "How to Run a Good Meeting," 3.

78. "How to Run a Good Meeting," 3.

79. "How to Run a Good Meeting," 3.

80. Saunders et al., "My Time or Yours?" 19–31.

81. "Minor Memos," *Wall Street Journal* (February 2, 2001), p. 1.

82. "Reacting to Difficult Types," *Communication Briefings* (2003), Vol. XX, No. 1, p. 8.

83. N. L. Torres, "Animal Instincts," *Entrepreneur* (February 2003), pp. 26–27.

84. Torres, "Animal Instincts," 26–27.

85. "Reacting to Difficult Types," 8.

86. "Reacting to Difficult Types," 8.

87. Torres, "Animal Instincts," 26–27.

88. T. M. Glomb, "Interpersonal Aggression in Work Groups: Social Influence, Reciprocal, and Individual Effects," *Academy of Management Journal* (2003), Vol. 46, No. 4, pp. 486–496.

89. Torres, "Animal Instincts," 26–27.

Chapter 11

1. C. Hymowitz, "In the Lead," *Wall Street Journal* (February 20, 2001), p. 1; "Communicating Better at Work," *Communication Briefing* (2003), Vol. XX, No. 1, p. 3.

2. P. G. Clampitt, R. J. DeKoch, and T. Cashman, "A Strategy for Communicating about Uncertainty," *Academy of Management Executive* (2000), Vol. 14, No. 1, pp. 41–60.

3. J. Diamond, "The Idea of Organization," *Wall Street Journal* (December 12, 2000), p. A26.

4. S. L. Rynes, A. M. Mullenix, and C. Q. Trank, "Do Behavioral Skills Increase the Employability of Business Students," *Journal of Career Centers* (Summer 2001), pp. 40–43.

5. Hymowitz, "In the Lead," 1.

6. "Got What It Takes," *Entrepreneur* (March 2003), p. 52.

7. Hymowitz, "In the Lead," 1.

8. L. Gratton and C. Truss, "The Three-Dimensional People Strategy: Putting Human Resources Policies into Action," *Academy of Management Executive* (2003), Vol. 17, No. 3, pp. 74–86.

9. "Why Goliath Needs David," *The Rhythm of Business* (October 31, 2003), p. 1; B. Kirkman, B. Rosen, C. Gibson, P. Tesluk, and S. McPherson, "Five Challenges to Virtual Team Success: Lessons from Sabre," *Academy of Management Executive* (2002), Vol. 16, No. 3, pp. 67–76.

10. M. Alavi and R. B. Gallupe, "Using Information Technology in Learning," *Academy of Management Learning and Education* (2003), Vol. 2, No. 2, pp. 139–153.

11. "Nua Internet Survey," *Entrepreneur* (April 2003), p. 30.

12. "Forbes.com," *Entrepreneur* (April 2003), p. 30; "Jupiter Research," *Entrepreneur* (April 2003), p. 30.

13. G. Van Der Vegt, E. Van De Vliert, and A. Oosterhof, "Information Dissimilarity and Organizational Citizenship Behavior," *Academy of Management Journal* (2003), Vol. 46, No. 6, pp. 715–727.

14. R. Daft and D. Marcic, *Understanding Management*, 4e (Mason, OH: South-Western, 2004).

15. W. Mossberg, "Clean Image Is So Key to Google's Success, Why Take Gmail Risk?" *Wall Street Journal* (May 6, 2004), p. B1.

16. J. Kickul and M. A. L. Troth, "The Meaning Behind the Message," *Mid-American Journal of Business* (2003), Vol. 18, No. 2, pp. 23–36.

17. M. J. McDermott, "Listening with a Purpose," *Chief Executive (U.S.)* (February 2001), p. 35.

18. B. Barry and I. S. Fulmer, "The Medium and the Message: The Adaptive Use of Communication Media in Dyadic Influence," *Academy of Management Review* (2004), Vol. 29, No. 2, pp. 272–292.

19. Kickul and Troth, "The Meaning Behind the Message," 23–36.

20. S. Shellenbarger, "Mental Gymnastics: Parents Share Tricks for Switching from Work to Home," *Wall Street Journal* (March 9, 2004), p. D1.

21. M. Hogan, "You've Got Mail," *Entrepreneur* (April 2004), pp. 51–52.

22. "Communicating Better at Work," 3.

23. "Selling Services," *Entrepreneur* (August 2003), p. 61.

24. "Selling Wholesale," *Entrepreneur* (August 2003), p. 60.

25. M. G. Seo, "Overcoming Emotional Barriers, Political Obstacles, and Control Imperatives in the Action-Science Approach to Individual and Organizational Learning," *Academy of Management Learning and Education* (2003), Vol. 2, No. 1, pp. 7–21.

26. Barry and Fulmer, "The Medium and the Message," 272–292.

27. "When You Write an E-Mail Policy," *Communication Briefing* (2003), Vol. XX, No. 1, p. 5.

28. "Communicating Better at Work," 3.

29. "Ideas to Use When Delegating," *Communication Briefing* (2003), Vol. XX, No. 1, p. 8.

30. "Becoming a Better Speaker," *Communication Briefing* (2003), Vol. XX, No. 1, p. 4.

31. G. Jaffe, "What's Your Point, Lieutenant?" *Wall Street Journal* (April 26, 2000), pp. A1, A6.

32. Margin note, *Entrepreneur* (April 2004), p. 29.

33. "The Five Major Time Wasters," *Communication Briefing* (2003), Vol. XX, No. 1, p. 5.

34. B. Farber, "People Who Need People," *Entrepreneur* (May 2003), pp. 76–77.

35. "Becoming a Better Speaker," 4.

36. S. Begley, "Gesturing as You Talk Can Help You Take a Load off Your Mind," *Wall Street Journal* (October 14, 2003), p. B1.

37. Farber, "People Who Need People," 76–77.

38. Begley, "Gesturing as You Talk," B1.

39. "Accountemps," *Entrepreneur* (April 2003), p. 30; Margin note, *Entrepreneur* (December 2003), p. 28; K. T. Gordon, "Words to the Wise," *Entrepreneur* (October 2003), pp. 91–92.

40. "Food Companies," *Wall Street Journal* (March 15, 2004), p. A1.

41. "Communicating Better at Work," 3.

42. T. Pollock, "Mind Your Own Business," *Supervision* (February 2001), Vol. 62, No. 2, p. 16.

43. "When You Write an E-Mail Policy," 5; "When Writing News Releases," *Communication Briefing* (2003), Vol. XX, No. 1, p. 3; "When Writing Copy for Ads," *Communication Briefing* (2003), Vol. XX, No. 1, p. 7.

44. "Double Your Brain Power," *Communication Briefing* (2003), Vol. XX, No. 1, p. 7.

45. "The Alcohol Industry," *Wall Street Journal* (April 22, 2004), p. A1; "A Law Firm," *Wall Street Journal* (September 2003), p. A1.

46. "Becoming a Better Speaker," 4; Farber, "People Who Need People," 76–77.

47. "When Writing News Releases," 3.

48. "Communicating Better at Work," 3; "How to Run a Good Meeting," *Communication Briefing* (2003), Vol. XX, No. 1, p. 3.

49. "Ideas to Use When Delegating," 8.

50. S. E. Moss and J. I. Sanchez, "Are Your Employees Avoiding You? Managerial Strategies for Closing the Feedback Gap," *Academy of Management Executive* (2004), Vol. 18, No. 1, pp. 32–44; N. L. Torres, "Playing Well with Others," *Entrepreneur* (February 2003), p. 30.

51. "Communicating Better at Work," 3; "How to Deal with Conflict," *Communication Briefing* (2003), Vol. XX, No. 1, p. 1.

52. Moss and Sanchez, "Are Your Employees Avoiding You?" 32–44.

53. "Communicating Better at Work," 3.

54. J. Ghorpade, "Managing Five Paradoxes of 360-Degree Feedback," *Academy of Management Executive* (2000), Vol. 14, No. 1, pp. 140–150.

55. Moss and Sanchez, "Are Your Employees Avoiding You?" 32–44.

56. Moss and Sanchez, "Are Your Employees Avoiding You?" 32–44.

57. Hymowitz, "In the Lead," B1.

58. "If You Must Criticize Someone," *Communication Briefing* (2003), Vol. XX, No. 1, p. 5.

59. "Selling Services," 61.

60. B. Farber, "All Ears," *Entrepreneur* (April 2004), pp. 83–84.

61. K. T. Gordon, "No Regrets," *Entrepreneur* (December 2003), pp. 104–105.

62. "Selling Services," 61.

63. Shellenbarger, "Mental Gymnastics," D1.

64. Farber, "People Who Need People," 76–77; "Selling Wholesale," 60.

65. Torres, "Playing Well with Others," 30; "Why We Don't Hear Others," *Communication Briefing* (2003), Vol. XX, No. 1, p. 1.

66. "Why We Don't Hear Others," 1; "How to Run a Good Meeting," 3.

67. Torres, "Playing Well with Others," 30.

68. "Ideas to Use When Delegating," 8.

69. Torres, "Playing Well with Others," 30; "How to Run a Good Meeting," 3.

70. "How to Deal with Conflict," 1.

71. Torres, "Playing Well with Others," 30.

72. "Why We Don't Hear Others," 1.

73. Farber, "All Ears," 83–84.

74. Seo, "Emotional Barriers, Political Obstacles, and Control Imperatives," 7–21.

75. A. A. Grandey, "When the Show Must Go On: Surface Acting and Deep Acting," *Academy of Management Journal* (2003), Vol. 46, No. 1, pp. 86–96.

76. D. Goleman, *Emotional Intelligence* (New York: Bantam, 1995) and *Working with Emotional Intelligence* (New York: Bantam, 1999).

77. Goleman, *Emotional Intelligence.*

78. "Carly Fiorina, Up Close," *Wall Street Journal* (January 13, 2003), pp. B1, B6.

79. Rynes, Mullenix, and Trank, "Do Behavioral Skills Increase the Employability of Business Students?" 40–43.

80. "If You Must Criticize Someone," 5.

81. Moss and Sanchez, "Are Your Employees Avoiding You?" 32–44.

82. C. Hymowitz, "How to Tell Employees All the Things They Don't Want to Hear," *Wall Street Journal* (August 22, 2001), p. B1.

83. Hymowitz, "In the Lead," B1.

84. "Why Goliath Needs David," 1.

85. M. Piszczalski, "GM's Smart New Portal," *Automotive Design & Production* (2002), Vol. 114, No. 2, pp. 14–15.

86. Hogan, "You've Got Mail," 51–52.

87. L. Abrams, R. Cross, E. Lesser, and D. Levin, "Nurturing Interpersonal Trust in Knowledge-Sharing Networks," *Academy of Management Executive* (2003), Vol. 17, No. 4, pp. 64–71.

88. R. Griffin, *Fundamentals of Management*, 3e (Boston: Houghton-Mifflin, 2003).

Chapter 12

1. M. C. Bolino and W. H. Turnley, "Going the Extra Mile: Cultivating and Managing Employee Citizenship Behavior," *Academy of Management Executive* (2003), Vol. 17, No. 3, pp. 60–71.

2. R. B. Pickett and M. M. Kennedy, "Career Development Strategies: Understanding and Using Organizational Politics. Part One," *Clinical Leadership and Management Review* (March/April 2004), pp. 120–122.

3. J. E. Bono and T. A. Judge, "Self-Concordance at Work: Toward Understanding the Motivational Effects of Transformational Leaders," *Academy of Management Journal* (2003), Vol. 46, No. 5, pp. 554–571.

4. R. E. Boyatzis, E. C. Stubbs, and S. N. Taylor, "Learning Cognitive and Emotional Intelligence Competencies Through Graduate Management Education," *Academy of Management Learning and Education* (2002), Vol. 1, No. 2, pp. 150–162.

5. C. Wittmeyer, "The Practice of Management: Timeless Views and Principles," *Academy of Management Executive* (2003), Vol. 17, No. 3, pp. 13–15.

6. Boyatzis, Stubbs, and Taylor, "Learning Cognitive and Emotional Intelligence Competencies," 150–162.

7. M. C. Bolino, W. H. Turnley, and J. M. Bloodgood, "Citizenship Behavior and the Creation of Social Capital in Organizations," *Academy of Management Review* (2002), Vol. 27, No. 4, pp. 505–522.

8. A. S. DeNisi and A. N. Kluger, "Feedback Effectiveness: Can 360-Degree Appraisals Be Improved?" *Academy of Management Executive* (2000), Vol. 14, No. 1, pp. 129–139.

9. Bolino and Turnley, "Going the Extra Mile," 60–71.

10. G. Chen and R. J. Klimoski, "The Impact of Expectations of Newcomer Performance in Teams as Mediated by Work Characteristics, Social Exchanges, and Empowerment," *Academy of Management Journal* (2003), Vol. 46, No. 5, pp. 591–607.

11. P. M. Senge, "Taking Personal Change Seriously: The Impact of Organizational Learning on Management Practice," *Academy of Management Executive* (2003), Vol. 17, No. 2, pp. 47–50.

12. P. Tierney and S. M. Farmer, "Creative Self-Efficacy, Its Potential Antecedents and Relationship to Creative Performance," *Academy of Management Journal* (2002), Vol. 45, No. 6, pp. 1137–1148.

13. B. Farber, "Get Over It!" *Entrepreneur* (October 2004), pp. 88–89.

14. R. Hogan and R. Warrenfeltz, "Education of the Modern Manager," *Academy of Management Learning and Education* (2003), Vol. 2, No. 1, pp. 74–84.

15. W. R. Boswell and J. O. Buchanan, "Experiencing Mistreatment at Work," *Academy of Management Journal* (2004), Vol. 47, No. 1, pp. 129–139.

16. A. E. Randel and K. S. Jaussi, "Functional Background Identity, Diversity, and Individual Performance in Cross-Functional Teams, *Academy of Management Journal* (2003), Vol. 46, No. 6, pp. 763–774.

17. Boyatzis, Stubbs, and Taylor, "Learning Cognitive and Emotional Intelligence Competencies," 150–162.

18. R. A. Guth, "Midlife Correction: Inside Microsoft, Financial Managers Win New Clout," *Wall Street Journal* (July 23, 2003), p. A1.

19. J. B. Miner, "The Rated Importance, Scientific Validity, and Practical Usefulness of Organizational Behavior Theories: A Quantitative Review," *Academy of Management Learning and Education* (2003), Vol. 2, No. 3, pp. 250–268.

20. Pickett and Kennedy, "Career Development Strategies," 120–122.

21. A. Maslow, "A Theory of Human Motivation," *Psychological Review* (1943), Vol. 50, pp. 370–396; *Motivation and Personality* (New York: Harper & Row, 1954).

22. J. Kickul and M. A. L. Troth, "The Meaning Behind the Message," *Mid-American Journal of Business* (2003), Vol. 18, No. 2, pp. 23–36.

23. J. G. Clawson and M. E. Haskins, "Beating the Career Blues," *Academy of Management Executive* (2000), Vol. 14, No. 3, pp. 91–102.

24. C. Alderfer, "An Empirical Test of a New Theory of Human Needs," *Organizational Behavior and Human Performance* (April 1969), pp. 142–175, and *Existence, Relatedness, and Growth* (New York: Free Press, 1972).

25. R. Daft and D. Marcic, *Understanding Management*, 4e (Mason, OH: South-Western, 2004).

26. F. Herzberg, "One More Time: How Do You Motivate Employees?" *Harvard Business Review* (January/February 1968), pp. 53–62.

27. N. W. Van Yperen and M. Hagedoorn, "Do High Job Demands Increase Intrinsic Motivation or Fatigue, or Both? The Role of Job Control and Job Social Support," *Academy of Management Journal* (2003), Vol. 46, No. 3, pp. 339–348.

28. Bolino and Turnley, "Going the Extra Mile," 60–71.

29. Kickul and Troth, "The Meaning Behind the Message," 23–36.

30. J. R. Rentsch and R. P. Steel, "Testing the Durability of Job Characteristics as Predictors of Absenteeism Over a Six-Year Period," *Personnel Psychology* (Spring 1998), Vol. 51, No. 1, pp. 165–191.

31. H. Murray, *Explorations in Personality* (New York: Oxford Press, 1938).

32. J. Atkinson, *An Introduction to Motivation* (New York: Van Nostrand Reinhold, 1964); D. McClelland, *The Achieving Society* (New York: Van Nostrand Reinhold, 1961); D. McClelland and D. H. Burnham, "Power Is the Great Motivator," *Harvard Business Review* (March/April 1978), p. 103.

33. S. E. Moss and J. I. Sanchez, "Are Your Employees Avoiding You? Managerial Strategies for Closing the Feedback Gap," *Academy of Management Executive* (2004), Vol. 18, No. 1, pp. 32–44.

34. N. L. Torres, "At Risk," *Entrepreneur* (January 2004), p. 23.

35. Moss and Sanchez, "Are Your Employees Avoiding You?" 32–44.

36. Van Yperen and Hagedoorn, "Do High Job Demands Increase Intrinsic Motivation?" 339–348.

37. Van Yperen and Hagedoorn, "Do High Job Demands Increase Intrinsic Motivation?" 339–348.

38. Boyatzis, Stubbs, and Taylor, "Learning Cognitive and Emotional Intelligence Competencies," 150–162.

39. J. S. Adams, "Toward an Understanding of Inequity," *Journal of Abnormal and Social Psychology* (1963), Vol. 67, pp. 422–436.

40. L. K. Scheer, N. Kumar, and J. B. Steenkamp, "Reactions to Perceived Inequities in U.S. and Dutch Interorganizational Relationships," *Academy of Management Journal* (2003), Vol. 46, No. 3, pp. 303–316.

41. W. R. Boswell and J. O. Buchanan, "Experiencing Mistreatment at Work," *Academy of Management Journal* (2004), Vol. 47, No. 1, pp. 129–139.

42. Kickul and Troth, "The Meaning Behind the Message," 23–36.

43. F. J. Flynn, "How Much Should I Give and How Often? The Effects of Generosity and Frequency of Favor Exchange on Social Status and Productivity," *Academy of Management Journal* (2003), Vol. 46, No. 5, pp. 539–553.

44. Scheer, Kumar, and Steenkamp, 303–316.

45. E. C. Hollensboe and J. P. Guthrie, "Group Pay-Performance Plans: The Role of Spontaneous Goal Setting," *Academy of Management Review* (2001), Vol. 25, No. 4, pp. 864–872.

46. Daft and Marcic, *Understanding Management*.

47. Miner, "Organizational Behavior Theories: A Quantitative Review," 250–268.

48. D. Knight, C. C. Durham, and E. A. Locke, "The Relationship of Team Goals, Incentives, and Efficacy to Strategic Risk, Tactical Implementation, and Performance," *Academy of Management Journal* (2001), Vol. 44, No. 2, pp. 326–338.

49. Miner, "Organizational Behavior Theories: A Quantitative Review," 250–268.

50. J. Welch and J. Byrne, "Jack: Straight from the Gut," *Journal of Small Business Strategy* (Fall/Winter 2002), Vol. 13, No. 2, pp. 97–99.

51. L. Holtz, "Setting a Higher Standard," *Success Yearbook* (Tampa, FL: Peter Lowe International, 1998), p. 74.

52. P. K. Mills and G. R. Ungson, "Reassessing the Limits of Structural Empowerment: Organizational Constitution and Trust as Controls," *Academy of Management Review* (2003), Vol. 28, No. 1, pp. 143–153.

53. "How to Be a Great Manager," *Communication Briefing* (2003), Vol. XX, No. 1, p. 5.

54. V. Vroom, *Work and Motivation* (New York: John Wiley & Sons, 1964).

55. Miner, "Organizational Behavior Theories: A Quantitative Review," 250–268.

56. Chen and Klimoski, "The Impact of Expectations on Newcomer Performance in Teams," 591–607.

57. D. E. Bowen and C. Ostroff, "Understanding HRM-Firm Performance Linkages," *Academy of Management Review* (2004), Vol. 29, No. 2, pp. 203–221.

58. P. Brandes, D. Dharwadkar, and G. V. Lemesis, "Effective Employee Stock Option Design: Reconciling Stakeholder, Strategic, and Motivational Factors," *Academy of Management Executive* (2003), Vol. 17, No. 1, pp. 77–93.

59. M. J. McDermott, "Listening with a Purpose," *Chief Executive* (U.S.) (February 2001), p. 35.

60. C. Gomez, B. L. Kirkman, and D. L. Shapiro, "The Impact of Collectivism and In-Group/Out-Group Membership on the Evaluation Generosity of Team Members," *Academy of Management Journal* (2000), Vol. 43, No. 6, pp. 1097–1106.

61. K. T. Gordon, "Sweet Rewards," *Entrepreneur* (August 2003), p. 75.

62. Bono and Judge, "Self-Concordance at Work," 554–571.

63. Daft and Marcic, *Understanding Management*.

64. B. F. Skinner, *Beyond Freedom and Dignity* (New York: Alfred A. Knopf, 1971).

65. Pickett and Kennedy, "Career Development Strategies," 120–122.

66. B. Beersma, J. R. Hooenbeck, H. Moon, D. E. Conlon, and D. R. Ilgen, "Cooperation, Competition, and Team Performance: Toward a Contingency Approach, *Academy of Management Journal* (2003), Vol. 46, No. 5, pp. 572–590.

67. P. G. Clampitt, R. J. DeKoch, and T. Cashman, "A Strategy for Communicating about Uncertainty," *Academy of Management Executive* (2000), Vol. 14, No. 1, pp. 41–60.

68. Bowen and Ostroff, "Understanding HRM-Firm Performance Linkages," 203–221.

69. W. R. Boswell and J. O. Buchanan, "Experiencing Mistreatment at Work," *Academy of Management Journal* (2004), Vol. 47, No. 1, pp. 129–139.

70. J. Ghorpade, "Managing Five Paradoxes of 360-Degree Feedback," *Academy of Management Executive* (2000), Vol. 14, No. 1, pp. 140–150.

71. S. McCartney, "The Tickets Airlines Don't Want You to Buy," *Wall Street Journal* (April 7, 2004), p. D1.

72. Bowen and Ostroff, "Understanding HRM-Firm Performance Linkages," 203–221.

73. Knight, Durham, and Locke, "Team Goals, Incentives, and Efficacy," 326–338.

74. Gordon, "Sweet Rewards," 75

75. Bolino and Turnley, "Going the Extra Mile," 60–71.

76. Mills and Ungson, "Reassessing the Limits of Structural Empowerment," 143–153.

77. DeNisi and Kluger, "Feedback Effectiveness," 129–139.

78. Bolino and Turnley, "Going the Extra Mile," 60–71.

79. K. Blanchard and S. Johnson, *The One-Minute Manager* (New York: William Morrow & Co., 1982).

80. "How to Be a Great Manager," 5.

81. G. Hofstede, "Motivation, Leadership, and Organizations: Do American Theories Apply Abroad?" *Organizational Dynamics* (Summer 1980), p. 55.

82. "Deming's Demons," *Wall Street Journal* (June 4, 1990), pp. R39, 41.

Chapter 13

1. R. Hogan and R. Warrenfeltz, "Education of the Modern Manager," *Academy of Management Learning and Education* (2003), Vol. 2, No. 1, pp. 74–84.

2. B. Bass, *Stogdill's Handbook of Leadership*, 3rd ed. (New York: Free Press, 1990).

3. D. A. Whetten and A. L. Delbecq, "Saraide's Chairman Hatim Tyabji on Creating and Sustaining a Values-Based Organizational Culture," *Academy of Management Executive* (2000), Vol. 14, No. 4, pp. 32–33.

4. C. Wittmeyer, "*The Practice of Management*: Timeless Views and Principles," *Academy of Management Executive* (2003), Vol. 17, No. 3, pp. 13–15.

5. S. A. Zahra, "Introduction: Peter F. Drucker's *The Practice of Management*," *Academy of Management Executive* (2003), Vol. 17, No. 3, pp. 7–8.

6. L. Bossidy, "The Job No CEO Should Delegate," *Harvard Business Review* (March 2001), Vol. 79, No. 3, p. 47.

7. D. Foote, "Don't Kid Yourself: Leaders Are Made, Not Born," *Computerworld* (March 12, 2000), p. 32.

8. "Carly Fiorina, Up Close," *Wall Street Journal* (January 13, 2003), pp. B1, B6.

9. R. J. Sternberg, "WICS: A Model of Leadership in Organizations," *Academy of Management Learning and Education* (2003), Vol. 2, No. 4, pp. 386–401.

10. J. P. Doh, "Can Leadership Be Taught? Perspectives from Management Educators," *Academy of Management Learning and Education* (2003), Vol. 2, No. 1, pp. 54–67.

11. J. Merritt, "The Education Edge," *Business Week* (October 20, 2003), pp. 86–92.

12. Information taken from the Web site of the Center for Creative Leadership at *http://www.ccl.org*, accessed June 8, 2004.

13. G. M. Pedroza, "Balancing the Books," *Entrepreneur* (March 2003), p. 25.

14. B. Barry and I. S. Fulmer, "The Medium and the Message: The Adaptive Use of Communication Media in Dyadic Influence," *Academy of Management Review* (2004), Vol. 29, No. 2, pp. 272–292.

15. "Got What It Takes," *Entrepreneur* (March 2003), p. 52.

16. R. E. Boyatzis, E. C. Stubbs, and S. N. Taylor, "Learning Cognitive and Emotional Intelligence Competencies Through Graduate Management Education," *Academy of Management Learning and Education* (2002), Vol. 1, No. 2, pp. 150–162.

17. R. Wolter, "Follow Your Leader," *Entrepreneur* (April 2004), p. 124.

18. Information taken from the GE Web site at *http://www. ge.com*, accessed June 8, 2004.

19. "Shining a Light Bulb on Leadership," *Wall Street Journal* (January 23, 2004), pp. A1, A14.

20. J. B. Miner, "The Rated Importance, Scientific Validity, and Practical Usefulness of Organizational Behavior Theories: A Quantitative Review," *Academy of Management Learning and Education* (2003), Vol. 2, No. 3, pp. 250–268.

21. Sternberg, "WICS," 386–401.

22. Bass, *Stogdill's Handbook of Leadership*.

23. E. Ghiselli, *Explorations in Management Talent* (Santa Monica, CA: Goodyear, 1971).

24. K. Boyers, "Why Am I Here?" *Association Management* (March 1998), Vol. 50, No. 3, pp. 63–66.

25. Doh, "Can Leadership Be Taught?" 54–67.

26. G. Williams, "Comic Belief," *Entrepreneur* (April 2003), p. 28.

27. For more information on Spirit at Work and its founder Dr. Judith Neal, visit the organization's Web site at *http://www.spiritatwork.com*.

28. B. Graham, "Leadership and Spirituality," *Success Yearbook* (Tampa, FL: Peter Lowe International, 1998), p. 54.

29. Z. Ziglar, "Formula for Complete Success," *Success Yearbook* (Tampa, FL: Peter Lowe International, 1998), pp. 30, 105; P. Lowe, "The Fifth Level of Life," *Success Yearbook* (Tampa, FL: Peter Lowe International, 1998), pp. 91–93.

30. Ziglar, "Formula for Complete Success," 30, 105.

31. V. U. Druskat and J. V. Wheeler, "Managing from the Boundary: The Effective Leadership of Self-Managing Work Teams," *Academy of Management Review* (2003), Vol. 46, No. 4, pp. 435–457.

32. Barry and Fulmer, "The Medium and the Message," 272–292.

33. K. Lewin, R. Lippert, and R. K. White, "Patterns of Aggressive Behavior in Experimentally Created Social Climates," *Journal of Social Psychology* (1939), Vol. 10, pp. 271–301.

34. R. Liker, *New Patterns of Management* (New York: McGraw-Hill, 1961).

35. R. M. Stogdill and A. E. Coons, Eds., *Leader Behavior: Its Description and Measurement* (Columbus: Ohio State University Bureau of Business Research, 1957).

36. Information taken from the Loews Cineplex Web site at *http://www.loewscineplex.com*, accessed June 7, 2004.

37. R. Daft and D. Marcic, *Understanding Management*, 4e (Mason, OH: South-Western, 2004).

38. R. Blake and J. Mouton, *The Leadership Grid III: Key to Leadership Excellence* (Houston: Gulf Publishing, 1985); R. Blake and A. A. McCanse, *Leadership Dilemmas—Grid Solutions* (Houston: Gulf Publishing, 1991).

39. J. E. Bono and T. A. Judge, "Self-Concordance at Work: Toward an Understanding of the Motivational Effects of Transformational Leaders," *Academy of Management Journal* (2003), Vol. 46, No. 5, pp. 554–571; Hogan and Warrenfeltz, "Education of the Modern Manager," 74–84.

40. Bono and Judge, "Self-Concordance at Work," 554–571.

41. "The Leadership Connection," *Entrepreneur* (March 2003), pp. 50–51.

42. Bono and Judge, "Self-Concordance at Work," 554–571.

43. D. Vera and M. Crossan, "Strategic Leadership and Organizational Learning," *Academy of Management Review* (2004), Vol. 29, No. 2, pp. 222–240.

44. M. C. Bolino and W. H. Turnley, "Going the Extra Mile: Cultivating and Managing Employee Citizenship Behavior," *Academy of Management Executive* (2003), Vol. 17, No. 3, pp. 60–71.

45. T. D. D. Eden, B. J. Avolio, and B. Shamir, "Impact of Transformational Leadership on Follower Development and Performance," *Academy of Management Journal* (2002), Vol. 45, No. 4, pp. 735–744.

46. L. Varricchionne, "Session Examines Transformational Leadership Skills," *Nation's Cities Weekly* (March 19, 2001), Vol. 24, No. 11, p. 13.

47. Vera and Crossan, "Strategic Leadership and Organizational Learning," 222–240.

48. Miner, "Organizational Behavior Theories: A Quantitative Review," 250–268.

49. J. Welch and J. Byrne, "Jack: Straight from the Gut," *Journal of Small Business Strategy* (Fall/Winter 2002), Vol. 13, No. 2, pp. 97–99.

50. D. A. Waldman, G. G. Ramirez, R. J. House, and P. Puranam, "Does Leadership Matter? CEO Leadership Attributes under Conditions of Perceived Environmental Uncertainty," *Academy of Management Journal* (2001), Vol. 44, No. 1, pp. 134–143.

51. W. P. Wan and R. E. Hoskisson, "Home Country Environments, Corporate Diversification Strategies and Firm Performance," *Academy of Management Journal* (2003), Vol. 46, No. 1, pp. 27–45.

52. G. Chen and R. J. Klimoski, "The Impact of Expectations on Newcomer Performance in Teams as Mediated by Work Characteristics, Social Exchanges, and Empowerment," *Academy of Management Review* (2003), Vol. 48, No. 5, pp. 591–607.

53. S. J. Shin and J. Zhou, "Transformational Leadership, Conservation, and Creativity: Evidence from Korea," *Academy of Management Journal* (2003), Vol. 46, No. 6, pp. 703–714.

54. Bolino and Turnley, "Going the Extra Mile," 60–71; Chen and Klimoski, "Newcomer Performance in Teams," 591–607.

55. D. E. Bowen and C. Ostroff, "Understanding HRM–Firm Performance Linkages," *Academy of Management Review* (2004), Vol. 29, No. 2, pp. 203–221.

56. C. Hyowitz, "Good Leadership Requires Executives to Put Themselves Last," *Wall Street Journal* (April 20, 2004), p. B1.

57. M. A. Boland and J. P. Katz, "Jack Gherty, President and CEO of Land O'Lakes, on Leading a Branded Food and Farm Supply Cooperative," *Academy of Management Executive* (2003), Vol. 17, No. 3, pp. 24–30.

58. Hyowitz, "Good Leadership," B1.

59. F. Fiedler, *A Theory of Leadership Effectiveness* (New York: McGraw-Hill, 1967).

60. D. J. Campbell, "The Proactive Employee: Managing Workplace Initiative," *Academy of Management Executive* (2000), Vol. 14, No. 3, pp. 52–66.

61. Shin and Zhou, "Transformational Leadership, Conservation, and Creativity," 703–714.

62. D. J. Ketchen, Jr., "An Interview with Raymond E. Miles and Charles C. Snow," *Academy of Management Executive* (2003), Vol. 17, No. 4, pp. 97–103.

63. R. A. Guth, "Midlife Correction: Inside Microsoft, Financial Managers Win New Clout," *Wall Street Journal* (July 23, 2004), p. A1.

64. R. Tannenbaum and W. Schmidt, "How to Choose a Leadership Pattern," *Harvard Business Review* (May/June 1973), p. 166.

65. Barry and Fulmer, "The Medium and the Message," 272–292.

66. Tannenbaum and Schmidt, "How to Choose a Leadership Pattern," 166.

67. Daft and Marcic, *Understanding Management*, 4e.

68. R. House, "A Path-Goal Theory of Leadership Effectiveness," *Administrative Science Quarterly* (1971), Vol. 16, No. 2, pp. 321–329.

69. Campbell, "The Proactive Employee," 52–66.

70. V. H. Vroom, "Leadership and the Decision-Making Process," *Organizational Dynamics* (2000), Vol. 28, pp. 82–94.

71. P. Hersey and K. Blanchard, *Management of Organizational Behavior: Utilizing Human Resources*, 4th ed. (Englewood Cliffs, NJ: Prentice Hall, 1982).

72. J. R. Schermerhorn, Jr., "Situational Leadership: Conversations with Paul Hersey," *Mid-American Journal of Business* (1998), Vol. 12, No. 2, pp. 5–11.

73. S. Kerr and J. Jermier, "Substitutes for Leadership: The Meaning and Measurement," *Organizational Behavior and Human Performance* (1978), Vol. 22, pp. 375–403.

74. S. Kerr, J. Jermier, and R. Gordon, "Substitutes for Leadership," *Supervision* (July 1994), Vol. 55, No. 7, pp. 17–20.

75. Wittmeyer, "*The Practice of Management*: Timeless Views and Principles," 13–15.

76. G. Dessler, *Management*, 3e (Upper Saddle River, NJ: Prentice-Hall, 2004).

77. J. Winter, J. Neal, and K. Waner, "How Male, Female, and Mixed-Gender Groups Regard Interaction and Leadership Differences in the Business Communication Course," *Business Communication Quarterly* (September 2001), p. 43; R. F. Martell and A. L. DeSmet, "A Diagnostic-Ratio Approach to Measuring Beliefs about the Leadership Abilities of Male and Female Managers," *Journal of Applied Psychology* (December 2001), pp. 1223–1232.

78. W. R. Boswell and J. O. Buchanan, "Experiencing Mistreatment at Work," *Academy of Management Journal* (2004), Vol. 47, No. 1, pp. 129–139.

79. C. Bendersky, "Organizational Dispute Resolution Systems: A Complementarities Model," *Academy of Management Review* (2003), Vol. 29, No. 4, pp. 643–656.

80. R. Johnston and S. Mehra, "Best-Practice Complaint Management," *Academy of Management Executive* (2002), Vol. 16, No. 4, pp. 145–154.

81. Margin note, *Entrepreneur* (December 2003), p. 33.

82. M. M. Davis and J. Heineke, *Managing Services Using Technology to Create Value* (Burr Ridge, IL: McGraw-Hill, 2004).

83. Johnston and Mehra, "Best-Practice Complaint Management," 145–154.

Chapter 14

1. A. S. DeNisi and A. N. Kluger, "Feedback Effectiveness: Can 360-Degree Appraisals Be Improved?," *Academy of Management Executive* (2000), Vol. 14, No. 1, pp. 129–139.

2. S. E. Moss and J. I. Sanchez, "Are Your Employees Avoiding You?," *Academy of Management Executive* (2004), Vol. 18, No. 1, pp. 32–44.

3. R. Zomke, "Systems Thinking," *Training* (February 2001), Vol. 38, No. 2, p. 40.

4. M. G. Seo, "Overcoming Emotional Barriers, Political Obstacles, and Control Imperatives in the Action-Science Approach to Individual and Organizational Learning," *Academy of Management Learning and Education* (2003), Vol. 2, No. 1, pp. 7–21.

5. R. E. Crandall and W. R. Crandall, "Managing Excess Inventories: A Life-Cycle Approach," *Academy of Management Executive* (2003), Vol. 17, No. 3, pp. 99–113.

6. EDS Web site *http://www.eds.com*, accessed June 11, 2004, and the second edition of this book.

7. C. Hymowitz, "How to Tell Employees All the Things They Don't Want to Hear," *Wall Street Journal* (August 22, 2001), p. B1.

8. DeNisi and Kluger, "Feedback Effectiveness," 129–139.

9. R. Wolter, "Take a Breather," *Entrepreneur* (December 2003), pp. 134–135.

10. J. S. Lublin, "How to Win Support from Colleagues at Your New Job," *Wall Street Journal* (November 25, 2003), p. B1.

11. J. Magretta, *What Management Is: How It Works and Why It's Everyone's Business* (New York: The Free Press, 2002).

12. S. K. Majumdar and A. A. Marcus, "Rules versus Discretion: The Productivity Consequences of Flexible Regulation," *Academy of Management Journal* (2001), Vol. 44, No. 1, pp. 170–179.

13. J. Welch and J. Byrne, "Jack: Straight from the Gut," *Journal of Small Business Strategy* (Fall/Winter 2002), Vol. 13, No. 2, pp. 97–99.

14. C. Argyris, "Double-Loop Learning, Teaching, and Research," *Academy of Management Learning and Education* (2002), Vol. 1, No. 2, pp. 206–218.

15. Welch and Byrne, "Jack," 97–99.

16. Magretta, *What Management Is*.

17. Magretta, *What Management Is*.

18. M. Crossan, "Altering Theories of Learning and Action: An Interview with Chris Argyris," *Academy of Management Executive* (2003), Vol. 17, No. 2, pp. 40–46.

19. Argyris, "Double-Loop Learning, Teaching, and Research," 206–218.

20. EDS Web site *http://www.eds.com*, accessed June 11, 2004, and the second edition of this book.

21. "How to Be a Great Manager," *Communication Briefing* (2003), Vol. 20, No. 1, p. 5.

22. Seo, "Overcoming Emotional Barriers, Political Obstacles, and Control Imperatives," 7–21.

23. S. Bacharach, P. Bamerger, and W. Sonnenstuhl, "Driven to Drink: Management Control, Work-Related Risk Factors, and Employee Problem Drinking," *Academy of Management Journal* (2002), Vol. 45, No. 4, pp. 637–658.

24. L. Gratton and C. Truss, "The Three-Dimensional People Strategy: Putting Human Resources Policies into Action," *Academy of Management Executive* (2003), Vol. 17, No. 3, pp. 74–86.

25. Bacharach, Bamerger, and Sonnenstuhl, "Driven to Drink," 637–658.

26. K. K. Mortland and D. B. Mortland, "Budgeting for Change," *Clinical Leadership and Management Review* (March/April 2004), pp. 127–130.

27. Magretta, *What Management Is.*

28. S. Pulliam, A. Latour, and K. Brown, "U.S. Indicts WorldCom Chief Ebbers," *Wall Street Journal* (March 3, 2004), p. A1.

29. "Communicating Better at Work," *Communication Briefing* (2003), Vol. 20, No. 1, p. 3.

30. "How to Be a Great Manager," 5.

31. Crossan, "Altering Theories of Learning and Action," 40–46.

32. E. K. Yakura, "Charting Time: Timelines as Temporal Boundary Objects," *Academy of Management Journal* (2002), Vol. 45, No. 5, pp. 956–970.

33. Information taken from the UPS Web site *http://www.ups.com*, accessed June 17, 2004.

34. Crandall and Crandall, "Managing Excess Inventories," 99–113.

35. C. J. Prince, "Number Rustling," *Entrepreneur* (March 2003), pp. 43–44.

36. Mortland and Mortland, "Budgeting for Change," 127–130.

37. Prince, "Number Rustling," 43–44.

38. Prince, "Number Rustling," 43–44.

39. N. L. Torres, "Playing Well with Others," *Entrepreneur* (February 2003), p. 30.

40. Seo, "Overcoming Emotional Barriers, Political Obstacles, and Control Imperatives," 7–21.

41. S. Thurm and K. J. Delaney, "Yahoo, Google and Internet Math," *Wall Street Journal* (May 10, 2004), p. C1.

42. Prince, "Number Rustling," 43–44.

43. Mortland and Mortland, "Budgeting for Change," 127–130.

44. Information taken from the PricewaterhouseCoopers Web site *http://www.pwc.com*, accessed June 17, 2004.

45. "PricewaterhouseCoopers Agreed," *Wall Street Journal* (December 22, 2003), p. A1.

46. Information taken from the IBM Web site *http://www.ibm.com*, accessed June 14, 2004.

47. Moss and Sanchez, "Are Your Employees Avoiding You?," 32–44.

48. Lublin, "How to Win Support from Colleagues at Your New Job," B1.

49. "How to Be a Great Manager," 5.

50. D. Foote, "Don't Kid Yourself: Leaders Are Made, Not Born," *Computerworld* (March 12, 2000), p. 32.

51. C. Bendersky, "Organizational Dispute Resolution Systems: A Complementarities Model," *Academy of Management Review* (2003), Vol. 29, No. 4, pp. 643–656.

52. Torres, "Playing Well with Others," 30.

53. "If You Must Criticize Someone," *Communication Briefing* (2003), Vol. 20, No. 1, p. 5.

54. S. Bazan, "Individual Performance Problems: A Diagnostic Protocol," *Clinical Leadership and Management Review* (March/April 2004), pp. 112–116.

55. M. C. Bolino and W. H. Turnley, "Going the Extra Mile: Cultivation and Managing Employee Citizenship Behavior," *Academy of Management Executive* (2003), Vol. 17, No. 3, pp. 60–71.

56. B. J. Tepper and E. C. Taylor, "Relationships Among Supervisors' and Subordinates' Procedural Justice Perceptions and Organizational Citizenship Behaviors," *Academy of Management Journal* (2003), Vol. 46, No. 1, pp. 97–105.

57. Bazan, "Individual Performance Problems," 112–116.

58. Moss and Sanchez, "Are Your Employees Avoiding You?," 32–44.

59. Bazan, "Individual Performance Problems," 112–116.

60. "If You Must Criticize Someone," 5.

61. A. E. Randel and K. S. Jaussi, "Functional Background Identity, Diversity, and Individual Performance in Cross-Functional Teams," *Academy of Management Journal* (2003), Vol. 46, No. 6, pp. 763–774.

62. "Communicating Better at Work," 3.

63. "Avoid Control Talk," *Communication Briefing* (2003), Vol. 20, No. 1, p. 8.

64. Bazan, "Individual Performance Problems," 112–116.

65. R. L. Ackoff, "Role of a University in Community Development," presentation at University of New Haven, May 23, 2002.

66. Information taken from the Wal-Mart Web site *http://www.walmart.com*, accessed June 16, 2004.

67. Bacharach, Bamerger, and Sonnenstuhl, "Driven to Drink," 637–658.

68. "Predicting Failure," *Wall Street Journal* (April 24, 2001), p. A1.

69. "Core Incompetency," *Wall Street Journal* (April 24, 2001), p. A1.

70. Bacharach, Bamerger, and Sonnenstuhl, "Driven to Drink," 637–658.

71. Bazan, "Individual Performance Problems," 112–116.

72. "How to Be a Great Manager," 5.

73. J. Zaslow, "Personal Life Coaches Need Help, Too, So They Get Together," *Wall Street Journal* (November 24, 2002), p. A14.

74. Gratton and Truss, "The Three-Dimensional People Strategy," 74–86.

75. Bazan, "Individual Performance Problems," 112–116.

76. A. A. Grandey, "When the Show Must Go On: Surface Acting and Deep Acting," *Academy of Management Journal* (2003), Vol. 46, No. 1, pp. 86–96.

77. "Leadership Test," *Communication Briefing* (2003), Vol. 20, No. 1, p. 2.

78. Bazan, "Individual Performance Problems," 112–116.

79. D. E. Warren, "Constructive and Destructive Deviance in Organizations," *Academy of Management Review* (2003), Vol. 28, No. 4, pp. 622–632.

80. "If You Must Criticize Someone," 5.

81. C. Penttila, "Tough Choices," *Entrepreneur* (May 2003), pp. 70–71.

82. J. A. Lepine and L. V. Dyne, "Peer Response to Low Performers: An Attributional Model of Helping in the Context of Groups," *Academy of Management Review* (2001), Vol. 26, No. 1, pp. 67–84.

Chapter 15

1. A. E. Randel and K. S. Jaussi, "Functional Background Identity, Diversity, and Individual Performance in Cross-Functional Teams," *Academy of Management Journal* (2003), Vol. 46, No. 6, pp. 763–774.

2. S. Hanschild, T. Licht, and W. Stein, "Creating a Knowledge Culture," *The McKinsey Quarterly* (Winter 2001), p. 74.

3. B. Beersma, J. R. Hooenbeck, H. Moon, D. E. Conlon, and D. R. Ilgen, "Cooperation, Competition, and Team Performance: Toward a Contingency Approach," *Academy of Management Journal* (2003), Vol. 46, No. 5, pp. 572–590.

4. K. Atuahene-Gima, "The Effects of Centrifugal and Centripetal Forces on Product Development Speed and Quality: How Does Problem Solving Matter?," *Academy of Management Journal* (2003), Vol. 46, No. 3, pp. 359–373.

5. S. A. Zahra, "Introduction: Peter F. Drucker's The Practice of Management," *Academy of Management Executive* (2003), Vol. 17, No. 3, pp. 7–8.

6. D. Harrison, K. Price, J. Gavin, and A. Florey, "Time, Teams, and Task Performance: Changing Effects of Surface- and Deep-Level Diversity on Group Functioning," *Academy of Management Journal* (2002), Vol. 45, No. 5, pp. 1029–1045.

7. L. A. Perlow, G. A. Okhuysen, and N. P. Repenning, "The Speed Trap: Exploring the Relationship Between Decision Making and Temporal Context," *Academy of Management Journal* (2002), Vol. 45, No. 5, pp. 931–955.

8. M. J. Waller, M. E. Zellmer-Bruhn, and R. C. Giambatista, "Watching the Clock: Group Pacing Behavior Under Dynamic Deadlines," *Academy of Management Journal* (2002), Vol. 45, No. 5, pp. 1046–1055.

9. D. C. Johnston, "Kodak to Reduce Its Work Force by Up to 15,000," *New York Times* (January 23, 2003), p. C5.

10. J. Shuman and J. Twombly, "Pearls by Peter," *The Rhythm of Business* (June 15, 2001).

11. G. DeSanctis, J. T. Glass, and I. M. Ensing, "Organizational Design for R&D," *Academy of Management Executive* (2002), Vol. 16, No. 3, pp. 55–61.

12. R. C. Ford, "Pierre Bellon, Founder and President-Director General of Sodexho Alliance, on Working Hard and Having Fun," *Academy of Management Executive* (2003), Vol. 17, No. 1, pp. 38–45.

13. Perlow, Okhuysen, and Repenning, "The Speed Trap," 931–955.

14. P. J. Brews and C. L. Tucci, "Internetworking: Building Internet-Generation Companies," *Academy of Management Executive* (2003), Vol. 17, No. 4, pp. 8–20.

15. Perlow, Okhuysen, and Repenning, "The Speed Trap," 931–955.

16. "Why Goliath Needs David," *The Rhythm of Business* (October 31, 2003), p. 1.

17. Information taken from the Apple Web site *http://www.apple.com*, accessed June 25, 2004.

18. "Apple Reports," *Wall Street Journal* (April 15, 2004), p. A1.

19. Information taken from the Apple Web site *http://www.apple.com*, accessed June 25, 2004.

20. DeSanctis, Glass, and Ensing, "Organizational Design for R&D," 55–61.

21. "Toyota Plans," *Wall Street Journal* (May 17, 2004), p. A1.

22. B. C. Skaggs and T. R. Huffman, "A Customer Interaction Approach to Strategy and Production Complexity Alignment in Service Firms," *Academy of Management Journal* (2003), Vol. 46, No. 6, pp. 775–786.

23. Randel and Jaussi, "Functional Background Identity," 763–774.

24. Randel and Jaussi, "Functional Background Identity," 763–774.

25. C. J. Collins and K. D. Clark, "Strategic Human Resource Practices, Top Management Team Social Networks, and Firm Performance: The Role of Human Resource Practices in Creating Organizational Competitive Advantage," *Academy of Management Journal* (2003), Vol. 46, No. 6, pp. 740–751.

26. DeSanctis, Glass, and Ensing, "Organizational Design for R&D," 55–61.

27. G. A. Fowler, "Technology Changes Game for Toymakers During Holidays," *Wall Street Journal* (December 18, 2003), p. A1.

28. Information taken from the Tyco Web site *http://www.tyco.com*, accessed June 29, 2004.

29. "Tyco," *Wall Street Journal* (January 12, 2003), p. A1.

30. A. Merrick, "Gap Offers Unusual Look at Factory Conditions," *Wall Street Journal* (May 12, 2004), pp. A1, A12.

31. C. Cummins, S. Warren, and M. Schroeder, "Shell Cuts Reserve Estimate 20 Percent as SEC Scrutinizes Oil Industry," *Wall Street Journal* (January 12, 2004), pp. A1, A10.

32. DeSanctis, Glass, and Ensing, "Organizational Design for R&D," 55–61.

33. E. K. Yakura, "Charting Time: Timelines as Temporal Boundary Objects," *Academy of Management Journal* (2002), Vol. 45, No. 5, pp. 956–970.

34. Yakura, "Charting Time," 956–970.

35. Yakura, "Charting Time," 956–970.

36. S. Chopra and P. Meindl, *Supply Chain Management* (Upper Saddle River, NJ: Prentice-Hall, 2004).

37. R. E. Crandall and W. R. Crandall, "Managing Excess Inventories: A Life-Cycle Approach," *Academy of Management Executive* (2003), Vol. 17, No. 3, pp. 99–113.

38. Chopra and Meindl, *Supply Chain Management.*

39. Brews and Tucci, "Internetworking," 8–20.

40. S. Karush, "Kmart Rebounds, Reports Profit," *The Republican* (March 19, 2004), Business Section p. 1.

41. C. Vitzthum, "Just-in-Time Fashion," *Wall Street Journal* (May 18, 2001), p. B1.

42. Crandall and Crandall, "Managing Excess Inventories," 99–113.

43. M. A. Razi and J. M. Tarn, "ERP System Solutions for Small Companies: Readiness & Selection," *Journal of Small Business Strategy* (2003), Vol. 14, No. 1, pp. 71–85.

44. R. L. Daft and D. Marcic, *Understanding Management*, 4th ed. (Mason, OH: South-Western, 2004).

45. Razi and Tarn, "ERP System Solutions," 71–85.

46. Information taken from the Harman Music Group Web site *http://www.harmanmusicgroup.com*, accessed June 29, 2004.

47. G. Dessler, *Management*, 3rd ed. (Upper Saddle River, NJ: Prentice-Hall, 2004).

48. Razi and Tarn, "ERP System Solutions," 71–85.

49. M. Henricks, "A Tight Ship," *Entrepreneur* (December 2003), pp. 95–96.

50. Crandall and Crandall, "Managing Excess Inventories," 99–113.

51. G. T. M. Hult, D. J. Ketchen, Jr., and E. L. Nichols, Jr., "An Examination of Cultural Competitiveness and Order Fulfillment Cycle Time Within Supply Chains," *Academy of Management Journal* (2002), Vol. 45, No. 3, pp. 577–586.

52. Chopra and Meindl, *Supply Chain Management.*

53. D. K. Berman, "Telecoms Embrace Internet Calling, but Is It Trouble?" *Wall Street Journal* (December 29, 2003), p. B1.

54. J. Magretta, *What Management Is: How It Works and Why It's Everyone's Business* (New York: The Free Press, 2002).

55. J. Bandler, "As Kodak Eyes Digital Future, a Big Partner Starts to Fade," *Wall Street Journal* (January 23, 2004), p. A1.

56. B. Schneider, S. S. White, and M. C. Paul, "Linking Service Climate and Customer Perceptions of Service Quality: Test of

a Causal Model," *Journal of Applied Psychology* (April 1998), Vol. 83, No. 2, pp. 150–164.

57. M. J. Benner and M. L. Tushman, "Exploitation, Exploration and Process Management: The Productivity Dilemma Revisited," *Academy of Management Review* (2003), Vol. 28, No. 2, pp. 238–256.

58. Schneider, White, and Paul, "Linking Service Climate and Customer Perceptions of Service Quality," 150–164.

59. M. J. Lankau and T. A. Scandura, "An Investigation of Personal Learning in Mentoring Relationships: Content, Antecedents, and Consequences," *Academy of Management Journal* (2002), Vol. 45, No. 4, pp. 779–790.

60. Benner and Tushman, "Exploitation, Exploration and Process Management," 238–256.

61. Benner and Tushman, "Exploitation, Exploration and Process Management," 238–256.

62. J. A. DeFeo, "Be a Six Sigma Leader!," Information taken from the Management General Web site *http://www.mgeneral.com*, accessed June 29, 2004.

63. DeFeo, "Be a Six Sigma Leader!"

64. Social Accountability International (SAI) Web site *http://www.sa-intl.org*, accessed June 29, 2004.

65. A. Berland, "Six Sigma," *Fortune* (February 19, 2001), p. 32.

66. Berland, "Six Sigma," p. 32.

67. DeFeo, "Be a Six Sigma Leader!"

68. Information taken from the Ford Web site *http://www.ford.com*, accessed July 2, 2004.

69. R. Zomke, "Systems Thinking," *Training* (February 2001), Vol. 38, No. 2, p. 40.

70. D. Wessel, "Capital: The Magic Elixir of Productivity," *Wall Street Journal* (February 15, 2001), p. 1.

71. S. D. Friedman and S. Lobel, "The Happy Workaholic: A Role Model for Employees," *Academy of Management Executive* (2003), Vol. 17, No. 3, pp. 87–98.

72. F. J. Flynn, "How Much Should I Give and How Often? The Effects of Generosity and Frequency of Favor Exchange on Social Status and Productivity," *Academy of Management Journal* (2003), Vol. 46, No. 5, pp. 539–553.

73. "U.S. Productivity Growth," *Wall Street Journal* (June 4, 2004), p. A1.

74. M. P. Brown, M. C. Sturman, and M. J. Simmering, "Compensation Policy and Organizational Performance: The Efficiency, Operational, and Financial Implications of Pay Levels and Pay Structure," *Academy of Management Journal* (2003), Vol. 46, No. 6, pp. 752–762.

75. S. K. Majumdar and A. A. Marcus, "Rules versus Discretion: The Productivity Consequences of Flexible Regulation," *Academy of Management Journal* (2001), Vol. 44, No. 1, pp. 170–179.

76. "Measures of Productivity," *SBANC Newsletter* (March 2, 2004), p. 2.

77. S. Shellenbarger, "Taking an 'Inner Vacation': How to Relax When You're Chained to Your Desk," *Wall Street Journal* (October 9, 2003), p. D1.

78. "U.S. Productivity Growth," A1.

79. "Outsourcing of Computer Work," *Wall Street Journal* (March 30, 2004), p. A1.

80. "U.S. Car Makers Are Close," *Wall Street Journal* (June 11, 2004), p. A1.

81. S. L. Rynes, K. G. Brown, and A. E. Colbert, "Seven Common Misconceptions about Human Resource Practices: Research Findings versus Practitioner Beliefs," *Academy of Management Executive* (2003), Vol. 16, No. 3, pp. 92–104.

82. Shuman and Twombly, "Pearls by Peter."

83. A. Gumbus and R. N. Lussier, "Developing and Using a Balanced Scorecard," *Clinical Leadership & Management Review* (2003), Vol. 17, No. 2, pp. 69–74.

84. R. Kaplan and D. P. Norton, "On Balance," *CFO* (February 2001), pp. 73–78.

85. R. Kaplan and D. P. Norton, "Using the Balanced Scorecard as a Strategic Management System," *Harvard Business Review* (January-February 1996), pp. 75–85.

86. R. Kaplan, D. P. Norton, and M. Witzel, "Great Believers in Balance: Guru Guide Robert Kaplan and David Norton," *The Financial Times* (August 2003), p. 11.

87. Gumbus and Lussier, "Developing and Using a Balanced Scorecard," 69–74.

88. L. Maholland and P. Muetz, "A Balanced Scorecard Approach to Performance Measurement: The Balanced Scorecard Provides a Useful Framework for Focusing Performance Measurement Efforts on the Critical Drivers of Success," *Government Finance Review* (2002), Vol. 18, No. 2, pp. 12–17.

89. Information taken from the Ford Web site *http://www. ford.com*, accessed July 1, 2004.

Glossary

A

acquired needs theory Theory that proposes that employees are motivated by their needs for achievement, power, and affiliation.

acquisition Occurs when one business buys all or part of another business.

adaptive strategies Overall strategies for a line of business, including prospecting, defending, and analyzing.

arbitrator A neutral third party who makes a binding decision to resolve a conflict.

assessment centers Places where job applicants undergo a series of tests, interviews, and simulated experiences to determine their managerial potential.

attitudes Positive or negative evaluations of people, things, and situations.

attribution The process of determining the reason for someone's behavior and whether that behavior is situational or intentional.

authority The right to make decisions, issue orders, and use resources.

B

balanced scorecard (BSC) A management tool that measures financial, customer service, and internal business performance, as well as learning and growth performance.

BCF statement A statement that describes a conflict in terms of behavior, consequences, and feelings.

behavioral leadership theorists Theorists who attempt to determine distinctive styles used by effective leaders.

behavioral theorists Researchers who focus on people to determine the best way to manage in all organizations.

benchmarking The process of comparing an organization's products or services and processes with those of other companies.

bona fide occupational qualification (BFOQ) An occupational qualification that may be discriminatory but that is reasonably necessary to normal operation of a particular organization.

brainstorming The process of suggesting many possible alternatives without evaluation.

budget A planned quantitative allocation of resources for specific activities.

business plan A written description of a new venture—its objectives and the steps for achieving them.

business portfolio analysis The corporate process of determining which lines of business the corporation will be in and how it will allocate resources among them.

business-level strategy The plan for managing one line of business.

C

capacity The amount of products an organization can produce.

capital expenditures budget A projection of all planned major asset investments.

career A sequence of related job positions, involving increasing responsibility and increased compensation and held over a lifetime.

career development The process of gaining skill, experience, and education to achieve career objectives.

career planning The process of setting career objectives and determining how to accomplish them.

centralized authority Important decisions are made by top managers.

charismatic leadership A leadership style that inspires loyalty, enthusiasm, and high levels of performance.

citizenship behavior Employee efforts that go above and beyond the call of duty.

classical theorists Researchers who focus on the job and management functions to determine the best way to manage in all organizations.

coaching The process of giving motivational feedback to maintain and improve performance.

coalition A network of alliances that help a manager achieve an objective.

collaborative conflict resolution model A conflict-resolution model that calls for (1) stating the problem in a BCF statement, (2) getting the other party to acknowledge the conflict, (3) presenting alternative resolutions to the conflict, and (4) coming to an agreement.

collective bargaining The negotiation process resulting in a contract between employees and management that covers employment conditions.

command groups Groups that consist of managers and the employees they supervise.

communication The process of transmitting information and meaning.

communication channel The means or medium by which a message is transmitted; the three primary channels are oral, nonverbal, and written.

communication process Process that takes place between a sender who encodes a message and transmits it through a channel to a receiver who decodes it and may give feedback.

compensation The total of an employee's pay and benefits.

competitive advantage Specifies how an organization offers unique customer value.

complaint An expression of dissatisfaction with a situation, often coupled with a request for change.

conceptual and decision-making skills The ability to understand abstract ideas and select alternatives to solve problems.

concurrent control Action taken to ensure that standards are met as inputs are transformed into outputs.

conflict A situation in which people are in disagreement and opposition.

consensus mapping The process of developing group agreement on a solution to a problem.

content motivation theories Theories that focus on identifying and understanding employees' needs.

contingency leadership model A model used to determine if leadership style is task- or relationship-oriented and if the situation matches the style.

contingency plans Alternative plans to be implemented if uncontrollable events occur.

contingency theorists Researchers who focus on determining the best management approach for a given situation.

control frequency The rate of repetition—constant, periodic, or occasional—of measures taken to control performance.

control systems process (1) Set objectives and standards, (2) measure performance, (3) compare performance to standards, and (4) correct or reinforce.

controlling The process of establishing and implementing mechanisms to ensure that objectives are achieved.

corporate growth strategies Strategies a company can adopt in order to grow: concentration, backward and forward integration, and related and unrelated diversification.

corporate-level strategy The plan for managing multiple lines of business.

creative process The approach to generating new ideas that involves three stages: (1) preparation, (2) incubation and illumination, and (3) evaluation.

creativity A way of thinking that generates new ideas.

criteria The standards that an alternative must meet to be selected as the decision that will accomplish the objective.

critical path The most time-consuming series of activities in a PERT network.

critical success factors The limited number of areas in which satisfactory results will ensure successful performance, achieving the objective/standard.

customer involvement The amount of input from customers, which determines whether operations are make-to-stock, assemble-to-order, or make-to-order.

customer value The perceived benefit of a product, used by customers to determine whether or not to buy the product.

D

damage control Action taken to minimize negative impacts on customers/stakeholders due to faulty outputs.

decentralized authority Important decisions are made by middle and first-line managers.

decision making The process of selecting a course of action that will solve a problem.

decision-making conditions Certainty, risk, and uncertainty.

decision-making model A six-step model that, when used properly, increases chances of success in decision making and problem solving.

decoding The receiver's process of translating a message into a meaningful form.

delegation The process of assigning responsibility and authority for accomplishing objectives.

departmentalization The grouping of related activities into units.

development Ongoing education to improve skills for present and future jobs.

devil's advocate Group members focus on defending a solution while others try to come up with reasons the solution will not work.

direct investment Construction or purchase of operating facilities (subsidiaries) in a foreign country.

discipline Corrective action to get employees to meet standards and standing plans.

divisional structure Departmentalization based on semiautonomous strategic business units.

E

empathic listening Understanding and relating to another's feelings.

employee assistance program (EAP) A benefit program staffed by people who help employees get professional assistance in solving their problems.

encoding The sender's process of putting the message into a form that the receiver will understand.

entrepreneur One who starts a new small business venture.

equity theory Theory that proposes that employees are motivated when their perceived inputs equal outputs.

ERG theory Theory that proposes that employees are motivated by three needs: existence, relatedness, and growth.

ethics Standards of right and wrong that influence behavior.

ethnocentrism Regarding one's own ethnic group or culture as superior to others.

expectancy theory Theory that proposes that employees are motivated when they believe they can accomplish a task and the rewards for doing so are worth the effort.

external environment The outside of an organization's boundaries factors that affect its performance.

F

facility layout The spatial arrangement of physical resources relative to each other—operations use product, process, cellular, or fixed-position layouts.

feedback Information that verifies a message.

financial statements The income statement, balance sheet, and cash flow statement.

first-mover advantage Offering a unique customer value before competitors do so.

forcefield analysis An OD intervention that diagrams the current level of performance, the forces hindering change, and the driving force toward change.

functional conflict A situation in which disagreement and opposition support the achievement of organizational objectives.

functional strategies Strategies developed and implemented by managers in marketing, operations, human resources, finance, and other departments.

functional-level strategy The plan for managing one area of a business.

G

Gantt chart A scheduling tool that uses bars to graphically illustrate a schedule and progress toward the objective over a period of time.

giving praise model A four-step technique for providing feedback to an employee: (1) Tell the employee exactly what was done correctly; (2) tell the employee why the behavior is important; (3) stop for a moment of silence; (4) encourage repeat performance.

global sourcing The use of worldwide resources.

global village Companies conducting business worldwide without boundaries.

goal-setting theory Theory that proposes that achievable but difficult goals motivate employees.

grand strategy An overall corporate-level strategy for growth, stability, or turnaround and retrenchment for some combination of these.

grapevine The informal flow of information in any direction throughout an organization.

group Two or more members with a clear leader who perform independent jobs with individual accountability, evaluation, and rewards.

group cohesiveness The extent to which members stick together.

group composition The mix of members' skills and abilities.

group performance model Group performance is a function of organizational context, group structure, group process, and group development stage.

group process The patterns of interactions that emerge as members perform their jobs.

group process dimensions Roles, norms, cohesiveness, status, decision making, and conflict resolution.

group roles Group task roles, group maintenance roles, and self-interest roles.

group structure dimensions Group type, size, composition, leadership, and objectives.

group types Formal or informal, functional or cross-functional, and command or task.

H

hierarchy of needs theory Theory that proposes that employees are motivated by five levels of needs: physiological, safety, social, esteem, and self-actualization.

horizontal communication The flow of information between colleagues and peers.

human and communication skills The ability to work with people in teams.

human resources management process Planning for, attracting, developing, and retaining employees.

I

information systems (IS) Formal systems for collecting, processing, and disseminating information that aids in decision making.

innovation The implementation of a new idea.

internal environment Factors that affect an organization's performance from within its boundaries.

international business A business based primarily in one country that transacts business in other countries.

International Standards Organization (ISO) An organization that certifies firms that meet set quality standards.

intrapreneur One who starts a new line of business within a large organization.

inventory The stock of materials held for future use.

inventory control The process of managing raw materials, work-in-process, finished goods, and in-transit goods.

J

job description Identifies the tasks and responsibilities of a position.

job design The process of identifying tasks that each employee is responsible for completing.

job enrichment The process of building motivators into a job to make it more interesting and challenging.

job evaluation The process of determining the worth of each job relative to the other jobs within the organization.

job specifications Identify the qualifications needed in the person who is to fill a position.

joint venture Created when firms share ownership of a new enterprise.

just-in-time (JIT) inventory An inventory method in which necessary parts and raw materials are delivered shortly before they are needed.

K

knowledge management Involving everyone in an organization in sharing knowledge and applying it continuously to improve products and processes.

L

labor relations The interactions between management and unionized employees.

large-group intervention An OD intervention in which members of an organization as well as key outside stakeholders come together to solve a problem or take advantage of an opportunity.

leadership The process of influencing employees to work toward the achievement of organizational objectives.

leadership continuum model A model used to determine which of seven styles of leadership, on a continuum from autocratic (boss-centered) to participative (employee-centered), is best for a given situation.

Leadership Grid A model that identifies the ideal leadership style as incorporating a high concern for both production and people.

leadership style The combination of traits, skills, and behaviors managers use in interacting with employees.

leadership trait theorists Theorists who attempt to determine a list of distinctive characteristics that account for leadership effectiveness.

leading The process of influencing employees to work toward achieving objectives.

learning organization An organization with a culture that values sharing knowledge so as to adapt to the changing environment and continuously improve.

levels of authority The authority to inform, to recommend, to report, and full authority.

levels of culture Behavior, values and beliefs, and assumptions.

levels of management Top managers, middle managers, and first-line managers.

line authority The responsibility to make decisions and issue orders down the chain of command.

M

management audit Analysis of the organization's planning, organizing, leading, and controlling functions to look for improvements.

management by objectives (MBO) The process in which managers and their employees jointly set objectives for the employees, periodically evaluate performance, and reward according to the results.

management by walking around (MBWA) A type of supervision in which the three major activities are listening, teaching, and facilitating.

management counseling The process of giving employees feedback so they realize that a problem is affecting their job performance, and referring employees with problems to the employee assistance program.

management functions Planning, organizing, leading, and controlling.

management role categories The categories of roles—interpersonal, informational, and decisional—managers play as they accomplish management functions.

management science theorists Researchers who focus on the use of mathematics to aid in problem solving and decision making.

management skills The skills needed to be an effective manager, including technical, human and communication, and conceptual and decision-making skills.

manager The individual responsible for achieving organizational objectives through efficient and effective utilization of resources.

manager's resources Human, financial, physical, and informational resources.

materials requirement planning (MRP) A system that integrates operations and inventory control with complex ordering and scheduling.

mediator A neutral third party who helps resolve a conflict.

merger Occurs when two companies form one corporation.

message-receiving process A process that includes listening, analyzing, and checking understanding.

message-sending process A process that includes (1) developing rapport, (2) stating your communication objective, (3) transmitting your message, (4) checking the receiver's understanding, and (5) getting a commitment and following up.

mission An organization's purpose or reason for being.

motivation The willingness to achieve organizational objectives.

motivation process The process of moving from need to motive to behavior to consequence to satisfaction or dissatisfaction.

multinational corporation (MNC) A business with significant operations in more than one country.

N

networking The process of developing relationships for the purpose of socializing and politicking.

new venture A new business or a new line of business.

nominal grouping The process of generating and evaluating alternatives using a structured voting method.

nonprogrammed decisions Significant decisions that arise in nonrecurring and nonroutine situations, for which the decision maker should use the decision-making model.

nonverbal communication Messages sent without words.

norms Expectations about appropriate behavior that are shared by members of a group.

O

objective A statement of what is to be accomplished that is expressed in singular, specific, and measurable terms with a target date.

OD interventions Specific actions taken to implement specific changes.

one-minute self-sell An opening statement used in networking that quickly summarizes your history and career plan and asks a question.

operating budgets The revenue and expense budgets.

operational planning The process of setting short-range objectives and determining in advance how they will be accomplished.

operations The function concerned with transforming resource inputs into product outputs.

operations flexibility The amount of variety in the products an operation produces, which determines whether products are produced continuously, repetitively, in batches, or individually.

organization chart A graphic illustration of an organization's management hierarchy and departments and their working relationships.

organizational behavior The study of actions that affect performance in the workplace.

organizational culture The values, beliefs, and assumptions about appropriate behavior that members of an organization share.

organizational development (OD) The ongoing planned process of change used as a means of improving performance through interventions.

organizing The process of delegating and coordinating tasks and allocating resources to achieve objectives.

orientation The process of introducing new employees to the organization and their jobs.

P

paraphrasing The process of restating a message in one's own words.

participative decision-making model A time-driven or development-driven decision tree that assists a user in selecting one of five leadership styles to use in a given situation to maximize a decision.

path-goal model A model used to determine employee objectives and to clarify how to achieve them using one of four leadership styles.

perception The process of selecting, organizing, and interpreting environmental information.

performance Means of evaluating how effectively and efficiently managers use resources to achieve objectives.

performance appraisal The ongoing process of evaluating employee performance.

performance formula Performance = ability × motivation × resources.

personality A combination of behavioral, mental, and emotional traits that define an individual.

PERT A network scheduling technique that illustrates the dependence of activities.

planning The process of setting objectives and determining in advance exactly how the objectives will be met.

planning sheet A scheduling tool that states an objective and lists the sequence of activities required to meet the objective, when each activity will begin and end, and who will complete each activity.

policies General guidelines to be followed when making decisions.

politics The process of gaining and using power.

power The ability to influence others' behavior.

preliminary control Actions designed to anticipate and prevent possible problems.

priority scheduling The continuing evaluation and reordering of the sequence in which products will be produced.

problem The situation that exists whenever objectives are not being met.

problem solving The process of taking corrective action to meet objectives.

procedure A sequence of actions to be followed in order to achieve an objective.

process consultation An OD intervention designed to improve team dynamics.

process motivation theories Theories that focus on understanding how employees choose behaviors to fulfill their needs.

product A good, a service, or a combination of the two.

productivity A performance measure relating outputs to inputs.

programmed decisions Decisions that arise in recurring or routine situations, for which the decision maker should use decision rules or organizational policies and procedures.

Pygmalion effect The theory that managers' attitudes toward and expectations and treatment of employees largely determine their performance.

Q

quality A measure of value determined by comparing actual functioning to requirements.

quality control The process of ensuring that all types of inventory meet standards.

R

reciprocity The creation of obligations and the development of alliances that are used to accomplish objectives.

recruiting Attracting qualified candidates to apply for job openings.

reflecting responses Responses that paraphrase a message and communicate understanding and acceptance to the sender.

reinforcement theory Theory that proposes that through the consequences of their behavior, employees will be motivated to behave in predetermined ways.

responsibility The obligation to achieve objectives by performing required activities.

rework control Action taken to fix an output.

routing The path and sequence of the transformation of a product into an output.

rules Statements of exactly what should or should not be done.

S

selection The process of choosing the most qualified applicant recruited for a job.

servant leadership Leadership style based on simultaneously meeting the needs and goals of employees and the goals of the organization.

single-use plans Programs and budgets developed for handling nonrepetitive situations.

situation analysis An analysis of those features in a company's environment that most directly affect its options and opportunities.

situational approaches to leadership Theories that attempt to determine appropriate leadership styles for particular situations.

Situational Leadership model A model used to select one of four leadership styles that match the employees' maturity level in a given situation.

small business A business that is independently owned and operated, is not dominant in its field, and has annual receipts not in excess of $500,000.

social responsibility The conscious effort to operate in a manner that creates a win-win situation for all stakeholders.

sociotechnical theorists Researchers who focus on integrating people and technology.

span of management The number of employees reporting to a manager.

staff authority The responsibility to advise and assist other personnel.

stages of group development Orientation, dissatisfaction, resolution, production, and termination.

stages of the change process Denial, resistance, exploration, and commitment.

stakeholders People whose interests are affected by organizational behavior.

stakeholders' approach to ethics Creating a win-win situation for all stakeholders so that everyone benefits from the decision.

standards Measures of performance levels in the areas of quantity, quality, time, cost, and behavior.

standing plans Policies, procedures, and rules developed for handling repetitive situations.

statistical process control (SPC) A statistical test that aids in determining whether quality is within an acceptable standard range.

status The perceived ranking of one member relative to other members in a group.

strategic human resources planning The process of staffing the organization to meet its objectives.

strategic levels Three levels of plans: corporate, business, and functional.

strategic planning The process of developing a mission and long-range objectives and determining in advance how they will be accomplished.

strategy A plan for pursuing a mission and achieving objectives.

stress The body's reaction to environmental demands.

stressors Factors that cause people to feel overwhelmed by anxiety, tension, and/or pressure.

substitutes for leadership Characteristics of the task, of subordinates, or of the organization that replace the need for a leader.

supply chain management The process of coordinating all the activities involved in producing a product and delivering a product and delivering it to the customer.

survey feedback An OD intervention that uses a questionnaire to gather data to use as the basis for change.

SWOT analysis A determination of an organization's internal environmental strengths and weaknesses and external environmental opportunities and threats.

symbolic leaders Leaders who articulate a vision for an organization and reinforce the culture through slogans, symbols, and ceremonies.

symbolic leadership Leadership style based on establishing and maintaining a strong organizational culture.

synectics The process of generating novel alternatives through role playing and fantasizing.

systems process The method used to transform inputs into outputs.

systems theorists Researchers who focus on viewing the organization as a whole and as the interrelationship of its parts.

T

task groups Employees selected to work on a specific objective.

team A small number of members with shared leadership who perform interdependent jobs with both individual and group accountability, evaluation, and rewards.

team building An OD intervention designed to help work groups increase structural and team dynamics performance.

team leaders Empower members to take responsibility for performing the management functions and focus on developing effective group structure and group process and on furthering group development.

technical skills The ability to use methods and techniques to perform a task.

technology The process used to transform inputs into outputs.

time-based competition The use of strategies to increase the speed with which an organization goes from creativity to delivery.

total quality management (TQM) The process that involves everyone in an organization focusing on the customer to continually improve product value.

training The process of teaching employees the skills necessary to perform a job.

transactional leadership A leadership style based on exchange.

transformational leadership A leadership style that brings about continuous learning, innovation, and change.

two-dimensional leadership styles Four possible leadership styles that are based on the dimensions of job structure and employee consideration.

two-factor theory Theory that proposes that employees are motivated by motivators rather than by maintenance factors.

types of change Changes in strategy, in structure, in technology, and in people.

types of managers General managers, functional managers, and project managers.

V

vertical communication The flow of information both downward and upward through the organizational chain of command.

vestibule training Training that develops skills in a simulated setting.

Index